Text editing

Text editing

a handbook
for students and
practitioners

Kris Van de Poel
WAM Carstens
John Linnegar

UPA
University Press Antwerp

GPRC
Guaranteed
Peer Reviewed
Content
www.gprc.be

The GPRC label (Guaranteed Peer Review Content) was developed by the Flemish organization Boek.be and is assigned to publications which are in compliance with the academic standards required by the VABB (Vlaams Academisch Bibliografisch Bestand).

UPA is an imprint of ASP nv (Academic and Scientific Publishers nv)
Ravensteingalerij 28
B-1000 Brussels
Tel. + 32 (0)2 289 26 50
Fax + 32 (0)2 289 26 59
E-mail: info@aspeditions.be
www.upa-editions.be

ISBN 978 90 5718 114 6
NUR 113 / 610
Legal deposit D/2012/11.161/050

The original Afrikaans edition of this work was published as *Teksredaksie* (WAM Carstens & Kris Van de Poel) by SUN MeDIA, Stellenbosch, South Africa (www.africansunmedia.co.za).

Cover design, text design and layout: Kerry Abramowitz
Proofreading: Deborah Cooper, Jean Kilroe, Ken McGillivray, Nikki van Rooyen
Index: John Linnegar

Printed by Digital Print Solutions, Cape Town, South Africa

Preface

It has been said time and again: communicating effectively can mean all the difference between making money and losing it. Text editing has never been more in evidence or important and has become a fully integrated phase in the pursuit of effective written communication. However, in practice, it is not enough to know the tricks of the text-editing trade; the text editor also has to be able to apply knowledge and skills sensibly, all the while being acutely aware of what they are doing.

Text editing: a handbook for students and practitioners is driven by the conviction that you turn out a better job when you know what you are doing, why you are doing it, and to what end. It draws on the experience and expertise of three diverse contributors with very different backgrounds. Indeed, the *Text editing* authors come from varying professional domains (public and private enterprise), take different approaches (theoretical and applied, hands-on and reflective), have different language backgrounds (even different types of English), are rooted in different continents (Europe and Africa), and they approach text editing with slightly different eyes (inward- and outward-looking). Each person in their own right has contributed to this book, which is primarily the product of a long-standing collaboration between two academics in the field of applied linguistics and has its roots in a 20-year research partnership.

Kris Van de Poel of the University of Antwerp (Belgium) Research Unit for Applied Language Studies is an applied linguist in the real sense of the word, always looking for challenges in the area of language in use. During her sojourns in Denmark and Scotland she ran a successful text-editing business called editek which aimed to make intercultural texts say what they were meant to say. Upon her return to Belgium she guided many generations of translators and linguists along the slippery slopes of effective and professional communication, trying to raise their communicative awareness. Moreover, she devoted a considerable portion of research time to text editing in academic and professional contexts, meanwhile developing writing scales (assessment requirements) and materials for teaching, learning and self-evaluation. Her strong pedagogical and didactic principles guarantee a systematic approach to writing.

Wannie Carstens, professor of Afrikaans linguistics and current director of the School of Languages at North-West University (Potchefstroom campus) in South Africa, has carried out some pioneering work on normative grammar and text linguistics. His many stays in the United States and Europe have led to interesting exchanges with colleagues and field workers. In the *Text editing* team he is the analytical reader and he has the most comprehensive overview of the theoretical and world literature on the topic, which, as a genuine scholar, he keeps expanding and updating. He has the unique capacity to absorb, digest and re-digest the literature on the topic in such a way that even the most intricate findings become accessible to an interested audience. His drive in teaching generations of students has ensured a place for qualitative text editing in the minds and professional lives of many of his graduates.

The third member of the team, John Linnegar of McGillivray Linnegar Associates based in Cape Town (South Africa), is firmly rooted in the publishing industry. Being a sought-after professional trainer of text editors, subeditors, proofreaders, project managers and index-ers, John was drawn into the team for his hands-on experience as a language practitioner in the publishing industry and his abiding passion for language. A strong advocate of professionalisation for practitioners in the field, he is immediate past chairman of the Pro-fessional Editors' Group in South Africa and has also been an associate of the Society for Editors and Proofreaders in the United Kingdom for a number of years. A former school-teacher, and also an inhouse copy editor/proofreader, subeditor, project manager of book and magazine projects, and author himself, he brings 30 years of experience to his role as co-author of the present volume.

What binds the three authors together is that through their experience and research they are avid believers in the need for text editing to have solid foundations, at the same time acknowledging that theory is firmly rooted in practice and that in turn practice can be perfected through teaching and training.

The current book has many fathers and mothers in the form of publications rooted in the lives, past and present, of the three authors. One book in particular should be mentioned as the basis of the current work: *Teksredaksie* (2010). The result of a long period of inten-sive conceptualisation, it has provided the original framework that has been meticulously converted and extended to serve another language, a slightly different purpose and a far wider audience.

We hope that you will find the present book as exiting to read as it was enjoyable to write. We invite you to share your views with us at texteditinghandbook@gmail.com.

Kris Van de Poel

Wannie Carstens

John Linnegar

May 2012

Acknowledgements

A project as massive and wide-ranging as *Text editing* has turned out to be, can reach its successful denouement only with the greatest degree of collaboration and teamwork. The production of this volume has been proof positive of this, and we authors wish to thank the following for their unselfish and unstinting collaboration in various ways and to varying degrees – all of which we sincerely appreciate:

- Catherine Grady, Althéa Kotze, Janet Mackenzie, Elizabeth Manning Murphy and David Owen for the contributions they have made based on their own researches into and keen observations of language usage;
- David Owen for his wonderful open-mindedness and insightful close reading of and comments on the first draft of a number of the chapters;
- the 11 volunteer text editors who put their reputations on the line and in so doing made chapter 12 possible: Wendy Barrow, John Deane, Anne Denniston, Eldene Eyssel, Joan Fairhurst, Denise Fourie, Catherine Grady, Jean Kilroe, Marina Pearson, Anni Protti and Pauline Visser;
- our countless students and trainees, who have been the inspiration for and driving force behind the book as well as being indirectly responsible for much of its content;
- Catherine Grady for her enthusiastic support and for fielding our many questions;
- Ken McGillivray for so willingly assuming responsibility for imposing consistency on the entire text while at the same time implementing innumerable tranches of corrections to the manuscript;
- Piet Swanepoel for the interesting chats about visual literacy and document design;
- Jan Renkema, the progenitor of the CCC model on which this text is premised, for his support en route;
- Kerry Abramowitz for providing us with an inspired – and inspiring – design for the book, and for laying out the pages so adroitly;
- the reviewers of our text for their wholehearted commitment to our enterprise;
- our publisher, Gert De Nutte, of ASP Editions, Brussels, for trusting in us and steering the project through international waters;
- all those well-wishers who offered us encouragement along the way.

We are really grateful for the privilege of having got to know so many interesting people through this project, all of whom have warmed to the subject-matter of *Text editing* and cheered us in the process.

The authors

May 2012

Contents

Chapter 4
Process and procedure: doing text editing

Chapter 5
The text editor and editorial project management

Chapter 6
Text editing in practice: content

Contents

Contents

Chapter 12
Text editing in practice: a comparative analysis of texts

Appendices

We dedicate this publication to our respective partners, Eddy, Wilma and Ken, who had to put up with all the seemingly endless 'words, words, words'.

Also to the likes of Catherine, a professional translator and editor; Chris, the director of a primary school who spends his spare time editing textbooks; Frederik, the secretary at the university who expertly weighs every word; and Bridget, an indomitable editorial spirit who has refused to allow disability to stand in the way of her passion for words. Each in their own way is an example to us all, doing what they can to make this world a more communicative place.

Introduction

Text editing: a handbook for students and practitioners attempts to answer three fundamental questions:

- What is a text editor?
- What does the process of editing texts involve?
- Which tools are available to make a text communicate effectively?

This volume gives full recognition to the role of the text editor in a wide range of guises, including that of freelancer, project manager, proofreader and 'ghostwriter', as well as of practitioner in corporate or educational environments, dealing with print and/or digital media. *Text editing* also details the critical, normative and text-linguistic challenges that are likely to confront English-language practitioners as they work through authors' writings. If there is a central message that forms a leitmotiv running through the 640 pages that make up the book, it is that, like weaving, text editing is a *process*, and one that should be undertaken systematically.

We've subtitled this book *a handbook for students and practitioners* because we believe it to be not only an important and useful point of entry into the profession of text editing for neophytes but also an essential back-to-basics guide to practising editors. Since human beings scan, skim, read and internalise knowledge in different ways, we have tried to present the content in diverse ways too. For both groups, we hope that the many lists, checklists, tabulated matter and diagrams will prove to be particularly supportive and useful as an easy reference. *Lists* are meant to give concise overviews of particular topics. More often than not, the listed items are enumerated by means of chevrons, but sometimes they are numbered when indicating steps or stages or for easy referencing later in the text. *Intext short lists* are as a rule bulleted and often exemplify a stated case. *Checklist* items are generally formulated as questions which are preceded by ticks. We have known students who copy checklists and stick them on the fridge door or keep them in the vicinity of their computer screen to consult whenever needed. These are for them, as well as for those practitioners who want to be sure they have performed a task thoroughly. *Tables* and *figures* are visual and summarised representations of some of the chapters' content. We have tried to be consistent in distinguishing between the different forms of presentation.

Bearing in mind that a work of this nature must surely have an international readership, we have also taken into account the needs of editors who are likely to have to edit texts written by non-native speakers of English (and cope with the challenges such texts present) and of text editors who themselves are not native users of English. For both groups, the detailed treatment of the grammatical, syntactic, morphological, spelling and punctuation facets of the editor's armoury may be helpful.

The overriding thread through the 12 chapters of *Text editing* is the idea that there are many facets to creating an effective or communicative text. Chapter by chapter, the different facets are presented as follows:

- Chapter 1 *From language practice to model building: the foundations of text editing*. This foundational chapter attempts to define language practice as an applied linguistic intervention by exploring the boundaries with neighbouring disciplines and identifying the text editor's role(s) in that process.
- Chapter 2 *Text as a domain of text editing – an applied model* essentially introduces the text-evaluation model by the renowned Dutch linguist, Jan Renkema, and explains how important a text's readability and accessibility are and what knowledge the text editor can rely on to determine text quality systematically. This chapter is firmly rooted in the established literature and wide-ranging academic research. The 15 evaluation points that arise from the confluence of text facets and the three criteria for analysis – correspondence, consistency and correctness – are ultimately illustrated in vivid detail in chapter 12.
- Chapter 3 *The profile of a text editor* attempts to describe the roles and responsibilities of the text editor as comprehensively as possible. In doing so, we describe the diverse circumstances and roles in which practitioners are likely to find themselves: language practitioner, translator, proofreader, editor of various types of text, from newspapers and magazines through marketing materials and reports to journals and books. We also address the vexed questions of what the differences are between a light, a medium and a heavy edit, and the distinction between text editing and proofreading.
- Chapter 4 *Process and procedure: doing text editing* focuses on how texts are edited in reality. We make the point that this craft has to be viewed and practised as a multilayered process, one in which many passes through a document are necessary to ensure that optimal communication can be guaranteed through a text.
- Chapter 5 *The text editor and editorial project management*. Because of the specialised nature of this function, the fact that it demands certain qualities and qualifications, and the reality that more and more publishers are requiring people to manage multiple projects (whether inhouse or as an outsourced function), we have treated the topic in a chapter of its own.
- Chapters 6 to 10 together form a grouping entitled 'Text editing in practice', but each chapter focuses on one particular text facet: content, structure, wording, presentation (spelling and punctuation; typography and layout). For the text editor or the text editor-in-training, these five chapters should probably be the most thumbed pages of the book. They contain an abundance of practical advice on and illustrations of the kinds of problem practitioners encounter daily – though we are fully aware that an entire book on its own could be filled with such content.

- Chapter 11 *Resources* is dedicated to the print and online resources that text editors will find useful from time to time in their day-to-day work. They include – importantly, we believe – the standards for editing practice of several professional bodies from around the world, and also tools facilitating professional text editing and proofreading. Those resources that appear only in this chapter and nowhere else in *Text editing* are not repeated in the bibliography.
- Chapter 12 *Text editing in practice: the editor's voice – a comparative analysis of texts.* Here the editor's voice is eventually heard! We have consolidated the critique, comments and corrections effected by a group of 11 practising text editors from the northern and southern hemispheres to present to our readers 'text editing in action'. We believe that chapter 12 will illustrate vividly the detailed nitty-gritty that comprise the workings of theory in practice.
- In addition, in the appendices, as supportive reading, we have added five brief exposés on a variety of Englishes and the pitfalls and challenges they present to text editors worldwide: text editing for the multinational client; English as encountered among students in an academic second-language environment; the characteristics of the English used in southwest Europe; the influences and constituents of South African English; and the problems thrown up (particularly for foreign visitors and settlers) by the English of Australia. These are in addition to sections on English as a lingua franca in chapters 3 and 6. We trust that they will prove to be useful pre-emptive material for those who venture into the arena of editing texts drafted in particular by English non-native speakers.

We hope that you'll find yourself drawn to this *vade mecum* on text editing that tries to promote communicative textual output and presents the tools needed en route. We also hope that you'll find yourself supported in delivering work to a level of professionalism you'll be proud to present to both your clients and the readers.

1

From language practice to model building: the foundations of text editing

Errors, like straws, upon the surface flow; He who would search for pearls, must dive below.
John Dryden, 'All for Love', 1678

An ounce of action, is worth a ton of theory.
Ralph Aldo Emerson

A fact is a simple statement that everyone believes. It is innocent, unless found guilty. A hypothesis is a novel suggestion that no one wants to believe. It is guilty, until found effective.
Edward Teller

The important thing in science is not so much to obtain new facts as to discover new ways of thinking about them.
Sir William Bragg

Contents

Objectives

Written communication takes place through text. This introductory chapter looks into the steps that need to be taken before a text can be made public. Attention is paid to (a) delineating the domain of text editing, (b) defining the foundations of the domain, (c) describing the process of intervention in a text and (d) describing the different roles that text editors fulfil in this process. In this way, this chapter is a prelude to and a stepping stone towards all the subsequent topics in this book.

1 Introduction: text presupposes tasks

> ... a copy editor makes certain that a manuscript becomes a published work, and that task requires an individual with knowledge, decisiveness, top-notch writing skills, and diplomacy.
> *Beene*

> ... books require professional editing ... editors make sure a publication is appropriate for its intended audience, stays accurate and consistent, adheres to standard grammatical conventions, presents an inviting design, and keeps the project on schedule.
> *Beene*

1.1 Communication in text

We are not merely individual beings, living in isolation like islands; we are social creatures who live among and with each other. Apart from our basic biological needs of eating, drinking and sleeping, we also have psycho-sociological and cultural needs in which communication plays a central role. Etymologically, the word 'communication' carries with it a sense of 'togetherness'. Indeed, communicating entails exchanging ideas, thoughts and emotions through a complicated system of verbal and non-verbal signs. From an evolutionary point of view, human beings have remained the only species that is able to communicate by using language and speech. Speech – the ability to convert language into sound and words – is the preferred medium for human communication and probably also the most essential medium for social interaction.

In the initial development of communication, parents act as an example to their children and their efforts at, for instance, correcting errors help children to develop their own language skills. In a way, parents are constantly 'editing' their children's utterances while helping them to discover and develop their competence in language usage. Editing takes on a different character when members of the same household write a text such as an advertisement for a car boot sale or a babysitter or an invitation to a celebration. Matters discussed are whether the style is appropriate, which words to select and how to hit the appropriate register to achieve a predetermined goal – namely, communicating a message to a defined audience. No wonder these cosy writing sessions often end in debate and clashes of likes and dislikes, and may lead to real bouts of graphophobia!

Not only in our personal history but also in time past, speech has always been important. In the pictographic writing stage of humankind's development, information was available to those who could see and understand the object represented. Those were the people who could place the object depicted in the right context and could recognise and interpret an image or a token. The use of symbols to represent concrete objects was easily understood by the in-crowd. However, as soon as the symbols started to be used to express more abstract ideas and were transformed into, for instance, an alphabetic writing system where written symbols represented the sounds of the spoken language, the chances of faulty communication increased. Although written products became more widespread and more accessible to a larger group of people, the presence of images decreased (except in children's books, manuals and reference books).

Nowadays, in an era where messages increasingly take on a written form supported by or integrated with visual and audio components, communication has become globalised. Gradually, written messages by themselves have become the sole possession of the members of a particular language group and have become accessible only to those in active contact with the same language.

Sound, image and text have to be adjusted to one another and to their receiver. In the next section, what is meant by the different phases of adjustment and fine-tuning is clarified.

1.2 Read, reread and amend

There are different ways to go about the final stage of the creative writing process: either authors correct their own text in a rereading phase in which they themselves determine what 'adapting' means (Bisaillon 2007: 76) or they can ask another person to read their text critically and correct it in return for payment; in the latter case, the instructions regarding professional text revision are determined by the client (Bisaillon 2007: 76; Mossop 2001, 2007). According to Beene (2009: 3), the text of a book is always submitted to a thorough process of evaluation: 'a book undergoes more review than any other information source.' Thus, before being published, a publication will be put through a comprehensive control process to make sure that it is 'correct'. In this process the text editor is only one of the many links in the production chain (see figure 3.1 in chapter 3).

During this quality assessment process, some of those critical readers will consider the communicative effect of the text as the most important aspect, while others will focus on 'dots and commas' in order to improve the text; yet others will focus on the form and the lexical appropriateness of the text. Whatever the focus, the goal is to make the transmission of the message as effective as possible.

In his work on the prophesied end of the printed book, Bolter's (1991: 239) concluding remark is: 'Printed books usually end, as they began, with a confession.' Indeed, at the beginning of a text authors more often than not confess to not having written their book on their own and go on to express their gratitude towards partners, friends and editors (in this order) for their having helped to write the book in question. Most often in a sepa-rate sentence, the person who has 'taken care of', 'edited' or 'corrected' the text or, in a minimalistic way, the language, is acknowledged. At the same time, authors safeguard themselves and their collaborators by adding that they, and they alone, are responsible for any shortcomings of their book.

1.3 The future

Even though, according to Bolter (1991), printed books may soon be a thing of the past, publishers and editors will apparently not be out of work for some time to come. A 1999 survey by the American Copy Editors Society (ACES 1999: 46) among 115 magazines, for instance, showed that 79 vacancies for copy editors were waiting to be filled. A more recent collaborative study (2009), conducted by ACES together with researchers from the University of Missouri and the American Society of News Editors (ASNE) (http://www.cop-ydesk.org/conference/2009/minne/entry/aces-survey/), looked into the need for text edi-tors in news groups in the United States. The result showed that two-thirds (66.2%) of the 278 respondents were optimistic about the future of the news industry. A third (32.3%) were expecting to remain in their present position for at least the next five years and more than a third (38.9%) wanted to keep their position until their retirement.

Thus, it seems that the profession does offer those involved in it a positive future. As long as texts will need to be produced, therefore, some form of editing and preparation for publication will be needed. The nature of this editing and preparation is explored in the following sections of this chapter.

2 Terms and terminology: the profession

2.1 Generally accepted definitions

Texts can be improved in many ways, which means that they can be made better or more meaningful, and they can be adapted to diverse readerships before they are released to the general public for reading and interpreting. In order to get a better insight into the nature and the form of the revising and editing process, it is important to understand what exactly is meant by 'revising and editing'.

The word 'text editor' can be found only in reference lists as meaning a type of computer program used for editing plain text files. If we focus on the word 'edit', the following two basic meanings stand out (*CALD* online):

- to prepare a text or film for printing or viewing by correcting mistakes and deciding what will be removed and what will be kept in, etc ….
- to be in charge of the reports in a newspaper or magazine, etc ….

According to the first dictionary meaning, 'editing' means manipulating a text in such a way that it yields a product which is as correct as possible and thus contains the fewest errors possible. 'Editing' here is regarded as a process that is normative at the level of sentence, word and letter (it is all about correcting), but also – and more seriously auto-cratically – it is the process in which an editor, on behalf of a publisher and/or an author, more or less autonomously determines the length, content and readability of a text (the deciding component of the definition) (for a detailed discussion see chapter 3). The second dictionary meaning above refers directly to the managerial tasks associated with being the 'editor' of a newspaper or magazine.

Preparing a text for publication, whether in print or electronically, presupposes linguistic decision-taking other than error correction and so the first definition carries a more central *language* implication. This is reinforced by the definitions of 'editor' (*Cambridge dictionary* – http://dictionary.cambridge.org):

- a person who corrects or changes pieces of text or films before they are printed or shown, or
- a person who is in charge of a newspaper or magazine, etc, and is responsible for all of its reports.

From these sources we can deduce that textbook editor and film editor are well-estab-lished compounds that indicate where the editor is entitled to correct but also change pieces of text before publication.

Merriam Webster (http://www.merriam-webster.com) adds another dimension, connect-ing as it does the activities of the text editor to 'editing' as a profession:

- Editor (1649)
   1: someone who edits especially as an occupation
   2: a device used in editing motion-picture film or magnetic tape
   3: a computer program that permits the user to create or modify data (as text or graphics) especially on a display screen

- Copy editor (1899)
   1: an editor who prepares copy for the typesetter
   2: one who edits and headlines newspaper copy

The verb 'edit' (1791) describes the process of editing in quite some detail, and description 1c below inparticular provides interesting insights:

   1a: to prepare (as literary material) for publication or public presentation
   1b: to assemble (as a moving picture or tape recording) by cutting and rearranging

1c: to alter, adapt, refine especially to bring about conformity to a standard to suit a particular purpose …

2: to direct the publication of …

When editors 'alter, adapt or refine' a text, they need an objective which aims at an outcome and a target audience and which corresponds to specified standards. To 'refine' or 'revise' a text refers to making it more specific for a well-defined target audience (cf Clouse 1992). If editing is the practice of selecting information (see definition 1b above), the editor will act as a gatekeeper who decides what to include and what not.

The tasks performed by an 'editor' when 'editing' are not spelt out clearly in the definition, but do seem to be quite diverse. Trying to pinpoint the reason for this looseness, Beene (2009: 6) summarises the problem as follows:

> … what an editor does is so varied and depends so directly on the company employing an editor that it is *a challenge to get a firm definition of editor*, to present a limited list of what an editor does, or *to define editing with certainty*.

In order to delineate the activity of adapting a text slightly more precisely, we have decided to use the term 'text editor' in this handbook to refer to someone who revises texts in order to improve their quality in the broadest sense possible. This approach is elaborated on further in chapter 3, and especially in section 5 of that chapter.

2.2 Defined by the domain and the market

Another way to delineate the profession of text editor is by investigating how professional organisations cater for the needs of the profession and then to use this information to define it. The Editorial Freelancers Association (EFA) (http://www.the-efa.org) is a New York-based national organisation for text editors in the broad sense of the word and those who employ them (the EFA terms itself 'The professional resource for editorial specialists and those who hire them'). Its members are employed in eight different countries and perform a wide range of activities. They are abstractors, copy-editors, designers, desktop publishing experts, editors, indexers, manuscript evaluators, picture researchers, project managers, proofreaders, researchers, textbook development editors, translators, and writers.

Similar organisations and associations exist in other language areas and are fairly widespread; they take different forms and offer different services. In South Africa, there are the Professional Editors' Group (PEG) (www.editors.org.za) and the South African Translators' Institute (SATI) (http://www.translators.org.za), which aim to protect and support the interests of language practitioners in South Africa. In Canada, the Editors' Association of Canada (EAC) (www.editors.ca) serves the same purpose, as does the Society for Editors and Proofreaders (SfEP) in the United Kingdom www.sfep.org.uk. In Australia (a federal state), each state has its own society of editors (eg Canberra, Victoria) but there is also an overarching national organisation, the Institute of Professional Editors (IPEd – http://www. editors-sa.org.au).

Text writers, editors(-in-chief), and proofreaders can be connected through mailing lists such as *Spits* (http://www.collegasintekst.org), while in other networking opportunities they would meet at conferences or workshops. Some organisations (eg IPEd) provide on-line help and others, such as PEG, offer a form of in-service training for their members. Obviously, the practitioners involved also cooperate across national borders and there are networks of language practitioners who keep each other posted on activities and issues in which there is a mutual interest. Attendance at one another's national conferences and workshops, and participation in training programmes, is also a fairly common occur-rence.

Since professional organisations reflect an established professional life, Pym (2000) looks at language-related tasks from the perspective of market demands. Here it becomes clear that more often than not professional language work goes beyond simply translating a text. He tries to define the language professional by using terms such as 'intercultural man-agement assistant', 'intercultural management consultant', 'language services provider', 'information broker', 'multitasking translator' or the extension of the IT term 'localisation' (that is, adapting a text from one cultural context to another). Whatever name is chosen, language professionals are 'called upon to do more than just translate' (Pym 2000: 2). For this reason it is useful to take a closer look at how some of the language professions com-pare. Doing so will allow us to make a more precise delineation of the editorial task.

3 Working with text

> Nor ought a genius less than his that writ attempt translation.
> *Sir John Denham*

> So you want to be a textual editor? Think again. Unless, that is, you fancy poring over a text, just to make sure that the person who keyed in the version you're using as your electronic text, didn't skip a period …
> *Isis*

> If you didn't get on well with grammar at school or if your spelling is poor, copy-editing is almost certainly not the job for you.
> *Society for Editors and Proofreaders (SfEP)*

Comparing the profession of text editing with some related occupations in which re-working written texts is central may give us a clearer idea of the tasks of the text editor. Even though the professions of editor, translator and copy-writer show resemblances, it is important to stress the differences. By doing so, it becomes clear that text editing is a profession in its own right (Plotnik 1982: 47–48).

3.1 The translator: cognitive and stylistic editor

Translators are not necessarily text editors, since they often rework texts which have al-ready been published in a target language. Moreover, the texts would not be accessible to the new target audience without the translators' intervention. In other words, translators are indispensable mediators in the communication process between author and reader (or speaker and listener in the case of interpretation) because they make texts accessible to new groups of readers who would not be able to understand the original versions.

Translating (interlingual rendition, rendering) can also be defined from the perspective of the text itself. In this case, it is a transmission of meaning which attempts to create a one-to-one relationship between the original text and the translation by trying to create 'a written communication in a second language having the same meaning as the written communication in the first language' (http://dictionary.babylon.com/translation/). When the target audience needs specific attention, the translator can receive an assignment that is strongly focused on register, for instance 'rewording something in less technical terminology' (http//dictionary.babylon.com/translation/).

Finally, the process of translation can also be defined from the meaning a text has in its specific context: 'Translation is the comprehension of the *meaning* of a text and the subsequent production of an *equivalent* text, likewise called a 'translation' that communicates the same message in another language' (www.en.wikipedia.org/wiki/Translation).

The way in which this communication process takes place in translation is not always transparent, but the above quotation indicates the important difference between translating and editing: without a translator, communication between writer and reader will be impossible because they operate within different linguistic systems. A text editor, however, will 'only' optimise texts in order to improve the transmission of the message, so that the document will be enhanced for the audience that communicates through the same linguistic system as the author.

Nevertheless, a translator will also have to do some cognitive revising (ie adapting the ideas and the way in which they are formulated) where the source text is of poor quality (Mossop 2001: 17ff, 2007). When investigating the entire process of text editing, the dividing line between translating and editing becomes artificial because – according to Cardinal (1992: 189) – a translator will also have to do editing '... in the final stage of translation as a *process*, where the proposed TT [target text] is actually examined as a product. This stage is known as *editing*. A TT is only really complete after careful stylistic editing.'

Thus, stylistic editing, or editing to clarify meaning, improve flow and smooth language, is an indispensable last step before publication and is therefore also part of the finishing touches applied in translating.

3.2 The textual editor: the faithful processing of text

In the English-speaking world, the concept of text editing can be applied to two different job descriptions, that is, the textual or supervisory editor and the copy-editor. The textual editor either works on the texts contributed to a multi-author publication in order to manage the individual authors and their contributions and impose uniformity on the individual contributions or is employed by a journal to manage both contributors of articles and their contributions, usually assigning the editing of the contributions to a copy-editor. Less commonly, a person (either an editor or the author themself) may be called upon to revise, update or correct a previously published text for the purposes of publishing a new edition; such a person would be referred to as a 'textual editor'. Editors of modern editions (usually with a scholarly commentary) of classics such as the plays of William Shakespeare would be termed 'textual editors'. The copy-editor, on the other hand, reworks texts *before* they are published, that is, they are still in the form of final-draft author's manuscripts (MS).

Both activities involve text meaning and language. The first kind of textual editor referred to above is often the lead author in a team of contributors, often the most experienced member in the particular field or the most senior among them. Their task is, first, to act as a go-between between authors and publisher: they obtain the individual contributions timeously, review them and, if necessary, liaise with each author about alterations; they check that the content supplied by the individual authors is not contradictory, either of the overall theme of the publication or of other writers' theses; and they play the role of copy-editor, to some extent, by imposing overall consistency or uniformity on the text as a whole (eg footnotes or endnotes; reference citation style; treatment of quoted matter and use of quotation marks; heading and subheading hierarchy; style and register; terminology and word meanings). It is with the textual editor that the publisher's copy-editor will liaise about matters they are unable to resolve and for consent to make certain material changes.

As with a translator, a textual editor can also work with a text which was published previously for a specified target audience. If after the author's death a new edition (annotated or not) comes on the market, the textual editor can make changes and independently add comments based on previous editions. They may even write an extensive introduction in support of their intervention in and emendations to the original edition. Authors can also play the role of textual editor of a text. They can apply changes in a first and a second edition of the work. Their alterations are primarily triggered by changes in the reality underpinning the text, for instance a new political or social situation has to be taken into account, more modern language usage is required. Thus, the text is brought up-to-date as far as a particular context is concerned, but also with respect to co-text, that is, the language used. Small & Walsh (1991: 6) maintain:

> *The textual editor relates the authorial time to the present.* Because the editor and hypothetical audience are contemporary, sharing cultural assumptions about the overall myth or

general Story within which the edited text occupies a proportionate position like plot, the textual editor's work can be described as canonical. The editor relates the plot (or text) to the overall Story, acting as talebearer within the culture, by virtue of having presented the text. Both author and texts are *other* to editor and audience, and this admits the necessity for interpretation, elevating the role of the editor to that of a critic.

This activity is known as 'textual scholarship' (which is a discipline in its own right). It involves reprinting a text and linguistically it refers to the transfer of one language system (usually an older one) to a (possibly) new(er) language system. In the case of scholarly editing, the original language used will be explained and commented upon and the significance of alterations over time will be illuminated. Without the intervention of a textual editor certain parts of these texts would be incomprehensible, inaccurate, incomplete and not even scientifically justifiable. Therefore, the language is adapted, (usually) with the help of explanatory annotations consisting of footnotes or end notes, glossaries or comments in the text. This results in a text that is 'owned' by both the author and the textual editor.

3.3 The copy-editor: accessibility guaranteed

The term 'copy-editing' (sometimes also spelled as 'copyediting' or 'copy editing') leads us to the core of this book. Copy-editors or text editors (the preferred term in this work) ensure that an edition is correct (in terms of grammar, style, punctuation and spelling) and accessible to its readers (in terms of content, structure, register and visual layout). Beene (2009: 6) summarises these activities as follows:

> While an editor may work on the specifics of grammar, spelling, and punctuation (the microcosm level), that same person will also work on the content, structure, style, illustrations, and production (the macrocosm level) for a text and will, simultaneously, work with the writer to produce an understandable, coherent document. *An editor is around to help make the writer's word readable.*

Text editors also check facts (insofar as they can) and help the publisher to resolve potential problems regarding defamation (or libel/slander), plagiarism, copyright and any further language editing required before a text is published – see the website of the Society for Editors and Proofreaders (SfEP) (http://www.sfep.org.uk/pub/faqs/fedit.asp) for further information. Kotze (1998: 2) captures the essence of text editing as follows: transforming an everyday text that is often too long, boring, disorganised and unstructured into the bestseller of the year.

Text editors utilise their education, training, skills, creativity and experience to perform their service and in so doing they become co-responsible for the published text (see also chapter 3, where this aspect is considered in more detail). Despite bearing this co-responsibility for the success of the final product, however, text editors usually remain anonymous – their contribution to the published product rarely being publicly acknowledged. In this respect, theirs is a kind of ghostwriter role (see more about this role in chapter 3, section 6).

The intervention in a manuscript is different for translators and text editors, for a number of reasons. First, text editors actively contribute to the creative writing process. Without their dedication, a text would be less accessible and readable because it is the text editor who adapts the original text in such a way that the most optimal communication transfer can take place for its readers. Secondly, unlike translators, text editors have the same audience in mind as the original writer.

The diversity of tasks that falls to text editors is discussed further in section 2 of chapter 3. These include activities that, strictly speaking, fall outside their responsibility: checking for copyright infringements, excising defamatory statements (or libel/slander), checking factual correctness, designing covers, briefing illustrators, doing page layout, proofreading and indexing (more about this in chapter 4). Text editing associations admit that quite a few professional text editors develop these skills in the course of their careers and that they can provide these services. However, if this is the case, then there ought to be clear agreement on what exactly should be delivered (see the SfEP website – http:// www.sfep. org.uk/pub/faqs/fedit.asp).

4 The scope of text editing

> In principle, no TT [target text] is ever 'finished' and 'polished' to the point where it could not be edited further. The practical question is whether further editing will actually improve it. In practice there must, sooner or later ..., come a point where one has to stop tinkering with a TT. However, there is *plenty of work* to be done before that point is reached.
> *Cardinal*

> You write to communicate to the hearts and minds of others what's burning inside you. And we edit to let the fire show through the smoke.
> *Plotnik*

> Generally, what do editors do? ... editors review, rewrite, and edit the work of writers.
> *Beene*

> ... writing, rereading, reviewing, rethinking, rearranging, repairing, restructuring, reevaluating, editing, tightening, sharpening, smoothing, pruning, polishing, punching up, amending, emending, altering, eliminating, transposing, expanding, condensing, connecting, cohering, unifying, perfecting.
> *Cheney*

4.1 The text-production process

The scope or field of text editing can be properly understood only in the context of the entire text production process, that is, from initial concept to final product (see chapter 4): in brief, the author's manuscript (text) is edited, the edited version is laid out (typeset or 'designed') and then the setter's proofs have to be read (at least once, but usually several times) before a (near-)perfect book can go for printing. At the outset of this process, moreover, the text editor may have been asked to put together a representative set of sample features from the manuscript, from which a book designer will create a design unique to the book and its readership.

Editing will take different forms. In some cases, the editor's brief implies following strict rules, for instance where spelling and punctuation are concerned (see chapters 2 and 9). However, in other cases, the focus lies elsewhere: for instance, when making a judgement on grammar, spelling and punctuation issues or when deciding on the efficacy of the page layout (see further chapters 2, 8, 9 and 10). Each stage of the production process involves activities or tasks that are part of the text editor's range of duties (see chapters 3 and 4).

4.2 Tasks and roles of the text editor

In practice, a whole group of people can be involved in the production process from the moment the text leaves the author's desk until the moment it is published (see Gilad 2007; Kotze 1998: 199ff). The process has a relatively fixed pattern:

- first, the text will be read by the content editor, who focuses on content and structure;
- alternatively, if a great deal of rewriting, reshaping and inserting of missing information or features is required, the text may be given to a development editor;
- then it is read by the text editor, who amends the language, grammar, punctuation, style and register, and ensures that the correct meaning is conveyed clearly;
- after that, the page layout and the typography are looked at, and
- finally, the proofreader and possibly the author will read through the text again, followed by the production editor.

The table below illustrates this process.

Tasks and activities	Responsible
Creative writing process	Writer/ghostwriter
Content and structure	Content editor/structural editor/ development editor
Layout	Graphic designer/typesetter
Spelling, grammar, punctuation, register and style	Text editor
Proofreading/corrections	Proofreader and designer/typesetter
Production/preproduction	Production editor/managing editor

Table 1.1 *Tasks and roles during the text-editing process*

The text editor in table 1.1 is often an idealised concept of a person who performs one nicely delineated task. In reality this is not always the case: in recent years, more and more diverse tasks have come to be allocated to one person, namely the text editor. In the correction process a number of important tasks can be combined, namely confirming the correctness of the content; adapting the style; ensuring correct grammar, spelling and punctuation; attending to the author's meaning, tone and register; and checking the typography and layout. Thus, the text editor focuses not only on grammar, but also on language-in-use issues (such as style and register), layout concerns and, most importantly, the clear and correct transmission of the author's intended message in the text. As a result, texture, as a basis for unity (see chapter 2), receives a lot of attention because the verbal and visual features are so tightly interwoven and integrated in the text.

As a consequence of allocating a number of different roles to one person, the terms referring to the profession have become confusing and the boundaries between them somewhat blurred. In the discussion above, it should already have become clear that there are various kinds of 'editor' (cf Beene 2009: 6–8; Judd 1990: 7–19; Kotze 1998: 121–123).

Authors agree that the responsibility of text editors (as people who improve texts until they become excellent) is a great one. In the first instance, text editors need to protect the reputation of authors by showing that they (the authors) are good communicators. Secondly, they also have to guarantee that publishers will not lose any money on the publication (by making sure that nothing of cardinal importance is either omitted or incorrectly stated). Furthermore, they have to ensure an optimal transmission of the author's meaning. Thus, the ideal text editor is someone who takes the audience's interests to heart.

After a thorough analysis of the text, text editing can take the form of editing (ie thoroughly correcting and proofreading the text), producing (helping to write (part of) the text) and providing advice (ie judging the text and proposing how to improve it). The text editor therefore plays an indispensable, though sometimes invisible, role in the complex process of meaning transfer (see chapters 3 and 6–10).

4.3 Types of text editing

Butcher (1992, 2006: 1–2) distinguishes four types of editing jobs that correspond to the demands and taks that were explained above: (1) substantive editing, (2) detailed editing for sense or meaning, (3) checking for consistency, and (4) visual editing (see chapter 3 for a more in-depth discussion of these types).

In the case of *substantive editing*, the editor tries to improve the representation and presentation of the work with respect to its content, length and structure or organisation. The text editor can present the improvements to the author or autonomously rewrite pieces of text. They also keep an eye on plagiarism and other legal problems (such as defamation or libel/slander). In other words, a code of ethics – whether of the individual editor or of a professional association – plays an important role here (see chapter 3).

When *detailed editing for sense* is being carried out, the text editor investigates whether every part is an exact representation of what the author intended to communicate (the intended *meaning*). The text editor also checks whether each part of the text follows logically from the previous one and whether these individual sections together make up a conceptual unity. The editor looks for gaps in the author's argumentation or contradictions in the text and fixes them as much as possible. Here, work is undertaken at a text level.

The third type is *checking for consistency*; it is regarded as vital to achieving a quality end product. It entails, among other things, checking for consistency of spelling and punctuation and adjusting a text to match the publisher's house style; ensuring the consistency of the author's numbering systems; making cross-references consistent; and checking both the design style and the relevance of tables and figures as well as references to illustrations.

Finally, Butcher (1992) distinguishes *clear representation of the material for the typesetter*, in which phase the editor checks whether the text is completely and correctly marked up for typographical treatment by the typesetter or designer. In some quarters this is known as a production edit or a production mark-up or tagging (see chapter 3).

If one person needs to assume all these tasks, then the question arises: What profile does this text editor need to respond to? And, allied to this, what kind of text edit is required?

4.4 Training

Clearly, text editors play a cardinal role in the process of information transmission, but Ezra Pound, writing as an author, remains critical: 'with plenty of printers, plenty of paper, plenty of ink, it is manifestly idiotic that we couldn't have the editions we want' (Pound cited in Bornstein 1994).

Is this complaint justified? And if this is a problem, then how should it be approached? What do companies do to train their text editors and to keep them up to date through offering further training opportunities and support?

The general impression is that text editors work intuitively and with the hindsight of experience (see chapter 3 for a more detailed discussion on this matter). This could create the impression that talent alone is sufficient. However, most text editors have had a solid education (with, among other educational inputs, a firm linguistic background), often in quite diverse fields. Language studies, often even advanced qualifications in languages, appear to be a required starting point. In more recent times communication scientists have also been taken on as text editors.

But as Butcher et al (2006: xii) remark in the highly acclaimed textbook for text editors, *Butcher's copy-editing*, 'new copy-editors could benefit from the accumulated experience of their predecessors rather than having to learn by making their own mistakes', because:

copy-editing is largely a matter of common sense in deciding what to do and of thoroughness in doing it; but these are pitfalls which an inexperienced copy-editor or text editor cannot foresee. This is why it is *learnable*.

Sadly, in most publishing houses that have adopted 'lean and mean' staffing models in recent years, the opportunities for on-the-job training between seasoned mentors and newcomers have been lost inhouse, probably forever, without conscious efforts having been made by the same publishers to put in place succession planning and upskilling in order to restore even some semblance of the skills pool that existed previously. One solution has been to outsource the training function or to send suitable candidates to university courses in publishing studies and the like. On the other hand, the professional associations of editors around the world have taken up the training/skills development/accreditation baton, allied to mentorship schemes, with a view to raising and maintaining professional standards and dealing with the problem of uninitiated newcomers not being able to make themselves (self-)employable as competent practitioners.

In this electronic age, other alternatives to training are possible: for example, a peer system could be beneficial and is quite feasible. This goes beyond the process approach (Gile 1995; Kruger 2007, 2008) that has been dominant so far and it corresponds to new educational views, tendencies and constructivist techniques (Spivey 1997) that focus on performing realistic and genuine tasks in a learner-centred environment (Massey 2005). Goal-oriented collaboration is central here.

The fact that the area of text editing is vast and is often experienced as merely intuitive handiwork is probably an important reason why almost no scientific research has been carried out on the topic. Yet it is precisely this all-encompassing nature of text editing that makes it a linguistically and empirically interesting research area. Most reference works on the topic focus on the practical, normative and prescriptive aspects of text editing or only cover certain practical components of the field (cf Butcher et al 2006; Einsohn 2005; Gilad 2007; Mackenzie 2011; Murphy 2011). The present book on text editing as a discipline is an earnest attempt to combine a theoretical account with practical content. In this way it could also serve as a handbook for the training of text editors. The theoretical basis that focuses on text quality is discussed in detail in chapter 2.

4.5 A profile

Escarpit (quoted in Nyssen 1993) has summarised the text editor's activities in three active verbs: *choisir*, *fabriquer*, *distribuer*: a text editor indeed has to select, create and distribute or disseminate, but Escarpit does not provide clear descriptions of who performs each of these activities. However, an extensive profile is provided on the University of Amsterdam's website http:///www.hum.uva.nl/redacteur_editor (2009), where the editor is described as a *Homo universalis*, because:

Text editors read the manuscripts received and agree with the authors about potential corrections that will improve the quality of the book. In other words, editors should not only have
an excellent and precise command of language but should also be able to grasp more extensive pieces of texts. Furthermore, they will also have to give thought to the cover design,
the target audience, title and price of the book. Editors also have to keep abreast of the real
world, know what other publishers are busy producing, where to find new talent and give
thought to (almost) anything that comes their way: Is there a book in it? [An editor] does not
sit behind a desk all day long, but also takes to the road to attend festivals, book launches, in
search of possible authors. Over and above all of this, text editors are avid readers.
(author's own translation)

Judd (1990: 1) sums up the skills needed for these different tasks: '... close attention to
everyday detail in a manuscript, a thorough knowledge of what to look for and the style
to be followed, and the ability to make quick, logical and defensible decisions.'

Text editing therefore presupposes a certain personality (inquisitive, questioning, with an
eye for detail), a unique knowledge (about linguistics, style and content) and special skills
(acquired through experience) with regard to texts. Plotnik (1982: 39) calls the text editor
a 'crafty editor', because they have to range over so many skills. Text editors are often described with these words: smart, intelligent, clever, bright, awake, willing, curious, sharp,
dedicated and witty – all characteristics that are fed by knowledge and skills. To be something of a detective (à la Sherlock Holmes, Poirot or Miss Marple) is also a useful asset.

Plotnik (1982) divides these skills into six categories: research, strategy, perception, organisation, linguistics and troubleshooting. Each of these skills can be paired up with certain
personality traits. For instance, curious text editors will automatically do research; alert,
thoughtful editors will be perceptive in their approach to the author's content and the
structure of a text; and if text editors lack the skills to organise their daily affairs, they will
probably be incapable of meeting their (often nearly impossible) deadlines.

4.6 Challenges

Text editors are 'the quality-control people; they add value to the final product ... when
quality fails, credibility crumbles' (Auman et al 2001: 140). They add value to the creation
of a written product. Nevertheless, text editing does not appear to be regarded as a high-
status profession. The reasons behind this perception are many, and include:

- *Job burnout* is the first reason why editors resign: 'Job burnout can be characterised as
  a type of withdrawal syndrome from work. ... One probable result of job burnout is to
  quit the job: in effect, to completely withdraw from work' (Cook & Banks 1993: 109).
- *Emotional tiredness* and high degrees of *depersonalisation on the job* are apparently
  more strongly present in editors than in reporters (Cook & Banks 1993: 113). The American Society of Newspaper Editors found in a 1989 research project that the copy desk is
  'the Mount Everest of newsroom discontent' (Gump 1997: 15).
- *Time pressure* is another factor that is increasingly complicating the profession of editing.

'... *time pressure*, new technologies and new duties ... have left less time for traditional editing and have made the copy editor's job more difficult' (Auman et al 2001: 141)

- *Stress* is augmented by the electronic changes, improvements and failures. Also, the lack of training opportunities or an insufficient amount of learning leads to bottled-up frustrations. Nightly shifts, irregular meal times, no or splintered holidays, long working hours and work at weekends seem to be the order of the day rather than the exception. Many text editors cannot deal with this pressure on private and family time. The average inhouse editor is not too satisfied with their salary either (Auman et al 2001).
- *Career prospects* do not seem to be too promising. Kotze (1997) describes the anonymous role of the editor as being very similar to that of a ghostwriter, which leads to the editor's being almost invisible in an organisation and not being considered for promotion as a result. Catalano (1987) describes the problems of editorial staff:

> Doing the majority of their work under cover of night is just one of the institutional factors that conspire to keep copy editors despondent. They are by nature invisible: their names don't appear in the paper like those of reporters, photographers and graphics people. If they do their jobs well, they don't call attention to themselves; it's only when they screw up and a story ends in mid-sentence that the spotlight shines on them.

Auman et al (2001: 145) studied the status of copy-editing within the framework of journalism and they found that creating quality texts rates much lower than finding and writing down interesting stories. This is often reinforced by teaching institutions, which rank writing and reporting much more highly than editing.

The decline in the number of professionals (from the 1990s onwards) might be linked to the status of the job being low. Initiatives towards remedying this perception include job swopping between editors and reporters (limited in time and duration). This is called 'cross-training', and it leads to mutual respect and understanding (Wizda 1997: 38). A more dramatic experiment entailed discontinuing the task of subediting and building topic teams to which were allocated reporters, designers and subeditors. Positive reactions from the participants were one outcome of this experiment (Wizda 1997).

Another initiative has been the 'maestro concept', 'in which big packages are handled by a team that includes all the relevant players' (Wizda 1997: 38). This concept ensures that subeditors have the opportunity to ask questions about sentences, content, etc within a less-demanding and less-intimidating context and that the work is less deadline-driven. Attributing a more central role to the text and with it to knowledge of text-linguistic concepts may also enhance the image of the profession.

Professionalisation of the job through the establishment of professional organisations and associations such as, for instance, SfEP in 1988, PEG in 1993 and ACES (the American Copy Editors Association, established in 1997), has given text editors a voice, but has also provided them with training, networking and information-exchange opportunities, and the possibility of obtaining work (through workshops, online troubleshooting as well as specialised newsletters) and access to resources worldwide (Wizda 1997: 38) (see chapter 3 for more about professionalisation). As Fitzgerald puts it:

> Copy editors need to be part of the decision-making process … They feel as if they are work-ing with their hands shackled, not able to get into a story – not to butcher it – but to be a professional. … Copy editors need recognition. They need a national spokesman. They need somebody standing up for them.

4.7 The text editor as a bridge between publisher, author and reader

There is no doubt that the competent text editor can be – and usually is – an important link between publisher and author. First, the editor is likely to get closer to the author's words than the publisher, and so operates on behalf of the publisher from a position of strength. Secondly, while many publishers (or commissioning editors) are drawn from the ranks of text editors, the latter are more likely to stay abreast of trends regarding editorial mat-ters (when to italicise, which referencing system to use, the introduction of neologisms, newly accepted idiomatic usage, etc) and are often called on for advice by publishers and authors alike. Thirdly, given publishers' own busy schedules and their focus on acquiring new authors and launching new titles to fill gaps in the market, editors tend to be relied upon to liaise directly with authors regarding the text itself. Fourthly, authors for whom writing is difficult or for whom the language of the text is non-native rely heavily on their text editors to 'get the words right' and even restructure fractured text. Novice authors will also value the text editor who plays the mentoring role that is normally the preserve of a publisher. Fifthly, the text editor is often transformed into the proofreader on certain projects, and may also be called upon to handhold the novice author in marking up a set of proofs, and then create a consolidated set of proofs for the typesetter to work from. Finally, in heavily illustrated books, both publisher and author may rely upon the experi-enced editor to play a project-management role in drawing up an artwork brief; editors of academic titles may be called upon to compile a brief for the indexer, if not to index the book themselves, should they be skilled in that area.

Given their often central position in the book-production process, the text editor is fre-quently pressurised from different sides: for one thing, publishers want to (have to) sell a product, but writers are sometimes very touchy about changes to their text. The tighter the production deadlines, the greater the pressure on the editor.

Another source of pressure is the tensions that can arise between writers and editors, which only enhance the feelings of depersonalisation and emotional exhaustion in the latter. Sometimes this is a by-product of the process itself; at other times it ensues from having to work with 'difficult' (ie inflexible or unreasonable) authors, some of whom don't take kindly to text editors 'messing with their words', however correctly or empathetically they do so. This is often the case when the text editor adopts a reader-oriented approach to interven-ing in the text and makes fairly sweeping changes to it, earning the wrath of a self-centred or arrogant author in the process. Such situations call for the utmost tact and diplomacy.

The management at newspapers and magazines have it in their power to change the unsatisfactory and often unhealthy environments in which writers and editors work (Cook & Banks 1993: 48):

> One area that seems to contribute to job burnout is poor newsroom management. Countless copy editors tell me they get no respect and their ideas are often ignored. Copy editors want to feel part of the team. They want to be included in news and packaging decisions. They want to know that their opinions and ideas count in producing the newspapers.

For different reasons and pressures, practitioners who work on learning materials for schools, in particular, which require exceptional attention to a high degree of detail for protracted periods in order to meet very unreasonable deadlines, may harbour similar feelings.

Project managers clearly have to adopt a more human face: in their interactions with text editors, respect, recognition, the valuing of inputs, team spirit, positive motivation and co-responsibility should be high on the agenda. Moreover, the expectations of the readers also have to be met (Butcher 1992: 2; Butcher et al 2006: 2):

> The main aims of copy-editing are to remove any obstacles between the reader and what the author wants to convey, and also to save time and money by finding and solving any problems before the book is typeset, so that production can go ahead without interruption.

The editor is presented with the same problem as the translator: the decision has to be made whether the text has to remain as close as possible to the original or the text has to be brought closer to the target audience. In the first case, as little as possible is changed in the original; in the second the style can be adapted if required and if the text editor deems it necessary. This dilemma, which concerns the degree of adaptation, is closely connected to the problem of the ethics that surround text editing: how much of the author's original text can be changed? To what extent are adaptations to the style acceptable?

In an attempt to answer these questions, Fryer (1997: 30) compares the task of a text editor (whom he calls a 'language editor') with that of a surgeon and claims that:

> text editing is a profession and the editor is a versatile and professional person, not only responsible for taking care of the text, but (like a surgeon) also playing a role in interhuman relations, here within the publishing world, for which text editors should be acknowledged. *(our translation)*

Both editor and surgeon play a mediating role and have to be recognised for it. The task of text editors is a complex one because they may carry out several tasks and have to take up a position in between the publisher, writer and reader. These roles may well be in conflict with one another and the text editor has to reconcile them. As Kotze (1997) explains: the reader wants a text that is reader-friendly, error free and interesting. It has to be the publisher's mission to produce quality products. The editor has to meet the expectations of the author, publisher and reader. A text full of mistakes and tiresome, irrelevant and outdated information may well upset the readers, perhaps even putting them off reading to the end. The text editor's brief should be to prevent that happening, even at all costs.

A considerable number of authors do not like the idea of a text editor going through their texts. The relationship between author and editor is therefore a delicate balancing act because both in different ways and degrees claim authorship of a text (Beene 2009: 6–7). Therefore, they are susceptible to each other's criticism (Clark & Fry 1992: 3):

> Writers hate editors who butcher prose, suppress creativity and turn exciting experiments into tired formulas. Editors hate writers who indulge themselves and forget the needs of readers. Traditionally both groups would rather bitch and moan than consult and collaborate.

The collaboration between the different parties is not always plain sailing all the time, as becomes clear from the following anecdote (Wizda 1997a):

> Red-markered copy in hand, he went back to the editor on duty, who promptly forbade him from changing a word unless it was spelled wrong. 'This has been approved by the lawyers, and so we're not going to make any of these changes …'

This is a pity, of course, because a harmonious, productive interaction between editor and author usually enhances the production process (speeds it up and facilitates it), and the final product might be more satisfying (qualitatively). In the end, a qualitative relationship between the text editor and the reader is the main objective and must thus occupy a central place in the text editor's professional aims (Plotnik 1982: 25):

> An editor's only permanent alliance is with the audience, the readership. It is the editor's responsibility to hook that readership; to edify it, entertain it, stroke it, shake it up – do whatever is necessary to keep the medium hot and desirable for the people who support it. The editor, not the author, best understands that readership.

So the question that remains is this: Which are the theoretical foundations that the editor can fall back on in order to fulfil all the requirements of their professional interventions?

5 Theoretical frameworks revisited

> … a copy editor makes certain that a manuscript becomes a published work, and that task requires an individual with *knowledge, decisiveness, top-notch writing skills, and diplomacy.*
> *Beene*
>
> I am drawn to those areas of linguistics that are concerned with *language in context* … applied linguists and typographers have much to learn from each other.
> *Walker*

In order to define the theoretical framework within which text editing functions, we must go back in history. Clouse (1992: 86) defines the task of the text editor more broadly than the traditionally subservient role, since the text editor plays an important part in helping to write a book: 'It is the primary task of the text editor to *rework* the text of an author in such a way that it becomes more precise, more consistent and more meaningful than the original text.'

In order to obtain this more precise, more consistent and more meaningful result, a number of (re)writing phases have to be gone through. Not only can there be many such phases, but the same holds true for the ways in which to edit, since they depend on the type of text: consider the differences between scientific publications and literary texts, press reviews, electronic media, multimedia, etc. The task of the text editor is therefore multi-faceted and relies, among other things, on a combination of text-linguistic insights and a mastery of the language in question (relying on one's normative and textual knowledge). The many-sidedness of the profession makes it difficult to define the text editor's role precisely or to define their tasks exhaustively (but see chapter 2, where a model for doing so is described); but their role can be summed up broadly as manipulating language, content and layout in such a way that the communication between author and reader is optimised, or at least facilitated. This suggests that the text editor's task is process-based and relies heavily on basic communication models that can be traced back to classical rhetorics.

5.1 Classical rhetorics

Classical rhetorics forms the basis of present-day disciplines such as sociology, linguistics, public relations and literary criticism (Howes 1965; Kastely 1997). It is seen as 'a politically and ethically established style of teaching effective public speaking' (Kastely 1997: 2). Aristotle, Cicero and Quintillianus distinguished five components of rhetorics: invention, arrangement, style, memory and delivery (Howes 1965: 4; Kastely 1997: 1–2).

According to Howes (1965: 4), rhetorics involves two activities: composition and rhetorics. Composition leads to discourse or text, a text that is read or listened to. It is the process leading to the product. Rhetorics aims at the analysis of the discourse in such a way that the structure can be determined; that is, it is the analysis of the product.

Text editing operates at two levels. The editor has to have an in-depth understanding of how a particular type of discourse works before touching or possibly re-orienting the process of composition and redesigning the final product. In this way, the editor can become part of the writing process and gain a certain degree of 'authorship' as ghostwriter and re-writer of a text. They also play an important role in the area of text analysis and evaluation, because the result of these processes can be presented as advice about the text which can lead to an adaptation of the original text to better fit in with its objective and readership.

Aristotle claimed that rhetorics does not necessarily have to be regarded as the art of convincing, that is, persuasive communication, 'but as the art capable of discerning the *available means of persuasion* in any given case' (cited in Kastely 1997: 11). These means include variables such as textual elements, adaptation of the message to a specific audience and its needs, the text's pragmatics or context and different types of style. So, if we follow Aristotle, text editing will be heavily involved in the textual aspects of documents. The text editor has to recognise the means of persuasion and bring them in line with the message, source or sender, the audience (readers or listeners), the channel along which the message is sent, and the code or the message. In other words, the text editor must be aware of the different components of the communication process and, consequently, also of the communication process itself as a whole.

5.2 Communication models

The most basic model representing communication leads us back to the Greek philosophers who proposed a threefold structure: a first person talks to a second person about a third person or thing in the presence or absence of a witness (a structure reflected in the Greek verb declination). This distinction was systematically developed within a linguistic framework by Bühler (1933). He distinguished three elements: representation (relying on a topic), expression (related to the speaker) and vocation (focusing on the listener). Jakobson (1960) renamed Bühler's concepts as referential (denotative or cognitive), emotive (attitudinal) and conative (focusing on the addressee) and linked them to the components of the communication process. Whenever language focuses on one of these components – that is, sender, receiver, message, field of reference, channel or code – a specific linguistic function is being activated. When studying the components, it becomes clear that language is not reduced or reducible to the above three functions, that is, denotative, emotive and conative. It can have different additional functions, such as the aesthetic or metacommunicative (both in their own way focusing on the code), appellative (focusing on the audience or addressee) and phatic (focusing on the (psychological) channel).

Lyons (2001) has distinguished three types of information transmission: descriptive, expressive and social. Halliday (1976) chose to use the labels 'ideational', 'interpersonal', 'expressive' and 'textual meaning'. Since language serves a general 'ideational' function, we are able to use it for all the specific purposes and situation types involving the communication of experience. We are able to use it for all the specific forms of personal and social interaction, since it also serves a general 'interpersonal' function. The textual function refers to text creation and is a prerequisite of the effective operation of the other two functions (Halliday & Hasan 1976: 25). If we look at the role of the text editor in the communication process, we can conclude the following: the text editor is one of the receivers in the original transmission process. The text editor is not the unique nor the intended receiver of the text, but the one member of the audience whose task it will be to enhance the text's communicative capacities.

After reworking the text (the text-editing process), the text editor will again become the sender of the text (Jakobson 1960). As such the text editor is a mediator or facilitator but also a referee in two communication systems which often are making use of the same code or language (Hermans 1996: 2; Jakobson 1960). They therefore act as a mediator in the tension between intended and received meaning (Hatim & Mason 1990: 223) and they have to weigh this tension and minimise it as much as possible so that the meaning can be transmitted to its fullest potential possible (Lefevere 1999: 75). As such, they will act as the director of the transmission process, aiming at optimising the communication attempt (cf Van den Broeck & Lefevere 1979: 10; Lefevere 1999: 75; Kotze & Verhoef 2001: 83–84).

The 'language practitioner' – a term that includes translators, interpreters and text editors – occupies a central position in the mediation of differences in approach towards communicative, pragmatic and semiotic (symbolic) meaning (Hatim & Mason 1990: 236ff). Language practitioners must have an insight into the ideological and cultural environment of meaning and into the way in which language communities interpret reality (Hatim & Mason 1990: 337). Communicative mediation deals primarily with correlating intended and received information. Pragmatic mediation focuses on finesses in language usage and the way in which context is included in language usage. Finally, semiotic mediation refers to the way in which the language practitioner and text editor succeed in incorporating the underlying socio-ideological sign system into the process.

The process of the transmission of meaning is studied in semiotics, 'the communication of any message whatever' (Jakobson 1960). Sebeok adds to this that it is about the 'exchange ... of the systems which underlie them' (1994: 106), something the text editor has to be aware of. He treats language and language usage not only in terms of their communicative value but also from the perspective of language as a modelling system (Sebeok 1994: 114, 125). Furthermore, semiotics deals with the question of how messages are generated, encoded, sent, decoded and interpreted, and the way in which language plays a role when reflecting the conceptual world of language communities (Dirven & Verspoor 1999: 1). According to Sebeok (1994: 125), the transmission of messages seems to move to the background:

> Languages – consisting of a set of features that promotes fitness – can best be thought of as having been built by selection for the cognitive function of modelling, and, as the philosopher Popper and the linguist Chomsky have ... insisted, not at all for the message-swapping function of communication.

For the purpose of text editing this means that not only normative language questions are an issue (eg the use of capital letters, full stops and commas; see further section 4 in chapter 2) but also whether the use of a certain language (style) is adequate in a given situation.

Indeed, text editing transcends the normative. It is possible for the text editor to analyse and assess the message in the widest sense of the word and not only get it right (by restructuring and remedying it) but also to formulate advice on how to enhance the communicative process. This process and these outcomes are typical not only of the profession of text editor, but also of the related professions that try to make language and texts more accessible.

5.3 Text editing and the study of text

The text itself takes up a central position in the text-editing process. Since text can carry both a personal and a social meaning, it can be a remarkably powerful instrument that ought to be used correctly. The realisation that a text can take on as diverse functions as being persuasive or manipulative depending on word choice and sentence construction emphasises the necessity of critical text evaluation and of knowing the target audience in order to ensure that a fair transmission of information takes place. The dangers of densification or obfuscation and oversimplification or conversationalisation are always at hand, and language is, of course, never value-neutral. The analysis of language and its effect on people is part of the study domain of critical applied linguistics (Cook 2003; Pennycook 2001; Seidelhofer 2003); and when text is placed within its social context as part of a process of social change, then it becomes part of the study domain of critical discourse analysis (De Beaugrande 2009):

Critical discourse analysis (CDA) is an interdisciplinary approach to the study of discourse that views language as a form of social practice and focuses on the ways social and political domination are reproduced by text and talk.

Texts reflect reality and reality in itself is in turn a reflection of texts. Because communication always takes place through the medium of text, a text-theoretical foundation is of increasing importance in language training, translation training, text-editing training, etc, or, as De Beaugrande quotes: 'The creation of a linguistic text theory is thus urgent not only for linguistics, but for society at large' (Isenberg 1976: 47, cited in De Beaugrande 2009).

According to this view, text theory is a core component of any study of text quality. If one combines this idea with the principles of textuality (as developed by De Beaugrande & Dressler 1981) that can be used to differentiate between a text and a non-text, then it becomes clear why the study of these determining principles of text formation is important to text editing and to the professional text editor.

5.4 Text editing as applied linguistics

As has been stated above, text is central to the concept of text editing, and a study of the creative aspects of intervention in texts is necessary. So is a problem-solving approach to the difficulties that can be experienced in the creation and understanding of texts. Such an approach is therefore a natural core component of the study of text editing. For this reason, the discipline of text editing is part of the study domain of applied linguistics.

This domain can be defined, on the one hand, as 'a discipline which can be used to investigate problems in many areas of language study' (Crystal 2008); on the other hand, the discipline also serves 'to propose a solution to social problems involving language' (Davies 2004). Both the investigation and the solution models of applied linguistics can therefore contribute to the development of text editing. Davies (2004: 100) summarises this view:

The correctness issue presents itself as a language problem to the applied linguist in two ways. First, as an issue which, as we have seen, is constantly drawn to the attention of students in particular and of the public more generally. *The applied linguist has a professional responsibility to take a serious interest in all aspects of the issue*, including public concern. Second, the applied linguist, in person or in writing, *is properly called on for guidance about the choices of usage* students, and indeed all of us, must make.

It is in this light that the linguistic disciplines which are important for acquiring more scientific insights into text editing as a developing discipline (eg the CCC model, text linguistics, normative linguistics and document design) are discussed in detail in the next chapter.

6 Summary

> Even if your grammar and spelling skills are good, copy-editing still might not be your cup of tea. If you find it frustrating to have to accept an author's style you don't like or a publisher's house style that you find sadly inadequate, or if you find it impossible to do a less-than-perfect job (if that's what the client wants), then again this probably isn't the job for you.
> *Society for Editors and Proofreaders (SfEP)*

The objective of this first chapter was to explore the fields of language and text editing by giving an overview of definitions of the domain and the profession; of the roles, tasks and profiles of people involved in it; and also of the theoretical models within which all of these facets are investigated. Rather than providing answers, this overview shows that there is a degree of vagueness about the precise role and task of text editors, about the domains providing the foundations for the study of the discipline, and about the best form of training.

This handbook is an attempt to flesh out some content to this relatively vague sketch; turning this vagueness into greater precision will be a task for many research projects to come. We have considered the complexity of the profession to be central to our argumentation. This complexity and versatility will become increasingly evident as we try to lend more weight to our arguments and assertions.

Text as a domain of text editing: an applied model

... information about the foundation of text editing as theoretical subdiscipline is virtually nonexistent.
Kruger

... prescriptivism – the view that one variety of a language has an inherently higher value than others and ought to be the norm for the whole of the speech community.
Crystal

The problem with defending the purity of the English language is that English is about as pure as a cribhouse whore. We don't just borrow words; on occasion, English has pursued other languages down alleyways to beat them unconscious and rifle their pockets for new vocabulary.
James D Nicoll

Contents

Objectives

This chapter aims to show (a) the importance of the accessibility and readability of a text and (b) how the text editor can be helped to determine text quality in a systematic way. To this end, we (c) present the CCC model as an objective tool for diagnosing textual problems and (d) introduce its foundational knowledge of normative linguistics, text linguistics and document design. Finally, we (e) indicate how these disciplines contribute to a better understanding of the application of the CCC model.

1 Introduction

This chapter focuses on text as an object of study and also as an applied manifestion of language practice. Editors work with texts daily, but what exactly is meant by the term 'text' and which approaches can be used to analyse and adapt a text to make it an optimal component that contributes to a body of writing as a communicative unit? Creating a good text is a dynamic and multifaceted process inspired by a combination of factors (eg the author and a deadline), skills (eg experience in writing for a particular audience) and technologies (familiarity with word processors, spell- and grammar-checkers and terminological databases).

In this chapter we show how the quality of an edited text can be evaluated and improved by and large with the help of the CCC model developed by the Dutch linguist, Jan Renkema (1996, 2004, 2005, 2008). We also demonstrate that a foundational knowledge of normative linguistics and text linguistics as well as document design is essential to applying the model in practice. In the life and work of text editors these aspects should therefore play a cardinal role.

2 Text as an object of study

2.1 Communication through texts

Before looking at different ways of treating texts, we have to introduce some basic terminology: text and communication, in particular.

Human beings typically use one or other form of text in order to express themselves and exchange messages (whether in speech or in writing) in the diverse contexts of everyday life. The word 'text' comes from the Latin *textus*, meaning the wording of anything written and the texture of a work, which literally refers to something woven. Communication is an activity central to human functioning and implies 'making common' (from Latin *communis*) or 'sharing, dividing out, imparting, informing, joining, uniting, participating in' (from Latin *communicare*) (online *Etymology dictionary*). A considerable part of communication is verbal (and oral), that is, making use of words; it is studied from different angles in disciplines such as:

- syntax (structure)
- morphology (word formation)
- phonetics and phonology (sound)
- semantics (meaning)
- pragmatics (usage)
- sociolinguistics (social or societal), etc.

The context in which language is used to communicate is dealt with by:

- semantics (the study of meaning)
- pragmatics (the study of usage)
- document design (the study of the integration of words and visuals)
- discourse analysis (the study of meaningful language units).

Communication involves at least two interacting parties: a sender (writer or speaker) and a receiver (reader or listener), which makes it by definition a social activity. Consequently, when human beings engage through language, social challenges are to be met which can be adequately discussed in an applied linguistics framework since this framework proposes 'solutions to social problems involving language' (Davies 2004).

Applied linguistics is mainly concerned with understanding knowledge-based skills in a diversity of domains, such as language education, computer-mediated language usage, languages in contact, translation and cultural mediation, speech therapy, language pathology, forensic contexts, and medical and business communication (cf Candlin & Sarangi (eds) 2011; Chen & Cruickshank 2009; Cook & Seidlhofer 1995; Cook & North 2009; Davies 2004, 2005, 2007; Davies & Elder 2006; Grabe 2002; Hall, Smith & Wickasono 2011; Hudson 1999; Hunston & Oakey 2009; Simpson (ed) 2011; Wei & Cook (eds) 2009). Since its establishment as an independent discipline in the middle of the last century, applied linguistics has grown in scope, which explains why it is so difficult to encapsulate the domain of applied linguistics in one definition. Spolsky proposes an overarching definition that leaves room for subdisciplines to develop autonomously (2005: 36, as quoted in Davies 2007: 2):

> The definition of a field can reasonably be explored by looking at the *professionals* involved in its study ... Applied linguistics [is now] a *cover term* for a sizeable group of *semi-autonomous disciplines*, each dividing its parentage and allegiances between the formal study of language and other *relevant* fields, and each working to develop its own methodologies and principles.

Hudson (1999) highlights the problem-solving capacities of applied linguistics with respect to different forms of authentic language use, which results in a diversification of domains to which it can relate (http://www.phon.ucl.ac.uk/home/dick/AL.html):

> The main distinguishing characteristic of AL [applied linguistics] is its concern with *professional activities* whose aim is to solve 'real-world' language based problems, which means that research touches on a particularly wide range of issues – psychological, pedagogical, social, political and economic as well as linguistic.

This broad applicability automatically leads to applied linguistics being interdisciplinary or, as Poole (2002: 73) puts it: 'Applied linguistics ... is widely seen as relevant to any *real-world, language-related* problem that an *interdisciplinary*, as opposed to purely linguistic, approach can address.'

The fact that the discipline is rooted in real life and in human interaction involving language from which it draws its data makes it possible for researchers to inventorise, systematise, describe and possibly present different explanations for the 'problems' that language users experience in their daily lives. In doing so, researchers rely on knowledge from other disciplines often unrelated to the world of language (such as facts about the surrounding world) in order to describe systematically and critically what is going on and to present potential solutions to real-life language challenges.

One of those potential language-related challenges is the quality of written texts. Texts are supposed to communicate as they are without subtitles, manuals or voice-overs. Unlike in face-to-face interactions, there is no opportunity to explain, highlight, redefine or defuse potential hostility because of miscommunication or misunderstanding. Even though writing and proofing processes are meant to produce an effective means of communication, not all texts are optimally accessible and understandable or appropriate to their recipients. Starting from the intended audience, a text can be a weak form of communication if it uses an inappropriate style, an inappropriate register, inaccurate grammar or spelling, exceedingly long or complex sentences, an incorrect paragraph division, an unsuitable typography, overtly complex terminology, etc.

Since different strands of meaning are intertwined in a text, the context and world it is embedded in and the medium and code it is transmitted through, understanding can be a complex undertaking on the part of the receiver who reads it from his or her perspective devoid of its original intention (Jakobson 1960). Any potential obstacle to effective understanding has to be removed by making use of knowledge of different linguistic insights. In this chapter we draw on three linguistic disciplines in order to try to understand the textual features that can improve this process and, consequently, the text quality. First, however, in the following paragraphs, the meaning of the term 'text' is briefly explained before the problems of text understanding and text quality are discussed.

2.2 The concept of 'text'

> Understanding a text is an active process of constructing meaning from the signals
> that a writer provides. And composing a text is an active process of constructing
> meaning from a text and using textual cues to signal meaning to readers.
> *Spivey*

Text as an object of research has mainly been studied within the context of text linguistics (De Beaugrande & Dressler 1981; Mellet & Longrée (eds) 2009; Trappes-Lomax 2006) or discourse analysis (Harris 1952; Van Dijk 1972, (ed) 1985, 2000, (ed) 2007, 2008, 2010). On the basis of the literature, Carstens (1997: 17–82) provides an overview of more than 80 possible definitions of the term 'text', which should make it clear that it is not easy to define the term precisely because of the multitude of possible interpretations from different angles. From these definitions, one can deduce that a text typically has the following features:

List 2.1 Text features

> › A text is the result of human activity: on the basis of a communicative process a product (ie the text) is created.
>
> › A text is a communicative and coherent unit.
>
> › A text has a specific semantic, syntactic and morpho-phonological structure.
>
> › A text has a specific texture (what makes text coherent) and it forms a unit (unity).
>
> › A text is created within a specific context.
>
> › The length of a text is unspecified.
>
> › A text has specific functions.
>
> › The nature and the form of texts differ depending on their function.

From these features one can deduce the following description of a text (Carstens 1997: 79):

> ... a *coherent* unit of language use which has a specific (syntactic and morphological) *structure* and fulfils a clear semantic *function* in a specific *context,* ie to enable communicative contacts between human beings. The *length* of a text, which can range from a word to a series of books, and the *form* in which it is delivered, which can cover diverse spoken or written genres, are solely determined by the ultimate *communicative purpose* of the text.
> *(our translation)*

Note that the concept of text in this definition includes both spoken and written genres. On the basis of this description it is possible to formulate the following linguistic working definition: 'A text is a stretch of language use which the textual partners involved experience and accept as a communicative unit on syntactic, semantic and pragmatic grounds' (Carstens 1997: 81, our translation).

This working definition corresponds to Enkvist's view (1991: 7–8) on the communicative features by which text quality can be measured, namely:

- *Intelligibility*: text has a unique syntactic, morphological and lexical structure.
- *Comprehensibility*: every text has a fixed meaning or a semantic structure.
- *Interpretability*: a text has to be placed within its context, that is, within the actual environment in which it is used.

It can be concluded, then, that each text has a fixed structure which reflects a recognisable unity that also fulfils the demand for comprehensibility. The goal of the text-editing process is to ensure that the final draft of the text is the most complete and polished product that can be attained before communication can take place without a problem.

The issue of cohesion, coherence and unity is clearly established, so we can state that a text has a typical structure that serves to transfer content and that it also has a certain communicative goal. This can even be taken one step further by stating that the aim also determines the ultimate structure of the text: a text communicates the message and the content that a creator (the writer) wants to transfer to a receiver (the potential reader) in a particular format.

Typically, a text is created in stages. First, every text has (or at least should have) a clear plan which determines how the text is to be created and what its aim is. Of course, that plan is built around the theme of the text, that is, around the topic to be discussed. For instance, a report (as an example of one text type) would have the following text plan: introduction, problem statement, explanation and discussion of the problem, and eventually a conclusion and, sometimes, recommendations. This plan is executed with the aid of functional text units (such as words, sentences and paragraphs) that are connected in certain ways (following the principles of coherence and cohesion). The plan is then implemented in different phases: the planning phase (determining the aim and how it can be attained), the conceptualisation phase (organising the ideas), the formulation phase (translating ideas into language), the structuring phase (putting language elements in the correct order) and, finally, the realisation phase (the final product – a number of drafts).

Following basic language principles, such as spelling and punctuation conventions (see chapter 9), helps to create order in the text and improve its quality so that it communicates optimally. A text, therefore, is more than a random collection of language elements; rather, it is the result of a number of intertwined processes, each consisting of different phases that result in a coherent text. The task of the text editor is to aid this process in such a way that the final product communicates perfectly, right away.

2.3 Measuring text quality

If you intend to write a text, decide beforehand what you want to write about, which information has to be related and how the information has to be ordered.
Tol-Verkuyl (our translation)

In truth, the communication of content does not always happen according to plan and steps often have to be taken to evaluate the quality of a text – and usually to effect amendments to improve it. In section 3 of this chapter we introduce and describe in detail a particular model as the basis for evaluating texts objectively and thoroughly; in sections 4 and 5 we describe some text-linguistic and normative approaches to evaluating and intervening in texts; for now we consider text quality generally and the criteria to harness when having to identify weaknesses and effect improvements.

Within the framework of text linguistics, there are seven principles (or criteria) of textuality to which language-in-use must adhere in order to be accepted as 'a text' (De Beaugrande & Dressler 1981). Any text of quality must display:

List 2.2 The seven principles (or criteria) of textuality

> › Cohesion: the unity of the text's surface elements, that is, the words and sentences on paper or onscreen.
>
> › Coherence: thematic unity and the logical flow of the text.
>
> › Intentionality: the intention of creating the text – What message does the creator want to transfer?
>
> › Acceptability: the willingness of the receiver to read the text and evaluate whether the goal has been achieved.
>
> › Contextuality: the context in which the text is written, including the intercultural competencies needed in order to understand it.
>
> › Informativity: the extent of information-sharing and the way in which information is presented.
>
> › Intertextuality: the way in which texts are interwoven and the similarities that they display.

In practice, it is not always possible for all seven criteria to be applied simultaneously to enable communication to take place (cf Renkema 1987: 295–296; Renkema 2001; Hubbard 1989), but the criteria (both individually and combined) are nevertheless considered to be a good starting point for determining text quality. For this reason, having a knowledge of text linguistics should be an important component of a text editor's armoury, because the discipline helps the practitioner to appreciate that a text does not just 'happen', but that it is the result of a complex process in which a diverse range of factors have to be taken into account. (This is discussed further in section 7 of this chapter.)

When discussing text quality in the context of normative linguistics, the focus should be on the importance of good and correct language usage in general (Bartsch 1987) and on how to make judgements about texts in particular. Research in the field of text quality has shown that the occurrence of language and spelling errors does not necessarily imply that a text is weak or that it does not communicate well; rather, it leads to readers' forming negative impressions of the text and its writer, and to the assumption that overall the text has been carelessly and unprofessionally put together (De Jong & Schellens 1997). Sloppiness in language, spelling and punctuation can even diminish readers' trust in a writer and the content. As a result, the writer is viewed as anything but serious and professional. In the light of these possible adverse effects, a text editor is justified in making sound judgement calls on the basis of a solid knowledge of the normative grammar of a specific language (see below).

Normative and text–linguistic insights also form the basis of the CCC model as developed by the Dutch linguist, Jan Renkema (1996, 2000: 27ff, 2004: 180–187, 2008: 37–47; Renkema & Kloet 2000). Since it has considerable potential as an objective tool for evaluating text quality and improving texts, this model is described in detail in the next section.

3 The CCC model and text quality

> One of the main causes of the failure to get information across to the reader is the lack of quality of a text.
> *Renkema*

3.1 The CCC model: background

During the text-editing process, practitioners must probe the text by asking themselves – and obtaining answers to – these fairly typical questions:

List 2.3 Questions about text quality

1. Is the text appropriate to the target group?

2. Is the information relevant, logical and correct?

3. Is the text logically structured?

4. Is the text coherent?

5. Is the text linguistically correct?

6. Are the word choice and sentence structure suitable for the language level of the target group?

7. Is the layout clear, meaningful and pleasing to the eye?

A little reflection will show that these questions can be organised and diversified to reflect the natural process that a critical receiver of a communication will go through. But they also give rise to more probing questions:

- Is there a foundational taxonomy or model?
- If so, how can it be applied to improve the reader's understanding of a text?
- Which criteria should be applied when amending a text?
- Are there any limitations to the model?

Direct answers to these types of question are provided by Renkema's CCC model, which takes its name from the three main criteria for diagnosing the quality of a text and implementing remediation: correspondence, consistency and correctness. What are the meanings behind these labels? Three simple questions should begin to reveal them immediately:

- Is there correspondence between the intention of the writer and the expectations and needs of the reader(s)?
- Does the text fulfil the requirement of consistency (ie are all like or similar elements treated in the same way throughout)?
- Are the language, grammar, spelling and punctuation usage and the content correct?

Moreover, the practitioner should also be aware that the following factors can be involved (and they sometimes interfere) in the process of diagnosing textual quality:

- interhuman factors (the message needs to be transferred between writer and reader);
- intertextual factors (the text has to be embedded in a context to which it refers), and
- the text itself (the message takes a particular form which can be dense or multilayered).

Renkema (1996, 2004: 180–183) has indicated that, without firm or meaningful guidelines, it is not always easy to judge the quality of a text and often only subjective opinions are involved of the kind: 'I like this text', 'This is just terrible, unreadable', 'There's nothing I can do to improve it' or 'This will need only a light edit' (whatever that means – see chapter 3). Indeed, there is no set-in-stone truth about the criteria for evaluating a text. Sometimes, for example, a text is simply too complicated for a particular audience, or it is too long; or it does not fit the expectations and background of the target group; or the structure is unclear, the pages are too full; or it is flawed by language errors.

Regardless of the reasons why texts do not work, there is a clear need to measure whether the author's final draft communicates as effectively as it should. Renkema devised his CCC model as a more objective tool for diagnosing any textual problems needing attention. The model is constructed so as to help the text editor evaluate well-defined textual elements so that clearly identified problems can be ironed out and the information transmission function of a text can be enhanced.

Renkema (1996: 325, 2008: 46–47) has also pointed out that the term 'model' should be viewed as a theory-based method that proposes a systematic approach to analysing a text with the aim of improving it. Apart from that, the model can also be used by authors as a means of verifying and, if necessary, adapting the different tasks and phases of the writing process. In the process, judgements about texts can be made more systematic. Inevitably, though, authors and editors will ask searching questions about the model such as:

- Does text revision on the basis of this model lead to better texts?
- Does the model help to identify and correct the problems that readers experience with texts?

The model largely succeeds in answering these questions in the affirmative – a reason it has become widely accepted for evaluating text quality.

3.2 Rationale behind the adoption of the CCC model

Not everyone agrees that the CCC model is the be-all-and-end-all of text evaluation. Blijzer & Kloet (1999), for example, question the categorisation of the evaluation points (see further below, where this term is explained) and argue that several evaluation points could be defined differently or could be elaborated upon, something which was done in a recent publication by Daniëls (2011). Elling & Lentz (2003) question the predictive strength of the model. They conducted an experiment where one participant group used the model while a second group did not, but relied on their own personal judgement instead. The results showed that the differences between the evaluations of the two groups were minimal, from which the researchers concluded that the model does not predict text quality sufficiently well and therefore does not significantly contribute to making text evaluation any more objective.

A further criticism is that the model is experienced by some as being too cumbersome or too abstract. Renkema (2008: 46–47) himself admitted that the model might be too abstract, and that it might be more helpful to use concrete linguistic features such as sentence length, the use of passives, or the number of subordinate clauses per sentence to evaluate text quality. However, these concrete examples are all covered by the model's evaluation points and can therefore be evaluated from within the model.

For text editors it is important to have a starting point (be it a model or a taxonomy) for determining either where a text succeeds in communicating or is less communicative and from there to fix whatever problems there may be. The CCC diagnostic model provides just this. For this reason, it can be used as a sound theoretical basis for judging the quality of a text, and identifing and rectifying flaws, based on a practitioner's sound knowledge of, for instance, normative linguistics (eg the conventions of grammar, spelling and punctuation), text linguistics (eg cohesion, coherence and informativity) and the basics of document design (eg font types and sizes, text widths and alignment, numbering systems and paragraphing) (about which see sections 6, 7 and 8 in this chapter).

Moreover, the model also offers a vehicle for verifying whether all the components of the writing process have been taken into account; and the evaluation points also point discreetly at which knowledge is needed. The nature of the knowledge needed to enhance text quality has immediate implications for text editors' profiles (see chapter 3) and, more specifically, for the skills they have to acquire in order to perform optimally. However, it will become clear in the next section that the practitioner must also have a broad range of knowledge (that is, knowledge about the starting points and application of normative linguistics, text linguistics and document design) and also that they have to acquire the necessary skills within an appropriate environment (for instance, training at an institute of higher education or with a skilled and experienced industry-specific training provider, or an internship with a professional language bureau or in the editorial department of a publishing house). In such contexts, this model can form a sound basis for teaching the trainee editing practitioner their craft.

3.3 The CCC model explained and applied

The CCC model consists of the following elements:

- Three criteria for the analysis of quality: *correspondence, consistency* and *correctness.*
- These three criteria can be measured through five text facets, namely *text type, content, structure, wording* and *presentation.* These text facets are the different perspectives from which we can view a text.
- The combination of criteria and text facets gives rise to 15 evaluation points on the basis of which text quality can be measured.

In reality, editing a text should be considered as a holistic intervention, but for reasons of quality control every text can be broken down into a number of components: the text facets, for instance, are always evaluated against the three criteria. In the following figure, the criteria and text facets are placed so that they relate to each other, which creates 15 benchmarks or evaluation points (eg 1: Appropriate correspondence between text type and readers; 8: Consistency through uniformity of structure; 15: Correct spelling, punctuation, layout and typography as elements of presentation) according to which texts are evaluated and the text editor then takes the appropriate remedial action. These 15 evaluation points have been defined to cover pretty well all the possible facets of a document that are likely to require the text editor's remedial intervention.

Text facets	Criteria for analysis of text quality		
	Correspondence	Consistency	Correctness
A. Text type	1. Appropriate text	2. Unity of genre	3. Application of genre rules
B. Content	4. Appropriate and sufficient information	5. Congruence of facts	6. Facts
C. Structure	7. Sufficient cohesion	8. Uniformity of structure	9. Linking words and argumentation
D. Wording	10. Appropriate wording	11. Unity of style	12. Syntax, vocabulary and meaning
E. Presentation	13. Appropriate layout and typography	14. Congruence between text and layout	15. Spelling, punctuation, layout and typography
	15 evaluation points		

Figure 2.1 *The CCC model for text quality (text facets × criteria for analysis)*

We first explain the model's main components, as illustrated in figure 2.1, and then consider the evaluation points in greater depth.

3.3.1 Criteria for determining text quality

When evaluating a document, the three main conditions, or criteria, for assessing its quality and where remediation may be required are these:

- *Correspondence*: The authors of texts always have an aim in mind that they would like to accomplish. If they succeed at achieving their aim or intention and manage to satisfy the need(s) or expectation(s) of the reader(s) at the same time, then the text will fulfil the quality condition for correspondence. For this to happen successfully, there must be agreement, or correspondence, between what the writer wishes to convey (eg information about a certain subject) and what the reader or readers want to know. The writer often has to make assumptions about what has to be conveyed to the reader (adopting a reader-centred approach) and the editor's role is to gauge whether correspondence has been achieved.

  This criterion is usually regarded as being the most important requirement that needs to be fulfilled in any communication process. There must therefore be a good balance between aim or intention and need in order to prevent the kinds of correspondence error that do arise when there is a lack of congruence. For instance, it may be that a reader receives too little information to respond appropriately, or even that poor wording makes the text inaccessible to the reader. In either case, the text is incomplete from the point of view of the reader and the required congruence between goal and need is not attained. Renkema (2000: 29, 2008: 358) has pointed out that correspondence errors are quite difficult to amend because there may be differences between what the writer understands the function of the text to be and what the target group needs to understand it (possibly based on different levels of knowledge or education, or different cultural backgrounds).

- *Consistency*: In the course of the writing process, a number of choices must be made and then adhered to consistently throughout the editing process: for example, text type and size, numbers and numbering systems, vertical lists, style of writing, register, spelling, punctuation and use of capital letters (or not) at the beginning of nouns. A text fulfils the requirement of being consistent if all choices that are made during the creation process are maintained throughout the entire text. For instance, inadvertently shifting from one text type (eg the format of a letter) to another (eg the format and structure of a report) seriously damages the quality and the effect of the text. Also, if someone begins by presenting the content thematically and then shifts to a chronological order without any reason or motivation, this can cause confusion and may negatively affect the quality of the text.

  Consistency errors therefore occur when choices that are made from the outset are not upheld to the end of the process or document. From the point of view of text editors, consistency is cardinal: they are its custodians.

  Another good example is the choice of either the American English or the British English spelling system (see chapter 9). If, following the American system, the text spells 'centre' as 'center' and 'harbour' as 'harbor', then it should also spell 'travelling' as 'traveling' and use 'license' for both noun and verb forms. The text editor's role extends to registering the preferred spellings and applying them consistently with the aid of a style guide, a reputable dictionary and a style sheet (see chapter 3).

- *Correctness*: This prerequisite of text quality tends to be more prescriptive in that it concerns the implementation of the rules of a specific language and the presentation of the correct content (facts). Correctness is about right or wrong; it is rare to have any grey areas. Errors involving correctness or otherwise occur when the conventions of good language usage, based on the 'rules' or norms of the language involved, are not adhered to or if facts are reproduced incorrectly.

  For instance, in English, a language rule is broken when the relative pronoun *that* is used in a non-defining relative clause (instead of *which*) or to refer to a person (when *that* should be used only for animals and things) (see chapters 6 and 8).

  *His house, *that* is painted blue, is very old. (correct form: *which*)

  *This is Naomi, *that* sells the tickets. (correct form: *who*)

Also, when a word like *accommodation* is spelled as *accomodation* or *accomadation* or *cemetery* spelled as *cemetary* a norm is being transgressed.

  A thorough knowledge of the grammar of a language is therefore essential if the practitioner is to fulfil this requirement. Answers to language problems such as these can be found in language reference books, language guides, grammar books and dictionaries and are discussed in detail in chapters 6 and 7.

  Correctness also applies to the content of a document. A content error would occur if, for instance, it is written that the Eiffel Tower in Paris was built in *1881* when in fact it happened in *1889*. Similarly, it is also a content error if an author writes that the *Titanic* sank on *12 April 1912,* since this happened in the early hours of **15** *April 1912*. It is also not true that all the passengers drowned, even though 1 552 of about 2 200 did. It is also a content error if one spells a name Macdonald when in fact McDonald is the correct spelling.

These kinds of error can be solved quite quickly and easily by using reference books and internet search engines, but correcting them presupposes that text editors have a broad general knowledge, are well up on current affairs, or have a questioning mind that takes no 'fact' at face value; but they also have to know when they are required to verify facts about historical events, dates, people or places and how or where to do so. Bowles & Bordon point out that it is important for text editors to know 'when to consult a standard reference work, probably within reach on the copy desk or just a few keystrokes away on the internet, and when a specialized book or electronic database is needed' (2011: 79).

The most common errors in this respect occur with the spellings of names, the correctness of dates and place names and the description of historical events. All these facts need to be confirmed accurately by the alert editor. Sometimes, however – as in fiction and narrative non-fiction – the only person who can verify the facts is the author him- or herself and then apparent errors must be raised with them for verification.

Renkema (2008: 39) stipulates that the three criteria for analysing text quality represent links between writer, text and reader:

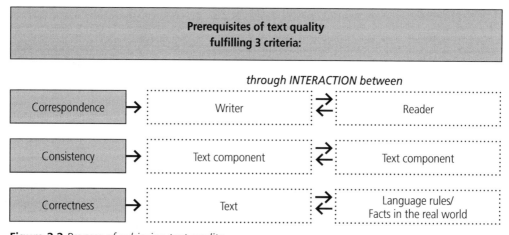

Figure 2.2 *Process of achieving text quality*

Essentially, this means that correspondence is achieved if the writer takes the readers' needs into account and composes the text in such a way that their needs are satisfied. Consistency is reached if the choices made in one part of the text are maintained or upheld in other parts too. Correctness is achieved if the language and the facts in a text are used in such a way that there are no disturbing instances of incorrectness.

3.3.2 Engaging with text facets to determine text quality

In this section, we discuss the five text facets that can be linked to the three broad criteria for evaluating text quality: *text type, content, structure, wording* and *presentation*. The combination of criteria and facets produces a matrix comprising a total of 15 evaluation points.

- *Text type*: Every text can be characterised as a certain type: letter (personal, business or in a newspaper), report, memorandum, dissertation, academic article, newspaper article or report, novel, short story, children's book, detective story, poetry, prose, drama, advertisement, user manual, business report, thesis or dissertation, recipe, etc. (One possible overview or typology of text types is presented in table 2.1.)

Main text type

1. Referential texts (descriptive)

SECONDARY TYPE	TEXT AIM	EXAMPLES
Informative	Presenting information: factual messages	• Travel guides • News messages • Articles in journals and newspapers • Bibliographies • Dictionaries
Argumentative	Presenting information: well-reasoned relationships between facts	• Academic articles • Reports • Essays • Theses • Memorandums • Specialised books
Instructive	Presenting information: systematically broadens knowledge	• Handbooks • Manuals • Directories • DIY books • Sports rules • Descriptions • Lists
Narrative/ descriptive	Presenting information: retells what happened	• Children's and other stories • Logbooks and diaries • Novels • Short stories • Reports

>>

2. Expressive texts

SECONDARY TYPE	TEXT AIM	EXAMPLES
Poetic/ literary	Expressing emotions, ideas, thoughts, opinions	• Prose • Drama • Poetry
Emotive/ affective	Expressing emotions, ideas, thoughts, opinions	• Diaries • Editorials • Love letters • Pamphlets • Greetings cards

3. Appellative texts

SECONDARY TYPE	TEXT AIM	EXAMPLES
Evaluative	Influencing opinions, thoughts, ideas: judgemental	• Reviews (of books, plays, etc) • Speeches • Legal judgments • Political pamphlets
Directive	Influencing opinions, thoughts, ideas: change in attitude and behaviour	• Election speeches • Political texts • Advertisements • Lectures (teaching) • Church sermons • Fundraising letters
Rhetorical	Influencing opinions, thoughts, ideas: provoking reflection (and action)	• Debates • Speeches • Literary texts

4. Interactive texts

SECONDARY TYPE	TEXT AIM	EXAMPLES
Social contact	Generating interaction during or just after speech contact	• Telephone conversations • Signing contracts • Doctor's visits • Social calls • Restaurant visits • Intervals during plays

Table 2.1 *Overview of text types*

From this table it should become immediately clear that some of the text examples could easily be attributed to a different or secondary text type and that sometimes the boundaries between text types are somewhat blurred. This makes it difficult to define clear rules for categorising texts into different genres. Some people will prefer a simple dichotomy: literary vs factual or fiction vs non-fiction; others distinguish between business and personal categories of text type. Another categorisation of non-fiction text types, taken from the Lancashire Grid for Learning (LGfL) which supports primary literacy, is:

- recount (retelling events in time order);
- report (describing the way things are);
- instruct (how to do things);
- explain (how or why things work or happen);
- persuade (why you should think this);
- discuss (reasoned argument)

(LGfL 2012, http://lancsngfl.ac.uk/nationalstrategy/literacy/index.php?category_id=72).

Whichever categorisation is used, there are broad indications of the rules that can apply and it is possible to define some typical features of specific text types that can be used to categorise a text (ie a text typology) as belonging to the same type. Daniëls (2011: 18) also states that each text type has specific distinguishable features (text type features or genre rules). In other words, a diary entry will be recognised as a diary entry only when it can be distinguished as such. However, it is possible to deviate from these features – and this is what sometimes makes wonderful pieces of literary art – but generally following the genre rules leads to more ease of reading and, consequently, to a better understanding of the writer's meaning and intention.

Having insight into text types is useful for obvious reasons: it allows people to produce, predict and process texts with the correct format in the correct context. It also helps to satisfy people's expectations about the structure of a text. For instance, writers will know what the typical format of a memorandum is and they will compose the text according to that format. Readers also know, based on their intertextual knowledge, what a memorandum looks like and they will therefore evaluate the text according to this typically expected format.

Each text type is characterised by a specific function or aim (eg persuading, informing or evaluating, which is what the sender wants to do with a text), content (how it is compiled; how the function is actually realised), context (in which wider setting the text is placed or embedded), and effect (the result of the text or whether the aim of the text has been achieved or not). In summary, a text is not written randomly; rather, it is the product of a complex number of factors that depend on and influence one another.

Now that we have explained text types in more detail, we can consider how writers make decisions when they want to communicate through a text. In this process, they formulate control questions at every intersection between text facets and the criteria of analysis. In doing so they use evaluation points to scrutinise the different aspects of text quality. It's now an appropriate point to introduce the evaluation points in the CCC model.

For ease of reference figure 2.1 is repeated here:

Text facets	Criteria for analysis of text quality		
	Correspondence	Consistency	Correctness
A. Text type	1. Appropriate text	2. Unity of genre	3. Application of genre rules
B. Content	4. Appropriate and sufficient information	5. Congruence of facts	6. Facts
C. Structure	7. Sufficient cohesion	8. Uniformity of structure	9. Linking words and argumentation
D. Wording	10. Appropriate wording	11. Unity of style	12. Syntax, vocabulary and meaning
E. Presentation	13. Appropriate layout and typography	14. Congruence between text and layout	15. Spelling, punctuation, layout and typography
	15 evaluation points		

Figure 2.1bis *The CCC model for text quality (text facets × criteria for analysis)*

Interpreting 2.1 bis

The evaluation points can be read from the perspective of the three criteria (vertically) or from the perspective of the five text facets (horizontally). This gives the text editor three different types of information:

1 • A1, B4, C7, D10, E13: evaluation points for *correspondence*
   • A2, B5, C8, D11, E14: evaluation points for *consistency*
   • A3, B6, C9, D12, E15: evaluation points for *correctness*

2 • A1, A2, A3: evaluation points for *text type* for the criteria correspondence, consistency and correctness, respectively
   • B4, B5, B6: evaluation points for *content* for the criteria correspondence, consistency and correctness, respectively
   • C7, C8, C9: evaluation points for *structure* for the criteria correspondence, consistency and correctness, respectively
   • D10, D11, D12: evaluation points for *wording* for the criteria correspondence, consistency and correctness, respectively
   • E13, E14, E15: evaluation points on *presentation* for the criteria correspondence, consistency and correctness, respectively

3 • 1 ... 15: evaluation points 1 to 15 for analysing text facets for quality.

The evaluation points can be interpreted as optimal outcomes, but they also reflect the process of evaluation and can be glossed in different ways.

- *Text type:* For text type this generates the following possible questions:

Evaluation point 1: *Appropriateness of the text:* Is the chosen text type appropriate to the communication's aim or intention?
- ✓ What is the aim or intention of the text?
- ✓ Who is the target group of the text?
- ✓ Is the chosen text type the appropriate genre to achieve this aim or intention?
- ✓ Is the text appropriate within the given context?
- ✓ ...

Evaluation point 2: *Unity of genre:* Is the genre correct for the aim or intention of the text?
- ✓ Which is the chosen text type?
- ✓ Why was it chosen?
- ✓ Is the genre used correctly?
- ✓ Is the text consistent with the genre choice?
- ✓ ...

Evaluation point 3: *Correct application of the genre rules:* Are the genre rules applied correctly?
- ✓ Does the text respect the rules of the chosen genre?
- ✓ Is the correct form of address used for this genre?
- ✓ ...

- *Content:* The text facet of content concerns the message itself. Again, a balance is required: if appropriate and sufficient information is transferred, the intention of the writer and the needs of the reader will correspond, and the text will be evaluated as good and informative. If there is insufficient information, then the text will be evaluated less positively. It is also important that the content is consistent throughout the entire text and factually correct. The following questions guide the process of quality control:

Evaluation point 4: *Appropriate and sufficient information:* Does the text give appropriate and sufficient information?
- ✓ Is all the information needed present?
- ✓ Is the information in line with the frame of reference of the readership?
- ✓ Are all concepts and terms explained?
- ✓ Is the reader left with questions after having read the text?
- ✓ If so, what kinds of question are they left with?
- ✓ ...

Evaluation point 5: *Congruence of facts:* Are the facts presented consistently?
- ✓ Is there any paradox in the text?
- ✓ Is there any overlap in the text?
- ✓ Are concepts and terms used consistently throughout the text?
- ✓ ...

Evaluation point 6: *Correctness of the data:* Is all the information factually correct?
- ✓ Are all the facts correct?
- ✓ Does the text use sources?

    ✓ Which referencing system has been used?
    ✓ Are the sources referred to correctly and consistently?
    ✓ Are the sources used qualitatively (cross-checked)?
    ✓ Are there enough sources?
    ✓ Has plagiarism been avoided?
    ✓ ...

- *Structure*: The structure (chapters, paragraphs, sentences, words) of a text must be logical (well reasoned and in the correct order) and the different parts must be connected to each other with appropriate linking words or phrases. The order has to be clear right from the start and has to represent the general line of thought in the text. What belongs together should therefore be presented together.

    The coherence of the text must be clear throughout and the connection between the different parts of the text must be visible. Cohesion, coherence and informativity – basic principles in text linguistics, play an important role here (see section 7) and can be checked through the following evaluative questions:

Evaluation point 7: *Sufficiently cohesive*: Are parts that belong together placed together, so the link between them is clear?
    ✓ Is there clear coherence between the different parts of the text?
    ✓ Are aspects that belong together placed together?
    ✓ Is it easy enough for the reader to follow the author's argument(s)?
    ✓ Is the text logically structured?
    ✓ Are there gaps in the argumentation?
    ✓ How are these gaps bridged?
    ✓ ...

Evaluation point 8: *Uniformity of structure*: Do consecutive parts follow each other and is this maintained consistently throughout the text?
    ✓ Is there a structural plan for the text (an outline)?
    ✓ Has this plan been followed?
    ✓ Is the structure of the text consistent – with respect to spaces in the text, matching font types and sizes, similar kinds of word, a similar length for all paragraphs and chapters?
    ✓ Has a fixed structure been chosen for the presentation of the content?
    ✓ Are components that are equally important also treated in a similar way?
    ✓ Is the difference between essentials and side issues clear and treated and indicated consistently?
    ✓ ...

Evaluation point 9: *Correct linking words and argumentation structure*: Do linking words correctly connect the different parts of the text? Is the argumentation correctly structured?
    ✓ How are different parts of the text linked?
    ✓ Are the words used for connecting different parts of the text, sentences or phrases correct?
    ✓ Do the linking words contribute to the meaning of the text and the argumentation?
    ✓ Are the linking words obvious?
    ✓ Is the argumentation structure easy to follow, consistent and correct?
    ✓ ...

- *Wording*: The wording chosen by the writer must align with the competencies of the target group. The syntactic/structural and lexical/verbal choices must also be aligned with the level of the communication. For instance, there is not much point in using the wording of an academic text in a textbook or a storybook for children: the word choice, phrases and sentence length will be above the readers' level of comprehension. It is also important that the chosen style is used consistently throughout the entire text – especially in multi-author documents and books, where the different authors' writing styles are likely to vary widely.

Evaluation point 10: *Appropriate wording*: Do the level and the choice of the wording agree with the abilities (framework, expectations, competencies, ...) of the target group?
- ✓ Does the wording correspond to the text type?
- ✓ Can the intended reader understand the text?
- ✓ Is the wording of the text accurate enough?
- ✓ Does the text have enough depth?
- ✓ Is the text attractive to read?
- ✓ Is there enough diversity in the text?
- ✓ Does the average sentence length accord with the abilities of the target group?
- ✓ Is the word choice appropriate to the target group?
- ✓ Does the text contain any prejudices (eg racism or sexism) or stereotypes that have to be eliminated?
- ✓ Is boredom prevented?
- ✓ Are there any clichés in the text?
- ✓ Is there any figurative usage that is likely to mislead or baffle the readers?
- ✓ ...

Evaluation point 11: *Unity of style*: Is the style maintained consistently?
- ✓ Is the style consistent throughout the entire text?
- ✓ Is the style appropriate to the chosen text type?
- ✓ Is the style consistently attractive?
- ✓ Is the style consistently concise?
- ✓ ...

Evaluation point 12: *Correct sentence structure (syntax), vocabulary or word choice (lexicon) and meaning (semantics and register):* Is the text's syntax and the selection of words with respect to meaning and register sufficient to promote optimal understanding?
- ✓ Are the sentences well formulated and structured for maximum accessibility?
- ✓ Are the sentences of adequate length (not too short and not too long)?
- ✓ Is there enough variation in sentence and paragraph length and sentence structure?
- ✓ Are the rules of the language adhered to?
- ✓ Are active and passive used adequately or appropriately?
- ✓ Are the correct words used?
- ✓ If foreign origin words are used, are they adequately indicated and, if necessary, explained?
- ✓ ...

- *Presentation*: This facet concerns decisions about the appearance of the text: Is the external or surface appearance of the text such that it helps the reader to understand immediately what is meant by it? It is important to be consistent in how the text is presented and this is especially important in the case of the typography and layout of the text, as both convey important visual messages to readers.

Evaluation point 13: *Appropriate and effective presentation and visual characteristics (layout and typography)*: Is the way in which the text is presented appropriate for transferring the content to the readers?
- ✓ Is the format of presentation of the text appropriate to the target group?
- ✓ Will the target group understand the text?
- ✓ Is the use of font types, font sizes, line widths and white space between and around lines of text optimal?
- ✓ Is the text visually appealing?
- ✓ Are the spelling and punctuation as clear and supportive of the text as the audience will expect them to be?
- ✓ Is the visual presentation correct with respect to the message and audience?
- ✓ ...

Evaluation point 14: *Agreement between text and presentation:* Is the chosen format and layout followed throughout consistently?
- ✓ Does the layout agree with the intention of the text?
- ✓ Do the layout and content complement each other?
- ✓ Is the use of font types, font sizes, line widths and white space between and around lines of text consistent?
- ✓ Are tables, illustrations, photographs and schedules labelled in the same way throughout?
- ✓ Are the contents, formatting, alignment and styling of tables and figures treated consistently?
- ✓ Are spelling and punctuation consistently dealt with throughout?
- ✓ ...

Evaluation point 15: *Correct visual presentation:* Is the look and feel of the text correct?
- ✓ Are all words spelled correctly?
- ✓ Is the punctuation correct?
- ✓ Is the punctuation functional?
- ✓ Is the visual presentation consistently correct with respect to the overall design of the document or book?
- ✓ ...

In the following section, a few practical reflections on the application of the model are discussed.

3.3.3 Application of the CCC model

Starting from the presentation of the model, some important practical reflections need to be shared:

- In order to determine the quality of a text, all the evaluation points should be taken into account and responded to.

- The model has to be read from left to right and from top to bottom, following the numbers.
- The position of the evaluation points determines their relative importance. Evaluation point 1 (*agreement between the goal of the writer and the needs of the reader*), for instance, is more important than evaluation point 15 (*correct visual presentation: spelling, punctuation and layout, typography*). Although the last point is not unimportant, achieving the intended communicative aim of the text is more essential than having perfect typography and layout. However, it should be pointed out that typography that is well married to the subject-matter and its treatment will enhance ease of reading and message transfer. It will, in turn, support the process of attaining the aim of the communication piece.
- Editors' experiences with measuring text quality indicate that the majority of the problems that occur in texts are covered by one of the 15 evaluation points. The function of the model, therefore, is to show where the problems are located and how they can be corrected. In this way, there is a ripple effect within the text: a problem that is treated under evaluation point 3 (*correct application of genre rules*) may also solve possible issues of *wording* (evaluation point 10), *style* (evaluation point 11) and even *appropriate presentation* (evaluation point 13). The issue of genre rules always affects these facets because each genre has its own rules for them.
- From the point of view of text editors, some evaluation points will probably be more important than others, precisely because it is their task to evaluate which aspects have to receive greater attention when they correct a text. In addition, by the time the text is presented to the text editor, some of the problems that occurred in the writing process may already have been solved by the author and a publisher (if one is involved), which is why the focus of the text editor may be mainly on aspects that are connected to the presentation of the text: the language, wording and layout (see chapters 6, 7, 8, 9 and 10).
- The evaluation points have to be specified further for each text type, since text types differ in terms of format and language usage.
- Certain evaluation points are therefore more relevant to certain text types and communication contexts than to others.
- Some evaluation points need to be defined further. For instance, evaluation point 10 (*appropriate wording*) is quite vague in itself, but it means that a text needs to be engaging enough for its intended audience or, in other words, the audience has to read it with ease. Moreover, it has to be understandable (and functional), concise and correct.
- The model can also be used as a template and checklist for writing a 'good text'. Adhering to the principles leads to the author's becoming better acquainted with the components that a text should consist of in order to be labelled as 'communicative'.

Finally, an illustration: a text, in this case an academic piece of writing (ie a paper, an essay or a dissertation) has an optimal quality if all the criteria and text facets accord in such a way that the text can be judged as follows:

An (academic) paper as a prototypical example of **text type**
corresponds if …
- ✓ the main message is *clear* and transparent
- ✓ the text corresponds to the target *audience*'s basic knowledge of the topic

is consistent if …
- ✓ the text does not jump around from one text type to another

is correct if …
- ✓ the text contains the required *text components* (introduction, body, conclusion, title page, table of contents, conclusion, references, …)
- ✓ the *title page* contains all the required information (title, author, affiliation, supervisor, date, …)
- ✓ the *acknowledgement* pays tribute to whoever has helped to carry out the project
- ✓ the *introduction* clearly presents a problem statement and a plan of action
- ✓ the *body text* is an elaboration and motivated discussion of the problem
- ✓ the *conclusion* derives logically from the argumentation (thesis statements and support) and contains an indication of how to answer the initial question
- ✓ the text contains some (self-)critical *reflections* and points to possible routes for the future (application and further research)
- ✓ *terminology* is (critically) explained
- ✓ a list of *references* is added and follows a set standard

An academic paper's **content**
corresponds if …
- ✓ the text contains all the information *required* to respond to the main question
- ✓ the text does not contain unnecessary and *superfluous* information
- ✓ the text contains sufficient information with respect to the target audience's *familiarity* with the topic

is consistent if …
- ✓ the content is *logically* structured
- ✓ all new and controversial *terms* are explained and the author's stance is explained
- ✓ all the reader's *questions* are being answered

is correct if …
- ✓ the information provided can be *checked* with the help of the sources used

An academic paper's **structure**
corresponds if …
- ✓ the information is being presented in a *logical sequence*
- ✓ the text structure becomes clear through *logical connectors* or *linking words*

is consistent if …
- ✓ the *structure* corresponds to the plan outlined in the introduction
- ✓ the chapters and *paragraphs* clearly reflect the text's structure
- ✓ every paragraph covers only one *topic*
- ✓ the *layout* is uniform

is correct if …
- ✓ linking words are used correctly
- ✓ the text components logically follow one another

An academic paper's **wording**
corresponds if …
- ✓ it is *accurate*
- ✓ it is *inviting* and *engaging*
- ✓ the style is appropriate to the target *audience*
- ✓ the style is appropriate to the *text type*
- ✓ there is enough *variation* in word choice
- ✓ the text is not *boring*

is consistent if …
- ✓ the writer does not deviate from the *topic*
- ✓ the *terminology* is explained throughout

is correct if …
- ✓ the *word choice* (register) is appropriate
- ✓ the *sentence structure* is in line with the grammatical rules of the language

An academic paper's **presentation**
corresponds if …
- ✓ the use of *typography* is functional and helps to communicate the content
- ✓ the target audience understands the text (and feels familiar with it)

is consistent if …
- ✓ the *illustrations* (figures, tables, etc) are treated consistently and support the text
- ✓ the illustrations have a *title* and a *reference,* and also *labels,* where necesssary
- ✓ the *typography* is kept the same throughout the text

is correct if …
- ✓ the spelling is in accordance with the rules of the language
- ✓ the punctuation is functional and supports understanding of the text
- ✓ the text contains only accepted abbreviations

As explained above, the evaluation points and control questions help editors to make informed decisions about the quality and effectiveness of text and to strategise where their remedial intervention is most needed. According to Renkema (2000: 88), good text quality is mainly determined by a proper selection of information expressed clearly and logically and its presentation in a good structure. When studying the CCC model and its applicability to the practice of text editing, it becomes clear that the evaluation points can easily be linked to the three discplines of normative grammar, text linguistics and document design (see table 2.2). Knowledge of these three domains is therefore crucial.

Text facets	Criteria for analysis of text quality		
	Correspondence	Consistency	Correctness
Text type	1. Appropriate text	2. Unity of genre	3. Application of genre rules
Linguistic disciplines:	Text linguistics	Text linguistics and Document design	Text linguistics and Document design
Content	4. Appropriate and sufficient information	5. Congruence of facts	6. Facts
Linguistic disciplines:	Text linguistics and Document design	Text linguistics and Document design	Text linguistics
Structure	7. Sufficient cohesion	8. Uniformity of structure	9. Linking words and argumentation
Linguistic disciplines:	Text linguistics and Document design	Text linguistics and Document design	Normative linguistics; Text linguistics and Document design
Wording	10. Appropriate wording	11. Unity of style	12. Syntax, vocabulary and meaning
Linguistic disciplines:	Normative linguistics; Text linguistics and Document design	Normative linguistics	Normative linguistics
Presentation	13. Appropriate layout and typography	14. Congruence between text and layout	5. Spelling, punctuation, layout and typography
Linguistic disciplines:	Document design	Document design	Normative linguistics; Document design

Table 2.2 *The knowledge base of the CCC model's evaluation points*

When assigning evaluation points to domains, there is quite a lot of overlap (see the shared evaluation points in figure 2.3 below). This shows that judging text quality is actually an integrated and a holistic process.

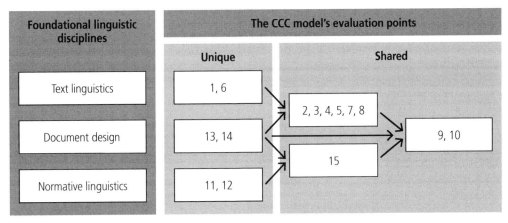

Figure 2.3 *Overview of the CCC model's evaluation points allocated to disciplines*

It is clear from the above that the skills needed to evaluate texts have a sound knowledge base and therefore can be learned and acquired. There are different ways to acquire these skills and the learning objectives can be formulated as follows:

• Increase your insight into the demands of effective communication by, for instance, making sure that you know what the demands of the different text types – emails, reports, technical manuals, ebooks – are with regard to structure, layout, wording and presentation.
• Improve your diagnostic skills, that is, your ability to locate, identify and correct errors. If you are acquainted with the three disciplines stated above, you will be able to detect and correct errors more easily.
• Acquire a knowledge of problem-solving strategies. Always try to think of more than one solution to a problem. Your broad knowledge will allow you to apply the best solution.
• Gain experience. It takes a while to get to the point where you have 'enough experience', but remember that 'lifelong learning' is an essential aspect of the training and working life of text editors: in this profession, you will not, you dare not, stop learning. The more you know, the more easily you will see problems and the easier it will be to correct them.

This leads to an integrated model that can be schematically presented as follows (figure 2.4):

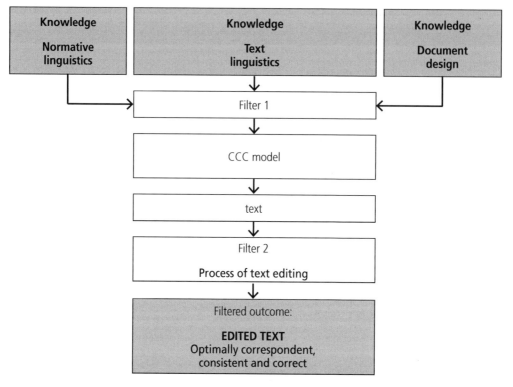

Figure 2.4 *Integrated process model of text editing*

In sections 4, 5 and 6 of this chapter foundational aspects of the model are discussed in greater detail.

4 Normative linguistics and text quality

> Writers or communicators who wish to use words clearly, powerfully, or effectively often use prescriptive rules, believing that these may make their communications more widely understood and unambiguous.
> *Wikepedia*

> Prescriptivism ... is an authoritarian view, propounded especially in relation to grammar and vocabulary, and often with reference to pronunciation. ... Those who speak and write in this variety are said to be using language 'correctly'; those who do not are said to be using it 'incorrectly'.
> *Crystal*

Normative linguistics is concerned with judgements about language use in terms of 'good' or 'correct' vs 'bad' or 'wrong' and how they contribute to a text's communicative effect. The fact that we are dealing with good and bad explains why this often generates emotional discussions, especially when deviations from what is generally considered 'good' are subjected to debate. Knowledge about and of language and the demands of communication is central to the editing function. The focus in the following concise explanation will be on the following questions:

- What does the term 'normative linguistics' refer to?
- What is a normative approach to language?
- What is a normative approach to English specifically?
- What is the impact of normative linguistics on the CCC model?

The aim of the following sections will be to show the importance of a knowledge of normative linguistics to applying the CCC model.

4.1 Normative linguistics as a field of study

> … 'normative' grammar instruction aimed to teach 'proper usage' common in primary and secondary school, which linguists call prescriptivism.
> *Nunberg & Wasow*

Early on in their careers, text editors have to become acquainted with and gain insight into the principles, rules and conventions that determine correct and effective use of the language they are working in. In practice nowadays, these principles, rules and conventions are known as the 'norms' of the language. Text editors typically apply their knowledge of norms in their daily linguistic practice when processing and polishing texts (see, among others, chapter 3). The success of the process is largely determined by how well they know the norms of the language, because this helps them to make motivated choices about the grammar, style and register to be used. Since the norms of a language – and, more especially, the deviations from the norm – can cause heavy debate among language users, an attempt at a definition is required at the outset.

4.1.1 A working definition of 'norm'

> Prescription aims to draw workable guidelines for language users seeking advice in such matters.
> *Wikipedia*

> The English-speaking world may be divided into (1) those who neither know nor care what a split infinitive is; (2) those who do not know, but care very much; (3) those who know and condemn; (4) those who know and approve; and (5) those who know and distinguish.
> *Fowler*

The word 'norm' takes on different definitions, depending on who is using the term. The following play a role:

- Norms have a double nature: on the one hand, they function as conventions or rules about the way in which language *should* be used. In other words, they provide guidance. On the other hand, they can also function as a measuring standard to check whether the postulated expectations are being realised, in which case they are also a source of control.

- A norm implies that there is always a choice and that an evaluation or value judgement needs to be made. One form is therefore better than another. A choice or evaluation can be made only if there are certain general rules that determine how you have to do this or how you can measure that.
- Norms in general play an important role in our daily social interaction with the people around us. From a social point of view, for instance, it is important to wear clothing appropriate to the occasion. For instance, one would not wear a T-shirt, swimming trunks and flip-flops when attending a formal function. Wearing a suit and tie to the beach would be really odd nowadays. In a similar way, people make choices about what forms of language are appropriate in specific language situations. For instance, it is not acceptable in French to address a stranger with *tu*. Instead, the more formal (and distant) *vous* has to be used. In German, the same convention applies to *du* and *Sie*, respectively. In English, the situation is different and the form *you* will be interpreted on the basis of the context (where titles accompany positions of rank, those replace *you*, as in Your Excellency for an ambassador; Your Highness for a member of royalty, Your Grace for an archbishop). Since particular forms of language are not acceptable in particular contexts, text editors must develop the knowledge and the ability to make the right choices.

The words 'acceptable' (satisfactory, tolerable) and 'appropriate' (suitable) have been used several times already. Important questions relating to these terms are: For whom is something acceptable or appropriate? On what basis is it acceptable or appropriate? Who determines what is acceptable or appropriate? Language is determined by conventions of use which have been 'approved' by someone for use in certain contexts:

- Any language rule is based upon observed language usage which – after a while – became the fixed pattern (or norm). The objective observation of language in use and the description of patterns that results from it are known as 'descriptive linguistics'. This refers to the careful perception and analysis of language in daily use, and recording such usage without passing judgement. After a while, the findings that result from observaton and analysis attain the status of language rules, which may create the impression that speakers always use language in this way. However, language rules are meant only as a starting point. When people want to be guided in how to use language, description – objective, empirical observation and analysis – becomes the basis for prescription, that is, directing people about how to use language. The language prescribed indicates the preference of the language community for how they want to use their language in order to communicate as easily and effectively as possible. In this way, preference has turned into a rule. Prescription always follows and is based on description (Mossop 2010: 49–55). We see this in the many Englishes that make up World English – American, Canadian, Australian, Indian, Scottish, Irish, South African, West African, and so on.

- Who takes the lead in the process of description? Usually educated people, such as linguists, are in charge of the process of description. These people (often organisations) take the lead, but they do not make random judgements on the basis of their personal preference for user rules. Rather they rely on their knowledge (about how language evolves diachronically and is used synchronically) and experience (about how language is used in reality) in order to judge these patterns and then they make a decision. It is clear that it is not the task of a single language user to decide 'this is how language should be used', but rather it is the task of several people who know how language works, how change is reflected in the way in which they indicate the existing user norms. Obviously, these norms are not static, since language communities change continuously and from one generation to the next. Norms will therefore also evolve, because language is and remains dynamic. The difference between descriptive and prescriptive is therefore a simple one: people who work descriptively say how language is being used (based on empirical control), whereas people who work prescriptively say how language should be used (in certain domains of language usage such as, for instance, education or publishing).

Within the framework of normative linguistics, prescription is important, though.

- On the basis of the discussion above, it is clear that language norms cannot be seen as independent of a language community, since language is the ultimate means for social action. As a consequence, language norms are in effect sociolinguistic norms, and actually it is obvious: language usage is in essence normative since the social situation determines which linguistic form is appropriate. The starting point in any normative approach should therefore take a sociolinguistic view into account: if people interpret language norms as sociolinguistic norms, then there is some room for interpretation of these norms. In this way, sociolinguistic norms have a social meaning: they play a role in communication and sometimes even determine the membership of a group on the basis of judgements about correct and incorrect linguistic behaviour (Swann, Deumert & Lillis 2004).
- For text editors the last point is especially relevant: when editing a text, they are confronted with questions such as:
    - Have I chosen the *correct* word?
    - Is my sentence structured *correctly*?
    - Is this the *right* spelling?
    - Do I use punctuation *correctly*?
    - Is this the *right* style for this piece of text?, etc.

For text editors it is therefore crucial to be aware of the prevailing language norms required in well-defined social situations. For text editors, knowing what is 'right' or 'wrong' is much more important than for other language users, since their success as text editors (and, consequently, as paid professionals) is determined by the degree to which they succeed in making 'correct choices'. In order to communicate effectively and economically, therefore, practitioners must be true to the lingusitic norms of their time. Therefore, proficiency in a language definitely demands a knowledge of the different norms of that language and also a knowledge of the situations in which certain utterances are appropriate or not.

In the next section we focus on correctness and appropriateness; in short, we focus more intently on 'norm'.

4.1.2 The standard language as norm

> A standard language is a dialect with an army.
> *Popular saying among linguists*

> Standard languages arise when a certain dialect begins to be used in written form ....
> *Encyclopaedia Britannica* online

For some people the term 'standard language' has a negative connotation, because it implies that other varieties of language are 'less standard or substandard and therefore less good' or inferior (Crystal 2003: 193, 366). However, in situations where people want to reach as many of their fellows as possible or where they want to make written contact with a large group, a language variety will be chosen that can be accessed by everyone in order to make the message understandable. This form is called the standard language, or standard variety, at the same time acknowledging that other varieties are not to be regarded as 'weak' or 'wrong'. In some professional situations a knowledge of standard language is almost part of the job description: this is certainly the case for teachers, lawyers, language professionals, etc. Webb (1985: 80) states that a language community needs an overarching variety that can serve as the linguistic reference framework or as a means of communicating at a higher functional level. If a community wants to function effectively, it will have to make use of a standard language, whatever form that takes.

The starting point for a practice-driven normative approach should therefore be obvious: it seems useful to focus on the variety that can be used for as many purposes as possible. The variety that is accepted as having the biggest user value across the entire language area will therefore be preferred. This is a sociolinguistic criterion. Of course, it does not mean that text editors do not need any knowledge of the other varieties of the language – they must be aware of those, too, because only then will they be able to use the language to its full extent and potential when processing and polishing texts.

The story of how Standard English emerged, as told by David Crystal (on the BBC Voices project website, November 2004), is in itself an interesting case study in sociolinguistics. During the Middle Ages (the time of Chaucer), a new era of multilingualism and multi-dalectism dawned in the British Isles. In addition to the five main Old English dialects, the Norman invasion had brought Latin and French to coexist with English. Educated people became trilingual as a matter of course, given the power of Latin (the language of the Church, most scholarship and some politico-legal areas) and French (the language of the court).

It was during the Middle Ages that the area of south-east England bounded by London, Oxford and Cambridge became a region of special social and economic influence. As a consequence of that, the speech of the inhabitants of that region who had routine contact with the worlds of courtly culture, commerce and learning increased in prestige and began to be evaluated as a more polished, elegant and altogether more desirable medium of communication than the varieties of English available elsewhere. As Crystal writes, 'Social change always has a linguistic sequel. ... The stage was set for the emergence of a standard language.' It was not too long before that dialect began to be described as 'correct', 'proper' and 'educated' and the non-standard varieties of other regions began to be ridiculed and condemned.

But it was only in the late eighteenth century (after some 300 years) that class distinction came to be expressed through language, especially through the way a person spoke. A new concern arose then to 'find the rules' governing polite usage, and writers such as Dr Johnson (dictionary), Lowth (grammar) and Walker (pronunciation manual) came to be recognised as authoritative prescriptivists. In fact, says, Crystal, during that period, under the influence of such writers, only by following their rules would speakers be perceived to be educated. The pressure to conform (and obtain the 'best' education) must have been enormous. By implication, if you did not conform to the standard dialect (then the norm), to the uniform mode of linguistic behaviour then dominant, you were considered uneducated and, to all intents and purposes, not 'one of us'. A century later, the legacy of the eighteenth-century preoccupation with class and correctness found form in one accent that attracted more prestige than others (the speech of polite London society), named 'received pronunciation' (or RP), that is, the kind of speech passed down from one educated generation to the next.

4.1.3 The boundaries of normative studies

> Normative research sets the 'normal way' for future improvements.
> *answers.yahoo.com*

Normative research is research that characterises what is usual in a defined population (O'Connor 1990). In language we would like to describe or characterise what is usual in particular domains.

As indicated above, there are two ways of dealing with language data. One is simply to describe occurrences in practice (descriptive), the other is to make a value judgement about what can be observed (prescriptive). Descriptive studies observe the way in which language is used by its users and try to analyse it and formulate generalisable rules from it. Descriptive studies do not deal with what is good or bad language usage, so these studies are based on how a language actually is, not on how it ideally should be (UsingEnglish.com). In a prescriptive context (often a professional context such as education, publishing, broadcasting, politics and law) linguists make decisions about what they believe to be right and wrong, good and bad language usage. For usability's sake, these decisions are laid down in rules.

But are normative studies the final word on language usage? What can they do, how do they help text editors? Where do such studies provide answers, if at all? Do editors have to make autonomous decisions? We can really only direct you to chapters 6 to 10, where you will see copious examples of correct and incorrect usage, and some 'grey areas', which we hope you'll find insightful. Looking at the position from a pragmatic (day-to-day working) perspective, we can conclude that text editors should know about the following issues:

> › Grammar: syntactic and morphological aspects.

> › Meaning: lexical (vocabulary) usage and the possibilities inherent in English words.

> › Writing conventions: especially those specific to the use of English, for instance, spelling and punctuation rules, preserving language purity, writing style, text types (letter and report writing), etc.

Being able to cling to something that others have established as sound and solid (that is, norms) creates a feeling of security. In order to know how much has been established by external sources and where there are gaps, how they should be filled or further investigated, as well as which options are available and how they have to be decided upon, you have to know the available sources and which side of the descriptive–prescriptive fence they sit on. The 'classic' sources to consult on such matters as norms and deviations were (and still are) (see also chapter 11):

• Fowler's *Modern English usage*, first published as a prescriptive style guide in 1926, updated by Sir Ernest Gower in the 1960s and completely revised under the editorship of Robert Burchfield as a descriptive usage guide in 1996 and 2004 and published as *The new Fowler's modern English usage and Fowler's modern English usage*, respectively;
• Gowers' *The complete plain words* (first published in 1954) as a guide to the use of English and revised by Greenbaum and Whitcut in 1996, is built on two pamphlets written for British civil servants, *Plain words* (1948) and *An ABC of plain words* (1951);
• Kahn (ed) *The right word at the right time: A guide to the English language and how to use it,* is a Reader's Digest publication;
• Quirk et al *A comprehensive grammar of the English language*;
• Leech & Svartvik's 1985 *A comprehensive grammar of the English language*.

Non-native speakers can rely on the above, but also have:

• Michael Swan's standard reference work *Practical English usage* (1980, 2005).

Fowler, though prescriptive in his aims in guiding users of the language, differs from his nineteenth-century contemporaries, the grammatical authors, in the way he combines a respect for tradition with a readiness to debunk the worst excesses of purism and underpins his remarks with an elegant blend of humour and common sense (Crystal 2003: 196). In *Modern English usage*, his general approach encourages a direct, vigorous writing style and opposed all artificiality by firmly advising against convoluted sentence construction, the use of foreign words and phrases, and the use of archaisms. He opposed pedantry and ridiculed artificial grammar rules unwarranted by natural English usage, such as bans on split infinitives and on ending a sentence with a preposition.

Like most practical guides to writing and speaking a language, the linguistics of *Modern English usage* mixes the prescriptive and the descriptive (http://en.wikipedia.org/wiki/A_Dictionary_of_Modern_English-Usage). In this respect, the Reader's Digest's *The right word at the right time* is in the Fowler camp. In dealing with points of grammar, punctuation, spelling and meaning, this publication indicates both acceptable and unacceptable usage, but also indicates words that are in a state of transitional, suspect or indeterminable usage.

5 Knowledge of sources

Possibly the most important aspect that has to be discussed here is: Which sources can I use to solve my language problems? And: Which sources are authoritative and reliable? The underlying idea is that language needs to be codified (in the form of language handbooks, language manuals and dictionaries, and so on) in order to create a starting point for problem solving. Language users want constancy and therefore they prefer clear (and understandable) explanations of how language can be used. Of course, it is not always easy to provide this kind of explanation, but that they are requested, and even looked for, is a fact (this is also why language blogs run by 'ordinary' language users are so successful, if a little precarious).

The general starting point is that a knowledge of the appropriate reference works and the theoretical assumptions underlying them leads to familiarity with the general norms that apply in language usage. For instance, text editors have to know whether the foundations of the works used are based on a description of linguistic forms, structures and usage or whether the authors formulate prescriptive rules based on norms of correct and incorrect usage (WordNet 2010).

5.1 Rationale for indepth knowledge of sources

> An active knowledge is always operating in the background, activating itself when it's needed.
> *Campbell*

Knowing *where* and *when* to look for answers to language questions is one of the most important competencies of text editors – perhaps even more so than knowing all the answers oneself (in the case of a living, dynamic language such as English, that's well-nigh impossible anyway). It is a skill that *must* be acquired, because, if it is not, a range of language problems may pass unseen and uncorrected. Possessing a knowledge of the types of norm will make text editors especially versatile as people who are knowledgeable and who know what to do with their knowledge. Moreover, having a knowledge of the appropriate reference works brings with it a familiarity with the general norms of English. The simple truth is that text editors – and language professionals in general – who are not educated in these matters and who do not keep abreast of linguistic trends may not be able to deliver truly good work. By trying to stay informed about what is new on the English language market, text editors can expand their knowledge and adapt it (if and where necessary). For contemporary practitioners, moreover, the challenge with online resources is to distinguish the really authoritative from the less so.

5.2 Criteria for the appropriateness of sources

What makes a source appropriate for evaluating language usage and for solving language problems? Experience has shown that the following criteria – presented in order of importance, starting with the most important – may be helpful:

- *Age*: Older sources are less indicative of modern language usage than more recent sources. If possible, the newest sources will have to be checked for solutions to language problems. For some languages it is difficult to find recent reference works; in such instances, older sources can be used, as long as the practitioner uses the most recent available edition of that work (working with a first or second edition if there is a fifth is inexcusable; it is a sign of laziness and a lack of professionalism if this still occurs).
- *Status of the author(s)*: Is the author an authority in the field or have they displayed evidence of experience and expertise in it?
- *User-friendliness*: This criterion is related to the accessiblity of the information in a text. Does the source have a good table of contents? Are there page numbers that can be tracked? Are the chapters (if any) presented in a logical order? Are the examples self-illustrative? Is there an index to help the user find information more quickly? Is there a good bibliography? Similar questions can be asked of online texts.
- *Appropriateness of the source*: Use a dedicated source that can answer language problems at the text level. For instance, a learner's dictionary might be too limited in vocabulary to have the weight of authority when it comes to field-specific terminology (jargon). In such cases, it is better to have at hand a technical or specialised dictionary or even a textbook on the topic when the need for a very detailed, specific source is great.
- *Manageability*: Reference materials have to be manageable. Sometimes a reference work is too heavy to be carried around and then it is used less often. When your internet connection is generally unstable, you cannot rely on online resources unless you are willing to put up with a certain degree of irritation. One solution is to use resources on highly portable CD-ROM or to burn online resources to CD-ROM.

- *Price*: Some sources are very expensive (eg highly specialised reference materials). This is usually a disadvantage for the individual user, since the more affordable sources are not necessarily the best. For professional text editors, though, price should not count as a real criterion – and, in any event, expenditure on the tools of one's trade is not only a sound investment but usually one that is tax-deductible (see chapter 3 section 5).

See also chapter 11 on resources.

Now that it has been established how important a good knowledge of sources is, we can find out in which normative areas to use them.

6 Types of language norm

> Writers who observe the poignancy sometimes given by inversion, but fail to observe that 'sometimes' means 'when exclamation is appropriate', adopt inversion as an infallible enlivener; they aim at freshness and attain frigidity.
> *Fowler*

> Display of superior knowledge is as great a vulgarity as display of superior wealth — greater indeed, inasmuch as knowledge should tend more definitely than wealth towards discretion and good manners.
> *Fowler*

Norms can be classified in different ways, but in general three main types of language norm can be distinguished (Carstens 2011: 24–26 – our translation):

- *Global or universal norms* apply to all languages: for instance, language users will generally avoid ambiguity (unless there is a specific reason for it) or they will do their utmost to select the correct or most suitable word for a particular context;
- *Language-specific or internal norms* are inherent in or unique to the structure or meaning of a specific language and are not necessarily valid in other languages: for example, the use of the genitive *-s* in English (the boy's shirt; girls' things; its, hers);
- *Situational or external norms* strive for pragmatic correctness: for instance, a formal situation will require a formal kind of language use (a dissertation; a wedding invitation); texting is reserved for messages sent via electronic devices.

The choices that language users make with regard to language forms and structures rely on these norms. For the practising text editor it is important to know what exactly these norms are and what effect they are likely to have on the text in hand.

When applying norms, you should keep in mind that you are meant to contribute to enhancing the text's communicative power. In this process, each bit of language that is being revised needs to respond to the requirements of the 4 C's, namely *clarity, coherence, consistency* and *correctness* (Einsohn 2011 2005: 3). If one refines and complements these demands by adding the need for *cohesion, accuracy, completeness* and *appropriateness*, the list of tasks becomes immense, complicated and somewhat obscure. In order to make the assignment manageable, the CCC model, with its three entry points ('criteria for analysis') applied to five text facets (see figure 2.1), can function as a taxonomy or even a checklist, since it presents a matrix of evaluation points and this principled categorisation can play an important role in keeping language practitioners both objective and focused.

The three major types of norm can be linked to the three objectives text editors should have in mind when applying norms, namely (1) to achieve grammaticality by respecting the grammar rules of the text, (2) to attain pragmatic correctness by using the right forms in the right context, and (3) to generate correct or appropriate language use so the text will communicate effectively. If text editors manage to attain each of these three objectives, they will succeed in making the (revised) text clear, coherent, consistent, correct, cohesive, accurate, complete and appropriate. Each of the three objectives therefore activates a particular norm, as shown in the next section.

In the following paragraphs the different types of judgement required to attain the respective objectives are described in more detail.

6.1 Judgements of grammaticality

Text editors are renowned for the fact that they agree that texts have to respect the grammar rules of the language in which they are written. But sometimes, grammaticality can be moved aside to generate a special effect (eg in advertising or in poetry), though in the majority of cases texts should or do aim at grammaticality (ie being grammatically correct). In English there is a clear difference between the syntactic and the morphological norms necessary to attaining the required grammatical standard.

6.1.1 Internal norms of English syntax

In *A dictionary of modern English usage*, Fowler's general approach encourages a direct, vigorous writing style and opposes all artificiality, by firmly advising against convoluted sentence construction, that is, simpler applications of syntax rules. He opposed pedantry and ridiculed artificial grammar rules unwarranted by natural English usage, such as bans on *split infinitives* and on ending a sentence with a *preposition*; rules on the placement of the word *only*; and rules distinguishing between *which* and *that*. Some examples of faulty or misleading syntax in contemporary usage are:

- The position of *only* in a sentence: I *only* want to attend the performance on Tuesday.
  Problem: In this sentence, to which part of the sentence does 'only' refer? The subject (I), the verb (want to attend), the object (the performance) or the adverbial phrase (on Tuesday)? When the precise intended meaning is blurred by the casual placement of 'only', then the syntax is not supporting good communication and the reader will be in some doubt as to the author's intended message.
  Solution: Move 'only' to the left of whichever word or phrase it's supposed to be relating to: Only I want to attend the performance on Tuesday (no one else does) OR I want to attend the performance only on Tuesday (not on any other day).

- The incorrect *tense of a verb*: I returned to my favourite restaurant, which I *visited* on many occasions before.

    Problem: Both verbs, 'returned' and 'visited' are in the same tense (simple past), which suggests that both actions took place during the same period of time. This is not true. The visiting took place further in the past, in a previous period of time. The form of the verb 'visited' (present or past perfect) should reflect this.

    Solution: I returned to my favourite restaurant, which I *had visited* on many occasions before.

- The *dangling* or *unrelated participle*: *Playing* football in the park, *the dog* bit me.

    Problem: This construction, involving a participial clause qualifying the noun that follows the comma, makes it appear as if the dog was playing football, when in fact the speaker/writer was.

    Solution: Place the subordinate clause after the main clause OR make 'I' the subject of the main clause (even though this leads to a passive voice construction): The dog bit me while I was playing football in the park OR Playing football in the park, I was bitten by the dog.

- The *ambiguous referent*: Botany is the study of the plant life around the earth. *It* first began to be studied more than 200 years ago.

    Problem: To which noun does 'It' refer back? 'Botany' or 'earth'?

    Solution: Replace 'It' with 'Botany'.

6.1.2 Internal norms of English morphology

When we look at potential morphological deficiencies in English, the norms enunciated by, among other writers and linguists, Fowler, become clear. He classified and condemned every *cliché*, while defending useful distinctions between words whose meanings were coalescing in practice, thereby guiding the speaker and the writer away from illogical sentence constructions and the misuse of words. He was also critical of the use of archaisms. Some examples of faulty or misleading morphology (word formation) in contemporary usage illustrate this point:

- *Irregular verbs* give particular trouble, for example, take, took, have taken; sing, sang, have sung; teach, taught, have taught: We have *tooken* that train before. (have taken) They *sung* that hymn beautifully. (sang) He *teached* us well. (taught)
- Addition of '*do*' to verbs, when emphasis is not intended: We *do* go there frequently vs We go there frequently.
- *Plural forms with apostrophe*: Closed on Sunday's. Peach'es $0,30. Fresh banana's.
- *Plural forms used as singular*: criteria (is) – criterias (are); phenomena (is) – phenomenas (are).
- *Comparative and superlative forms of adjectives*:
    - Using the incorrect form: good, better, best: Who is the *gooder* between us? (better)
    - Combining the *-er* suffix with 'more' (or the *-est* suffix with 'most'): I'm *more happier* now that I am reunited with my family. (happier) This container is the *most fullest* of them all. (fullest)
    - Using the adverb intensifier 'more' and 'most' instead of the *-er* or *-est* suffix. She is the *most dear* person I know. (dearest)

6.2 Pragmatic correctness (appropriateness)

The concept of pragmatic correctness is concerned with text editors' ability to choose the correct word that is appropriate in the situation in which it is used. Knowledge about, amongst other things, the following norms is necessary here.

6.2.1 Internal norms of semantics

Language professionals' ability to select the right words determines their success as practitioners to a great extent. For instance, they need to know which pragmatic synonyms have to be used in which context: discrete vs separate vs different vs diverse; relevant vs appropriate vs germane; joyful vs joyous; circumscribe vs delimit vs restrict. Is there any difference in meaning between flammable and inflammable?

Malapropisms (ie words that sound or look similar to the word or meaning that is intended): create significant problems of meaning for inexperienced authors and text editiors, especially those whose mother tongue is not English or who have not learned how to use the indispensible explanatory dictionaries. For instance, it is important to be aware of and alert to the difference in meaning between (confusing) word pairs such as those in this small selection:

different vs diffident	memorial vs memorable
elusive vs illusive vs illusory	precede vs proceed
ingenuous vs ingenious	recoup vs recuperate
inoculate vs innocuous	respectful vs respective vs respectable
impatient vs inpatient	season vs seasoning
it's – it is – its	there – they're – their

Idioms: To have the cat by the tail. In my mind's eye. As the crow flies. Like a fish out of water. Don't be a fly in the ointment. Make hay while the sun shines. Play fast and loose. I'll move mountains to make it happen. The investment broker sold me down the river. It's a dog's life. I wish I were a fly on the wall at that meeting. He's at sixes and sevens ... All of these sentences and phrases enrich a language by drawing, usually, on local 'wisdom' or customs to provide figurative alternatives to run-of-the-mill literal phrasing. They tend to be characterised by their pithiness and their innate wisdom, and are often based on people's keen observation of the world around them.

However, as a text editor one has to be aware of the several problems that can arise in connection with the use of idioms, including these:

- The target readers may not understand the idiom used at all, so it has to be 'translated' into a clearer literal form if they are to understand the message being conveyed. For example: 'He's at sixes and sevens at present' means He's in a state of turmoil or confused or irrational at present. This means that the text editor has to be even clearer about who the intended readership of a document is if they are to deal with idiomatic usage appropriately.

- The author may misquote an idiom, getting it only half-right – in which case, the message it is intended to convey can be distorted. Even the slightest or sublest of misquoting can be damaging. For example: 'As the bird flies' doesn't have the same resonance as 'As the crow flies' (ie in a straight line – a particular characteristic of a crow's flight, presumably). The remedial action required of the editor here is either to look up the correct form in a dictionary of idioms (of which there are many) or to provide a literal 'translation' of the idiom if the readership is unlikely to understand the idiom anyway.
- Some idioms are so localised or obscure that only a fraction of the intended readers will understand them (so much so that they may not even be listed in dictionaries of idioms). They should then either be replaced or 'interpreted'.

6.2.2 External norms of English spelling and punctuation

It should go without saying that text editors must be able to spell correctly and that they must, as a starting point, be able to apply the appropriate norms for punctuation effectively and functionally. If they cannot do this, then they will be unable to complete a piece of work correctly or to the satisfaction of their client, as is expected of a professional.

Spelling errors are among the most obvious flaws in texts and are easy to correct, so there should really be no excuse for their appearing in print. The help of a good spell-checker (see further in chapter 4, section 3.4) contributes to eliminating such errors, as does the eagle eye of a thorough proofreader – for we cannot depend upon electronic spell-checkers alone, which will not see the spelling of *trial* instead of *trail*, *their* instead of *there*, as an error.

6.2.3 External norms of standard language

The existence of a norm does not imply that only the standard language is 'acceptable'. Rather, it means (1) that text editors must be aware of and sensitive to the concept of diversity in language, (2) that there is a diversity of varieties of English, and (3) that every variety is good in the circumstances for which it is intended. Text editors must make sure that they choose the correct variety – especially in terms of style and register (see chapter 8). For instance, books for children require a different style from books for teenagers. Therefore, it is important to decide beforehand which variety is required and make the correct choice in terms of register and style before starting to revise the text.

6.2.4 External norms of language purity

Experienced text editors will know how to handle language purity issues, and this is essential because there is an important difference between borrowings that are 'good' for a language (loan words) and borrowings that are bad. Text editors need to know that sometimes it is necessary to cross the bounds of purity to increase the effectiveness of a text, and that language purity is not a 'holy cow', that it is sometimes also necessary to take a stand. Text editors must know enough about the problems of language purity and how to check whether there is any question of the 'purity' of a certain word or expression. Insufficient knowledge about this and passing over problematic cases can make employers lose their trust in the ability of text editors – and can, consequently, lead to a loss of clients and income.

6.2.5 External norms of style

One of the most important areas in which language professionals need extra training is the area of style, and no one should be embarrassed to ask for help or to learn from more experienced language professionals if it means mastering this elusive aspect of writing. Stylistic polishing contributes towards the success of a text, but what makes it a particularly challenging facet of an editor's work (especially when editing multi-author works and works of fiction or narrative non-fiction) is the fact that the editor has to try to stay true to the original style of a piece of writing while at the same time correcting stylistic errors if and when they occur. You should keep in mind at all times that the author's style of writing has to be sacrosanct: it is, after all, their text, not yours. Your job is to enhance it, not mould it to your preferred style.

6.3 Normative linguistics and the CCC model

In the previous section the principles of normative linguistics were explained and illustrated. From this it should have become clear that an all-round knowledge of language and language usage is necessary and that text editors must make a conscious effort to acquire as much of this knowledge as possible. A text cannot be acceptable when the text editor does not manage to underpin their intervention with a thorough knowledge of normative linguistics.

The CCC model's evaluation points 9, 10, 11, 12, 15 are firmly embedded in normative linguistics and are all located in the lower half of the taxonomy. This means that they pertain to the second part of the revision process, after text type and content have been assessed. Normative matters that require discussion are *structure* (evaluation point 9), *wording* (evaluation points 10, 11, 12) and *presentation* (evaluation point 15).

This is the stage where the wheat is separated from the chaff and therefore it is important to be accurate and precise about norms when polishing and finishing a text. Schematically, this process can be presented as follows:

Text facets	Evaluation points	Text quality To be guaranteed through …	Normativity Norms pertaining to …	
Structure	9	Correct linking words Argumentation structure	Syntax Lexicon	
Wording	10	Appropriate wording	Style Use of standard language Lexicon	Knowledge of sources
	11	Unity of style	Style	
	12	Correct sentence structure Correct lexical meaning	Syntax Semantics Use of standard language	
Presentation	15	Correct spelling Correct punctuation	Spelling Punctuation	

Table 2.3 *Text quality and normative linguistics*

Since texts are cemented not only through norms but also through textual features, we now need to look at how text linguistics supports text quality. In the next section, the importance of a knowledge of text lingusitics in the process of text editing is discussed.

7 Text linguistics and text quality

> Text analysis analyzes the text somewhat like a forensics lab analyzes evidence for clues: carefully, meticulously and in fine detail.
> *http:// utminers.utep.edu/omwilliamson/engl0310/Textanalysis.htm*
>
> The core questions of textual analysis: 'Who (says) What (to) Whom (in) What channel (with) What Effect.'
> *Harold Lasswell*

Text linguistics views texts as communication systems and helps us to understand the diversity of texts. The question is: What makes a study of text linguistics so special for text editing? A knowledge of texts and how they are composed can help to determine what is being said in a text and how it is being communicated to the reader, and for this reason text editors need to know about the nature of this discipline and the principles underlying it.

Texts are important sources of information that are used for both oral and written communication. Having a knowledge of texts as multilayered unities can help text editors when they have to examine the correctness of a text when judged against the context in which it communicates. Knowledge of text composition will help them to determine whether a text is correct when judged against the purpose it intends to fulfil. In this respect, there is a direct connection with the CCC model.

7.1 Text linguistics as a field of study

In this section, the following topics are discussed:

- What is studied in text linguistics?
- How is a knowledge of text linguistics valuable for text evaluation and editorial intervention?
- What impact does text linguistics have on the CCC model?

7.1.1 'Text' as a linguistic unit

Over the years, several approaches towards the study of texts or units bigger than a single phrase have developed. The approaches range from text grammar to text linguistics (De Beaugrande 1995, 2009; De Beaugrande & Dressler 1981), to discourse analysis (cf Bhatia, Flowerdew & Jones (eds) 2008; Brown & Yule 1983; Gee 2010; Van Dijk (ed) 1985, 2007; Schiffrin 1994; Schiffrin, Tannen & Hamilton (eds) 2001; Renkema 2004; Renkema (ed) 2009: Trappes-Lomax 2006), to critical discourse analysis (cf Bloor & Bloor 2007; Coffin, Lillis & O'Halloran (eds) 2010; Davies 2007: 140–148; Fairclough 1995; Seidlhofer (ed) 2003: 125–168; Toolan 1997; Van Dijk 2008; Wodak & Meyer (eds) 2009), to conversation analysis (Sidnell (ed) 2009; Sidnell 2010). This indicates that it is hard to find one 'right' approach to studying texts and it is therefore necessary to make a distinction between the different approaches:

- A *text grammar* attempts to create a model that can be used to describe and explain the grammatical structures in texts. This approach is similar to the Chomskyan starting point and it is probable that this is the reason why it does not usually receive a lot of support as a workable model (Van Dijk 1972). Text linguistics is 'devoted to describing how texts are *created* and *understood*' (Donnelly 1994: 18) and by such description the different features that determine textuality can be studied (De Beaugrande & Dressler 1981; De Beaugrande 2004, 2009; Mellet & Longrée (eds) 2009).
- *Discourse analysis* traditionally involves the analysis of written and spoken texts, especially the analysis of utterances as social interaction (Schiffrin 1994: 419). It turns out that it is difficult to determine the concept 'discourse' more accurately and this creates problems. Schiffrin (1994: 42), for instance, states that discourse analysis is 'one of the most vast, but also least defined, areas in linguistics' (cf Alba Juez 2009; Bhatia, Flowerdew & Jones (eds) 2008; Coffin, Lillis & O'Halloran (eds) 2010; Dontcheva-Navratilova & Povolna (eds) 2009; Dytel (ed) 2009; Gee 2010; Renkema 2004, 2009; Renkema (ed) 2009; Sidnell (ed) 2009; Van Dijk (ed) 1985, 2007).
- *Critical discourse analysis* (CDA) focuses on power relations (caused by ideology, racism, dominance, inequality, lies, denial and political rhetorics) as they are reflected in language. Language not only expresses the relationships between people, but also whether one or the other dominates (cf Bloor & Bloor 2007; Breeze 2011; Coffin, Lillis & O'Halloran (eds) 2010; Davies 2007: 140–148; Fairclough 1995; Hart (ed) 2011; O'Halloran 2003;

Pennycook 2001; Renkema 2004; Renkema (ed) 2009; Seidlhofer (ed) 2003: 125–168; Toolan 1997; Van Dijk 2008; Van Leeuwen 2008; Wodak & Meyer (eds) 2009; Wodak & Van Dijk (eds) 2000).

The approach used by De Beaugrande & Dressel (in their well-known *Introduction to text linguistics*, 1981) seems to be the preferred approach in text linguistics (De Beaugrande 1995, 2004, 2009; Mellet & Longrée (eds) 2009). This does not mean that De Beaugrande & Dressler's approach is the only or even the perfect starting point for a study of text linguistics. However, it does appear to be a useful and well-defined method and therefore it is also used in this book as a point of departure.

Before we consider text linguistics, however, there are a few questions that need to be answered first. For instance, What exactly is text? And also, How can the 'textuality' of a text be studied?

- About the concept 'text': it is extremely difficult to give an exhaustive, inclusive description of what text is (Trappes-Lomax 2006: 149–151). Carstens (1997: 82) uses the following working definition for this term (see also subsection 2.2 in this chapter): 'text is a component of language usage that text participants experience and accept as a unity on syntactic, semantic and pragmatic grounds.' For text linguistics it is important to know that there is a large variety of text types, which makes it impossible to give a perfect description of the concept 'text'.
- The problems surrounding 'textuality' and its specific nature form the actual focus of text linguistics. According to De Beaugrande & Dressler (1981: 3), a text can be considered a communicative event that fulfils the seven standards of textuality (later renamed as 'principles' by De Beaugrande in 1995) and it is possible to evaluate a text's acceptability or validity on the basis of these principles: cohesion, coherence, intentionality, acceptability, informativity, contextuality and intertextuality.

In the next section, these principles are explained briefly.

7.1.2 The principles of textuality

> The most salient phenomenon of discourse is the fact that *sentences* or utterances are *linked* together.
> *Renkema*

There are many sources that describe the content of the seven principles of textuality – compare, among others, De Beaugrande & Dressler (1981), Donnelly (1994), Carstens (1997) and Renkema (2004). The core aspects of cohesion, coherence, intentionality, acceptability, informativity and contextuality are explained below.

7.1.2.1 Cohesion

> ... *cohesion*, referring to the connections which have their manifestations in the discourse itself.
> *Renkema*

Broadly speaking, cohesion is about the way in which the surface components of the sentences in a text, that is, the individual words in a sentence or between successive sentences, are mutually connected. According to Halliday & Hasan (1976: 11), whose book *Cohesion in English* is generally accepted as a standard work, cohesion occurs 'where the interpretation of any item in the discourse requires making reference to some other item in the discourse'. De Beaugrande & Dressler (1981: 3) state that '... *surface components* depend upon each other according to *grammatical* forms and conventions, such that cohesion rests upon grammatical dependencies'. Renkema (2004: 51) sees cohesion as 'the connectivity that is *literally detectable* in discourse, for example, by synonyms or pronominal words such as *she, it,* etc'. This suggests that the syntactic knowledge of language users plays a central role in the creation of these relationships. Jackson (1990: 205) also refers to the fact that 'a *bond* is formed between one element and another because the interpretation of a sentence either depends on or is informed by some item in a previous – usually the previous – sentence'. Halliday & Hasan (1976: 8) claim that this connection has a semantic nature:

> Cohesion is a *semantic relation* between one element and another in the text and some other element that is crucial to the interpretation of it. This other element is also to be found in the text; but its location in the text is in no way determined by the grammatical structure. The two elements, the presupposing and the presupposed, may be structurally related to each other, or they may not be; it makes no difference to the meaning of the cohesive relation.

Halliday & Hasan (1976: 13) further believe that 'the concept of cohesion accounts for the essential semantic relations whereby any passage of speech or writing is enabled to function as text'. They also claim that this concept can be systematised on the basis of different categories that offer a practical method for describing and analysing texts:

> Each of these categories is represented in the text by particular *features* – repetitions, omissions, occurrences of certain words and constructions – which have in common the property of signalling that the interpretation of the passage in question *depends* on something else. If that 'something else' is verbally explicit, then there is cohesion.

These categories (known as 'cohesion markers') are: referencing, substitution, ellipsis, conjunction markers and lexical cohesion. The relationships of meaning that occur between these cohesion markers are called 'cohesion chains', which refers to the creation of chains or links between words in previous or following sentences (cf Baker 1992: 180–215; Christiansen 2011; Halliday & Hasan 1976, 1985). Cohesion as such is the result of a process that is realised through several methods (cohesion markers forming cohesion chains). These categories are explained by means of examples below.

- *Referencing*

Referencing is the most common cohesion chain in language usage (Halliday & Hasan 1976, 1985; Kibrik 2011). It relies on the principle that two (or more) elements in the same part of a text can be associated with each other at a semantic level because they both refer to the same referent in reality. The concepts 'antecedent' (that which is referred to) and 'anaphora' (that which refers to the same referent in a shorter way) are especially important here. Some examples will illustrate referencing:

> You can use *any bent pin* as **a hook** when you want to catch *a fish*. On *that pin* you put a little worm. If **the fish** then notices the curly worm on **the hook**, *it* will bite soon.

Explanation:
- *Any bent pin* (antecedent) is in a referencing relationship with *that pin* (anaphora).
- *A hook* (antecedent) is in a referencing relationship with *the hook* (anaphora).
- *A fish* (antecedent) is in a referencing relationship with *the fish* (anaphora) and *it* (anaphora).
- *A little worm* (antecedent) is in a referencing relationship with *the curly worm* (anaphora).

Thus: antecedents can consist of various language forms, as can anaphoras. It is true, though, that pronouns are in general used more frequently than anaphoras, but that does not exclude the possibility that other language forms can fulfil the same function. For text editors it is important to know which language forms are used.

Further examples:
- Please put *this table* in the corner, but try not to knock *it* against the wall.
- *This coat* is years old, but is still nicer to wear than *my new one*.
- *The government* wants to use this to make it clear: *The government* will not allow *itself* to be prescribed to by anyone.
- A long, long time ago, *an evil leprechaun* lived in a big forest. *This leprechaun* did not like it when **naughty children** played in *his* forest and for this reason *he* laid several sly plans to keep **them** out of *his* forest.
- *The group of children*, who played soccer on **the grass** the whole day, returned home eventually. *They* were thirsty and *they* were thoroughly grumpy because *they* were all itching from having played on **the grass**. We could have sworn we had told *them they* should not go and play **there**!

It is essential for text editors to know about the concept of referencing and especially about the elements involved in the referencing process, because the issue of congruence (ie agreement in terms of number and gender) is so fundamentally important to clear and correct communication. Compare, for instance:

> – *Annie,* stand still for a moment. Suzie, look how wonderful *he* looks in *his* dress. (Annie is typically a woman's name and the pronouns used as anaphoras should therefore be female (*she, her*) rather than male (*he, his*).)
> – *Ministers* should receive a housing allowance, so *he* can take care of *his* own accommodation. (*Ministers* is a plural noun whereas *he* and *his* are singular; it would be more correct to choose either 'a minister' and 'he/his' or 'ministers' and 'they/their'.)

- *Substitution*

As a cohesion marker, subsitution is quite rare in formal written language. It refers to the replacement of one element by another element (a replacing word or phrase) without a change in meaning. The element replaced does not refer to the same referent as the antecedent (as is usually the case with referencing). Some illustrative examples:

> – *My pencil* is already too short to write with. I will have to get *another one.*
> – We had searched for *a house* for ten months before we found *the perfect one* by accident.
> – Please sort through *this bag of apples* for me. You can throw the *rotten ones* out.
> – Laura will do the *dishes* if she is ordered to, but John will never do *this* at all.

- *Ellipsis*

Ellipsis occurs rather infrequently in written language, though it occurs more often in spoken language where the context can clarify the language forms. This phenomenon (also known as omission, deletion or eclipsis) implies the omission of certain elements from the text because within the context of the selected sentence these deleted elements can still be deduced and interpreted. With substitution the part that is replaced is still present, but in the case of ellipsis it must be inferred. Some examples illustrate this:

> – But I thought he was …
> – Count Dracula says: 'I never drink … wine.'

- *Conjunction*

The phenomenon of conjunction occurs often in texts. It helps to make the flow of the text clear (and through this it also helps to achieve coherence) by connecting consecutive sentences with each other using cohesion markers that express certain relationships (for instance, contrasting, coordinating, reasoning, indicating time, summarising, ordering, analysing, illustrating, interrupting or agreeing). The word classes known as 'conjunctions' and 'adverbs' (see chapter 7) typically act as markers of conjunction relationships:

> – *Adverb of consequence:* Text editors have been provided with all the tools they need. *Thus,* they will be able to polish almost any text.
> – *Subordinating conjunction: Unless* we act now, the text quality will be lost.

– *Conjunctive adverb:* The text will not function optimally. *Moreover*, it will create the wrong impression.

- *Lexical cohesion*
Lexical cohesion is the underlying connection between so-called 'content words' (nouns, verbs, adjectives, adverbs) in consecutive sentences. There are two possible kinds of lexical relationship (meaning relationships), namely repetition and collocation. *Repetition* occurs by means of direct repetition of words through synonyms, superordinates, epithets, etc. *Collocations* (ie words that can be associated with each other on the basis of their meaning, even though the nature of this relationship is not clear) also occur in the form of synonyms (eg *calm, quiet, peaceful*), antonyms (eg *small*), complementary terms (eg *true, false*), oppositions (eg *parent, child*), meronyms (part–whole relationships) (eg *leg, body, arm*), ordered series (eg *day, week, month, year*), combination possibilities between words (eg *drive + motorcycle, dog + bark*). The nature of these special relationships is not always equally clear, but there is always a kind of relationship that contributes to the bonding of these words. These connections lead to a better understanding of the text and help to increase cohesion and therefore also coherency.

Text editors must be aware of the potential that words have at a lexical level. Since it is assumed that more than 40 per cent of the cohesion chains are based on lexical cohesion (Hoey 1991: 9), this is an important area for the practitioner to immerse themselves in.

The abovementioned relationships help to create cohesion chains that can make surface connections clear and controllable. Baker (1992: 211) and Christiansen (2011) point out that cohesion can also be achieved by other means. These include continuity of tenses, consistency of style and register, punctuation (for instance, like conjunction markers, semicolons indicate how parts of sentences connect or simply state that they are connected). A knowledge of the nature of these markers and the chains they create should be indispensable to language practitioners.

7.1.2.2 Coherence

> ... *coherence*, referring to the connections which can be made by the reader or listener based on knowledge outside the discourse.
> *Renkema*

'Coherence is a product of many different factors, which combine to make every paragraph, every sentence, and every phrase contribute to the meaning of the whole piece' (Kies 2000). Coherence as a principle of textuality (and of writing in general) is accepted as one of the main components of any form of language study. It is considered to be 'the single most important principle of textuality' (Werth 1984: 7), because if a text cannot be understood, then it is not a 'good text'. The main objective of research in text linguistics is to determine what makes one text 'acceptable' but another 'unacceptable'. In other words, 'what makes a sequence of sentences or utterances a discourse' (Renkema 2009).

It is difficult to define what exactly makes a text 'coherent', because Brown & Yule (1983: 199) claim that 'texts are what hearers *treat* as texts' and in this way it is quite indeterminable. Text receivers are just as likely to accept a text as valid or as invalid, based on their experience with language in general and with the context in which a statement occurs. Neubert & Shreve's (1992: 94) description of this matter is insightful: 'A coherent text has an *underlying logical structure* that acts to guide the reader through the text' so 'it "sticks together" as a unit' (Hatch 1992: 209) and creates the idea that the text is coherent, makes sense and is more than a random collection of words. It is all about the connection of ideas and concepts – in other words, about a conceptual link. If the ideas are not related to one another – if they do not have an underlying, logical structure – then the text cannot be good (see Donnelly 1994: 75).

For text editors, textual unity is the outcome to which they strive, both at a structural and at a conceptual level. A text will be accepted and experienced as coherent if (Yancey 2004):

- all the sentences in the text relate in some way to the same discourse topic;
- all the sentences (and paragraphs) follow one another in a logical order;
- the sentences and paragraphs are conceptually linked.

If a text does not possess these features, it will be hard to achieve effective communication (see further sections 12 and 13 in chapter 6 for a discussion on the importance of coherence in a text). Coherence is therefore largely concerned with interpretability or with the ability text users have to build a world around the text and interpet it. Text users' communicative competencies are challenged daily. They have to try to understand texts on the basis of their predicted nature and structure and by relying on shared experiences with similar texts.

7.1.2.3 Intentionality and acceptability

Intentionality and acceptability are two principles usually considered as one 'pair' because they are so attuned to each other. For every text there is a producer who has the intention to transfer a piece of information and a receiver of information who must be willing to accept that the presented text is intended as a communicative event. Symbiosis can be achieved only when both producer and receiver adhere to the Gricean cooperative principle (1975), which determines that each participant in an interaction will normally deliver maximum effort to make the intended communication successful (Blake 2008: 113–118). Thus, sender-writers and receiver-readers must work cooperatively and must mutually accept each other in order to reach an optimal communicative effect. In other words, they have to correspond properly (see the correspondence criterion above for analysis of the CCC model). If the writer succeeds in achieving the predefined objective of his text and at the same time manages to fulfil the need(s) and expectation(s) of the readers, the text has met the correspondence criterion.

This condition is considered to be the most important demand made on the text editor: make sure that what the writer wants to communicate (information about a certain topic) corresponds to what the reader would want to know about the topic.

7.1.2.4 Informativity

Informativity is the way in which text components transfer specific communicative information. For instance, an identifying statement such as *The man with the golden watch* has more communicative value (and hence more informative value) than a personal pronoun such as *he* or even *the man*. Because so much of what practitioners work on involves information transfer and identifying a text's readership first and foremost, a knowledge of informativity systems is essential, as is knowledge about the informative value of syntactic expressions. It is also important to know that information is organised in terms of known (old or given) and unknown (new) information (Clark & Haviland's 1977 *Given–new contract*). Text editors have to know that in a text there must be a balance between what its readers know and what they do not. Knowledge of this balance helps text editors to make responsible decisions about the correct distribution and place of information that has to be communicated.

7.1.2.5 Contextuality

> We develop on the idea that everything is related, inside, and therefore determined by a context.
> *Gershenson*

Contextuality as a principle focuses on the extremely important role of context in any form of communication. Trask (1997: 68) states that '*Every text* – that is, *everything* that is said and written – *unfolds in some context of use*'. This means that in any situation where language is used, the quality and effectiveness of the communication are determined by the contextual knowledge of the text participants: for instance, background information, role patterns and social demands. This aspect of language usage is studied within the framework of both sociolinguistics and pragmatics. Sociolinguistics studies how language is influenced by its sociocultural context, whereas pragmatics focuses on how meaning is produced and comprehended by language users.

Communication can never be disentangled from its context (cf Skehan 1995: 91; Fetzer & Oishi (eds) 2011; Trappes-Lomax 2006: 144–146; Van Dijk 2010; Woods 2006: ix–x; Renkema 2004: 41). Well-founded decisions have to be made about target group, style, register, content and structure of the text, because discourse, after all, is more than merely a matter of transmitting a message to a receiver. Aspects involved are, for instance, the plan of the discourse, the physical environment in which it takes place, the cognitive skills of the receiver to make the right inferences and the development of the receivers' communicative competence.

Text participants should find common ground so that communication remains 'a form of social action, of *joint* action' (Renkema 2004: 42) that needs to take into account the 'appropriateness of language use' (Skehan 1995: 91) to a specific context. Text editors have to contribute to unfolding this common ground clearly so that contextual equivalence (Neubert & Schreve 1992: 85–88) can be attained.

7.1.2.6 Intertextuality

> Intertextuality ... is central to a definition of what a text is.
> *Slembrouck*

> This principle literally means that the formation and interpretation of a text are influenced by the structure of other, similar texts; in other words, 'texts often ... *respond* to *prior* texts, and at the same time, *anticipate subsequent* ones'.
> *Auer*

One text is never exactly the same as another, but it can belong to the same broad category and often this, usually hard to define, relationship leads to the acceptance of a text within a certain context of use. For instance, if people read a poem, it is reasonable to assume that they 'understand' this poem (at least in terms of its structure) because they have read and understood other poems before. That is also the reason why a newspaper is accepted as a newspaper: because it corresponds to previous experiences with this genre of news coverage. And so it is that experiences with one text type open up a world of similar texts for their readers.

In a similar way, language users have so much mutually shared background knowledge (about as diverse matters as those that cover the social, cultural, political, religious, economic, literary and linguistic fields) at their disposal that it is in fact quite natural that their experience and evaluation of a text is to a large extent based on this knowledge. Language users, too, implicitly build a sort of genre knowledge in their daily interactions with language in this way, and this knowledge is activated when a text is presented as a certain type. The expectations of what a text should look like, based on previous experiences with similar texts, determine how they will interpret a new text: Is the structure as it should be? Is the content appropriate to the type of text? Are the style and register correct for the genre? and so on.

Intertextuality is therefore also the starting point for distinguishing between different text types (see again section 3.3.2 above) and for the production of text types on the basis of certain features (for instance, the fact that a poetry anthology and a textbook differ in their content and structure). Intertextuality is therefore an important cognitive precondition for the production and the reception of texts (Fetzer & Oishi 2011; Slembrouck 2007: 3–4).

7.1.2.7 Perspective

Text linguistics feeds on theoretical knowledge from a variety of research fields – syntax, semantics, pragmatics, sociolinguistics, literary theory, etc. In this respect, it adopts an interdisciplinary approach to language study, which accounts for its broad, all-encompassing perspective.

7.2 Text linguistics and text editing

The main goal of text linguistics is to study textuality, that is, whether a text or passages of text are acceptable and successful or not, as judged through the lens of the seven principles of textuality. Viewed from this perspective, the purpose of the text-editing process (see later in chapter 4) is to shape an effective text that communicates to the full from the outset. Text linguistics and text editing therefore pursue a common objective: the creation of a successful text. In due course, we shall demonstrate how a knowledge of text linguistics – and, more specifically, of the principles of textuality – helps practitioners to achieve the objectives of the text-editing process.

7.2.1 Cohesion

In section 7.1.2.1 above, it was pointed out that text cohesion refers to the way in which the surface structure of a text is created, in other words, the way in which words are combined in line with the structural patterns of a language. The aim is to form effective sentences that promote unity and effective communication with the aid of cohesion markers such as referencing, substitution, ellipsis, lexical cohesion and conjunction.

Cohesive elements contribute to the creation of an understandable text because they help to draw attention to connections between concepts and words by making them verbally explicit (Donnelly 1994: 96). This, in turn, promotes textual continuity and also contributes to making 'text comprehension proceed more efficiently'. As Donnelly puts it '... cohesion emphasizes the *syntax* of sentences and indicates how cohesive devices can be used to make a text more *compact*, so that the text is easier to *comprehend*' (1994: 96–97).

In effect, the surface structure (syntax and semantics) is usually the most visible text structure and a good indicator of text quality. Having a sound knowledge of the cohesive elements and techniques that contribute to an effective text will enable text editors to do this structure justice, in the process highlighting the chains that link words and sentences and facilitating an author's subtle linguistic connections.

7.2.2 Intentionality and acceptability

Intentionality and acceptability focus on the contributions of the participants in the information-transfer role of documents of various kinds. Texts are always produced with a certain intention in mind: their originators want essentially to transfer information. For their part, on the other hand, the recipients (readers) must be willing to accept the good intentions of the text producer and ultimately find the product of both author's and editor's labours acceptable.

In this process, then, text editors act as mediators between the originator and the intended reader. Consequently, they have to be able, first, to understand the originator's intention and interpret it in such a way that effective communication can take place. If they conclude that the author's intention is not being successfully transmitted, or that their product is not acceptable as is, the practitioner needs to make the necessary adjustments to the text in consultation with the author, even if this means intervening in a heavy-handed way akin to performing 'surgery' on the text (Fryer 1997: 30). Sometimes, it is only through the hard work of a 'heavy edit' (see chapter 3), that is, by correcting the text's cohesive structure and content fundamentally, that the intended information can be transferred successfully.

Text editors are therefore facilitators in the full meaning of the word, because they have to be able to imagine themselves both as originator and as reader. It is their task to identify and correct any and all errors and infelicities that could inhibit the successful communication of the writer's intention.

7.2.3 Contextuality

No piece of information can be conveyed outside a context or, as Trask (1997: 68) has put it: 'Every text – that is everything that is said or written – unfolds in some context of use.' Donnelly (1994: 159) adds that we must remember that '*grammar* alone does not offer all the information we need to know in order to speak or write in every given situation'. In every communicative situation, then, we have to look further, beyond pure language structure. Woods (2006: ix) supports this view as follows:

> The ability to communicate competently requires us to learn and understand the dynamic and shifting system of *communication in context*, and we learn it by becoming familiar with patterns and routines of language usage.

Consequently, contextuality covers the entire spectrum of knowledge that can be used to evaluate a given text: the time and place of communication, who the text editor is, the language form used, the shared background knowledge, and so on (De Beaugrande & Dressler 1981). If the text is an academic one, for instance, the reader will know which aspects of their contextual knowledge are involved: a specific register and style, a characteristic typography, layout and structure, etc. Each text is evaluated through the recipients' knowledge of that text: for instance, Who is the target group?, What is the content? and What is the format? For the reader, therefore, all possible knowledge that influences the interpretation of a given text matters when they come to determine whether or not it is successful within its context of use.

Text editors aim to present a successful text to a specific target group in a specific context. This often requires sound choices about what is appropriate in which context, in which case the personal contextual background of the text editor does play a role. For this reason, if text editors are aware of what contextuality means as a text-linguistic principle, they will be better able to distinguish between what is appropriate to a specific text and what is not.

7.2.4 Informativity

Informativity is mainly concerned with the way in which language elements are used to provide information in a text. It is an accepted fact that not everything that is conveyed either verbally or visually is equally informative: we have to decide which is and which is not. For instance, a third person pronoun such as *he* has less informative value than a proper noun (the Ambassador). The text editor has to ensure an effective spread of information throughout a text, in other words, that a balance is struck between old/known information and new/unknown information, because this balance makes the text readable and interesting (Bell 2000: 168). Establishing this balance is particularly important in expository texts such as school and university textbooks, where authors often experience difficulty dealing with or juxtaposing the known and the unknown, or enabling learners and students to acquire knowledge deductively.

The degree of familiarity/unfamiliarity of information for a particular reader group should determine the method of communication and the language elements to be used in the knowledge transfer process. If a text becomes boring as a consequence of the information not being new to or of great interest to the target group and loses thematic coherency, it must be made more interesting without its content being altered. If a text carries only known information, the informative load is too low to make the text attractive to a potential readership. In this respect, the key role of the text editor as intermediary between author and editor should not be underestimated: it requires not only a keen and critical eye for gaps and imbalances in texts but also a good grasp of the needs of the intended readership.

7.2.5 Intertextuality

Previously in this chapter, intertextuality as a principle of textuality was related to the influence of other (older, different) texts on the interpretation of a given text. An understanding of intertextuality – or of text types, of the requirements for specific texts and of the way in which one text can influence another – is important because texts have to be assessed as valid examples of the specific genre into which they purport to fit. Therefore, a knowledge of genre (or genres) is essential to the work of text editors, for it is they who have to know what the final version of a text should look like in terms of its presentation.

7.2.6 Coherence

Coherence, or the way in which a text makes sense and shows coherency to the reader, is another non-negotiable facet of text editing: striving for coherence must at all times and at all costs be the objective of the professional text editor's intervention. They must take care that the exposition of a topic is logical and continuous, so that consecutive sentences, paragraphs and sections follow each other logically and link up meaningfully, and that there are no hiccups in the development of the author's train of thought. Through this intervention, the practitioner will be contributing to text unity and texture (ie the heart of coherence) (Forey & Thompson 2008).

Coherence is one of the most important criteria by which to evaluate any kind of text. There is no point in presenting a collection of beautifully formulated sentences containing wonderful ideas if there is no logical connection between those sentences. If readers cannot move from one sentence to another fluently, then they will stop reading and the result will be a breakdown of communication. The text editor must prevent this eventuality by reading a manuscript with an eye solely focused on coherence.

7.3 Text linguistics and the CCC model

Text linguistics – which by definition attempts to clarify how a text is produced and understood – strongly focuses on written texts, and knowledge of aspects of text formulation is indispensable for text editors. Accordingly, in the course of the preceding discussion, we have indicated what a knowledge of text linguistics entails for the practitioner, specifically the principles of textuality and their value and role, and the value it can bring to editorial interventions. Text linguistics provides a valuable foundation for text editors because it allows them to make more well-founded (or 'correct') and also more nuanced (regarding 'consistency' and 'correspondence') judgements about the validity or the success of a text.

Having a knowledge of text linguistics also enables text editors to shape cohesive and coherent texts that are contextually relevant, intertextually appropriate and sufficiently informative. This also means that the original text originator's intention has to come clearly to the fore and also has to be accepted. The text will be considered to have succeeded provided it does not have to be read more than once in order for the content to have been absorbed and understood. If through their intervention the text editor does not help the author to achieve this objective, then they will not have performed to an acceptable standard. In the training of professional text editors, therefore, the value of theoretical knowledge – especially of text linguistics, but also of normative linguistics (see section 4 in this chapter) and document design (see section 6 in this chapter) – should not be underestimated.

In section 3.3.2 above, the appropriate evaluation points in terms of Renkema's CCC model were pointed out. The following evaluation points are particularly relevant to text linguistics.

Text facets	Evaluation points	Text quality To be guaranteed through …	Foundations of text linguistics Norms pertaining to …	
Text type	1	Appropriateness of text	Contextuality Intentionality Appropriateness	
	2	Unity of genre	Intertextuality	
	3	Correct application of genre rules	Intertextuality Informativity	
Content	4	Appropriate information Sufficient information	Appropriateness Informativity	Knowledge of sources
	5	Unity of information	Informativity	
	6	Correct facts	Informativity	
Structure	7	Sufficient cohesion	Cohesion Coherence Informativity	
	8	Uniform structure	Informativity Cohesion Coherence	
	9	Correct linking words Correct argumentation	Cohesion Coherence	
Wording	10	Appropriate wording	Cohesion Contextuality Intertextuality	

Table 2.4 *Text quality and text linguistics: evaluating text*

The above evaluation points play an important role in assessing how understandable and coherent texts are. Text-linguistic principles and their implications for text structure take up a prominent position in text editors' theoretical baggage.

In the next section, we pay attention to the nature of document design and its importance in the process of understanding, intervening in and polishing texts.

8 Document design and text quality

> Readers deserve documents that meet their needs, and (…) the people who create prose and graphics play a central role in making this happen.
> *Schriver*

> Design is an editorial tool ... used to manipulate the raw materials: space, words-in-type, pictures, colour ... Good design should make the reason for publishing the message flare off the page at first glance. This should be the editor's primary goal: clarity in communicating ideas – as they are defined by the writer.
> *White*

Documents or texts in documents play an important role in almost everyone's daily activities, but, as Schriver (1997: 3) points out, rather surprisingly, 'knowledge about creating documents for audiences is not yet well developed. Most ideas about writing and design are based on intuition, lore and personal experience.'

Not surprisingly, many documents fail because they are so unattractive or inaccessible that readers do not understand them well enough, even though people have for a long time been insisting on *readable* texts. According to Schriver (1997: xxiii), the theory of document design should aim to determine how texts can be made 'less ugly and less confusing', where the words themselves can take their rightful place. If that aim is realised, texts will have become 'good' documents that are likely to be more readily easily read and bring about effective communication.

In this section we provide an overview of what document design entails, mainly focusing on:

• how knowledge of document design can be valuable in evaluating text quality;
• the impact of document design on the accessibility, readability and communicative value of a text.

8.1 Document design

> Designing effectively means thinking about *who* is going to use a document, *how* it is going to be *used*, how it is going to be *produced* ....
> *Walker*

> Document designers ... need to understand that a document should be designed in such a way to make it as easy as possible for the reader to consume the information.
> *De Stadler et al*

> One of the myths in the field of publication making is that readers are readers. In actuality, they start out as viewers. They scan, they hunt and peck, searching for the valuable nuggets of information. Reluctant to work, saturated by media, and a bit lazy, they literally need to be lured into reading. Then, they need to be gently but purposefully led through the information.
> *White*

The title of the book *Document design: Linking writer's goals to readers' needs* (Maes et al 1999) provides a good indication of what document design aims at (see also cf Felker et al 1981; White 1989; Campbell 1995; Jansen & Maes 1999; Delin, Bateman & Allen 2002; De Stadler 2004, 2005). Document design tries to harmonise the goal(s) of the text originator with the need(s) of the receiver, the underlying thought being that many documents are presented in a format that does not help to achieve this balance between goal and need, and therefore fail as communications media, largely because they don't marry a clearly defined textual message with the visual and design elements (images, sequencing, contrasts of size, scale, typefaces) that contribute to a 'visually unified and intellectually consistent whole' (White 1989: 8).

In other words, the relationship between the individual contributions of the participants of the communication process – author, text editor, book designer, reader – is a core factor in determining the visual presentation of the text, the way in which it is 'packaged' (cf Campbell 1995; De Stadler 2004, 2005; De Stadler, Basson & Luttig 2005; Shriver 1997: xxv–xxix; Walker 2001: 3).

Knowledge of the target group is therefore the absolute starting point: if you do not know who is going to read the text, the publisher will not know how to design the 'package' in order to make it communicate optimally. For some readers, a text-heavy book may be more appealing (as being 'serious', 'authoritative'), whereas for others a stronger visual element will be required to induce them to read on. A consideration of the reader – with all their perceived strengths and weaknesses – plays a central role in the planning and creation of the text, and here two central questions have to be answered: Does the reader experience the text as accessible, readable and communicative? How can the text be adapted to become more attractive, accessible and communicative?

Document design helps to ensure the creation of good documents and it is the process in which good writing (content) and good visual design (typography and layout) almost coalesce to make a joint contribution to bringing readers into contact with documents and texts that communicate well (White 1989: 9–12, 36). In this respect, Schriver (1997: 10) also talks about the integration of writing and visual design or, in other words, about the way in which content (writing) and presentation (graphics and typography) can be reconciled in order to achieve the chosen objective of a particular text with the projected target group. Document design can thus be defined as '... the field concerned with *creating texts* (broadly defined) that integrate *words* and *pictures* in ways that help people to achieve their specific goals of using texts at home, school or work'.

Walker (2001: 3) maintains that effective design is impossible if the following parameters are not taken into account:

> No description of visual organisation, or effective designing, can take place without knowing something about the *intended* readers, circumstances of use, means of production, and the *content* of the information, as each of these parameters offers its own constraints and opportunities.

Since document designers must strive to balance readers' expectations with the function, content, structure and style of a specific document type (De Stadler, Basson & Luttig 2005), the central question to be addressed is: How will choices about graphics (tables, illustrations and pictures) and typography (font, spaces, etc) contribute to the optimisation of text understanding?

Graphic techniques and the judicious use of space play an important role in this process of making texts accessible and readable, since they will articulate text and thus greatly influence how pages of words are interpreted by readers (Walker 2001: 12). The introduction of the personal computer has created many new possibilities for document design, word processors lending themselves to experimentation with the concepts of page, space, variation in fonts types and sizes, and the like, all in the interests of creating 'the perfect document'. The visual development of electronic texts and text types as diverse as websites, annual reports and blogs has given a new lease of life to document design. Yet the danger always exists for design to predominate over words (a common failing of many websites and blogs), at which point the author's intention and message suffer.

8.2 The process of document design

> Editors and designers need to have clear guidelines for how information should be presented, should pay attention to consistency, and should respect the basic principles of design.
> *Bowles & Borden*

> ... words have to be turned into visible marks on paper if the ideas are to be transmitted to someone else. And once you have those visible marks, you cannot help but have design.
> *White*

Document design principles have to be taken into account when evaluating a text for editing. Obviously, text editors do not have to be experts in the area of document design in order to be able to edit a text, but their ability to distinguish between what makes a text's presentation effective or not (whether that involves questions of type style choice or layout, or even the positioning of illustrations in relation to the text) may go a long way towards helping to improve the edited final product (White 1989: 7–12). To this end, they will need to know – even if only at a basic level – about which design and layout processes a document has to go through in order to achieve the objective to make it as attractive and accessible as possible so that effective communication can take place.

According to Bowles & Borden (2011: 175; cf White 13–14, 33–36), a decent text design has certain advantages for its readers, since it:

• attracts their attention;
• reads more easily than a text that is not well designed;
• wards off boredom in the reader;
• structures the content of a text in terms of relative importance.

Analysis and design play a prominent role in the document designing process, since they help identify and clarify the advantages of good text design in different ways.

Each document has to be contextually analysed. In other words, the following have to be determined: the objective of the text, the intended target audience, and the topic or theme of the text. The following questions need to be answered in the course of this process:

› Who is the target group?
What, among other things, is the audience's educational and social background, interests and profession?

› How much knowledge do the readers already have on the subject?
Do they know anything about it? If so, how much do they already know?

› How complete should this document be?
Will leaving out information be detrimental to understanding the topic or the author's thesis?

› Is it supposed to be a long or a short document?
What is common practice in this area or domain? How much will potential readers be willing to pay for such a document?

› What needs to be achieved with the text?
Does the text aim at changing the opinion of the readers, informing them, or motivating them to act?

› What is the target group supposed to do with the text?
For instance, if the text is a pamphlet on HIV/Aids, what should the reader learn from this pamphlet? Is behaviour change an important outcome?

› How does the document need to be approached in order to attain its intended objective?
For instance, how should a pamphlet on the dangers linked to substance abuse be approached in order to induce a change in behaviour in the readers?

› Does the document need to be illustrated?
Does the inclusion of tables, drawings, sketches and photographs enhance the document's intention or message?

The answers to these kinds of question help the document designer, together with the text editor, to make important choices with regard to the approach of the document, the style and the register of the document, the language and the visual elements (layout and typography), the genre it belongs to. This aspect is discussed further in section 2 of chapter 4.

The result of an analysis largely determines the approach the design should take, since it is now clear what the text intends to achieve. The outcome is the document's blueprint and the focus is on its features or components and how each of them contributes both individually and together to balancing the intention of the writer and the needs of the reader (ie so that they correspond – one of the three model CCC criteria).

8.3 The principles of document design

> It is often at the level of typographic detail that formal-looking documents fall down.
> *Walker*

> Typography is one of the most influential elements on the character and emotional quality of a design. It can produce a neutral effect or rouse the passions, it can symbolize artistic, political or philosophical movements, or it can express the personality of an individual or organisation.
> *Ambrose & Harris*

> *Fonts* are part of the twenty-first-century document examination ... what they are and why someone may pick them for a specific communication, can be telling and significant.
> *Cornwell*

Content, structure, style, typography and layout are facets of the delicate balancing act of document design. Text and illustration, and to a lesser extent typography and layout, contain a predetermined, fixed content (ie an intended message), a specific structure and a certain style. They all support the text's accessibility and readability. Some organisations use house style or a stylesheet (a prescribed structure) for the design, which makes it relatively easy to create a document. In other cases, the result of an analysis of a particular document's attributes and readership (see above) will determine what the design will look like. The design facets are introduced briefly below, but are discussed in detail in chapter 10.

8.3.1 Content

The content of a document depends on its function (to inform, motivate, evaluate, etc). Knowing about how much the audience already knows, is familiar with, is used to and is expecting is imperative and will inform the document design brief (regarding the page size, text types, line spacing and width, structure, style, special typographical features and layout).

8.3.2 Structure

When audience and content have been decided upon, the next step is to arrange the content along internal (how the text is structured, eg aim-approach or problem-solution) and external (linguistic and graphic) structural lines. The internal text structure is commensurate with the argumentative or persuasive structure of a text and this is closely related to the genre. For external structure we can distinguish between, on the one hand, text elements (such as titles, table of contents, introduction, paragraphs, summary) and, on the other hand, sentence elements (such as thesis statement or topic sentence, structuring sentences, the use of link words such as adverbs and conjunctions, vertical lists).

8.3.3 Style

Style is the way in which a theme is expressed through language. Style defines the degree of difficulty, precision, density, coherence of the text, and the degree of reader involvement.

The two components that are typically associated with the surface realisation of document design are typography and layout, which is why they are discussed in more detail below. A knowledge of these components is required every time document design is talked about, because it allows text editors to use clear criteria for systematically analysing and designing documents.

8.3.4 Typography

Typography pertains to those visual features of text that make it easier for people to read and understand a text. There is an extensive literature on typography as a discipline and as a concept, but since the purpose of this text is merely to provide an introduction, only a few views are discussed here.

Ambrose & Harris (2005: 6) define typography as the way in which a written idea takes on a visual form (ie through choice of font, size of font, degree of contrast between fonts on a page, the amount of white space between and around the type, and so on). Walker (2001: 2) adds to this that typography is concerned with the rules that influence people when they make choices about the visual organisation of a text. From this perspective, a typographer is someone who uses specific visual techniques to help express the meaning of a text and so ensures that the text is easily accessible to the readers (White 1989: 39–45). For this reason, Bowles & Borden (2011: 175) consider typography as 'the art of designing and arranging *type* to have *desired effects* on readers'. The use of white space and type, and layout generally (see further below), are important aspects of any document and they work together with the following aims of good document design:

List 2.6 The effect of typography on text

> › to determine the tone, visual impact and the feeling of a text (however formal or informal the style or register);

> › to clarify the structure of a text (eg ideas are grouped together to form paragraphs);

> › to invite and motivate readers to navigate within the text (eg from top to bottom, from left to right, column by column, by clicking hyperlinks);

> › to indicate the text genre;

>>

> › to suggest how a text should be interpreted (Is it important, should it be saved, or is this just an introduction?);
>
> › to determine and indicate what is important to the reader (by means of spacing, type styles (bold, italic, regular) and sizes, titles and sub-titles, and the use of special effects to give prominence to certain features).

Typography is therefore mainly concerned with the following details of design:

- **The use of space on a page**
  This includes margin width, white space between lines, paragraphs and sections, size of illustrations and space around them, placement of illustrations, etc.

- **Type styles/fonts**
  These include graphic design of the type of letters used, some of which have serifs (short, horizontal strokes at the bottom and the top of the letters; these fonts are generally preferred for more conservative, 'serious' communications, as in academic articles; examples are Times Roman, Courier and Garamond).

  Other fonts do not have serifs (sans serif). Sans serif typefaces allow a larger variation in form and in contrast than letters with serifs. They tend to be regarded as more modern and easier on the eye; examples are Arial, Calibri and Century Gothic.

  Most fonts have differences in slope and weight (variants): roman (normal, straight text), **bold, extra bold** and *italics*. It is tiring on the eye to read long pieces of text in either italics or bold; however, italics is often used to indicate emphasis, foreign words, a translation, and the like.

- **Type families**
  This refers to a number of fonts that are related to each other, for instance all the different sizes and variants of Times New Roman or Arial or Courier. There are several variants of Arial, for instance: Arial, Arial Narrow, **Arial Rounded**, **Arial Black**.

- **Type weight**
  Fonts can be indicated in different ways, in terms of light (Arial) or dark (**Arial**), light italics (*Arial*), black italics (***Arial***), ultrablack (**Arial**).

- **Type sizes**
  The size of a letter or other character is usually measured in points (there are about 72 points in one inch (or 2.5 cm)) and can be quite large. As a rule of thumb, 9 to 13 point is regarded as legible and therefore readable for body text. Sizes bigger than 13 point are generally reserved for headings and subheadings.

- **Flexibility of typefaces**

  Preferably choose a flexible typeface. Times New Roman and **Arial** are typefaces that are flexible and can easily be used in the different ways described above.

- **Indication of contrast**

  In some texts, it is necessary to change typefaces in order to stress certain things, or to distinguish different features on a page. For instance, typefaces with a bigger size and a heavier weight are reserved for titles, headings and subheadings so that they stand out from the smaller and lighter typeface of the body text.

It all boils down to how appropriate a certain choice is or, as Quinn (2001: 73) puts it: 'A publication's choice of typeface directly influences how easily people read it ....' Several typographic devices (eg space between lines of type, spacing between words, typefaces, letter size, letter weight) can be used to realise this objective, and text designers have some freedom here. Walker (2001: 12) points out that graphic devices and space have an important distinguishing role because they help to unfold the different elements in a text (clearly) by presenting them visually:

> Words or phrases may be differentiated for a number of reasons: to show emphasis, quotation from another source, distinction (eg of a book title). Access structures such as headings, notes, commentaries, lists may be treated in particular ways so that readers can distinguish them.

Thus, typography has to be used in such a way that it increases the accessibility and attractiveness of a text. In this respect, it plays a cardinal role in how readers experience the content of the text cognitively (White 1989: 12), how they organise it and how they remember it. In short: a well-chosen typographical style contributes to the accessibility and readability of a document.

As Bowles & Borden (2011: 175) confirm, text editors rarely play a role in the choice of typographic means. (After all, this is the task of a specialised typographer, graphic designer or book designer.) However, they do *evaluate* the effectiveness and consistency of the typographical choices and in this way they do influence the readability of a text. If a text – whether in print or on a website or a blog – is a typographical 'miracle work' but is not reader-friendly, the designing process has missed the mark. Text editors must therefore evaluate whether the typography is appropriate in relation to the objectives of the document. In this way, text editors contribute to the success of texts as communicative media.

Bowles & Borden (2011: 185) point out further that:

> Editors and designers who develop an aesthetic appreciation of the differences [between] styles, weights and families, as well as a *practical knowledge* of type sizes and widths, will always be in demand.

8.3.5 Layout

> ... a good layout will *support* your copy, not dominate it.
> *Ferreira & Staude*

> Good layout is one whose whole is greater than the sum of its parts. If ... the layout tells its story and manages to look attractive while doing so, then you've got a synergistic wonder that makes one plus one equal three.
> *White*

Layout is the 'language' of line, mass, space, size, colour, pattern and texture. With modern technology texts can be easily livened up by underlining, using italics, bold fonts and shadows. However, too much enthusiasm will hamper the accessibility and readability of the text (White 1989: 35). In order to use these elements wisely in the layout process, it is necessary to identify and respect certain fundamentals of sound design and page layout, including:

List 2.7 Fundamentals of design and layout

› *Continuity of choice:*
If a specific format and shading is chosen for tables, then the design should apply to all tables consistently. If a typeface or type size is chosen for certain headings and subheadings, then it should be used like that throughout the entire text. Try, too, to be consistent in the use of line spacing ('leading'), and also with graphics, tables and illustrations. For text editors, this aspect deserves special attention.

› *Contrast:*
Use the advantages of, for instance, different weights of type and different rule widths or, where affordable, use colour to differentiate or to show contrast. Differences can consistently be indicated with different treatments. Even just two colours on a printed or web page provides sufficient contrast.

› *Emphasis:*
Certain elements are emphasised more in the design than others. To do this, several typographical devices are available, including the use of bold or italics (or both), different font sizes, and the use of colour or greyscale shading.

› *Simplicity:*
Too much contrast is disturbing. With the target group in mind, choose a layout that is effective and workable and stick to that choice. Limit the different typographical devices that are used, but use them effectively.

List 2.7 continued

› *Culture and experience:*
Culture and experience largely determine people's view on matters
and experiences. Be sensitive to symbols that can have a special value
or generate negative feelings in certain cultural groups and those that
may lead to cultural misunderstandings or tensions.

From the fundamentals of good design flow some basic layout principles that need to be
adhered to:

List 2.8 Principles of effective page layout

› *Chunking:*
Break sections up into acceptable parts; group like elements together.

› *Hierarchy:*
Organise information on the basis of its importance.

› *Filter information:*
Put together what belongs together, having filtered it out of the totality of elements.

› *Colour:*
If you use colour, make sure that it is used functionally. Colour can
help to ease searches and it can also help with the internal organisation of information in documents. Too much colour can be distracting,
though.

› *Illustrations:*
If illustrations are used (graphics, tables, sketches, silhouettes, pho-
tos and cartoons or comics), decide on their purpose beforehand
and make sure that the level of understanding required matches the
knowledge and the abilities of the target group. People differ in
terms of background, education and ability in their understanding
of abstraction, culture and age. There must be a balance between
the purpose of an illustration and the assumed level of understanding of the document's target group. Illustrations trigger the readers'
interest and are often remembered long after they were first seen. A
comic-type text would, for instance, be more effective in transferring a
message about HIV/Aids to a semi-literate community than a pamphlet
with a lot of text (Swanepoel 2005). Research has also indicated that
text with illustrations communicates better than plain text, provided
that the drawings support or complement the words. Text and illustrations must therefore complement each other and together contribute
to a better text understanding.

Obviously, only the main points have been covered above and they deserve to be further elaborated on, both in training and through experience. For more about typography and layout, see chapter 10.

8.4 Document design and the CCC model

Good document design is the act of bringing together prose, graphics (including illustrations and photography) and typography for the purposes of instruction, information or persuasion. *Good document design enables people to use documents in ways that serve their interests and needs.*
De Stadler et al

Communication is a two-step process, requiring presentation from the givers and interpretation from the receivers. We must learn to use our shared language, be it verbal or visual.
White

The previous section explained those aspects relevant to an understanding of document design as a discipline and the knowledge required for evaluating text. As with normative linguistics (section 4 in this chapter) and text linguistics (section 5 in this chapter) some knowledge of document design is necessary to understanding the bigger picture so that sound choices can be made concerning *content, structure, style, typography* and *layout* and to help create communicative texts. There are quite a few advantages to such an argument: 'There is considerable potential for exchange of ideas, and for collaborative projects between typographers and applied linguists ...' (Walker 2001: Preface).

The composition requirements of a document justify a comprehensive view and the CCC model creates the ideal framework to do this in. Here, text editors should evaluate the presentation of a text on the basis of a set of criteria that determine how the content and the visual presentation of the text complement each other. The content will always exert a strong influence on what form the structure and layout of the text will take.

When considering the facets content, structure, style, typography and layout in the process of document design, the following CCC evaluation points are relevant:

Text facets	Evaluation points	Text quality *To be guaranteed through …*	Foundations of document design *Norms pertaining to …*	
Text type	2	Unity of genre	Structure	Knowledge of sources
	3	Correct genre rules	Style	
Content	4	Appropriate information Sufficient information	Content	
	5	Congruent facts	Content	
Structure	7	Sufficient cohesion	Structure	
	8	Uniform structure	Structure	
	9	Correct linking words Correct argumentation	Structure	
Wording	10	Appropriate wording	Style	
Presentation	13	Appropriate layout Appropriate typography	Layout Typography	
	14	Congruence between text and layout	Typography Layout	
	15	Correct layout Correct typography	Layout Typography	

Table 2.5 *Text quality and document design*

The evaluation points highlighted here match the appropriate features of document design. On the basis of this similarity, it is clear that the principles of document design and the facilitation of communication through texts should be harmoniously married.

9 Summary and conclusion

In this chapter we have shown that the CCC model provides a solid starting point for the daily practise of text editing. In our opinion, the model passes the test as both a practical and a pedagogical model. It provides a basis for bringing together three quite diverse disciplines that require an integrated approach. A knowledge of normative linguistics offers insight into making well-founded judgements about right and wrong at a linguistic level. A knowledge of text linguistics offers a foundation for making judgements about the structure and texture of texts (and their components) and how they can be formed into coherent units. In addition, a knowledge of document design helps with judgements about the way in which a text is put together and how it is physically presented in order to help optimise communication. Together these three disciplines provide the foundational knowledge necessary for the demanding task of text editing. The knowledge required and the text quality assured are presented in the following table:

Text facets	Evaluation points	Text quality To be guaranteed through …	The foundations of … Norms pertaining to …	Knowledge of sources
Text type	1	Appropriateness of text	Contextuality Intentionality Appropriateness	Text linguistics
	2	Unity of genre	Intertextuality	Text linguistics
			Structure	Document design
	3	Correct application of genre rules	Intertextuality Informativity	Text linguistics
			Style	Document design
Content	4	Appropriate information Sufficient information	Appropriateness Informativity	Text linguistics
			Content	Document design
	5	Unity of information Congruence of facts	Informativity	Text linguistics
			Content	Document design
	6	Correctness of facts	Informativity	Text linguistics
Structure	7	Sufficient cohesion	Cohesion Coherence Informativity	Text linguistics
			Structure	Document design
	8	Uniformity of structure	Informativity Cohesion Coherence	Text linguistics
			Structure	Document design
	9	Correct linking words Correct argumentation	Syntax Lexicon	Normative linguistics
			Cohesion Coherence	Text linguistics
			Structure	Document design

>>

Text facets	Evaluation points	Text quality To be guaranteed through ...	The foundations of ... Norms pertaining to ...	Knowledge of sources
Wording	10	Appropriate wording	Style Use of standard language Lexicon	Normative linguistics
			Cohesion Contextuality Intertextuality	Text linguistics
			Style	Document design
	11	Unity of style	Style	Normative linguistics
	12	Correct sentence structure Correct lexical meaning	Syntax Semantics Use of standard language	Normative linguistics
Presentation	13	Appropriate layout Appropriate typography	Layout Typography	Document design
	14	Congruence between text and layout	Typography Layout	Document design
	15	Correct spelling Correct punctuation	Spelling Punctuation	Normative linguistics
		Correct layout Correct typography	Typography Layout	Document design

Table 2.6 *The theoretical foundations of the CCC model*

The profile of a text editor

More than ever, editors are needed to *add value* to information and to rescue readers from boredom and confusion.
Mackenzie

Good editors may be likened to those *crystal-clear prisms* which form a vital part of a pair of binoculars. They are not there to alter the view or change the scene, but to make it *clearer* and *closer*.
Mackenzie

A good editor is worth their weight in gold.
Kuitert (translation)

To be a really good editor, you have to be a really good listener. I don't only mean to the author .... You have to listen to what you're reading.
Ellen Seligman

Contents

Objectives

The following aspects of being a text editor are covered in this chapter: (a) the text editor as language practitioner (as communications specialist, as someone who espouses lifelong learning, and who often performs the role of ghostwriter); (b) the role of the text editor in language practice (in the publishing process, where does their work fit in?); (c) the text editor and ethics (and therefore their role as protector of a text); (d) the training of text editors (both generally and specifically); (e) how an individual becomes active as a professional text editor; (f) the advent of self-publishing and e-publishing and the changing role of the text editor in those milieus, and (g) the process of professionalising text editors. The purpose of this chapter is also to describe everything that's necessary (competencies, knowledge and qualities) in order to perform the role of a text editor.

1 Introduction

The purpose of this chapter is to answer a number of important questions with a view to obtaining clarity about who and what a text editor is. What does a text editor actually do?, is one such question. Or, to put it differently: What can be expected of a text editor? What types of text editing can be done? Is it only language that they work on? What impact is the introduction of electronic media having on the role and modus operandi of the text editor? In which industries or sectors is there work for the text editor? Is the text editor really a kind of ghostwriter? What ethical requirements must they meet? How are text editors trained? Is training at all necessary (even possible)? (Anyone with a language qualification can do it, is the general belief.) How, then, do individuals enter the realm of professional text editing? What are the characteristics of a typical text editor, and is there such a thing as a 'typical' text editor? And in the realm of self-publishing, is the text editor's role any different? These types of question are raised – and answered – in this chapter.

2 The work of a text editor

> Editors improve written communication.
> *Anonymous*

> The main aims of copy-editing are to remove any *obstacles* between the reader and what the author wants to convey and to find and solve any problems before the book goes to the typesetter, so that production can go ahead without interruption or unnecessary expense ... *The copy-editor is the reader's advocate and the author's ambassador ...*
> Butcher, Drake & Leach

... editors strive to rid the text of all errors.
Bisaillon

The copy editor's job, then, is to ferret out the remaining infelicities in a manuscript. We do this in order to help the writer forge a connection with the reader based on trust – trust that the writer is intelligent and responsible. ... And we do it ... because we derive satisfaction and pride from knowing how.
Saller

Anyone who keeps him- or herself busy with the improvement (or editing) of a text (see chapter 4 for more about this) will be acutely aware of the fact that a multiplicity of tasks fall on their shoulders and that a variety of demands are placed on their competence. Plotnik (1982: 11) says, for example:

When told to 'edit' a manuscript, no two editors in the world will go about it in the same way. *The **act** of editing means many things to many people: it is seen as an art, a craft, a catharsis, a crusade.* Editing becomes all these and more eventually, but to professional editors it is first a *job* that results in a *product. Editors are paid to 'process' words into communication 'packages'.* (our italics)

Beene (2009: 11) adds

Copy editors ... have the liberty to rewrite an author's text. In fact, a copy editor's most important job may be to screen out bad writing even if that writing is grammatically acceptable. Hence a copy editor will work to tighten a manuscript's rambling prose; smooth awkward transitions; suggest more appropriate wording; restructure disorganized information; query the writer for additional information or clarification; ensure a consistent style; add headings, subheadings, or captions; and, in some instances, suggest completely rewriting sections.

For what reasons would a text need to be improved? Why would anyone take the trouble to create better 'communication packages' as products? Billingham (2002: 7) gives the reasons for this below, though there are clearly a lot more than are given here.

List 3.1 Reasons for editing text

> No matter how well a writer plans or how thoroughly they work, the first draft of a piece of writing is seldom the perfect or final version.

> There may be too little space on the page to say everything that the writer wants to say. So the text has to be cut.

> Documents have to be made appropriate to different target groups. One version will probably not suit everyone.

> The contents of a document must be made as clear as possible.

> Long documents are often less effective – and lose the readers' interest – and therefore have to be adapted to communicate more effectively and still remain compelling.

>>

List 3.1 continued

› Even though spell-checkers and grammar- and style-checkers are used in the preparation of a document, errors can still occur, because these electronic aids are not yet able to detect and indicate every single mistake. A thorough check still requires human intervention.

› An organisation's style guide has to be applied to a document so that its preferences regarding language, style and register can be implemented.

› It is of cardinal importance that at least facts, numbers and names are correct.

› Sometimes a document needs to be manipulated so that readers will be persuaded to read it.

› Everything about a document must be consistent – including the language, the layout, the typography, the paragraphing and the content.

It sounds challenging to be able to achieve all of these tasks, and in practice this is usually the case. However, no two text editors will work in the same way to perform these tasks (for one editor it is a 'work of art' that is being created; for another it is a matter of practical competence). This creates a demand to function in an environment in which, despite efforts to impose uniformity (so that the text can communicate more clearly), that ideal cannot necessarily be guaranteed. This creates a kind of anomaly. An anonymous source (2006a) puts it as follows:

> ... a good copy editor has a comprehensive range of interests, a passion for good writing, a ready knowledge of where to find answers, an eye for graphics, and the ability to pull it all together into an attractive, credible package of words and pictures.

The text editor must, as a result, possess the personality and the following competencies/skills in order to deliver a faultless product (insofar as that is humanly and practically possible):

List 3.2 Traits and skills of text editors

1. A practitioner has to have a thorough linguistic ability, command of language and feeling for the language being worked in in order to perform competently as a text editor.

2. Practitioners need to be multi-talented (Auman 2000).

3. They must have wide interests and an instantaneous knowledge in order to be able to cover the multiplicity of subject-matter they are likely to encounter (Baskette, Sissors & Brooks 1986: 6):

Copyeditors, even if mediocre, must of necessity accumulate a warehouse full of facts, facts that they have gleaned from the thousands of stories they are compelled to read and edit or from the references they have had to consult to verify information.

4. They have to know where to obtain answers to the array of questions (about content, style, language and facts, for example) that are likely to arise while editing a text. They also have to have a broad knowledge of sources (Cleaveland 1999; http://www.writershelper.com; Einsohn 2005: 17):

    At the basic level, copy editors need up-to-date reference books, internet access and improved electronic library systems.

    You should be familiar with a variety of resources like style guides and dictionaries and know when to use each one.

    … you should look up anything that you are unsure of. With your dictionary, style manual, usage guide, thesaurus, and other reference books at your side, this is the time to read up on troublesome mechanical issues, brush up on tricky grammar and usage controversies, and verify your suspicions about factual inaccuracies or inconsistencies in the manuscript.

5. They have to be prepared to explain and motivate the changes they make (Anonymous 2006a):

    … to teach you to articulate and *justify* your editing decisions … they must be able to explain. They know that *justifying* their decisions by citing references enhances their professionalism and thus their influence.

6. They must have a sense of thoroughness and detail (the proverbial 'eagle eye'): '… the copyeditor is required to *read* and *weigh* every letter, number and punctuation mark' (Derricourt 1996: 112).

7. They must have an eye for detail (especially for whatever may have been omitted) (Anonymous 2006a; Gilad 2007: 61):

    Copy editors must have or must develop a *careful, precise mindset* and a *compulsive attention to detail*. Calling a copyeditor a *perfectionist* will be taken as a compliment.

    Getting the details right doesn't matter to everyone. But for some people, everything they read is like a game of gotcha. Copyeditors should be among those people.

8. They must be passionate about good, effective language usage (including spelling, punctuation, grammar and the avoidance of ambiguity).

9. They must be able to hone an author's style (pruning where necessary) (Baskette, Sissors & Brooks 1986: 5):

> The copyeditor is a *diamond* cutter who *refines* and *polishes*, removes the flaws and shapes the stone into a gem. He or she searches for the ills in copy and *meticulously* scans the product for *flaws* and *inaccuracies*, ever searching for the maximum power of words.

10. They must have a 'sixth sense' for seeing errors (such as content, style, language, facts and typography): a kind of nit-picking and a tendency towards fault-finding are required here.

11. They must be able to recognise inconsistencies (of style, spelling, punctuation and typography).

12. They must be creative and imaginative and through their contribution act as co-creator in the total creative process (but not co-owner) of something that sparkles (Baskette, Sissors & Brooks 1986: 5):

> The copyeditor knows when to prune the useless, the redundant, the unnecessary qualifiers. The copyeditor adds movement to the piece by substituting active verbs for passive ones, specifics for generalities. The copyeditor obtains color by changing faraway words to close-up words. The copyeditor keeps sentences short enough so that readers can grasp one idea at a time and still not suffer primer prose. The copyeditor strives for pacing. If the sentence clothes several ideas majestically and in good order, he or she has the good sense to let the writer have his way. The copyeditor realizes he or she is not the storyteller. *His or her talent is in what can be done with another's copy to make it sparkle.*

13. They must have the ability to look at the writing of others critically, to identify the weak points, and to correct them so that the text flows.

14. They must be able to judge writing.

15. They must have an inborn inquisitiveness (so that they keep learning): '... the basic lifelong education of an editor is *reading* – reading everything and anything at every opportunity' (Plotnik 1982: 3).

16. They must have the cognitive skills to make connections that are apparently not there, to ascertain the nature of the connection and to clarify it – in order to facilitate cohesion.

17. They must have a clear mind (Glover 1996: 3; Butcher, Drake & Leach 2006: xii):

> Common sense is having an *intuitive sense* that something needs to be done and then doing it.

> Copy-editing is largely a matter of common sense in deciding what to do and of thoroughness in doing it ...

18. They must be able to bring the end product together as a unit, as an 'attractive, credible package'.

19. They must have strong powers of endurance and determination (to complete, in the agreed time, whatever has been started on).

20. They have an exceptional ability to concentrate because they have to work in a focused manner.

21. They must have efficient analytical skills because they must be able to identify problems and solve them in a thoroughly thought-out manner.

22. They must have a strong sense of diplomacy and tact that enables them to deal with people with empathy for example when a text requires heavy adaptation (Kuitert 2008: 28, 29 – our translation):

> The editor must work like an amateur psychologist, because authors are often oversensitive where their work is concerned.

> Ideally, the editor knows how to inspire the author, to fire him with enthusiasm so that the author can be led to approach the manuscript in a positive manner.

23. They have to have a sense of justice (in other words, don't make changes where they are not necessary).

24. They must naturally be intelligent, because they have to know a lot about seemingly useless things.

25. They must have the ability to admit their faults and always to learn from their mistakes.

These innate or acquired personality traits and competencies combined with and nurtured by acquired talent are all integrated harmoniously in the editorial process. This phenomenon can be summarised schematically as follows (Note: the numbers in the table below correspond to the numbers listed above):

General profile		Aptitude and attitude to learning	
2.	Multitalented	2.	Predisposed to multitasking
3.	Broad interests	3.	Eager to fine-tune available knowledge
24.	Intelligent		Able to search and find
4.	Inquisitive - a high degree of interest in almost anything	4. 5.	Know (of and about) sources where and how to search
24.	Intelligent	15.	Committed to lifelong learning
7. 16.	A specific cognitive make-up	13. 14.	Metacognition about what makes good writing
6.	Thorough	4. 5.	Able to decide and explain with reference to sources; argumentative skills
7.	Sense for detail	7.	Able to spot errors
	A natural tendency towards perfectionism	10.	Positive nit-picking
		18.	Able to see the unity of a text, able to maintain, strive for and re-create a text
		11.	Able to spot inconsistencies
8.	Passion for language - native language with a sound theoretical basis or outstanding command of the target language	8.	Develop thorough language competency Strive for effective language usage
12.	Creative and able to engage with the text	18.	Able to recognise the unity of a text, maintain it and re-create it
17.	Sound judgement	18.	Able to be moved to action, and do so thoroughly
19.	Perseverance and endurance	21.	Able to work within a given context
22.	Sympathetic	22.	Able to acquire tact if it isn't inborn
23.	Fair	23.	Able to acquire/develop sound judgement based on knowledge
25.	Unassuming	25.	Able to appreciate limitations in knowledge and ability

Table 3.1 *Attributes of a text editor*

It is in fact a demanding task that makes the text editor a kind of 'Superman' or 'Super-woman' of language practice, a 'passionate magician with words' (as one advertisement for the position of subeditor at a periodical once put it). This is because the craft of the text editor blends *talent*, *competence* and *knowledge* in a unique way. Butcher, Drake & Leach (2006: 4) describe such a person as follows:

> The good copy-editor is a rare creature: an intelligent reader and a tactful and sensitive critic; someone who cares enough about perfection of detail to spend time checking small points of consistency in someone else's work but has the good judgement not to waste time or antagonize the author by making unnecessary changes.
>
> Copy-editors need not be experts on the subject of the work, but they must be able to interest themselves in it in order to try to put themselves into the position of the intended readers.

According to Baskette, Sissors & Brooks (1986: 173), the text editor's primary task is 'to correct and refine copy'. This includes 'checking copy for accuracy, clarity, conciseness, tone and consistency of style'. This accords with what Van de Poel & Gasiorek (2006: 76) identify as the qualities of a good text, namely, that a text must communicate, convince and be clear, concise and correct. Einsohn (2005: 3) says the text editor's work – by applying the competencies stated above – is typically intended to promote easier communication (cf also Murphy 2011: 4ff). This is achieved by ensuring that every passage of language that is edited meets the requirements of the '4 Cs', that is, clarity, coherence, consistency and correctness. Add to these accuracy, completeness and appropriateness and then the demands and the work that accompanies them become great indeed.

In this regard, Combrink & Blaauw's (1998) point of departure of '100% communication, first time' is fundamental precisely because it is the principal goal of the text editing process to facilitate smooth and successful communication between the original intention of the originator of the text (the author or writer) and the recipient (the reader or listener) of the product offer or message. In this process, the text editor acts as an intermediary, as a facilitator between the two participants in the process of communication. In reality, then, the text editor becomes the first real reader of the intended product offer and their role is to ensure that effective communication takes place (whatever its role, extent and aim are).

This the text editor must do by working on the product offer or message in such a way that communicating the originator's message succeeds (Murphy 2011: 4–5). This is achieved by improving the language (structure), making the meaning of the words clearer, checking the spelling and punctuation (and adjusting it where necessary), defining the typography to be used in the page layouts, double-checking facts and grammatical correctness, and so on. Einsohn (2005: 4) says that in this regard 'excruciating care and attentiveness' are expected of the text editor – it is almost like sitting an examination of your competencies and knowledge: 'At any given moment, your knowledge of spelling, grammar, punctuation, usage, syntax, and diction is being tested.' Van Rooyen (2005: 199) summarises the text editor's task as follows:

> The fundamentals of copy-editing cover matters such as editing for grammar, usage, spelling, punctuation, and other mechanics of style; checking for consistency of style and internal consistency of facts; inserting sub-heading levels and approximate placement of illustrations; editing tables, figures, and lists; and notifying the designer of any unusual production

requirements. It also includes the following: [localisation] of spelling, names, etc; metrication; editing the illustrations in a manuscript; providing or changing the system of quotes and references; editing an index; writing or editing captions or credit lines; inserting running heads; obtaining or listing permissions needed; and providing front matter (prelims).

That is quite a list! But by doing all of these things, the text editor is simply performing the basic tasks of each text-editing process (cf AVS 2006; Butcher, Drake & Leach 2006: 3–4; Clark 1994: 73–75; Einsohn 2005: 3–10, 2005: 4–10; Flann & Hill 2004: 11–12; Gilad 2007: 62ff; Judd 1990: 20; Mackenzie 2011: 1ff; Merriam-Webster 2001: 225, 235–238; Murphy 2011; Tarutz 1992: 14ff; Van Rooyen 2005: 123–124, 199–200), namely:

List 3.3 Tasks to be performed during the editing process

> › Check the suitability of the text to the intended target audience. Is the language pitched at the appropriate level (eg the level of difficulty, style and register)?

> › Check the indicators of language and structure by doing mechanical editing: spelling, punctuation, checking figures and numbering as well as quoted matter (where possible).

> › Check the elements of the text by ensuring that all the component parts and sections those actually present and those that should be present are in place: check headings and subsections, the table of contents, bibliography, list of illustrations and tables as well as the footnotes or endnotes.

> › Check the style and register and improving the language usage where necessary: errors of syntax have to be eliminated, the preciseness of word usage must be improved, the correct patterns of word formation must be adhered to, and style and composition generally must be refined. As Einsohn puts it: '… copyeditors set right whatever is incorrect, unidiomatic, confusing, ambiguous or inappropriate without attempting to impose their stylistic preferences or prejudices on the author' (2005: 7).

> › Check the content while this is not the primary function of the text editor, it does include checking facts (dates, names and events), sums and cross-references.

> › Check the accuracy of the information in the text: Is the spelling of names of people, places, institutions and so on correct? This includes asking critical questions such as: Is there anything unnecessary in the text? Or, conversely: Is there anything missing from the text? Are footnotes necessary, for instance? Billingham (2002: 64–68) says that accuracy determines the quality of a text. Inaccuracies in any form

>>

List 3.3 continued

(whether of facts, statistics or statements) can cause doubt to be cast on the text as a whole.

› Check that consistency is maintained throughout in terms of spelling, punctuation, capitalisation, hyphenation, numbering, headings and subheadings, and paragraphing.

› Check the paragraphing, including the length of paragraphs and the highlighting of new themes.

› Check the use of quoted or other borrowed material for what requires permission: quoted matter, drawings, graphs, tables, photographs. Also check for instances of plagiarism and, where they are detected, informing the client about them.

› Providing feedback to the client, primarily by handing them the edited text for further processing.

These tasks are also summarised schematically below:

Level	Task	Activities
Reader (Target audience)	Check suitability of text	Checking whether the language is appropriate: • Style • Register • Level of difficulty
Language	Check language and structural indicators	Mechanical editing of: • Spelling • Punctuation • Numerals • Numbering • Correctness of quotations
Language	Check style and register	Polishing language usage: • Eliminating errors or omissions of syntax • Improving precision of word usage • Adhering to patterns of word formation • Broadly refining style and composition
Language/text	Check paragraphing	• Comparing length of paragraphs • Highlighting new themes

Level	Task	Activities
Text	Check the parts of a text	Identifying all text components: • Part titles (where applicable) • Headings and subheadings; sections and subsections • Figures and tables • Captions and labels • Preliminary matter: title, imprint, foreword, preface, acknowledgements, table of contents • End matter: glossary, bibliography, annexures, index • List of illustrations and tables • Footnotes or endnotes, etc
Content	Check content	• Facts (dates, names, events) • Sums, numbers and numerals • Intext references and cross-references • Libel or slander/defamation
Content	Check accuracy of information	• Spelling of people's names, places, institutions, etc • Asking questions such as: is there anything superfluous in the text? Or, conversely: is there anything missing from the text? For example, are footnotes necessary?
Text/language	Check consistency in text	• Spelling • Capitalisation • Use of italics • Punctuation • Typography • Layout • Paragraphs • Numbering
Text, content	Check for permissions	• Copyright • Intellectual property • Plagiarism
Complete text	Provide feedback to client	• Raise and respond to author queries

Table 3.2 *Tasks and activities to be performed during the editing process*

If the text editor can manage to perform all these tasks, then they will have done their job correctly and have contributed towards transforming the original unpolished document into a well-honed product. This is a product that will withstand the test as a communications tool and that will be a product that reads fluently, that makes sense, that is correct and that will cause the client no legal or other problems (LLTD 2006).

By attending to these matters, text editors fulfil their core function: namely to execute their brief by undertaking the technical preparation of the material the author has presented for publication (cf Murphy 2011: 4–5; Ritter 2005: 26; Tarutz 1992). In this respect, the text editor promotes optimal communication between the author and their reader(s).

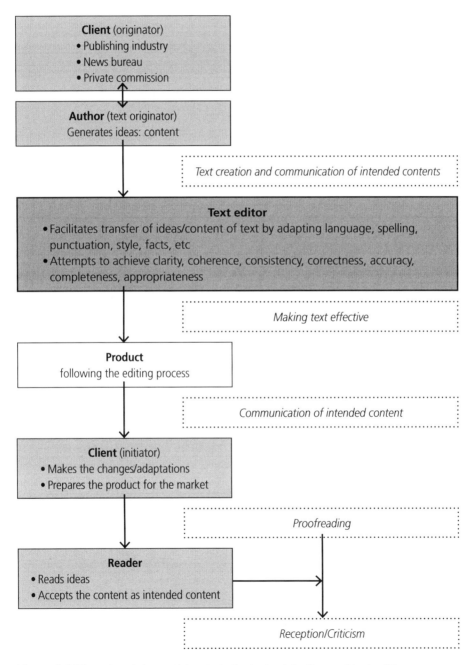

Figure 3.1 The roles of the participants in the text-origination and text-editing processes

This entire process can be presented schematically, as in figure 3.1 above (cf Baskette, Sissors & Brooks 1986: 4; Einsohn 2005: 3, 14–21; Mackenzie 2011: 6–7; Murphy 2011: 4ff; O'Connor 1978: 150). It seems that there is a predefined role for each participant in the text-creation and the text-editing processes: the originator (initiator) of the text (eg the publisher or client), the author as creator of the text, the text editor as the first criti-cal reader of the text, and the intended reader as recipient of the text. Ultimately it is an integrated process that has as its objective an error-free product. That this is not always possible is a given ('every copyeditor misses errors here and there' – Einsohn 2005: 4), but both the point of departure and the goal itself of all the participants in the process should be to strive after the perfect text. Therefore, as Murphy (2011: 5) puts it: 'The editor's job is as big or small as you want to make it. Having an interest in all aspects of the process of getting ideas into print makes the actual editing all the more interesting and satisfying.'

3 Types of text editing

> ... the copyeditor acts as the *author's second pair of eyes*, pointing out – and usually correcting – mechanical errors and inconsistencies; errors or infelicities of grammar, usage, and syntax; and errors or inconsistencies in content.
> *Einsohn*

> This is what I love about copyediting: When I'm faced with something that doesn't quite work, I get to suggest fixes. Fun.
> *Gilad*

> Editing is a multifaceted occupation, involving all aspects of the publishing industry, working with others in specialist areas, having confidence in your own understand-ing of acceptable English grammar, and so on. And it's great fun.
> *Murphy*

In view of what has been highlighted in section 2 above about the variety of competencies and knowledge that can be expected of a text editor, we now also have to consider the types of text editing there are, so that particular competencies can be associated with dif-ferent certain types of text editing. Einsohn (2005: 4–10) distinguishes the following steps in the text-editing process (see also table 3.2 above): (1) mechanical editing, (2) checking that the component parts of text fit together, (3) the improvement of language usage, (4) the editing of the content of the text, (5) checking for copyright permissions (and plagia-rism) and (6) the delivery of the text to the client.

Mossop (2010: 27) takes this a step further and distinguishes the following types of text editing: (1) copy-editing; (2) stylistic editing; (3) structural editing, and (4) content editing.

3.1 Copy editing (or copy-editing or copyediting)

This entails adapting a piece of writing in accordance with previously set rules: 'the gen-erally recognized grammar and spelling rules of a language community, rules of good "usage", and the publisher's "house style"' (Mossop 2010: 27). The purpose of this type of editing is to achieve consistency in language, terminology and layout (including headings, the numbering of sections and subsections as well as the labelling and styling of tables and figures). Mossop (2001: 21) says it is 'tedious work' whereas in 2010 he replaces these qualifications with 'copyediting requires close attention to small details' (Mossop 2010: 37). Regardless the description of the task, it has to be done: while it is essential (and its absence is often so visible), it is also relatively unexciting. What we have here is arduous and time-consuming 'line-by-line work', work with the fine detail in the text, but work that no manuscript can do without. The occurrence of spelling and punctuation errors, for example, has a negative effect on the reader, distracts the reader's attention from the content of the text and sows doubt about the quality of the work generally. As a result, readers can lose confidence in the content communicated via the text, and the text can fail in its attempt to communicate effectively, even at all.

Spelling errors can also lead to the meaning of a text becoming distorted and to confused readers – there is a world of difference in meaning between *discrete* and *discreet*, *aptitude* and *attitude*, *sever* and *severe*, and, for example *quite* and *quiet*. Spell-checkers can, of course, play a role in identifying spelling errors and correcting them, but only to a limited degree (see section 3.4.6 of chapter 4).

Many grammatical errors can be detected quite easily, for example *is* or *was* instead of *are* or *were* when the subject of the verb is plural ('Those boys *is* my friends'; 'The noise of the drills *were* deafening.') or when an unrelated participle is used ('*Having* finished the shopping, *the weekend* was mine to enjoy').

Other obvious errors include the incorrect use of plural forms (*mediums* versus *media*; *phenomenas* versus *phenomena*) or the incorrect expression of degrees of comparison ('She's the *most happiest* person I've ever met' instead of 'the *happiest* person') or adjective forms used instead of adverb forms ('He sings so *beautiful*' instead of 'He sings so *beautifully*').

Conveying the incorrect meaning through selecting the wrong word (either a homonym or a homophone, or simply the wrong word entirely) from among easily confused doublets or triplets is a fairly common occurrence. Compare, for example, *their* versus *there*, *practical* versus *practicable*, and *social* versus *sociable* versus *societal*. (More examples of these kinds of problem are set out in section 3 of chapter 8.)

Copy-editing therefore entails putting one's shoulder to the wheel to perform work that is not always exciting but which has to be done to ensure that documents succeed in their purpose. And if the editing is not done well, it stands out like a sore thumb.

3.2 Stylistic editing

This form of editing aims to make a text more readable by making sentences read more fluently, by removing any vagueness resulting from poor sentence construction and by eliminating ambiguity. The editorial intervention must add clarity to the text so that the language used does not obscure the author's intended meaning and prevent their message reaching the intended reader(s). As Mackenzie (2003, 2011: 3) puts it, 'editing adds value by providing clarity and precision.'

There is always a danger attached to stylistic editing, of course: that the text editor imposes their own stylistic preferences on the author's text, in the process causing the author's voice to be lost. Einsohn (2005: 9) puts it like this: '... copyeditors are not hired for the purpose of imposing their own taste and sense of style on the author.' This is where the accomplished text editor will know where to make changes to the text and where not. It is important that the author's voice be heard. Most authors have a distinctive style, and even substantial changes have to be made without their voice being lost. In this respect, it has been said that the good text editor has been everywhere and is revealed nowhere (Davies & Balkwill 2011: 170). Or as Baskette, Sissors & Brooks say (1986: 5): 'the text editor knows that he/she is not the storyteller. His or her talent is in what can be done with another's copy to make it sparkle.' The text editor therefore has to maintain a fine balance between that which *has* to be corrected and that which doesn't *have* to be changed at all.

3.3 Structural editing

This form of editing is mainly about reorganising material to provide a more logical and flowing sequence in the narrative or exposition. It takes place at two interconnected levels: conceptual and physical level. Mossop (2010: 74) states it thus: 'The structural editor's job is to help the reader follow the conceptual structure by making adjustments to the physical structure.'

For the text editor this means taking the requisite steps that will cause the physical structure of a text to flow conceptually.

By 'conceptual' we mean the manner in which, for example, an argument is structured: statement of the problem, the hypothesis for solving the problem, the arguments in support of the hypothesis and those against it, and the solution. In contradistinction, the physical level comprises setting out the conceptual flow on paper, such as the prescribed structure of a report or proceedings: title, table of contents, abstract, chapter 1 (with a corresponding prescribed structure), chapters 2, 3, 4 up to the chapter that summarises the entire contents, recommendations, bibliography. In this structure, the distinct components have their set places in the build-up of the structure and argument so it is important that the format be maintained. Typically, incorrect or inappropriate paragraphing (see chapter 7, section 2) should also receive attention to bring it into line structurally and conceptually.

3.4 Content editing

Apart from ensuring (as far as possible) that the facts are true and correct, this form of editing includes careful checking that the text fulfils the ethical requirements. For example, are the requirements of truthfulness, correctness, fairness and appropriateness to the potential readers fulfilled? Can crude language in a text aimed at children under the age of ten be approved of without any remarks being made about its inappropriateness? Is there any chance that an individual or an institution has been defamed?

Content editing also includes such matters as the correct spelling of names, correct dates and names of events, physical or postal addresses, web addresses, telephone and facsimile numbers, names of organisations and associations, and also numbers and calculations. A lack of control over these matters can lead to problems for clients and even to their embarrassment when inaccurate or incorrect information is published.

Traditionally, it is the job of authors to take care that these aspects of the content are correct, but there is unfortunately no guarantee that this will always be the case. Therefore, for safety's sake, the text editor should always check that they have been attended to and, if nothing else, draw the client's attention to any potential problems with the content. This sound, cautious approach will not only prevent subsequent embarrassment but also prevent the text editor from earning a bad name in the industry in which they operate.

In addition to Mossop's four categories of editing, Butcher, Drake & Leach (2006: 1–2; cf Clark 2001: 74–76; Flann & Hill 2004: 10, 11–12; Einsohn 2005: 11) state that the following types of text editing also occur: (1) substantive editing, (2) detailed editing for meaning, (3) checking for consistency, and (4) presenting the edited text to the client for layout and preparation for printing.

3.4.1 Substantive editing

The aim of substantive editing is to improve the overall coverage and presentation of a piece of writing, its content, scope, length, level and organisation. In this phase, the editor may suggest improvements for the author to make (or may by agreement with the author rewrite and rearrange the material), suggest better illustrations, and so on. A normal editorial function here is to look for legal problems such as defamation (or libel/slander) and plagiarism, and also for quotations and illustrations that may need reproduction permission from the copyright owner.

3.4.2 Detailed editing for meaning

Similar to Mossop's standard editing, this means checking whether each section follows on logically from the previous one, whether each expresses the author's meaning clearly, without gaps and contradictions. Also, do the sections together form a conceptual whole? Editing for meaning also involves looking at each sentence, the author's choice of words, the punctuation, the use of abbreviations, and checking whether tables and text and also illustrations and text are in agreement with each other.

3.4.3 Checking for consistency

This is a mechanical aspect of text editing, but nevertheless an important one if the text is to be a visibly well-rounded product. It involves checking the spelling, punctuation (eg the use of single or double quotation marks and whether full stops are used with abbreviations or not), numbering and styling of sections and subsections (eg the numbering system and whether bold or italics), the consistency of the bibliographical references (both in-text and in the bibliography itself), and references to tables and figures to ensure that they are treated consistently throughout the manuscript; and also that the table of contents mirrors the text itself (eg wording) exactly. The knowledgeable and experienced text editor knows, for example, that alternatives can take more than one form and meaning (eg *altogther* versus *all together*; *flammable* versus *inflammable*), and that it is important not only to choose between the two but also to use the same form consistently.

3.4.4 Presenting the edited text to the client for layout by the typesetter

Here the text editor makes sure that the manuscript is complete ('Is everything in its proper place?) and that all the parts are clearly identified (eg the different subheading levels, the positions of tables and illustrations), and which text should be distinguished typographically from the body text (eg bulleted lists, long quotations).

Nowadays, with word processing not only being the norm but also being integrated (or at least compatible) with page make-up DTP software (eg PageMaker, InDesign), it has become one of the text editor's duties to make up (or tag) the different features in a manuscript to distinguish them from one another. Thus making up (or production edit) can take various forms, for example:

- [CH head] Chapter title
- [A head] First-level subheading
- [B head] Second-level subheading
- [CAP] Caption to an illustration

or

- <CH> Chapter title
- <A> First-level subheading
- <B> Second-level subheading
- <CAP> Caption to an illustration

The typesetter or designer then converts each tag into the code required to implement the Style for each feature set out in the Styles or design spec supplied by the client.

For Butcher, Drake & Leach (2006) 'copy-editing' consists of the first three types listed above.

Then there is also a category of text editing known as *development(al) editing* (Clark 2001: 73–74; Einsohn 2005: 11) that is largely restricted to textbook production. It is usually employed when inexperienced authors, who may be subject specialists, have problems conveying information in a coherent, structured manner and/or experience difficulty with providing all the elements required to meet the requirements of a particular curriculum (content, activities, glossaries, projects, consolidation exercises, etc). Then the developmental editor is expected to introduce a logical flow to each chapter and to fill the gaps left by the author either by raising author queries (to prompt the author to write the missing copy) or more likely by writing the text and sending it to the author for approval. Together with the authorial team, developmental editors can help to shape a project from conception to completion (Clark 2001: 74).

In extreme cases – especially where the writer is a non-native speaker of the language of the text – the text editor's role may be labelled 'overwriting' or 'rewriting' and they are given licence to rewrite a text line by line and to restructure it as necessary to make it flow correctly (cf Butcher, Drake & Leach 2006: 35; Davies & Balkwill 2011: 170; Einsohn 2005: 11, 13). Some refer to this extreme intervention as 'ghostwriting' (Davies & Balkwill 2011: 170) (see section 6 below) because little of the original author's text remains visible – either structurally or in terms of the content, and yet the author's input remains invisible to the reader. To others, this would be a matter of 'heavy editing' (see section 4 below).

At all times during this process, however, the text editor's guides should be the intended audience and the publisher's brief (because such extensive text editing is likely to have both scheduling and cost implications). In addition, this type of editing requires the editor and the author to communicate frequently and to deal openly with radical changes to content and structure, and the editor should not be seen to be riding roughshod over either the author or their text, but able to justify every major change made to the manuscript. Moreover, in these circumstances the editor should be acutely aware that tact is of paramount importance, because authors vary greatly in their sensitivity to having their work edited and many are quick to take offence at what they may consider to be high-handed editing, even if the text editor considers it to have been 'light' or 'medium' (see section 4 below). At the same time, the text editor must remember that the book is essentially the author's and a certain amount of sensitivity and humility towards both author and text is required (Davies & Balkwill 2011: 170; Merriam-Webster 2001: 234–235).

On the other hand, what if the text editor him- or herself is a non-native speaker of the language of the manuscript, as is happening more and more nowadays. This presents several challenges, the principal of which are:

- The text editor not necessarily being able to recognise spelling errors, ungrammatical constructions, inappropriate word choice and unidiomatic usage in the author's original manuscript, and therefore not doing the text justice.
- The text editor making changes to the text that lead to misspellings, ungrammatical constructions and unidiomatic usage based on the conventions and rules of the editor's

native language and, for a similar reason, introducing inappropriate words and consequently doing the author's text an injustice in a different way.

• The text editor disturbing the natural flow of the author's original text by making unnecessary changes to words and sentences, and in so doing interfering with the author's style and register.

As a result, there is a good case in this sort of situation for non-native speakers to limit their editing to the more substantive, mechanical and consistency-related aspects of a manuscript, and even possibly to the coding of the different features, but to leave the editing for sense as described by Butcher, Drake & Leach (2006) to native speakers (NS) of the language. This is in no way to suggest that non-native speakers are in any sense less effective producers of English, or to imply that their own variant of English is sub-standard compared to that produced by a native speaker. But it is a pragmatic recognition of the fact that language production and language editing are separate skills, with separate requirements. An editor is called on to have a profound understanding of the language in its many variants, both NS and NNS, and a failure to meet these requirements may result in a text that does not meet the expectations of a very broad and critical readership. What this does mean for editors, however, is that they must be highly sensitive to the issue of non-native speaker-produced English, and decide carefully about when and how to modify such language. See chapter 6 for further discussion of this question.

Irrespective of how one approaches text editing and what types are distinguished, what is clear is that as an activity it is a combination of the types listed above: it is the editing of the language, style, content, typography and layout. In the light of what has been said above, one can give a unique content to each of these facets (summarised in checklist 3.1 below).

All of these components are needed in order to do a proper editorial job on a text as a whole. One component is not necessarily more important than another, but on its own each is an important part of the whole activity known as 'text editing'.

To ensure that each and every aspect of the text editor's intervention is given due attention, one can develop a practical checklist of the many tasks they are required to perform (cf Butcher, Drake & Leach 2006: 432–452; Einsohn 2005: 421–429; Gilad 2007; Merriam-Webster 1998: 235–238; Murphy 2011: 4ff):

Checklist 3.1 Text-editing tasks

Editing of the content: *check particularly*
1. Correctness and accuracy
2. Consistency
3. Starting point: the client's house style

   ✓ Facts
   ✓ Events

>>

✓ Names of people and places
✓ Names of institutions, associations, societies, organisations and companies (spelling and correct style of writing them)
✓ Addresses

✓ Numbers
✓ Sums and mathematical formulae
✓ Statistics
✓ Percentages
✓ Dates

✓ Quotations/extracts (correctness and accuracy)
✓ Cross-references to other parts of the text

✓ Plagiarism
✓ Copyright declaration
✓ Instances of defamation

Editing of the language: *check particularly*
1. Correctness and accuracy
2. Consistency
3. Starting point: the client's house style

✓ Sentence structure (syntax)
✓ Word structure (morphology)

✓ Meaning of words and phrases (semantics)

✓ Purity of language (avoid a mixture of languages, unless it is required)

Editing of the spelling and punctuation: *check particularly*
4. Correctness and accuracy
5. Consistency
6. Starting point: the client's house style

✓ All aspects of spelling
✓ Abbreviations and acronyms
✓ Punctuation

Editing of the style and register: *check particularly*
1. Correctness and accuracy
2. Consistency
3. Starting point: the client's house style

✓ Strive towards cohesion generally
✓ Paragraphing
✓ Logical structure of arguments
✓ Construction of sentences generally (both within and between paragraphs)

✓ Length of sentences
✓ Ambiguity in sentences and the use of words

✓ Choice of register (per subject and generally)
✓ Formality of language (suitably pitched at the readership level): formal vs informal
✓ Vagueness of expression
✓ Redundancies and repetitions

Editing of the layout and typography: *check particularly*
1. Consistency
2. Starting point: the client's house style

✓ Front and back covers
✓ Title page
✓ Table of contents
✓ Headings and subheadings
✓ Running heads and footers
✓ Sections and subsections
✓ Numbering generally
✓ Page numbering
✓ Tables (placement and references to)
✓ Diagrams (placement and references to)
✓ Illustrations (placement and references to)
✓ Appendices
✓ Bibliography
✓ Index
✓ Glossary

✓ Font/typeface
✓ Font/type size
✓ Spacing
✓ Mirrored or asymmetrical double page spreads?
✓ Page depth: rigid or floating?
✓ Page layout/design (including the use of white space)

✓ Footnotes and/or endnotes
✓ Cross-references (textual and bibliographical)

✓ Textual patterns (does the text adhere to the typical composition of a particular type of text (eg, an annual report, a school textbook?)
✓ Widows and orphans

In the literature on the subject, a variety of these checklists are to be found (see the sources at the end of this chapter). An example of such a checklist is provided in section 11 of chapter 5. In the next section, we deal with the levels or degrees of text editing.

4 Levels (or degrees) of text editing

> No one tells copyeditors how to edit – they have to experience it for themselves.
> *Baskette, Sissors & Brooks*

> Before you start a job, talk to the author or managing editor. ... you may want to find out what he or she expects of you. Specifically, you need to ask how *light* or *heavy* an edit is required on the document.
> *Gilad*

> 'What do you charge for editing?' That depends upon what is to be edited, the complexity of the document, the level of edit required ... among many considerations.
> *Murphy*

Einsohn's (2005: 13) thoughts on this subject are an appropriate start to this section, as they sum up the dilemma experienced by publishers, corporates and editors in a wide range of spheres:

> If time and money were not an issue, copyeditors could linger over each sentence and paragraph in a manuscript until they were wholly satisfied with its clarity, coherency, and correctness – even with its beauty and elegance. But since time and money are always an issue, many book and corporate publishers use the terms *light*, *medium*, or *heavy* to let copyeditors know how to focus and prioritize their efforts. ... [even though there] are no universal definitions for light, medium, and heavy copyediting.

In practice, because of the complexity and extent of the editing process, (especially if everything listed in checklist 3.1 above has to be taken into account), it is essential that the text editor consider the level of editing required on the text submitted even before they begin editing the manuscript.

In an ideal world, every time editing must be done the text editor will refer to all the aspects above and evaluate the degree of editing required by considering only (a) the quality of the writing in the manuscript and (b) the target audience. In practice, however, this is not always possible, for reasons that include time constraints (a tight deadline) and/ or financial constraints (there are only very limited funds available for this project). As a result, it is not always possible to give the same sort of attention to every text. Consider Mossop's view (2010: 34) that '[p]rofessional editors do not apply equal editing effort to every text'.

This means that text editors always have to make a choice regarding the level of editing, taking into account the abovementioned (and possibly other) reasons. Mackenzie (2011: 14) sums it up as follows: '... some jobs call for intervention, some for a delicate touch.' Therefore the text editor sometimes has to perform the job of surgeon and to make deep incisions to remove the canker and on other occasions a 'balm' is adequate to cover up an ugly patch.

According to Davies & Balkwill (2011: 170), Einsohn (2005: 13) and Mossop (2010: 34), the levels of text editing are: (a) *light* editing, (b) *medium* editing or (c) *heavy* editing. The level is largely determined by:

List 3.4 Factors that determine the level of editing

> › the quality of the author's writing;

> › the intended target audience;

> › the production schedule;

> › the available budget for the project;

> › the author's reputation, their attitude towards editing generally, and their own schedule (and therefore their availability to work on the editor's changes, especially if they are likely to be heavy);

> › the size of the print run;

> › the importance of the publication to the client (ie a publisher or a magazine or newspaper editor);

> › the reputation of the client (eg a publisher);

> › the nature of the publication (eg textbook, periodical, youth fiction, children's storybook, novel, newspaper article or encyclopaedia);

> › the author's reaction to the changes made to their text.

Mossop (2010: 34) gives as an example here the inhouse newsletter of a smallish business:

> there is not much point in spending vast amounts of time on the stylistic editing of a text which is relatively ephemeral, like an in-house staff newsletter, which only a limited number of people within an organization will look through, fairly quickly, and discard.

The readers of this kind of publication will endure errors more readily than would be the case in other, more comprehensive publications (such as annual reports) intended for other target audiences within the same business.

What, therefore, is the ideal, taking into account the factors listed above? How thoroughly and comprehensively must such a project be tackled? Einsohn (2005: 16) considers that at least two passes through the text are adequate to find and correct the most important and most obvious errors:

> Two passes seem to be the universal magic number. No copyeditor is good enough to catch everything in one pass, and few editorial budgets are generous enough to permit three passes (unless the text is only a few pages long).

In every instance, the text editor should try to answer the following fundamental questions up front (based on Einsohn 2005: 14–15) before a decision is taken about the level of editing.

Target audience
- ✓ Who is the primary target audience for the text?
- ✓ How much must readers know about the subject?
- ✓ How will readers use the publication? Is it intended for professional reading or for pleasure? Is it a reference work or a throw-away publication? Will only sections be read or will the entire text be read?
- ✓ Does it need to be stronger visually for a more visually literate audience?

Text
- ✓ How long is the text?
- ✓ In what physical format is the text?
    - – Editing the hard copy: Is the text in 1.5 or double spacing or single spacing? How many words are there on a page? What font and font size have been used? How readable is it? How wide are the margins? Is the text printed on one side of the page only? (The text editor can, of course, change all of these settings to suit themselves.)
    - – Editing onscreen: Which word-processing program has the author used? Is the software or format compatible with the text editor's?
- ✓ How will the text be processed?
    - – Editing the hard copy: Must the entire document be keyed in again, or is it a case of only correcting errors? In the latter case, the changes will have to be made neatly, clearly and in a strong colour that contrasts with the text (and which will be photocopiable, if necessary). Pencil should be used to highlight and make author queries in the text and the margin. How, and in what form, should the end product be delivered to the client?
    - – Editing onscreen: How must the changes be indicated: by using MS Word's Track Changes and Comments (for queries) functions or by using a second colour (eg red) for all alterations? Or should they not be visible at all? How compatible will the procedure followed be with the typesetter's page make-up software (eg InDesign)? How, and in what form, should the end product be delivered to the client?
    - – Editing both on hard copy and onscreen: If both are combined, which will the client want to see: both versions or only the edited electronic text? Will the client still want MS Word's Track Changes to be used when the changes are all visible on the hard copy?
- ✓ Does the manuscript comprise more material than just text (eg tables, figures and illustrations)? Should they be delivered separately from the text or embedded in it? Should the tables be converted to a different/smaller font than the body text? If the documents are very large (ie they take up a lot of memory), can the memory-intensive images be removed to make the documents more workable, and place-holders be typed in the spaces left by the removed images?

Level of editing

✓ What level of editing is required: *light, medium, heavy*? (Because of their ill-defined nature, it's worth probing a little to determine exactly what the client means by the level stipulated. See table 3.3 below.)

✓ Is the author a NS of the language of communication? If not, the text editor's level of intervention is likely to be somewhat heavier.

✓ Has this decision been based on time or financial constraints, or both?

✓ Has the person who briefed you read the text themselves, or simply skim-read it?

✓ What funding is available for the project?

✓ Is the text editor expected to shorten (or lengthen) the text? If so, by how much?

✓ Must the text editor check the worked examples in mathematics or will this task be allocated to another expert (eg a teacher of the subject)?

✓ In a medical textbook, must the text editor check the names and dosages of drugs and other medication or will this task be allocated to a medical expert?

✓ Must the text editor check bibliographical references?

✓ Do quotations (extracts) have to be checked?

✓ Are there preferences or restrictions regarding, for example, typography, references to tables, figures and illustrations, the layout and numbering of exercises in columns, the treatment of case studies or lengthy extracts, and footnotes or endnotes?

✓ Must in-text references be checked against the bibliography?

Approach to editing

✓ Have particular style guides, dictionaries and encyclopaedias been prescribed?

✓ Does the client have a house style guide? If so, how strictly must it be adhered to?

✓ Are there equivalent texts or even previous editions of the text to be edited that the editor can refer to?

✓ Is the manuscript part of a series, the style, structure and format of which have to be followed?

Author

✓ Who is the author? Are they an experienced writer? Or is this their first publication?

✓ Is the author an NS of the language of communication?

✓ Has the author placed any restrictions on what may or may not be done to the text?

✓ Has the author seen a sample of the text edited by the text editor? And have they given their feedback, either negative or constructive?

✓ Has the author been briefed about the type or level of editing that will be applied to their text? If so, what is the author's reaction or opinion?

Administrative details

✓ To whom must the text editor direct questions that arise during the editing process?

✓ What is the deadline for completing the project? How cast in stone is this deadline?

✓ In what format must the manuscript be returned to the client?

Ensure in advance, therefore, what the client expects regarding the level of text editing and consider it before you start work on the project, because doing so will determine for how long you will have to work on the manuscript and what producing the final product will ultimately cost (Mackenzie 2004: 144). The information required, according to this checklist, will determine the amount of time and attention that is devoted to the manuscript, and therefore to the level of editing: light, medium or heavy.

Whichever level the text editor is working at, the three degrees of editing have certain elements or tasks in common (Einsohn 2005: 12; Davies & Balkwill 2011: 170), namely:

Task/element	Details
Mechanical editing	• Ensure consistency in spelling, capitalisation, punctuation, hyphenation, abbreviations, format of lists, etc. • Check that treatment of embedded and displayed quotations (extracts) is consistent. • Check that style of bibliography or reference list is applied consistently (use of and or &, full stops, publication dates, order of publisher/place of publication, use of bold and italics, use of upper- and lowercase). • Optionally: allow deviations from house style if the author consistently uses acceptable variants.
Correlating parts	• Check contents page against chapters; check numbering of footnotes or endnotes, tables and figures. • Check numbering system used (if any) for headings and subheadings throughout the chapters. • Check that standard components of chapters are all in place (eg statement of objectives, introduction/background and summary/conclusion). • Check that tables, figures and other illustrations are correctly and consistently referred to in the text and correctly/sensibly placed. • Check in-text, footnote or endnote references against details in bibliography (names, dates, etc). • Check alphabetisation glossary of bibliography or reference list, and index.
Permissions	• Note any text, tables, figures or illustrations that may require permission to reprint. • Coding for style ('typecoding'). • Typecode or tag all elements appropriately. (See section 3 above.)

Table 3.3 *Tasks/elements of the three degrees of text editing*

It is really to the language editing and the content editing components (and a little structural editing) of the text editor's brief that the different levels really apply (Davies & Balkwill 2011: 170; Einsohn 2005: 12):

	Light text editing	Medium text editing	Heavy text editing
Language editing	• Correct all indisputable errors in spelling, grammar, syntax and usage, but ignore any locution that is not an outright error. • Point out paragraphs that seem too wordy or convoluted, but do not revise. • Ignore minor patches of wordiness, imprecise wording and jargon. • Ask for clarification of terms likely to be new to readers.	• Correct all errors in grammar, syntax and usage. Point out or revise any infelicities. • Point out any patches that seem wordy or convoluted and supply suggested revisions. • Ask for or supply definitions of terms likely to be new to readers.	• Correct all errors and infelicities in grammar, syntax and usage. • Rewrite any wordy or convoluted patches. • Ask for or supply definitions of terms likely to be new to readers.
Content editing	• Query factual inconsistencies (eg cross-referencing) and any statements that seem incorrect.	• Query any facts that seem incorrect. • Use desktop reference books to verify content. • Query faulty organisation and gaps in logic.	• Verify and revise any facts that are incorrect. • Query or fix faulty organisation and gaps in logic.
Structural Editing	• Possibly help standardise the organisation and headings by pointing out discrepancies and gaps in typography and layout.	• Suggest changes to the organisation and headings that the author should make.	• Make the necessary changes to organisation and structure for the author to approve.

Table 3.4 *Degrees of text editing*

Authors with a reputation for submitting well-prepared manuscripts will often need only a light edit; also, authors who are likely to be hostile or hypersensitive to more major changes may fall into this category. A light edit may be quite cursory, and the text editor's billable hours will be expected to reflect this. Medium editing is naturally the norm to which most manuscripts conform (Merriam-Webster 2001: 235). Heavy editing means giving broad latitude to shape, among other things, the manuscript's prose. It is used if the work is in need of significant improvement, usually in the opinion of either the commissioning editor or an external reviewer, or sometimes of the text editor (Davies & Balkwill 2011: 170). When this decision is taken, the next question that arises is: Will the author be capable of making the book acceptable to its target audience or should a detached professional text editor be asked to undertake the necessary improvements?

Mossop (2010: 37–38) is of the opinion that a distinction between micro- and macro-editing includes all these aspects of the text editor's work. *Micro-editing* includes the editing of the language of a text (including grammar, spelling and punctuation), word choice, style, register, and so on. Macro-editing is more applicable to the editing of the layout and the typography. Macro- relates to the presentation of a text generally and micro- to the detail of language usage. Mossop (2010: 37) also says that the macro-editing on a manuscript should be completed before work starts on the micro-editing.

Regardless of what you call the level or type of editing, according to Einsohn, the process is underpinned by the following important principle: '*Do not machete a manuscript or rewrite a document unless you are explicitly asked to do heavy editing or rewriting.* If the author's sentences are clear, correct, and serviceable ... let them be' (2005: 27).

Do not change something simply because it's not written the way you would have written it, but rather because the sentence is incorrect and communicates poorly. Therefore: 'Don't change things that don't need to be changed' (Wallraff 2004). It is therefore better to use the 'axe' sparingly rather than liberally.

In this regard, Saller offers sound advice (2009: 64–66): she urges text editors to ask themselves three questions about the current state of the manuscript *before* they begin 'surgery' on it:

1. *Is it wrong?*
   Often the way a writer organises/styles/formats his work isn't incorrect; it's just different. ... If it doesn't seem to follow any guide you're familiar with, but it's more or less consistent and makes sense, seriously consider leaving it alone. ...

2. *Is it confusing?*
   'Confusing' is a lesser form of 'wrong' and calls for intervention. When all the legends to a series of pie charts list the percentages in alphabetical order instead of in order of quantity, it's not wrong – it just makes it harder for the reader to see at a glance who gets the biggest piece of the pie. ...

3. *Is it ugly?*
   There is the occasional instance in which a writer's decision isn't wrong or confusing, but, aesthetically speaking, you know it will lie badly on the printed page and thereby hinder the reader. For instance, a surfeit of numbers in running text can be an eyesore and difficult to make sense of. The information might be better cast as a chart or table. ...

Once you've considered a complex editing issue and decided it must be done, lean on two virtues: carefulness and transparency. The first (having knowledge of issues that matter) helps prevent mistakes, the second (making your changes visible) will help you to check your work and undo it if you get into a fix.

5 The text editor as language practitioner

> ... copy editors fail to understand that style rules (which pertain to punctuation, capitalisation, hyphenation, preferred spelling ...) are often by nature arbitrary and changeable. ... grammar rules are more strict and less negotiable. ... Flouting the rules of grammar creates an impression that the writer is incompetent or uneducated. Most writers are grateful when we correct their grammar.
> *Saller*

> Without considering the basics of ... grammar – the morphology involved ... and syntax – an editor cannot do justice to any author's work. ... We can be meticulous in our checking of grammar in everything we edit.
> *Murphy*

In reality, the text editor is a language practitioner who performs a variety of language-practice functions and who in the process also performs a number of other roles. The term 'language practitioner' is used as an inclusive term for those who work daily with language while they carry out their duties as translators, interpreters, text editors, proofreaders, full-time language practitioners employed at universities and in government institutions and businesses, copywriters at advertising agencies, writers of news bulletins for radio and television, subeditors in the editorial teams at newspapers and magazines, dictionary compilers and a host of other roles.

Language practice is an old profession, but it lacks professional acknowledgement, and this book is an attempt to put that right. Good language practitioners (with a natural flair and sound training) can make a respectable living, but poor practitioners (with inadequate training and skills) do harm to the profession.

It can be said, in view of clients' (and reviewers' and readers') expectations of a text editor's output, that the core function of a practitioner is to fix the grammar and language, possibly above all else, though probably on a par with the imposition of consistency throughout a text. If an error of grammar, punctuation or spelling is detected, the usual response is that the text was 'badly edited' (regardless of the restraints imposed upon the editor in pursuit of the shortest possible production schedule or through a 'difficult' author's wanting the editor's changes reversed!). Given the state of most manuscripts presented to text editors for 'improvement', aspects of grammar and language are, yet again, those issues that need to be addressed first and foremost – if only because little else can be done to the text without heavy editorial intervention at that level. Very often, it's left to the text editor to decipher what an author is trying to convey through mangled and garbled sentences, and only then can the veneer of structural order, logical reasoning, consistency and meaningful numbering systems be applied.

As a language practitioner, a text editor is a *facilitator*, someone who has to succeed daily in building bridges between two poles: on the one hand, the creator of the text (the author) and, on the other, the recipient of the text (the reader). Here, the text editor plays the role of trained expert in communications, someone who knows (as a result of their training) how to handle the needs of the author (to create a unique text) in such a way that their intended (unique) message reaches the intended target audience after the text editor's intervention (with the aid of light, medium or heavy editing).

This means that the text editor has to remove the language from the picture a little (quite ironically, because they represent language practice) and has to focus on the smooth transmission of the message. The language may therefore act only as the instrument that transmits the message, and the language as such may not be the most important factor in the communication. The total offering (content plus language) is what puts the message across successfully, and it demands a lot of the text editor to get everything to click together (Bisaillon 2007: 90–92).

If the text editor cannot facilitate this smooth transition, the effectiveness with which the message is conveyed will be hindered. The role of the text editor in this process is therefore an explicit one in making possible the 'communicative success of the text as a coherent unit' (translated from Kotze 1998: 56).

But the text editor's work doesn't stop here, because they constantly have to play the role of lifelong learner, of someone who never stops learning about how to make the smooth transfer of messages possible. This means that text editing is an ongoing concern, a job which demands that the practitioner not only keeps up with new publications in their field of specialisation and generally, but also keeps up with trends in language. The text editor is by definition someone who is involved in language practice to add technical and linguistic lustre to an author's material as far as possible with a view to having it published (Kotze 1998; Murphy 2011: 4ff).

Today, the text editor is engaged in this process primarily in five sectors: *publishing* (as editor of publications generally, and in particular of books of every possible type), *journalism* (in the editorial offices of newspapers and magazines), the *corporate environment* (such as insurance companies, banks and universities), the *public service sector* (municipalities, national and provincial language services, semi-state institutions) and as *freelance* practitioners (often hand in hand with work as translators and/or interpreters).

In the first four sectors, text editors often enjoy the luxury of devoting themselves entirely to editing manuscripts (of whatever kind and extent they are) routinely from nine to five, whereas those who work as freelancers mostly work under the pressure of time and financial constraints and are not confined by a nine-to-five routine.

5.1 The text editor in publishing

> [Copy editors] are the people who turn messy manuscripts into legible books. They edit books in such a way that the reader will find them easy to understand, that the author's errors are eliminated, and that the DTP operator will know what to do with the manuscript.
> *Van Rooyen*

> The main aims of copy-editing are to remove any *obstacles* between the reader and what the author wants to convey and to find and solve any problems *before* the book goes to the typesetter, so that production can go ahead without interruption or unnecessary expense.
> *Butcher, Drake & Leach*

> ... most evidence suggests that a badly edited book is unlikely to secure the approval of critics or the confidence of its readers.
> *Davies & Balkwill*

There is no doubt about the importance of the publishing industry (in the broadest sense) in the professional life of text editors. Mackenzie (2011: 3) states it quite clearly: 'Although editors work in many sectors, *the book industry is the origin and the core of the profession* ....' Einsohn (2005: 4) confirms that text editing is really only one step in the entire process in which a manuscript is transformed into a published product (whatever form it may take: book, annual report, newsletter, article in a periodical, dictionary, press release, research report, technical report, proceedings, thesis or dissertation, legal document, product information document, catalogue, pamphlet, brochure, business letter or memorandum). Walker (2002: 190) adds that text editing fulfils one of the most cardinal roles in the production process, namely that it is the last quality assurance phase in the process (cf Auman 2000; Greer (ed) 2008: 221; Kotze 1998: 205; Stepp 1989: 2, 32; Van Rooyen 2005: 201–206). In this respect, the text editor's work contributes by adding value to the final product. Frequently, therefore, it is the text editor's task to get the author's manuscript into the final format in which it will be published.

Without this process, the quality of publications will be seriously threatened because they will fail to attain the necessary expertise in the process of adhering to the principles of correctness, accuracy, completeness and consistency. In publishing, it is therefore expected of text editors to edit manuscripts and to fine-tune them with a view to publishing them. Derricourt (1996: 112) for example, says the following in a letter to an author about the advantages of having a text editor make their special contribution:

> There are many advantages to you, as an author, of a professional copyedit. *In fact, the copyeditor is the only person that will have read every word of your book with care* – the publisher's acquisitions editor and our outside readers and advisors may at best have read quickly or even skimmed parts. *But the copyeditor is required to read and weigh every letter, number and punctuation mark*. You can assume they can look at your manuscript from the viewpoint of your future readers, while remaining sympathetic to your goals as author. Their aim is to help you communicate with your readership.

This raises an important matter, namely that there is an implicit acceptance that manuscripts are seldom completely ready for publication. Every manuscript is therefore gone through very carefully, as a 'golden rule', to determine whether it is in fact ready for the publishing process to run its course. In this connection, the following questions are often asked: How much editing is needed to prepare the text for publication? How much time is there in which to do it? What will it cost? Derricourt (1996: 113) attempts an answer:

> From the publisher's viewpoint, their copy editor is simultaneously undertaking a number of separate tasks on the manuscript, all directed towards *making the manuscript as good as possible for the needs of the eventual reader*. That means, particularly, *removing barriers that may stand between the author and the reader, between the purpose of the manuscript and the fulfilment of a printed book*. That often means that good copyediting is invisible, because it brings the book to an *expected standard*.

Given Derricourt's views, it is the publisher or commissioning editor's job to convey to the text editor what their level of responsibility is regarding fixing the structure of the material, checking the factual accuracy of the content, ensuring that the authors are expressing themselves clearly, and similar matters (Murphy 2011: 4–5; Ritter 2005: 27). What, then, is expected of the text editor if they are to fulfil their responsibility? It is worth the text editor's while to nurture a good relationship with the author in order to ensure that the author's needs are met. The author must therefore be informed what the editor will be doing, the role of the rules of house style should be explained to them (see chapters 4 and 11), and they should be told how many stages of proof there will be to read, and the order in which the different proofreading will be required to occur.

It is important that the publisher confirm whether the author wishes to be kept informed of the editor's changes and the production process and, if so, to what extent. Identify the book's target market; in consultation with the author and the editor, establish what type and level of editing will be necessary.

Kotze (1998: 52) says that, from a text editing point of view, the publication process is really about the extent to which page make-up programs, text-editing software and text-editing techniques can lead to more economical, well-edited and market-oriented books and at the same time make the job of the writer, the typographer and the text editor easier. In other words, focused work in which the text editor by definition plays a central role.

The editorial process (that is, the process in which a manuscript proceeds to the stage of a final product) comprises five basic steps (cf Davies & Balkwill 2011; Kotze 1998: 52–60; Van Rooyen 2005: 201–206):

- The *evaluation* or *selection process*: If a text is not commissioned by a publisher, then a manuscript is presented to a publisher; the publisher (or someone appointed by them) evaluates the manuscript in terms of particular criteria (content, readability, potential impact in the market, the type of language usage and style), and the publisher takes a decision whether to publish or not.

- The *production process*: a format or design for the book is decided upon in consultation with the author, and also the typographical style, including the font or typeface and the font size (see chapter 2, section 8; chapter 10); also the number of pages the book will make is estimated; the edited text is subsequently made up according to these specifications. Other than perhaps providing the publisher with a representative set of manuscript pages that illustrate all the main features of the manuscript, the text editor usually doesn't have much to do with this process (Kotze 1998: 53). However, they should know about the technicalities of the process because of the impact that it will have on the editorial intervention.

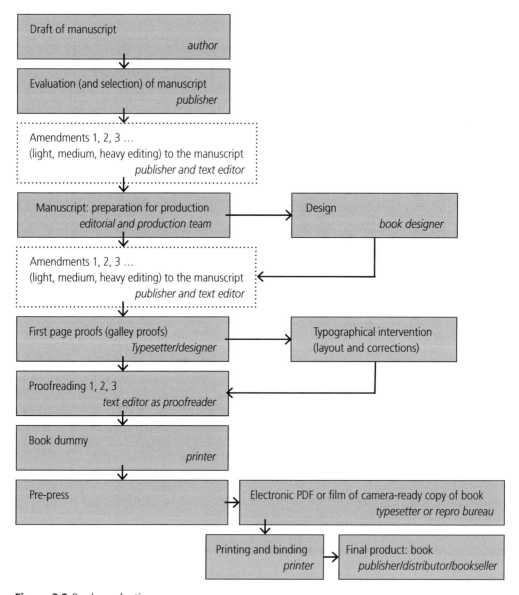

Figure 3.2 *Book production process*

- *The design of a cover and/or the creation of graphics* by graphic designers and artists.
- *The text editing process*: it includes quality control over correct language usage and content as well as structural appropriateness, consistency and suitability of the typography, page layout and text type; the writing of a title and a subtitle and of a blurb (advertising copy) for the back cover as well as checking the suitability of the front cover design and checking the preliminary matter (Kotze 1998: 55). It also includes intensive reading, reworking and working through the manuscript on the part of the text editor, after which the typesetter can make the necessary changes and corrections. The text-editing process should be repeated at least four times until the editor and the head of the typesetters are satisfied with the content and the appearance of the pages. If heavy editing is done, the author is kept informed throughout the process.
- *Preparation of the final copy for printing:* A number of additional checks always occur at this stage, especially whether the intended editorial amendments were in fact effected and whether they were incorporated in the final text (clear filenaming of the edited documents is essential here).

5.2 The text editor of a multi-author or multi-volume work (or compilation)

> In multi-author works, there are usually two editors: the volume editor, who oversees the team of authors and ensures that they write to a set of consistent house style guidelines, and the copy-editor, who is expected to respect the individual authors' 'voice' but also to 'iron out the wrinkles' in the reading experience by imposing the kind of consistency that will facilitate ease of reading ....
> *Inga Norenius, Editorial and Production Manager*

> The volume editor is responsible for providing a clear and consistent text in exactly the same way as if he or she were the author of the book. ... [and] for the quality of the book and for obtaining the contributors' agreement to any changes made before the text reaches the publisher. ... If the contributions are not consistent when they reach you, your decision as to how far to make them consistent will depend on the kind of book it is.
> *Butcher, Drake & Leach*

In the scientific and academic worlds, it is fairly commonplace for text editors to have to grapple with variances between authors' style of writing, voice and adherence to house style guidelines in multi-author and multi-volume works. In such instances, the text editor's task is made much easier when the team of authors has been thoroughly briefed before the writing starts and where there is a volume editor to oversee the team of contributors – the more so when they are committed to imposing consistency on the text as a whole and apply (or get their co-authors to apply) the publisher's house style to the papers or chapters before handing them over to the text editor. It is therefore important for the text editor to know from the outset the extent of the volume editor's brief and to what extent they have fulfilled that brief. This will enable them to know how extensive and intrusive their intervention needs to be. Also, the degree of urgency with which the book or volume has to be published will determine the scope and intensity of the text editor's work.

Whether the publication comprises conference proceedings, a set of independent pieces (as in a festschrift) or a series of chapters written jointly by two or more authors, the same kinds of problem tend to arise: the style, structure and content of the text are likely to be inconsistent and the text editor needs to know whom to consult about queries – the volume editor or the individual authors. If the latter, then the volume editor should be kept informed about decisions made and any delays, disagreements or unresolved problems (Flann & Hill 2004: 41).

How much needs to be done to the text, however, will also depend on the kind of book it is. If it is the kind that has a beginning, a middle and an end and was conceptualised to be read right through, then it should be treated as a single unit and consistency should be imposed throughout. Although papers from conference proceedings may have been penned by inexperienced or non-native speaker contributors, and be in need of a medium or heavy edit, time constraints may limit the text editor to correcting only those pieces that are really ambiguous, misleading or obscure. Such volumes usually have a consistent style for subheadings, bibliographical references, abbreviations, spelling, spelling-out of numbers, etc, although you may have to settle for consistency within chapters rather than across the entire book (Butcher, Drake & Leach 2006: 297–298).

Style problems could include different language levels and uneven styles (varying from breezy to formal) between sections. The most practical solution in such cases, though often not ideal, is usually to make changes to the least prevalent style to bring it into line with the majority. However, this could require rewriting by the authors and could lead to (often costly) delays, and so should only be a last resort.

Structural problems could include: (a) variation in the depth of treatment of sections of the text (signalled by widely differing chapter lengths or divisions within chapters); (b) different formats and content elements within chapters (some having bibliographies, others not; some footnotes, others endnotes); (c) unnecessary repetition of information between chapters or some important information having slipped between the cracks (inadequate division of work), and (d) variation in language level and writing style (voice or tone).

It is therefore important for the text editor to obtain a very clear brief as to the nature and ambit of their work on a multi-author or multi-volume publication, to dovetail closely with what the volume editor has already completed, and not to work in isolation or to intervene inappropriately.

5.3 The text editor in the newsroom

> The copy editor serves as a professional reader for the good of a very special client – the reader of the newspaper.
> *Berner*

> Overall, nothing will contribute more toward better journalism than better editing.
> *Stepp*

Good sub-editors are compulsive about serving readers.
Nel

A good sub is one of a publication's most valuable assets.
Müller

Text editors who work in newspapers and magazines are sometimes referred to as the readers' 'watchdogs' (Bowles & Borden 2008: 4), as people who jealously stand guard over the way in which news is conveyed linguistically and who help to package the story or report so that it is conveyed to the reader in the most effective manner. Bowles & Borden (2011: 5) sum this up as follows:

> Copy editors are a rare breed, and they are scarce. Just ask any editor or publisher to hire one. And they are dedicated, intelligent individuals, whose love of language and penchant for precision make many reporters look good. Copy editors are the very heart of the media organization, supplying the lifeblood for healthy existence and serving as gatekeepers of the news for the public.

The text editor in the news media – in most cases known by the name 'subeditor', or 'sub', in the bureaus of newspapers and magazines – is for all practical purposes only one link in the entire process of creating a news report, but there's no doubt that, in view of the nature of their work, theirs is among the most important functions in the newsroom (Greer (ed) 2008: 221). Each publication also has its editor-in-chief (or editor), the executive editor (for the arts, sport, business and politics), the journalist (who must write the required report) and the typographer (cf Beene 2009: 6; Conley & Lamble 2006: 216–228; Cotter 2010; Greer (ed) 2008: 219–220; Kotze 1998: 121–123; Tarutz 1992: 3–8). Each of them has a demarcated role to play, and it is also important that it is always carried out so that every issue of the publication sees the light of day. (For more about the types of editor, see sections 2 and 3 in chapter 1.)

Stepp (1989: 32, 97–114) points out that these people, the subeditors, have to fulfil a large number of secondary functions in the course of their work:

- As someone who must help to make decisions about the manner in which the *content* will be conveyed and also the quality of the article or report. For example, they have to consider: Is the content accurate (so far as it can be determined), correct, fair, clear, consistent, logical and thorough? Is the text interesting? Does it contain sufficient information about the origin of the information itself? Is there anything in the text that could be regarded as defamatory? The central question is always: what is the newsworthy angle? 'As the "copy doctor", the editor needs the skills of an intellectual surgeon, and the wisdom to know what to leave alone' (Stepp 1989: 32).
- As someone who must help to make decisions about the *structure* of the news. What should the report look like? Stepp maintains that '... to inspect copy word for word and mark by mark. This is fine tuning. It is *nit-picking*. And it is *quality control* at its most precise' (1989: 32).

- As someone who must pass *judgement* on the way in which the news is presented: the length of the report, the prominence it is given, the style and register of the writing, the spelling – that is, how to prepare the report so that it will have the maximum effect on the target readership. Is the text complete? Is there not perhaps an element missing? Does the text form a totality, a unit?

The sub's main function is therefore clear: to prepare a story or report for publication once the other processes have been dealt with.

This boils down to decision-making in a newsroom, often under pressured circumstances. Subeditors' contributions to the 'tidying-up process' account for the most important difference between' … excellence and mediocrity in journalism' (Stepp 1989: xii); remove this role from the publication process and quality and accuracy are threatened.

The responsibilities of the subeditor – as text editor and as 'tracker down of errors' – include the following (cf Baskette, Sissors & Brooks 1986: 39; Bowles & Borden 2011: 6–7; Fryer 1988; Greer (ed) 2008: 220–222; Nel 2001: 231ff; Quinn 2001: 15–18):

List 3.5 Responsibilities of a subeditor

› Helping to ensure accuracy: 'Of all the copyeditor's duties, editing for accuracy is probably the most important' – accuracy is therefore non-negotiable (Nel 2001: 231). In a report of the American association of newspaper editors it says: 'Every spelling error, poor apostrophe, poor sentence construction and incorrect graphic or map erodes the public's trust in the newspaper's ability to get things right.'

› Removing unnecessary words (the sub is therefore a 'pruner').

› Working on language usage (correct spelling, punctuation, style and grammar). In this regard, the beginner journalist with adequate training and poor skills stands out like the proverbial sore thumb.

› Checking for consistency (of language, content and presentation).

› Assessing the newsworthiness of the report.

› Refining the style in collaboration with the journalist (does the text read fluently?).

› Checking for defamation (or libel/slander), and for gender and racial bias.

› Ensuring that the publication has kept abreast of ethical issues in journalism.

› Deleting articles or reports that are in bad taste.

>>

List 3.5 continued

› Protecting the newspaper/magazine's reputation indirectly.

› Ensuring that the copy is readable and complete.

› Helping to select headlines that will attract the attention of the reader, introductions, subheadings and pull-quotes.

According to the literature, the subeditor has to perform the following tasks (cf Berner 1982: 44–61; Bowles & Borden 2011: 6–7; Greer (ed) 2008: 221–222; Nel 2001: 226–252):

Help to retain the flow of the story.

List 3.6 Tasks of a subeditor (1)

› Check for readability, which will lead to a coherent report.

› Make it easier to read the report fluently by rewording poorly constructed sentences, or even by shortening them.

› Turn weak writing into exciting writing (sometimes rewriting).

› Fill gaps in the story.

› Be wary of believing everything in news reports and therefore question facts and statements.

› Get the facts right (accuracy) where it is achievable (the final responsibility for this remains the reporter's).

› Send the report back to the writer (reporter) if they are in any way unsure.

› Check for typing and spelling errors.

› Maintain a consistent style (but also don't change the reporter's touch and style unnecessarily).

› Check for defamation (or libel/slander) and language issues relating to gender matters and racism. (Try to avoid litigation by being proactive.)

› Respect people's privacy.

› Always keep the needs and preferences of your target audience (potential readers) in mind.

› Check for ambiguity.

› Avoid repetition.

› Check for accuracy (eg of figures and calculations).

List 3.6 continued

> Check names (spelling, the correct person or institution).

> Avoid stereotypes as far as possible.

> Remove whatever matter doesn't illustrate the story. Ensure that whatever is removed does not affect the central message or theme.

> Help to provide a headline for a story.

> Apply time management skills and meet deadlines.

> Adhere to the publication's house style.

Auman (2000) and Bowles & Borden (2011: 7–9) supplement this list further. According to them, the subeditor must:

List 3.7 Tasks of a subeditor (2)

> Know the target market (the applicable reading public).

> Be versatile (multi-faceted – able to do many things).

> Have a positive attitude towards work.

> Have a fresh pair of eyes (that can see afresh and critically).

> Have self-confidence (in their levels of knowledge, writing ability, and knowledge of the demands and nature of the publication in question).

> Have a critical disposition (so that statements/facts can be questioned).

> Be able to appreciate good writing.

> Be knowledgeable about a large number of events (both recent and even less recent) – therefore be well read and well informed.

> Be willing to (help) find solutions.

> Be willing to remaining a lifelong learner.

> Be trustworthy/reliable.

> Be innovative and creative.

> Be diplomatic (so as not to lose the trust of journalists).

> Have a good sense of humour.

> Be able to work hard and fast.

> Be a team player.

Regarding the language of a story specifically, the following questions need to be asked. Nel (2001: 233–234) calls this the 'language checklist':

Checklist 3.3 Language

- ✓ Is the information presented in such a manner that the reader will be drawn by its revelation?
- ✓ Is the style of the writing appropriate to the intended medium?
- ✓ Is the headline likely to make you want to read the article?
- ✓ Is the headline clear and explicit?
- ✓ Has the journalist used everyday words? Or does the emphasis in the text fall on technical language instead? If so, how can the report be adapted to make it accessible to a reader?
- ✓ Is the writing direct, without superfluous words?
- ✓ Are the sentences well constructed to ensure an optimal reading experience?
- ✓ Are the sentences largely written in the active voice?
- ✓ Do linkages connect the sentences and ideas?
- ✓ Has the grammar regarding the words (diminutives, plurals, degrees of comparison and inflections) and the sentences (sentence construction) been checked?
- ✓ Have the spellings and punctuation been checked? If available: has a spell-checker been used to check the spelling?
- ✓ Have all the typos (typographical errors) been detected and corrected?
- ✓ Does the writing conform to the house style guide?

From this, one can clearly infer why the subeditor is frequently considered to be the most valuable person in the process of distributing the news, as the so-called 'last line of defence' for the newspaper (LLT 2006) before a story is published, as the person who knows how to pull everything together (Anonymous 2006a) – as the person who stands between the bald telling of a story and the telling of a credible story (Cleaveland 1999). Along these lines, good subs have the technical skills of a language expert, the sense of a good journalist and the qualities of a good leader. For these reasons, no newsroom (in fact, no media publication) can function without subeditors (as text editors). It is they who prevent 'bad things' happening: '... bad things like mistakes, inconsistencies, omissions, libel [or defamation], hidden meanings and gaffes of all sorts' (Anonymous 2006a). To provide this function takes subeditors/text editors who have at their fingertips a vast pool of knowledge, who display a diligence and passion for good writing, who know where to find answers to potential questions quickly, who have the ability to use graphics to good effect and who, finally, have the ability to bring everything together in the form of the final product – '... an attractive, credible package of words and pictures' (Anonymous 2006a).

To conclude this section, here are some hints (from Bowles & Borden 2011: 5–16; Greer (ed) 2008: 221ff; Stepp 1989: 114–115) about how the subeditor's attitude towards the editing of reports can contribute to a higher standard of editing:

› The subeditor's job is to help the journalist write a good story and not to write it themselves. The story remains the journalist's and the subeditor simply helps to package it well. The subeditor 'must make the story readable and ensure that it fits the requirements of journalistic writing', in the view of Greer (ed) (2008: 221).

› Good subeditors know how the news-gathering and -writing and the production processes work at a particular publication and edit in accordance with those in-house processes.

› Do not alter copy without consulting the writer.

› Apart from your text-editing function, you'll also be expected to wield your well-honed expertise in writing the creative 'furniture' that will pull the reader into the story or report (headlines, introductions, sub-heads or cross-heads, captions and pull-quotes) (McKay 2006: 122ff).

› Coach writers by helping them to write their stories. This approach helps to bring writer and subeditor closer together.

› Regard each story as special in its own right.

› Remain involved in the news-generation process.

› Find ways of also saying 'yes' to writing. Be a writer of reports yourself and not simply a critic of others' writing.

› Treat writers as colleagues.

› Be critical without simply being negative.

› Do your homework: be sure that you know about what you're passing judgement on.

› Enable journalists/writers to feel that they can seek your advice – and then give it.

› Always read the entire text before you begin to engage with it. (Before a text can be refined, you first have to establish what the story is about – even good grammar, perfect spelling and accurate facts aren't of much use if the story itself doesn't make sense.) But more than that, you have to have read the entire story or report before you can add the 'creative stuff' such as headlines, introductions, subheads, captions and pull-quotes that will draw the reader into the piece (McKay 2006: 128–130).

Remember: Readers take good, accurate subediting for granted, and those same readers very seldom realise how good it sometimes is. But when errors appear in print, then the attitude towards the editorial contribution changes rapidly, because (Greer (ed) 2008: 221):

> ... *bad copy editing can make or break a newspaper's hard earned reputation*. Readers always remember the mistakes. You, the journalist, represent the first line of defence against inaccuracy and misinformation. *Sub-editors are the publication's last line of defence against errors*.

It is indeed an enormous responsibility and undertaking.

5.4 The text editor as technical editor

> Technical editors frequently write, edit, and manage written documents such as books, pamphlets, quick reference cards, reports; electronic materials from online documentation to web pages; video scripts; and computer-based materials.
> *Beene*

> What a technical editor needs more than any other advanced skill is a thorough understanding of multiple audiences ...
> *Beene*

Technical editing mainly involves getting to grips with descriptive and expository writing, often composed by technical experts. Typically, it describes products or processes: how a computer programme should perform certain tasks when we interact with it; the steps involved in servicing a motor vehicle; the leaflet inserted in every box of medicine. Often they have to follow a rigid format and layout prescribed by the industry or the client; certainly, when such texts describe processes they must flow logically and not be flawed by omissions or warnings about incorrect usage, etc. In these respects, theses and dissertations often qualify as technical documents that require the expertise of a technical editor when intervention is called for. The same could be said of that specialised genre, recipe books, where attention to detail and cross-checking between ingredient lists and methods are the order of the day.

By their very nature, technical documents also contain a great deal of jargon with which authors are familiar, but not necessarily their multiple target audiences (which may also be multilingual) are familiar. The text editor of technical documents, therefore, has to focus particularly on:

- the logical sequencing of information (looking out for gaps where the author has assumed knowledge or understanding on the part of the reader);
- the clarity of the text as presented by the author (including explanations of jargon, where necessary), and
- whether the content and layout conform to the strictures imposed by the industry or the client.

These requirements make technical editing painstaking work, especially since the editor has to ensure that the steps and descriptions are complete, correct and coherent every step of the way. And on top of that they have to check for consistency – of spelling, word choice, capitalisation, hyphenation, the use of vertical lists – too.

As the world has moved closer to 'global village' status, so formerly unilingual environments have become multilingual with the movement of nationals across national boundaries in search of employment opportunities. In Europe, Polish builders and nurses now rub shoulders in the workplace with Belgians and Swedes, Greek and Turkish artisans with German- and French-speakers. In South Africa, since 1994 there have been 11 official languages, (only one of which – English – having international status). In all such contexts, the need for technical editors to scrutinise technical documentation extremely critically and carefully is great. But at the same time, despite differences and barriers, all languages must develop terminology that keeps up with the latest trends and innovations, and so concepts such as English for the Workplace and English for Academic Purposes have arisen to help non-native speakers understand notices, instructions and user manuals. Editors of such documents have to maintain a keen awareness of the profile and limitations of the intended readers, at times applying the principles of plain language to the texts they edit.

Particularly in multilingual environments and contexts – such as in offices where dictionaries are compiled, the offices of insurance companies and banking groups, and in the realms of government documentation, legal documents, pamphlets, brochures and manuals – where the same documents have to be translated into any number of languages, the text editor must ensure that the terms and phrases used in each language are indeed equivalent and do not convey contradictory or different messages to their audiences.

In the opinion of Garbers (2007), there is little glory in technical editing: it is usually hard work and sometimes feels like 'writing an eight-hour-long examination every day'. It is exhausting, can be soul-destroying and boring, and it can alienate the non-dedicated editor. It does present many challenges though and many editors do find this work fascinating, fulfilling and exciting. As with other forms of editing, it demands discipline, patience, good interpersonal relationships, good manners, humility (everyone makes mistakes) and a heavy dose of curiosity. Often, a newcomer to a particular field makes the best technical editor because they bring a freshness and objectivity – a tabula rasa – to the subject-matter that those immersed in the field lack. Such technical editors are usually a more suitable intermediary between technical writers and non-technical readers. You also develop a 'sixth sense' that helps you to sort out tough terminological issues. And, here too, you will make constant use of reference works on the widest possible front: general dictionaries, subject dictionaries, word lists, internet chat groups and personal contacts in particular industries. The objective of the entire process is always to contribute to an accurate, technically correct and user-friendly document (taking into account the field within which the subject is being communicated) that is also as cost-effective and on time as possible (Garbers 2007: 18).

5.5 The text editor in the corporate sector

Language practitioners (in particular translators and text editors) do not always enjoy the luxury of choosing what they will be doing from one day to the next, particularly if they are freelance. However, there are those who work in the corporate sector – that is, for companies or organisations that are linked to a particular undertaking or sector, such as banks, advertising agencies, insurance companies, universities – whose work is at least demarcated to some extent and where there is a limited degree of choice and focus. One advantage of this is that the work revolves mainly around the content of the particular undertaking or sector in which the institution resorts. A disadvantage is that, particularly in the longer term, the work develops a sameness year in, year out, and the practitioner has to find ways of counteracting the setting in of boredom.

There are three main advantages to working in the corporate sector: (1) that the language practitioner acquires the business or institution's way of doing things and is able to make use of the sector's support and infrastructure; (2) that the language practitioner builds up subject knowledge over time because they work within a certain discipline, and (3) that the language practitioner enjoys a fixed, regular income and usually works set hours. The value of having knowledge of the business, institution or sector is that the practitioner gets to know the prevailing corporate ideology. There are also disadvantages attached to working in the corporate sector, namely that whatever crosses the practitioner's desk usually has to be done irrespective of personal preferences. Pearce (in Mackenzie 2005: 163–164) says that a key point to bear in mind about corporate editing is to recognise that you are working in an organisation whose key business is not publishing, and which doesn't readily recognise the benefits of the text editor's contribution to the overall success of the enterprise – often because what you do is intangible and a bit of a 'mystery' to colleagues.

McLachlan (2009), supported implicitly by Pearce (2005), on the other hand, is of the opinion that within a specific sector the practitioner will encounter a great variety of text types on which they will have to work. For example, someone who works in the language bureau of a university can work daily on a variety of texts, from policy documents, financial statements and annual reports to speeches, articles about certain subjects, study guides and international agreements. Pearce herself, in her public relations role in a multinational organisation, edits media releases, newsletters and glossy journals; handles both internal and external communications, which entails preparing material for the organisation's internet (marketing) and intranet (internal communications) sites. Also within the ambit of her job are researching and writing copy for journals, mapping out marketing campaigns for managers worldwide and even something as mundane as proofreading batches of business cards. This work may well be prescriptive as well as repetitive and predictable, but it nevertheless presents challenges for being creative with language and a wide variety of texts. Pearce advises corporate editors to tailor the job to fit the budget and says that it is important for corporate editors in her position to sell communications within their organisation.

These types of text still have to pass the test of good communications (Bisaillon 2007: 77–78), where the needs of the reader are taken into account while the communicator concentrates on the formal quality of the text. They have to do so because the texts have to be effective and correct. As a result, boredom and predictability may actually not be a problem, even when you are familiar with the language and documents of your environment.

In most cases, texts will have to be edited as part of the job specification of the general language practitioner, which in a way presents opportunities to specialise in a particular sector. With this comes a large measure of familiarity with the language of the business, institution or sector and with the way in which its documents are formulated. An important advantage of this is that it gives the language practitioners the necessary background knowledge, to enable them to work faster. As a result, the practitioner will then not have to set aside time to acquire information in a certain field before being able to tackle an assignment.

5.6 The text editor as freelance language practitioner

> If you want to make some extra money while you work at another job, freelance copyediting is a good way to do it.
> *Judd*

> Not everyone is suited to self-employment: being good at editing is not enough. Do not think of becoming a freelance editor unless you have the personal qualities that make editors such paragons.
> *Mackenzie*

> A freelancer has to be one and a half times as good as an in-house editor.
> *Arms*

The administrative aspects of editing are no less important than the editing itself – certainly not 'inconsequential' at all (Murphy 2011). It is indeed the case that text editors are able to make a good living by applying their special skills in and aptitude for language practice. They can do so in two ways: either as a full-time language practitioner (which can include translation and text editing at a publishing house or as a member of the editorial team at a newspaper or a magazine) or as a part-timer (that is, as someone who holds a less permanent position and carries out well-defined assignments). In the latter case, the individual offers their services as a freelance language practitioner, whether as translator, interpreter or text editor, or by combining these services.

Others again hold down permanent positions (eg at a university or as a teacher or a librarian) but take on editing assignments (including translation and proofreading) in their private capacity after hours. Sometimes this arrangement is preparatory to going freelance completely, in which case it is viewed as 'testing the waters' or making the necessary contacts prior to leaving full-time employment or retirement. Post-retirement, such individuals find that, having made contacts in publishing (whether they've taken on another full-time job or not – we're all living much longer nowadays and most pensions are inadequate for sustaining one's pre-retirement lifestyle), they are able to occupy their working days with editing manuscripts, proofreading proofs, writing, compiling indexes, and so on, all from the comfort of their home and more or less according to a schedule that suits them (Judd 1990: 278; Boland 2008).

Then there are those practitioners who, preferring or being obliged to spend more time with their families (White 2005; Butcher, Drake & Leach 2006: 1), constitute possibly the majority of freelance language practitioners nowadays. Typically, they work for a variety of clients, who are usually restricted by fixed budgets and inflexible schedules. The US Department of Labor (2006) calculated that approximately one-third of all language practitioners in the United States work for themselves (are 'self-employed'). This could possibly be the case in other countries, but there are currently no statistics available to support this assertion.

Freelance language practitioners are obviously not only text editors. They obtain work either exclusively or in addition to text editing as proofreaders, translators, interpreters, writers, even indexers. It is true that translators in particular cannot escape the demands and responsibility of text editing (see section 5.10 in this chapter). By definition, they busy themselves with the transfer of content from one language into another (cf Gouadec 2007; House 2009; Newmark 2003; and see also section 3.1 in chapter 1). As part of the polishing or rounding-off phase of the translation process, the target document has to be thoroughly edited – a non-negotiable component of any form of translation (Mossop 2010).

There are also individuals who as freelance language practitioners do only text editing or proofreading (or sometimes both), and who prefer to specialise in particular fields or disciplines. The traditional freelance text editor seldom permits themselves the luxury of specialisation because of the risk that holds of certain work not coming their way – and it is not always possible for the freelance to turn work down (cf Boland 2008; Game 2005; Gilad 2007: 289–314; Liebenberg 2008; Selyer 2008; Tarutz 1992: 53; White 2005).

Mackenzie (2004: 171, 2011) notes that some practitioners consciously choose freelance text editing as a career, whereas others take it on for a variety of reasons: the loss of a permanent position (as a result of retrenchments), having to supplement their income after retiring, as well as wanting to combine family and work commitments (if the text editor has young children, for instance).

What is actually important to know is that not everyone is prepared or equipped to make a success of being freelance, because of the uncertainty that being freelance brings with it. Not everyone, for example, is able to handle the constant pressure of meeting deadlines and having to bring in a regular income (added to possible family pressures) – and having to cope with the accompanying administrative burden of quoting, invoicing, complying with legislative requirements, etc. And there are those without sufficient financial resources to be able to survive clients' late payments.

Mackenzie (2004: 171) refers to the advantages and disadvantages of life as a freelance:

The freelance lifestyle offers both the pleasures and the irritations of working at home. As a no-collar worker you wear what you like, you control your working environment and equipment, you don't have to commute, you avoid meetings and office politics. The disadvantages are equally obvious: you need to obtain enough work to survive, your income is uncertain, it is difficult to maintain a smooth schedule, there are no workmates down the corridor, and you need to separate your work from the demands of the household.

Van der Merwe (2007) and Jones (2005) suggest the following additional advantages and disadvantages of freelance practice:

List 3.9 Advantages and disadvantages of freelance practice

Advantages:

› You yourself choose which documents you want to accept or reject. (But when there's a shortage of work, you'll probably accept anything you're offered.)

› Greater freedom: you choose your own working hours. (But when the pressure is on, again you have little choice but to work long hours.)

› You are no longer directly involved in (often unpleasant) office politics.

› You gain experience across a wide range of subjects and disciplines.

› You work with a wide variety of clients and texts.

› Freelance work can be combined with permanent work elsewhere (though to a limited degree) or with your family commitments (though it doesn't always work out that way).

› If you work hard, the freedom and the income are much greater than they would be were you in a permanent position.

› Often the remuneration is better than if you were in a full-time position as a language practitioner.

› More favourable taxation, because your business expenses are tax-deductible from your income.

› You take control of your own professional development and create your own business networking opportunities.

Disadvantages:

› Irregular income.

› No work, no remuneration, and therefore minimal security.

› No paid leave and no sick leave.

› No pension fund or medical aid funding. You have to make provision for them yourself.

› Loneliness and social isolation.

› Competition for the same work among a number of language practitioners (although if you can maintain good relationships with clients by fulfilling their needs, you can usually ensure a relatively constant flow of work).

› Uncertainty about work prospects.

› The 'feast or famine' syndrome: you sometimes have to wait a long time for work and then it arrives all at once, sometimes more than you can cope with.

› You have to pay for your own professional development (although it is tax deductible).

› You have to provide all your own business infrastructure (furniture, telephone, internet connection, cellular phone, facsimile machine, computer, scanner and printer, stationery) (again, tax deductible).

› You run the danger of falling behind with training and refresher courses – both in the area of language usage and terminology and technologically. You also allow your reference works to become out of date (Murphy 2011: 19).

This would seem to suggest that those who choose to try out life as a freelance language practitioner should possess a number of special qualities (cf Game 2005; Holden & Hardie 2005; Murphy 2011: 18–24; Wood-Ellem 2005):

> Self-discipline (for example, to work set hours, but also to sit at a job until it has been completed).

> Confidence in their ability (skills and knowledge).

> The ability to learn from their mistakes.

> Self-motivation.

> The ability to work without supervision (must be able to function alone).

> Dedication (considering the hours it can take to complete a job).

> Complete absence of laziness.

> An ability to manage time (Selyer 2008).

> A sense of orderliness and organisation.

> Being meticulous and crystal clear in approaching projects.

> The ability to handle tension (sometimes from having too much work, sometimes from there being too little, or even none).

> Knowing how to solve problems in a text (includes a knowledge of sources).

> Being able to plan (and meet deadlines as a result).

> Being able, also, to say 'no' and to stand by that decision (when, for example, an unreasonable deadline is set or too much work is expected for the limited payment offered).

> Being able to evaluate the level of work required and to make a reasonable estimate of the time and cost.

> Diplomacy (to be able to work with clients and to retain them).

> The ability to work with money, accounts and contracts (Murphy 2011: 52–58, 71).

> The ability to market your services. Excessive modesty is consequently not to be recommended (Bishop, Linnegar & Pretorius 2011: 26; Linnegar, Marus & De Wet 2012).

List 3.10 continued

› A willingness to remain a lifelong learner (constantly developing your professional skills and knowledge by, for example, purchasing new reference materials and attending relevant training courses).

› The ability to ask the right questions at the right time.

› The ability to form, maintain and even to expand networks – with fellow practitioners as well as clients and other potential business contacts (Bishop, Linnegar & Pretorius 2011: 56–57).

› The ability to assume a mentorship role at times to help develop younger or less experienced language practitioners (Murphy 2011: 8).

Apart from these attributes, the freelance text editor should also have wide experience and a good reputation (characterised by professional conduct); possess the ability to manage projects (see chapter 5); should work in a pleasant working environment (with computer, printer, internet access, good lighting and ergonomically suitable furniture) (Liebenberg 2008; Bishop, Linnegar & Pretorius 2011: 27–39); and a well-stocked library (dictionaries, reference works, etc, including the applicable electronic aids such as the internet (for browsing) and spell-checkers) (see chapter 11).

In addition to what has already been enumerated above, the following hints for the freelance text editor cannot go unmentioned (cf Arms 2005; Boland 2008; Gilad 2007: 289–314; Greenfields 2007; Holden & Hardie 2005; Judd 1990: 278–295; Liebenberg 2008; Mackenzie 2004: 171–188, 2011; Murphy 2011; Saller 2009; Wood-Ellem 2005):

List 3.11 Additional hints for freelance text editors

› Produce quality work (this is non-negotiable).

› Be thorough in and proud of your work.

› Plan your workflow as far as you can (so that everything doesn't have to be done at once); and plan every day (to prevent chaos), dividing it into time slots for administration, research for the creative aspects of your work and personal time.

› If you care for your service providers, then your clients and the income will follow almost automatically.

› Ensure that you work in an optimal working environment (such as a pleasant and restful workspace).

› Conduct yourself professionally at all times: when giving quotations, meeting deadlines, signing off a well-produced product and when delivering an invoice (Waddingham 2008).

>>

> Create a climate for mutual communication, including with the author and your client.

> Build sufficient relaxation into your routine to counteract the tension that builds up in meeting deadlines, keeping clients satisfied and fulfilling your personal commitments (Selyer 2008).

> Join professional associations. Accreditation with such an association broadens your network and also sends out the signal that you meet the minimum quality standard (Jones 2005; Murphy 2011: 6–7, 20–21).

> Quote according to agreed-upon professional tariffs (cf Bishop, Linnegar & Pretorius 2011: 48–49; Gilad 2007; Murphy 2011: 52–56). Overpricing leads only to short-term profits. Remember that you deliver a specialised service and are entitled to remuneration commensurate with the quality of the work you deliver, the urgency with which it needs to be completed, the degree of complexity of the content, and the demands placed on the text editor's knowledge of the subject.

> Do not accept work that you cannot handle, for whatever reason (Bishop, Linnegar & Pretorius 2011: 52).

> Know your limitations and be honest with your clients about them.

> View your limitations as opportunities for growth. Don't be afraid to take on work that's outside your frame of reference: just do the necessary research and budget for extra time to complete it (Van der Merwe 2007; Bishop, Linnegar & Pretorius 2011).

> Always enter into written contracts to secure the conditions under which you accept work. (See chapter 5.) Doing so could ensure that you're properly paid for hard, dedicated work.

> Don't enter into contracts for work for which you are not fit. (This is very important!)

> Provide quotations and invoices as requested by due date (Lightfoot 2005; Murphy 2011: 52–58).

> Don't be ashamed to speak about money – that is why you do the work: to earn an income (Bishop, Linnegar & Pretorius 2011: 53–55).

> Don't be afraid to seek legal assistance when clients don't pay you (Capstick 2008).

> Impress potential employers with your professionalism (Murphy 2011: 607).

It seems possible to add much more to this list, but Mackenzie (2004: 188, 2011) puts in a nutshell what needs to be said in general: 'If you are *flexible*, *autonomous* and *disciplined* and can *adapt* to the particular requirements of freelance editing, you will find your career is a real possession in the changing fortunes of time' (cf Bishop, Linnegar & Pretorius 2011; Linnegar, Marus & De Wet 2012).

To these attributes we can add what Saller (2009) calls the 'three paths to editing enlightenment': carefulness, transparency and flexibility: carefulness is about possessing knowledge (for example, of the current trends and rules of style and grammar) when going about meticulously editing a text. For Saller, 'the first step toward carefulness is to study your style manual' (2009: 24). Transparency is all about making our editorial changes clear to the author and the client on the manuscript (or the electronic document) and also in our communications with them; it should 'invite the participation of the author' rather than your presenting the edited manuscript as a fait accompli (2009: 26). Track Changes in MS Word makes transparency that much easier. Flexibility pertains to the text editor's attitude when approaching a manuscript: are you going to apply the often arbitrary 'rules' as you know them doggedly (especially regarding matters of style, as opposed to grammar) or are you prepared to be more negotiable on such questions, having discerned your author's preferences in your initial reading of the text? Armed with these three attributes, you're bound to present yourself to clients and authors as professional, reasonable and accommodating without compromising standards.

In summary: freelance text editing is a practical and viable possibility, but the practitioner needs to be aware beforehand of the demands that it makes and the responsibilities that accompany the freelance existence. If you can stay the pace, freelance work should become and remain a rewarding business. If not, look elsewhere.

5.7 The text editor as 'sub' or proofreader for magazines

Much of what has been said of the text editor in the newsroom applies to the subeditor working in the world of magazines and journals; but some specifics are worth recording here. First, magazines can be either text-led (in which case the text predominates and the visuals are of lesser importance) or picture-led (in which case there's minimal text and the visuals dominate the pages to tell the story). Each has its challenges to varying degrees: more text editing has to be done in the former type of magazine, naturally; more credit- and caption-checking and checking of the suitability of the visuals are the order of the day in the latter type. In both, headlines, introductions, subheadings and pull-quotes usually have to be written by the sub and checked by the proofreader once the pages have been completely designed or laid out, and suitable cover lines written. So, either way, there's a great deal of creative work for the sub to work on.

Essentially, the magazine sub's tasks include the following:

› Edit the text supplied by the commissioned journalists and other specialist writers.

› Apply the in-house house style to every article or report, updating it where necessary with each issue of the publication.

› After reading each article, write (or rewrite) suitable headlines, introductions, side heads/cross-heads, captions (for whichever pictures are available at subbing stage) and pull-quotes.

› Check that the copy fits the available space: if too little, look for opportunities to fill blank space; if too much (this is 'over-matter'), try various strategies to fit all the text into the available space.

› To fill space, try these options:

› Create additional lines in selected paragraphs by replacing shorter words with longer ones or replacing words with phrases.

› Where possible, split a paragraph into two.

› Insert subheads, where practicable.

› Replace personal pronouns with their noun equivalents (eg, *it* with *tyrannosaurus rex*).

› If all else fails, request the designer to increase the word and letter spacing in specified paragraphs, if doing so will help to create an additional line of text here and there.

› To fit over-matter into the available space, try these options:
  – Eliminate widows by cutting words or phrases or flowing text back.
  – Where possible, combine two paragraphs into one.
  – Remove subheads, where practicable.
  – Replace phrases with single words or long words with shorter synonyms.

› If all else fails, request the designer to reduce the word and letter spacing in specified paragraphs, if doing so will help to save a line of text here and there.

› Check that every article or report ends in an endmark.

>>

List 3.12 continued

› Check that every picture which requires a caption in fact has one (or a temporary placeholder).

› Check that every picture or other graphic has a credit line (and the correct one, too).

› Where a tag line (or strap line) is required for each different story, ensure that the correct one accompanies each story (eg health, lifestyle, travel, education).

› Draw up the table of contents for the issue, checking especially that page numbering and wording correspond to the text in the magazine. Often this requires a degree of creativity too, since exactly the same wording should not be used in headlines, contents list and cover lines.

› Check that the paragraphing style for the publication is followed consistently (either first line indented or block style).

› Check that sidebar copy is clearly marked as such and is treated consistently by the designer.

Once the pages have been designed or laid out, in most cases with both text and visuals in place, the process of proofreading can commence. This is often a task assigned to an eagle-eyed text editor. These are the items to check at proof stage (bearing in mind that in most cases the page proofs will be in full colour, and that the colour work will also have to be proofed):

Checklist 3.4 Magazine proofreader's tasks

• Addresses and contact details of publisher and management staff:
   ✓ Are they suitably formatted and correct?
   ✓ Are these a post box or a street address?
   ✓ Email addresses: are they correct and consistently formatted?
   ✓ Are telephone and fax numbers in the correct format?

• Contents list:
   ✓ Do wording and page numbers correspond to the actual fall of pages?
   ✓ Check at every proofing stage, especially in the case of late insertions or pulls of stories.

• Picture credits:
   ✓ Are they present, updated to reflect the source, and correct?
   ✓ Are they in the correct position? Are they facing the right direction?

• Cross-references:
   ✓ Are they correct in text and in cover lines?
   ✓ Are they correct in the editor's letter?
   ✓ Is the format as per house style?

>>

- Diacritical signs (ü, ô, à, õ, ç, ê, ø, etc):
  - ✓ Are they all where they're supposed to be?
  - ✓ Are they the correct signs (especially check ê, è, é)?

- Drop caps (if applicable):
  - ✓ Are they the right size (3, 4 or 5 lines deep) and font?
  - ✓ Are they used in the right places?

- Edition:
  - ✓ Are the number and date correct on front cover, spine, contents list, inside pages (eg Winter 2012, 21 February 2012, Second quarter 2012)?

- Endmark (if applicable):
  - ✓ Is it there at the end of every story? Is it correct?

- Fonts and style:
  - ✓ Check carefully: tag/strap lines, headlines, introductions, body text, captions, pull-quotes, side heads/cross-heads, sidebars, tables, figures

- Full stops:
  - ✓ Are these used for abbreviations, initials? Exceptions?
  - ✓ Are they used at the end of introductions?
  - ✓ Are they used at the end of captions?

- House style (follow style sheet):
  - ✓ Spelling
  - ✓ Capitalisation
  - ✓ One word/hyphenated/two words
  - ✓ Numbers
  - ✓ En-rule vs em-rule

- Italics:
  - ✓ Are they used correctly, as per house style or the style sheet?

- Names of people and places:
  - ✓ Are the spellings correct?

- Orphans and widows (cuts and fills):
  - ✓ Have these been attended to/eliminated?

- Page numbers (folios):
  - ✓ Are format and font correct?
  - ✓ Is the position on the page correct?
  - ✓ Have they been omitted on pages comprising visuals/advertisements only?
  - ✓ Have they been omitted on preliminary pages?
  - ✓ Have cross-references been corrected (check at every proof stage)?

- Phone numbers:
  - ✓ Are they suitably formatted and correct?
  - ✓ Are national or international codes required?

>>

Checklist 3.4 continued

    ✓ Should they be spaced or unspaced?
    ✓ Is the mobile number format correct?

- Websites:
    ✓ Has the full, correct url been used?
    ✓ Is the format correct?
    ✓ Do they start with http:// or www.?
    ✓ Are websites within < > given?

See also section 9 in chapter 4 on the why and how of proofreading.

If the text editor is asked to check printer's proofs (Epson or Rainbow proofs) prior to printing, these items will need to be proofread:

Checklist 3.5 Pre-press proofing

- Diacritical signs (ü, ô, à, õ, ç, ê, ø, etc):
    ✓ Are they all where they're supposed to be?
    ✓ Are they the correct signs (especially check ê, è, é)?

- Folios and headers/footers:
    ✓ Are they present and correct?

- Italics and bold:
    ✓ Have they been used for the correct purpose (following style sheet)?
    ✓ Are they in the correct font?

- Has copy fallen off any pages?

- Visuals:
    ✓ Are they corrupt?
    ✓ Have they become reversed?
    ✓ Are they pixellated?

5.8 The text editor as trainer or mentor

> What's the difference between a teacher and a mentor? ... Teaching means passing on specific skills, actively helping the learner to acquire a set of skills, testing them on their understanding, and making sure that they are competent to use those skills. A mentor guides and encourages a person and allows them to develop along their own lines. ... It is the mentor's role to help the mentee to see stumbling blocks and get over them ... but never by actually doing work for them. A good mentor will know when to let go and allow the mentee to take off on their own.
> *Murphy*

In many instances and situations, the experienced text editor plays the role of mentor and trainer of younger and inexperienced individuals. In a study of professional editing, Bisaillon (2007: 84) points out the important role that experience plays in doing text editing

– it helps, among other things, with the types of text that are taken on and also with the tempo at which the work is completed. When the experienced editor plays the role of mentor and supportive companion towards more inexperienced individuals in the industry, effectively they are training them. In this way individuals are groomed for the job of text editing and gain a better idea, from a practitioner, of how to tackle editing projects; they become involved in existing networks, they learn the do's and don'ts of text editing, and so on. There is no counterpart for the role that the experienced – and wise – language practitioner can play in the training of other practitioners. One could even say that in view of the shortage of really well-trained editors, it should be the duty of the more experienced practitioners to fulfil this important function whenever the opportunity presents itself. If, as a novice text editor you can find a mentor to guide you while you gain experience and build editing skills, so much the better, but a mentor won't be able to do the work for you – that's up to you (Murphy 2011: 8).

Unfortunately, the way in which developments have forced formal publishing to realign itself and in the process shed full-time permanent staff during the past decade (the emergence of ebooks and ereaders, and of digital media, quite apart from economic factors globally) has led to the demise of the time-honoured practice of on-the-job learning in the manner described above, where more experienced staff members were available to guide and support newcomers to the industry. Now, most of the experienced practitioners are freelancers, not in the same position to mentor and train colleagues as before. For colleagues and for the industry as a whole, this is a seriously retrograde step: Where will new entrants obtain their (formal and informal) training, other than from courses presented by tertiary institutions, private trainers, or associations of professionals who have a direct interest in helping their members upgrade their skills? (Murphy 2011: 8).

One of the consequences of the lack of on-the-job training opportunities or the absence of more experienced practitioners in publishers' offices and newsrooms is that more and more errors are creeping in to the media in which we had become used to seeing high standards of language, grammar, punctuation, spelling and typography upheld. Many of these errors can be ascribed to ignorance, to non-native speaker writing and editing in what is essentially a 'foreign' language, to a poor grounding in such matters at school and university level, and to an arrogance that shouts 'don't try to teach me my craft; I know it all'. And it's not only newspapers that are guilty of this drop in standards; many a reviewer has felt bound to refer to errors of fact, language, grammar, spelling, syntax, and so on that can frequently be detected in books that have – contrary to what seems – been edited and proofread. Is this the result of overhasty publishing schedules or the use of inexperienced or inadequately trained practitioners, or a combination of both? Often, quality is sacrificed on the altar of profitability ....

Fortunate, then, indeed, are those inexperienced text editors and journalists who are able to work in a thriving newsroom or editorial office (regardless of the sector or the industry) and who are able to be mentored by more experienced people in their industry. They should be thankful for the formative training and the support they receive, in a place where language is practised daily. On the other hand, the experienced text editor who patiently plays the role of mentor and trainer is quietly helping to prepare a new generation of experienced practitioners and, in the long term, promote quality in what the profession delivers daily, weekly, monthly and indefinitely.

5.9 The text editor as checker of language in texts

In certain working environments or situations the experienced text editor serves as a checker of others' work (such as translations – see 5.10 below). This is especially the task of more seasoned language practitioners in language bureaus in businesses, corporate offices, the banking and insurance sectors as well as among the subeditors at newspapers and magazines. In these setups the experienced text editors go through the work of junior translators and text editors to check it for correctness, accuracy and appropriateness to the audience and the medium. Often the work of junior colleagues is returned to them and has to be redone. Most experienced language practitioners have been along this road in their careers; and what started out as a disappointment has often turned out to be an invaluable lesson, namely, that there's no substitute for either experience or quality work.

In general, newcomers to language practice and text editing are well advised to grasp every opportunity for on-the-job learning from their peers, as few other opportunities exist among practitioners for such learning to take place. This is particularly true of the contemporary situation, in which many publishers and language bureaus largely outsource the editorial and language practice functions, denying countless practitioners the opportunity to learn on the job. Any contacts with more experienced text editors should therefore be cherished, particularly those opportunities afforded by professional associations.

In the realm of text editing, (of which language forms such an important part) in particular, the concept of lifelong learning, which is central to current knowledge- and skills-acquisition thinking and practice, makes complete sense: the really professional text editor will freely admit to learning something new with each document they're called upon to work on. To apply a little artistic licence to an excerpt from a famous poem: 'Dull would he be of soul who could pass by an opportunity so touching in its majesty' (Wordsworth's sonnet 'Composed upon Westminster Bridge'). Who better to learn from than one's more experienced and worldly-wise peers.

5.10 The text editor of translated texts

> When people are translating into their native language, they often write ungrammatical and especially unidiomatic sentences, under the influence of the source text.
> *Mossop*

It is important not to lose sight of the fact that translated texts have to be edited as much as the original manuscript. Also, that a translation should not be attempted on an unedited manuscript – even though some publishers consider doing so to be a shortcut that should help speed up the production process. To their peril, they learn too late that translating from an unedited text is in practice a long and costly route that can throw out a schedule and blow a budget. Translating an unedited document can mean, for example, that the translator has to deal with many unresolved restructuring issues, including rewordings of sentences, word choice changes and unidiomatic usage. It may even be that the translator works on sentences or paragraphs that should have been deleted – a waste of time, effort and expenditure.

With translations, the text editor's role should be twofold:

• First to edit the source document (the first language).
• Then to edit the target document (the second language).

When it is known that a document will be translated, there is a greater need to ensure that all author queries and other problems involving syntax, semantics and idiom have been resolved, because unresolved matters should not be carried over to the translated document. Indeed, the uncertainty caused by unresolved matters will complicate the translator's task and could lead to delays in delivering the final translation – and exasperation at the wasted effort.

When the text editor begins their edit of the translation, they should have in their possession both the edited original document and the translation: thus equipped, they will be better able to resolve any queries they may have regarding the meaning of words and expressions in the translation. Also, non-native speakers of English, or less educated people, may well experience problems with syntax, word choice and idiom, sometimes translating literally from their mother tongue or source text.

The example below illustrates how tightly connected a paragraph in a translation can be if it is well planned – in this case by incorporating the use of logical connectors (*two accidents, In the first accident, In another accident, In both accidents*), syntactic repetition (*lost control of his vehicle*) and synonyms (*motorist, man, passengers*) (*Die Burger* newspaper, 21 December 2009: 2 – our translation):

> A Netcare 911 spokesperson said that two accidents occurred in George yesterday. In the first accident a motorist lost control of his vehicle near the Pacaltsdorp offramp. In another incident a man lost control of his vehicle on the N2 near the Garden Route Mall. In both accidents the passengers suffered only light injuries.

You as text editor will usually need to know the writer's native language to make sensible corrections. The original edited document should be the more reliable guide to the use of terminology and other words and phrases should queries arise. Armed with the original document, the text editor will also be better placed to check whether any text, or any part of the message being communicated, has not been carried across to the target language during translation.

A perennial problem with editing translations is the differences of interpretation and word choice that can occur or exist between editors and translators. This is sometimes related to a lack of authorities or references or to the imposition of practitioners' personal preferences should there be room for differences in interpretation. When such personal choices are made, they must be recorded in the editor's style sheet for the text. In this way, the style sheet grows organically, helping to impose standardisation and consistency on a text or a series of texts. Here the text editor should be guided by the best, most suitable meaning in a given context and, if necessary, check the possible meanings of words carefully in a dictionary or in another reliable word list. In the case of specific disciplines, the editor should also be supplied with a terminology list, if possible, to help them standardise on the terms used.

For a number of reasons, the text editor of translated text should also receive a copy of the house style or the style sheet for the particular title so that any inconsistencies or unusual word usages can be checked (Mossop 2010: 38ff).

5.11 The text editor and self-publishing

As Flann & Hill (2004: 14) point out, the availability and flexibility of modern desktop publishing systems has created a boom in self-publishing, particularly in the areas of family and local history, but also among writers unable to find a publisher for their 'great novel' or that story 'for which there just has to be a market'. The more recent release onto the market of 'print on demand' (POD) printing technology, which operates as sophisticated digital printers that output printed matter in formats suitable for binding up as books, has had the effect of accelerating the trend towards self-publishing by making the printing of books much more affordable to the person in the street. POD makes it both feasible and affordable for authors to print as few as 50 or 100 copies of their book at a time at a price that no longer depends upon large economies of scale. These developments have led to a steadily increasing demand for the services of freelance text editors to help private individuals (usually) prepare their work for publication.

In these circumstances, while opportunities are many for text editors to develop an additional income stream through this innovative growth area and the temptations are great to edit individuals' manuscripts, the attendant risks are also high, because so many authors are quite ignorant of the processes, the costs and the tasks involved in the production of a book once they have written it and many a collaboration between author and text editor has come to grief as a result of (a) the author's ignorance and (b) the editor's failure to educate their client from the outset and/or (c) both parties' neglect to pen an editing agreement prior to commencing work.

Think of it. Virtually since the invention of printing presses in the West, when an author has approached a publisher who then accepts their manuscript for publication, the publisher has traditionally taken on what were originally the author's responsibilities (and financial risk): having the text edited, typeset and proofread; having illustrations drawn, and having an index compiled. In return for taking on these expenses and marketing the book, the publisher is entitled to make a profit on the sale of every copy, from which the author is paid a royalty (an agreed percentage of the book's selling price). Other than write and possibly check the edited manuscript and read a set of proofs, the author is usually given little or no insight into the workings of a publisher.

Take away the publisher and you should begin to understand the nature and extent of the problems the author who decides to self-publish (and their text editor-cum-'publisher') is faced with. First, the typical author in this position usually doesn't understand the difference between text editing and proofreading – that's where the first area of conflict often arises. Nor do they understand the various types and levels of editing; and, for their part, the unwitting text editor is, unfortunately, not shielded by either the publisher or a formal author–publisher contract that lays down responsibilities, standards and boundaries (publishers often specify to authors that they will not publish a manuscript until it is in an 'acceptable' (ie well-edited) state) (Davies & Balkwill 2011: 169). Such authors also have little or no idea of the book publishing process (write, edit, typeset, proofread, print-ready document, print and bind – see figure 3.2), and so have only a limited conception of the time-scale and the production costs involved. And, absent the publisher, the text editor often takes on the role of publisher, editor, proofreader and project manager all rolled into one. Expect to be asked a wide range of questions about the production of the book; respond to those you are able to as honestly as you can; for those you cannot offer answers, refer the author to the authorities (such as professional and industry associations). As a result, what usually starts out as a cordial and creative collaboration often degenerates into an acrimonious conflict involving finger-pointing and counter-claims ('the proofreader has destroyed my text, changed all my words', 'they don't deserve to be paid the balance of their fee for what they've done to my novel') – and sometimes an out-of-pocket text editor when the client has refused to honour the practitioner's invoice.

For all these reasons, text editing for authors who self-publish is not for the novice practitioner; and even the seasoned editor would be well advised (and well prepared) to educate the author from the outset by spelling out the steps in the production process (see figure 3.2 in this chapter), putting time frames to each step, and attaching a fee to each task. And then, of course, committing to writing the terms agreed to. But once the work starts, there's even more reason for the text editor and the author to have open communication and to work closely together on polishing the text – as Davies & Balkwill (2011: 172) put it: 'authors respecting editors' needs and constraints as much as editors responding to author demands.' Lowenstein (in Mackenzie 2005: 250–252) offers the following tips for editors who work with self-publishers: know where to draw the line, because the self-publishing author often may not; also, be precise about the services provided so that confusion between author and editor does not occur. 'Caught up in the enthusiasm of producing their own book, [such authors] are apt to be mortally wounded when the final invoice charges for all those late-night phone calls and last-minute changes arrives. Not to mention their distress when they realise that the object that has occupied their lives for months on end may be "just another job" to the freelancer.'

There are two aspects to the personal and difficult task of fashioning an author's manuscript, which tend to become more acute in a self-publishing context. Some authors need more than just friendly encouragement while they are writing; they may benefit from someone with a critical eye (and loads of tact) who has the courage to judge whether or not ideas are working, making judgements that the author is willing to accept and trust. The second aspect is to criticise a completed manuscript and suggest ways in which it could be improved – a role those in the formal publishing industry take for granted as being the editor's (Davies & Balkwill 2011: 169). Setting up a modus operandi with your author and developing a good working relationship with them are therefore fundamental to making the editing of an author's manuscript work well in the exposed circumstances of self-publishing.

An editing agreement should state either an hourly rate, a per page rate or a per 1 000 words rate, or a price for the whole job (in the form of a quotation) – professional associations of editors should be able to give guidelines regarding fees. It should also spell out clearly what services will be included (Flann & Hill 2004: 14). Of course, all the terms used in the check list below will usually have to be explained to the author as part of their 'education' – your written agreement may even have to include a 'definitions' section:

Checklist 3.6 Self-publishing author: services to be agreed

✓ Will it include substantive (structural) editing and mechanical (style) editing or basic text editing only (alternatively, a light, a medium or a heavy edit), based on an assessment of the manuscript? (See above in this chapter.)
✓ Who will be responsible for checking factual data?
✓ How will author queries be handled?
✓ Who will be responsible for creating a book design? What will they charge?
✓ Who will compile the preliminary pages and the end-matter if the author has not done so?
✓ Who will be responsible for doing the corrections to and the formatting of the manuscript?
✓ Who will be laying out the pages, following the book design?
✓ Who will design the cover? Who will write the back cover blurb?
✓ Will the proofreading of the final page proofs be part of the job (and therefore billable)?
✓ Who will organise permissions requests for photographs or other material used from other sources, and how will permissions fees be paid?
✓ Who owns the copyright in the text, the illustrations, and so on?
✓ Who will apply for an ISBN for the publication?

>>

Checklist 3.6 continued

✓ How will the service providers be acknowledged in the book? (Usually on the imprint page, but sometimes in the preface or the acknowledgements.)

✓ Will the author accept your services to project manage the process (over and above your text editing/proofreading role)?

✓ Who will be printing the book, and how many quotations must be obtained if a printer hasn't already been secured?

✓ If pictures have to be researched and artwork briefed and executed, who will be responsible for these functions? Is there budget to cover the costs to be incurred? (There should also be agreement that 'free' images cut-and-pasted off websites will not be acceptable in print media.)

✓ If design advice is required (and to be given), this should be quoted for and included in the terms of agreement.

✓ If an index is required, who will compile it and how much will this cost?

✓ If work on any aspect of the manuscript exceeds or falls short of the schedule or budget, what steps will the parties be entitled to take? Can the fees be either increased or decreased accordingly, or will it remain fixed?

✓ Are service providers such as the text editor, the proofreader, the typesetter, etc, each entitled to a copy of the printed book?

A fairly standard checklist of all the possible publishing production tasks, as part of the written agreement, would help to simplify matters and also help with specifying those tasks that have been agreed upon.

Until the author has signed the written terms of agreement, including the various fees for the tasks agreed upon, the text editor is advised not to commence work. It would also not be unreasonable, in these circumstances, for the text editor to require a deposit to be paid (usually up to 50% of the total fee for the project) prior to the commencement of work – the balance to be paid on presentation of an invoice upon completion of the work (payment terms to be specified).

5.12 The text editor's intervention in web page/website text

While most of the tasks a text editor performs in print media apply equally to electronic media such as websites and social networking sites such as Facebook, Twitter and blogs, the particular requirements of and conventions associated with such electronic media require some adaptation on the part of the practitioner and, ideally, a much closer collaboration with web designers (cf Arnold 2007; Butcher, Drake & Leach 2006; Craig 2005; Dorner 2000; Flann & Hill 2004; Gilad 2007; Hart 2007; Kaashoek & Simmons 2000; Lee 2005; Marsen 2007; Jansen & Steehouder 2001; Treebus 1995, 1997; Waddingham 2006; Wallace 2004).

Some of the conventions peculiar to electronic media (which distinguish them from print media), and of which text editors operating in the web space should be aware are:

› Sans serif fonts are more readable onscreen than are serif fonts.

› Headlines and headings should be short and clear (preferably not cryptic).

› Shorter sentences and paragraphs are preferable.

› Bulleted lists are considered more desirable than long passages of continuous text.

› Italics is less readable onscreen, and is generally avoided.

› Bold is preferred for emphasis.

› Underlining (or bold and underlining) is reserved for links between web pages and to other websites.

› Text should be arranged in narrow columns for ease of reading. A reader should not have to scroll across or down a page to take in the full text.

› Text on a page should be as 'visual' as possible, that is, not appear as a sea of indigestible words.

› Readers tend to place more emphasis on the left side of a column or a page, so the really important information should preferably be located there.

› Information in an article should be prioritised and arranged according to the shape of an inverted triangle. In other words, place the really important information at the head of an article, where readers are likely to focus most of their attention. Some readers may never read to the end of an article, so important information placed there will be lost on them.

› The principles of plain language apply even more pertinently to electronic media than to print, because of the greater need for brevity, clarity, correctness and consistency.

› Articles that are more factual and informative, rather than having a sales or marketing ring about them, tend to be taken more seriously and therefore be read more thoroughly. Remove hype from web text if its purpose is to inform, not sell.

› Unfortunately, much copy that gets presented as web-ready was originally written for a print medium and therefore usually doesn't

List 3.13 continued

meet the criteria for good web text and layout; it therefore has to be edited to make it meet the criteria.

› Text that has simply been translated into English for use on a web page or website must be carefully edited to render it more suitable to the electronic medium. Often the weaknesses inherent in such texts are: substandard grammar and idiom; misspellings; inappropriate punctuation; inconsistencies; inappropriate tone or register (either too formal or too informal, depending upon the entity, product or service being promoted on the website).

The modus operandi for editors and proofreaders of electronic text is, as a result, somewhat different from that of print media:

• Website 'publishing' tends to be design/visual-driven rather than text-driven. This means that the text is made to fit into the design template for the web pages.

• It is rare, therefore, that the text editor will see the text to be edited before it has been laid out in the format of a particular web page or website. The usual problems of logical flow, consistency, spelling, punctuation, overlong sentences and paragraphs, accuracy and clarity should nevertheless be ironed out on the pages of the beta site.

• Text editors will make use of Content Management Applications/Systems (CMS) that are designed specifically to allow webpage editors/proofreaders and translators to access web text onscreen.

• The text editor could also be shown or given access to a draft or beta version of the relevant pages, will usually be unable to manipulate them onscreen, and will consequently have to print individual pages out, edit the hard copy, and then hand the marked-up pages to the designer, who will then implement the corrections.

6 The text editor as 'ghostwriter'

> Editors ... tend to be introverts, carrying out off-stage duties outside the spotlight and without the gratification that accompanies public credit.
> *Stepp*

Is the text editor a 'ghostwriter' or not? The debate about this question has a number of sides to it. On the one hand, there are those who believe that the text editor's brief and job are only to improve text and that they are paid to do just that; and that by adhering to their brief text editors fulfil their responsibility. In an older source, Rae says (1952: 104):

> The copyreader, who remains anonymous as far as the public is concerned, does not write stories or rewrite those given him, except in emergencies. He is *hired* for his technical knowledge and editing ability acquired by long years of experience.

Einsohn (2005: 11) adds to this by claiming that text editors cannot be ghostwriters, because they '... do not have *licence* to *rewrite* a text line by line'. There are two arguments in favour of this assertion: (1) the text editor is paid for their work (whereas a writer is not) and (2) text editors are not, by definition, briefed to rewrite texts. By paying the text editor for their services, the client acknowledges that their work has been completed and that 'rewriting' is regarded as the job of the author him- or herself and not that of the text editor. For these reasons also, the text editor does not need to receive any further recognition for their contribution to the production process.

On the other hand, there are those who believe that text editors, precisely on the ground of their training and experience, play a professional role in the publication process, and that, on that basis, they can act as co-writer or co-creator of the final product and can then certainly be considered to be an active role-player. Research by Kotze & Verhoef (2003) into the text editor's function as a ghostwriter indicates that writers in general know little about the different phases through which a publication has to pass and that thus eventually provides text editors with the job (and challenge) of transforming an often long, disorganised, unstructured, boring and mundane text into a bestseller. In these circumstances, the practitioner's intervention becomes a heavy, substantive and content edit that is tantamount to writing or rewriting. In this way text editors do an exceptional job of perfecting the text in their professional capacity by drawing on their qualifications, experience and creativity. Consequently, they become jointly responsible for the published text.

Clearly, this makes the text editor a kind of 'ghostwriter'; in other words, someone who helps to refine a raw product by applying their unique skills, knowledge and experience to a manuscript (Kotze & Verhoef 2003; Einsohn 2005: 11ff). Without this, a text often runs the danger of remaining 'often too long, disorganised, unstructured, boring and mundane', and one that does not 'sparkle and shine'. By unlocking the text's potential, the editor transforms it, improving it substantially. Therefore, the text editor remains largely responsible for the quality and appearance of the final product in a fruitful collaboration with the author.

Nevertheless, some authors can and do feel that they bear the full responsibility for the final product in co-operation with the client (eg a publisher) and that the text editor plays only a technical role – and therefore a secondary one – in the process. But there are also writers who see things differently, and Kotze's (1998: 202) research mentioned above also points to the belief among most authors that the text editor should receive professional recognition and that the good ones should also enjoy much wider exposure among authors (Kotze & Verhoef 2003).

The reason for this appears to be an acknowledgement of the quality-control role that editors perform, thanks to their professional training and broad experience. Without their input, any manuscript runs the danger of becoming (and remaining) an average product rather than something closer to perfection.

This brings us to the question of rewriting (sometimes called 'overwriting') as opposed to ghostwriting. At a time when the quality of manuscripts received from authors is deteriorating, largely because their authors are not NS of the language in which they write (with the accompanying problems of expression), editorial intervention is expected to be more penetrating in the interests of a more acceptable end product. The degree of editorial intervention may well lead to a number of positive outcomes for the text editor in terms of both payment and recognition of their contribution to the text:

- Pay the text editor a higher fee for the heavier editing or rewriting and acknowledge their role simply as editor.
- Split their payment between an upfront editing fee and a later share of the author's royalties and also acknowledge their input as either editor or co-author.
- Elevate them to co-author status and reward them only in the form of a share of the royalties (this obviously has to be discussed and agreed upon with the other author(s)).

Related questions that must be asked in such circumstances include: What kinds of rewriting are there? What basic principles may usefully be employed when rewriting? To what extent should the original author(s) be involved in agreeing to the extent of rewriting deemed necessary? How does the text editor, as the reader's champion, go about identifying the problems that rewriting will be able to solve? Or, looked at differently, to what extent is the text editor required to intervene to 'save' the author's manuscript?

Whatever one's view on the role of the 'ghostwriter' played by the text editor, it is clear that text editors play a penetrating and integral role in bringing the end product into being. The decision whether to give visible acknowledgement or not (and not just a monetary reward) to their behind-the-scenes role lies largely in the client's hands. More recently, in many publications (excepting works of fiction) it is becoming more common to acknowledge the editor in print together with the names of the other role-players in the production process. This is already a good measure of acknowledgement of the invaluable intervention of the text editor.

7 The text editor's role in ebooks/digital media

> Today, if you think you're in the print-layout industry, you can worry, but if you're in the publishing, or content, industry, you'll be fine. There is going to be a lot of paying work.
> *Attwell*

> If you think editing is about correcting spelling and grammar, you're not doing enough and you'll be out of a job before long. In this way, ebooks actually create an incentive for greater quality in editing, by making good editors more valuable, and mediocre ones unnecessary.
> *Attwell*

> Highly literate editors accustomed to the fixity and authority of print are adapting to the evolving interactivity of the web. … 'editors are probably best placed to start building the framework for XML publishing' … the editor who has traditionally done some mark-up in MS Word, should complete that task by formatting in XML, thus taking control of the whole production process. This will require 'expertise in document design, preparation of graphics and development of style sheets'.
> *Mackenzie*

Although the text editing required for digital media is in essence no different from that for printed publications, there are some important considerations to be taken into account when preparing texts for the digital environment – the subject of this section (cf Attwell 2010; Butcher, Drake & Leach 2006; Flann & Hill 2004; Gilad 2007; Knowles 2011; Mackenzie 2011: 84–93; Quinn 2001; Sunshine 2009). For one thing, screen publications have two important features that print lacks: they are both dynamic and interactive (Mackenzie 2011: 84). For another, the substance and structure of screen publications must be premised on a continuing relationship with readers, providing for feedback, alternative views, updates and revisions. Also, screens are harder to read than print is, so readers rarely take in the material word by word; instead, they scan a page, looking for points of interest. It follows, then that the screen should contain plenty of signposts, giving prominence to the main points; in addition, the body text should be structured according to the inverted triangle that journalists use for reports and features, where the most important information is at the start, in the heading and the first sentence. What this means, in essence, is that the structure of web pages is dictated by the users' needs rather than the structure of the organisation that created it. In fact, the connections between parts are just as important as the content in creating an effective publication for the screen. Text editors who work in this environment have, of course, to be conversant with all of these factors (and more) unique to web pages.

In recent years, the convergence of print and digital multimedia has led to the emergence of 'single-source publishing', an efficient way of preparing a single digital document that can be published in several versions: printed book, ebook, website, or for a handheld device. Electronic tags in a single source document code the text and illustrations in such a way that a page reference appears in the print version whereas a hyperlink appears onscreen, for example. And because the markup language used stores data in plain text format independent of both software and hardware, it can be shared by different applications and platforms, making upgrades between different versions of a document a lot easier. In environments in which there is considerable overlap in the content of different versions and the information is likely to be revised or updated frequently single-source is ideal.

What does this mean for editors currently wedded to print media? Well, it would seem that those with a bent for IT and document design are likely to become one of several compatible freelances who could form a creative team on single-source publishing projects.

Gardiner (in Mackenzie 2011: 93) claims that 'infrastructure and expertise within the publishing industry is underdeveloped to support XML production. So ... editors (who are increasingly diversifying into desktop publishing and graphic design) are probably best placed to start building the framework for XML publishing.' This is good news for text editors, particularly freelances, wanting not to be left behind by the technological changes sweeping through the publishing industry.

What is XML? Well, digital publishing relies on markup that determines how the content is displayed onscreen, differentiating text into headings, paragraphs, lists and links and dictating the size and positions of pictures. Think of MS Word's Styles function without thinking of a traditional book format and you've more or less got the picture, only in computer code instead. Now, single-source is made possible by the best-known markup language – hypertext markup language (HTML) – which is supplemented by extensible markup language (XML) and cascading style sheets (CSS). CSS provides the instructions for the design and layout aspects of digital documents, whether for print or the web.

One of the multimedia made possible by the e-troika of HTML, XML and CSS is ebooks. Regarding the nuts and bolts of editing practice in a digital environment, text editors should be interested in what Shuttleworth Fellow Arthur Attwell (2010), whose specialty is pioneering the publishing of ebooks in Africa, has to say. Like Gardiner, he believes that there is still a place for the human input that text editors offer in an industry in which production processes are becoming increasingly automated, but that the nature of the editor's intervention has had to change. He points out that the traditional role of the editor – of mechanically correcting spelling and grammar, for example – is falling by the wayside as more of the editor's functions become automated and the emphasis in book production shifts to preparing texts for a digital environment. The editor's focus, he says, should be on the content and on preparing it more creatively for electronic media. This means focusing on styling documents so that they can be adapted for any digital or print format. The reason for this shift is that in order to add enough value to the publishing process to be able to charge money for their products, publishing companies are having to offer creative, human input to the content they gather from authors. That's where editors are invaluable.

One spinoff of this shift in functional focus is that the quality of texts should improve as editors focus on creativity, leaving automatons to deal with the mundane aspects of the editors' traditional brief. Says Attwell: 'As competition among publishers for readers intensifies, editorial quality is one of the few value-adds that will distinguish them, because really good, really involved editing cannot be automated.' He offers four pointers to text editors who want to join the 'digital revolution':
• First, the most important thing is to make sure that you're focusing on the part of your work that can't be automated: using your imagination to improve the quality of the text.
• Secondly, you must automate every part of your editing process that you can. Make time

to learn about the tools that offer you automation of any sort. Most editors hardly use the automation features that MS Word offers. If you understand them and control them, they are powerful tools.

- Thirdly, think of your book content as flowing strings of plain text, not as laid-out lines on pages. Learn how to represent anything in plain text – in an editor like Notepad, for instance.
- Fourthly, try reading ebooks. If you can afford it, get an e-ink ereader. If not, get your next dictionary or reference book as an ebook on your computer, so you've got a reason to use an ebook, and to learn how ebooks work.

That's the text editor's perspective on ebooks. How are the readers of digital media's needs catered for, and what should the practitioner know about it?

Perhaps more so than with print media, the profile and needs of a book's audience need to be taken into account when writing and editing a text intended for electronic publication (either exclusively or in addition to a print format). This is particularly true where the readers are likely to be newcomers to the digital environment and need to have the parts of the ebook clearly mapped out. This makes navigation possibly the most important of their needs; and, closely allied to it, logical connections between the sections and elements of a text, and meaningful structuring. Knowles (2011), supported by Mackenzie (2011: 85), says that the digital medium requires an ebook to be consistently well structured, consistently styled, granular (divided up into many meaningful, logical interconnected subdivisions), unambiguous (wording must be direct, clear and obvious in order to help the only reader navigate directly to the text they want to read) and to have the functionality in place that is easy to anticipate. This approval and these criteria present different challenges to the text editor.

For an ebook to be consistently well structured, the headings, sections and substructures both within and between the chapters must be logically structured, equivalent, consistent in their content, consistently meaningful, and comprise wording that clearly indicates the content to which it refers. On the ebook's home page, for example, should the first-level headings be positioned across the top of the page or down the left side? How are the various levels below them indicated (both typographically/visually and geographically)? How flat (or deep) should the structure of an ebook be? Should a limit be imposed on the extent of the 'contents list' so as to avoid it becoming unwieldy? Furthermore, headings and subheadings must do the same kind of work in every chapter (Introduction, Conclusion, Summary, for example) and also between chapters: if chapters 1 to 4 constitute section A and chapters 5 to 9 form section B, that breakdown should be reflected in the 'contents list' on the home page and the reader must know, clearly and quickly, where to click to get to the text they want to read.

To achieve this consistent structuring, the author should, in the first instance, be requested to incorporate it into the manuscript from the outset, even if it means training them to think and write in this digital-friendly way. Next, the text editor has to know what the structural requirements of a particular digital publisher or ebook are and their brief should specify the nature and extent of the structural straightjacketing they have to do. Experience during the past ten years, during which time digital has been gestating, has shown that the text editor can play a big part in helping to optimise the digital format of publications, and that, try as one might, it remains challenging to convert authors to the 'digital' way of thinking and preparing their manuscripts, so the need for editors who are able to do so has increased substantially.

Unlike with print media, where the structure and contents list usually evolve from the delivered manuscript, with digital media a logical structure has to be worked out and agreed upon from the outset and the individual chapters massaged to fit the structure. This approach is greatly aided by MS Word's Styles function, which the text editor will have to master if they are to intervene most effectively in the preparation of the manuscript for a digital format.

Consistently more specific (rather than vaguer) wording is better in ebooks, too. This is a characteristic feature of ebooks that are consistently styled. But the need for descriptive headings that state explicitly what the content is has to be weighed up against the need for shorter rather than longer headings, which are preferred for practical reasons. As Knowles (2011) reminds us, headings organise; body text describes. For example, if several sections of a chapter deal with blood disorders, it is regarded as more useful to readers to repeat these key words in subheadings:

– Introduction: blood disorders
– Diagnosis: blood disorders
– Stenting: blood disorders
– Summary: blood disorders.

The text editor also has to ensure that between chapters there is also a constant depth of information. If one chapter comprises 42 pages and another more than 100 pages, how can and should such unevenness be dealt with? Is there not a case for splitting the longer chapter into two or more shorter chapters to achieve an even depth between chapters? And are features within chapters also used – and labelled – consistently (mini-contents list, abstract, figures, tables, etc)?

The text editor also has to ensure that functional consistency is imposed on digital texts. For example, numbering schemes have to be consistent between and within chapters, and boxes, callouts and video clips not only have to be clearly distinguishable but also have to fulfil functional expectations. Moreover, the targets of callouts must be unambiguous. Also, both author and editor must understand that digital products don't have a 'geography' in the sense that print books do, and so cross-references such as 'see above' and 'see infra p 419' are less helpful in ebooks; and a cross-reference such as 'see pneumothorax, p 246' is less ambiguous, and therefore more helpful, than 'see p 246'. However, 'see table 4.5' is acceptable because it is unique (the text editor will have ensured that it is a reference to the fifth table in chapter 4). It is also important for text editors to be aware of whether a title is part of a series, so that the title they are currently working on can be made to fit structurally into the series model (on the understanding that any deviations will be flagged).

Other aspects for the text editor to consider when preparing manuscripts for digital publishing include:

- Text editors will be required to fit text into preconfigured templates that impose uniformity or standardisation on it.
- The use of colour needs careful attention: colour usually has meaning attached to it in a digital environment (eg green symbolises useful information; red signifies critical information or danger or emergency). Also, some media (eg ereaders) don't work in colour. If a text is being prepared for both digital and print media, the former can probably afford the use of colour, the latter not; and one needs to consider whether a colour illustration originated for a digital environment will work as well or at all in a grey-scale print environment.
- Numbering of headings: this could be more of an impediment in ebooks, because digital media place more emphasis on the meanings of words and phrases.
- Special handling or features for new media types: for example, movements such as scrolling or alternating text/images.
- The appropriateness of artwork: for example, the size, any scaling, 3D versus 2D.
- Not allowing print terminology to be used inadvertently in digital media (eg references to cover, endpapers, prelims, end-matter).

What, then, are some of the key implications of digital media for publishing?

- In the first instance, the onus for expert copy preparation will continue to fall on the text editor, though with a shift in emphasis, because authors will increasingly be required to write texts more specifically for the digital format after having received intensive briefing.
- Secondly, for a while to come, a great deal of the optimisation of manuscripts needed for ebooks is likely to continue to be done by text editors.

This means that both authors and text editors (and their publishers) will have to undergo a change in thinking, right from the commissioning stage, so that before the handover of a manuscript into production most of the preconditions for digital publishing will have been met.

8 The text editor and the importance of ethical controls

> The editor must set standards not just on *technical* matters but also on *ethical* matters.
> *Morrish*

> Copyediting is largely a matter of common sense in deciding what to do and of thoroughness in doing it; but there are *pitfalls* an inexperienced copyeditor cannot see.
> *Butcher, Drake & Leach*

> Ethics is a serious matter, and unethical behaviour by just a few people can undermine the whole editing profession. ... [An editor's stated ethical stance] usually amounts to a short statement about confidentiality and privacy issues, work standards, policy on accepting or not accepting jobs, and perhaps their proposed action in the event of a conflict of interest or other difficulty. It helps the client to get a full picture of the sense of professionalism of the editor.
> *Murphy*

In the literature on what text editing encompasses and how the editor should go about it, it is often said that everything possible should be done to ensure that ethical pitfalls are avoided and that a manuscript meets the ethical demands expected of it (see sections 2 and 3 in this chapter; cf Einsohn 2005: 10; Butcher, Drake & Leach 2006: 28ff; Murphy 2011: 38–41).

Ethics can be defined as (*Macquarie dictionary*, cited in Murphy 2011: 38):

> a system of moral principles by which human actions and proposals may be judged good or bad or right or wrong; the rules of conduct recognised in respect of a particular class of human actions; moral principles, as of an individual.

Ethics in this context has three aspects to it: (1) a general attitude in the profession towards handling problems (eg in books and newspaper and magazine articles); (2) the manner in which a text editor should do their work to avoid ethical problems arising; and (3) the code of ethics to which language practitioners in general – and text editors particularly – bind themselves. In this section we go into each of these aspects of the ethics of text editing.

8.1 Ethics in an industry or profession

> *Ethics* is the branch of study dealing with what is the proper course of action for man. It answers the question, 'What do I do?' It is the study of right and wrong in human endeavors.
> *http://www.importanceofphilosophy.com/Ethics_Main.html*

This matter receives a lot of attention in the literature, especially the literature about ethics in the media (cf Bishop 1984: 74ff; Greer (ed) 2008: 101–115; Hyde-Clarke 2011; Kruger (ed) 2004; Morrish 1998: 13ff, 2003; O'Connor 1978: 149ff; Painter-Morland 2011; Plotnik 1982: 50ff; Stepp 1989: 151ff; Wasserman 2008). In the case of journalism (see section 5.2 above), it boils down to the following general ethical issues:

› Respect people's privacy.

› Don't gather information under false pretences.

› Be honest when conducting interviews.

› Ensure that statements and assertions are backed up with firm evidence.

› Don't be the spokesperson for others' ideas.

› Be sure of your facts.

› Be honest, fair and objective in your reporting.

› Avoid a conflict of interests.

These kinds of issue, and obviously many others, are concerned with the ethical choices that the publisher and the text editor have to make in the workplace: When difficult situations arise, how should they respond to them and how should they be reported on? The 'golden rule' in such instances seems to be: Do not do to others anything you would not like to have done to you.

Stepp (1989: 157) points out the positive and cumulative effect that ethical choices have in the newsroom: '*Decisions* about how to finance, *organize*, and *operate* newsrooms have an *ethical dimension* that publishers and editors should not overlook.'

These kinds of ethical reality are determined to a large extent by the judgements of people about what is right and wrong; and these judgements are based on two facets: those that people know intuitively to be wrong and those that journalists are taught. People are therefore ethical beings who don't live in isolation but who live instead in close association with others in a restricted social community, and that entails a constant process of making choices between right and wrong, between what is permissible and what is less permissible. In this respect, people are '... more than the sum of their situational ethics' (Stepp 1989: 158). Bishop (1984: 74) concludes as follows:

> Ethics are the *principles of morality*, the *rules of conduct*, or the *duties and obligations associated* with a *particular activity* or *association of people* ... Ethics are essential to all human activities in bridging the gap between punishable crime and chaotic laissez-faire ... Ethics are enforced, not in any formal sense, but by the social pressure that the affected community applies to unethical behavior.

It is therefore not possible for people to escape making many ethical choices as they go about their daily lives. This applies to all industries and professions, including the media and publishing industries.

8.2 Dealing with ethical questions in the course of editing

Text editors constantly have to take decisions about the correctness, suitability, reasona-bleness and acceptability or otherwise of the material they encounter in manuscripts. For example, by definition, editors are expected to draw the writer's and/or the client's atten-tion to any material (whether in the text or in tables, diagrams or illustrations) '... that might form the basis for a lawsuit alleging libel [or defamation], invasion of privacy, or obscenity' (Einsohn 2005: 10). This can include pointing out to the writer or client whether a section in a manuscript has been correctly quoted or not, whether a statement an author has made can be interpreted as defamatory (or libellous), whether permission has been obtained to copy material from one or more other writers (in terms of the prevailing copy-right laws), or whether all the necessary acknowledgements have been recorded (thereby helping to reduce or prevent plagiarism – see section 9 in this chapter), where the lan-guage used in a text can be experienced as racist, sexist, ageist or labelling in some other way, and so on. There are also ethical questions surrounding the use of photographs of people in published works without their consent, especially if their image is associated with anything negative (eg alcohol or drug abuse, rape, family violence).

The text editor must therefore keep an eye out for any potential legal problems (such as libel/ defamation, breach of copyright and plagiarism) and to try sooner rather than later to prevent them occurring (Butcher, Drake & Leach 2006: 28; Murphy 2011: 30–31).

8.3 Living up to a code of ethics for text editors

> Few ethical decisions are clear-cut, and many are quite complicated.
> *Bowles & Borden*

> ... ethics offer[s] us a set of *professional guidelines* to follow as we exercise our 'agency'. They give us a *reference point* outside the immediate hurly-burly of the job, one that is inspired by the highest ideals.
> *Krüger (editor)*

In section 8.2 above we stated that text editors constantly have to make decisions about the correctness, suitability, reasonableness and acceptability (or otherwise) of material in documents on which they work. They therefore have to judge whether facts stated or opinions expressed by the author are correct or not. Underlying such decisions is the issue of ethical control, which can form the basis of the text editor's judgements. The question is this: What is meant by this and how can the ethical problem raised in the context of text editing be resolved?

It is a characteristic of any professional environment that a form of ethical control will be put in place. This usually happens in one of two ways: through either internal or external con-trol (cf Blaauw 2001; Blaauw & Boets 2003: 69–71; Murphy 2011: 38–41). What is meant by external control (the so-called 'external locus of control') is the regulation of a profes-sion by means of legislation (a set of control measures, including regulations, as pertains, for example, in the legal, auditing and health fraternities). Legislation usually sets up a professional council (such as a Council for Health Professionals) to regulate the manner in which professional services are rendered. Such a council or institution exercises control over the members of the particular profession in terms of the relevant legislation. If the rules governing a profession are transgressed, such as through unprofessional conduct, then the member involved may be punished and then, in terms of a prescribed procedure (following a complaint, a hearing and possibly a verdict of 'guilty'), denied the right to practise or to be associated with the professional body. If an auditor defrauds clients, for example, they can be punished and denied the privileges of council membership; if a doctor fails to follow the correct procedure for an operation and a patient dies as a result, the professional council may proceed against the doctor. Almost daily, such steps are taken worldwide. But what recourse do dissatisfied clients have against errant editors in terms of an external locus of control?

On the other hand, internal control (the so-called 'internal locus of control') affects those individuals who associate themselves with the underlying values and principles that are reflected in the execution of the external measures referred to above. This means that people identify themselves with the rules of the professional body and live and work according to them to the extent that those rules become part of their lifestyle. When this happens, the rules are usually set out in the form of a code of conduct or a code of ethics that serves as a guide to the manner in which its adherents conduct themselves both professionally and in their daily lives. This is tantamount to self-regulation: upon joining, members of a professional association bind themselves to adhering to the association's code of conduct and they can be held to it in the event that they transgress it in any way. In addition, clients should be made aware of the code of conduct before committing themselves to a particular practitioner, and should have recourse to it should the practitioner conduct themselves in an unethical or unprofessional manner.

This suggests that the professional's implicit knowledge of right and wrong will be played out in the way they exercise their profession daily. Bowles & Borden (2011: 148) state clearly that ethics is a personal matter and that each of us is both bound and driven by it:

> ... it can provide us with certain *basic principles* by which we can *judge* actions to be right or wrong, good or bad, responsible or irresponsible. Because of this background, we make many *moral* judgements without much thought or deliberations.

An advantage of having a professional council for language practitioners in place – it underlines the professionalisation of practitioners (see also section 12 of this chapter) – is that it promotes the imposition of control over training, accreditation, examining, rates/fees for services rendered and the registration of members so that those who don't deliver work of an acceptable standard (ie those who don't qualify for membership) can be excluded from the professional body until such time as they do meet the requirements for qualification. A downside is that such councils tend to impose a bureaucratic burden on their members, which has the effect of weighing down further already burdened freelance practitioners.

By as late as 2011, Australia, the United Kingdom and Canada had made greater progress towards the establishment of professional bodies to serve the interests and impose controls on text editors and other language practitioners; in South Africa, besides the existence of the South African Translators' Institute (SATI), the Professional Editors' Group (PEG), the Academic and Non-fiction Authors' Association of South Africa (Anfasa) and the South Afrcan Freelancers' Association (Safrea), all of which might be termed 'self-regulatory internal controls', there is as yet no professional controlling body in place for language practitioners.

Important aspects of the move towards fully fledged professionalisation are the introduction of an accreditation examination (according to which the proficiency levels of individuals can be tested and possibly confirmed) and adherence to a code of conduct (ie universally agreed-upon principles and values). In a number of countries codes of conduct have been in place mainly for translators and interpreters, but not for text editors, though professional organisations in Australia, Canada, South Africa and the United Kingdom have had codes of conduct in place for some time. A study by Blaauw (2001), based on empirical research supported by practising text editors, stimulated interest in the development of a code of conduct for the profession as a whole (Blaauw & Boets 2001, 2003).

This code mainly relates to the three general aspects that Hinkkanen (2006) views as being of cardinal importance when professional language practitioners apply ethics in practice (see also section 12 below in this chapter, where these aspects are dealt with in connection with professionalisation).

8.3.1 The relationship between text editor and client

Mackenzie (2011: 41) refers to the editor's having 'a three-way responsibility to the publisher, the author and the reader'): here the principle of mutual respect for each other applies in the main. This encompasses matters such as (Murphy 2011: 39–41):

• respect for concluding an agreement with a client and fulfilling it;
• respect for deadlines and adhering to them;
• respect for trust regarding the material being worked on; this would include adopting an objective stance on content that you as editor may disagree with;
• respect for the client's requirements;
• accepting work that is within their capability;
• maintaining a respectful relationship with your author, no matter how exasperating they are;
• not disclosing details of current or recent projects to other (rival) clients;

- if you find yourself working on books for different clients that are in competition with each other, either withdraw from one of the projects (explaining why) or exercise scrupulous discretion;
- when editing theses and dissertations, resisting the temptation to edit substance and structure, which should remain the province of the student;
- not accepting work intended for dishonest or immoral purposes.

As Mackenzie points out, in all projects the text editor is constantly making a trade-off between what the publisher can afford and what the reader needs.

8.3.2 The relationship between one text editor and another

If, for instance, the work is subcontracted, certain rules must be upheld, such as:

- having mutual respect for each other's skills;
- meeting agreed deadlines and the quality of the work required;
- expecting that only quality work will be delivered;
- exercising mutual solidarity by, for example, not speaking ill of each other or of clients;
- sharing the income from published works equally, according to a contract;
- not 'stealing' work from each other.

8.3.3 Personal ethics

This includes the respect that text editors have for themselves. It also affects the manner in which practitioners put these values into practice in their daily work routine. These include (Murphy 2011: 39–41):

- not accepting impossible deadlines set by clients;
- not accepting work that you lack the experience to undertake;
- not abandoning your personal values: honesty, reliability, punctuality, professional delivery and sincerity;
- not endangering your health by taking on too much work; work overload usually leads to poor performance because the work receives uneven attention;
- learning from your mistakes;
- acknowledging your shortcomings and work on improving or eliminating them;
- persisting with obtaining continuous training;
- acknowledging that you really do want to be viewed as a professional person.

These and many more aspects are contained in this suggested code of conduct (Blaauw & Boets 2003):

A code of ethics for text editors

As a professional text editor, I undertake to remain true to the following code of ethics:

1. To fulfil at all times my obligations to maintain the highest professional standards and to resist any conduct that will harm the profession, the client or the reader.

2. To strive to deliver the highest quality work continuously and to remain at the forefront of developments in my area of expertise in pursuit of self-improvement.

3. To take on only such work as I am competent to complete in terms of the language, the subject-matter and the time frame, and if it were at all possible, to accept such work only after I have spelt out the limitations to my client, or else to pass it on to another competent person after liaising with my client.

4. To accept responsibility for all the work that I undertake to do, subject to any limitations that may be agreed upon with my client.

5. To respect my client's rights and to regard all work that I take on as confidential, not to pass on any information in connection with the work to any other person, and not to use any information thus acquired to my advantage, except as agreed with my client.

6. To negotiate with the client the remuneration for the work agreed upon before commencing the editing on it, in the spirit of fairness and reasonableness and bearing in mind the prevailing market trends.

7. To share professional knowledge with other members of the profession, wherever reasonable, without breaching confidentiality.

8. Not to accept any work intended for dishonest purposes or for what might appear to be dishonest purposes.

9. Always to fulfil my duty, in consultation with the parties concerned, to strive towards a product that meets the communication needs not only of my client but also of the reader of the text.

The contents of this suggested code of ethics should be something that every text editor strives after in pursuit of continuously delivering a high-quality service. There should be no mistaking that. In the process the values (including respect, honesty, loyalty, precision and correctness) associated with professionalism should be evinced at a personal level. Doing so will help the text editor traverse the 'ethical highway' (Jeffreys, cited in Krüger (ed) 2004: ix), having first made the code of ethics their own. Through this the text editor will become an extremely important link in the text-production process.

9 The text editor, plagiarism, copyright and permissions

> Plagiarism on the grand scale has been made more and more tempting and easy for lazy [writers] by people who provide whole essays on all manner of subjects on the web.
> *Murphy*

Whereas until the late twentieth century the focus of most publishers, authors and text editors was on copyright per se and any infringements of copyright law, since the advent of the internet and the greater accessibility of and ease of copying and pasting information it has engendered, the more widespread problem of plagiarism – whether inadvertent or intentional – has reared its head. This possibly stems partly from ignorance of the law of copyright (which in itself tends to be found wanting for vagueness and complexity) but also from the misguided belief that any and all material published on websites is in the public domain and therefore freely available for use without acknowledgement. This is to misunderstand the spirit and intent behind the concepts of copyright and intellectual property: that is, copyright exists to protect authors' intellectual property that takes the form of an expression of an idea (not the idea itself). Intellectual property includes trademarks, designs and patents, so permission must first be obtained to use any of these in publications. Understandably, much has been written recently about this pervasive problem, particularly in the sphere of academic writing (cf Butcher, Drake & Leach 2006; Einsohn 2005; Gilad 2007; Mawdsley 1994; Neville 2010; Pecorari 2008; Saller 2000).

However, the first question we have to ask is: What is plagiarism? The answer should be of considerable interest to professional text editors.

Plagiarism is (PLC Melbourne 2000; The Learning Centre 2004):

> using other peoples' [sic] words and ideas without clearly acknowledging the source of the information.

> using the words or ideas of others and presenting them as your own. Plagiarism is a type of intellectual theft. It can take many forms, from deliberate cheating to accidentally copying from a source without acknowledgment.

This makes plagiarism a potentially serious multiple offence. Since the original author is not acknowledged when an author passes their work off as his or her own, it is effectively the theft of another's intellectual property (IP); if that IP is copyright protected, then the act of plagiarism is also a breach of copyright law (plagiarism may also occur where copyright protection has lapsed or the original work is in the public domain (Butcher, Drake & Leach 2006: 29)); and, thirdly, if the information is passed off as the writer's own when it is not, that act contains an element of deceit and therefore constitutes fraud (PASA 20ll).

Plagiarism at the academic level can take many forms, including:

- Buying a paper or essay from a research service or online paper-mill.
- Handing in another person's work with or without the author's or creator's permission.
- Copying an entire source and presenting it as one's own.
- Copying sections from a source without appropriate acknowledgement.
- Paraphrasing material from a source without appropriate acknowledgement (PLC Melbourne, cited in Murphy 2011: 30).

But such forms of plagiarism are not limited to academia: they can, and do, occur everywhere.

Copyright exists to protect an author's IP from being copied without permission or compensation. In terms of international copyright law, only the copyright owner may do or authorise the doing of the following: reproduce a work in any manner or form; publish the work; perform the work in public; broadcast the work; transmit the work in a diffusion service (eg cable television), or adapt the work. Anyone who performs any of these actions has infringed copyright (PASA 2011). If the text editor is in any doubt as to what copyright is all about, follow this rule of thumb: someone owns the copyright on anything that's been written and copyright is not freely available for at least 70 years after the death of the author. Before that period has expired, authors have to seek the permission of the owner of the copyright before using anything, wherever in the world it has been written. Only when copyright has expired can a work be said to be 'in the public domain', not requiring permission for it to be used (Murphy 2011: 31).

Before a writer can publish another's text or visual material in their own publication, they also have to decide whether its use constitutes 'fair dealing'. Defining this concept is like trying to grasp the proverbial slippery eel! But it has been described as follows (PASA 2011):

> … copyright is not infringed by any fair dealing with a literary or musical work for the purposes of research or private study by, or the personal or private use of, the person using the work. 'Fair dealing' is a difficult concept to explain because what is 'fair' in any given situation will always depend on the circumstances of that situation. However, it is reasonable to expect that making a single copy of part of a work, for your own use, will qualify as 'fair dealing'.

Using the text or visuals of others in a published work tends to put a different complexion on 'fair dealing', because there is the element of personal financial gain (in the form of author's royalties) to consider. Here test for fair dealing is both quantitative (ie the extent of the text copied) and qualitative (the importance of the extracted text in the context of the work as a whole). Thus, fair dealing is a test applied after the fact in which all the circumstances are taken into account. For example, copying eight lines of a poem of 40 lines has been held to be an infringement of copyright (PASA 2011).

While 'fair dealing' is written into most copyright protection legislation, it is often difficult to define in practice: four lines of a short poem may be regarded as a substantial borrowing, as would one line of a haiku; on the other hand, 50 to 100 words in total from a textbook or a novel would normally not be regarded as extensive and is more likely to be viewed as 'fair dealing' that would also serve the purpose of promoting the original author's publication.

Publishers depend upon professional, competent text editors to play the role of watchdog in detecting occurrences of plagiarism and breach of copyright, and to know when to point out where permission to use copyrighted material (whether visual or verbal) is required. This task is usually written into a text editor's brief. In view of the preceding text on plagiarism and copyright, both authors and text editors should be encouraged to err on the side of caution when considering whether a breach of either plagiarism or copyright, or both, has been committed.

In order to detect transgressions, the text editor should be on the lookout for changes in writing style from what is clearly the author's own natural style to that of others. Often the difference is quite marked. The text editor should note such lapses from the author's own style, and ask the following questions about them:

- Has the author acknowledged the source from which the text was taken? If not, this should be noted and it should be drawn to the client or publisher's attention. In addition, the text editor may run the passage through plagiarism-detection software (such as www.turnitin.com, www.duplichecker.com and www.plagiarism.org) in order to verify instances of plagiarism by finding hard evidence.
- If the author has quoted another source and acknowledged it correctly, how extensively have they 'borrowed' from the source? Is it little enough for 'fair dealing' to apply (in other words, a permissible 'fair' number of words/thoughts borrowed from another source)? Or have extensive passages been lifted from another source (even if acknowledged)?
- Even if such another source has been acknowledged, if the borrowings are more extensive than what is considered 'fair dealing', must the copyright holder's permission be sought to reproduce their text? The answer is an unequivocal 'yes', and the client or publisher should be informed of this.
- Does even paraphrasing another author's words (or adapting another's drawings or graphics) require acknowledgement of the source from which the ideas or concepts were obtained? Again, an unequivocal 'yes', and permission will need to be sought from the copyright holder.

Nowadays, it is so easy to copy and paste text from websites and ebooks that many writers either give no thought to the 'crime' they are committing (stealing others' IP and passing it off as their own) or consider anything published on the internet to be in the 'public domain' and therefore not needing acknowledgement. In both cases, however, an author's thinking is erroneous and likely to land them in trouble once the copyright holder of such borrowed text becomes aware of the fact that their published work is receiving little or no acknowledgement. If you read the fine print on most websites carefully, you will usually find a privacy statement, copyright information or other material that prevents copying more than once for personal reference purposes only (Murphy 2011: 30).

What writers (and editors) must keep in mind is that copyright usually subsists in published written and visual material for 70–75 years from the date of publication (or 70–75 years from the death of the author or creator, in certain circumstances).

Even slight adaptations of visual material lifted from other sources will not enable one to escape requesting permission to copy such material. And although someone like Shakespeare is long since dead, if an author borrows text/ideas from, say, a twentieth century commentator's text on Shakespeare's comedies, then we have both to acknowledge our source and to ask the copyright holder for permission to reproduce extensive passages from their commentary.

The profession has acquired more profile and formal training in recent years, but there is still no recognised pathway into it (Mackenzie 2011: 18–19).

10 How to get into text editing professionally

> Some experienced freelancers say that word of mouth is their most effective method of finding new clients.
> *Saller*

> People pursue careers in editing from many different starting points. Some study professional writing, communications or journalism in university, and move right into full-time editing careers. Others work in completely unrelated fields, and then, their interest piqued, combine that experience with an education in editing to move into new positions.
> *Editors' Association of Canada*

> Proofreading can be especially instructive if you are given the edited manuscript to proof against ... If you can get work proofreading, you might be able to use that as a stepping-stone to work as a copy editor.
> *Saller*

According to the Editors' Association of Canada (EAC 2011: 6):

> Most people become professional editors because they're intrigued by language. They enjoy finding just the right word to convey a point, making sense of a complicated piece of information and manipulating text until it flows flawlessly. They have a passion for detail and accuracy. They find themselves drawn into editing because they can't ignore the mistakes they see in publications. They notice illogical arguments, inaccurate statistics and poorly constructed sentences.

The basic 'equipment' an individual needs to be a competent editor includes an instinct for recognising patterns, organising ideas and creating categories; a willingness to question assumptions, theories and facts; and an interest in learning new things (EAC 2011: 6). Mackenzie (2011: 11) cites a study of editors' training needs: '… much of the knowledge and skill in editing comes from people's natural instinct for and love of words and books … and from their highly developed reading skills …'.

Getting into text editing professionally should involve four or five steps:

List 3.16 Steps to entering text editing professionally

1. Obtain *an academic or similar qualification* appropriate to the field you want to work in, for example language studies or applied linguistics, communications, publishing studies, manuscript writing, the humanities or the social or pure sciences. Also consider those disciplines in which there may currently be a shortage of practitioners with the requisite knowledge and skills (eg mathematics and science; accountancy and auditing; environmental law; business studies; medicine). Your background will usually play an important role in your marketability: for example, schoolteachers are generally favoured for writing, editing and proofreading school textbooks, academics for higher education texts; librarians generally make suitable indexers, and so on. Any relevant experience should also count towards your suitability: for example, you may have worked in an NGO environment, or for a financial services organisation, or have a passion for cooking and baking that leads to your gaining an intimate knowledge of recipe books.

2. Master *the language, text editing and proofreading skills* required of a competent practitioner. If necessary, attend appropriate training courses in these subject areas to ensure, first, that you have all the requisite skills and, secondly, that your knowledge and skills are at the cutting edge of current practice. A basic, non-negotiable competency for any text editor or proofreader is a thorough knowledge of the grammar, punctuation and spelling of the language in which they operate, so ensure that these skills are really well honed.

   You will also have to be computer literate (MS Word is the industry standard word processor, as is working with PDFs) and be able to access and use the internet and email – the standard electronic tools on which the publishing and communications industries operate.

   Do not assume that, because you have a teaching background or a degree in a language or communications, or you have some specialist knowledge (you're a medical practitioner), for example, that you can commence work as a text editor without acquiring formal editing and proofreading skills: that approach will inevitably lead to disillusionment.

>>

3. Join *a professional association of text editors* specifically or language practitioners generally. Doing so offers the new practitioner several benefits and advantages: networking opportunities; exposure to work offers; information sharing; professional learning experiences through events such as workshops and conferences; opportunities to enhance your qualifications and experience through voluntary testing and accreditation; and opportunities for being mentored (important during the initial phase of practising as a text editor).

4. If you prefer to enter into *full-time, permanent employment, identify potential employers and be proactive about approaching their human resources departments* to make yourself known to them, and possibly to set up an appointment for an initial interview. You may be required to write an editing and/or proofreading test to prove your competence prior to taking the process further (Saller 2009: 118). Alternatively, surf the internet or scour the print media for possible positions vacant and follow up on them (Editors' Association of Canada 2011: 11).

   Choosing between freelance (self-employed) and inhouse (part- or full-time) editing work comes down to two key questions: 'How important is a regular paycheque?' and 'How important is control over your schedule?'

   A freelance editor's flexible schedule can be ideal for night owls and parents of young children. Freelance editors can also choose their colleagues and clients, to a degree. They can also focus on marketing their services to industries they are interested in.

5. If you intend operating *as a freelance practitioner, market yourself to potential clients*, which could lead to your being required to write an editing and/or a proofreading test to prove your competence (Saller 2009: 118). If you need to have some 'real' editing or proofreading assignments on your curriculum vitae, then, if you have to, offer to do pro bono work for family, friends or organisations such as charities, church groups and associations of volunteers. They always need help with letters, newsletters, fliers, reports, minutes, and so on.

Saller (2009: 117) recommends that newcomers to editing and proofreading offer themselves as unpaid interns at publishing houses or other institutions in order to gain invaluable experience in a broad range of areas: text editing, proofreading, evaluating unsolicited manuscripts or updating efiles of edited manuscripts.

Mackenzie (2011: 19) mentions that work for online editing services could be a good way for learner editors to gain experience and confidence that's almost equivalent to an apprenticeship.

It is encouraging that, during the past few years, worldwide (EAC 2011: 12):

> [t]here has been a marked increase in demand for freelance editing because of the blossoming of technology used in publishing and the changing marketplace. Today, CEO's often see hiring an independent contractor as an economical alternative to hiring full-time staff.

In addition, as an independent small-business entrepreneur, you'll also have to put some typical small-business systems in place: a work area or dedicated office; registration with the inland revenue service (or equivalent); accounting or bookkeeping support; a backup system for all your electronic files; the correct furniture and equipment; business cards or marketing materials and e-stationery, including templates for quotations and invoices (Bishop, Linnegar & Pretorius 2011: 27–47).

11 The training of text editors

> Significant numbers of people who want to become editors today are graduates of in-depth editing and publishing programs taught by respected instructors ... Rigorous professional training in an editing program is now becoming essential ... and is producing editors who maintain high standards in their work.
> *Editors' Association of Canada*

> Like exercising new muscles, *learning* to edit can prove painful, especially for the novice.
> *Stepp*

> ... if you aren't trained and confident in at least the basics of copyediting ... you can't hope to give the readers what they deserve – or gain the respect of your writer.
> *Saller*

The first question to ask is this: Are text editors born or do they have to be trained? Because, to quote Stepp (1989: 47; Mackenzie 2011: 18): 'Short of a saint, what kind of person can have, or acquire, the *many qualities* demanded of good editors?'

These 'many qualities' and abilities include, according to the Editors' Association of Canada (2011: 7):

> visualising the end product while focusing on and remembering details; thinking logically and exercising good judgment; reorganising a document to achieve clarity and momentum; recognising what's missing in a passage; using a wide range of reference materials; working within deadlines; keeping an eye on the budget, and working well with the many other people who are part of the publication process.

Clearly, it is a combination of these two perspectives that is required here: without talent, text editing of any quality is virtually impossible; yet, without training, latent talent cannot be developed and refined. Broadly speaking, training can actually contribute meaningfully to better editing, so there are some positive remarks/observations that can be made about training programmes for text editors (Kruger 2007, 2008).

Berner (1982: v) takes this further: text editing is also an art form, and to develop it two things are required of the text editor. First, they need the conceptual framework within which text editing is viewed (a combination of talent and knowledge of the theoretical points of departure about what text editing encompasses). Secondly, they must understand the basics of the text editor's craft (Saller 2009: 7–8). Text editors *can* be trained, therefore; in fact, they *must* be trained if they are to realise their full potential (Kruger 2007, 2008). According to the US Department of Labor's website (2006), tertiary training (such as a degree in language and literature, communications, journalism, translation, language practice, and so on) is a prerequisite for further professional training. This is not always necessarily the case: many an editor is widely read, has an inquisitive mind, is mature enough to have received a solid grounding in language and grammar at school or college, and as a result fits into text editing like a hand in a glove. All they really need to do is hone and expand their editorial and technical skills periodically to remain at the top of their game.

In this section we focus on the training of text editors, on what they have to do, and on the demands they have to meet in order to be able to fulfil their role.

If ever there were a profession to which the concept of 'lifelong learning' applied, it is text editing. The editor who fails to keep up with trends, with new or revised knowledge and with new technologies – primarily through constant training and retraining, through fearless trial and experimentation, and through avid reading – will fast become an unserviceable dodo. (Only recently has the scientific community downgraded the number of planets in our solar system from 9 to 8, for example (Pluto having been downgraded from planet status); and in 2011 questions were beginning to be raised about the validity of Einstein's long-held theory of relativity ($E = mc^2$). In fact, it could be argued that it should be an essential, integral part of a text editor's responsibilities and service offering constantly to expand their knowledge through a process of lifelong learning (Murphy 2011: 19–21).

Mackenzie (2011: 18–19) refers to the fact that text editors' training should not emphasise only the *what* and the *how* of editing, but that the person's personality and qualities in particular should form the point of departure for training. That is, a text editor is by definition 'a wordy sort of person', someone who loves words, books and language, someone who reads extensively and avariciously, and in such a case the training builds on this foundation. We come back to the background of the person who will be undergoing training: and two aspects should be dealt with during training – the person (inherent competencies) and the sharpening of their (external) competencies.

So what should the training comprise? From Kruger (2007 & 2008) we can infer that any training programme should ideally 'aim to *develop*, within the framework of continuing education, a series of *skills* and *competences* that are relevant to both the trainees' *professional status* and their *future work*'.

Training that makes this type of professional development possible and which is relevant to the individual's future professional status and work can take place in different ways: (a) as training courses at tertiary institutions (for example, as part of a course in journalism or as part of a degree programme in languages); (b) as inhouse training courses or programmes (where, for example, an inexperienced person has already acquired elementary competencies but then requires further training from an experienced person (often a senior language practitioner – such a person acts as a mentor of sorts); (c) courses to hone particular skills (offered by training institutions such as universities or colleges or by experienced private trainers or by professional associations). Included in these specialist skills could be: grammar and punctuation usage; the effective use of word processing software; project management of, for example, books and magazines; editing and proofreading in specialist areas such as mathematics, science, medicine and the law; converting texts to plain language; book design and production; writing, editing and proofreading web-based text; and editing fiction and narrative non-fiction).

All these forms of training ultimately lead to the relevant competencies being performed more competently, and this in turn leads to activities such as editing being carried out to a higher standard – the aim of any training programme. In reality, therefore, training is indispensable in the preparation of text editors for practising their craft, though it must commence with '... a solid education in the basics' (Glover 1996). By this, of course, is meant, in the case of text editors: language (grammar, spelling and punctuation), style (how to write), typography and graphics (layout, the use of space on a page, and typefaces (or fonts)). To these basics must be added computer skills – essential in twenty-first-century practice (Mackenzie 2011: 17). And if a text editor wishes to enter the world of book or magazine publishing, they have to be trained in the relevant production processes (see section 5.1 above); and if they begin work as a subeditor at a newspaper or a magazine, they will have to undergo training in the functioning of a newsroom (see section 5.2 above). Add training in newspaper law and copyright for subs; plagiarism/copyright and permissions, and also project management, for text editors. Fundamentals of book design; plain language; referencing systems also need to be learned/revised or have skills in them sharpened.

From what has been said above, training programmes for text editing should include these components (practice in skills and the acquisition of knowledge) (broadly based on Kruger 2007; Mackenzie 2011: 1–3; Murphy 2011: 20ff; Roberts 2004; Stepp 1989: 169):

> The theoretical points of departure on which text editing is based: normative language, the application of a knowledge of linguistics and of document design, methods and techniques of textual analysis (see chapter 2, where these topics are discussed extensively) (see also Kruger 2007, 2008).

> The basic aspects of language usage: the exactitude of word usage, formulation and good grammar has to be emphasised and put into practice (see chapters 2 and 6). Those who are being trained must be made aware of their strong and weak points regarding language usage in general:
>   – Grammar (principles of syntax, morphology and semantics)
>   – Punctuation
>   – Spelling
>   – General ability to use language correctly (making judgements about language purity, the use of different registers and the use of formal or informal language)
>   – The principles of good paragraphing.
>   (These are all discussed in chapters 6 and 9.)

> Skills in determining the coherence of a text: knowledge of linguistics and the principles upon which it is based (compare section 7 of chapter 2).

> Knowledge of the manner in which a document is designed and the role that graphics and typography play in document design (compare section 8 of chapter 2).

> The broad spectrum of editing in practice. Ensure that the different types of text editing are dealt with:
>   – Editing for linguistic correctness (language, punctuation and style).
>   – Editing for style and register (formulation and clarity of expression).
>   – Editing for content (accuracy, correctness of information, completeness and structure of argumentation).
>   – Editing typography and the use of graphics (layout in broad terms).

In addition, text editors should be expected to:

> › practise exercising their editorial judgement based on reference materials; according to Einsohn (2005: 4), this relates to an editor's intuition and instinct about when to intervene in a manuscript and how deeply to intervene – in other words, the development of a kind of 'sixth sense';

> › determine the level of text editing (how deeply to intervene);

> › use the proofreading marks correctly;

> › distinguishing between types of text and the unique demands that each makes (regarding structure, register, style and formatting);

> › apply plain language principles to texts;

> › use sources when dealing with editing problems (how to identify and then to resolve them);

> › appreciate the importance of ethical controls and working according to a personal code of ethics;

> › maintain an overview of the various language practice functions (including the book production process and how a news bureau operates);

> › develop professionalism generally (which includes how one behaves towards clients, presents quotations and invoices, adheres to deadlines and expands one's professional competencies);

> › hone their computer skills;

> › obtain training in effective writing skills (including the use of effective paragraphing techniques);

> › master and apply the principles of sound book design.

> › The interpersonal skills required by the industry ('At the heart of good editing are people and ideas, powerful, living forces worthy of respect and recognition' – Stepp 1989: 179):

'Interpersonal skills' encompasses the total being of the text editor and the demands that they place on an individual at the social, cognitive, and creative levels, and also on their ability to concentrate:

› *Social skills:* respect and empathy for authors and readers; skills of diplomacy and tact ('diplomatic skills to help them deal with writers and a thick skin for when diplomacy fails' – LLT 2006); patience; a sense of humour; caution; justice; motivation; energy; enthusiasm; team work vs working alone; perfectionism ('calling a copyeditor a perfectionist will be taken as a compliment' – Anonymous 2006a); a nitpicky nature; an ability to handle tension; drive and persistence.

› *Cognitive skills:* a very broad general knowledge, building self-confidence; an ability to organise and plan; honing the editor's instincts (refining talent) and effectiveness; honing one's analytical skills; to be a problem-solver in all respects; powers of observation; skilled at creating/introducing coherence into texts; alertness; thoroughness; flexibility when necessary; the development of reading skills.

› *Skills of creativity:* the ability to be generally creative; the ability to put oneself in the position of the reader; vivid imagination; curiosity ('... if you are not curious enough even to check a dictionary for a word you are not sure of, you can't really claim to be a copyeditor at all' – Judd 1990: 17); a desire to know the answers to questions ('A good copy editor can't resist the challenge of finding the correct answer to an obscure question' – Judd 1990: 17); questioning facts and events.

› *The skills associated with concentration:* dedication; decisiveness when having to make decisions; thoroughness; eye for detail; disciplined; an ability to identify inconsistencies.

› The demands of the industry include:
  – handling administrative demands that the workplace places upon people (managing a business, dealing with accounts and providing quotations) – for which training can be given;
  – a willingness to work hard;
  – pressure (often) being exerted on family commitments, and
  – handling long and irregular working hours.

See further chapter 4.

Roberts (2004) summarises these facets nicely by answering this basic question: 'Why train?'

List 3.20 Why train?

> › To acquire the core editorial skills, to put them into practice and to improve.

> › To deliver a good professional service to all your clients and superiors.

> › To have regular opportunities to evaluate your skills (and to improve) by obtaining feedback on the work you deliver.

> › To keep up with developments in the world around you: linguistically, technologically and through a constant flow of new sources.

> › To create networks among your colleagues in order to learn from one another and to keep up the learning process together.

12 The professionalisation of text editors

> The good copy-editor is a rare creature: an intelligent reader and a tactful and sensitive critic; someone who cares enough about perfection of detail to spend time checking small points of consistency in someone else's work but has the good judgement not to waste time or antagonize the author by making unnecessary changes.
> *Butcher, Drake & Leach*

> We always want to aim to be extremely competent, to have impressive competence and to aspire to reach the highest standards that the public has the right to expect from us.
> *Kemisho*

> ... professional editors strive to do their work quickly and efficiently ...
> *Bisaillon*

> Professionalism and accreditation go hand in hand but are not joined at the hip. ... My earnest hope is that accreditation will be a rite of passage from 'learning to be a professional editor' to 'being a professional editor'. But remember that accreditation can't teach you professionalism – it's something, like adulthood, that you grow into.
> *Murphy*

The concepts 'professional' and 'professionalism' have been used variously in this chapter without their having been properly explained. So the time has come to do just that, since we are about to deal with the matter of the 'professionalisation' of the job of text editing. Let's start with a reputable definition of the words 'professional', 'professionalisation' and 'professionalism' from the *Shorter Oxford dictionary* and proceed from there:

> **professional** *noun*. **1** A person who makes a profession of an occupation or activity usually engaged in as a pastime (as opposed to an amateur). **2** A person engaged in a profession, especially one requiring advanced knowledge or training. **3** A person highly skilled or competent in some activity or field.

> **professional** *adjective*. **1** Engaged in a profession, especially one requiring advanced knowledge or training. **2** Engaged in a specified occupation or activity for money or as a means

of earning a living, rather than as a pastime. **3** Having or showing the skill of a professional person, competent; worthy of a professional person. **4** Of, done by, or of a type or standard used by a person in a (particular) profession.

professionalisation *noun*. The action of professionalising an occupation etc.

professionalism *noun*. The body of qualities or features, as competence, skill etc, characteristic of a profession or professional.

There is much to be drawn from these definitions and applied to the task of text editing:

- an occupation or activity is elevated to the rank of profession;
- requiring advanced knowledge or training;
- highly skilled or competent in some activity or field;
- a means of earning a living, rather than a pastime;
- skilled, competent, worthy of a professional person.

A professional editor is clearly competent, in possession of advanced knowledge or training, highly skilled in their field and earning a living from their work, to the point of being worthy of the appellation 'professional'. The question this begs, though, is: 'How does a practitioner attain the status of professional?' (see section 13 in this chapter).

In considering what the professionalisation of language practitioners means, Kemisho (2006) uses the following definition drafted by the British Computer Society: 'Professionalism is an *aspiration* to meet the *highest standards* that the *public has the right to expect* rather than a set of minimum requirements.'

It is therefore the aspiration to meet the highest possible standards in order to provide a service (admittedly for an agreed-upon remuneration) that will be both of high quality and effective that makes the difference between amateur and professional. Du Plessis (2007) adds the thought that the use of these competencies also has to be to the advantage of the wider public. Without such an objective in mind, neither exceptional training nor the pursuit of high standards will count for much.

Mackenzie (2004: 7, 2011) takes this point further by referring to text editors specifically: 'we need editors with high standards to produce texts [that] readers can trust.' Editors (those who have been trained) must therefore be trained and equipped with the necessary skills without which the readers of edited texts (ie the public, in the British Computer Society's definition) cannot do. It is therefore necessary for editors to be 'committed to *quality* and *excellence*'. That is not negotiable. If this requirement cannot be met, one cannot expect too much of the work that the editor delivers. In this connection, Combrink & Verhoef (2002) use Tseng's (1992) model to describe the process of professionalisation:

- *Phase 1*: A need exists in the market to remove entrants whose incompetence and substandard work bring disrepute to the craft as a whole. Those who continue to operate in the market choose to use their particular skills and training to advantage to gain the upper hand over other operators. What emerges is a kind of consensus that they must protect both their own interests and themselves against poor workmanship.

- *Phase 2*: A need develops to consolidate the industry or profession and in that way to generate a greater demand for quality services. Furthermore, the need to provide and offer focused training emerges.
- *Phase 3*: Professional association with others who deliver the same services become important and the collective image of the group contributes to the value attached to such services. This leads to the emergence of the requirement that those who belong to the group have to show the same level of dedication in the execution of their craft.
- *Phase 4*: Usually what follows is the formulation of standards of ethics that everyone in the industry or profession has to adhere to. On the one hand, this contributes to public confidence in what the operators deliver; on the other, such standards serve as an internal control against which other operators can be measured. Eventually this process can lead to the formation of professional bodies that receive statutory recognition.

Following on from these phases in development towards more professional status, it becomes clear that the professionalisation of an industry or craft (any one) rests on two components: (1) the nature of the training on offer and (2) the text editor's commitment to meeting their personal standards when putting their training into practice. A number of comments follow regarding each of these components.

12.1 Training

The minimum level of training must be attained.

- This usually includes a tertiary qualification (or equivalent) such as a degree or a diploma in linguistics, literature, translation/interpretation, language practice/applied linguistics, journalism, communications, or whatever other discipline is applicable as background (Law & Kruger 2008; see also section 10 above).
- Without training, it is simply not possible for a text editor to have the desired knowledge and skills that enable them to practise their craft competently: these have to be acquired. Training (see section 10 above) comprises active processing of and practice in a variety of skills that are supported by substantiated knowledge; it should lead to the practical application of the relevant competencies.
- Training can be obtained in a variety of ways (see section 11 above): in the form of training courses, inhouse training (eg mentorships) and refresher courses designed to hone particular skills continuously. To earn the title 'professional person', the individual concerned must possess the applicable 'up-to-date *skills* and *abilities* appropriate to the particular task' (Kamisho 2006: 39). It is also typical of someone who pursues an occupation earnestly to keep up to date with developments in their field of work after having attended initial training; they do so by attending further courses, seminars, symposiums and workshops, and in that way keep up with trends in thinking and methodologies and

the latest reference works (for example, regarding the latest language conventions, guide books and dictionaries (Kotze 1998: 137, 2012; Murphy 2011: 19, 20, 77, 79, 81)).

- One can even compile a rating scale for training according to which skills training can be measured (roughly based on Wilkinson 2006: 40):
    - The skill to be learned must be present.
    - Natural talent is necessary ('an ingrained ear for language', for example (Plotnik 1982: 37), but must be built upon.
    - You must have a love of language and languages – if you find grammar and spelling a 'pain', consider another occupation.
    - Formal language training (in grammar, punctuation, style and register, the strictures of typography and graphics) is required.
    - Informal language training is recommendable: continuous training opportunities – do not allow learning opportunities to pass you by; make a habit of lifelong learning.
    - Never stop reading (about anything and everything, at every possible opportunity: 'the basic lifelong education of an editor is reading' – Plotnik 1982: 37), so that you become a 'walking encyclopaedia of useless information'.
    - Develop routines for explaining why changes must be made in a text, 'to articulate and justify your editing decisions' (Anonymous 2006a). Poor editing is characterised by the lack of a reference work to back up an editorial decision or the inability to give an explanation for a correction (Stepp 1989: 94 – '"It just does not sound right" does not count').
    - The text editor must identify their own limitations and work actively at overcoming them. Learn to compensate for the areas where you are less strong by focusing more on and taking up opportunities for training (Stepp 1989: 113) – text editors '... must recognize when they need to supplement their knowledge skills' (EAC 2006).
    - Join associations and language bodies that are related to your chosen occupation or specialisation: in the United Kingdom, the Society for Editors and Proofreaders (SfEP); in the United States, the American Copy Editors Society; in Canada, the Editors' Association of Canada (EAC) (or Association canadienne des réviseurs), in South Africa, the South African Translators' Institute (SATI), the Professional Editors' Group (PEG), the South African Freelancers' Association (Safrea); and in Australia, not only the overarching Institute of Professional Editors (IPEd), but also the state societies, such as the Canberra Society of Editors and the Victoria Society of Editors; and so on.

        Characteristic of these kinds of association is the fact that they remain involved in the professional training and positioning of their members. In this way they help to inculcate uniform (and even minimum) standards (see, for example, Mackenzie 2004, 2011: 10, 11 on the work done to establish CASE in Australia, and its activities; CASE 2001; 2011), to institute guidelines on tariffs, to promote networking among their members, and so on.

- Accreditation or certification usually forms part and parcel of professional associations' efforts to professionalise their members by encouraging them to sit a test. Passing such a stringent examination in editing, proofreading, and so on lends prestige to successful candidates and helps to distinguish them from those who remain unaccredited or uncertified both in the eyes of potential clients and among their peers.
- Act, in addition, as trainers by helping to give other, possibly less-experienced, text editors guidance and support. Such editor-trainers are then playing the roles of both 'teacher' and practitioner (Anonymous 2006a; Murphy 2011: 7–8).

- Text editors would do well to have a liberal dose of self-knowledge if they are to develop: by gaining insights into their strengths and weaknesses, they become aware of where they need to beef up their knowledge and/or undergo further training. Get to know, and overcome, your limitations, constantly.
- Glamann (2000) contends that the training of text editors should not form part of general training – it's not something that can arbitrarily be tacked on to a degree course, for example, merely as an add-on. Instead, it should be unique, focused training – aimed at giving text editors optimal training opportunities (Law & Kruger 2008: 485) and building pride and professionalism into the training itself – that has been designed specifically to meet the professional needs of text editors.

12.2 The person behind the training: setting and achieving personal standards

In general, language practitioners should comply with the following requirements inasmuch as they affect them as individuals:

- Be *reliable* at all times (that is, deliver consistently good work and be trustworthy).
- Be *focused* in the work you do (sloppy work is unacceptable).
- Be *adaptable* (not everything runs according to plan).
- Be involved in the *extension* of your professional competencies and do whatever you can to expand your skills and field of knowledge.
- *Comply* with the code of ethics that applies to text editors specifically and to language practitioners generally (see section 8 in this chapter).

In short, these requirements boil down to this important point: avoid unprofessional conduct as you go about fulfilling your professional commitments and dealings (cf Kotzé 2012; Mackenzie 2011: 41–42; Waddingham 2008). This includes:

> dishonouring an agreement about a deadline;

> underestimating the work to be done as well as over-estimating your own ability to do it;

> not honouring the confidential nature of the information contained in manuscripts;

> underquoting for work (and then subsequently requiring payment amounting to more than was budgeted for);

> asking to be paid excessive amounts for work, or excessive deposits before work will be commenced;

> gossiping about colleagues.

12.3 In pursuit of the professional ideal

In the bigger scheme of things, writes Kotze,[1] professions function like any other commodity in a free-enterprise society. These occupations develop from satisfying a need in society at large and follow the law of supply and demand that governs any other commodity. Certain occupations successfully ascend the ladder to professional status provided that they meet the criteria of 'profession'. This professional status places them at the pinnacle of the occupational hierarchy and grants special rights, status and benefits worthy of a profession's all-important inherent service ideals.

The occupation of text editing has not yet risen to this desired status, despite the complex, multifaceted nature and important mediating role of the editor as language practitioner evident from the discussion in this chapter. From the point of view of the sociology of professions, language practitioners, and especially text editors, are an extreme example of a neglected, manqué professional occupation (Law 2011; Kotze 2012). In an increasingly competitive market-dominated, multi-cultural, multi-lingual, service-oriented and globalised society the role, responsibility and nature of the work of the text editor develop into a mission extraordinaire. Apart from their core functions, the professional text editor as language practitioner:

• becomes a project manager in the freelancing market that services the publishing sector when in charge of the overall production of a publication, whether a single volume, a multi-volume or a multi-author work;
• turns into a co-writer and quality controller of all facets of language usage in news bureaus, in the corporate sector, in technical editing, in journals, magazines and ebooks or digital media;

---

[1] We are grateful to Althéa Kotze for contributing to this section.

- plays a key role as a trainer of or mentor for young, would-be language professionals;
- intervenes in website text to ensure that it is concise, correct and consistent, and upholds plain language principles;
- is often the ghostwriter who transforms mundane texts that are often too long, boring, disorganised and unstructured into bestseller material.

If service excellence is the desired goal, this multifaceted nature of the mediating role of the editor as language expert translates into the need for professional attributes unique to the 'true profession' (cf Abbott 1988; Barber 1963; Freidson 1983, 1994; Goode 1969; Hughes 1963; Larson 1977; Macdonald 1995; Torstendahl & Burrage 1990; Wilensky 1964). Professional attributes in text editing – professionalisation – are demonstrated by very detailed attributes associated with a professional text editor:

- an altruistic service ideal;
- a well-developed ethical code;
- occupational autonomy, jurisdiction and monopoly;
- professional training institutions;
- specialised, career-oriented education and training, as well as structured continuous education;
- a professional body;
- a viable income congruous with expert status.

The altruistic service ideal lies at the very heart of the activities of the professional text editor. Altruism – or selfless service – focuses on the needs of society and implies a professional responsibility and trusteeship to each and every client or product. But no text editor can enter into such a relationship without the necessary courage of their conviction to serve the client's needs.

A well-developed ethical code and the need for a viable income commensurate with expert status go hand in hand with the altruistic service ideal. The ethical code provides a professional framework in a specific time and place (Pym 2000) to guide the professional text editor in their career.

Such a framework gives the public a legitimate point of view of the values, norms, standards and ideals of the profession; it functions as a disciplinary mechanism (where necessary), ensuring the general public that the standards of the profession will be upheld. It also serves as a socialisation mechanism to promote homogeneity between members of the profession.

Whereas the characteristics of selfless professional service typical of a professional calling imply personal commitment and service orientation (altruism) as opposed to profit orientation and commercial greed, this does not mean that the concept of altruistic service should outweigh the earning of a prestige income typical of professional status. Altruism carries with it an economic as much as a symbolical attribute. In an increasingly complex and competitive market-dominated society, the economic nature of language services provides a significant income for language professionals. Therefore practitioners should place more emphasis on undergoing the kind of specialised, career-oriented training that will enable them to earn an income becoming of a professional, preferably a 'long course of professional instruction and supervised practice' (Becker et al 2009: 4).

Furthermore, the control of admission to training programmes and control over students' socialisation into the practice of text editing in the socio-economic market creates the very foundation for the professional mindset needed for a practice-based and altruistic work ethic.

Occupational autonomy, jurisdiction and monopoly denote the all-important occupational regulation and sanctioning of professional status from within the community – public and legitimate state sanctioning and elite group endorsement – that ensure occupational stability and autonomy. Regulation consequently becomes the decisive factor in the professionalisation process. Without this public recognition, the text editor as language practitioner remains an invisible, run-of-the-mill practitioner in society. Thus, '[t]he effect of regulation will inevitably be to make the certified language practitioner the automatic preference of the serious client' (Bell 2000: 147).

A statutory professional body with full control of the processes of examination, certification, accreditation, licensing and admission control and the discipline of the profession is a prerequisite of regulation (Bell 2000: 149; Tseng 1992: 75).

The professional body, alongside standardised training and qualifications, therefore plays one of the most critical roles in the setup and work ethic of the text editor as a language professional. Such a body is responsible for measures of control over professional competence and the formal mechanisms of discipline in respect of professional standards. They have been called the 'powerhouse of all professional endeavours' (Tseng 1992: 75).

A text editor who strives to fulfil the professional ideal is one who functions within a professional work ethic where the core element is work based upon the mastery of a complex body of knowledge and skills. The task of text editing develops into a vocation in which knowledge is science, learning and practice used in the service of others. The text editor, moreover, is governed by a code of ethics and professes a commitment to competence, integrity and morality, altruism and the promotion of the public good within their domain.

These commitments form the basis of a social contract between the profession of text editing and society, which in turn grants it a monopoly over the use of its knowledge base, the right to considerable autonomy in practice and the privilege of self-regulation. Without these commitments the text editor will never be worthy of the inherent, all-important mediating task at hand.

From the discussion above it should be clear that professionalism depends upon two principal factors: the nature, quality and extent of the training that individuals receive (and the pursuit of the best possible training) and the human factor. The ability of these two factors to be reconciled is what makes professionalism a reality. But be aware, also, that you will never really be fully 'educated' and that lifelong learning should be an integral part of the active text editor's way of operating as a professional.

13 The profile of a text editor

> ... editing demands many intangibles – judgment, scholarliness, background, memory, aggressiveness, motivation, curiosity, imagination, discretion, cynicism, scepticism, and even some genius.
> *Baskette, Sissors & Brooks*

> Most of us labor into the night in anonymity, happy to check facts and catch errors, fix grammar and make stories conform to conventions of style and usage.
> *Cleaveland*

> Editors come from a variety of different backgrounds, but they are all skilled at developing communications tools by identifying the most appropriate structure, format and content for each audience and purpose. Ultimately, editors are people who think, and they do so on behalf of both the writer and the reader.
> *Editors' Association of Canada*

According to the Editors' Association of Canada (EAC 2011: 8):

> Editors can be found everywhere. The fields they work in include – but are not limited to – publishing and desktop publishing, sales and marketing, manufacturing, government and education. Editors can be specialists who, for example, edit only scientific or medical documents, or they can be generalists who deal with a wide range of content. Editors often work with a wide range of people, including writers, publishers, web developers, designers, artists, photographers, project managers, printers and other editors.

A fair question to ask is: What does the profile of a typical text editor look like? In other words: Who is the most typical person who does this sort of work?

The literature on this subject is reasonably clear: the typical text editor is a woman in her forties, someone who is well qualified (mostly graduated, often with focused supplementary qualifications) and who runs her own business as a freelance language practitioner (Mackenzie 2011: 4, 17). Mackenzie (2011: 4) points out that in Australia approximately two-thirds of the text editors in book publishing are female and in general only one in every nine text editors is male. Responses to a 2009 EAC member survey provided the following snapshot of the average EAC member: 88% are female; 89% are university educated, 85% work freelance, 70% from an urban home office; 66% work full-time as freelance editors, 12% work inhouse (as employees); 20% of members reported that they work both freelance and inhouse. Corresponding statistics for South Africa, the United

Kingdom and the Netherlands are currently not available, but they would probably correspond to a large extent with other countries.

The typical text editor is also someone with thorough experience and has probably also worked in the industry (as journalist, subeditor, publisher's assistant, publisher, language teacher, librarian, academic or language practitioner at private firms and institutions), but for personal reasons they prefer to work from home; furthermore, they are someone who takes the trouble to keep well informed about developments in the area of language by attending extra classes or grasping other educational opportunities.

On the website BigBrainEditing (http://bigbrainediting.com; Anonymous 2006d) the following marketing question is posed: Why should the services of a text editor be used? According to the marketing proposition, the answer is simple: the client (a) saves time and money (by not using a single one of their own staff because they receive a complete, polished product from the text editor); (b) they receive a better product (this has a positive effect on the potential reader(s) because it has been rounded off well), and (c) the client gets a better night's sleep (because the work is completed by a professional and the client certainly doesn't have to have sleepless nights over possible errors and the consequent negative impact that could have on the business). Apparently, this is to state the case too simplistically for obvious marketing reasons, but there is still an element of truth in these reasons for retaining the services of a professional text editor. Apart from any other considerations, they fulfil the '4 C's' of effective communication (Einsohn 2005: 3; see also section 2 in this chapter): clarity, coherence, consistency and correctness. In other words, an edited document should succeed as a text that communicates. This is what text editing is about: to convert a rough, often raw text into a neat, polished communications piece.

Typically, this kind of work is done by a person (mainly female) from whom professional conduct can be expected (punctual, prompt, thorough, accurate, reliable and trustworthy), who has been properly and thoroughly trained and who possesses the requisite personality traits (who can uphold personal and professional codes of ethics). This person has an exceptional professional profile (Kotze 2012) that in turn incorporates a combination of the following skills (Kotze 1998: 137):

List 3.22 Skills required of the text editor

> research skills (knowing where and how to find the answers to potential problems in a text);

> strategic skills (knowing how to approach a text to maximise its potential);

> perceptual skills (to formulate ideas about texts; to allow the human aspect of text editing to come to the fore in the best interests of the text);

>>

List 3.22 continued

> organisational skills (the ability to plan, to organise and to re-arrange in order);

> language and problem-solving skills (to be in such control of language and language usage that sound reasons can be given for any changes made).

The particular combination of these skills in fact make the text editor someone with a unique nature, as Butcher, Drake & Leach (2006: 4) say: a rare person – an intelligent reader and a sensitive and tactful critic; someone who cares enough about perfection to spend time searching for a seemingly trifling detail; someone who knows when to change and when not to; someone for whom consistency of usage is important; someone who knows when not to antagonise an author by fiddling unnecessarily with the text. They are also someone who knows a lot about many things and who is multi-faceted; someone who can take responsibility for tasks and can deliver them by deadline; someone who is disciplined; someone with the eye of a hawk (and who also sees errors quickly); someone who is not lazy; someone for whom 'I think so' is by no means acceptable as a reason for making a change; someone who can transform disconnected and loosely knocked together words and sentences into jewels that sparkle; someone who is passionate about language usage; someone who appreciates good writing; someone who derives pleasure from the successful completion of a seemingly impossible task – therefore, someone who derives satisfaction from what they have done to a text or a language so that it communicates better. It is hard work, but also work, driven by altruism, that provides satisfaction when the end product is there to savour.

Glover (1996) investigated what the ten 'most typical attributes' of the 'perfect copy-editor' are. In the light of the discussion above, it is appropriate to list them briefly here. The 'perfect copy editor' is someone:

List 3.23 Typical attributes of a text editor

> who is passionate about their work;

> who has had firm training in the basic aspects of the industry: language and language usage, and also typography;

> with experience;

> who is creative;

> who is informed about the environment in which they function (the publishing and media industries);

> who can justify a decision with conviction, and who can also defend their decision;

List 3.23 continued

> › who is flexible (can do many things);

> › for whom detail is very important;

> › who is inquisitive;

> › with a liberal dose of healthy intelligence.

Linking up with this list of attributes, Quinn (2003) suggests a sort of credo for text editors. When people encounter text editors, they should know in advance what kind of 'package' awaits them:

We as text editors ...

Checklist 3.7 A credo for text editors

- ✓ Care a lot about accuracy and creditworthiness.
- ✓ Are here to help – we are not the enemy!
- ✓ Are oriented towards detail because our authors (yours, actually) are too.
- ✓ Have wide experience and competence – if this were not the case, we could have done something else with our time!
- ✓ Ask questions because we don't have all the answers and, in any event, in the best interests of the reader(s), we want to know.
- ✓ Work hard at improving our own skills because we know we work in challenging terrain.
- ✓ Like good writing, because our (and your) readers also like it.
- ✓ Are able to deal with matters with humour and humility, even when under pressure.
- ✓ Have the determination and ability to take on work and to pursue it to the end.
- ✓ Correct errors without rubbing your (or anyone else's) nose in them.
- ✓ May possibly be anonymous, but we nevertheless want to be heard and recognised.
- ✓ Are the people who can carry through the vision in a text from start to finish.
- ✓ Accept responsibility as the proverbial 'last line of defence' for you or your text.
- ✓ Are often the glue that holds together the production process.
- ✓ Are able to work in a team, if so required.
- ✓ Do our very best at all times to give you (and your readers) a good text.

14 Summary

Copyediting is not fun, it is *hard work*!
Judd

Editing – *the art of ensuring that a writer's words and meanings can be understood by intended readers* – is seldom routine. Yet the best editor is inconspicuous in the final work. For the reader, the work must bear the stamp of its creator, not its editor.
http://www.editors.ca

If a copyeditor does her job correctly, *the mechanics are invisible to the reader*, so that nothing interferes with the reader's experience of the story or with the message.
Gilad

In this chapter we have attempted to give greater clarity to who and what the text editor is in reality: what the profile of a text editor actually is. In the process, we have highlighted the profile of the typical text editor: female, equipped with special skills and knowledge (thanks to sound training), experienced, and able to deal with the practical issues that beset text editing.

In describing this profile, we have also laid emphasis on the types of editing that are expected of such a person, on the different levels of editing; we have also considered the different occupations that text editors can engage in; we have given attention to some of the challenges with which text editors are faced almost daily, including being a watchdog for authors' commissions of plagiarism and breaches of copyright; then, too, the importance of ethics in our day-to-day dealings with authors and publishers or other clients has been highlighted, which is often part and parcel of joining a professional association with its own code of ethics that members are required to adhere to. The need to undergo expert and ongoing training, as part of lifelong learning, in order to maintain one's professional edge (Kotze 2012) is also highlighted in this chapter. Joining a professional association is just one of several steps the new entrant to the world of text editing can take, and we consider what newcomers should do to enter the world of professional language practice as well as what the professionalisation of text editors and related practitioners means in practice.

In the next chapter the emphasis falls more on the demands that practising as a text editor places on the practitioner: precisely how text editors have to go about executing an editing commission, and everything that they have to keep in mind during that process.

Process and procedure: doing text editing

Editing is *hard work*, calling for special capabilities, distinct from those of reporting and writing.
Stepp

Copy-editing is largely a matter of common sense in deciding what to do and of thoroughness in doing it; but there are pitfalls an inexperienced copy-editor cannot foresee. ... I have found that it is more difficult for inexperienced copy-editors to recognise a potential problem than it is for them to discover the appropriate solution.
Butcher, Drake & Leach

The skilled editor pays ruthless attention to detail ... which can mean the difference between your writing being understood or misunderstood, being accepted or rejected ... between a reader finishing an article or becoming bored.
Kaplan

Editing is an examination of the smaller issues in writing.
Enquist & Oates

4

Contents

Objectives

The following matters are discussed in this chapter: (a) what the text editing process entails; (b) how to go about (the procedure) editing a text (both on hard copy and onscreen); (c) the types of knowledge editors should have at their disposal in order to do justice to a text; (d) what the difference is between proofreading and text editing; (e) the appearance and use/purpose of proofs in the text editing process; (f) the errors that a text editor can make; (g) what a text editor does (or should) not do; (h) the role that text editors can play in managing large-scale projects. The chapter concludes by stating a number of rules that should be applied during the editing process.

The use of electronic tools and the role and function of house style and style guides are looked at in detail in chapter 11.

1 Introduction

In this chapter, we focus on the tasks a text editor must perform to produce an edited text. It includes how the editor performs these tasks, the knowledge and skills they need to edit a text, the steps to be followed when editing, and also what text editors do not do (or should not do) as part of their intervention.

2 What does the process of text editing involve?

> Copyeditors serve their *readers* best by ensuring that copy conforms to accepted standards.
> *Baskette, Sissors & Brooks*

> An editor's only permanent alliance is with the *audience*, the *readership* ... The editor, not the author, best understands that readership. Authors know their subject. Editors specialize in knowing the audience.
> *Plotnik*

> Good copy-editing is invisible.
> *Butcher, Drake & Leach*

> Editors must read texts from the point of view not only of evaluators but also of *potential readers*.
> *Bisaillon*

In chapter 3 (figure 3.3), we point out which people are involved in the complicated process of text editing and which phases apply to the creation of the product (that is, a well-rounded, -edited and -produced book). The author (as the original creator) writes a text with a particular goal in mind (they want to convey certain information; they want to convince someone of an alternative point of view or they want to guide someone as to how to tackle something, and so on) and the text editor performs the role of facilitator or intermediary in helping to realise this objective optimally. The text editor achieves this by means of macro- and micro-editing (about which see section 3 of chapter 3), by effecting certain adaptations to the language (grammar, spelling and punctuation), style, register, content and layout so that the text as a whole is able to answer to the four important C's of communication, that is, clarity, correctness, coherence and consistency (about which see section 2 of chapter 3). To these can be added completeness and appropriateness.

During this process, the text editor must not lose sight of the cardinal role of the reader(s) (that is, the projected target readership of the particular text) (about which see section 4 of chapter 3). What the text offers (including language) has to be attuned to what the text editor knows (or can establish) about the background of the reader. It makes sense for the text editor to know in advance what the reader's knowledge of the subject is, what their attitude is towards the content and how they will want to use the text. All of this will help to determine the profile of the reader – which is essential to enabling the process of text editing to proceed as smoothly as possible. The types of question that should be asked in this connection include these (cf Billingham 2002: 16–25; Mossop 2010: 60; Ruddock 2001):

- *What motivates the readers to read the text?*
  If they are highly motivated (highly interested), they will supposedly be more tolerant of a poorly edited text because they're more focused on the content. If they're less motivated (less interested), they're likely to be less tolerant of errors and a poor text. In the case of a poor text, much more trouble must be taken to make a text attractive or user-friendly, including ensuring that the layout is good.

- *How much do the readers know? What is their background knowledge of a certain terrain?*
  Text aimed at specialists will naturally include more technical language. It can be insulting or affronting to a specialist to have such a text literally spelling everything out (Mossop 2010: 60–61). For such an audience, knowledge overload and over-explicitness have therefore to be kept in mind – and avoided – throughout the text. On the other hand, those who lack specialised knowledge prefer explicit detail that is expressed simply. Therefore, the text editor should adapt the nature and extent of the text to the type of reader and their background knowledge of the subject. This means that not only the language usage but also the content and the format must be matched to the identified readers. Here, once again, the text editor has to make an important choice from the outset.

- *What is the readers' level of training or education?*
  Mossop (2010: 60–61) says that readers without a secondary education, for example, will find it difficult to read a text that, among other difficulties, contains words of foreign origin (Latin and Greek) – for example, cognition as opposed to thought; semantics instead of meaning. If the text is aimed at the mass market (which then includes people with a lower level of academic literacy), the text editor must ensure that all the intended readers will in fact be in a position to be able to read it. Clearly, this includes a choice about style (including sentence length) and register (the choice of higher-frequency (or better-known) words in preference to words of foreign origin). It is even possible to use the results of tests of the text's readability to help decide on what is suited to and appropriate in a particular text. (Further on this see Baskette, Sissors & Brooks 1986: 11–18; Mossop 2010: 62.)

- *What is the nature of the relationship between author and reader?*
  An informal relationship naturally leads to more informal language; for example, a company's internal newsletter will communicate more directly, personally and informally. But where the author does not know their readers – for example, in the case of an article in a newspaper or a periodical – the language, style and register should be adjusted to the medium, which entails the good use of language, a neutral style and register, as well as good layout.

- *What will the readers' intention be in using the text?*
  Here Mossop (2010: 63) distinguishes three appropriate questions: How is the text being used? Where? and Why?
    - *How?*: Will the text be read aloud, for example a story book for children? Will the book be read silently? Will the text be read from beginning to end in its entirety (like a thriller or a detective story) or will only sections be consulted (like a dictionary or a textbook)?
    - *Where?*: Will the reader be standing while reading the text, as in a lecture theatre, a courtroom or a church? Will they be relaxed as they sit and read, for example at home or in a bus, on a train or on an aeroplane? Will the reader read the text in privacy?
    - *Why?*: Will the text be read for pleasure or to pass the time (as on public transport)? Or will it be read to help the reader make a decision or issue an instruction?

What this all comes down to is that the text editor must constantly take into account the potential readers of the text. In reality, the reader must be put in a position where they can process the text easily – to experience the magical '100% communication' at the first reading. Plotnik (1982: 43) adds that the text editor must hear an 'identifiable reader voice' at which they must aim in order to make 'complex, crucial decisions'. This makes the text editor a many-faceted and accommodating person who:

› knows how to make the right choices in order to achieve effective communication;

› knows enough about the language to be able to deal with language problems and to take responsibility for their decisions;

› knows enough about style to recognise and deal with potential problems relating to formal and informal language;

› knows enough about register to make the right choices regarding it in good time;

› knows when to check the content for correctness and accuracy;

› knows, understands and can apply at least the basics of typography;

› by definition, is disposed to providing the reader with the best possible communications package.

In this way, the text editor will be able to make possible the most effective written communication.

We can now return to answering the question posed at the beginning of this section: In the text-editing process, which people are repeatedly involved in preparing and polishing the 'product'? They are:

• the original creator (author);
• the person instructing the editor (mainly the client – such as the publisher, or even the author);
• the facilitator (the text editor, or as participant in the translation process on the basis of their knowledge and experience);
• the reader (who has to find the text as accessible as possible, or who has to recognise the text as special or unique).

In the next section we set out how you should go about editing a text in order for the process of editing (see figure 3.3) to be accomplished.

3 Methods of working: how to edit a text

> ... the secret of good editing lies in the use of a velvet glove, as well as – occasionally – an iron hand.
> *O'Connor*

> ... a computer and a pencil are the same, albeit at different levels. They are different tools. The creative source they both need to function well is a human brain.
> *Berner*

Some people can look at a document and immediately spot the problems – the subject–verb agreement errors, the inconsistencies in tense, the undefined terms. To many other people, though, such errors are invisible ...
Eisenberg

The editor's first task will be to identify what is missing, what has not been done well, and what is excessive ...
Davies & Balkwill

There is no absolutely prescribed manner in which to go about editing a text. According to Eisenberg (1992: 29), no book exists that prescribes universal and accepted practices ('How do I do it?') for actively editing a text. In a number of sources, there are tips and guidelines for doing text editing, but that is about as far as the 'advice' on sources goes.

The reason for this is that while some of the errors in texts are easy to identify and correct, others are difficult to detect and some of those will remain invisible – for example, the subtle smoothing over of the structure of an argument in a text. As a result, it takes special skills and prior knowledge to sit down and start doing this work. Moreover, practising text editors pursue their own methods and techniques, mostly based on experience, test runs, a process of hit-and-miss, and the advice of other language practitioners, and often it boils down to a case of 'so many heads, so many opinions'. The literature on the subject actually guides us here and we draw on this source material in this section.

It is clear that there are at least three methods according to which text editing work can be done: (1) by hand, using a pen or a pencil on a hard copy (a printout) of the text (also known as the paper-based method – see section 3.2 below), (2) by taking advantage of what the computer and technology have to offer (the electronic format; also known as the onscreen method – see section 3.3 below) or (3) the combined method (where both a hard copy of the text and a computer are harnessed – see section 3.4 below). In reality, the third method is probably the most popular nowadays (for a number of practical reasons).

The ascendency of the computer and technology has over time contributed to the fact that the personal computer and products based on developments in electronics have led to a situation in which in they are used almost exclusively to edit texts (Bisaillon 2007: 85–88; Gilad 2007). Some text editors actually still prefer to work on hard copy, or on hard copy and onscreen, however, and so guidelines on how to use these methods are given.

Obviously, the practical implications of the text-editing process will be evident in the specific tasks performed by the editor. We have already indicated in section 2 of chapter 3 the particular tasks that a text editor is expected to carry out to produce a text that communicates well. These tasks include (see also list 3.2 and figure 3.1 for a more comprehensive picture):

> › Checking the suitability of the text to the intended target audience.

> › Checking the indicators of correct language usage and structure.

> › Checking that all the connected parts of a text as presented and evident are in place.

> › Checking the style and register of the text.

> › Checking the content (as far as possible).

> › Checking the accuracy of the information in the text.

> › Checking that consistency has been maintained throughout the text.

> › Checking the paragraphing in the text.

> › Checking for copyright permissions.

> › Giving feedback to the client.

The text editor performs these tasks with precision by carrying out, comprehensively and indepth, all the required activities – these aspects are illustrated fully in figure 3.1. Text editing entails editing the language, style, register, content and typography of the text as a whole. In reality, these activities are carried out regardless of the medium – paper or electronic. It is the task of the text editor to ensure that the result of the editing process (that is, the final copy of the text) will result in a quality publication, one that serves the best interests of both reader and client.

3.1 Practical aspects of the process of text editing

How does one go about practically editing a text? First, you prepare your work area in preparation for starting work (Billingham 2002: 102; Bisaillon 2007: 81); secondly, agree with the client in advance in what format the text will be delivered to you; thirdly, follow the steps in the process, at least so far as they are applicable to the work at hand.

Preparing your work area:

> › A well-lit surface on which to work.

> › A clear working surface.

> › An isolated work area (to ensure that you are able to sustain your concentration).

>>

› A good chair (which offers firm back support), at which you will be able to sit at length without discomfort.

› At least the primary reference works (such as dictionaries, word lists (such as spellers and dictionaries for writers and editors, style guides and books on grammar and punctuation) should be within arm's reach. (For more about this, see chapter 11, where sources of importance to the text editor are discussed.)

› Pencils (and a good quality eraser) or pens for making corrections on hard copy. A pencil is strongly recommended for raising author queries in the text and/or margin space, since the pencil can be easily erased once the author has responded to a query (or it can be made more permanent with ink, if necessary). Pens are permanent and much more visible (and also photocopy better than pencilled corrections). (Judd 1990: 203–204.)

› Decide on which text editing symbols you will be using when you work on hard copy. These constitute the editor's shorthand. You can use either the standard proof correction marks (see more about this in section 9 of this chapter), or a list of your own symbols. These marks are very helpful in practice, and save time, as they help the editor to avoid constantly having to indicate corrections in long hand.

› A stapler, paper clips, a pair of scissors (possibly for cut and paste) and extra writing paper (for queries to the author and the client, among other uses) are also essential items of stationery that you should have to hand. Post-it or other sticky notelets can also be useful as bookmarks.

› Possibly a pocket calculator, for checking figures, totals or percentages, as necessary. Or use the calculator in your PC, mobile phone or laptop.

› A personal computer or a laptop connected to a printer.

› Access to the internet, which can be used to check entries in online dictionaries, official websites and encyclopaedias very quickly. MS Word's thesaurus is also useful. (For further information, see chapter 11.)

› If you work with a computer or laptop (PC or AppleMac), you will have less need for some of the items listed above. For instance, the different colour combinations of Track Changes can be used to indicate corrections, adaptations or insertions.

Requirements of the text editor when working with hard copy – some suggestions:

> › Ask for the manuscript or text to be laid out with 1.5 or double line spacing. This gives you sufficient space to write in the text and to fit in your text-editing symbols.

> › Ask for the margins (left, right, head and foot) to be at least 2.5 cm wide. This also gives you sufficient space in which to write and to fit in the text-editing symbols.

> › Ask for the type size (font size) to be at least 12 point of a readable font – for instance, Arial, Times New Roman or even Courier. For headings, subheadings, tabular text and artwork captions and labels, the font should stand out clearly from the body text – that is, either a contrasting font or a bolder variant of the body text.

> › The text must be printed crisply and clearly so that it is easily readable.

> › The text must be printed on only one side of the manuscript pages, both making the text and corrections clearer and more readable and giving you more space to write if you have to rewrite or reformulate text.

> › The text must be handed to you in as complete a form as possible. An important reason for this is that it is easy for consistency to be compromised when text is supplied to the editor piecemeal (ie bit by bit) or incomplete. This problem is compounded when the client then requires the edited text to be handed back in small batches.

> › The client must state clearly whether a house style guide exists that must be adhered to. If one does exist, a copy should be given to the text editor to consult. If not, the editor should be briefed to compile a style sheet for the particular manuscript and hand that in together with the edited manuscript (Linnegar, Schamberger & Bishop: 2009).

> › The client must also indicate their preferred standard reference works: for example, the *Oxford, Collins, Cambridge* or *Chambers English dictionary*; and the *Oxford manual of style, Butcher's copy-editing* or the *Chicago manual of style*; and the *Oxford dictionary for writers and editors* or the Collins or Penguin titles of the same ilk.

Einsohn (2005: 14–15) considers the process to begin only when a number of core questions are asked and answered, namely, who the target audience is, what the nature and extent of the text is, the degree of text editing needed, the approach that should be adopted to the editing (for instance, is there a house style guide that has to be followed?), the author's background, and what the administrative demands of the job are likely to be.

These matters have already been taken into account in list 3.2 in chapter 3, so we shall not deal with them again here; but one could view them as a first, evaluating step prior to work commencing on the manuscript. Certainly, practising text editors consider it idealistic to think that all projects can begin in this manner, because there is seldom time for such a (somewhat detailed and elaborate) preliminary phase (McLachlan 2007; Blaauw 2008). It is rather a case of: obtain the text, read it through thoroughly first, then make the necessary corrections as effectively as possible, hand the text back to the client (by the agreed deadline). And then the process starts all over again, with the next brief ...

In order to provide a measure of guidance, typical steps in the text-editing process, as they appear in the literature on the subject, are set out (especially in Butcher, Drake & Leach 2006, 2009; Einsohn 2005, 2005; Gilad 2007; Grossman (ed) 1993; Judd 1990; Mahan (ed) 2003; Morrish 1998; Mossop 2001, 2007, 2010; Plotnik 1982; Renkema 2005; Ritter 2003). Obviously, some of the steps in the different processes are repetitive and therefore, where relevant they are either adapted or left as is.

3.2 Text editing: hard copy format

The text or manuscript lands on your desk in hard copy format. You asked to make it fulfil the requirements set out in list 4.4 above. This has (you hope) been done. Then you start working systematically ...

What now?

The first objective is to determine how much work needs to be done on the manuscript. You therefore try to establish what the level of difficulty of the text is and approximately how long it will take to complete the task. The first step in this process is:

1. Find out from the client precisely what needs to be done to the manuscript – you have the right to know what is expected of you. (Butcher, Drake & Leach 2006: 3–4, 2009; Davies & Balkwill 2011:166, 168–169.) Your brief should spell out the details.
2. Ensure that you know who the intended target market for the text is – knowing this affects a considerable number of editorial choices, such as word choice, style and register.
3. Ensure that the text is readable. If it is slipshod, having to edit it will undoubtedly affect the completion time (Linnegar 2008: 28).
4. Make sure that the complete text has been received (or, as an alternative, an agreed part of the complete text) (Butcher, Drake & Leach 2006: 3, 2009).
5. Texts should preferably not be received piecemeal (bit by bit) because this can lead to problems with maintaining consistency during the editing process – for example, the

different ways in which words can be spelt, conveying different meanings (altogether versus all together; everyday vs every day; lose vs loose; no-one vs none; any one vs anyone).

6. Check for completeness:
   - Whether all the pages of the manuscript are present.
   - Whether all the pages are correctly numbered.
   - Whether copies of all the tables, figures, illustrations, drawings and pictures have been supplied.
   - Whether all the footnotes and/or endnotes are in place.
   - Whether (if applicable) the bibliography or a list of references (depending upon which is supplied) has been included with the manuscript.
   - Whether all the relevant additional material, such as the title page, imprint page, foreword, preface, table of contents, addenda, questionnaires and glossaries have been included.

To see whether everything that should be there is in fact in the manuscript, parts of the text are read. In this regard, Einsohn (2005: 16–17) talks about a 'preliminary skim', that is, a sort of skim read through the text to determine the content, organisation and quality of the language usage; and, in this process, to establish if there's any aspect that will require more than the usual attention: for example, the style in which the text is written is poor and there is a good likelihood of a rewrite. Are the chapters logically arranged or arranged in accordance with a curriculum? Do the parts within the chapters fit together? It is good to know these things up front, because you can then make provision for dealing with them in planning your work schedule. This step is usually the first of the macro-editing stages of engaging with a manuscript.

Mackenzie (2011: 68) says that this is also an opportunity for determining the author's voice; in other words, it gives you a chance to establish how the author thinks and plans, and also how they express themselves on paper. That's how one gets the first 'feel' of the text. This browsing around the manuscript helps the text editor to form an impression of the task that lies ahead. It also enables them to determine the nature of the text, for example, if it forms part of a series of publications or is a standalone title; whether there's a house style guide that must be followed; whether it's possible to complete the required work in the stipulated time or whether that needs to be renegotiated; or whether the quotation (see the sample quotation on page 222 below) for the job is on target or needs to be renegotiated (Grossman (ed) 1993: 64; see also Bisaillon 2007).

Arrange the text so that the job becomes clearly divided up. Save parts (such as chapters) in separate files (or, electronically, as documents), each marked differently for the sake of distinguishing one from the other. Other possibilities include using different-coloured paper clips per chapter or placing the chapters in separate piles on your work surface. Doing so also gives you an impression of the extent of the job, and it helps with conceptual

JANE SMITH
Language practitioner
Email: janes@gmail.com · Cell: 803 123 4999

QUOTATION

Date:

To: Ms Emmah Gimani

Quote number:

Electronic language editing of MBA dissertation

Date on which job is to be delivered to client:	15 June 20XX
Total word count:	26,184 words
Rate:	R0.30 per word
*Total payable:	**R2,834.27**

* No VAT is payable.
Terms and conditions:
1. The service includes electronic language and grammar editing, corrections, professional layout and applying academic/professional style.
2. The service does NOT include critical reading from an academic point of view, eg logical structure, flow, research methodology. These aspects are the writer's responsibility.
3. Electronic queries inserted by the editor are for the client's attention and decision.
4. No responsibility is taken for any occurrences of plagiarism, which may not be obvious to the editor.
5. Since editing work is done part-time, time constraints must be taken into consideration. An additional fee may be required for 'rush jobs'.
6. Email transmission and the editing process may lead to changes in formatting, such as in pagination and layout; in font, line and paragraph spacing; or in tables or graphs. In addition long documents, complex graphics and tables may lead to further corruption or difficulty in handling documents.
7. No responsibility is accepted for delays or problems caused by the complexities of the electronic editing and/or emailing processes as described above.

JANE SMITH
Language practitioner
Email: janes@gmail.com · Cell: 803 123 4999

INVOICE

Date:

To: Ms Emmah Gimani

Invoice number:

Electronic language editing of MBA dissertation

Total word count:	26,184 words
Rate:	R0.30 per word
*Total payable:	**R2,834.27**

* No VAT is payable. Payment terms: 30 days from invoice date.

JP Smith   XYZ Bank   BCD Branch (575 775)   Savings account no 9876 5431

Figure 4.1 *Examples of a quotation and an invoice*

planning. Also keep the table of contents (if it is available) to hand: it will help you to check whether the text is in the correct sequence and complete, according to the contents list, though be forewarned: if the author prepared the contents list too early in the process or made substantial changes to the text itself after compiling the table of contents, then the list itself will have to be updated. The contents list can also be used as a checklist for measuring one's progress.

The next step is of considerable practical importance: With a pencil or a pen in your hand (according to your preference), start reading the text – 'plunge in', to quote Einsohn (2005: 17). But at this stage focus on the reading, not so much on the correcting, as getting bogged down in the correcting will distract you from obtaining the overview you need of the entire manuscript at this stage. By all means circle or underline any 'problems' you detect as you're reading (as an aide memoire of things to return to when you do begin editing in earnest), but move on quickly once you have done so.

There's a lack of unanimity in the literature on how many times a text should be read. Some reckon that twice is enough, others three times. Einsohn (2005: 16) says that, ideally speaking, one cursory read through and two, more indepth readings are sufficient: 'Two passes seems to be the universal magic number.' In reality, though, no text editor is so good that they will detect and correct every error (of whatever kind) at the first read-through, which means that only one read-through is insufficient. Normally our brain is not able to cope with so much information all at once. Three indepth read-throughs are also seldom attainable for perfectly normal, practical reasons, such as the pressure of time and financial constraints (in simple terms: the longer you spend on a document, the lower your hourly rate, the less you earn). The most attainable approach is to read through once quickly (to evaluate the text – see paragraph 2 above again) and then to give the text two more thorough passes.

1. With the first indepth read-through it is necessary to read slowly: v-e-r-y s-l-o-w-l-y and t-h-o-r-o-u-g-h-l-y. Einsohn (2005: 17) puts it like this:

   > On the first pass through the text, most copy editors read very, very slowly. Let me say it again, because it is crucial to your success as copyeditor: You must *train* yourself to read v-e-r-y, v-e-r-y slowly – slowly enough to scrutinize each comma ('Ok, comma, what are you doing here? Do you really belong here? Why?'), to interrogate each pronoun ('Hey, pronoun, where's your antecedent? Do you two agree in gender and number?'), to cross-examine every homophone ('You there, 'affect'! Shouldn't you be 'effect'?'), and to ponder each compound adjective, adverb and noun ('Does our dictionary show 'cross section' or 'cross-section'?'). Moreover, you must read slowly enough to catch missing words (a dropped 'the' or 'a'), missing pieces of punctuation ('We need a hyphen here'), ambiguities in syntax, and gaps in logic. On the first editorial pass through the manuscript, then, you will want to *read as slowly as you can.*

   During this read-through it is important to look up everything you're in any way uncertain about. With the help of your reference works (see chapter 11 for more about references) you must perform a competent mechanical edit, that is, read line by line and look out for aspects such as: the use of initial uppercase letters, spelling generally, sentence construction, ambiguity, inverted commas (quotation marks – the convention for the use of singles and doubles), unfamiliar terminology, repetition, spacing, and so on. These are the aspects that can rob a text of its shine if they are not attended to and put right. (See also lists 2.9, 2.10, 2.11 and 2.13 for a detailed indication of what is relevant here.)

Obvious factual inaccuracies must, wherever possible, be followed up on and resolved, and consistency (whether in language usage, style, typography or context) must be ensured. This phase is considered to be the most time-consuming in the entire text-editing process. According to the *Chicago manual of style* (Grossman (ed) 1993: 663–664), it is at the same time also the most important phase, because it is then that serious attention is given to detail and also when text editors have to push their knowledge and experience to the limit and take quick, logical and defensible decisions. To a large extent, this phase determines the success of the entire editing process.

Einsohn (2005: 30) focuses attention on a very important matter: whether done on hard copy in pen or pencil, the editing must be neat, especially readable, otherwise during the process of transferring corrections major errors are likely to creep in as a result of misunderstandings of the author's or text editor's intended changes. Writers on this subject are agreed that (especially if corrections are handwritten) with text editing neatness is all important; and that text editors must ensure that every sign, word, letter and numeral must be unambiguous (cf Butcher 1993: 45; Einsohn 2005: 30; Judd 1990: 204, 225; Mossop 2010: 101). Of course, editing onscreen avoids this problem almost entirely.

2. The second indepth read-through consists of reading for the sake of implementing checks. Was something perhaps overlooked during the first read-through? This phase can even warrant rewriting, reformulating or restructuring the text, or parts of the text, in the interests of better communication. In this phase, for example, paragraphing and style are given particular attention, because these are subtler aspects that need to be followed up on. The focus at this stage is on the broader picture. Einsohn (2005: 17) also suggests that the second indepth read-through should be undertaken – if possible – with as little interruption as possible, because this helps the text editor to detect and fix inconsistencies more easily. At this stage the text is still in a practitioner's short-term memory, which makes it easier to spot errors. This is the primary reason why an assignment should not be dealt with section by section; the result is usually unavoidably contradictory editorial decisions.

3. Some text editors reverse the process: the first read-through is fast and all about getting an overview of the manuscript; the second slow and indepth. During the first read-through, all the obvious errors (of the mechanical type) are identified and corrected

and during the second the subtler errors are dealt with. Each text editor eventually embraces a method that works for them, so which method they use can't be prescribed. In most cases the result is the same.

4. It is often necessary, as a result of time constraints (the publication must be published by a certain date or time) or financial limitations (insufficient funds are available for the project), to set priorities. Tarutz (1992) says that questions such as the following can help to determine the nature and extent of the list of priorities:
    – What matters to the readers?
    – How important is the document to the readers?
    – What types of error are the readers likely to spot which will bother them?

It is not always possible for the ideal text-editing process (in terms of the reading strategy discussed above) to occur in reality, but it is possible to determine what is most important for a given project (despite certain weaknesses or flaws) and what can be overlooked for the time being, even if doing so leaves the text editor feeling uneasy. In this respect, Einsohn (2005: 18–20) gives some practical advice and guidance. The list of priorities is naturally determined by the project itself. There is a list of minimal tasks that include those aspects of the job that, if they are not attended to in a text, will cause embarrassment to the client, and which will probably also confuse the reader. This list of minimal tasks is:

Checklist 4.1 Minimal editorial tasks

✓ As far as possible, correct every spelling error.
✓ Correct obvious grammatical errors (such as the wrong form or tense of a verb, an incorrect plural form or misused comparative or superlative forms of adjectives).
✓ Correct obvious punctuation errors (such as commas, semicolons and exclamation marks).
✓ Question obvious factual inaccuracies or contradictions.
✓ Indicate those pages on which copyright permission is lacking.
✓ Read the title page (especially the title itself and the names of the author(s), copyright notice, foreword, preface and table of contents for errors and inconsistencies.
✓ Check the numbering of footnotes and/or endnotes.
✓ Check the numbering of headings and subheadings, main and subsections, tables, figures, illustrations, diagrams and sketches.
✓ Attend to basic paragraphing. (No paragraph should extend over two pages.)
✓ Shorten long sentences. The use of a full stop or a semicolon is to be recommended.
✓ Eliminate excessive use of the passive voice.
✓ Eliminate occurrences of repetition, redundancy and, where possible, ambiguity.

The text editor could also decide to work through the text quickly only twice or, alternatively, to skim-read it only once, following that up with a slower read. The decision regarding the number of times a text is read depends entirely on the type of text, the extent of the list of priorities given above (either the entire list or only agreed upon priorities), and the text editor's own style and tempo of working.

It is clear that by giving attention at least to the tasks itemised in checklist 4.1, the editor will deliver a considerably better text (according to estimates, by at least 60–70%). Doing so makes a difference to the quality of a text.

Check that the content of the text or manuscript is in agreement with the title. There are often subtle imperfections in a text in this respect. Mackenzie (2011: 69) gives as an example the case where she had to edit a book that was supposed to be about Australia the country as a whole, but in which the only examples there were illustrated only two of the six federal states. The title was consequently not an accurate reflection of the content. This fact was pointed out to the client and the title was changed as a result.

Sometimes the level of writing in a book or the nature of the readership is such that it can be understood only with the aid of a glossary. The text editor has to draw the client's attention to words and expressions in need of a gloss. In the process, the text editor's reputation should be affirmed, which can possibly lead to future work from appreciative clients.

Always draw up a checklist or a follow-up list of matters that must still receive attention during the text-editing process. For example, a particular reference has to be checked out, either to verify the spelling of an unknown word or to establish its usage frequency. The matters included in the list have to be followed up one by one and the results of your researches incorporated into the text (*Chicago manual of style* 1993: 79–80). All of this makes the text editor's task more complex and difficult, but also more challenging and even interesting.

Take the intention and requirements of the client and the author into account throughout the process. If there is any doubt about any aspect of the manuscript, it is the text editor's moral duty to ask the client or the author questions about it. The text editor's unique aptitude lies in unlocking information for the potential reader, and it is therefore important that they ensure that the intended information, as it appears in the manuscript and as interpreted by them, accords with the intention and requirements of the author and/or the client (*Chicago manual of style* (1993: 79–83).

The text editor must also bring obvious errors in the text (such as the spelling of place names, facts, numbers, statistics and assertions) to the attention of the author or the client. One question that can arise is, for instance, whether names should or should not contain accents or other diacritics (is it Riga or Rīga in English?). And if there's a reference to an event that occurred on a certain date in the past (such as 19 October 1899) and the next reference to the same event indicates another date (such as 29 October 1999), the editor must mark or query both with the author.

Another frequent error occurs in bibliographic references, where, for example, in one place there's a reference to Johnson 2006 and in another there's Johnson 2006a or Jonnson 2006. Which is correct? A sharp eye (the proverbial 'eagle eye') is of great help here. This is just further proof of how important concentration and concerted attention on one topic in one text are.

The text is returned to the client. After the text-editing process is completed, the manuscript is handed back to the client for further processing. But this is not necessarily the end of the road for the text editor; it could be that they will be approached to go through the text again with a fine-toothed comb to refine it further after the author has responded to all the text editor's queries, comments and suggestions. At this stage in the process it is appropriate for the text editor to confirm with the client, either in a letter or by email, the work that has been completed.

Mackenzie (2011: 138–141) sets out the ten steps that she takes when she edits text on hard copy. According to her, it is not a fixed method, but rather a workable and tested model (a) that can increase your effectiveness (because you then know how you will proceed in an orderly and organised manner) and (b) that can be adapted according to the needs, level of competence and experience of the text editor as well as according to the nature and extent of the assignment. The steps involved are first given in summary form below; after that each is discussed in greater detail.

Step	Activity
1	Evaluating the manuscript
2	Organisation: deciding how changes will be marked
3	First editing of the text: the textual component
4	Second editing of the text: the non-textual component
5	Checking and cross-checking Production markup: indicating to the typesetter/designer special typographical treatment of the text
6	Raising and responding to queries to the author/client
7	Finding additional documentation, if necessary
8	Incorporating the author's feedback
9	Final checking and proofreading the final edited pages
10	Signing-off of the project prior to printing

Table 4.1 *Steps and activities for hard-copy format editing*

Step 1: Evaluating the manuscript

Once the manuscript is in your hands, ascertain whether you have received all the parts of the manuscript, as indicated in checklist 4.1 above. Read through the text quickly and ascertain what the quality (or the lack of quality) of the work is and how much time it can be expected to take to perform the text-editing work. At all times, the objective remains to produce a publishable text. Therefore you must first gain a global view of the text. Then draw up a project plan to indicate how the work will be tackled – for example, the dates on which work will be done and the manner in which the schedule will be met. Also establish precisely what the client expects of the editing process: a light, a medium or a heavy edit. Knowing this will help to flesh out the project plan. But bear this in mind: no text is ever like any other, neither in form nor in format, structure, subject-matter, style, language usage or register. For each text therefore, the editor will have to take a unique approach.

Step 2: Organising how the changes to the hard-copy text are going to be marked

- This happens mainly according to the client's way of working and often also in collaboration with the designer/typesetter or the printer who will finally print the publication.
- The changes can either be marked in a variety of dark colours or (much less commonly nowadays) by using dark and light pencils.
- It is also customary to use a number of text-editing symbols (or proof correction marks) to indicate corrections in the text. In the past, the standard proofreading symbols were used for this purpose, but nowadays an increasing number of text editors are resorting to drawing up a list of their own symbols (most of them based on the standard BSI proof correction marks – see section 9 of this chapter for more details) and using them in the text. In such cases it is extremely important that the recipient of the hard-copy text has the editor's list to consult so that they can implement the corrections accurately.

Step 3: First editing of the text: the text component ('rough edit of the text')

Start by doing a basic edit of the text component of the manuscript (excluding, that is, the non-text component at this stage). Correct obvious errors (such as spelling and punctuation) as far as possible. Make decisions to impose consistency within and across the chapters (spelling, punctuation and the use of space on the page), recording your decisions on a style sheet (see section 2.5.2 of chapter 11) as you make them. At this point, compile lists of problems you encounter that you cannot resolve immediately or that only the author can resolve (linked to prompts in the margin): problematic spellings, unfamiliar words or terminology that you will have to look up in hard-to-access references, things (of whatever nature) that you will have to ask the client or author about (such as facts or figures that appear to be incorrect). Effect the major changes at this stage, if you can: spacing, font, font size, the use of space on the page, the format of headings and subheadings and of sections and subsections, abbreviations and contractions, acronyms, the use of uppercase letters, spaces after full stops and commas (and spaces before punctuation), double spaces between sentences, the way of writing dates and numbers, and so on.

Step 4: Second editing of the text: the non-text component ('rough edit of everything else')
Check references (both internal cross-references and those to sources), quoted matter (typing and formatting errors crop up frequently in quotations – do not disregard them), bibliographic references, tables, figures, diagrams, illustrations, sketches, table of contents and the title page.

Also ensure that the headings and subheadings are correct and that they are logically numbered, that the figures or tables are placed and referred to in the correct positions in the manuscript, and that the wording and page numbers in the table of contents, list of illustrations, list of figures, and so on, correspond to what is found in the text.

Step 5: Checking and cross-checking ('smooth edit of everything else')
The editing of the document is now almost completed, but you should read it through one more time to track down those last few imperfections in the manuscript (often things you got sidetracked from by becoming preoccupied with other corrections that need your attention).

Also ensure that the entire manuscript (both the text and all the other components, such as the tables, front matter such as the table of contents and end-matter such as the bibliography and the glossary) constitutes the complete and unified text.

Mackenzie (2011: 141) advises that text editors should put themselves in the position of the reader at this stage in order to check 'whether the text works'. If possible, build into the editing process a 'cooling-off period': when you look at your edited version of the text with a fresh eye, you might detect errors that you yourself introduced into the manuscript or which you overlooked and remember the management rule: every *change is not always an improvement* (Langley et al 1992), so avoid making changes for change's sake.

Step 6: Raising and responding to queries to the author/client
As you will have worked through the manuscript, you will have raised and flagged queries that only the author is able to answer. At the end of your edit, compile a set of these and present them (tactfully) to the author, in the form of an email (or email attachment), a letter or a fax that they will be able to respond to. Make it as easy as possible both for the author to understand the nature of the problem or query and also for them to respond with the appropriate answers to your questions. (If necessary, refer them to a specific manuscript page, paragraph and line for each query.) When they receive this document, the author should be in no doubt about the deadline for the return of their responses, otherwise the process can become too drawn out and deadlines missed as a result.

The following document is an example of a standard format that copy editors should use when raising queries with authors:

Author queries relating to (book title):

The edited manuscript is attached for your reference. Please check that all changes made by the editor are acceptable to you. In addition, we'd appreciate it if you would respond to the specific queries listed below by fax/email/letter by (date):

Page	Line	Query	Response
General		I have reduced the frequent use of italics because in print it could be distracting. Are you happy with this?	
		Because footnotes are expensive to set, I had to take them into the text. Please check pp 30, 46, 110, 136 to make sure they are integrated acceptably.	
26	10	May 1969, or 1967 as references?	
30	3 up	'constructing ... to' – incorrect English or correct jargon?	
36	4		
		Koesterbaum, or Koestenbaum as references?	
42	10–11		
		Please check my rewording.	
46	7		
		'a reminder ... for their subject area' – sense?	
49	2		
		Graham, 1984 not in refs; Husserl, 1931: a or b?	
51–53			
		Tables 3.1–3.3: Please give details of sources (they appear to be photocopies of printed material).	

Figure 4.2 *A copy of your correspondence with the author must, of course, be sent to the client for their attention, if the client and author aren't one and the same person.*

Step 7: Finding additional documentation

Ensure that all the additional documents pertaining to the manuscript are included at this stage. This will help to ensure that everything has been covered and that the client's briefs and requests are clear, and clearly understood. Have the client's briefs regarding the typography and the placement of figures, tables, illustrations (including photographs, sketches and digital drawings) and footnotes or endnotes been implemented? Have all the illustrations been provided with captions and numbered, where applicable?

These documents include notes and suggestions to the designer/typesetter and the printer. Make especially sure at this point that everything you're supposed to have done has in fact been done.

Step 8: Incorporating the author's feedback

The author's feedback should be incorporated clearly into the hard-copy text (the working document), perhaps in a different-coloured ink or a darker pencil to make it stand out. This usually entails either erasing a pencilled author query in the margin or replacing it with a more permanent correction. Where, however, the author rejects your query or suggested change, you would simply erase the pencilled query.

Where the author supplies written responses (corrections, insertions, replacements) in response to your queries, ensure that they are edited for correctness, completeness and consistency – do not simply accept them without any editorial intervention – because you cannot expect the author to follow the spelling, capitalisation, punctuation and hyphenation conventions you decided upon during the editing process. Sentences will also have to be checked for grammatical correctness and their correct fit into the edited text.

Step 9: Final checking and proofreading

Make sure that you obtain answers to every question regarding the manuscript and check that they have been incorporated into the correct places in the manuscript. A useful control mechanism at this stage is to tick off each answered query with a different-coloured pen. This helps you to ensure that all such queries have been dealt with.

Step 10: Signing off of the project

The manuscript is eventually handed over to the client in its final form. This is the time to write a letter or an email confirming that the work has been completed. The style sheet the text editor compiled for the manuscript should accompany it (see chapter 11). The invoice for the work done (see the example on page 222) should also be handed to the client at this point.

The section above has dealt with the ways in which text editing on a hard copy of the manuscript should be done. In the process, we have provided some useful hints and several discrete steps have been highlighted. Every text editor develops their own way of working according to their experience, knowledge and personality; in the majority of cases their method parallels those described above. We advise you to choose the method that works best for you and to pursue it with commitment. In the next sections we will discuss the electronic editing process and a combined method of hard copy and electronic copy editing. They only differ insofar as part or all the editing is done onscreen instead of on hard copy, by implementing the changes electronically either with or without MS Word's Track Changes function. In the case of electronic editing only, the client is likely to want to see Track Changes used (see 3.3 below). In the 'combined' process, you will first edit on the hard copy and then transfer the corrections onscreen onto the electronic version of the text. This method would be employed when a client specifically asks for both the hard copy and the electronic copy to be submitted (see 3.4 below).

In conclusion, Mackenzie (2011: 157) offers a number of guiding principles to take into account when you edit texts. They are not in any particular sequence, but we hope they will serve as a point of departure when you have to take decisions during the text-editing process.

› Don't antagonise the author. Focus rather on building up a good working relationship with them. Tact and diplomacy are essential to doing so, considering the number and extent of the changes you are making to an author's manuscript, and the number of author queries you are likely to raise.

› Don't create unnecessary work for yourself. In this regard, it helps to know what your normal pages-per-hour rate of working is on a particular genre (for example, textbooks, theses or fiction), so that you can work out when you're taking longer to complete an edit of the normal number of pages and therefore reducing your earning power.

› Eliminate meaningless variation.

› Do not be pedantic (or rigid). Amongst other things, this often leads to the author's voice and/or intention being lost.

› Avoid responsibility: rather find someone else (ie the author or the client) to take decisions.

› Get the book done.

› Get it right.

› If it can be lived with, leave it well alone.

› Every word must count.

› Remove ramblings or deviations (anything that is not relevant).

› Remove unnecessary words.

› Determine what will best serve the interests of the reader.

› Decide whether the publication will sell better as a result.

3.3 Computer-based text editing

> We must ponder what human editors can do best for authors in the computer age. For computers have learned not only to store, find, sort, and deliver text, but to enhance it.
> *Plotnik*

> Most material accepted in electronic form – just like most of that accepted in hard-copy form – will need full copy-editing.
> *Butcher, Drake & Leach*

> The skills of the editor will be more necessary than ever as the information explosion continues.
> *Morrish*

According to Mackenzie (2007: 610; 2011: 71), the difference between the process of editing text on hard copy, on the one hand, and that aided by the advantages offered by computers, on the other, is not so great (see also Billingham 2002: 96–97; Mossop 2010). In reality, the same steps in the process – evaluate, read, reread, correct, check, correct, raise queries about problems, incorporate the answers to queries into the text, round off and hand in – pertain (see table 4.1 above). With the aid of a computer, the process tends to be less untidy or random and a lot more systematic.

The difference lies largely in the speed (at least as far as text adaptation and putting the finishing touches to text are concerned) that computer-based text editing makes possible, and consequently also the shorter production time that it contributes to (Mossop 2010: 101). Electronic aids such as spelling- and grammar-checkers (if and where they are available) help us largely to spot basic spelling and typing errors and to correct them with a click of a mouse, and in doing so save us an enormous amount of time (Anonymous 2006a; Mossop 2010). In particular, they eliminate the time-consuming word-for-word check, although electronic aids do not solve all the problems a manuscript is likely to expose. For example, at present they are not able to check all the possible spellings in a language. (We return to this subject in section 3.4 of chapter 11.) The negative role of a flickering computer screen in this process must not be underestimated, because it can place considerable strain on the eyes.

Butcher (1993: 8) says it is important to remember that everything handed in for processing in electronic format – just as in the case of the paper-based format – still has to be subjected to the full editorial process. The fact that it is available electronically certainly does not mean that it is well written, that there are no spelling errors, that there are no stylistic lapses or that the typographical layout is perfect. Quite the contrary, in fact.

The text editor is still expected to deliver the same level of text editing as for any other format. It is obvious that a whole lot more adaptations still need to be made. This pertains to *every* level of the text: language, contents, style, the accuracy of the information, the correctness of facts, an evaluation of the suitability of the text, the paragraphing, and so on. The difference is just this: it is no longer a question of taking a pen or a pencil in the hand, or using coloured paper clips or folders; but with the assistance of a computer mouse and the facility of MS Word's Track Changes (Gilad 2007; Hart 2007), the Comments function, or a variety of colours the text editing can proceed smoothly onscreen. In this way, even a team could work on one text without a mix-up arising because each member can be identified by means of a separate colour.

Changes can also be stored more easily and more safely, and it is by and large also easier to work more directly on the text. The corrections can be made immediately and this helps to speed up the completion of the work. And faster completion also contributes to reduced costs. Even illegible handwriting doesn't matter anymore, because a computer does not read handwriting. Towards the end of the editing process, it makes sense to make one further printout of the full hard-copy manuscript so that the final text can be viewed in its edited state, with none of the corrections visible.

It would be important to follow the steps listed below if you wanted to edit a manuscript electronically (onscreen).

Before you begin editing (cf inter alia Billingham 2002: 96–100; Bisaillon 2007: 85–89; Butcher, Drake & Leach 2006: 15–16, 400–417, 427, 2009; Einsohn 2005: 16–17, 37–45; Hart 2007; LEO (Literacy Education Online) 2007a, 2007b; Mackenzie 2011; Sunshine 2009; Waddingham 2006: 404–410) here are some hints and suggestions:

List 4.7 Practical hints: editing onscreen

› First and foremost, run the original document through an anti-virus scanner to detect and remove any viruses it may have picked up. The reasons for this are obvious. You really do not want a virus on the document you are working on, or to infect all the documents or software on your computer.

› Then make a working copy of the original document and store the original in a safe place. The reasons for this are obvious too.

› It is neither good nor responsible practice to save a document to your computer's hard drive as well, especially not if the working copy has already been saved there. Should the hard drive crash (for whatever reason; but it does happen fairly often), you will be left with nothing to work on and all the editing you will have done electronically will have been lost permanently. You should therefore *store the working copy and the original document in different ways and in different places.* Do this for every document you receive.

› Use only the working copy to work on. Work on this copy of the document from start to finish.

› *Save your work regularly.* You can set your computer to autosave the open document every few minutes; this way, if, say, a sudden power failure shuts your computer down, the version of the document saved in the last few minutes will have been saved and not too many of your edits will have been lost. In any event, ensure that the document is also saved elsewhere – for example, on a memory stick or as an attachment to an email. Doing so will help avoid any unnecessary stress later.

› At the end of *every* work session, make a copy of the document you've been working on and store it elsewhere. Some text editors regularly send themselves emails with the saved document as an attachment.

› The golden rule in executing the editing process is: Rather be overcautious than extremely sorry later.

› Check that you have received every component of the manuscript: chapters, diagrams, tables, footnotes/references, bibliography, table of contents, etc. This is especially important when the entire document is delivered as a number of separate electronic documents and components such as diagrams and tables have been supplied separately.

› Mark every document clearly and save it separately rather than combining them all as one large document. Label the folders or documents meaningfully; for example: Chapter 1, Chapter 2, Foreword, Contents, Bibliography, Questionnaire 1, Questionnaire 2, Addendum 1, Addendum 2, Glossary, Table 1, Table 2. As you begin working on each one, add something like '_edAN' (where AN is your initials as an extension). This helps to distinguish the copy you're working on from your untouched original – both for you and your client.

› Some text editors prefer to work on one large document, but that can be risky because of the possible large size of the document – particularly if it has images (illustrations) embedded in the text. Such large documents can be very slow and tedious to work on. An advantage of having one large document to work on, however, is that it's easier and more efficient to perform a thorough Find and Replace function on the entire text.

› Ensure that the electronic document is compatible with the software and programs you currently have on your computer (eg different versions of MS word). If this is not the case, arrange with your client to achieve compatibility At times, accessing or printing special characters (the pound sterling symbol or a particular accented character or bullet) can be a problem, but one that is usually overcome with a bit of pre-planning.

› If you do not receive a printout of the complete manuscript from your client, it is good practice to print it out so that it can be compared with the electronic version. Especially if the client has supplied a print-out, compare a sample against your electronic documents: check, for instance, whether the opening and final paragraphs correspond, then choose any other paragraph or paragraphs in the same document at random. If there is no correspondence between the two versions, let your client know right away – there may be a versioning problem they weren't aware of. The other advantage of hard copy is that it is easy to look up things (as opposed to scrolling) or to mark up. A hard copy is also handy alongside the copy on the computer screen.

› A printout of the manuscript also enables you to ensure that all the parts of a document are in place, and also to see what the text looks like when printed out. If you are aware of this beforehand, it is easier to implement the changes onscreen.

› Make doubly sure that the document(s) you receive are actually the latest copy or copies. Do this, for example, by *dating* each document upon receipt and comparing each against the client's copy. If they are not checked, it is possible that you could discover later on in the process that you've been working on an earlier (instead of the latest) version. This can result in a lot of time being lost, a deadline being missed, and loads of frustration.

› It is easier to read documents onscreen when the text is black on a white background. Configure the screen so that the appearance is easier on your eyes.

› There are writers who say that the computer screen is more difficult to read than the version on paper (Mackenzie 2011: 71; Mossop 2010: 101). First, people are inclined rather to view the screen than the pre-cise text, and that can lead to errors being transferred. Then the flicker evident on many computer screens is often tiring on the eyes. Also the eye is designed for distant rather than close vision, so constant star-ing at a computer screen will lead to eye strain, dryness and soreness. To counteract theses effects, take regular breaks and treat your eyes regularly with a sterile ophthalmic solution. See section 3.4 of this chapter for views expressed about the advantages and disadvantages of using computers for editing text.

List 4.7 continued

> It is not always so easy to remember where corrections have been made in an electronic text. Therefore don't go ahead with the editing without first activating a program that will indicate all your changes on the screen. Here, MS Word's Track Changes and Comments utilities are exceptionally helpful to authors and editors. You can also search documents for changes (or for instances requiring the same changes) using MS Word's Find and Replace function, or use this function to implement changes throughout a document. To highlight words you will want to return to later, use MS Word's Bookmark function, accessed via the Find dialog.

> Indicate every alteration you make. If a word must be transposed, delete it at its original position and insert it where required elsewhere, but in the process indicate where it has been inserted. The process can otherwise become unbelievably confusing.

> Use MS Word's Comment function to indicate passages that lack clarity, to comment on specific matters, to make comments, to point out matters that will need to be followed up later with the author or client, to highlight terms that will need to be found later, and so on.

> On the toolbar, you will be able to access some useful shortcuts, such as adding electronic dictionaries or opening up websites on the internet.

Now we begin to tackle the onscreen editing process and realise that, step by step, it differs very little from the hard copy process. Before you start, make very sure that you understand precisely what the client is expecting of the text. If the editing required is light, medium or heavy, what are the time constraints and what does the typesetter/designer expect?

3.4 Text editing: the combined method

A computer will assuredly make the job easier, but a human will have to know what the job is.
Berner

Software might eliminate 90% of errors, but that is not much consolation when you distribute copy that is only 90% correct.
Anonymous

I ... saw that word processing is not relied on by all professional editors and that *it is possible to integrate word processing into the editing process in a variety of ways.*
Bisaillon

From these statements it is clear that an individual and their particular skills and abilities play the central role in any text-editing process. Waddingham (2006) clearly supports this view: in spite of the extraordinary contribution that technology can make to editing texts, the computer cannot do the work singlehandedly. A person must still interpret, weigh up, judge and negotiate; as against that, a computer can merely carry out an instruction. It is quite possible that a combination of man and machine will deliver the best product: the former during the creative work, the latter able to perform only the mechanical tasks (Attwell 2010). Texts are already being improved with the help of technology (typed using a particular word processor) so that they are available as documents that can be worked on. It is rare nowadays for a handwritten document to be handed over for editing. By harnessing the advantages of the computer (see more about this below) we can complete the editing process more quickly, more thoroughly and more consistently.

Mossop (2010: 100–103) and Bisaillon (2007: 85–89) have investigated the pros and cons that are discussed whenever the choice has to be made between working onscreen versus hard copy:

- *Speed*: Working onscreen can be a faster alternative to writing out corrections long hand. Untidy handwriting is also not a problem. Using a spell-checker also helps to detect and correct the more mechanical spelling errors more quickly, consistently and comprehensively. One disadvantage of a computer screen is that reading can become difficult and lead to eye strain (see below). Another is that, for some text editors, scrolling is not as efficient as paging through hard copy.
- *Accuracy*: A poor-quality screen can make reading difficult, and that can lead to errors in the text being overlooked. On the other hand, a major advantage is that, by using, for example, the spell-checker or the Find and Replace function, corrections can be made across documents more systematically and comprehensively, leading to greater consistency in the edited text.
- *Eye strain*: The glare and the flicker inherent in most computer screens can lead to tired, dry and strained eyes – something less likely to happen with hard-copy editing. If the screen is smaller than an A4 sheet, this can affect the eyes adversely, but the new flat screens present less of a problem in this respect. In LEO (2007a) it is stated that the delimitation of a screen can lead to reduced reading productivity (Bisaillon 2007: 89). According to LEO (2007a), research has shown that text which is edited onscreen is more likely to be 'digressive, unfocused, chattier, and less concise'.
- *Geometry*: The placement of different windows on a screen can be confusing and can lead to difficulty with reading a text when the editor has to switch from one window to the other: 'flipping back and forth between six and seven windows is very likely to prove a nuisance' (Mossop 2010: 102). Doing so can also be time-consuming, whereas paging back and forth through hard copy is more natural and therefore possibly more efficient. Onscreen switching between windows seems to be less of a problem with the latest software and screen sizes, though.

- *The removal or undoing of corrections*: Whereas on paper it is messier and sometimes more tiresome to undo corrections that you have reconsidered (unless they were made in pencil and can easily be erased), and it can take time to track them down, with onscreen editing, undoing corrections is simply a matter of using the Find and Replace function to locate them and then pressing a few keys. Moreover, if you have used MS Word's Track Changes function, then (in MS Word 7) it's simply a matter of selecting the Review option and then Reject to have a correction undone and the original text restored (or Confirm to accept a change).

- *Costs and the environment*: Using a computer for editing can obviously save paper, and in the process a few trees, provided you don't keep printing out drafts. But Anonymous (2006a) says that this is not entirely true, because so much text editing is still done on hard copy:

> Even when electronic copyediting becomes routine, we suspect that a good deal of work will continue to be done on paper. One of the worst jokes in computing is the promise of a 'paperless office'. *The computer has generated more paper than ever before*. Some of the paper will be used to communicate changes in copy between writers, editors and the production staff.

There doesn't seem to be a clear preference for either of these methods. Gilad (2007) asserts that the advantages of the technology era should be exploited because doing so leads to things being done faster and more effectively (Bisaillon 2007); therefore 'wrap your arms around your computer and kiss it ...'. Just remember, though, that you are the pilot, the computer your co-pilot.

The advantages of using a computer and related technological advances generally have made it easier for text editors to get their work done at greater speed and to a professional standard (cf www.wordbytes.co.au; Gilad 2007: 255–272; Demoor, Lernout & Van Peteghem 1998). Certainly the technological developments listed below have made a major contribution to faster, more efficient and more professional interventions in texts.

3.4.1 Word processing software

These types of program (eg the different versions of MS Word; other open source programs are also available) can make a great contribution to polishing a text (Hazelton 2009). They can, for instance, be used to:

List 4.8 'What a computer can do for the text editor

› box, frame or tabulate text;

› generate word breaks electronically at the end of lines;

› move sections of text from one place to another;

› expand sections of text by using the Find, Cut, Copy and Paste functions to insert text from elsewhere in a document;

>>

List 4.8 continued

> delete sections of text;

> generate paragraphs;

> indent paragraphs;

> set margins;

> look up spellings, meanings, synonyms and antonyms of words in other external electronic sources, such as spell-checkers and electronic dictionaries, thesauruses and internet search engines (or browsers);

> check the spelling and grammar in a text (see sections 3.4.6 and 3.4.7 below);

> create or insert text boxes and tables;

> create columns;

> create bulleted or numbered lists;

> insert special signs and symbols (such as phonetic symbols and diacritics and mathematical characters, such as the operators) from an almost unlimited list;

> insert illustrations of various kinds;

> draw lines through words or sections of text;

> underline or italicise words or sections of text;

> make words, letters, figures or sections of text (eg headings) bold;

> superscript or subscript characters;

> insert page, section or column breaks automatically;

> set and apply styles to text;

> set fonts and font sizes from a wide variety;

> left align, right align or centre text;

> insert headers and footers;

> insert page numbers (folios) in the correct sequence;

> insert footnotes and endnotes;

> enable automatic numbering.

3.4.2 Creating styles in MS Word

Styles or codes are built in to word-processing software. Existing styles can be modified or new ones added. They contain information about the document's structure and formatting that is required for page make-up and which is present electronically, making subsequent layout in the publishing software more efficient (Butcher, Drake & Leach 2006: 402, 2009).

In MS Word, for example, there's a set of default styles that apply to most documents as a matter of course, unless the author or the text editor overrides them with a set of styles that pertain to the font variants and sizes, justification, indentation, leading (line spacing), and so on of a particular publication. These would apply to every feature of a text, from the chapter heading through the various levels of subheading, the body text and displayed quotations, to the bulleted lists, table and figure headings, artwork captions and labels, and even the footnotes or endnotes. In short, every different feature of the design must have a unique style attached to it. Styles are therefore a powerful way of adding structural as well as formatting information to a document.

There is no need to edit onscreen in the font that the author has chosen, or even the one that will be used in the final output, so use styles formatted in a way that you find most comfortable to work with (especially a more readable-sized font). The typesetter's own styles will override yours when the document is imported into their page makeup program (Butcher, Drake & Leach 2006: 423, 2009).

3.4.3 Tagging or coding text (production markup)

If word-processor styles or codes are not implemented in a manuscript, the text editor's brief may include the instruction to tag or code the text in such a way that the typesetter or designer does not have to guess how to structure and format the different features in the manuscript. This is done by inserting a simple set of 'tags' in the text, each tag being unique to a particular structure and format. The typesetter or designer then searches the manuscript for each kind of tag and replaces it with a matching string of computer code that will cause the correct font, font size, justification, indentation, leading, and so on to be output. For example, the three different levels of subheading might be tagged [H1], [H2], [H3]; at the head of a bulleted list, the text editor would insert [bul]. Caption text might be preceded with [Cap]. Italic text would be preceded by a tag such as [i]. Tags that terminate these initiating codes would be something like [/H1], [/H2], [/H3], [/bul], [/Cap] and [/i]. Instead of square brackets, angle brackets could be used: <H1>, <bul>, <i>, etc (Mackenzie 2011: 162–163).

When such tags or codes are used, the text editor should provide a printed legend explaining what each of the tags means when the completed manuscript is handed over for typesetting/design so that the typesetter will be able to implement the styles correctly and consistently. Structural codes can be adapted depending upon their destination – for example, a printed page, a website, a handheld computer or a screen reader. The same codes can therefore be used for different media (Butcher, Drake & Leach 2006: 415, 2009; Mackenzie 2011: 86, 92–93).

3.4.4 Using macros in MS Word

In the words of Waddingham (in Butcher, Drake & Leach 2006: 422, 2009), 'competent on-screen copy-editors use macros – it is the feature that distinguishes efficient copy-editors from the rest more than any other.'

A *macro* is an instruction to perform a series of actions – for example, to perform a sequence of global Find and Replace operations (eg replace double spaces with single spaces; or to insert a space either side of an ellipsis in the middle of a sentence; or to replace unaccented characters with accented equivalents). Macros perform actions in a fraction of the time a text editor would take, and will probably do so more consistently than a text editor. One of the most powerful and easiest to use is FRedit, which is a powerful scripted find-and-replace system for use in MS Word; it is known to reduce editing time significantly (Beverley 2011). They really come into their own during the pre-editing clean-up process and when you want to apply house style decisions across a document (this is one time when, in the interests of greater efficiency, you would want to create one document for the entire text). Using macros frees the text editor from having to correct mundane errors manually, saving you considerable time but, perhaps more importantly, enabling you to focus on the more creative and enjoyable aspects of the content without distractions (Butcher, Drake & Leach 2006: 422, 2009; Beverley 2011).

Word processors such as MS Word usually have built-in macro-recorder. To create a macro, turn the recorder on, perform a series of actions, stop it, then store it for future use – it's as simple as that. To repeat the same operation (eg find and replace), simply run the macro.

3.4.5 Predictive text (autocorrect function)

Traditionally, the autocorrect function in a word processor is used to correct predefined spelling errors (though not *all possible* errors) automatically (eg *teh* vs *the*; *speling* vs *spelling*). However, it can also be used to save keystrokes where the same text must be input repeatedly: microorganism; the International Monetary Fund, the Periodic Table, and so on.

The text to be automatically inserted is stored by the word processor and linked to a unique key combination of your choosing: pressing Ctrl + Alt + I, for example, may cause 'the International Monetary Fund' to be inserted at the position of the cursor.

Clearly, predictive text can be a useful time-saver for inputting repetitive standard text (Butcher, Drake & Leach 2006: 424, 2009).

The possibilities opened up by and the advantages of word processors are legion, and text editors who do not use them to the full when editing electronically are really foolish. These functions normally help you to prepare and polish a document to a higher standard and they make a wise saving of time and costs possible.

From the point of view of the text editor, probably the most useful function is Find and Replace (cf Beverley 2011; Billingham 2002: 100; LEO 2007a; Mossop 2010: 103). The Go to function is a close second in usefulness, taking, as it does, the editor directly to the exact page number, section, word, table, etc specified in no time at all. Mossop (2010: 103) calls Find and Replace the single most useful function that a word processor can offer a text editor. At the same time, however, he warns that the text editor must be extremely cautious when using the Find and Replace function, especially the overhasty and unthinking use of Replace All. For example, you never know what kinds of change will be made if you instruct the computer to replace all occurrences of 'ise' with 'ize': 'wise' will become 'wize', 'prise' will become 'prize' – and neither new spelling will be correct! Or globally replacing 'eg' with 'e.g.' will probably lead to absurdities such as 'ille.g.al'! The worst thing about having done this sort of global replacement is that it's impossible to reverse – unless you close the document without saving it (in which case you might lose other unsaved changes too).

The best advice, therefore, is this: 'it is probably best to avoid the Replace All option' (Thill & Bovée 2002; 2005: 150–151). It is usually safer to search case by case using the Find Next option and then to decide whether each item should be replaced or not. If it should be replaced, select Replace; if not, select Find Next and move on.

By first taking the trouble to check, for instance, capital letters, spaces and punctuation, you will save an enormous amount of time and frustration later in the process – and your doing so could also lead to much greater consistency. LEO (2007a) suggests that it makes sense to activate the Find and Replace function before you start editing the first draft (that is, once it has been read through quickly). LEO argues that once this technical stage has been completed early on in the editing process, it leaves the text editor free to focus on how the author's meaning is conveyed.

This approach can be adopted, among other things, to do the following (once you have decided to effect changes to the manuscript):

List 4.9 Possibilities for electronic checking

> › To detect and correct generally incorrect words and phrases. For example: it is easy to misuse the homophones bare vs bear; wait vs weight; dye vs die. The context in which each is used in a sentence determines which is the correct form, of course: it is not usually a question of either the one or the other. The same applies to alternatives such as all together vs altogether and any one vs anyone.

>>

> This approach is also helpful in tracking down the numerous preventable typing errors that occur in texts: seh instead of she; onw instead of own; litttle instead of little, and so on.

> To automate the recognition of errors.

> To check punctuation. Are there two spaces after the full stop at the end of a sentence, or only one? Are there spaces before colons, semicolons, commas and full stops? These can be corrected quite mechanically and easily throughout the text. If the dash, the exclamation mark or the semicolon are overused, check and, if necessary, reduce the number. The incorrect use of the comma in connection with adjective strings (strings of classifying adjectives ('geometric, enviro-friendly, German'), and strings of qualitative adjectives ('tall, dark, handsome') must be separated by commas; when the two types are mixed, there should be no comma between them ('tall French gentleman') must be corrected. And either defining or non-defining clauses will also need the editor's attention ('The house that is painted green is mine' – no commas around the defining clause; 'My house, which is painted blue, is Victorian' – a pair of commas must enclose the non-defining clause).

> To identify sentence patterns. Writers often lapse into stereotypical writing patterns, and in the long term that can become stylistically disturbing. Identify these forms individually and correct them.

> To detect and correct incorrect spellings of names, acronyms, contractions and abbreviations. This would include the spelling of words generally.

> To detect particular terms and to arrange them in lists.

> To correct an initial uppercase character (President) to lowercase (president) and vice versa, select More on the Find and Replace dialog, then check Match use on before starting to find occurrences.

> To replace italics with, say un-italics or bold, select Format in the Find and Replace dialog. Then specify the font style for the Find item, then the font for the Replace item before starting to find occurrences.

In conclusion: use the function with good judgement, but also with the conviction that it can make a difference to the time it takes to complete a project, while at the same time relieving you of the tedious, repetitive aspects of text editing.

3.4.6 Spell-checkers

> When you consider that the spell-check function has been around since the beginning of desktop publishing history, it is amazing that more people don't use it. I know I can't spell, and ... I know that other writers can't either. *There is no excuse for releasing documents that contain spelling errors. Do a spell-check!*
> *http://www.docsymmetry.com*

In general, spell-checkers are regarded as particularly useful tools in any text-editing process (cf Anonymous 2006a; 2006d; Billingham 2002: 97–98; Jansen & Steehouder 2001: 12–36; LEO 2007a; Mossop 2010: 103; Van de Poel 2006: 146–147). The spell-checking function is particularly handy because it can identify spelling and typing errors easily and then, with a few clicks of a mouse, they can be corrected onscreen. Research by Du Plessis (1999: 117) indicates that about 34% of the language errors that text editors identified in a study were spelling or orthographic errors. So, by correcting 40% of the immediate errors using a spell-checker, a manuscript can be improved considerably.

It is important to appreciate that spell-checkers are merely tools that are activated consciously and in a planned manner in order to improve a document: they do not activate themselves automatically. The text editor therefore has to take a firm decision to use a spell-checker. Moreover, we advise you not to place too much trust in this tool, because it can easily miss errors. As Anonymous (2006a) put it: electronic tools have serious limitations. They are useful, but not comprehensive. Text editors should use them 'but dare not rely on them because they miss too much'. They are only as good as the purpose for which they are programmed, that is, the extent of the data (words in the dictionary of the spell-checker) and their potential to recognise errors determines how good they are. (See chapter 11 for examples of spell-checkers.)

It is not possible for spell-checkers to cover the full vocabulary of a language as global as English: there are just too many variables that prevent it doing so. How spell-checkers work is this: the software goes through text word for word to check whether every one is correctly spelled (Billingham 2002: 96–97). It does so mechanically, checking every word in isolation; it cannot, therefore, highlight context-sensitive errors. Spell-checkers do not know, for example, when homophones such as *die* vs *dye* and *bate* vs *bait* differ in their meanings; they also don't 'understand' the use of pleonasms (eg the semantic meaning of the expressions *revert back* and *necessary prerequisite*). As far as a spell-checker is concerned, if a word is correctly spelt, it is correct – whether the meaning is appropriate in context or not. This is problematic, because it can lead to the incorrect spelling being used in a particular context (eg *form*, not *from*; *trail*, not *trial*). Such software can therefore merely check what *has* been written and not what the writer *intended* to do with the text.

Spell-checkers are not perfect, because a computer is simply an apparatus that is utilised to look up words in an electronic alphabetical list and to test whether a particular word matches one in the list. Consequently, this is the dilemma with spell-checkers: they offer a great number of possibilities, but not *all* possibilities. Furthermore, they do not always understand precisely what the user wants to do or have (Craig 2005: 149–152). Anonymous (2006d) says: 'Spell checkers are the copy editor's worst nightmare' – precisely because they can't always be completely trusted. They are wonderful tools when they are used correctly and consistently (LEO 2007a), but texts must still be read after spell-checkers have been used on them to ensure that other language and grammatical errors have been corrected.

These days the majority of spell-checkers have built-in thesauruses that indicate synonyms while the software is working through a text. The larger the thesaurus, the greater the chances of an incorrectly spelt word being detected and corrected with the press of a key. In this process, there should be no need to have another program, such as an electronic dictionary, running.

In this way, text editors should not hesitate to make spell-checkers a habit-forming part of their editing process, because they detect so many obvious errors and correct them so quickly. But don't rely on them as the alpha and omega of text editing – they are still not currently sophisticated enough to correct all errors (Billingham 2002: 96–97). Enquist & Oates (2009: 21) say that users should not become too complacent about spell-checkers, because even 'the best computer software does not know a "trail" from a "trial"'. It remains a good habit always to run a spell-checker through an electronic document as soon as you receive it. And before you finally hand in a document, it makes sense to run the spell-checker through it again, for the sake of checking at a more refined level that the document which leaves your hands has at least had the spelling and typing errors, as well as repeated words, removed from the manuscript. Your reputation as text editor could depend upon it.

In conclusion: use the function with discretion, as an aid, and don't allow it to become a crutch.

3.4.7 Grammar- and style-checkers

Spell-checkers are frequently used as a crutch rather than as a tool (Billingham 2002: 98; Craig 2005: 150). Anonymous (2006e) says this is even more the case with grammar- and style-checkers, the primary purpose of which is to evaluate whether the language usage in a text meets the requirements of the language of the currently open document.

It is difficult to test whether the word usage of and the sentence construction in the text corresponds to the often complex grammar rules of a particular language. It is also difficult for any grammar- or style-checker to perform its function 100% correctly because the checker doesn't know exactly what the language is trying to convey to the reader. Even if the rules of grammar have been correctly applied, the checker still can't indicate whether the message has been successfully conveyed (Thill & Bovée 2005: 149–150). Its use can create the expectation that the grammatical and stylistic errors can be identified electronically and consequently that they can also be corrected with the click of a mouse. Usually this is not possible, and the excessive use of a grammar-checker remains highly risky, at least until products that can detect and correct every possible error become available.

Mossop (2010: 104–106) asserts that these types of checker are not so effective in tracking down syntactical problems, for example; they are, he says, sometimes more of a nuisance than a help.

In conclusion: this type of software can offer a degree of help, but it has to be used with discretion and used to check errors jointly with the human text editor. There are already grammar- and style-checkers for a number of languages (including English) that are achieving reasonable success, but in a number of languages such checkers do not yet exist or they are still in development.

Some of the uses of a grammar- and style-checker are:

List 4.10 Advantages of a grammar- and style-checker

› *Syntax:*
  – Determine the correct grammatical constructions, for example the use of *well-known man* vs *man is well known; could not have* vs *not could have* or *could have not.*

› *Lexicon:*
  – Determine the word choice, for example the correct use of *sin* vs *seen* vs *scene.*
  – Highlight offensive words (by labelling them).

› *Spelling*:
  – Determine whether words are one word, hyphenated or two words, for example: *cooperate* vs *co-operate* and *no one* vs *no-one.*

› *Punctuation*:
  – Determine the correct use of punctuation marks, such as: single vs double quotation marks (inverted commas); in quotations that form a part of sentence, whether the final punctuation precedes or follows the quotation marks; whether there should always be a comma before 'but also' and 'because'; whether 'however' is followed by a comma at the start of a sentence, is surrounded by commas mid-sentence, and is preceded by a comma at the end of a sentence.

› *Consistency*:
  – Prevent inconsistent language usage, such as: *in addition* vs *additionally; paediatrician* vs *pediatrician; agriculturist* vs *agriculturalist.* Choose one form and adhere to it throughout the manuscript.

These advantages can be expressed as follows:

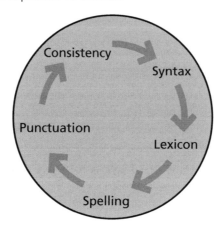

Figure 4.3 *The use of a grammar-checker*

3.4.8 Thesauruses

Another useful software tool for the text editor is the thesaurus. Typically, in a word processor such as MS Word, this tool will search a database for and display words similar in meaning to a word the text editor has selected in the text. This can be very useful when the author has used a word repeatedly and the text editor feels that one or more synonyms are needed; or a verb form instead of a noun (or vice versa), for instance, might be required. Once activated, the thesaurus window will display the various available options for the editor to select from. There's sometimes even a pronunciation key that activates a list of synonyms with their phonetic spellings to help the text editor decide whether the word selected is indeed the correct one.

Again, this is rather a mechanical tool: it certainly will not replace the human brain of the text editor; but it is accessible electronically, quick and easy to use, and helpful in displaying a number of synonymous options almost instantaneously.

3.4.9 Resources (such as dictionaries) on CD or online

Nowadays, there's almost no need for the text editor to possess a print version of a dictionary, because there are so many good ones built in to word processing packages or available on compact disc or the internet (eg see www.dictionaries.com).

The advantages of these resources are that they're rarely out of date (they're updated regularly to incorporate new words and meanings), quickly and easily accessible, and sometimes it's possible to cut-and-paste words from the resource into the manuscript, which helps to eliminate author's or text editor's typing or spelling errors.

Most of the major dictionary publishers (including Oxford, Cambridge and Merriam-Webster) have their word lists available in electronic format in addition to print versions. These tend to be more up to date than published print editions.

Note, however, that reliance on the online 'resource' known as Wikipedia is risky at best (Lih 2009). It is by no means authoritative or reliable, because any user in the world is able to 'contribute' to its content. Before any information on this site can be relied upon, therefore, it should be checked against and verified by that in other encyclopaedic websites, such as *Encyclopaedia Britannica*.

3.4.10 Google and other search engines

Possibly one of the key roles a text editor can play on behalf of the author and the publisher is to check spellings, accented characters, brand names, dates and other information, which occur in texts. A really quick and easy way to do so is via a reputable search engine.

Google is one such search engine. It explores the entire internet for key words that match the character string you enter into its search window. (Other search engines, or browsers, are Internet Explorer and Mozilla Firefox. A technique known as 'search engine optimisation' (SEO) makes such exploring and searching for key words possible.)

Ironically, while the time to taken to access information can be very short and information can be found very quickly, surfing the internet for information can turn out to be very time-consuming, for a number of reasons, so text editors should keep a close eye on the time whenever they do browse the internet – especially if time is money. One of the reasons for internet-browsing being so time-consuming is that there can sometimes be literally tens of thousands of websites to choose from. Another is that the user can become distracted by the plethora of fascinating information revealed by the browser.

But the information available is usually only as good and reliable as its creators, so make it a rule of thumb that you will consult at least three websites to corroborate information before deciding on a particular spelling (Amritsar and Chhattisgarh in India) or an accented character (raison d'être, mañana and façade) or a version of a brand name (DaimlerChrysler, smart car and TagHeuer).

Before deciding on which websites to enter, consider their authenticity or reliability: 'official' sites (eg of fan clubs and learned societies) are likely to render much more reliable and accurate information than non-official ones; corporate websites are more liable to put out detailed and reliable information about themselves than not.

Another important use to which the internet can be put is to run plagiarism-checks on selected text or entire manuscripts. This has become standard practice at many tertiary institutions, where student papers, dissertations and theses are all checked for unattributed wholesale 'borrowings' from sources (using software such as *ithenticate* and *turnitin*)

(Shober 2011: 115–117); the practice has become almost as common for manuscripts heading for publication, whether in magazines or in books. As a result, it has become the task of the text editor to check manuscripts for plagiarism, whether inadvertent or intentional (see section 9 in chapter 3).

The abovementioned advantages of electronic advances are obvious and a combination of them makes the editing of texts much easier and quicker.

The steps that are taken in the process of combined electronic and hard-copy editing (cf Butcher, Drake & Leach 2006: 6, 15–16, 2009; Clarke 2001: 74–76; Einsohn 2005: 4–10; Merriam-Webster 2001: 235–240) are virtually identical to those in hard copy format editing (see table 4.1 above). The detail of the process is described below. Before you begin, make doubly sure that you know precisely what the client expects you to do to the text.

Step 1: Evaluate the manuscript

Once an electronic copy of the manuscript has been made, someone must check that all its parts are present (see list 4.5 above again).

- Go through the text quickly and determine what the quality (or lack of quality) of the text is, and how much time the editing can be expected to take. Obtain a macro view of the text in the process.
- Compile a project plan that can and should be adhered to so that progress can be measured in terms of steps, goals and deadlines.
- Every text is unique and requires a unique approach.

Step 2: Organise the text: Decide how the changes will be indicated

- This has to tie in with the client's way of working and often also with the deadline that the printer has set for the printing.
- The combined method involves the text first being subjected to a spell-check and a grammar- and style-check if these functions are available. Excessive word spaces should also be eliminated at this stage. (Sentences should be separated by a single space only.) Only then should the hard copy be worked on. After this step, the text can be printed and the corrections made first by hand.
- The text editor could, alternatively, perform the lion's share of the work onscreen and only later print the manuscript out so that it can be checked by hand, using a pencil or a pen. Their preferred mode of working will determine the order in which the onscreen and the hard-copy editing are done.
- Determine the procedure:
    - Ensure that the brief is clear and that client requests have been understood.
- Agree on how the changes to the text will be made:
    - with the client: by hand and/or electronically.
    - with the typesetter/designer (if necessary).

- Agree on the process:
    - Run spell-, grammar- and style-checkers throughout the complete manuscript. (Step 3)
    - Make additional corrections by hand. (Step 4)
    - Incorporate all the additional corrections into the electronic text. (Step 4)
    - Check one last time: either electronically or by hand on a printout, or both. (Step 5)
    - Always make an electronic copy of the revised text (or part of it) and store it safely.
    - Incorporate the author's feedback (in response to your queries) into the text electronically. (Step 8)

Step 3: First edit of the text: the text itself ('rough edit of the text')

- First check the parts of the text.
- Activate the spell-checker and check all obvious errors (such as typing ('typos'), spelling and punctuation errors). As far as possible, correct these errors. This is quite a mechanical process that can be made easier onscreen by the use of a macro or the find and replace function in MS Word.
- If they are available, a grammar- and a style-checker can also be used here.
- Make choices that help you to achieve consistency (spelling, punctuation, word spacing, capitalisation, hyphenation, parallelism, numbers, dates and currency, etc).
- If a large document has been supplied as a number of separate files, it is often a good idea to combine them all while the mechanical–electronic checks are conducted. In this way, the text editor is more likely to make the same kinds of correction throughout the document. Where this is not possible and the documents have to be checked separately, it is a good idea to make a list of the errors that have to be searched for and corrected to ensure consistency across the entire document.
- Make lists of potential problem cases: problematic spellings, unknown words or terminology that it's almost impossible to look up in sources, and things (of whatever nature) you want to ask the author about (such as facts or numbers that appear to be incorrect or contradictory).
    - The 'Comment' function in MS Word is especially helpful for indicating corrections that need to be made, problem cases that need to be followed up on and raising queries (such as about facts or numbers).
- Make changes affecting (Merriam-Webster 2001: 235–240):
    - spacing
    - font style (typeface)
    - font size
    - the format of headings and subheadings, and of sections and subsections
    - abbreviations and acronyms
    - the use of uppercase and lowercase

- the deletion of spaces after full stops and commas, and before other punctuation marks
- the reduction of spaces between sentences to one only
- the way of writing dates, numbers, currency and SI units and symbols
- the indentation of text
- displaying long quotations (instead of embedding them)
- the use of single and double quotation marks
- the use of the ellipsis
- the use of (or conversion of text to) bullets – whether numbered or not
- a lack of parallelism or incorrect sequencing
- the style of any intext references.
- Type provisional instructions to the typesetter, for example colour sections and capital letters between square brackets.

Step 4: Second edit of the text: the non-text parts ('rough edit of everything else')

- With the more mechanical changes made, now print the text and continue to work on the hard copy. At this stage the text has already been 'cleaned up', that is, obvious errors have been identified and corrected.
- Check:
  - title page and table of contents
  - tables, figures, diagrams, illustration and photographs (that is, all illustrative matter)
  - references
  - quotations.
- Bibliographical references
- Cross-check:
  - the numbering of headings and subheadings (are they correct and logical?).
  - figures or tables (are they (indicated) in the correct places in the manuscript?).
  - that the wording in the table of contents agrees with that in the text itself.
- At this stage, all the corrections done on the hard copy can be transferred to the electronic version of the text.
- Always make an electronic copy of the revised text (or part of it) and store it safely.

Step 5: Checking everything ('smooth edit of everything')

- The document is, to all intents and purposes, complete; but the text editor should go through it once more to remove any lingering errors, such as potential inconsistencies or conflicts in the manuscript.
  - This can be done either onscreen or manually on the printout, or both.
- Ensure that the entire manuscript (the text plus all the other non-text components, such as tables, figures, table of contents, footnotes and bibliography) forms a single textual unit.

Step 6: Production markup: Indicating to the setter special typographical treatment of the text

A production markup (or type coding) entails identifying those elements of the manuscript that are not regular body text. This is done by means of simple 'tags' or 'codes' (such as <H1> for a first-level heading or [ital]word[/ital] to indicate the start and end of italics). Typically, this coding is applied to:
* part and chapter numbers, titles and subtitles;
* headings and subheadings;
* lists, extracts and displayed quotations;
* table and figure numbers, titles or captions, source lines;
* footnotes or endnotes;
* special characters (Greek, mathematical) that can't be inserted or should be highlighted;
* any other special features (sometimes italic and bold type, for instance)
  - On hard copy the 'tags' are normally written in the left margin of the manuscript; onscreen the codes are usually inserted at the beginning and end of each element. The typesetter searches through these codes, replacing them with code strings that result in each element being formatted correctly.

Step 7: Queries to the author/client

* Author queries have to be (tactfully) presented to the author (electronically, or on hard copy).
* Give a copy of the document to your client.
* Set a limit on reacting to the proofs to ensure that the process doesn't become too drawn out.

Step 8: Additional documentation

* Check all additional documentation connected to the manuscript. Is it present? And accurate?
* Ensure that the client's briefs and requests are absolutely clear.
* Check all the specifications for the typographical design of the manuscript.
* Check the captions and numbering of all the tables and schemata.
* Check that all the client's instructions have been carried out.

Step 9: Incorporation of the author's feedback

The author's feedback (mostly in response to the text editor's queries) is incorporated directly into the electronic copy of the manuscript.

Step 10: Final check of everything

* Ensure that you have received responses to all your queries in the manuscript.
* Check if the corrections have been incorporated in the correct places in the manuscript.

- At this stage, the text editor should consider running the spell- and grammar-checkers through the manuscript once more. This will ensure that the corrections and other changes have not introduced new errors.

Step 11: The final edited manuscript

- In addition to supplying the electronic version of the edited document, you may also have to print out two copies of the final edited pages, depending upon whether your client has indicated they want to receive only the final electronic version or that plus a printout of the 'Final' Track Changes document, or both the Final and the Final Showing Changes versions. Before you hand over anything at this stage, first check with the client what exactly they're expecting to receive.
- Check:
    - whether all the parts of the manuscript are indeed present
    - whether they are in the correct sequence.
- Keep an electronic copy of the final edited manuscript in a safe place.

Step 12: Proofreading

- After the client has manipulated the document (by sending it to a typesetter to be laid out per the design specifications), the text is usually proofread (see sections 5 and 6 of this chapter).
- The proofreading can be done either by the text editor themself (for a fee, unless another arrangement has been agreed upon) or by the fresh (and often less expensive) pair of eyes of a separate proofreader (Einsohn 2005: 11). With some justification, some text editors feel strongly that they should see the proofs at least once before the document is published, just so that they can resolve any outstanding problems or inconsistencies before printing (it is usually the editor, not the proofreader, who comes under fire from reviewers and readers who detect errors in the printed document!) (Flann & Hill 2004: 13).

Step 13: Signing-off of the complete book prior to printing

- Hand over the final form of the manuscript to the client.
- The client will have decided at the outset in what format (electronic and/or hard copy) they wanted to receive the manuscript.
- The text editor writes a letter or an email confirming that the work has been completed (see annexures B1 and B2 for examples of letters of confirmation).
- Submit your invoice (see page 222) for the completed work to the client.
- Start looking for the next assignment.

This method is, of course, not infallible, nor is it prescriptive. But it is a useful guide based on the experience of practising language practitioners and on the literature on the subject. As text editor you yourself should decide which of the three options works for you and your client: the hard-copy method, the electronic approach or the combination of the two. It is probably not worth using the combination for short documents, though (Butcher, Drake & Leach 2006: 404, 2009): it really comes into its own on long, complex manuscripts.

The advantages of the onscreen method combined with the broader view of the text that paper-based editing affords usually leads to this method being more effective in practice. Waddingham (in Butcher, Drake & Leach 2006: 403) supports the view that this approach is especially useful when a large manuscript has to be edited, because the conventional correction marks don't have to be used and the text editor mainly works with the text, so that you (as the intermediary between the author and the reader) can understand it. This in turn considerably reduces the chances of misunderstandings slipping through to the printed book. The use of a computer also enables the text editor to use a spell-checker to detect and correct a large number of errors in a very short time – a much more effective use of the text editor's time, plus they are more likely to correct more errors consistently throughout a manuscript. On the other hand, it is certainly important to be aware of the strengths and weaknesses of electronic aids and not to rely exclusively on them (Craig 2005: 152) (see sections 3.4.1 to 3.4.10).

4 The knowledge needed to be able to edit a text

Editors have upgraded their skills in response to the revolution in information technology; they are proficient in word processing and electronic file management, and some of them have mastered layout and graphic design programs as well.
Mackenzie

The copy editor will sometimes be more of a specialist in the subject ... It is therefore often left to a first-rate copy editor to turn an awkward, eccentric, incoherent manuscript into a cogent and credible text. ...

A copy editor must naturally have mastered the standard rules of English style. But he or she should also be an avid reader of good prose, since wide and thoughtful reading is what most reliably produces the kind of taste and critical discrimination that form the solidest foundation for an editor's judgment.
Merriam-Webster

So far in this book (compare chapter 2; also section 8 in chapter 3) mention has been made a number of times about the kinds of knowledge and skill a text editor must be in command of in order to meet the requirements of their work. It has become clear that what is meant are the kinds of knowledge dealt with in this section. Such knowledge becomes integrated into the text editor's professional offering to get the job done; and not just one or another aspect of it, but all of their knowledge should come into play during the editing process.

In summary, the combination of knowledge comes down to the following list. Immediately thereafter, we consider each aspect in greater detail.

› *General background*:
  • General knowledge
  Subsidiary inputs:
  • Knowledge of relevant sources
  • Knowledge of networks where you can obtain quick answers

› *Pragmatic or occupation-related knowledge*:
  • Knowledge of the language practice environment
  • Knowledge of the publishing industry
  • Knowledge of the private sector
  • Knowledge of the freelance world

› *Knowledge of the text*:
  • Knowledge of the language of the text
  • Knowledge of communication models
  Genres:
  • Knowledge of literary theory/theories
  • Knowledge of the texts of business communication
  • Knowledge of journalism
  Content:
  • Knowledge of relevant specialist areas (specialisms)

› *Knowledge of language theory*:
  • Knowledge of general language theory
  • Knowledge of normative language theory

› *Language proficiency*:
  • Knowledge of the particular idiom
  • Knowledge of how to write

› *Knowledge of argumentation*:
  • Knowledge of the structure of argumentation
  • Knowledge of paragraphing

› *Technical aptitude*:
  • Knowledge of the relevant editorial techniques
  • Knowledge of technology that applies to the process of text editing
  • Knowledge of bibliographical referencing techniques

› *Visual aptitude*:
  • Knowledge of document design
  • Knowledge of typography

The more detailed version is:

General background

- General knowledge: needed so that authors can be protected from their own errors (Mackenzie 2011: 60).

Subsidiary inputs

- Knowledge of relevant sources: you must know where to find answers to (a) enquiries about all sorts of applied linguistics issues and to (b) questions about facts, dates, events, and so on (Cleaveland 1999; Judd 1990).
- Knowledge of networks where you can obtain quick answers to your numerous questions. Botha (2008) says that these kinds of network (via internet chat groups or associations of language practitioners) do indispensable work to make the task of a text editor easier, because members of a network will usually have already posed questions about the same matter, have investigated it, and are able to elicit quick responses. In this way, networks save both time and effort.

Pragmatic or occupation-related knowledge

- Knowledge of the language-practice environment in which language practitioners (translators, interpreters, text editors, indexers) operate when you have to perform as an editor: it makes sense to be familiar with the full context of the language practice profession in order to be able to grasp the unique role that the text editor plays.
- Knowledge of the publishing industry if you work in that industry, so that you're better placed to understand the demands that the industry places on the production and polishing of texts (cf Butcher, Drake & Leach 2006: 3, 2009; Davies & Balkwill 2011; Einsohn 2005; Greco 2005; Haynes 2010; Hendry 2011; Mackenzie 2011; Morrish 1998, 2003; Murphy 2011; Treebus 1995, 1997 – see also section 5.1 in chapter 3).
- Knowledge of the private sector (Mackenzie 2011: 30–31).
- Knowledge of the freelance world (cf Bishop, Linnegar & Pretorius 2011; Linnegar, Marus & De Wet 2012; Mackenzie 2011: 199–217; Murphy 2011: 71–72).

Knowledge of the text

- Knowledge of the language of the text in order to be able to understand (a) how text has to be composed so that it forms a textual unit (ie, how texts form fixed structures) and (b) the number of text types that can be distinguished. Also a knowledge of intertextuality which helps us to understand the influence that different texts have on one another (Carstens 2003; Renkema 2004, 2009; see also section 7.1 in chapter 2).
- Knowledge of communication models.

Genres

- Knowledge of literary theory/theories if you are likely to work on literary texts (Mackenzie 2011: 25, 71–73).

- Knowledge of the texts about business communications (Murphy 2011).
- Knowledge of journalism as a genre if you are likely to work as a subeditor in a newspaper or a magazine's editorial bureau (cf Bowles & Borden 2011; Conley & Lamble 2006; Greer (ed) 2008; Leiter, Harriss & Johnson 2000; Nel 2001; Stepp 1989):

Content
- Knowledge of relevant specialist fields (such as the business sector, medicine, the law, the environment, and so on) if you are likely to work in these areas, as well as knowing where to find the solutions to problems when they crop up during the editing process.

Knowledge of language theory

Knowledge of general language theory: a knowledge of syntax, morphology, semantics, sociolinguistics and pragmatics (see again chapter 2). According to the website http://www.gotlinks.com (AVS 2006), the text editor sits an 'examination' in the language theory of each subject they edit in, and their subject knowledge gets tested in the process of putting theoretical knowledge into practice.

Knowledge of normative language theory: knowledge of the latest rules of spelling and punctuation; of language standards, that is, about what is right and wrong in language and the ability to argue about it; knowledge of style and register (see again section 4 of chapter 2 and sections 4 and 5 of chapter 8).

Language proficiency

- Knowledge of the particular idiom of the target language.
- Knowledge of how to write: so that advice can be given about good and effective writing techniques (Mackenzie 2011: 59; also Alamargot & Chanquoy 2001).

Knowledge of argumentation

- Knowledge of the structure of argumentation: so that you can understand how an argument should be built up and sustained; and what should be avoided in the process (cf Janssen & Steehouder 2001; Mossop 2010: 74; Van de Poel 2006; Van de Poel & Gasiorek 2007; compare chapter 7 section 3).
- Knowledge of paragraphing: so that the text is divided up into paragraphs in order to communicate most effectively (Cheney 1990. 2005; Mossop 2010: 76–77; see also chapter 7 section 2).

Technical aptitude/proficiency

- Knowledge of the relevant editing techniques: you must know how to go about editing a text – see section 5 in this chapter.
- Knowledge of technology that applies to the process of text editing (Mackenzie 2011: 192; see sections 3.3 and 3.4 above as well as section 6 in this chapter.

- Knowledge of bibliographical referencing techniques: so you can determine whether the correct bibliographical system or style has been followed and whether cross-references to sources are correct (cf Anderson & Poole 2009: 12–15, 98, 130–133; Einsohn 2005: 49, 290–292; Lipson 2011; Lourens 2007; Turabian 2007, 2010: 147–159, 160–173, 168, 177–178, 199–202; see also chapter 11 section 4).
- Electronic techniques for compiling bibliographies are fairly readily available. These include <http://www.endnoteweb.com> and <http://www.easybib.com/>. Word 2007 and later contain an equivalent technique: click on 'Insert', then on 'Document element' and finally on 'Bibliography'.

Visual aptitude/proficiency

- Knowledge of document design: so that you can understand how to compose documents in the most optimal way (Campbell 1995; Schriver 1997; see also section 8 of chapter 2 and section 3 of chapter 10).
- Knowledge of typography: you must know how the space on a page is affected by the editing process; how typeface, font size and the placement of headings affects the text and the overall appearance of a page (cf Mackenzie 2011: 191–192; also Ambrose & Harris 2005, Cheney 1990: 118–125; Felici 2003; Jansen & Steehouder 2001; Mitchell & Wightman 2005; Walker 2001). See further on this topic section 2 of chapter 10.

In fact, the text editor must *know* a lot – and then *do* a lot with it!

5 Author queries: when to raise them

> For a copyeditor, *good querying skills* – knowing when to query (and when not to query) and how to query effectively – are as important as a solid grasp of punctuation and grammar.
> *Einsohn*

> A good copy editor will spot everything that is *questionable* or *inconsistent*, and will ask you, politely, if this is what you really mean, and perhaps it might be better to rephrase this sentence ...
> *Allen*

> *Willingness to check* is one of the surest signs of competence.
> *Anonymous*

At both the editing and the proofreading stage, the text editor is expected to detect problems that only the author can resolve, and to raise author queries.

Closely related to the debate about whether the text editor should be a good generalist who is able to adopt a questioning approach to the texts they work on or whether they should take on only those texts whose subjects they have a commanding knowledge of is this reality: it is impossible for a text editor to know everything. They must therefore be expected to raise queries about a range of matters during the course of editing a manuscript (some would even argue that to have a questioning mind is more useful to an editor than subject knowledge – and this includes not being intimidated by one's author but rather putting yourself in the position of the average reader and asking whether they would have difficulty understanding the author's text):

- Saller (2009: 16) suggests that there are some important benefits to asking questions before you begin editing a manuscript: they showcase your capability; they can save you work later; and the writer's answers give you clues to their personality and preferences. But in managing your relationship with an author, questions also serve another important purpose: they can foster a collaborative environment rather than an adversarial one.
- If there is (any) doubt about the factual correctness of content that is being worked on, you have to raise a query. This usually includes dates, places, events, addresses, the correct registered names of companies, internet addresses, the completeness of assertions or statements – whatever the case may be. As text editor you cannot be held responsible for correcting all of these matters (Einsohn 2005: 9), but it would be unprofessional if you were to allow obvious errors to slip through. At least you should have raised an author query to obtain the correct information from the author.
- If your common sense and experience indicate that something in a manuscript is incorrect, the matter or statement concerned must be dealt with (Einsohn 2005: 41). It is important to know that your judgement has not let you down.
- If you are uncertain about a particular form of language usage, irrespective of what type it is (spelling, punctuation and/or grammar), you have to follow up to resolve it. It is the text editor's duty to look for the correct form to use in an appropriate source and then to implement it. Doing so can involve the text editor in contacting the author to ascertain for certain what the author actually means (Merriam-Webster 2001: 233–235; Saller 2009: 26–27).
- When uncertainty arises over style issues, before you consult any other reference works, you should seek the answer by first consulting the appropriate house style guide. But exercise flexibility when you do so: perhaps the author's or the particular discipline's way is not incorrect and has been applied consistently anyway.
- When inconsistencies occur, for example if an author expresses their views on an issue in one way in one reference and then they contradict themselves when referring to the same issue, then something is wrong and the contradiction must be resolved. The editor must then ascertain why it has arisen and solve the problem.
- If parts of a text are missing, such as footnotes that are referred to but cannot be found in the manuscript, or if bibliographical references in the text refer to a source that cannot be found in the bibliography, the editor has to query it with the author (and should certainly not try to provide the solution or fill in missing information themselves).
- Furthermore: anything about which the editor has doubts must be checked. It is a sign of professionalism when that which 'does not look correct' is re-read and either

corrected or justified. It's not for nothing that Anonymous (2006b) says that 'a willingness to check is one of the surest signs of competence'. Each text editor therefore needs to be equipped with well-developed editorial intuition as well as more than a modicum of editorial judgement – they will come in handy whenever something in a text niggles or causes concern.

Einsohn (2005: 41–43) suggests that the manner in which author queries are raised deserves special attention.

List 4.12 Raising author queries

> Make a special effort to nurture a good (working) relationship with both the author and your client or publisher (Linnegar 2008: 63–64). Doing so helps to make it easier to deal with matters should conflict arise. As far as possible, also keep the author informed about how the process will pan out and what they can expect to happen or to contribute along the way. It is also a good idea for you to have sight of correspondence between the author and the client or publisher so that you are better prepared to work with the author.

> Remember that writing and editing are not competing or competitive pursuits: they should complement each other. You should not be trying to prove you are better or wiser than your author; you should simply be helping them to publish a near-flawless product (Merriam-Webster 2001: 233–235; Saller 2009: 32, 34–35).

> Raise any questions with the author from the perspective of the reader. The fundamental question should be: 'Would the reader understand it better if it were expressed differently?'

> Frame questions positively rather than negatively: positive questions are more conducive to collaborative relationships; negative questions to adversarial ones (Saller 2009: 16).

> Author queries should not alienate your author. They should therefore not be demanding, intimidating, sarcastic, conflictual or belittling (Merriam-Webster 2001: 234–235). Indeed, the manner in which questions are posed can lead to problem-solving outcomes rather than the alienation of the author – the example below illustrates this point.

> > Problem: A certain statement can, in the judgement of the text editor, be interpreted as sexist. It would be injudicious of the editor to let it stand without raising a query with the author about their concern; but a tactful, diplomatic approach is required when approaching the author, especially about a matter as sensitive as this.

>>

Incorrect approach: *It is sexist to state this and you will look like a fool if you let it go through as it stands.*

Preferable approach: *Your statement could possibly be interpreted as sexist. What about considering one of these possible alternatives?*

› If an author annoys you, you could be tempted to make snide remarks while raising queries with them. You are allowing your ego to get in the way of your professionalism (Saller 2009: 27, 34–35, 37, 99). Doing so will not do either you or the reader any good, so resist the temptation: rather allow yourself to calm down first and then to approach the text afresh. There are better ways of approaching problems with authors and texts than by getting involved in petty and unproductive disputes. Murphy (2011: 5) says: you 'must have respect for the client'. Do not forget this.

› Einsohn (2005: 45) points out the following to text editors: if all authors were first rate, careful, dedicated and highly trained when it comes to writing, editors would be out of jobs. Therefore, she says, value an author's (honest) attempt at writing – it will give you the opportunity to hone it into the instrument it can be!

6 What the text editor should actually do and not do

The main function of the copy-editor is to ensure that the typesetter receives complete, clear and self-explanatory copy.
Foster

Given that there is no consensus about how to spell *copyediting*, it is not surprising that the meaning of the term is somewhat unsettled. In the world beyond book and journal publishing, *copyediting* is sometimes loosely applied to cover a range of editorial tasks.
Einsohn

Your first goal isn't to slash and burn your way through in an effort to make it conform to a list of style rules. Your first goal is merely to do no harm. ... [do not] take a fresh and well-voiced text and edit the life out of it.
Saller

6.1 What the text editor actually does (in summary)

In the excerpt from Einsohn above, the author refers to the looseness that exists in English regarding the spelling of the word 'copyeditor' (text editor). The varied spelling of the English term in numerous British, Australian and American publications (as *copy-edit, copy edit* and *copyedit*) points to the confusion that prevails between publishers and the various forms of English. As Einsohn asserts (2005: 11), if the British, Australian and American forms of the word lack uniformity, it would seem only logical that people will not attach the same meaning to the word. To link the term to a vague 'series of editing tasks' is indicative of this.

Saller (2009: 14–15, 23–30) pleads for *carefulness*, *transparency* and *flexibility* in text editors' approach to authors and their texts – the 'three paths to editing enlightenment', as she calls them (2009: 23). Exercising care is about possessing knowledge of a kind that will prevent you doing harm to an author's manuscript, that is, knowing which house style and grammar rules to apply, weighing them up against the author's (acceptable) preferences, knowing also when to resist making changes for change's sake, and using your own experience as a reader to inform your work as an editor. 'Meticulous' is synonymous with 'carefulness', but it should not be the blind variety.

Transparency happens before, during and after the editing, and at all three stages involves the author in a collaboration (using Track Changes and generating author queries are just two facets of transparency) rather than working in isolation on your own and presenting the edited manuscript as a fait accompli. The text editor sometimes has to try hard to work transparently with an author because they may not have the opportunity to meet face to face, to talk or sometimes even to email. That is the time to work through an intermediary such as a project manager or a commissioning editor, but communicate openly with your author you must (Foster 1993: 18, 22; Mackenzie 2011: 35).

The text editor has to avoid clinging too inflexibly to 'standards' and style conventions, almost as a point of honour. For example, you know a rule and have applied it consistently throughout a manuscript, only to have the author insist on changing it back. What do you do? Allow professional pride to take over and resist the author's rebuttal? If the text editor recognises that style conventions are often by their nature arbitrary and changeable, they'll realise that style is open to interpretation (there are also so many different interpretations of house style) and that style rules are a convenience created to make the editor stop and ponder less frequently in applying conventions consistently. 'They're used for the text editor's convenience in serving the reader,' says Saller (2009: 29). So if an author has a preference that you can tolerate, consider retaining it; if, on the other hand, there's a reason why that style is inappropriate to the document, make your arguments and perhaps the writer will see reason. You will then have displayed the necessary flexibility.

The text editor of today is someone who oversees a comprehensive series of tasks – and is someone who has the necessary competence (based on training and experience) to undertake the technical polishing of the material an author presents as effectively as possible with an eye on publication (see chapter 2 section 10–13 in this regard). This 'technical improvement' entails a great number of tasks that include checking:

✓ the appropriateness of the text to the intended target audience;
✓ the indicators of language and structure;
✓ that all the component parts of a text have been submitted;
✓ the style and register of the text;
✓ the content (as far as possible);
✓ the accuracy of the information given in the text;
✓ that consistency has been maintained throughout the text;
✓ the numbering and paragraphing;
✓ that copyright permissions have been obtained, where necessary;
✓ that feedback from the author and the client or publisher has been received.

As a result, text editing is not simply a random 'series of editing tasks', but it is much more than that. In the remainder of this section we explore what 'much more than that' entails.

6.2 What the text editor does (or should) not do

It is also important also to know what the text editor does or should not do (or is not supposed to do). These are some of them:

• *The text editor is by definition not a proofreader.* Although the job of proofreading can be an additional brief that the text editor is able to fulfil, it is really not their primary role (Mackenzie 2011: 35). In the nature of their work text editors also do a degree of proofreading because they must check texts for correctness and they are expected to detect and correct errors. Editing and proofreading are actually two diverse functions, but the distinction between them is not really understood by some authors and clients. It is as well, at the outset of a project, therefore, for the text editor to spell out the differences to the author or client so that there can be no doubt about the editor's deliverables. This step is especially necessary in self-publishing projects, where the author-client may well be unfamiliar with the publishing process and therefore possibly confused by it, or else may have unrealistic expectations as regards its results. See the discussion about this in section 5 of this chapter.

• *Text editors are neither ghostwriters nor overwriters.* It is possible that in the process of editing they will rewrite parts of the text to improve it, but it is really not the text editor's job to be a writer on behalf of the original author (and not acknowledged as co-author). Text editors are entitled to recognition for their contribution towards making a promising text into a really good one. See section 6 of chapter 3 for a fuller discussion of this topic.

• *Text editors are not developmental editors.* They are expected to query the structural and organisational problems that form the basis of developmental editing, not fix them (Einsohn 2005: 11).

• *Text editors cannot accept responsibility for factual errors in the text.* That is unquestionably the author's domain. If the text editor happens to have the appropriate knowledge that enables them to solve factual problems in the manuscript, that will be a bonus which will be appreciated by both client or publisher and author. On the other hand, text editors must not allow obvious factual errors (dates, names of individuals, incorrect names in the captions and titles of books, totals in tables) to slip through. Basic research and checking can reasonably be expected, but not much more than that: is it Mother Theresa or Mother Teresa? Was the title of the film *The Passion of Christ* or *The Passion of the Christ*? If the author claims that the name 'Abraham' occurs 80 times in the New Testament of the Bible, the figure can be checked against the electronic edition of the Bible. Do all you can – within your power – to correct the content of a document. In this regard, Bowles & Borden (2004: 147) say that if they want to be 100% accurate, text editors are expected to 'need a librarian's working knowledge of reference materials in both printed and electronic format'. That is indeed a tall order!

- *Text editors are not legal or medical practitioners.* In other words, it is not their primary job to obtain copyright permission or to detect instances of plagiarism. Of course they can help to obtain this kind of permission and they can point out those instances of plagiarism that they do detect, but these tasks are actually the responsibility of other specialists.
- If text editors detect instances of defamation, genderism, ageism or racism, they should bring them to the attention of the author and/or the client or publisher. Such instances cannot knowingly be ignored. In the end, however, the text editor never has the legal responsibility for the content of a text.
- Similarly, in medical textbooks, the dosages of medicines are details that only a medically trained person should be checking for accuracy; though, once again, if the text editor detects a suspected inaccuracy they should report it. The text editor will be more likely to spot misspellings of medical terms and drug names, or to look up those that seem suspect.
- *Text editors are not typographers or graphic designers.* This is the domain of other experts, although, of course, experienced text editors with a good knowledge of typography and book design principles are able to point out errors in these areas and contribute in other ways (Mackenzie 2011: 46). In fact, the nearest the text editor will get to typography and design is in marking up ('tagging' or 'coding') the various headings and subheadings to indicate the various levels to the typesetter so that the process of treating them typographically is made easier and more clear cut. The same would apply to coding bulleted and numbered lists, to indicating displayed quotations, and sometimes to indicating italics and bold within text.
- It is also their task to check the typography and graphic design elements and to speak out when those don't help a document to communicate effectively. It is certainly not the editor's task to design a document or even its cover.
- *Text editors are not indexers.* This is once again the work of specialists in this area. Which is not to say that text editors cannot compile indexes; they can, of course, do so in addition to their editing work, if they are suitably experienced and qualified to do so. But indexing is, without question, a distinct function in the publishing and document-generation processes.

- *Text editors are not copywriters or marketers.* The writing of marketing copy – for example, the back cover blurb that tells the potential reader about the content and the author – should be in the hands of specialist writers. If text editors have an ability to write marketing copy, then, following the principles of writing good back cover copy, or advertising copy generally, they could be called upon to do that as an independent brief; but doing so should not be an aspect of the text editor's core brief, despite their intimate knowledge of the text.
- *The text editor may not subcontract editorial work to another editor without the express written permission of the client or publisher.* In most instances, a publisher will try to match a text editor either to a text or to an author, or both. They do so based on the strengths, abilities, previous experience and personality of a particular text editor – some or all of which attributes another text editor may not possess, which could lead to a mismatch. So the freelance editor who is serving many masters simultaneously would be better advised rather to turn down a project for good reason (communicated to the client) than to take on something they know they cannot cope with (for whatever reason), only to pass it on to a third party.
- *The text editor must not spring surprises on the author* (Saller 2009: 17–18). Whether it's the deadline for returning the edited manuscript or for handing something in; or deciding on who will be compiling the index (and paying for it); or the actual cost of all the additional author corrections at proof stage, or of including those digital images in the book – don't spring this information on authors in the form of late or last-minute 'surprises'. Keep your author informed all along the way, communicating openly right from the beginning.

Most professional text editors possess the skills and capabilities that enable them also to perform these (secondary) tasks, but then they do so according to a separate agreement with the client (Mackenzie 2011: 4, 28–29; Murphy 2011: 4–9). Text editors would really be neglectful professionally were they to take note of these opportunities for intervention and yet remain silent, if by doing so the final text turns out to be less successful as a communications tool (Carstens 2003).

7 Errors that a (freelance) text editor is capable of committing

> Copy editors are charged with preventing bad things from *happening* ...
> *Anonymous*

Text editors certainly cannot know everything or indeed do everything, even though clients and publishers may think otherwise at times. Their training and experience stand them in good stead to perform a large number of tasks simultaneously (Bisaillon 2007: 84; Murphy 2011: 4–5). But it is possible that text editors will make mistakes before and during the text editing process, and so it is important both to highlight them timeously and also to be aware of what can go wrong.

7.1 Before the editing commences

• *Quoting for the job:* Freelance text editors are prone to presenting ill-considered and overhastily compiled quotations for work (see the example on page 222). This becomes a contract to which the parties are bound and which must be adhered to. Make absolutely sure beforehand what the work entails before you tell a client what the job will cost, and preferably have sight of all or a major portion of the manuscript at the quoting stage (Murphy 2011: 52–53, 55–56). Fortunately, with the passage of time we all learn from our mistakes, even in this area. One usually makes this kind of error of judgement only once.

When putting together a quotation, typical questions that should be asked are: What is the standard of language usage? How intensively must the manuscript be edited: a light, a medium or a heavy edit? (cf Flann & Hill 2004: 35–36; Einsohn 2005: 12, 13–15; Murphy 2011: 52–53; Saller 2009: 105–109). Must the editing be done on hard copy or electronically, or both? Will the editor receive only a printout or will the text be supplied electronically too? How many hours of work will it take to complete the project? Einsohn (2005: 21–23) gives extremely valuable advice in response:

List 4.13 Presenting quotations

> › Never provide an estimate of how long a project will take to complete until you have seen the document yourself. The emphasis here falls on *never*.

> › Make provision in your time estimate for unforeseen problems and delays. The language can be more technical than expected, you could fall ill, questions about problem areas could take longer to resolve (perhaps your contact person at the dictionary bureau is on leave and the online dictionary doesn't have the answer you seek), and so on.

> › Allow time for activities that are not directly related to the editing itself, such as photocopying, following up carefully on an enquiry, pointing out (diplomatically phrased) queries to the author, or arranging for courier services.

> › You know your own work tempo and know what you are capable of doing, but always build a buffer into your estimate. If you, for example, estimate that you can process 150 pages at five pages per hour, then the task will take 30 hours to complete. Build in a buffer of at least 20% here, that is, an additional six hours.

> › Be realistic about how many hours per day you are able to deliver quality work. It is unrealistic to work 15-hour days and still to expect to be working at your peak throughout.

>>

List 4.13 continued

> › Rather over-estimate the time you will need to complete the work than underestimate it. Deadlines that are not met (and which are based on your estimate) can have a major impact on the production process – and your reputation.

- *Underestimating the nature of the job:* In the first place, you should ask to see the entire manuscript if it has not all been given to you. Alternatively, ask for the total word count and seek an assurance that the unreceived balance of the text is in more or less the same condition as that you've received (Murphy 2011: 52–53, 54–56). Never be forced into quoting a fee (or, for that matter, accepting a client's fee) for editing a manuscript you have not seen: you are bound to under-quote.

  Multi-author works can be particularly demanding, because of the wide variations of writing style, numbering systems, division of chapters into sections and subsections, footnoting/endnoting systems, illustrative matter, and referencing systems. As a result, the text editor should charge a higher fee (based on longer hours) for bringing the different chapters into a uniform shape, as if they had been written by one author.

  Some text editors make the mistake of accepting work for which they are ill-suited or ill-prepared. Taking it on can lead to your delivering substandard work, which will in turn lead to your no longer receiving any further commissions from that client (rather than calling you in and talking you through where and how you underperformed, most clients simply cut off the supply of work to you without any explanation). So, if you are incapable to taking on a particular project, say so and move on – at least that way you might get other projects from the same client.
- *Underestimating the time required to complete the job:* Text editors can neglect to meet deadlines. That is a deadly sin throughout an industry driven by deadlines, for obvious reasons: 'Missing deadlines is an editor's worst nightmare, considered the proverbial kiss of death for future work' (Anonymous 2008).

  To self-manage the remedy to this problem, closely monitor yourself as you edit samples of a variety of manuscripts while you're working on them. This will give you an average page per hour rate, which can then be translated into a number of words per hour rate. No two editors work at exactly the same pace, and what you need to know is that there will always be jobs that will require slower reads but for which the schedules are more flexible; by the same token, there will always be opportunities for text editors who are able to take on the rush jobs effectively. Also try to work out from your samplings when your more productive times of day (or night) are and when not; and for how many hours are you able to maintain optimal productivity before you are forced to call it a day. Sit with a stopwatch, if need be, while you are sampling your pace.
- *Working with out-of-date reference materials:* It is possible that text editors find themselves using outdated reference materials, sometimes because replenishing them is regarded as a heavy expense, but also because it can be difficult to keep up with revised

editions and new publications. This can have a negative influence because the editing one does and the changes one makes are based on outdated trends and information, and the results are highly visible (cf Mackenzie 2011; Murphy 2011: 19; Saller 2009: 40).

Nowadays, this can largely be overcome by using online resources that are constantly updated (see chapter 11), but also by purchasing materials online at considerably lower prices. The text editor therefore needs constantly to be scanning the internet for the latest resources in order to keep up to date with important areas of their work.

- *Signing a contract:* As a freelance, you will in all probability be expected to sign some sort of document that sets out, among other things, the deadline for handing in the completed work, the fee for completing it to the required standard, and a brief setting out the tasks you are expected to perform for the edit (Mackenzie 2011: 206–207; Murphy 2011: 54). It could take the form of a Letter of Appointment (with or without a schedule), an Editorial Brief or even a more formal Memorandum of Agreement (see chapter 5 for examples of these documents).

  You should not be required to sign the document at the handover, but should be given 48 to 72 hours to read through both it and the full manuscript to see whether you are reasonably able to fulfil the terms and conditions. Start by scanning the manuscript in a fair amount of detail in order to ascertain the standard of the writing, the degree of editorial intervention required, the number of pages and the number of words per page (or the total word count), whether you are required to edit a large number of tables and figures, whether you are expected to draw up an artwork brief; and how many footnotes or endnotes and bibliographical references there will be to check. The more of these you need to tick off on the checklist of tasks, the longer you can expect the editing to take.

  Then, based on the number of hours per week you devote to text editing and the number of pages you estimate you'll be able to edit per hour or day, work out whether you'll be able to complete the full manuscript by the stated deadline. If you think it will be difficult or impossible, you'll need to negotiate the schedule with the client.

  Usually a client will base your fee (if you have not been asked to compile a quotation or estimate for the work – see above) for the job on the number of pages or the word count (taking into account the level of complexity of the text) and you'll have to measure that against your standard rate per page or per 1 000 words; if there's a gulf between the two, you'll have to consider negotiating the fee for the project or turn it down. Only when these important considerations have been agreed upon or renegotiated will you be in a position to sign the (amended) quotation, which will then be countersigned by the client and become legally binding.

- *Serving too many masters:* As a freelance, you are likely to be briefed by several clients, each of whom has a different style manual or set of procedures for preparing manuscripts, and also different deadlines. For this reason, your record-keeping must be thorough and well organised (Saller 2009: 104–105). The more infrequently you receive work from clients, the more you will need to keep track of the way they want things done – which dictionary they standardise on, which style guide they prefer, and the exceptions to both.

You will also have to juggle your workloads very carefully (inevitably, work is going to come your way simultaneously from different clients) to ensure that you do not let any of your clients down, as that could be your undoing. As a freelancer, you'll also have clients' schedules and deadlines imposed upon you, with little room for negotiation. If you decline this time round, you run the risk of another freelance getting not only this job but also future work that would otherwise have come your way.

In these circumstances, it's better to be open about your availability: either you say no, you aren't able to fit in the job, or you take it on, prepared to lose sleep trying to deliver. (Whatever you do, don't then miss the deadline or allow the quality of your work to suffer: either would annoy the client sufficiently to remove you from their list of freelancers.)

7.2 During the editing

- Text editors can sometimes challenge unnecessarily the reader's ability to make connections between words and sentences. In such instances the connection may well be clear to the text editor, but then they neglect to convey the connection clearly to the reader. In such cases, the text editor will not have done their job well enough to make the text coherent.
- Text editors are sometimes inclined to think that they have to make many changes to a document; thus, they believe, the more they change in a manuscript, the more important their task becomes in the process of text editing. The opposite is true: change only what is necessary (Einsohn 2005: 27; Saller 2009: 40).
- Text editors can rewrite sentences because they think their own sentences are better than the author's. That's not necessarily true. Change is not always better.
- Text editors can change an author's style in such a manner that the author's stamp on the text disappears, so much so that the author's personality disappears from the text. This is described by Linnegar (2008: 20) as 'the worst error an editor can make ...'.
- Text editors can over-edit (Linnegar 2008: 32). Avoid doing so at all costs, because on the one hand it devalues the character of the text and can undermine the author's voice and on the other it leads to a lot of unnecessary work (and a waste of time).

8 General rules of text editing

Gilad (2007: 317–324) says there are ten matters that together constitute a sort of recipe for success for anyone who wants to edit texts as an occupation:

List 4.14 Recipe for success when editing text

1. Get to know your client or publisher. Also make doubly sure that you've understood precisely what they expect from you.

2. Always meet deadlines.

3. Before you tackle the manuscript in detail, read through it to gain an overview of it.

4. Respect the writer (even if you don't always agree with them).

5. 'If you have an iota of doubt about anything you read, look it up.' Put differently, don't take everything you read as gospel or at face value.

6. Use the internet (Google, Mozilla Firefox, Internet Explorer and other search engines), if you're in any doubt about anything.

7. As you proceed, write everything down (so that you can follow it up later).

8. Proofread your own editing. It can do no harm to read the text a second time.

9. Read, read and read again about anything you can in order to broaden your horizons.

10. Keep up with changes in your profession. Therefore buy those new references, follow internet links and expand your network.

Eisenberg (1992: 29) writes that there is no such thing as an all-in-one book that deals with enquiries about text editing:

> No single, universally accepted book of editing standards exists. Indeed, editorial style in the sense of convention, and even in the sense of grammar, punctuation, and usage, varies considerably among publications.

How do we go about giving guidelines for implementing the editing process, then? The rules and guidelines that are indicated below are a collection of hints based on the experiences of language practitioners and on looking up countless resources on the discipline. Some of the hints have already been set out elsewhere, but they are given in consolidated form below. Applying them can make life much easier for the text editor. Two types of rule are distinguished: rules of principle and rules of practice.

8.1 Rules of principle

The Brief

The challenges

1. As regards the text, make sure from the start precisely what is expected of you. Are you expected, for instance, to deliver a light, a medium or a heavy edit?
2. Before you accept a manuscript for editing, first find out if the client has a house style guide to which you have to adhere. If one exists, then adhere to its contents (cf Flann & Hill 2004: 48–52; Merriam-Webster 2001: 240–241; Saller 2009: 27–30, 40–41).
3. Specialisation is not unusual. You really don't have to know everything; you also cannot.
4. Never be rigid; by definition, text editing requires flexibility (Saller 2009: 27–30).
5. Keep on learning (via courses, colleagues, the internet, language discussion groups, radio and your own reading) – you can really never know enough.

The editing process

The envisaged quality

1. The text editor is the proverbial 'last line of defence' against poor writing (Williams 1978). Make sure that you take on the 'defensive work' in all earnestness.
2. The text editor is considered to be a custodian of good language usage. But it's not just about good language usage for the sake of it; on the contrary, good language usage contributes to conveying the author's meaning more precisely and consistently. It is not just another task for the editor to perform: it is central to the text editor's contribution (Anonymous 2006a).
3. Simplify complex, wordy or poor sentence constructions on the basis of your own knowledge of and experience with clear and comprehensible language usage. If a decision can be supported by referring to an appropriate source, all the better.
4. If you are accused of being nit-picky, regard it as a great compliment (Mackenzie 2011). For the text editor, being nit-picky is not a luxury but a necessity. Just avoid being pedantic, arrogant or inflexible (Saller 2009: 27–28; 39–40).
5. As far as possible, always read through the text before you begin the editing. Doing so provides you with background and also gives you an early indication of the quality of the text. It is seldom possible to adopt this approach, but if you can plan for it, and actually do it, you will be implementing good practice.
6. Distinguish between editing and proofreading. Always proofread the hard copy for a last time. Also take into account that text editing occurs in different ways, even when one is freelancing, precisely to ensure a quality end-product to hand over to the client.
7. Dealing with factual errors is not your primary responsibility, but keep an eye out for them anyway. If you do spot any, draw the author's or client's attention to them: it is the author who should correct them.

8. If you notice anything in the text that could be considered defamatory, racist or sexist (or any of the other -*ists*, for that matter), draw the client's or author's attention to it immediately.
9. Do not lose or damage parts of a text (especially if you do most of your work on a computer) (Einsohn 2005: 4). It could be the only available copy and its loss or damage could be incalculable. For this reason, always ensure that you back up every file you work on at least daily, storing it in a safe place external to your PC or laptop, and that your computer autosaves regularly during the day (preferably at 20-minute or shorter intervals). If you do not, a power failure or a hard drive crash could have a dire effect on your productivity.

Respect for the text
1. Never change the author's meaning (at least not without their permission) (cf Einsohn 2005: 4; Flann & Hill 2004: 37–38; Merriam-Webster 2001: 234–235; Saller 2009: 32–33, 40). That is, it is the text editor's task to hone the packaging of the author's ideas and not their intended meaning (Plotnik 1982: 32).
2. Every text has its own character. Do not alter that character while editing the text, unless you are clearly instructed to do so (Wolff 2008).
3. Do not change that which does not need to be changed (Wallraff 2004).
4. Do not ask yourself whether a sentence can be improved; rather ask whether it's really necessary to change it (Mossop 2010: 182). It is often clear that sentences can be correct but that they do not communicate well because they are clumsy or inelegant, and therefore stylistically incomplete. In such cases the sentences should undergo some or other refinement. Sound judgement and healthy appreciation (you know that something is wrong and you know intuitively how to fix it) are as a result sometimes needed in the process of editing (cf Baskette, Scissors & Brooks 1986: 52; Judd 1990: 20; Glover 1996).
5. Never change text in order to 'prove' the importance of your editorial contribution. Some text editors feel that the more you change, the more will have justified your editorial brief. This is untrue (Plotnik 1982: 32; Einsohn 2005: 27; Saller 2009: 8–9).
6. Don't correct something that is essentially correct (Einsohn 2005: 4).
7. Don't create unnecessary work for yourself – if you can live with something, then leave it alone. Be careful, therefore, to guard against hypercorrection, that is, the over-use of the editorial pen. In attempting to be (hyper)correct, you could be tempted to replace correct words or expressions.
8. Keep your editing simple and straightforward.

Checks
1. Never ignore your 'sixth sense' (a feeling of discomfort) about anything; instead, check it to be certain about it. Your willingness to cross-check or double-check is one of the most important indicators of competence and professionalism (Anonymous 2006b).

2. Don't accept that everything in print is necessarily correct or true (Judd 1990: 17). Again, check it – doing so for the sake of certainty can do no harm.
3. Don't leave anything to coincidence. If something is in a text, it is there for a specific reason; make sure you understand what the reason is before you make any changes.
4. You have a (strange) obsession with correctness: you really do care if a comma is in the right place, if there is a space before or after the parenthesis or full stop, what the correct spelling of a word is, and what the correct degrees of comparison of a certain adjective are.

Respect for source materials
1. Background knowledge of the discipline or area covered by the text is of great help.
2. Know your source materials very well. If you don't know where to look for answers, you will not produce quality work. That's an accepted reality.
3. Ensure that yours are the authoritative sources for a particular area (Wolff 2008).
4. Ensure that you use the most recent sources. Out-of-date source materials provide outmoded answers. The fourth edition of *Butcher's copy editing*, for instance, contains much new and revised information that is not to be found in the third edition.
5. Know your sources well enough that you can attribute responsibility for the changes you make to the manuscript.
6. Expand your knowledge constantly and as widely as possible by reading everything you can lay your hands on: books, encyclopaedias, periodicals, newspapers, academic and popular articles, pamphlets, brochures, notices about particular matters, annual reports, church and other newsletters, comic strips, instruction leaflets, advertising boards, product labels, and so on. Also watch television programmes and listen to radio programmes. These are all sources that can be of use to attune one's eye and ear to new information (Stepp 1989: 149).
7. If you ever have any doubt about something (fact, language or any other aspect), look it up in a reference work. Consult every possible source, conduct internet searches. Be critical of the text in front of you, therefore, and don't accept anything at face value. Accept the fact that the author is fallible and will have made mistakes until the opposite is proven to be true. Therefore you should check everything that you possibly can: spelling of names, dates, quotations, sums, the contents of tables and figures, biblical text as well as the captions to photographs and illustrations.
8. If you don't have the answer to a problem, don't hesitate to acknowledge it and to seek help: 'If you hit a stalemate, don't be afraid of consulting a referee' (Stepp 1989: 94) – or a professional colleague, one might add.
9. Compile a list of the problematic issues that you have to look up in your references. Always indicate the source of the solution to a particular problem, then

you won't have to consult your own style guide again and you also won't have to go to all the trouble of consulting the source repeatedly.

Aids
1. Don't hesitate to use accessible electronic language aids (such as spell- and grammar-checkers, where they are available); they help with checking a text, whether it's before you begin the editing or as a final check after you have finished editing.
2. Master electronic editing. Increasingly, language practitioners are being required to receive documents electronically, to do the editing electronically and to return the edited work electronically – even to save it to a writable CD. But be very careful when using the Find and Replace function – never do so globally (Blaauw 2001, 2003).
3. As you work through a particular document, draw up a list of the preferred alternative forms used in it, especially in the case of longer documents. Then, subsequently, you can look up the terms more easily than by having to search through the document.
4. Draw up a list of discipline-specific terminology so that you can subsequently refer to it easily. Doing so promotes consistency and can also prevent unnecessary, repetitive and time-consuming work.
5. Consult electronic chat groups, terminology networks and national databases to remain abreast of new terms and to resolve problems with terminology.
6. Draw up a list of the names, contact details (at least a telephone number and an email address) and specialisms of (language) experts in the area in which you work. But always consult your own sources before you approach the experts.

Communicate your changes
1. Do not make changes without motivating or justifying (if only to yourself) why you did so (Mossop 2010: 5). Ensure that you always give a reason. 'I think so' or 'It sounds better as ...' or 'It feels as though ...' are no longer good reasons. Stepp (1989: 94) says 'A hallmark of bad editing is making changes for which you cannot cite a rule or offer succinct explanation'.
2. Never rewrite a sentence simply because it's not the way you would have written it. If the author's sentence communicates well, leave it as it is (Einsohn 2005: 27).
3. Be honest with your client or publisher. If you can't solve a problem, tell them directly, and certainly don't create expectations through your silence.

8.2 Rules of practice

These rules have to be read together with the usage hints and tips included in the relevant sections of chapters 6 to 10. See also sections 6 (What the text editor should actually do and not do) and 7 (Errors that a (freelance) text editor is capable of committing) in this chapter, which complement this section.

1. Read word for word, sentence by sentence, paragraph by paragraph.
2. If you have changed something in one place, ensure that you also change it in other places where the same error occurs (Mossop 2010: 182).
3. Be consistent in your choices (regarding spelling, the division of words, the use of uppercase letters, italics, underlining, dates and time, money, numbers and measurements, abbreviations and acronyms, the use of punctuation marks, the use of numerals, quotation marks (single or double), register, terminology, style, typography and page layout (cf Butcher 1993: 67–68, Butcher, Drake & Leach 2006: 126–128, 130–131, 135, 137–139, 141–146, 150–157, 158–162, 434–436; Einsohn 2005: 5, 6, 8, 12, 15, 421–429; Flann & Hill 2004: 48–52, 112, 171–172; Merriam-Webster 235–236; *New Hart's rules* 2005; Saller 2009: 27–30).
4. Keep your eyes peeled for typing errors. Letters and numerals are often swapped around by accident, characters are doubled, spacing errors occur and words or characters are left out.
5. Check the accented characters (diacritics) in words (Butcher, Drake & Leach 2006: 34, 46, 133, 135, 139–140, 148, 160, 436, 2009; Einsohn 2005: 48, 129).
6. Check the use of abbreviations and acronyms. In general, the correct usage should be that the full form of acronyms in particular is given at the first mention and after that the acronym is used on its own. Sometimes, however (eg in non-fiction textbooks and manuals), this rule is applied differently, that is, it applies to the first mention in each chapter, not to the first mention in the book as a whole. In some publications, on the other hand, an alphabetical list of the abbreviations and acronyms is printed at the front of the book together with the full form, and only the abbreviations and acronyms are used throughout the text. Follow the client or publisher's preferred house style. If an abbreviation or acronym is used only once in an entire text, abbreviating it usually cannot be justified. (Cf Butcher, Drake & Leach 2006: 117–122, 434, 2009; Clark 2001: 75; Flann & Hill 2004: 171–172.)
7. Always ascertain for sure what the house style is (if relevant) regarding the style of writing.
8. Check the correctness of titles and headings. There is nothing more embarrassing than a spelling error that persists in the title of a publication after the text editing has been completed.
9. At all times check the quotations from other sources, but do not edit them. This does not mean checking them against the original – that's the author's responsibility, and the original source is usually not available anyway – but that, as presented in the manuscript, they meet certain criteria: Have they been correctly cited? Are there missing words? Does the sentence structure relate to the previous section of the text? Is the punctuation correct? In that case, ensure that you at least do some superficial checking (such as reading to detect typing errors or accidental lapses). Also check the following: if ellipses (...) have been used, are they only three points (and not more)? Are they correctly spaced left and right? And where quotation marks are used, do they precede or follow the end-punctuation correctly? And if there are footnote or endnote indicators, do they follow the end punctuation, not precede it? Where an author has added their own emphasis within a quoted passage, have they indicated this after the quotation, and in a standard format? Where editorial insertions have had to be made, has the correct form and style be used? How are multi-paragraph quotations styled? (Cf Butcher, Drake & Leach 2006: 34, 43, 269–278, 445, 2009; Einsohn 2005: 77–78, 197, 198, 205, 206–211; Flann & Hill 78, 166, 282; Foster 1993: 40; Merriam-Webster 2001: 4, 163–167, 260–261.)

>>

Checklist 4.3 continued

10. Check page numbers, both on the text pages and in the table of contents.

11. Check the references to the sources. Is the format (spelling, abbreviated or full form, method of referencing (eg books versus periodicals), indication of one or more authors, and the date and/or place of publication each publication) correct? (Cf Butcher, Drake & Leach 2006: 45, 49, 231–268, 298, 430, 443–444, 2009; Flann & Hill 2004: 109–115, 179–181, 275, 294, 306; Einsohn 2005: 49, 222, 225–226, 278–292; *Chicago manual of style* 1993: 79, 2003; Mahan (ed) 2003; Merriam-Webster 2001: 173–174, 200–210, 214–218, 229, 237, 261–262.)

12. Check the bibliography for spelling, punctuation, typographical elements (spacing, typeface and type size, margin widths and italicisation of titles or not). Is the pre-scribed bibliographic style (eg Harvard style, Oxford style) maintained? (Cf Butcher, Drake & Leach 2006: 45, 49, 231–268, 298, 430, 443–444, 2009; Flann & Hill 2004: 109–115, 179–181, 275, 294, 306; Einsohn 2005: 49, 222, 225–226, 278–292; Grossman (ed) 1993: 79; Mahan (ed) 2003; Merriam-Webster 2001: 173–174, 200–210, 214–218, 229, 237, 261–262.)

13. Check the notes, numbers and numerals in tables too. (Cf Butcher, Drake & Leach 2006: 183, 219, 225–226, 310, 2009; Einsohn 2005: 244, 253–255; Flann & Hill 2004: 81–82.)

14. Check that the numerals (numbering) in sections, subsections, headings and subheadings follow one another logically (Butcher, Drake & Leach 2006: 213–214, 2009).

15. Ensure that there is congruence in the use of pronouns.

16. Ensure that there is congruence in number: if you use the singular form in one place, make sure that whatever relates to it is also in the singular form (whether it's a verb, a noun or another pronoun).

17. Avoid the repetition of words in successive sentences. 'However' should not appear in three sentences one after the other; there are, for example, good synonyms that can be used instead ('but', 'conversely', 'on the other hand'). Make sure that the stylistic synonyms include the same sense, though.

18. Avoid clichés.

19. Avoid foreign expressions (which could mislead or mystify the reader) where good English equivalents exist. Here the text editor should play the role of custodian of the language but also take into account the needs and limitations of the readers.

20. Check sentences for ambiguity in the meaning they convey. Identify the cause of ambiguity (poor word usage or poor sentence construction) when it does occur and revise a sentence so that its meaning is unambiguous.

21. Punctuation marks are not inserted in sentences to make them look good; they are functional, so make sure that their use helps to convey or support the meaning of sentences.

22. Excessive punctuation marks must be avoided. The exclamation mark, for example, must be used for a specific purpose only; and, when used, there should be only one at the end of a sentence, not more. The question mark (query) should be used only when a direct question is posed. Also avoid the use of too many commas; the modern trend is to use fewer.

23. Be careful not to tinker with an author's style. If you can't do otherwise, then intervene, but ensure that you are able to continue to do so consistently. In any event, if you do make changes to the author's style, you must consult them about your changes (*Chicago manual of style* 1993: 78, 79; Saller 2009: 26–27, 32–33, 40–42, 51–52).

24. Ensure that standardised terms are used in order to promote consistency.

9 Proofs in the process of text editing: the proofreading stage

> Proofreading is an exacting task. Those who can do it well ... are real artists.
> *Baskette, Sissors & Brooks*

> Proofreading means unlearning all the habits you have developed to read and make sense of a piece of writing. ... Train yourself to read proofs slowly, seeing every letter in every word and noting the punctuation of every sentence.
> *Foster*

> ..., we prefer the fresh eye of a new proofreader, who may pick up errors the copyeditor missed at the manuscript editing stage.
> *Derricourt*

> A copy editor is 'someone who decides where the commas go'. A proofreader is 'someone who decides where the commas should have gone'.
> *Sylvia Sullivan*

Once the text editing has been completed, the client (eg a publisher) will send the edited manuscript (incorporating the queries resolved by the author) to a typesetter or designer for the desktop publishing process to be implemented. Every time such a person intervenes in or manipulates the text, someone has to check that (a) any errors the editor and author allowed to slip through (called 'author's') and (b) any further errors the typesetter may have introduced (called 'literals' or 'typos') are detected and corrected (Van Rooyen 2005: 236). This process of reading and marking up corrections on proofs is called 'proofreading' or 'proof correction' (cf Clark 2001: 77–78; Davies & Balkwill 2011: 171–172; Foster 1993: 105–113; Legat 1991: 91–92; Mackenzie 2011: 12, 19, 74, 78; Mossop 2010: 30; Van Rooyen 2005: 235–240). That 'someone' is either the text editor performing the role of proofreader or an independent proofreader contracted by the client.

But proofreading is not editing: it's a matter of detecting and correcting what is obviously incorrect (nowadays especially in the areas of formatting and layout), not tinkering with 'nice to haves' that are not patently incorrect. To quote Burton (Mackenzie 2005: 74), 'Edit the manuscript, not the proofs.'

9.1 The process of proofreading

Usually, following desktop publishing, both the author and a proofreader receive copies of the same galley or page proofs to read, depending upon the nature of the book (ie heavily illustrated or exclusively text); thereafter, the author's corrections are usually incorporated into the proofreader's set and one consolidated set is returned to the typesetter for correction. There was a time when typesetting (literally retyping the author's edited text (which had either been handwritten or committed to paper using a typewriter)) was the preserve of the printer, who offered a one-stop inhouse service of typesetting, proofreading and printing (Foster 1993: 105–106; Legat 1991: 91). Nowadays, that traditional system has largely been replaced by independent desktop publishing carried out by freelancers and by freelance proofreaders engaged by publishers (Clark 2001: 78–79).

Based also on the pre-computerised technologies in use then, a printer's typesetter would produce one of two kinds of proof (cf Butcher, Drake & Leach 2006: 96–8, 2009; Clark 2001: 77–8; Foster 1993: 107; Legat 1991: 91–2; O'Connor 1978, 1986, 1993: 37):

- *Galley proofs*: These are a continuous version of the entire text of the manuscript without any divisions into pages. In the case of complicated books with a lot of illustrations, tables, figures, footnotes, and so on, these proofs simply provide an opportunity (particularly if the publisher is expecting there to be many corrections) for errors to be eliminated before the potentially more costly process of making corrections to pages is undertaken, with the possible added consequence of text having to be reflowed between pages, illustrations having to be moved and both (plus footnotes, possibly) having to be refitted to pages.

- *Page proofs*: In this case, the text will already have been divided up into page lengths according to the design specifications for the book (eg font size, text width, number of lines of text per page). Page proofs also give a more accurate estimate of the overall 'feel' of the publication and also the total page count (or 'page extent') upon which many input costs for the book are based.

Nowadays, first page proofs have largely replaced galleys and second and third page proofs have superseded the page proofs of yesteryear. This is confirmed by Mackenzie (2011: 124): 'Modern production methods have dispensed with galley proofs; the first round of proofs is usually laid out as pages.' This means that the first proofs are already in page format and that the second proofs become yet a further check on the first proofs. Going straight to page proofs also makes a meaningful contribution to finalising the text, because from the outset everyone gets to work with the text in its final published format. To keep control over budgets, publishers also prefer to know the actual page extent up front, which means that the proofreader's brief may include a requirement to save pages through text cuts. (Most service providers' fees are based on the estimated or actual number of published pages.)

Irrespective of what we call 'the proofs', in book production they have to go through a minimum of two stages: (a) the first layout of the text as it's supposed to look when published and which has to be carefully read in accordance with the relevant guidelines and instructions; and (b) the second version of the text on which the suggested corrections of the first set of proofs have been implemented. This second set must be used to check whether the errors of omission and commission apparent in the first proofs have in fact been corrected, and correctly so. In heavily illustrated books, the illustrations may be inserted only at this stage, once the text corrections have been made and artwork spaces created. This usually means that a third set of proofs will be necessary, if only to check that the correct illustrations have been placed, and inserted the right way round and up – and that the captions match them. And also, of course, that the table of contents now reflects the latest actual fall of the text exactly.

Publishers, however, usually opt for the minimum number of proof stages appropriate to the complexity of the book and the production method; and authors should be encouraged to keep corrections to a minimum at proof stage (Butcher, Drake & Leach 2006: 96, 2009). Magazine publishers, in contrast, mainly to meet very tight deadlines but also to keep a tight rein on costs, usually allow for only one proofread – usually of colour proofs, so that even the colours on each page or for each article can be checked for both suitability and readability. (For more on proofreading see also chapter 10 section 3.1.2.)

9.2 What a proofreader does

9.2.1 The nature of the task

What must happen during a proofread? In general, the proofreader's brief differs markedly from that of the text editor (cf Enquist & Oates 2009: 20; Judd 1990: 142; Mackenzie 2005: 7, 74, 2011), but exactly what needs to be done at this stage in the process depends in large measure on the production method chosen. For books that have been:

- *rekeyed by the typesetter*, the proofreader will have to ensure that the typesetter has followed the edited manuscript faithfully.
- *set from the author's electronic files*, the proofreader should check that the text editor's markup has been implemented successfully and that no problems have arisen in translating the author's disk into a desktop publishing package (eg special characters, changes of font, spacing, indenting).
- *edited onscreen*, the text editor is more likely to send the author a copy of the edited files (with or without tracked changes) as a kind of 'proof' prior to the documents' being sent to the typesetter for formatting and page makeup and being run out as first page proofs (Butcher, Drake & Leach 2006: 95, 2009).

Whatever the method chosen, the first proofs will be sent to the author and a proofreader to read and mark up independently. When the author's set of proofs is returned, the proofreader's task is then to collate the two sets of corrections into one consolidated set for the person making the corrections. Collation can involve:

- labelling the separate piles of paper to identify them clearly;
- disallowing author's corrections that are excessive ('rewriting the text at proof stage'), because proofreading is about correcting the typesetting, not improving or augmenting the prose (Mackenzie 2011: 155);
- streamlining duplicate marks where both author and proofreader made identical corrections – this entails transferring only the author's marks correctly made to the proofreader's set of proofs, ignoring duplicate marks;
- editing any author's corrections or additions for grammatical correctness, spelling, punctuation and consistency with house style.

The typesetter should receive only one consolidated set of proof corrections to work from.

If there are long corrections (assuming such corrections are permitted and charged to the author against their royalties), they should be typed up separately and saved as individual documents, named, for example, 'BookTitle Insert A page 17', 'BookTitle Insert B page 62'. These individual documents should be keyed in to the proofs clearly so that the typesetter/designer who receives them either via email or on CD will know where to insert them.

9.2.2 Proofreader vs text editor

Whereas the text-editing stage takes place before the text has been made up into pages, the proofreading stage takes place afterwards (Butcher, Drake & Leach 2006: 95, 2009). For print media, the former typically involves an electronic intervention; the latter is still largely paper-based (but see section 9.2.5). The text editor's role is namely to edit the first draft of the document (well before it is made up into proofs) with an eye on grammar, spelling and punctuation, the author's thinking and argumentation, style and formulation, facts and typography (see list 2.13). It is comprehensive, detailed, demanding and responsible work. They are also strongly advised to proofread their final draft before handing it back to the client.

The proofreader, in contrast, focuses on checking whether what the editor has done to the text is reflected in the page proofs. AVS (2006) says that proofreading means literally 'the reading and checking of proofs' against the original text. Judd expresses herself as follows: 'The proofreader must read *every character* in the proof, looking for typographical errors, spelling or punctuation errors, errors of fact, inconsistencies, and other discrepancies' (1990: 263). This would apply also to reading second proofs against first proofs, and third against second.

Saller adds to this: 'Proofreaders must have a copy of the [copy editor's] style sheet of whatever they proof. Otherwise they might start undoing the editor's work' (2009: 9).

Sometimes, an author presents the text in handwritten or typewritten form. Given the recent advances in electronic writing, editing and desktop publishing, neither format is suitable, so the publisher will usually engage the services of a so-called 'data capturer' to capture the author's words in an electronic form that's compatible with the software the typesetter uses. The data-captured version must then be proofread against the hand- or typewritten version *before* the text editing can commence.

It is clear that text editing and proofreading are carried out at entirely different levels: the text editor ensures that the author's message is clearly conveyed and effects their changes electronically, whereas the proofreader's eye for detail ensures that errors have not crept in and to prevent them detracting from the author's message; their work as proofreader is still exclusively paper-based. Consequently, the two practitioners have different objectives and tasks to fulfil in their interaction with the manuscript; as a result, each intervention requires different skills and levels of experience. Mackenzie (2011: 124) sees proofreading in reality as imposing quality control at an advanced stage in the publishing production process, and accordingly regards the proofreader as having a greater responsibility than the editor: namely, to ensure that the edited manuscript corresponds in all respects to the specifications set for the published work (house style, formatting, font and font size, use of italics and bold, etc). The proofreader's job is not to focus on content and structure (which is what the text editor should have done), but rather to ensure that the text editor's and book designer's instructions have been implemented faithfully and that they complement one another.

At first, the proofreader usually has two texts in front of them (though nowadays, since the advent of PDFs and with email being so convenient, the 'blind' or 'cold' reading of only one text is fast becoming the norm (see below)): the edited manuscript and the laid-out text divided up into pages (Mossop 2010: 30). Saller points out that, for newcomers to text editing: 'Proofreading can be especially instructive if you are given the edited manuscript to proof against, since it will give you a chance to see and learn from the editor's corrections and queries' (2009: 118).

9.2.3 The proofreader's main tasks

The proofreader now has two main tasks to fulfil – a letter-by-letter proofread, ignoring the sense, and a second proofread for sense only:

- To do a basic proofread of the entire text – by far their more important and more time-consuming task: compare the two texts feature-by-feature and word-for-word against each other. Have all the typing, spelling and punctuation errors in the manuscript been corrected? In implementing the corrections, have any new errors been introduced? Have all words that have been repeated unnecessarily been eliminated, for example two articles (*the the* or *a a*) or two prepositions (*on on* or *for for*), especially at the end of one line and the beginning of the next. Have the marked typographical corrections been done, including the space after punctuation marks, the use of space on a page, the font and the font size? Does every element conform to the design specifications throughout? Are numerical and alphabetical sequences correct? Is the vertical and horizontal alignment of set-off text correct? (Merriam-Webster 2001: 275–276.) Only by comparing every instance of the same feature in one pass (eg all the tables or all the captions) is the proofreader likely to detect deviations from the design specification. Revisit list 2.13, which enumerates such errors.
- To do an editorial proofread – which should not constitute more than 5–10% of their time and effort, and which should comprise making only essential changes, not 'nice to haves', to keep the cost of corrections down (Merriam-Webster 2001: 273–274) – observe the following:
    - Look carefully at the word usage (eg *pertinent* vs *relevant* vs *appropriate*; *some* vs *several* vs *numerous*; *born* vs *borne*; *a lot* vs *alot*).

- Word breaks at the ends of lines (follow a reputable spelling dictionary that indicates permissible word breaks) or at the ends of pages (by convention, the last word on a page should not be broken).
- The grammatical correctness of the text (is *who* used instead of *whom*, *what* instead of *which*, *which* instead of *that*?) should be scrutinised.
- In particular, check the consistency of the use of initial uppercase letters, the use of abbreviations, contractions and acronyms, accented characters, numbering, paragraphing, the use of italics and bold type, underlining, measurements (numbers and symbols), dates and the indication of dates, the names of people and places, inverted commas (quotation marks), gender and number congruency (he/she/they), cross-references, and bibliographical references. (Cf Billingham 2002: 128–129; Butcher, Drake & Leach 2006: 98–101, 2009; Enquist & Oates 2009: 20–21.)

You need, therefore, to read for more than mere spelling, punctuation and elementary typography and page layout. One guideline for effective proofreading is this: read the text from right to left (ie backwards) at least once, so that you can focus on each word or expression and not on the sense.

9.2.4 The 'blind' or 'cold' proofread: combining basic and editorial proofreads

If there is only one text to proofread (a so-called 'blind' or 'cold' proofread, usually of a PDF), then the requirements of the job are a little different, and possibly more demanding. It can be done either onscreen or on paper (Mackenzie 2011: 154–155, 186–188; also section 9.2.5 below). Essentially, the proofreader combines the basic and editorial proofreads and is given much more licence to make editorial changes, in some cases assuming the role of the editor to a greater extent. The 'blind' proofread is somewhat more demanding, too, since the proofreader does not have a point of reference against which to read: they simply have to read through the text in several passes, each time focusing on one or more particular aspects – for example, literals or typos in the first pass; grammar, punctuation and sentence syntax/length in another; formatting aspects in yet another. Looking out for inconsistencies may require a further read-through, for example, to check the spellings of names in the text against those in maps, tables and figures.

Content issues may also arise: if the text states that City A has the highest crime rate in the country, for example, is this borne out by the accompanying table or graph? Or if two captions terminate in a full stop but the only other two do not, which two do you mark as erroneous, especially if the client's style guide is silent on the matter? With no accompanying text to refer to, you have to look out for evidence internal to the document itself and resolve differences yourself, guided by house style or a style sheet.

9.2.5 Proofreading screen text and onscreen

Copy should preferably be proofread in its final medium – print or screen (Mackenzie 2011: 154). However, the distinction should be made between proofreading text that is destined eventually for online use and proofreading text that is already online (as on websites) (Butcher, Drake & Leach 2006: 426, 2009). In the former case, HTML/XML files are created from publishing or word-processing software and therefore this practice does not usually make the way the proofreader works much different from working on a printed product.

If you are sent a PDF (portable document format suited to both printing and multimedia use and created using Adobe Acrobat®) to proofread, you will need to have loaded Adobe Acrobat Editor or a PDF editor, which can be bought as a standalone product. 'Editing' consists of marking up and annotating the pages with various commenting and markup tools, such as highlighting and crossing out text and adding notes and comments (Butcher, Drake & Leach 2006: 424–425). Later versions of Adobe Acrobat Pro provide tools for simulating proofreader's marks (Text Edit tool or Stamps tool). Another product, Paperlessproofs™, also makes it possible to proofread PDFs onscreen, using the Adobe Acrobat Reader: you click on an onscreen keypad to select a proof correction symbol and then click again to place it on the page. Text changes are typed in the margin, and files containing longer text corrections and replacement images can be attached as part of the paperless proof (2012) (see figure 4.4 below).

In the latter instance (proofreading text that is online), if you are not required to attend to the markup language itself, print a copy of each web page and mark it up like a conventional proof; if the pages have not previously been edited, as proofreader you will need to combine the editing and proofreading functions. In addition to the usual text editor's duties (checking for consistency, accuracy, logicality and house style), it is necessary to perform several online tasks to test that the site functions properly (cf Butcher, Drake & Leach 2006: 426–427, 2009; Flann & Hill 2004: 328; Mackenzie 2011: 147–148):

- Check all pages against the website inventory list to ensure that none are missing.
- The text, visuals and layout should all be checked as for print; check also for visual consistency, relevance, placement, resolution, size, download time and colour.
- Ensure that special characters are displaying correctly; that the text is wrapping correctly at different browser font size settings.
- Note any pages that are slow to load.
- Check that all navigational elements and hyperlinks function and take you to the appropriate page or connect to the right site. Do the external links open in a new browser window? Are all hyperlinks the same colour and underlined, and do they comprise the smallest appropriate amount of text? Does the colour change when a link has been used?
- Ensure that forms (eg registration) work correctly.
- Does the search function do its job correctly (try a number of test searches)?

- Note any errors in images, video, animation, audio and rollovers (website graphics that change when the cursor moves over them).
- In lists and tables, check that indents, line wraps and column width display correctly on various popular platforms.
- Is the standard information at the bottom of a page (copyright notice, terms and conditions, privacy policy, etc) correct and up to date?

9.2.6 Proofreading preliminary matter and end-matter

Once the text itself (starting from page 1) has been proofread and corrected at least once, the client will probably supply you with first proofs of the preliminary pages and the end-matter to proofread against the manuscript. This is probably the first time you will have seen them, and they could comprise some or all of the following:

Checklist 4.4 Preliminary matter and end-matter

Preliminary pages

Pagination
✓ Where pages are numbered (and not all of the prelims pages are), the convention is to use lowercase roman numerals: iv, v, … ix, x, …
Half-title
✓ Correct short form of the title; no folio (page number)
Title page
✓ Correct title and subtitle (also check against cover); correct names and order of authors; correct publisher's logotype; no folio
Imprint page (verso)
✓ Correct publisher name, address and date of publication; correct publishing history (editions and impressions); correct name(s) of copyright holder and copyright date; correct ISBN; copyright statement; credits of service providers; and printer's name; no folio
Contents list
✓ Check text and folios against actual headings, subheadings and page numbers; correct folios
Other lists (tables, figures, plates)
✓ Check text and folios against actual table/figure/plate headings and captions, and page numbers; correct folios
Foreword
✓ Spelt correctly; correct fonts for heading and body text; consistency with house style in all respects; correct folio(s)
Preface
✓ Correct fonts for heading and body text; consistency with house style in all respects. Check that it starts on a right-hand page, if it's supposed to; correct folio(s)
Acknowledgements
✓ Spelt correctly; correct fonts for heading and body text. Check that it starts on a right-hand page, if it's supposed to; correct folio(s)
Introduction
✓ Correct fonts for heading and body text; consistency with house style in all respects. Check that it starts on a right-hand page, if it's supposed to; correct folio(s)

>>

End-matter

End-matter
✓ Commences on the next right-hand page following the last page of the text
Bibliography or list of references
✓ Authors' names in alphabetical order; turnover lines indented uniformly; punctuation, italics and uppercase used uniformly according to the referencing style followed; starts on a right-hand page
Addenda or appendices
✓ Each to start on a right-hand page?; uniform font type and size
Glossary or word list
✓ To start on a right-hand page: terms in correct alphabetical order; uniform typographical treatment (eg bold or italic); uniformly punctuated; turnover lines uniformly indented
Index
✓ Two or three columns on a page, depending upon the page size; font about two points downsize from the body text; entries and sub-entries in correct alphabetical order; turnover lines of entries indented two ems/tabs; sub-entries indented one em/tab; turnover lines of sub-entries indented three ems/tabs; locators (page numbers) in correct numerical order; italics for locators that indicate illustrations on a page; comma+space between locators; see and see also cross-references in italics

9.2.7 Summary of what proofreading entails

The list below summarises aspects of the text and other elements that should be checked during a proofread – there could even be much more to it than what is indicated here.

› **Text language, content**
  – **Pages: Are all the pages present? Are any sections of the text missing?**
  – **Headings: full or elliptic sentences; no final punctuation; logical numbering**
  – **Captions: uppercase or lowercase; alignment; final punctuation or not**
  – **Paragraphs: length; linking words/connectors**
  – **Sentences: length; degree of complexity; appropriateness/ correctness**
  – **Grammar: correct prepositions; no missing verbs, subject–verb agreement (concord); correct pronouns, degrees of comparison, plural and diminutive forms; dangling participles; ambiguous referents; symmetry or concord in bulleted lists; position of only (and other adverbs), etc**

>>

List 4.15 continued

- Words: any words missing?; degree of complexity ('difficulty') and accessibility (eg jargon); meaning
- Quotations: properly embedded or displayed?
- Spelling: uppercase or lowercase; hyphenation/one word/two words; word breaks at the ends of lines and the end of the last lines of pages; spelling of foreign words; explanation of all abbreviations, contractions and acronyms; indication of signs and symbols (phonetic symbols, mathematical symbols, etc); people's given names and surnames; geographical place names; names of businesses and institutions
- Punctuation: spaces before and after punctuation marks (commas, full stops, semicolons, colons, exclamation marks, question marks; spaced or unspaced dashes); single or double inverted commas; position of final punctuation vis-à-vis inverted commas
- Typing errors: transposition of letters and numbers; repetition of words; excessive spaces (especially between sentences, between words, before punctuation)
- Obvious errors of fact

› Layout
- Covers: is the title correct; are the authors' initials and names correct and in the correct hierarchy (if there is one); has the house style been applied consistently to the text on the back cover? Does the ISBN on the back cover agree with that on the imprint page?
- Spine: logotype; wording reading in the correct direction; correct author and title
- Title page: titles and authors' names
- Headings and subheadings
- Running heads and footers
- Numbering: in text, headings and subheadings, main and subordinate sections
- Page numbers (folios): preliminary pages; page 1 first page of text, and on right-hand page; sequence correct and complete
- Use of space: excessive spaces in sentences or between words; line spacing (leading); presence of widows (a paragraph-ending line on next page) and orphans (a paragraph-opening line at bottom of page)
- Table of contents: an accurate mirror of the book contents?
- Index: comprehensive, accurate, consistent with book text?
- Addendums/annexures/appendixes: placement; design treatment; each to start on right-hand page?; cross-references in the text

- Bibliography/List of references: spelling; format; cross-checks (is each source in the text also in the bibliography?)
- Explanatory (terminological) lists
- Tables, diagrams and illustrations (reference to and placement of); notes; source acknowledgement; style for column headings; alignment; missing data
- Footnotes and/or endnotes
- Cross-references (bibliographical)
- Type page (including the use of blank space)
- Indenting of paragraphs
- Typeface (font): consistent for each feature?
- Font size: consistent for each feature?
- Italics, bold and underlining

› Consistency
- Spelling: uppercase; names; alternative forms (eg any body vs anybody); word division; abbreviations; contractions and acronyms; dates; symbols, etc
- Punctuation: inverted commas (quotation marks) and spaces before and after punctuation marks, etc
- Layout and typography: italics; underlining; typeface and type size; placement of end notes and/or footnotes; spelling and format of bibliography; numbering in text, etc
- Internal cross-references in the text
- Client's house style

On this subject, compare Billingham (2002: 128–129); Butcher, Drake & Leach (2006: 432–452, 2009); Gilad (2007: 112–113); Mackenzie (2011: 198–199); Merriam-Webster (2001: 271–288) and Van Rooyen (2005: 235–240).

The question is whether at this stage further corrections of any magnitude can be made or even proposed. The literature is reasonably clear about this: however, for further discussion, see Butcher, Drake & Leach (2006: 96, 2009); Derricourt (1996: 125); Merriam-Webster (2001: 274); O'Connor (1993: 137–138).

As a rule, corrections that are likely to have an impact on the pagination are rarely accepted because of the cost implications. Major errors (that should have been detected and resolved during the text-editing process, but which possibly slipped through) should obviously be corrected, despite the potential costs, because doing so will result in a better and more correct text. Derricourt's (1996: 126) advice is sound: be careful and conservative concerning possible amendments at this stage.

9.3 Specifics of proofreading practice

Finally, here are some comments about some specifics of proofreading practice:

- Proofreading must be carried out in a suitable environment that's conducive to concentrated work. It doesn't help if it's done, for example, at the dining room table if the family's movements in that area are likely to be a distraction or a disturbance.
- Try to position yourself so that you are disturbed as little as possible. Tiresome interruptions caused by a ringing telephone, family members (young children?) who constantly ask questions, and so on, can cause lapses in concentration and, as a result, errors not to be corrected.
- Do not try to proofread when you are tired. It is an activity that requires a high level of concentration, which will be diminished or lost when you are fatigued and which will affect the accuracy and thoroughness of your work adversely.
- Ensure that you have a backup copy of the text to hand. If you proofread electronically, always make sure that you save a copy as you're working.
- Remember: to proofread is *to read for errors.* You should therefore read slowly and attentively. Enquist & Oates (2009: 20; cf also Butcher, Drake & Leach 2006: 99, 2009; Foster 1993: 106) advise proofreaders to read at their slowest reading speed. Butcher, Drake & Leach (2006: 99, 2009) say that the skill of reading slowly must be exercised consciously: '*Train yourself to read slowly*, so that you can see every *letter* in each word and note the punctuation of every sentence.'
- It can help you to focus on the section of the text you're reading if you use an opaque ruler or a clean sheet of cardboard to help your eyes focus on one line at a time (cf Enquist & Oates 2009: 20–21; Mackenzie 2011: 130; Merriam-Webster 2001: 272–273). If possible, compare every passage that you read against the original copy, especially during the first proofread.
- Read the entire manuscript, including headings, tables, quotations, page numbers (folios), footnotes, appendices, bibliography, and so on, in as many passes as there are major features to check. Do not try to cover all the features in one read-through, because that way you are less likely to detect inconsistencies between occurrences of the same feature (eg that full stop at the end of every caption).
- Proofreading is seldom done on or with the aid of a computer (the exceptions are described in section 9.2.5 above); instead, it's done on a printout of the text using a pen or a pencil. If it is at all possible, it can do no harm for the typesetter or designer to run the appropriate spell- and/or grammar-checker over the laid-out document prior to printing it out (Enquist & Oates 2009: 21).
- Ensure that you know in advance of a proofread what exactly you must check: the client must brief you precisely on what is required of you. A clearly set out contract between you and the client should then be drawn up for a specific project.
- Obviously, one read-through is the ideal (from the point of view of cost, time and earning power), but experience has shown that this minimal approach is not always

advisable in practice, and that at least a second reading, even a third or fourth, should also be carried out – one reading will not be sufficient to spot every single error.

- Once you have corrected an error, reread the line in which it occurs to ensure that you have not missed any other errors close by.
- Begin the proofreading assignment as soon as possible after receiving the proofs. You should always meet your deadlines scrupulously, otherwise severe 'slippage' (ie delays) in the production chain will ensue. If you yourself wrote the text, create a distance from it before you begin proofreading, otherwise you won't be able to see the errors.
- Divide long passages of text into smaller sections and proofread the sections one by one. Experienced proofreaders recommend that the proofs be read page by page, with breaks in between.
- Use colour coding when making corrections to differentiate between typesetter's errors, author's alterations and editor's alterations in order that the publisher might allocate the costs of typesetting changes at proof stage (Butcher, Drake & Leach 2006: 103–105, 2009; Merriam-Webster 2001: 276–277).
- Consider using a pencil for author queries and uncertain changes or corrections (instead of ink); once responses have been obtained, either the pencilled marks are inked to make them permanent or they get erased.
- It is generally acknowledged that it is not possible for one person to spot every single error. At least two pairs of eyes should ideally proofread the same text, though that is not always practically possible (Grossman (ed) 1993: 108).
- Some publishers believe it is better that the text editor does not also proofread the text; others take the contrary view. The reason for the first view is simple: the more you distance yourself from the original text, the more easily you will spot errors. The converse is also true: the closer you are to the text (that is, the more familiar you are with it), the more difficult you will find it to see errors because you have an image in your head of what *should* be there (Mackenzie 2011: 123). The contrary view is often adopted by publishers of highly complex, picture-intense publications, such as school textbooks. In such books there are so many elements to look out for on virtually every page that the familiarity made possible by text editing is usually a great help to a proofreader.

    But publishers who use the text editor to proofread the same text (which many include three or more proofreads of the same pages) take the precaution of bringing a completely fresh pair of eyes to the project: a so-called 'second-eye proofreader'. Their brief is usually to conduct a multi-layered proofread of the entire document and to mark or query whatever seems to be incorrect, inconsistent or in some way amiss. Their marked set is then usually presented to the original proofreader, whose task it becomes to respond to every one of the second-eye's marks: accepting, rejecting or holding over corrections till the first reprint.

- Proofreaders should not focus on content and structure (that is the text editor's task), but rather on ensuring that the text editor's instructions and the book designer's rendering of them correspond.

- Keep your instructions about corrections brief and to the point.
- Write clearly and plainly.
- Proofreaders use proof correction marks to indicate their corrections. In figure 4.3 below a number of proof correction marks are given; this is by no means a final or exhaustive list, but it merely illustrates the apposite standard proof correction symbols that play an important role, namely, to indicate in the text where there is an error and what kind of error it is. If you would prefer to compile your own list of marks (probably a selection of signs from the available lists of proofreading symbols), you are free to do so; just make sure that the client receives a copy of it (for themselves and for the typesetter or designer to follow). Some publishers provide their own little list (as in a house style guide) and expect the proofreaders to follow it closely.
- *Note: The majority of text editors use these same symbols when they are editing, because they find it unnecessary to write everything out in full (it is time-consuming to write out the same correction in detail every time). The symbols are a convenient shorthand for indicating corrections, both in the text and in the margins, when one is working on paper.*
- It is important that a symbol used in the text is also mirrored in the margins and accompanied by the actual correction (see figure 4.3, a sample marked-up proof): that's where the typesetters will look for it (cf Billingham 2002: 130; Butcher, Drake & Leach 2006: 102, 2009; *Chicago manual of style* 1993: 110; Merriam-Webster 2001: 275).
- Do not mark the same correction twice; it can cause confusion in the correcting process.
- When two or more corrections occur in a single line, the corrections/symbols are written in the same sequence as the errors in the line, reading from left to right, slash marks (obliques) should separate the symbols in the margin. Proofreading symbols may be written in either margin; if several corrections must be made in a single line, they may begin in the left margin and continue in the right margin (Merriam-Webster 2001: 275), evenly distributed either side of an imaginary central vertical line (see figure 4.3).
- While you're proofreading be extremely cautious. The major problem with proofreading is that your eye often sees what it wants to see and not necessarily what stands in the text. It is, for instance, easy to read *occurence* as *occurrence*; *seperate* as *separate*. These kinds of error make a text look unfinished and unpolished. Therefore avoid proofreading when your level of concentration is low: you will almost certainly miss errors.
- Read word for word, line for line.
- Some proofreaders read the text backwards as a last pass.
- If you hesitate over anything at all, look it up rather than simply correcting it by following your gut. In this respect, homophones can be particularly troublesome, for example: *bear* vs *bare*; *site* vs *sight*. Don't let these elude you.
- Keep your reference works at hand so that you can check things easily and quickly.
- Proofreading is very good preparation for people who want to become text editors. It teaches them the importance of discipline, the ability to concentrate and to read in a focused manner – and it also helps to develop a sensitive appreciation of language and errors in texts (Judd 1990: 263–265; Saller 2009: 107–108, 117–119).

- Be aware of your weaknesses as a proofreader and do something about overcoming them.
- Don't forget Murphy's law (or, rather, 'Muphry's Law'): if things can go wrong, they will (Mackenzie, 2005: 74–6, 143; 2011: 123). Errors will occur where you least expect them to. When an author thanks the proofreader for the quality of their work, you can bet

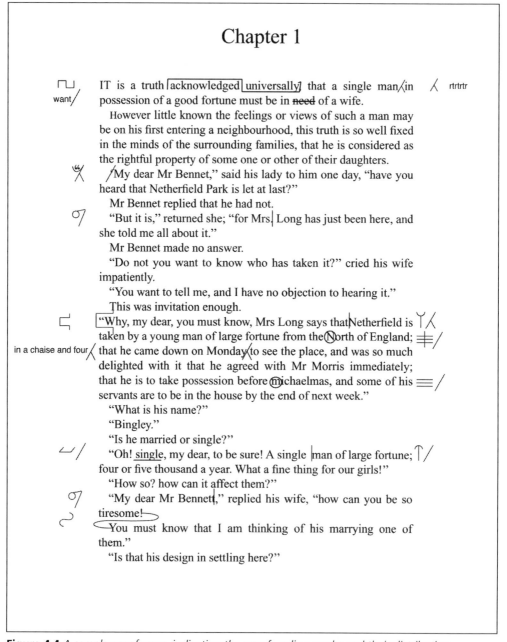

Figure 4.4 *A sample proof page, indicating the proofreading marks and their distribution*
Source: Paperlessproofs Ltd. <www.paperlessproofs.com>

that a 'printer's devil' will occur in some very noticeable place, such as on the title page! And in a book such as this, on text editing, there will no doubt be inconsistencies, even though every reasonable attempt was made to eliminate them.

Gilad (2007: 325–332) lists ten aspects that, in her judgement, form the basis of a proof-reader's brief and will ensure a continuous flow of work:

List 4.16 The recipe for effective proofreading

1. Reading through once is insufficient.

2. Also give attention to the table of contents at every stage of proof-reading (and ensure that it mirrors exactly what stands in the final text).

3. Don't forget to look at the headings and subheadings carefully, preferably in one pass.

4. Don't forget the running heads and footers.

5. Ensure that the graphics are all correct.

6. Work neatly.

7. Look out for literals (or typos) and author's errors.

8. You must not re-edit the text – that is not your job.

9. Read and read and read to expand your knowledge as widely as possible.

10. Meet your deadline.

9.4 Proofreading second, third or subsequent proofs

In feature- or illustration-heavy books it is usually the norm to go to two or three sets of proofs before the great majority of errors and omissions have been corrected and late additions proofread. The first proofread is always the most laborious and demanding, as you will have read in this section so far. The second and subsequent are less so, but at the same time they also introduce new elements to be checked.

For example, at second page proofs the illustrations and captions are likely to have been inserted for the first time; some of the preliminary matter (eg title, imprint, preface, fore-word, introduction) may have been added, as may some of the end-matter (eg appendices, glossary, bibliography). These elements will have to be proofread against the edited documents supplied, plus there will be the 'clean', corrected text to check against the corrections implemented on the first proofs.

At third proof stage, not only is the number of corrections to be checked reduced quite substantially, but the reader no longer has to proofread every single space and character. In addition, the typeset table of contents will have to be proofread against the author's or editor's original, and the typeset index (if there is one) will need a careful proofread for internal errors but also against the actual third or final page proofs. Checking the index itself can be an exacting undertaking because of all the detail it usually comprises and the conventions that have to be followed by indexers (main entries (in alphabetical order), subentries (indented uniformly), locaters, punctuation, en-rules for page ranges, italics/ bold for special purposes, and so on). Always perform a spot check of the locators against the actual pages to see that they are accurate. If the number of mismatches is too high, the index must be returned to the indexer for repairs.

At both second and third proof stages, it should be necessary to check running heads and footers as well as the pagination/folios (remember that blank pages are considered part of the numbering). And all intext cross-references will need highlighting and careful checking for accuracy and consistency.

What follows is a brief summary of the importance of proofreading and the demands that it makes on a person: 'A proofreader *examines* text, *discovers* what's wrong, and *fixes* it' (Gilad 2007: 14).

At this point, the subject of proofreading has now been thoroughly dealt with. It is clear that no editor can venture into the broad field of text editing without this skill, because the discipline of close and focused reading that it engenders is indispensable. Indeed, it can often be, as Saller (2009: 118) puts it, 'a big step toward working as a copy editor.' It is at the same time the last check in the publishing process and precisely for that reason it is important that it must be done so accurately and systematically (Beene 2009; Enquist & Oates 2009: 20–21). It is, in fact, as Baskette, Sissors & Brooks (1986: 473) have stated: a task that requires accuracy and precision and those who can do proofreading well can call themselves and be viewed as experts (sometimes even as 'artists'). You become really good at this 'art' if you continue to practise. As Ferreira and Staude (1991: 107) have put it, 'Proofreading is an art ... it is one that you only perfect after much practice.'

10 Summary

The common impression is that (editing) consists of correcting grammar and punctuation, which it does, but the job has many other aspects that make it endlessly absorbing. *If you are suited to it, editing is the best fun you can have at a desk.* Mackenzie

> When you are tempted to change your career, you realise there is no career as stimulating or rewarding as that of a language practitioner, and you bravely face a new day with its new challenges.
>
> *Greenfield*

Text editing is not exactly the simplest activity anyone can undertake to earn an income. Certainly not. Too much is asked of the person who has to do it: intensive and comprehensive training, the accumulation of relevant, useful experience over the years, exposure to a large variety of texts in the process, clients who frequently subject the text editor to impossible deadlines, clients who want to pay as little as possible for a professional service, and so on.

But in spite of all this, it remains a stimulating and rewarding challenge to be a text editor. The industry itself sorts out those who are not good enough, and for those who are really good the rewards are quite substantial – a constant supply of work, the satisfaction of seeing a completed product in print and the knowledge that they made a sound contribution towards turning an idea into a publication to be proud of.

The text editor and editorial project management

It doesn't matter how large or small the project is – if it's a real project, it needs project management.
Murphy

What does a managing editor do? People who come to this role have sometimes previously worked as a 'desk' or 'content' editor. The danger for them is knowing when to stop doing and when to stick to managing.
Davies & Balkwill

A 'good' schedule allows sufficient time to enable everyone involved to produce work to the required standard within normal working hours. One of the project manager's main responsibilities is to ensure that schedules are adequate and are maintained.
Horn

A smart project editor pads her schedule to allow for some lateness, but that isn't always possible ... There's room for a variety of work styles on [a project] editor's freelance list, but in her mind, reliability and good work will trump speed for any project where speed isn't an issue.
Saller

5

Contents

Objectives

In exploring the role of the editorial project manager in this chapter, we consider (a) the basic management functions they should perform and (b) distinguish line management from matrix management, the modus operandi that the project manager is likely to pursue when managing the production team members. Then the four principal responsibilities of the editorial project manager, namely, (c) scheduling, (d) budgeting, (e) briefing service providers and (f) quality control are described, before we consider (g) editorial project management in language bureaus. Finally, the special position and requirements of the freelance text editor as project manager are described.

2 The role of the editorial project manager

> The management of the editing process may be the responsibility of a managing editor, a project manager or a production controller, but is often the responsibility of a copyeditor.
> *Flann & Hill*

Editorial project managers are responsible for coordinating all the work on a publication, from receipt of text to publication. (In the world of magazines, their title is usually managing editor.) They, of course, don't perform all the functions themselves, but ensure that a team of specialists produce work on time, within budget and to an acceptable quality standard. Their real value lies in the overview they can have of the whole production process (Davies & Balkwill 2011: 173). The principles of a project manager's job are the same regardless of the content of the publication – whether the title is a new book or a reprint, or a journal, report, or magazine; or whether the final output is printed on paper, produced on a disk or displayed on a website (Horn 2006: viii).

They are, by definition, managers of people, of paperwork and of processes. This means they're expected to perform at least some of the classic roles of management: planning, organising, controlling and leading (or motivating):

- *Planning* (putting together a management plan)
  - Assessing the available materials in order to plan what must be done and how to do it.
  - Analysing the schedule and the budget (and, if necessary, revising them) to ensure that they are adequate to produce work of the required standard.
  - Identifying all the tasks that have to be performed to complete the project, and the requirements/specifications (audience/readership, extent, style, etc).

reprint, or a journal, report, or magazine; or whether the final output is printed on paper, produced on a disk or displayed on a website (Horn 2006: viii).

They are, by definition, managers of people, of paperwork and of processes. This means they're expected to perform at least some of the classic roles of management: planning, organising, controlling and leading (or motivating):

- *Planning* (putting together a management plan)
    - Assessing the available materials in order to plan what must be done and how to do it.
    - Analysing the schedule and the budget (and, if necessary, revising them) to ensure that they are adequate to produce work of the required standard.
    - Identifying all the tasks that have to be performed to complete the project, and the requirements/specifications (audience/readership, extent, style, etc).

- *Organising*
    - Selecting the most appropriate practitioners to work on a project (Flann & Hill 2004: 11).
    - Briefing the team members to enable them to do their work to the required standard.
    - Making the working relationship with service providers legally binding.
    - Saller (2009: 87) writes about the usefulness of logs as good organising tools: project managers, for example, can keep a spreadsheet log of freelances, with dates in and out, rates per hour or page, invoice totals, contact information, and anything else that is useful.

- *Controlling*
    - Supervising the work to ensure that schedules are met, budgets adhered to and quality delivered (Flann & Hill 2004: 11).
    - Setting out protocols for the accountability of each member of the team.
    - Establishing, maintaining and facilitating communications between all the team members.

- *Leading*
    - Providing feedback to the team, acknowledging work done well and providing constructive criticism of shortcomings, to build good working relationships and a strong team (Flann & Hill 2004: 18; Horn 2006: viii). Leading should therefore include a strong motivational element.

2.1 What is a project?

Murphy's response to this question is to point out the four defining features of projects (2011: 44–45):
- Each project has a definite beginning and a definite end.

- Each has direction – it's goal-oriented.
- Each consists of connected or interrelated activities or tasks – everything that has to be completed before you can say that the project is finished to satisfaction.
- Each is unique: no two projects are exactly the same.

Of projects and project management, Murphy (2011: 45) has the following to say: 'The principles of project management remain the same for every project, large or small, but the components change every time, so each new project is a different ball game.'

But project management is a special kind of management, different from the usual line management found in typical organisations. This is known as 'matrix management'.

Matrix management involves managing a team (or matrix) of skills, whether inhouse or freelance, specifically required for a discrete project that also has a fixed term. In it, the players are drawn from different disciplines – and sometimes from other teams, or they may serve two or more teams simultaneously – and as soon as the project is completed, the team dissolves and the players go their separate ways, often to join other project teams. This usually means the players cannot be motivated in the same way as salaried individuals working in 9–5 jobs; it also means that the team players and the project manager often have to cope with competing demands from different projects. Editorial project managers have to build these constraints into their planning, organising and controlling to ensure that they can realistically deliver an acceptable product on time. If, for example, one practitioner (the ideal choice for a certain project) is overburdened or unavailable when required, the project manager either has to have a backup service provider in place or has to see whether the practitioner's services can be used earlier or later in the production schedule.

Who are the team members referred to above? A variety of titles are used in the industry, indicated by the alternatives in the list below:

List 5.1 Possible members of a project matrix

> Publisher/commissioning editor/acquisitions editor

> Production manager/production editor/production controller

> Publishing services manager

> Managing editor/editorial manager/project manager

> Text editor/copy-editor

> Overwriter/rewriter/ghostwriter/copywriter

> Translator

> Proofreader

>>

List 5.1 continued

> Typesetter/designer

> Book designer

> Photo researcher

> Permissions administrator

> Book illustrator/artist/DTP artist

> Indexer.

The management of this team can – and often does – take any number of forms, depending upon the organisation and the project itself. On the one hand, the project manager may manage each of these individuals directly or, on the other hand, do so indirectly by relying upon a competent, experienced copy-editor to manage, say, the proofreader (or to do the proofreading themselves), to brief and manage the book illustrator and/or the photo researcher, and possibly to brief and manage the indexer.

Many text editors take on the role of editorial project manager at some stage during the course of their careers, but in order to be able to manage people and processes competently, the attributes (or key performance areas) of a project manager must include:

List 5.2 Attributes of a project manager

> an understanding of the basic role of authors, commissioning editors, text editors, overwriters, proofreaders, indexers, picture researchers, designers, typesetters, illustrators and production managers;

> familiarity with the principles of editing and marking up copy;

> a knowledge of the standard proofreading symbols and how they are used;

> an ability to collate proofs;

> a basic knowledge of copyright law;

> a knowledge of the basics of what constitutes a contract;

> basic numeracy (for scheduling, budgeting and processing invoices);

> an understanding of the stages and processes of book or magazine production;

> having access to and being able to use a personal computer, wordprocessor, email and the internet;

>>

List 5.2 continued

> strong organisational skills, including being deadline- and quality-driven;

> an ability to manage people with confidence, firmness, tact and empathy.

This is certainly a wide range of competencies, so it should not be a role the text editor should take on lightly. Some exposure, at least, to each of them is essential if you are to perform this key role effectively.

If the project manager is not working inhouse, a contract must be drawn up between them and the publishing house. This contract should include such matters as (Flann & Hill 2004: 19):

• Is it a fixed contract or can changes be made if the project runs over budget? Are there penalties for exceeding the budget?

• Who is responsible for paying the contract/freelance staff?

• When will the project management receive payment(s), especially if the project has a very long time frame? Can they claim for reasonable out-of-pocket expenses directly related to the project?

• Is there provision for compensation or rescheduling if the project is delayed by an outside agency (such as the typesetter or the printer) over which they have no control?

The principal stages in the production process which the editorial project manager must understand if they are to draw up meaningful, workable schedules and manage projects effectively are these (Horn 2006: ix):

List 5.3 Principal stages in production

1. Project proposed, costed and publication date agreed before acceptance.

2. Author's materials received by commissioning editor.

3. Author's materials handed over into production, edited and marked up; author queries resolved. Separate CD-ROM materials are identified and dealt with in preparation for replication.

4. Design and layout of content finalised; cover designed; cover blurb written.

5. Textual matter typeset, illustrations created and/or scanned.

>>

6. Proofs produced and proofread (as many times as required, until a print-ready master set is attained).

7. Proofs corrected (as many times as will be required to attain a flawless master set). These are distributed at least to the proofreader, the author and the publisher.

8. Master set sent for PDFing or scanning, in preparation for printing.

9. Publication printed and bound, or content uploaded to website; occasionally, a complementary CD is burned.

10. Advance copies received from printer, one of which becomes a correction copy.

Once a project has been initiated, the plan must be implemented. During this phase the four principal responsibilities of a project manager in publishing are keeping the project and its subprojects on schedule, ensuring that the allocated overall budget and sub-budgets are not overrun, briefing and liaising with service providers and maintaining quality control throughout (Murphy 2011: 48). This can be rather demanding when, as typically happens, the project manager is allocated several projects simultaneously. Each of the responsibilities is described below.

2.2 Scheduling

> A proper schedule is the foundation for the success of each project. When you plot the schedules of all your projects showing the critical and subsidiary paths, you have a tool that helps you manage your resources and control your work.
> *Horn*

Planning begins with putting a schedule for the project together. It is a framework of time and activities delimited by when the document must be published, on the one hand, and when the manuscript is received, on the other. Some of the project manager's main responsibilities as a planner are to ensure that schedules are realistic, that all members of the team are aware of the time frame for their particular contribution, and that, through monitoring each person's progress, the time frames are maintained once they have been set (Flann & Hill 2004: 21; Horn 2006: 1–2). Some of the factors that can affect the schedule include:

- the form in which the author delivers the manuscript (ie well or badly written; handwritten or in electronic format);
- the number of pages the book will make (ie its extent);
- whether the book is to be printed in one colour or four colours;
- the complexity of the content (eg how many hand-drawn or DTP illustrations and photographs there are);

- whether the book has an index or not;
- how many authors are involved; and
- how close the checking of the text needs to be (eg a medical book with many diagrams and medicine dosages will need very careful checking by several pairs of eyes, including those of medical/pharmaceutical experts).

The most common way of presenting a schedule is the classic Gantt chart (Murphy 2011: 46–47), where each stage in a process is represented by a 'step' that also indicates the time allocated to it. Nowadays, such a chart is easily created using MS Excel worksheets:

Time (weeks)	1	2	3	4	5	6	7	8	9	10	11	12	13	14
Activity 1														
Activity 2														
Activity 3														
Activity 4														

Figure 5.1 *A Gantt chart representing the tasks or activities in a production schedule*

But, simple and clear though this type of chart is, it seldom lends itself to more complex schedules where, for example, tasks performed simultaneously or in parallel have to be taken into account.

Accordingly, critical path analysis is a technique used most frequently in putting together production schedules for print media. The critical path is the chain of events that determines the minimum amount of time needed to complete the overall task (Davies & Balkwill 2011: 181, 182); an analysis of the production process entails looking for ways to shorten

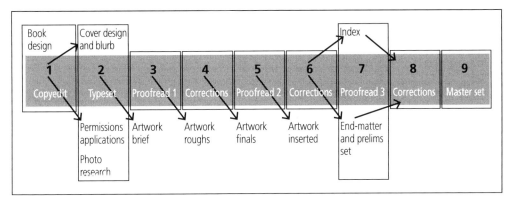

Figure 5.2 *The critical path (shaded stages 1–9) of the production of a book*

the time taken to complete a project, usually by looking for opportunities to perform overlapping tasks simultaneously. This interpretation of a production schedule could look something like figure 5.2 above.

So, for example, a project manager will analyse all the tasks and see which can happen simultanously (or in parallel, such as doing the photo research while the text is being typeset) and which can only be done in series (stages 1–9 in figure 5.2), because one must be completed before the next can begin (as in typesetting following editing, and in turn being followed by proofreading). Something like the cover design, for example, can be executed at any time during the production period, as long as it's ready at the time the book is due to go for printing. The critical path (shaded in figure 5.2) will be the time it will take for the serial tasks to be completed.

Typically, a schedule comprises a collection of subschedules (or subsidiary critical paths) – one for each of the production tasks, for example, copy-editing or artwork briefing and execution. The good project manager will build in to the schedule a bit of 'fat', that is, a day or two extra here or there to allow for any delays along the way. If it's not used, all the better; but it's nevertheless built in to buffer subschedule delays; though, as Davies & Balkwill (2011: 181) caution, one should guard against scheduling contingencies leading to a false sense of confidence or even complacency. However, each task is expected not to overshoot its deadline (including fat), because that is likely to have a knock-on effect on the other tasks, which will have the potential to make the project as a whole run behind schedule. Having said that, though, it's essential that delays be communicated to the project editor or managing editor so that they can strategise with the rest of the team, especially those immediately affected by the delay (Saller 2009: 34).

When schedules are being compiled, the project manager must start at the publication date and work back to the present (that is, the manuscript due date). The reason for this can be that a book launch is planned for a specific (immovable) date; that the issue of the journal will be needed at an international conference; that the books must be delivered to schools or universities in time for the new term; or there's some or other celebration for which the title will be required. In such cases, the longer the time frame between project commencement and estimated publication date, the easier it will be for the project manager.

When assembling schedules, the project manager must take into account unproductive public holidays and times when, for example, typesetters and printers are at their busiest and therefore turnaround times will be slower than normal.

Having started out as a planning tool, the schedule soon becomes a means of both organising the role-players and controlling the progress of the project. By consulting the schedule, you're able to specify when the different service providers' services will be required – the text editor's, the illustrator's and the typesetter's, for example – and book their time accordingly. This is precisely why editorial project managers must, as far as possible, have a good working knowledge of the tasks that each of the players in their team performs.

Moreover, most projects are monitored continuously, if only for weekly management reporting meetings. The schedule then becomes the 'master plan' against which daily, weekly and monthly progress can be measured. Project managers must therefore inculcate in their service providers an awareness of the need to meet their deadlines and to forewarn the project manager as soon as they become aware of any delays that are likely to occur.

With illustrated books, if the text editor has been tasked with managing the creation of the illustrations, then they will be required, as part of their editorial role, to:

- draw up the artwork list for the book;
- create a set of artwork briefs (one brief per artist);
- receive, distribute to the author and sign off the artwork roughs (or visuals);
- return them to the artist, and then to manage the process of producing the final artwork.

If digital or photographic images have to be sourced or photographs taken, it often falls to the text editor to manage this process too.

If copyright permissions are required for any materials used in a book (ie illustrations or quoted matter), the text editor should be alerted to the fact that they have to identify where permissions will be required while they are editing the manuscript, and provide the project manager with a comprehensive list of whatever needs permission, including the full publishing details of the source.

2.3 Budgeting

A budget for a publication is an estimate of the maximum costs to achieve a particular qualitative result – the budget for a novel is likely to be lower than for a full-colour recipe book, for example, because of the higher quality and more complicated inputs required in the latter. The budget should include a contingency amount (that is, an amount for unforeseen expenses), since it's often very difficult to predict the problems that are likely to beset a book while in production.

It is usually the commissioning editor (or publisher) who puts together each book estimate, an important document which indicates whether publication, and therefore production, should be proceeded with at all. The editorial project manager may be asked to estimate certain costs or they may simply be given a budget to work with. Either way, you have to appreciate the input costs that go into a budget and how those costs will determine whether a project is to remain financially viable or not. It's precisely the reason why you should not allow any of your service providers to exceed the agreed-upon budget for their service without an exceptionally good reason. The direct costs attached to each task must remain sacrosanct (Horn 2006: 19, 29), though Flann & Hill (2004: 20) point out that project managers usually have some leeway about deciding how to allocate their resources while working within a fixed budget.

In the budget below (figure 5.3), the significant figures as far as the project manager is concerned are the external costs (also known as work in progress costs), because they relate to the fees to be charged by the team members they will manage. Together with the cost of printing and binding, these constitute a significant input cost that will ultimately affect the profit that the publisher is able to make on each copy of the book sold (unit selling price minus unit costs). The higher these input costs, the lower the profit margin, the greater the chances of the book not being financially viable and therefore not a publishing proposition.

Costed quantity		2,000
Specimen copies		50
Net total sales		**1,950**
Sales Year 1		**1,200**
Print & bind		60,000
Origination		0.00
Total		**60,000**
Sundries		
External costs:		
Edit/proofread		24,000
Typesetting/DTP		20,000
Illustrations		500
DTP illustrations		2,000
Recoup DTP illustrations		–2,000
Scans		200
Cover artwork		800
Cover design		2,500

Index		9,600
Recoup index		−9,600
Total:		**48,000**
Total production cost:		**108,000**
Print cost per unit		30.00
Production cost per unit		24.00
Total unit cost:		**54.00**
Markup		3,.50
Price VAT incl		215.46
Price VAT excl		189.00
Extent		800
Production cost per page		0.07
Selling price per page		0.27

Deductions from SP:		
Royalty (%)		12.00%
Trade discount (%)		35.00%
Publishing overheads		30.00%
Editorial/Distribution		7.00%
VAT rate		14.00%
Price less discount	189.00 − 66.15	122.85
Price less royalty	22.68	100.17
Turnover		100.00%
Prime cost of sales	108,000	
Royalties	21,546	12.00%

>>

Distribution		
Gross profit		
Publishing overheads		
Nett profit		
Break even (no of units)	720	
Cost/discount breakdown		
Value per copy	**SP/(VAT/ex-VAT)**	**W/sale price**
VAT		
Trade discount		35.00%
Author's share		12.00%
Production costs		
Advertising		
Overheads		
Nett profit		
Total:		

Figure 5.3 *A sample book budget*

Moreover, when deciding between competing quotes, the cheapest option is not always the most cost-effective – an experienced freelance with a higher rate is likely to work efficiently and to time, will know how to present copy for designers and printers, and will often be able to detect and deal with potential problems before they cause disruption to the budget and schedule. To make sure that the budget is maintained:

• Ensure from the outset that it is adequate for the project you have to manage, based on prevailing rates.
• Negotiate payments for work with external suppliers in line with the budgeted amounts.
• Control the quality of the work while in progress – in order not to cause undue extra expenditure at a later stage.
• Maintain the schedule, which is directly related to costs insofar as slippage at one stage could lead to pressure at another stage, with additional costs being incurred to improve the quality of rushed work or because higher rates are charged for working overtime.

In practice, it is the editorial project manager who has to ensure that external suppliers do not exceed the budgeted-for fees by closely examining all part-invoices submitted to them. In the final instance, the sum of their invoices must not exceed the budgeted-for and agreed-upon fees. Service providers must also be encouraged to speak up sooner rather than later when they find cause for a budget to be revised – for example, when the state of the manuscript handed over by the author is substandard and will require a heavier edit than anticipated; or the number of illustrations turns out to be much less or greater than what had originally been indicated. With early advance notification, and before the work is actually undertaken, a project manager is usually able to 'make a plan' to find extra funds, but not ex post facto.

2.4 Briefing service providers

The publishing house will have briefed the project manager on the anticipated readership for the title. This information must be conveyed to the author(s), the editors, the designers, the permissions administrator, the illustrator(s) and anyone else working on the text in the form of detailed specifications of the extent, language level, writing style, house style requirements and special issues. If the project includes ancillary materials such as CD-ROMs or web content, it is important that they are compatible in style and language level with the publication (Flann & Hill 2004: 21).

Briefs give service providers the essential information they need to perform tasks to your satisfaction. While there is always a degree of assumed knowledge (for example, that a text editor has a mastery of grammar or is fully conversant with word processing software or has an eagle eye for inconsistencies – that's why you selected them to work on a particular title in the first place), a brief should be limited to information relevant only to a specific job. It should include all the information a service provider would require to produce the results you want.

When compiling a brief, you should draw on the commissioning editor's original brief to you (about the book as a whole), the publishing contract, a synopsis of the book and any other relevant documentation (such as the advance information sheet or the proposal to publish form), and your own assessment of the materials you've received. (Inhouse project managers will usually have access to the publishing contract; freelances will have to ask for access to only the relevant sections that will affect the scheduling, for example.)

According to Horn (2006: 72), there are five elements to the brief for all text editors (or proofreaders), and a sixth one for freelances:

1. A list of the materials supplied: recipients should always be asked to check that they have received exactly the materials listed as soon as possible after the briefing.
2. Relevant background information: this might include how the subject is being dealt with; changes either agreed to or rejected by the author; the main problems with the text (including whether it needs cutting or expanding, and by how much); implications of the target audience and the sales market; relevant author information.

Proofreading brief	
Title:	ISSN:
Publication date:	Issue number:
Flat plan supplied: Yes/No	Extent: pages (incl prelims and end-matter)
Publisher:	Editor:
Managing editor:	Production manager:
Designer:	Copy editor/subeditor:
Proofreader:	Picture researcher:
Background information: Author: Readership profile: Special features and problem areas: Proofreader's brief: House style manual/style sheet provided: Yes/No Design specification provided: Yes/No First proofs: Second proofs: Third proofs (including/excluding preliminary pages and end-matter): Prelims comprise: End-matter comprises: Colour coding required: Yes/No Special features/characters to note:	
Deadline(s): First batch of proofs:	Second batch of proofs: Third batch of proofs:
Queries: • Resolve with author • Send to managing editor	Permissions: • Check • Prepare detailed list of items needing
Liaise with: • Managing editor only • Designer • Picture researcher • Proofreader	
Other:	

Figure 5.4 *A sample proofreader's brief form*

3. The level of the text editing task: is it a light, a medium or a heavy edit? (See chapter 3 section 4.) Will the text editor work on hard copy or e-files, or both?

4. Alternatively, for the proofreader: the type of proofreading to be done – on hard copy or on PDFs ('blind' or 'cold'). In the case of PDFs, you will need to agree with the proofreader whether the document will be read onscreen or printed out; if the latter, what their per-page rate for printing out PDFs will be; how to return the corrections to you

5. A checklist of specific tasks or responsibilities.

6. The schedule: confirm in writing the freelances' availability to meet the agreed-upon deadlines.

7. The agreed fee: confirm in writing the agreed-upon fee for the task.

The briefing document may take the form of a letter of appointment (see figure 5.5) drafted by the client; once it has been read and signed by both parties (with or without amendment), it constitutes a legally binding document.

Both text editor and proofreader should be handed a copy of the house style guide or the style sheet for the series, if the title is part of a series.

After an initial briefing session, it is a sound practice to follow up a few days later to check that the practitioner has fully digested and correctly understood the brief, or that further information may be required or questions answered. This period will also be one in which the freelance will have an opportunity to (re)consider the brief, the schedule and the fee and return to negotiate any adjustments, if necessary.

When the covering letter of appointment, the brief and its accompanying documentation are accepted by the freelance service provider and countersigned by the client's representative, they form a binding contract.

2.5 Quality control

Another important facet of the editorial project manager's role is to assess the quality of service providers' output. Here again, experience in or exposure to the different tasks required to bring a title to fruition is essential to effective management. Effective project management also depends upon an individual's ability to delegate, but three key elements will contribute towards your achieving your goal:

- Your selection of the most suitable and qualified service providers for the job.
- The quality of your briefs.
- Your ability to monitor the service providers' work (Murphy (2011: 48).

PUBLISHER'S LETTERHEAD

[Editor's name and address]   [Date]

Dear X

[TITLE OF PUBLICATION] [EDITION]

Thank you for agreeing to [copy-edit/proofread] the above publication for us.
The specifications are as follows:

Title: [Book title]
Author/editor: [Author/editor name]
Book format: 228 x 152 mm
Extent: 320 pages
ISBN: 978 1 91998 023 7
Copy-edit: [Copy-editor's brief spelt out here, including a reference to the House Style that should be
                  followed.]
Background: [Description of the authors, the purpose/objective of the book and the target audience;
                  also the level at which it is pitched]

Please pay particular attention to the following aspects of the author's writing:
- Passive voice: convert, wherever possible, to active voice
- Unnecessary punctuation: use minimal stops and commas (Dr, eg, ie, Mr, Prof, Rev)
- Initial cap or lowercase letter in headings: will differ, depending on heading level
- No serial commas: red, white and blue, not red, white, and blue
- All 'ise' should be 'ize'
- Single quotes instead of double quotes (also secure the tools required)
- Cross-references to specific terms/words: italics, not quotation marks
- Spell out century numbers (eighteenth century)
- Racial labels: do not capitalise black, coloured, white; but Asian and Indian must take an initial cap
- 'Among', not 'amongst'; 'while', not 'whilst'; 'amid', not 'amidst'
- Adverbial participles (eg warmly received, freshly ground): do not hyphenate.
Pay close attention to consistency in the use of symbols (*, #, etc) and the formats of words (abbreviations,
bold, italics, alternative fonts, etc). The unedited hard copy will be supplied as a reference.

Target readership: Academics in the field of [subject field] but also to non-academics interested in the
                     subject. It will be distributed through bookstores nationally.
Editorial style sheet: To be supplied at handover.

Tasks to be undertaken:

Task	Yes/No
Author queries: mark up for the author's attention	Yes
Check spelling, punctuation, consistency, language	Yes
Check artwork labelling, especially against conventions in text	No

>>

Check bibliography in detail, and against intext references	Yes
Copyright permissions	Possibly; flag if detected
Proofread up to 2nd pages	Yes
Check typesetting style for consistency – use of different fonts, bold, italics, etc	Yes – at all proofreading stages
Check prelims, including contents pages/folios against body text	Yes – at final proofs
Check that line breaks and paragraphing are acceptable	Yes – at first proof stage
Check and eliminate widows and orphans	Yes – at all proofreading stages

Deadlines & production schedule: [insert dates for copy-editing and/or proofreading here]
A timeline for the project will be supplied.

Fee: [insert fee here for the copy-editing or reading two sets of proofs]
The publisher deducts/does not deduct 25% for income tax from the invoiced amount.

Please read this document carefully prior to initialling all but the last page and signing the last page to indicate your acceptance of the project. If you have any questions regarding any of the details, please raise them with the undersigned.

Yours sincerely
[SIGNATURE OF PUBLISHER OR PROJECT MANAGER]

Figure 5.5 *A sample letter of appointment for a text editor or proofreader*

It starts with your attending key meetings such as the handover and then checking the work done by each team member before you pass it on to the next player. During the implementation phase, you constantly have to evaluate the quality of the deliverables.

Checking the text editor's work: While you really do need to know how to edit text in order to be able to assess or check the work of your service provider, avoid the temptation of tampering with the text simply because you've found things that, while not incorrect, you would have done differently. Errors, of course, have to be corrected, but other changes to satisfy your preferences will be counter-productive. Rather focus on when, or how often, or to what extent, you will check the text editor's work – for example, an initial sample so that appropriate corrective action can be taken early on. Furthermore, encourage the text editor (and all your other team members) to raise any problems with you at any stage – there must be no stigma attached to doing so.

Next, create a checklist of the key tasks you require the text editor to perform, check a few random paragraphs and, if Track Changes has been used, assess both the number/

extent of the changes and whether they correctly interpret your brief. If the text editor was required to rewrite where specified, and either cut or expand text, check that they have done so according to your specifications. Similarly, check that they have prepared a permissions list and a set of artwork briefs, as required.

Then check randomly selected passages for the standard of general text editing: does the edited text pass the tests of clarity, conciseness, correctness and consistency in the way headings, tables, quoted matter, notes and cross-references have been edited, for example? Also conduct random checks that the house style has been applied (Horn 2006: 106).

Checking the proofreader's work: As with text editing, your job as editorial project manager is to *check*, not proofread. The difficulty here, though, is that proofs are typically returned as one complete batch, which makes the job of checking more onerous and time-consuming. Counteract this by breaking up the task of checking into parts and focus on each one at a time (Horn 2006: 114):

- Check that the standard proofreading marks have been used correctly, and the pages marked up correctly and clearly.
- Has colour coding been applied correctly? What is the proportion of red (typos) and blue (editor's and author's literals)? Does too many blue marks indicate that the proofreader is making too many unnecessary marks? Or that the editing was not thorough?
- Look at the queries raised by the proofreader. Have they been correctly marked? Are they reasonable (ie not requiring responses the proofreader could have found in references)?
- Are there any messages to the designer or the typesetter? What do they tell you about the work done by either?
- At page proof stage, have blank cross-references (000 or XXX) been left blank or filled in?
- Check any paragraphs that have remained unmarked: do you spot any errors the proofreader missed, or are they error-free?

2.6 The editorial project manager as communicator

An important skill that an effective project manager must possess is the ability to communicate with their team and, allied to that, to be able to anticipate or pre-empt deadlines and problems and communicate about them before they're likely to occur. Lines of communication will have been set up with all the team members by the time you have completed the briefings – which should, ideally, be both written and face to face (Horn 2006: 99). Where they can be conducted only via email or Skype, the communications should be at least as detailed as a face-to-face meeting should be.

As a manager, you have to inculcate a culture of open and honest communications from the outset: so you should be as good at listening to what others have to say as at imparting information. Doing so will help you to stay on top of your projects and the participants in them: for example, telephoning, SMSing or emailing a service provider 72 or 48 hours before deadline to check whether they're on track for a delivery on deadline. And having service providers notify you well in advance (and for good reason) that a deadline will not be met or they've struck a problem that's likely to hold delivery up. If individuals fail to report at the specified times, contact them, and take note of it: you may want to use them again because of their other skills, and it's best that you be forewarned and prepared for their inability to meet this part of the brief (Horn 2006: 99).

3 Editorial project management in language bureaus

Despite the fact that every language bureau has its own unique way of managing editorial projects, the general principles of editorial project management apply across the board. The principles of and guidelines for project management form the basis of the decision whether to use a group of inhouse or freelance/contract text editors.

Usually the head of the language bureau performs the role of editor-in-chief and project manager, but this function can also be delegated to a senior text editor, or it can even be contracted out. If the text-editing project is multilingual, then a separate editor should head up the work on each language. The importance of using an experienced project coordinator can also not be overemphasised.

Once the instruction to proceed has been received and it has been established that the language bureau has the capability to execute it, the project team is assembled. The project leader then collaborates with the client in putting together a project plan. Regular meetings, work sessions or Skype/telephone conferences are scheduled during which every aspect of the project plan is discussed.

The project plan should take account of aspects such as:

List 5.4 Tasks of the project team

> planning and project coordination;

> making a decision about the form of the text editing, for example whether it should be done on hard copy, electronically, or using a combination of both;

> compiling an overall project plan and index;

> assembling the translation and text editing team(s);

> internationalising the product (eg when a product is designed and implemented so as to be as culturally and technically neutral as possible so that it can be localised for specific cultures);

>>

> localisation of the product (eg to modify a product such as a software application or hardware component so that it meets the language, cultural and other requirements of a specific target environment or market);

> the compilation of terminology lists and style sheets (or word lists);

> the scheduling of the work;

> the allocation of resources for every aspect of the process;

> the completion of milestones in the production process;

> quality control;

> the financial aspects of the project;

> Liaison with the layout artist/designer and the printer.

In addition, all the aspects of text editing dealt with in chapters 6 to 10 apply also to editorial project management.

4 Editorial project management and the freelance text editor

There was a time when the editorial project management role was considered to be a core function of a publishing house that could not be outsourced, for a number of reasons. However, in recent years, with publishing houses being forced to downsize and rely more heavily than before on freelance service providers for what are now considered to be non-core functions, increasingly, more experienced freelance text editors are being approached to take on complete project management assignments – from handover of the manuscript right through to the PDF stage prior to printing. Such assignments can range from prescribed textbooks and annual reports to a large corporate's website origination or upgrade.

In such cases, the text editor must ensure that they possess the necessary technical knowledge and resources to take on such a large-scale project involving management roles such as planning, organising and controlling as well as scheduling, budgeting, quality control and constant supervision of and communication with the team members.

4.1 Contractual matters

Your contract as freelance project manager would also have to spell out your *rights* and *obligations*, as well as the *specifics* of your brief, clearly. These should be incorporated in a written contract, signed by both the publishing organisation and you (Flann & Hill 2004: 19). Matters that may have to be negotiated include the following:

- Is it a fixed contract or can changes be made if the project runs over budget?
- Will penalties be imposed if the budget is exceeded, even if for reasons beyond the project manager's control?
- Who is responsible for paying the contract or freelance service providers? If the project is expected to run over an extended period, will provision be made for payments at regular intervals?
- If the project is delayed by an outside agency, is there provision for compensation or rescheduling?
- When will payments be made to the project manager? May they claim for out-of-pocket expenses?
- Is there a clause covering professional liability? (The contractor may have to take out costly insurance if this is the case.)

We provide below (figure 5.6) a standard contract (memorandum of agreement) used by some publishers for engaging the services of contract or freelance practitioners. It can be adapted to suit the individual circumstances of a variety of freelance practitioners involved in wordsmithing and publishing.

4.2 Staffing the project team

Some or all of the team members will be recruited from outside the organisation, and this responsibility will normally fall on the project manager's shoulders. The question then arises: Who has the final say in the choice of service providers – the client or the contracted project manager? A number of scenarios can pertain. In some cases the external project manager may be expected to assemble their own team for a project, in which case their contract and remuneration will include provision for payment of contract and freelance staff. In other instances, the project manager will be responsible for the recruitment of practitioners and for keeping costs within budget, but the practitioners' actual payment will be the responsibility of the client.

Where a project manager is unable to source the most experienced or reliable or expert people, they could either put the positions out to tender or approach professional societies for lists of members' names, skills, specialities and experience. 'Word-of-mouth' recommendations might also be obtained from professional colleagues. When choosing between candidates, it is vital to make sure that all are given exactly the same detailed brief in order to ensure equitable treatment and allay any hint of favouritism or nepotism (Flann & Hill 2004: 20).

MEMORANDUM OF AGREEMENT
(Standard contract)

Memorandum of Agreement made and entered into by and between

_____

(hereinafter referred to as the '_____' on behalf of himself/herself and his/her heirs, executors, administrators, legal personal representatives and assigns, of the one part, AND

_____

(hereinafter referred to as the 'Publisher') on behalf of itself, its successors in business and assigns, of the other part.

Whereby it is mutually agreed as follows:

1. SERVICES TO BE SUPPLIED

The _____ agrees to supply services listed on the Schedule to the Agreement with respect to an original work at present entitled

_____

(hereinafter referred to as the 'Work'). The _____ agrees not to subcontract any of these services without the written permission of the Publisher.

2. PRESENTATION OF TYPESCRIPT

The Publisher will provide the _____ with the typescript of the Work on computer disk in MSWord or another Microsoft Office programme, and the _____ will return the edited typescript to the Publisher in the same form unless otherwise agreed. The Publisher will also provide the _____ with a printout of the typescript and may require the _____ to indicate all editorial changes on this print-out. When preparing the typescript electronically the _____ will strictly follow the rules contained in the Publisher's document entitled 'Guidelines for the preparation of documents on disk'. The _____ undertakes to do daily back-ups of the Work and to exercise the greatest possible care in all other ways during the electronic preparation of the Work to prevent the typescript from being erased or becoming corrupt.

3. STANDARD OF WORK

Should the Publisher within its sole discretion consider that the work produced by the _____ is not of a sufficiently high standard, the _____ shall be informed of the Publisher's objections to the said work and shall be given a reasonable opportunity to rectify such deficiencies. Should the _____ within an agreed reasonable time not sufficiently rectify such deficiencies, the Publisher shall be entitled within its sole discretion either to cancel this Agreement and claim expenses, including damages, from the _____ or, alternatively, to instruct a third party to rectify the deficiencies and subtract any expenses thereby incurred from any payments due to the _____.

The Publisher will pay for the corrections to _____, which may reasonably be considered to be as a result of misunderstanding in or alterations to the original briefing, but is not responsible for corrections which occur as a result of the _____'s not following the art brief. The latter will be done at the _____'s expense.

>>

4. COPYRIGHT AND OWNERSHIP

The _____ hereby assigns to the Publisher, for the full term of copyright and without limitation, the ownership and copyright of the said work, including any special characters or features which may have been specially created for the Work.

5. DEADLINES

The _____ agrees to provide each of the services listed on the Schedule by the specified deadlines. Should the _____ fail to meet these deadlines, without reasons which are acceptable to the Publisher within its sole discretion, then the Publisher may withhold the payment specified in this Agreement, or a pro-rata portion of the payment (such portion to be determined by the Publisher), or cancel this Agreement and commission another _____ to perform the work required.

Should the Publisher have made payments to the _____ in advance and in anticipation of receiving the services specified in the Schedule and should the _____ subsequently fail to provide such services, the _____ shall refund all such monies advanced to him/her by the Publisher.

6. PAYMENT

The Publisher shall pay the _____ the sum of R_____ (in words as well) (specified in the Schedule) within 30 days of receipt and approval of the agreed services on receipt of invoice from the _____. In the event of changes being made to the Publisher's brief, the _____ shall notify the Publisher of any extra costs likely to be incurred before proceeding.

The payment specified in this clause and on the schedule is a one-off fee covering all editions and impressions of the Work, and the _____ acknowledges that no further payments of any kind shall be made to him/her in connection with the services supplied in terms of this Agreement, unless the Publisher at a later date should require the _____ to work on a new edition of the Work, in which event a separate Agreement shall be entered into between the Publisher and the _____ for such work.

7. ATTRIBUTION OF WORK

The _____ will receive due credit in the Work on the imprint page. The form of the credit shall be at the Publisher's discretion.

8. FREE COPY

The _____ shall be entitled to receive on publication ONE free copy of the first impression of the Work.

9. ARBITRATION

This Agreement shall be subject to the laws of the Republic of South Africa and if any difference shall arise between the Publisher and the _____ touching the meaning of the agreement or the rights and liabilities of the parties hereto or any matters arising herefrom, the same shall be referred to the arbitration of two persons (one to be named by each party) or their umpire, in accordance with the provisions of the Arbitration Act No 42 of 1965 or any subsisting statutory modification or re-enactment thereof. Such arbitration shall take place in Cape Town.

10. DOMICILIUM CITANDI ET EXECUTANDI

It is agreed by the _____ and the Publisher that their respective addresses as set out above shall be the addresses to which all notices, processes or other documents may be served or sent in terms of this Agreement.

>>

SIGNED AT _____

This _____ day of _____ 20___

PUBLISHER _____

SUPPLIER _____

In the presence of the undersigned witnesses

WITNESS 1 _____

WITNESS 2 _____

Please supply copies of all correspondence with the author(s) for our files. On completion of the job, return all proofs, briefs etc, as well as originals of all correspondence.

Figure 5.6 *A standard contract (memorandum of agreement) between a publisher and a service provider*

5 In conclusion

As a result of a growing trend in publishing houses and other institutions to shed full-time editorial and production staff, the need to manage book, magazine and special projects in newspaper publishing has increased and the role of project manager has become critical to the successful conclusion of publishing projects.

The role of the project manager is to plan, organise and control projects staffed by a matrix of specialists that include text editors, proofreaders, translators, illustrators, typesetters and indexers. In order to manage projects effectively, the incumbents have to be able to create and manage schedules and budgets, and also exercise a quality control function over all deliverables.

Whereas, traditionally, project management was seen to be a full-time function usually assigned to an experienced inhouse text editor (for example, in publishing houses and language bureaus), increasingly, publishers have come to realise that it is a function that can be outsourced to capable text editors with a proven track record, and this chapter looks in some detail at what the attributes and responsiblities of the text editor who assumes the role of project manager are.

Text editing in practice: content

A really good copy editor is a great prize. A bad one is an unbelievable pain in the
***.
Allen

Unto those Three Things which the Ancients held impossible, there should be added
this Fourth, to find a Book Printed without errata.
Alfonso de Cartagena

English is a rich and fluid language and ... one person's unbreakable rule is another
person's insufferable pedantry.
Taggart & Wines

6

Contents

Objectives

The following five chapters focus on the application of the principles that were introduced in chapter 2. We aim to (a) provide guidelines for implementing the knowledge, (b) indicate the challenges, and (c) provide tips and insights with respect to personal preferences.

Chapter 6 introduces the chapters on the application of the principles with some reflections on norm and deviation before looking at the textual level of content. In chapters 7 to 10, we focus on how to apply the knowledge of normative grammar, text linguistics and document design raised in chapter 2. Chapter 7 discusses the practice of text editing from a structural point of view and points back to text-linguistic principles. More particularly, the role of paragraphs and of coherence in argumentation is discussed. The textual level of wording is the focus of chapter 8, where we shine the spotlight on grammar, meaning, style and register. Finally, chapters 9 and 10 look at the textual level of presentation, and the subject-matter of these chapters ranges from the attention that must be accorded to spelling and punctuation (chapter 9) to that which must be given to typography and layout (chapter 10).

Chapter 11 complements the preceding chapters, providing as it does some hints and tips on the tools available to facilitate the editing process. This series of chapters leads ultimately to chapter 12, in which concrete examples of text editing are presented, thanks to the voluntary interventions of a number of text editors from varying backgrounds.

1 Introduction to text editing in practice (chapters 6 to 10)

The concept of language errors is a fuzzy one. I'll leave to linguists the technical definitions. Here we're concerned only with deviations from the standard use of English as judged by sophisticated users such as professional writers, editors, teachers, and literate executives and personnel officers.
Paul Brians

The fact is that the world is full of teachers, employers, and other authorities who may penalize you for your nonstandard use of the English language. Feel free to denounce these people if you wish; but if you need their good opinion to get ahead, you'd be wise to learn standard English.
Paul Brians

The word *error* has different meanings and usages relative to how it is conceptually applied.
Wikipedia

In the course of this book, it has become clear that text editors should have a command of more than just a superficial knowledge of a wide variety of subjects in order to be(come) solid and sound practitioners. They require an indepth knowledge of the grammar, word usage, spelling, style and register of a particular language, as well as broad knowledge of the principles of typography and layout, and of how to go about presenting a text as a coherent whole, bearing in mind all of its component parts. For this reason, text editing means constantly judging a wide array of related matters. The editor's level of acquired and implemented knowledge, which is constantly being updated and completed, will determine their judgements on these matters and also the degree of success of the editing process.

Not only do text editors have to acquire the required levels of knowledge and insights; they also have to upgrade their skills in a lifelong learning process, even though it is almost impossible for a text editor to range over all the required levels of knowledge (Murphy 2011: 4, 8). There is just too much to know, and a human being's brain is just not capable of storing and making available all of this on demand! Consequently, we find that some text editors will definitely know more about certain aspects of the editing process than about others. That is both understandable and acceptable, but they do at least have to know where to find answers. In any event, the point is that text editors should know *where* to look for information rather than have an encyclopaedic knowledge of a wide range of topics. That frame of mind begins with an alert and enquiring mind, one that almost takes nothing at face value, no matter who has written it (see section 3.1 below). With experience, knowledge levels will increase and editing may well turn out to be easier over time. This, in turn, will have an impact on the quality (number and ways) of the adaptations to be made to texts (Bisaillon 2007: 84), primarily because more mature, experienced human beings can often solve language problems more easily or know better where to look in order to solve a problem.

Judgement calls about the quality of a text based on the editor's experience and knowledge will normally lead to a fair and reasoned analysis of a text and will result in its improvement – the ultimate aim of a text editor's work. In chapter 2 section 5, we have already indicated the importance of the text editor's possessing a knowledge of sources when disentangling editorial knots, and we elaborate on this topic in the following three chapters – and provide a number of sources that deal with these challenging areas of the text editor's craft.

1.1 The role of norm and deviation

It has been shown repeatedly in the literature (eg Brains 2008, 2011; Mossop 2007: 23) that texts are capable of communicating despite the language errors they may contain. Human beings are capable of reading between the lines and will understand passages of text, despite errors being present – no matter what kind they are. A language user will be able to understand a letter such as the following, the literature tells us, even though some processing will be required and problems might be experienced en route:

Hello,
My name is Susan. I'm forteen and I life in Germany. My hobbys are go to discos, some-
times I hear music in the radio. In the summer I go bathing in a lake. I haven't any brothers
or sisters. We take busses to scool. I visit form 9 at my school. My birthday is on Friday. I
hope I will become a new guitar.
I'm looking forward to get a email from you.
Yours,
Susan
(Learning English Online, http://www.englisch-hilfen.de – consulted 15 April 2011)

The same argument would apply to this email from a Chinese correspondent, received
recently by one of the authors:

Dear Manager
DO YOU INTERESTED IN A4 COPY PAPER?
Hope you have a nice day.We get your information form internet.
This is Jone from China, specialized in all kinds of papers ,such as A4 copy paper
A3 copy paper.The detailed information in the attachment ,please check it.
If you are interested in any terms ,please fell free to contact us.
We would like to send you our best price upon recieved detailed requirements.
Thanks&warm regards
Qiang

There are, of course, many more extreme examples, but the above fragments illustrate
the argument that even weak sentences riddled with errors can be deciphered and understood because readers interpret linguistic tokens.

It has also been pointed out that an important aspect of the communication problem
that arises in cases such as the above is the impression that text producers create about
their capability and about the quality and correctness of the text itself. The occurrence of
deficiencies in a text creates an impression of sloppiness, messiness and carelessness. As
a consequence, if the text editor allows such errors and deficiencies to slip through, their
ability to assess what's wrong with a document and what needs to be corrected will be
seriously questioned. Moreover, errors such as these draw attention away from content
and create a negative image of the intellectual capacity of the text's creator (not to mention the editor). Mossop (2010: 39) points out that, for instance, spelling mistakes are bad
because of the effects they have on the reader. For those who prefer polished language,
the following example will be a challenge:

Mispelings [sic] and typograhpical [sic] errors produce a very *bad impression*. They suggest
that the author and editor are *sloppy thinkers*, and that the publisher tolerates *carelessness*.
As a result, readers may *lose confidence* in the actual content of the work.

Of course, spelling mistakes should not automatically imply that factual errors should also
be expected to occur or that mistakes in argumentation and style will be present in the

same text. However, their presence in the text does unconsciously raise the suspicion that this could be the case, which is already sufficient to cast doubt on the quality of the text, quite apart from the irritation that readers experience with the text and the greater time it takes to process an error-ridden passage. The point is that obvious and blatant errors can draw the reader's attention away from the text and when this happens the author and editor lose part of their mandate and trustworthiness. Also, there is a risk that the reader's trust in the product itself will be diminished. As a consequence, the text editor who lets errors slip through will become an object of suspicion too. Hope (2005) claims that substandard language usage can be expensive to society in terms of lost opportunities:

> Bad spelling and grammar could be costing UK businesses up to £41 billion in lost sales, a new report has claimed. *More than 70% of customers would not trust businesses with poor communication skills*, according to a survey commissioned by Royal Mail.

Similarly, when your language lets you down, especially on paper, this can lead to the communicator being shamed. Text editors are easily criticised by their clients if the former have allowed something incorrect or obviously inconsistent to slip through – particularly when this is first discovered only at the time the final proofs are being read.

However, most often text editing is not simply a matter of right and wrong, but instead a delicate balancing act required to do justice to the dynamic nature of language. Influences from, for instance, sociolects (eg youth language, hip-hop lyrics), work contexts (eg terminology, jargon, slang), electronic media (eg blogs, games, chats), and other languages (loan words) have to be weighed and scrutinised in the context in which they are used. In this regard, the following guidelines may be useful:

- When in doubt whether a word is acceptable, consult *reliable* sources such as dictionaries and other word lists (both print and online). Human sources should be carefully chosen for their advice, interpretation or opinion: they should not only be subject experts who can explain terminology or jargon but they should also be fluent enough in the language to ensure that they offer the most appropriate solution in context.
- *Youth language* should be used only in texts addressing this target group. Check that the tone of the text is not inappropriate.
- *Professional contexts* often favour words with an international ring to them. Check that the usage and resultant tone are appropriate to a polyglot international readership.
- *Jargon* and *terminology* specific, for instance, to the legal and medical professions, and to the mining industry or the banking sector, have to be understood not only by the narrow target readership but also by 'outsiders', and this latter group has to be taken into account in communications that are compiled for their benefit.

In the rest of this section, we give a short overview of what is regarded as 'error', and the types of error that can occur. Sometimes errors can be made intentionally, especially in creative texts such as those found in literature (eg see Mark Twain *The adventures of Huckleberry Finn* and Sheridan's *The rivals*), and advertising. In these cases, language conventions are purposely breached in order to achieve a certain effect. This type of error is not discussed here, because it will not require editorial emendation. Instead, we study genuine errors of the kind that occur in formal texts.

1.2 Whose norm is it anyway? (section written by David Owen)

When discussing norms and deviation (see chapter 2 section 4), we are implicitly making reference to language thought of as being 'correct' and whose rules and expectations are said to have been broken or undermined when forms that do not correspond to this are produced. By 'correct', this generally means language that conforms to that produced by native speakers (NS), such as US or UK speakers of English, for example. For many people, and not only the NS, this will appear to be nothing other than common sense; in certain ambits such as writing in English for publication, the use of NS language may even seem to be a fundamental prerequisite – for accuracy, for pragmatic and discourse sophistication and for the general image that 'proper' English may project.

But the reality is far more complex. English is now – and has been for some considerable time – an international language, spoken, written, read and listened to by millions of people whose first language is something else. These 'other' users of English are known as non-native speakers (NNS). Indeed, English has many more NNS speakers than it has NS. Traditionally, the norms of English – semantic, grammatical, orthographic, phonetic – are 'generated' by its NS, and these norms are then learned and applied by NNS, who are said to make errors if they fail to produce the language expected by NS rules. Over time, though, a feeling has gradually developed that such a situation, in which a small inner core of speakers effectively produce and then 'police' the language that is also used by a huge outer core,[1] is unreasonable, and that NNS English should be recognised as valid in its own right (Kachru 1985; Canagarajah 2010. See also Quirk 1985).

Within international English (called, variously, English as a Lingua Franca: ELF; English as an International Language: EIL; and World English(es): WE), this has led to initiatives such as the development and promotion of core elements of pronunciation in ELF (Jenkins 2000, 2002; Mauranen 2003), in an effort to reach some sort of agreement on how internationally accepted variants – in this case, phonetic – might attain some sort of accepted similarities. Inevitably, though, for those who feel that anything other than strict adherence to NS norms results in sub-standard language (since it results in forms that may be at considerable variance with NS expectations), international English is difficult to validate. In contrast, those who feel that an insistence on such NS norms is restrictive and unfair (since most NNS users of English would therefore always be kept in a position of linguistic inferiority), international English facilitates meaningful communication without the need to feel constantly insecure in its production.

For editors who are working with NNS writers, this brings additional responsibilities: on the one hand, you may well be expected to act – by clients or by the profession at large

---

[1] In fact, linguists describe three 'ambits': an inner circle (English is a first language); an outer circle (English is a second language, sometimes official); and an expanding circle (English as a foreign language or a lingua franca). See Kachru 1985.

– as a sort of gatekeeper of 'correct' English; on the other hand, you must at all times be sensitive to the conditions and contexts of your authors, and will want to avoid any suggestion of being complicit with what many NNS users of English may perceive as linguistic imperialism (cf Phillipson 1992, 1997; Flowerdew 2001, 2008; Mišak 2005). Be aware of the fact that, although standard English may vary with an NNS author's own usage, such usage may be considered entirely acceptable in that author's environment. Where you feel that this usage is not acceptable (eg for your readership or because of inhouse guidelines), discuss this openly with your author and find an acceptable solution. The sensitive editor will avoid the heavy-handed imposition of rules and norms on any writer, as this would simply create tension. A far more productive approach is to be open to reasonable variance, to talk through any difficulties with your authors and to resolve all issues diplomatically and amiably.

1.3 The concept of 'error'

There's nothing ambiguous about the term 'error'. More often than not, an error is considered to be a deviation from what is accurate or correct (cf Brains 2008; Carstens 2011; Corder 1981; Ferris 2002; James 1997; Norrish 1983). This means that text containing an error does something different or is something different from what is expected or is incorrect in a given sentence structure, message or context. An 'error' can be regarded as a deviation from what is considered to be accurate or correct; in other words, it is a deviation from a dominant form or pattern that is widely accepted and established.

Seen in this light, deviations can take the form of language errors (deviations from what is accepted as correct in a language), spelling mistakes (deviations from accepted writing or spelling conventions), style problems (deviations from what is regarded as acceptable and appropriate in certain contexts, bearing in mind the writer's purpose and readership), content errors (a deviation from what is regarded to be the truth), etc. Of these classes of error, the most ill-defined and difficult to pinpoint are problems of style – precisely because one form may be appropriate to one context but inappropriate to another (see chapter 8 section 4).

In most cases, language errors are committed inadvertently and innocently: there is no intention on the part of the sender (the writer or speaker) to commit them. In this way, we can distinguish such errors from 'mistakes', which are errors caused by a fault – 'the fault being misjudgment, carelessness, or forgetfulness' (Robinson nd). However, in some cases, language users knowingly violate the norms – either as a consequence of laziness, snobbery or wilfulness, or as an outspoken preference for the alternative form, or (as we have already suggested) in order to achieve a particular goal or play on words, such as in advertising copywriting or dialogue in plays and novels.

There are different ways of categorising errors and the 'cognitive study of human error is a very active research field, including work related to limits of memory and attention and also to decision-making strategies' (Wikipedia: Human reliability – consulted 14 April 2011). The occurrence of errors can also be ascribed to a number of other varying factors, such as neurological defects (as a consequence, for instance, of aphasia or dyslexia) or barriers in the learning process, where language learners learn a certain pattern or form in an incorrect way (eg 'between you and I we should ...', instead of the grammatically correct 'between you and me we should ...'). Both in language acquisition (the natural learning process every child goes through) and in second-language learning, the fine nuances of a language are mastered at a later stage (if at all) and error is a perfectly normal part of the process of learning.

In section 4.1.1 of chapter 2 we introduced the concept of 'norm' and explained how, through a process of standardisation, certain usages of language have gained such a status that they have become the background against which something is judged as either right or wrong, acceptable or unacceptable. (That used to be the case in English with splitting the infinitive and ending a sentence with a preposition, but those are no longer considered to be hard-and-fast norms.) A deviation will count 'as an error if its occurrence is viewed as a violation of the norm and, as such, warranting negative sanctioning and/or correction' (Brains 2008; Ochs 1985: 785). Daily, the text editor has to make well-informed and well-considered judgements about right and wrong in a text. This covers the total range of the text: language (that is, argumentation), grammar, spelling, punctuation and style as well as typography and layout. So, for example, fairly common linguistic deviations nowadays are:

- *The ambiguous referent*:

    Astronomy is the study of the heavenly bodies in our universe. It began billions of years ago.

Here it is ambiguous what 'It' is referring to in the previous sentence: astronomy or our universe? The solution that brings the sentence construction or usage back to the norm is to replace 'It' with 'The universe'.

- *The dangling participle*:

    Walking along the promenade, the cruise liner made a splendid sight.

Here the construction (adjectival clause qualifying a noun) makes it seem as if the cruise liner was walking along the promenade – which, of course, is absurd. The problem is that the subject of 'Walking along the promenade' (ie 'we' or 'the group') has been replaced by 'cruise liner'. The solution that brings the sentence construction back to the norm is to reword the main clause or idea to read: 'We watched the splendid sight of the cruise liner sailing past' (or words to that effect).

- *The incorrect determiner*:

    Anyone person should be able to lift that load.

Here 'Anyone' should be two words (two separate determiners): 'Any one person should be able to lift that load.' (As opposed to 'Anyone who can lift that load is really strong.')

- *The comma splice*:

> Martin is healthy, that couldn't happen to him.

The solution to restoring the norm could be either 'Martin is healthy; that couldn't happen to him.' or 'Martin is healthy, so I don't think that could happen to him.' or 'Martin is healthy. I don't think that could happen to him.'

- *The incorrect spelling*, leading to the wrong meaning being conveyed (often due to homonymy or homophony):

> My favourite relative is my ant.

It can only be hoped that the aunt is not a picnic pest!

Other problematic words include (Van de Poel 2006: 135–137):

adapt/adopt	(=adjust/begin to have, eg a new policy)
affect/effect	(=have an effect on/to bring about)
ambiguous/ambivalent	(=an ambiguous letter/I am ambivalent about …)
amount/number	(=for non-countable things/for countable things)
beside/besides	(=next to/in addition to)
co-operate/collaborate	(=work together physically/mentally, eg research)
disinterested/uninterested	(=impartial/lacking interest)
economic/economical	(=related to the economy/cheap to operate)
ensure/insure	(=make certain/getting financial protection)
especially/specially	(=particularly, more than other things/for a special reason)
fewer/less	(=for countable things/non-countable things)
historic/historical	(=important/old, belonging to history)
opportunity/possibility	(=chance/option)
principal/principle	(=main, most important/standard, rule)

- *Typography and layout*:

> ***WELL, IF AN ENTIRE PARAGRAPH OR SECTION OF TEXT WERE TO BE TYPESET IN BOLD ITALIC CAPITAL LETTERS (LIKE THIS), IT WOULD PROBABLY BE CLEAR THAT THIS TYPOGRAPHIC STYLE IS NOT CONDUCIVE TO READING AND ACCESSING INFORMATION.***

Good book design therefore requires the body text to be in a certain font weight and size that is most readable to the age group, literacy level and visual acuity of the projected readers; and, furthermore, that not more than two fonts should appear on a page, if the reader is not to be confused by clutter and mixed messages. (See chapter 10 for more on this topic.)

When properly trained with respect to the components discussed in chapter 2 – that is, knowledge of normative grammar and basic knowledge of document design and text linguistics – the text editor simply has to be capable of judging the use of the components that occur in a text. Added to training, experience plays a significant role, because the longer professionals work with texts, the more familiar they become with the requirements of each text they encounter and with what is needed to make informed assessments.

Regarding linguistic errors, several writers have studied how a text editor distinguishes between linguistic deviation and an obvious language error. The nub of their reasoning can be summarised in the following list:

List 6.1 Language deviations vs language errors for text editors

› When text editors have to distinguish between *error* and *deviation*, they will first and foremost study the context. What is the norm for one context is not necessarily the norm for another. Pragmatic correctness is the foundation of sound judgement.

› The grammaticality[2] of a language is determined by its use and by the acceptance of that use by the community involved. Because language is dynamic and therefore in a state of constant change, norms can change over the years too. What is an error now will not necessarily be an error in 20 years' time.

› The occurrence of errors can hamper communicative effectiveness, unless the errors serve a communicative purpose and are aimed at the text's audience. An exclamation such as 'Why, Tom! *Where you been* all this time, you rascal?' (Twain *Huckleberry Finn,* chapter XLI) is regarded as adequate language, because it echoes the southerner dialect registered by Twain to reveal the antagonist's social background. Although on the one hand the construction 'Where you been' could, strictly speaking, be viewed as an error of grammar, is this not better understood in this context as an example of a deviation that reflects the spoken word in this part of the world? And therefore acceptable in this context?

› The language community in general will expect good language use in good texts. However, what counts for one language does not necessarily count for another. Every language has its unique usage.

---

[2] Grammaticality is the quality of a linguistic utterance of being grammatively well formed.

> › Language error and deviation are not always easy to distinguish between. Language deviations are not necessarily errors; they are often less frequent occurrences. Errors and deviations present themselves in the daily practice of the text editor and the editor has to have the capacity to make the right decisions when confronted by them.

(Based on Bartsch 1987 and Carstens 2011: 8–14.)

Whatever the reasons for the occurrence of what can be regarded as a deficiency in a text, a common core of what is right and what is wrong exists in language-practice circles: there will always be errors in texts. In other words, the 'ideal' of a perfect text will never ever be realised in practice. However, it is the task of the text editor to reduce the errors to their minimum in order to minimise the level of irritation on the part of the reader and to maximise reading effectiveness and efficiency. The kind and intensity of the editor's education and training will determine their success in identifying and correcting errors (see chapter 3 sections 11 and 12.1).

1.4 Types of error in the editing process

Types of error have been discussed in several ways in the course of this book but let it be said here that errors can be categorised in many different ways depending on what the taxonomy is used for. For present purposes, we distinguish between *text type* errors (regarding the function, purpose and audience of the text – see below in this chapter), *content* errors (facts, quotations, plagiarism – see below in this chapter), *structural* errors (text, paragraphs and coherence – see chapter 7), *wording* errors (grammar and meaning, style and register – see chapter 8), and *presentation* errors (spelling and punctuation, typography and layout – see chapters 9 and 10).

The types of error likely to be encountered in texts are summarised in table 6.1 below. We discuss each component in detail, below, as well as in chapters 7 to 10.

The remainder of this chapter, and chapters 7, 8, 9 and 10, provides insights into how different types of error can be identified and solved. The emphasis will constantly be on self-knowledge (based on training and experience) and continuous in-service training (based on the concept of lifelong learning). By and large, this will be the (ideal) recipe for the text editor's work. But before embarking on this journey, we first have to reflect on how to determine textual quality.

Text facets	Aspects	Potential errors
Text type Chapter 6	Function	• Categories • Subcategories
	Purpose	• Context • Effect
	Audience	• Background • Expectations
	Format	• Pen-and-paper or electronic • Length • Structure
Content Chapter 6	Text level	• Quotations • References and sources • Cross-references
	Word level	• Facts and context • Figures and tables • Names and titles • Places and addresses • Numbers and statistics
	Cross-cutting issues	• Ethics: plagiarism, slander or libel/defamation • Copyright and intellectual property
Structure Chapter 7	Text coherence	• Logical connectors • Transitions between sentences, paragraphs
	Text level	• Beginning, middle, end • Argumentation build-up
	Paragraph level	• Length • Topic sentences • Hooks • Support sentences
Wording Chapter 8	Grammar	• Syntax: structure, length, phrases, negation, congruence … • Morphology: word types, declination, tense, demonstrative, interrogative …
	Meaning	• Word usage • Synonyms, homonyms, metonyms, metaphors • Tautology, pleonasms, homonyms and homophones
	Style	• Level of formality, vagueness, stiltedness … • Length of sentences • Double meanings, clichés, jargon, slang, terminology • Active vs passive voice
	Register	• Grammar • Lexis: idioms, loan words, metaphors

Text facets	Aspects	Potential errors
Language presentation: spelling and punctuation Chapter 9	Spelling	• Word boundaries: hyphens … • Abbreviations and acronyms • Apostrophes
	Consistency	• American English vs British English • Uppercase vs lowercase • Italics • Hyphenation • Numbers …
	Punctuation	• Commas (splice), colons … • Parenthesis • Possessives • Quotation marks
Visual presentation: typography and layout Chapter 10	Typography	• Fonts: types, weights and sizes • Suitability to reader and medium • Readability
	Layout	• Page layout/design • Margins and spacing: widows/orphans • Headers and footers • Title(s) • Table(s), illustrations • Captions and labels • Notes • Numbering • Appendices • Index

Table 6.1 *Overview of the domains of potential errors allocated to text facets (chapters 6 to 10)*

2 The role of text type in text editing

2.1 Determining textual quality in practice

As indicated earlier (chapter 2 section 3.3), textual quality can be determined at five levels, namely, *text type, content, structure, wording* and *presentation*. At every level, the three quality criteria of correspondence, consistency and correctness have to be applied (as introduced in chapter 2). However, the different textual levels cannot exist in isolation and text type can influence a text's content and presentation considerably. In document design it has been shown that it is possible to raise people's awareness, convince or motivate them if you have an insight into how they think and how they process new information (Schriver 1997; Swanepoel & Hoeken (eds): 2008). In other words, as part of their knowledge of the text type, text editors also need to know as much as possible about a document's audience. If text editors are aware of this intricate relationship between the various levels of knowledge, they will then also know how to approach the text's content, structure, wording and presentation and be able to gauge how heavily to intervene in a text (see chapter 3 sections 3 and 4). Consequently, the content of a book on the rainforest for specialists in the field will differ considerably from, say, that of a book targeting 10–12-year-olds, and therefore it will require an altogether different approach.

In the remainder of this section the text-type facet and its interactions with other textual levels are discussed in more detail. Knowledge of text type allows the practitioner to employ clear criteria in systematically designing and analysing texts.

2.2 The components of text type

Every text belongs to a particular type that has to be appropriate to a well-defined purpose and audience (eg different age groups, literacy levels and familiarity with a specific subject) and has to respond to particular textual characteristics (ie genre) in which the rules of the genre are correctly applied. For instance:

An academic article, paper or thesis has to be written in accordance with certain norms or conventions, such as a particular style of writing and the use of a preferred system of referencing one's sources; also, such a document must conform to certain prescribed content requirements (abstract or executive summary, thesis statement, introduction, main body comprising findings and analysis, conclusion and possibly recommendations) (Flann & Hill 2004: 233–235). Tabular matter, figures and maps should all be checked carefully for completeness, correctness and consistency.

- A school or tertiary textbook will require certain characteristic components to make up the content: a statement of learning outcomes at the start of each chapter, practical/ assessment features such as exercises and activities, glossed terms, illustrations with or without captions, footnotes or end notes, case studies and so on.
- A recipe book has inherent demands of its own (Flann & Hill 2004: 221–223, 235): lists of ingredients that have to correspond to the ingredients mentioned in the method (and vice versa) and which all have to be styled in the same way (eg metric vs imperial units); plus a particular style of writing the method of each recipe and arranging the steps in vertical lists, the items of which are written in telegramese, verbs in the imperative form (eg 'Sift flour. Stir in eggs and sugar. Beat until firm.'); preparation and cooking terms; serving suggestions.
- In a work of fiction, the text editor will be required to look out for lapses in characterisation, plot, setting, names, places and dates.

The text editor's approach to each of these genres (and, of course, many others) will in all likelihood be somewhat different. The type of text being edited will fundamentally determine the nature and level of the editing required. In the first place, the language level and the style of writing will be a strong determinant of the editorial intervention. Secondly, the degree of jargon and/or technical content will exercise a strong influence, especially with regard to factual accuracy and the accessibility of the content to the target readership. Thirdly, the complexity of the text and the number of features will determine the level of the editing required. Word choice (vocabulary difficulty), sentence length and structure, the presence (or not) of tabular matter and the sequencing of information will all play a role – to a greater or lesser extent – in dictating the nature of the editorial intervention.

What, ultimately, these elements contribute to is the *readability* of text. Text readability is a measure of how well and how easily text conveys its intended meaning to a reader, and a number of factors additional to those listed above influence it: reader factors such as prior knowledge, reading ability and the motivation of the reader; physical factors such as font (typeface) style, font size, spacing and layout; text coherence and cohesion, and so on.

These textual considerations (and more) are outlined in the following table, under the five categories Function, Purpose, Audience, Format and Language – all of which are closely interconnected:

Function	Purpose	Audience	Format	Language
Categories Should this be a referential or descriptive text? ↓	**Objective** Should the text provide information or persuade? ↓	**Background** • What knowledge can we presuppose: intertextual, intercultural, etc? • What is the	**Length** Is the text in line with the audience's span of attention? ↓	**Type of language** • Should it be straightforward or rather complex? • Should it be prose or brief
Subcategories Should this be an informative, argumentative, instructive or narrative text?	**Context** In which environment will it be used? ↓	audience's level of education? • What experiences have they had with texts of this type? ↓	**Carrier** Is the text paper-based or online: from website to Twitter? ↓	point style (bulleted)? • Should it be factual statements only? • What degree
	Effect Will it inform the intended audience?	**Expectations** Does the audience want to be informed or convinced?	**Structure** Is it appropriate for the genre?	of jargon or formality is possible? • How should terminology be dealt with?

Table 6.2 *Examples of aspects of text types to be considered in error analysis*

What this speaks to is an approach in which, by considering the five categories together and weighing up the effectiveness of each, the text editor is able to contribute towards a much more textually cohesive document that is reader-centred; in other words, one which is based on the reader's expectations, their background knowledge, the medium through which they will be able to receive the information, the structure that will best serve the reader's needs, and their reason for reading the text. (A reading of chapter 12 will illuminate this point.)

2.3 The structure of a text

As soon as it has become clear who the target group of a text is and what their needs are, what the function or functions of a text are, and what the content should be, decisions have to be made about the organisation of the materials and it must be decided whether the content will be organised alphabetically, thematically or chronologically. The structural organisation is largely determined by the contextual analysis (see chapter 2, list 2.4; also chapter 7). Take, for instance, a pamphlet on Aids prevention: if you know who the target group is (eg people with a certain level of literacy, but who have basic reading skills) and what their needs are (the fact that they want to know more about the dangers attached to HIV/Aids), what the purpose of the text is (to persuade people to take active measures to prevent Aids) and what the actual content will be (scientific information on the dangers of Aids and how it can be prevented), then the process of planning the structure can begin.

Two structural aspects can be distinguished here: internal and external. The *internal structure* largely determines the way in which the information is organised. This can be done in a variety of ways, following the principles of specific arrangement – for instance, the so-called 'goal–means structure':

› Marketing pamphlet:
- Goal of the paper (marketing an insurance product)
- Problems motivating the goal (under-insured people)
- Advantages of achieving the goal (people will survive setbacks financially if they take out insurance)
- Means necessary to achieving the goal (for instance, taking out a specific insurance policy (eg householders, comprehensive insurance on a motor vehicle, and so on)

› Medical texts:
- Goal of the chapter (treating patients with diabetes)
- Problems motivating the goal (an increase in the incidence of diabetes, with few alternative medical solutions)
- Advantages of achieving the goal (reducing the inevitable consequences of non-treatment or inadequate treatment, such as unnecessary amputations or even death)

>>

List 6.2 Examples of internal text structure

- Means necessary to achieving the goal (educating doctors about the efficacy of alternative medical treatment/therapies)

› Academic text types:
  - Goal of the pamphlet (writing up research on a phenomenon not previously investigated)
  - Problems motivating the goal (a lack of understanding of the phenomenon and its possible connection to improving the quality of life)
  - Advantages of achieving the goal (the phenomenon can possibly help to improve the quality of life in several revolutionary ways)
  - Means necessary to achieving the goal (conducting research into the phenomenon and publishing research findings).

Often, the authors of such documents are experts in their specific fields but are not accomplished at conveying the information (even at a structural level) in the most readable way to their identified readership. Very often, they are self- rather than reader-centred. This is where the text editor has an important role to play, and identifying the structural type that a document exemplifies can help you to improve the document in a fundamental and material way. Where you have to be cautious, however, is in not intervening too heavily in the text to the point where you ride roughshod over the norms and conventions of a particular discipline. Sensitivity should guide you in your approach to such documents.

Other structures that also could be applied to this example are the problem–solution structure; the evaluation structure; the procedural structure; the inverted-pyramid structure; the hourglass structure; and the *Wall Street Journal* structure. Each of these is a specific structure that aims to attain a chosen goal (Cataldo & Oakhill 2000).

Apart from these different structuring options, there are also genre-specific rules that have to be followed, that is, conventional ways to organise and order information. Again, a pamphlet on HIV/Aids aimed at the general public, for instance, will be approached differently from a specialist book on the same topic aimed at clinicians. Text editors always have to know what these rules imply, because that will guide them in making informed judgement calls about the appropriateness of a chosen method of structuring.

The *external structure* is concerned with the linguistic and graphic elements used to realise the internal structure, that is, the manner in which the text is organised and set out on paper. Two levels are involved here: the text level and also the sentence/word level. With regard to the text level, the following aspects deserve attention:

List 6.3 External structural principles at the text level

› Subheadings in a text (these are mainly determined by the function of the text)

› The table of contents (which typically occurs in longer documents in order to help find information quickly)

› The introduction (which must stimulate, ie arouse curiosity or interest in reading the remainder of the content, and also introduce the structure, ie prepare the reader for what follows)

› Paragraphs and sections (this concerns delineating and joining sentences into paragraphs, and also organising the paragraphs themselves. For example: in an argumentative text, a statement is usually made first and then followed by the arguments that support it)

› Conclusion (summary and/or recommendations).

At sentence and word level the following are important:

List 6.4 External structure: sentence and word level

› Structured sentences (how a text is joined together)

› Signalling phrases (the words and expressions that express connections in a text):
  – Conjunction markers (conjunctions such as thus, consequently, and, but, and yet; numeric determiners such as first, second; adverbs such as before, please, and lastly)
  – Referential words and phrases (referring to a thing, person or event that has been mentioned earlier in the text, by using pronouns such as he, she and those, and other referential expressions such as that man with the green overcoat, the previously mentioned affair, etc)
  – Lists of items (usually enumeration lists, where a colon is used to organise words next to or underneath each other).

3 The attention to be given to content

Fiction editors are a very special breed. They need impeccable judgment, consummate tact, a perfect memory for trivia, the ability to hold several themes and subplots in their minds at once, and the stamina to endure the phone call at two in the morning from the irate author who has just discovered the semicolon you altered on page 104.

Flann & Hill

3.1 Introduction

The content (prose element) of a document is determined by its function (among other functions, to inform, motivate, persuade and evaluate (see table 6.2)). Of course, the needs of the target group are relevant here. However, in order to compose the document's content (regardless of its format: specialist book, story book, children's book, popular article in a newspaper or magazine, academic article in a specialist magazine, instruction pamphlet, election information or tax form), the text editor should understand what the readership's background and expectations are – in other words, what the readers know, think, hope for and, possibly also, which values and opinions they hold.

When having to deal with the content of documents, the text editor must be equipped with a questioning disposition and alertness, combined with healthy scepticism (not accepting all the content at face value), as well as a broad general knowledge. This must all be to the fore despite the status or experience of the author, for are authors not frail and fallible human beings too? Authors sometimes have to think and write under pressure or in conditions that are far from ideal, or while distracted by personal or professional matters, and while they might be on top of their subject, external circumstances often prevail to cause them to spell a name they know well incorrectly, type an incorrect date or misplace a digit in a number. These are precisely the sorts of content problem the text editor should be vigilant for, and where their hawkish eye for detail is an indispensable attribute.

On the other hand, the text editor who is on top of their subject-matter can also play a key role in saving an author's reputation by detecting (and either querying or correcting) factual errors, misquotations, incorrect information in text and tables and instances of plagiarism and defamation (or libel/slander), however innocently committed.

3.2 Levels of content errors

Content errors can broadly be grouped into three categories: those occurring at the level of single words and numbers; those affecting a document at a textual level, and then a number of matters, which we can label 'cross-cutting issues' (or transversal matters) that relate to broader ethico-legal issues. These levels of error in the content of a text that can require the editor's attention are outlined in table 6.3, and are then elaborated upon below that.

Word (micro) level	Text (macro) level	Cross-cutting issues Ethico-legal
• Facts and their context • Contents of figures and tables • Names and titles • Place names and addresses • Numbers and statistics • Index entries and locators (eg page numbers) • Correctness and consistency of names of characters, places and events	• Quotations • References • Intext cross-references • Sources • Numbering and styling of figures and tables • Table of contents and lists of figures accurately mirroring the contents of the text • In works of fiction, consistency of dialogue particular to characters	• Plagiarism • Libel or slander/defamation • Copyright • Intellectual property

Table 6.3 *Content errors*

Some of the editing at the word level will contribute to the content of the text. When, for instance, checking the name of an author, the editor's intervention can range from checking the spelling of that person's name to finding their first name or initials, affiliation and status with respect to a reference, and try then to reconcile the intext reference details with those in the bibliography or list of references. Even the date of publication of the author's text should be checked when such an opportunity arises. Other content errors at a word level include (cf Butcher, Drake & Leach 2006: 1–2, 31, 32, 403, 2009; Flann & Hill 2003: 52, 215–216; Mackenzie 2005: 25; 2011: 163, 164; Merriam-Webster 2000: 54–158, 292–311):

- *Facts and their context*: These can include dates and events given in non-fiction texts; in particular, look out for anachronisms (when events referred to could not have occurred when claimed, or are given out of their actual sequence).
- *Contents of figures and tables*: Do the numbers add up to the given totals? Do the percentages add up exactly to 100% and, if not, is an explanation given for the total exceeding 100%? If data is missing from cells, is it not available (in which case, this must be indicated somehow) or has it been omitted in error?
- *Names and titles*: Are people's names correctly spelt? Is the correct person referred to? Is their title correct (general vs major-general; chairman vs president; secretary-general vs general secretary, etc)?
- *Place names and addresses*: Are place names correct? Are they spelt correctly? Is the native or the anglicised version given (München vs Munich; Antwerpen vs Antwerp)? Are diacritics correctly used, where necessary (São Paolo)?
- *Numbers, dates and statistics*: Are the numbers correctly styled (decimal point or comma; thousands comma separator or space separator)? Is the percentage symbol or 'per cent'

used? Is a convention followed for numbers from 1 to 10 and from 11 upwards? Is the date format 16 June 2012 or June 16, 2012? Are statistics in the form of decimal fractions all rounded to the same number of decimals?

- *Index entries and locators (page numbers)*: Are the entries and sub-entries arranged in the correct alphabetical order? Are first letters of entries correctly uppercase or lowercase? Are entries and sub-entries correctly spelled/hyphenated and with correct diacritics? Are locators correct, correctly elided (or not)? Are they in the correct numeric sequence? Are they correctly punctuated and spaced?
- In works of fiction, are the names of characters, places and events correct and consistent? (Flann & Hill 2004: 215–217). Has the lead character's name, Jerry, become Gerry in places? Is the street in London Jermyn or Germyn or Jermin? Is it the Second World War or World War II? Do we have Pearl Harbor or Pearl Harbour?

However, some content editing is more mechanical and pertains to the surface structure and format of the text, such as, for instance, ensuring the consistent numbering of subheadings, tables and lists. So, apart from editing at a word (micro) level, the text editor will also carry out some editing out at a text (macro) level (cf Butcher, Drake & Leach 2006: 43–44, 129, 181–183, 199–200, 220–229, 269–278, 2009; Flann & Hill 2004: 75, 78–82, 103–104, 110–115, 166, 179–181, 187–188, 207, 225, 274, 275, 294, 296, 297, 300, 306, 318–319, 338; Mackenzie 2011: 77, 119, 125–128, 131–132, 135–142; Merriam-Webster 2000: 43–49, 176, 230–231, 237, 259–261, 263).

- *Quotations*: are these quoted (ie between quotation marks) or unquoted? Are they inset or not? Is there a change of font size? Are ellipses spaced? Are errors either placed between square brackets or followed by '(sic)'? How is the current author's decision to emphasise certain words or phrases dealt with? If footnoted, is the superscripted number present and correct?
- *References*: does the intext reference agree in detail with the reference given in the bibliography or the list of references? Are the references complete? Is a reference missing (possible plagiarism or breach of copyright)? If the short-title method of referencing is used, is it consistent and complete?
- *Intext cross-references*: if a cross-reference is along the lines of '(see the example on page 49)', does the example actually appear on page 49?; are the cross-references consistent in their wording?
- *Sources*: are sources for figures and tables given below them? Do they agree with the data given in the bibliography or the list of references?
- *Contents, numbering and styling of lists of figures and tables*: does the wording and do the page numbers given in the table of contents exactly mirror those in the text itself? Is the numbering and styling of the figures and tables consistent and sequential? Have any numbers been skipped or duplicated? Are the numbering systems correct and consistent between chapters?
  - Are the data in columns arranged in ascending or descending order?

- Is the most important column of data (ie usually the whole point of the table) on the extreme right?
- When there are notes in tables, are they numbered correctly and consistently, and is there a one-to-one correspondence between indicators in cells and notes below the tables?
- Are the data in columns left justified, centred or right/decimal justified?
- Are the column heads of all tables throughout the document formatted in the same way (ie bolded, italicised, left aligned or centred)?
- Are the table/figure headings/captions numbered and, if so, are they numbered correctly in sequence?

• Is the style for the table/figure headings/captions consistent across all the tables/figures? In figures, is the same font used for labels throughout?

• *Intext references and cross-references to figures and tables*: are these accurate and do they appear in the text before the figure or table they refer to? Are they on the same page as the visual material? If not, is the cross-reference appropriately worded?

• *Contents and styling of maps*: are the spellings and use of diacriticals and hyphens in place names consistent between the maps and the text?

• *In works of fiction, is the dialogue* particular to characters credible and consistent?

Overarching text-level and word-level editing, there are legal and ethical matters such as copyright in intellectual property (of authors, publishers, songwriters, scriptwriters, copy-writers, etc), plagiarism or issues of libel/slander or defamation that the text editor (more especially in their role as subeditor) will be required to attend to and draw to the attention of their client or publisher (cf Butcher, Drake & Leach 2006:2, 29, 61–64, 2009; Davis & Balkwill 2011: 194–195, 196–205, 202–203; Flann & Hill 2004: 52–57, 325–326; Mackenzie 2011: 35–36, 38, 45):

• *Plagiarism*: Although the matter of plagiarism is more the prime responsibility of both author and publisher, the text editor can play an important role here, too, in identifying instances and pointing them out to the publisher (see chapter 3 section 9).

• *Libel/slander or defamation*: And if they do detect instances of libel/defamation, editors will be making a significant contribution to the publishing enterprise by drawing them to the client's attention, citing specific instances. More than this they're not required to do. In these two respects, the text editor's function is much like that of the subeditor in the world of newspapers and magazines.

• *Copyright in intellectual property*: Related to plagiarism (and in some ways the other side of the same coin) is the question of copyright infringement. Here, the vigilant text editor who is sensitive to changes in writing style, word usage, and so on, can play an important role in identifying possible infringements and refer to these fully so that the publisher can take them up with the author. Having done that, they've done their (very useful) duty. (See chapter 3 section 9.)

Now, editing text with a focus on content can also be viewed from another perspective: Is the information sufficient, correct and consistent? We discuss each of these aspects of text editing below.

3.3 Sufficiency of information

Not only does the text have to be factually correct, it should also be complete.

First and foremost, there has to be sufficient information for the reader to understand both text and context. The text editor must therefore be on the lookout for errors of omission (gaps) in a text, as much as for errors of commission. This is particularly true of information that describes processes and procedures (eg instruction manuals, repair guides, recipe books). The information also has to be tailored to the needs of the readership in order to achieve an adequate and appropriate understanding of the text. The manner of presentation (see chapters 9 and 10) also makes an important contribution in this regard. It hardly needs pointing out that the text editor plays an important facilitating role here as a bridge between source and target text.

Checklist 6.1 Ways in which content should be sufficient, consistent and correct

Check:
- ✓ Is the information complete: for instance, within tables (totals in columns, missing data, lack of data indicated)?
- ✓ Are all data in graphics accurately and completely supplied (eg pie charts and graphs)?
- ✓ Data in tables and graphs: do the cross-references in the text correspond?
- ✓ Intext cross-references: are they accurate/do they correspond with actual page references?
- ✓ Do the table of contents and the actual text correspond?
- ✓ Do the lists of tables, figures and illustrations correspond to the actual items in the text?
- ✓ Do the text and the index correspond with each other – both wording and locators (page numbers)?
- ✓ Do cross-references correspond with end-matter (eg addenda, appendices, glossary)?
- ✓ Do the intext references correspond with the list of references/bibliography?

Facts and their context
- ✓ Are all numbers correct: dates, telephone numbers (with international prefix), statistics, weights, sums, …?
- ✓ Are figures, graphs, tables, and the like, correct and correctly cross-referenced?
- ✓ Are the following correct: names of people and their professional capacity (titles), institutions, firms, …?
- ✓ Are places and their geographical references correctly spelled and capitalised?
- ✓ Are references to any of the above and more correct: titles of books, plays, musicals, operas, songs, poems, films, …?

3.4 Consistency of content

Information also has to be provided in a consistent form. A range of examples is given here to illustrate this important consideration. There has to be agreement between facts (events, dates, names, etc) when they are repeated in the text. There must also be accuracy and a consistent style in the format of telephone, fax and mobile numbers (eg +0033 123 4567) and dates (eg 15 January 2013 vs January 15, 2013) when used repeatedly, otherwise an unimpressive appearance of carelessness and sloppiness is conveyed.

In fiction, characters' names and the names of places and events must be given and spelt consistently (Sara must not become Sarah later; and is the English county Somerset or Somersetshire?). Unusual or foreign spellings, in particular, and name changes (Peking to Beijing; Bombay to Mumbai, and so on) must be noted by the vigilant text editor and checked for consistent usage in manuscripts. It is strongly recommended that editors keep a 'little black book' (indexed) in which place names and other foreign terms are recorded for future use. (Again, the editor should know where to find such information, and not try to store it all in their head.)

The titles of publications such as newspapers, and their standard abbreviations (common among journals) also have to be given consistently: for example, these titles illustrate one aspect of the challenge facing text editors: *Frankfurter Allgemeine Zeitung (FAZ)*, *The Times*, *Vanity Fair*, *The Wall Street Journal*, *The Times Literary Supplement (TLS)*, *Washington Post*, *Mail & Guardian*, *Armidale Express*, *The Advocate*. When is there a definite article as part of the title (and therefore warranting italicisation) and when not?

So far as journals are concerned, are the standard abbreviations used in citing them: J for Journal, Soc for Society, Med for Medical, LJ for Law Journal, and so on?

Regarding the acronyms and abbreviations used for organisations, medical terms, and so on, which convention is to be followed: all uppercase or initial-letter uppercase only? So, for example: UNESCO or Unesco? MERCOSUR or Mercosur? ECOWAS or Ecowas? HIV, but Aids or AIDS?

The consistency issues are far too many and varied to list all of them here, but there are resources such as dictionaries for writers and editors and online checklists that should be used when the house style manual being followed is silent.

3.5 Correctness of content

Last but not least, the information has to be *correct*. This includes the following:

- Names of people, events and places: correct names, correct spellings
- Numbers, dates, telephone/fax/mobile numbers.

As could be expected, some overlap is inevitable between correspondence or sufficiency of information, on the one hand, and correctness, on the other. In other words, information can hardly be sufficient and yet not correct, or vice versa. The way to ensure that information is in fact correct is to consult a wide range of reputable references, both print (less up to date, but sometimes more detailed and authoritative) and digital/online (usually the most up-to-date sources (see chapter 11); but note that both authors and text editors should exercise particular caution with open-authored sources such as Wikipedia: although these may be extraordinarily up to date, their content may not always be the most authoritative):

- Atlases
- Encyclopaedias
- Books of facts
- Dictionaries
- Geography texts and official texts of place names
- Official reports of reputable organisations and research institutes: United Nations, Small Arms Survey, USAID, Africa Institute, Oxfam reports, and the directories of press associations, publishers' associations and other professional bodies
- International treaties
- National legislation.

The text editor would use these references to check, amongst other things, that:

- all data in tables are present and correct;
- all data in graphics have been accurately and completely supplied (eg pie charts and graphs);
- addresses (etc): that street and/or postal addresses are correct and that the latest telephone and fax numbers, and website and email addresses, are given in the correct format;
- title page: author's or authors' names are correctly indicated;
- numbering of chapter, sections and subsections is correct;
- references to sources: names, dates and publishers' details are given;
- titles of books are correctly indicated.

Where the text editor is of the opinion that any errors of omission or commission can or should be made good only by the author(s), then they should highlight such instances and draw the client's or publisher's attention to them, or write a memorandum to the author requesting resolution of the queries raised.

4 Summary and conclusion

Expanding upon the theoretical framework set out in chapter 2, in this chapter we have tried to draw closer to the actual practice of text editing. We began by examining the concepts of error and deviation and distinguishing between them. We then proceeded to focus on error and deviation in the context of the content of a manuscript, and considered the extent to which the text editor should intervene first to detect them and then to eliminate them from documents. Regarding content, there are three levels at which a text editor could potentially engage with texts: at the word (or micro) level, at the text (or macro) level, and in the area of ethical and legal considerations.

Word level entails a variety of factual errors, including the spellings of names, places and events; dates, numbers and the symbols that often accompany them. Text level entails a consideration of errors and problems at a sentence, paragraph and broader level. For instance, the logical sequencing of paragraphs and the use of appropriate linking words in context; and the correspondence between textual references and the list of references in the bibliography, or between intext cross-references to tables and figures and the actual tables and figures themselves. Incorrect sentence constructions (such as the dangling participle and the comma splice) also fall into this category of error. Ethical and legal considerations include checking whether the author has plagiarised texts, whether the requirements of copyright law as they apply to intellectual property and fair dealing have been observed, and whether any statements or opinions in the text could be construed to be libellous/ slanderous or defamatory.

Finally, editing the content was viewed from the perspective of sufficiency (has the author included all the necessary information?), consistency (have similar features, spellings, the use of capital letters, and so on been rendered in such a way as to create a veneer of consistency throughout a document?), and correctness (are the stated facts correct, and are devices inherent in the book, such as references, cross-references, tables and figures, as well as the table of contents, accurate?). These aspects of a document are critically important to the veracity and integrity of the author's text, and it should be a core element of the text editor's brief to ensure that the document is shipshape in all these respects.

We now move on to considering structural problems within a text, the next facet of error and deviation in which the text editor has to intervene, and which is described and elaborated upon in chapter 7.

7

Text editing in practice: structure

Structure cannot be considered in the abstract: it exists in relation to those familiar considerations, the needs of the readership, the author's intention, the available resources, and the type of publication.
Mackenzie

The most common structural problems are illogical arrangement of chapters or sections, imbalanced treatment of different aspects of the subject, and sections omitted or inadequately covered.
Flann & Hill

A book can contain many elements besides solid blocks of type. ... It is the editor's job to make all these elements work together to present the content effectively to the intended reader.
Mackenzie

Contents

Objectives

The following four chapters focus on the application of the *principles* that were introduced as *knowledge* of normative grammar, text linguistics and document design in chapter 2. We (a) provide *guidelines* for implementing this theoretical knowledge, (b) indicate the challenges, (c) provide tips and insights with respect to personal preferences and (d) highlight useful sources. Chapter 7 looks at text editing from a *structural* point of view. In particular, we discuss the attention that should be given to paragraphing and coherence in the process of text editing. In Chapter 8, the focus is on the textual level of *wording* from the perspective of grammar, meaning, style and register. In chapter 9 we see how spelling and punctuation are important elements of documentation affecting their *presentation* that the text editor must attend to. Finally, chapter 10 deals with the textual level of presentation in the form of typography and layout.

1 The attention to be given to structure

> The structure of a book cannot be imposed in a rigid, formulaic manner: its logic emerges out of the content.
> *Mackenzie*

> The contents page is a good place to start when assessing the structure of a manuscript.
> *Flann & Hill*

Textual quality can be approached from the five angles of *text type, content, structure, wording* and *presentation*. In this chapter we discuss structure, to which the three quality criteria of correspondence, consistency and correctness have to be applied (see chapter 2 section 3.3.1). We discuss in detail how a thorough knowledge of text structure can enable the practitioner to apply clear criteria to *develop* texts *systematically*.

From a communications perspective, the correct structuring of a text is the reader's lifeline: well-defined text types generate well-defined content that has been cast in a well-defined structure – a total communications package.

Mackenzie (2011: 73–75) believes that structure cannot be considered in isolation: it exists in relation to the needs of the readers, the author's intention, the available resources and the type of publication. She considers there to be four main aspects to the structure of a publication that should be taken into account: the nature of the publication, its elements, the proportions and the arrangement. A book by its very nature has a set of conventional structural elements that make it recognisable as such: chapters, subheadings, quotations, bibliography, diagrams, illustrations, endnotes or footnotes, maps, glossary, index, and so on. The text editor's task is to ensure that the edited end product takes the correct physical form according to the author's content and intention.

So far as the elements are concerned, the text editor's challenge (supported by the design and typesetting) is to make all of them work together to present the content effectively to the intended reader. And whereas the structure of a book cannot be imposed in a rigid, formulaic way (its logic emerging out of the content itself rather than the other way round), the text editor should see to it that the breadth and depth of the coverage should match the purpose of the publication.

Finally, the content of the publication should follow some logical arrangement, recognising the various ways in which readers might try to find their way around it – apart, that is, from the purpose that the table of contents and the index serve.

Table 7.1 below itemises the hierarchy of divisions, the principles of arrangement and the connections that make a book an effective, accessible and communicative whole (Mackenzie 2011: 75):

Hierarchy of divisions	Principles of arrangement	Connections

• Volumes
• Parts
• Chapters
• Sections (with or without headings)
• Sub-sections and sub-subsections
• Paragraphs
• Numbered and bulleted lists
	• Chronological or narrative
	• Alphabetical
	• Hierarchical
	• Thematic or topical
	• Deductive – from the particular to the general
	• Inductive – from the general to the particular
	• Thesis, antithesis:
	  – theory and practice
	  – problem and solution
	  – statement and critique
	  – the case for and against
	• Any combination of the above
		• Headings
		• Signposts
		• Transitions
		• Previews
		• Summaries
		• Cross-references
		• Headers and footers
		• Text features: breakout quotes, boxed text, marginal notes, etc

Table 7.1 *Hierarchy of divisions, principles of arrangement and connections for a book*

Structural problems can be compounded in multi-author works when the lead author or title editor did not brief the team of authors thoroughly enough, as Flann & Hill (2004: 40–41) remind us. The problems that can arise include:

On the one hand, text structure pertains to formatting; on the other, it ranges from how larger text parts are organised and the linking of paragraphs (and sentences) to the use of logical connectors (or linking words and phrases, such as *however*, *consequently*, *in other words*, *in addition* and *finally*). These are all vital to making a text genuinely communicative.

Even when the text is a bulleted list, the list has to make sense, it has to follow the rules of concord, and the grammar and punctuation of its constituents must promote understanding and clear communication. Linking becomes a more important component of structure when the text type has to reflect the author's need to argue the pros and cons of a topic (*on the one hand, on the other, from this/that perspective, alternatively, conversely*).

The following table is an overview (by no means comprehensive) of potential errors that the text editor will be required to put right with respect to the paragraphing and logical structure (coherence) in a text. They are elaborated upon further in this chapter and in chapter 12.

Type of error	Specific error	Remedy
Paragraph errors • Length • Topic • Topic sentences • Structure • Support • Conclusion	1. Only one sentence 2. Too uniform (approx. equal length) 3. Two or more topics in a paragraph 4. No topic or theme sentence (thesis statements) 5. No hooks (sentence/paragraph drawing reader into the text) 6. Absence of structuring or plan sentences 7. Absence of signalling words (to show steps) 8. Supporting sentences absent or insufficient 9. Concluding sentence absent 10. Missing transitions between sentences (logical relation: pronouns, synonyms, order, parallel forms) 11. No transitions between paragraphs (logical connectors)	1. Convert to at least two sentences 2. Vary the paragraph lengths 3. Limit to one paragraph, one idea 4. Ensure each paragraph begins with a topic sentence 5. Ensure that hooks are in place 6. Insert structuring sentence 7. Insert signalling words where needed 8. Insert supporting sentences where needed (or suggest some to author) 9. Insert concluding sentence (or suggest one to author) 10. Insert/make transitions between sentences 11. Insert appropriate logical connectors between paragraphs

Coherence errors
• Macro-structure
• Topics
• Type of argument
• Order of arguments
• Flow of arguments
	12. Macro-structure of introduction, body, conclusion not always in place
	13. Topics not clearly identified or identifiable
	14. Type of argument inappropriate or unclear. Most frequent types of academic argument:
	  – explain or analyse;
	  – discuss;
	  – compare or contrast;
	  – define
	15. Order of arguments not logical
	16. Author's argument not flowing
		12. Ensure macro-structure adhered to by either writing the missing components or requesting the author to do so
		13. Ensure topics are clearly identified
		14. Ensure that the correct type of argument is put in place by analysing the author's text
		15. Reorder text to make the argumentation logical
		16. Reorder the text to make the flow of the author's argument logical

Table 7.2 *Overview of potential text-structural problems and their remedies*

2 The attention to be given to paragraphs

> Each paragraph of an essay is a self-contained unit. Each paragraph should contain one (and only one) idea.
> *Van de Poel & Gasiorek*

> A paragraph is a unit of thought, not of length, so don't let the writing of your client ramble on and on.
> *Murphy*

> Writers need paragraphs to help them stay *organized* and *in control* of what they are writing.
> *Enquist & Oates*

Before we consider the nature and extent of the editorial intervention required at the level of paragraphing, it is as well to consider the role and effects of meaningful paragraphing on the readability and accessibility of text as a communications medium.

2.1 The effects of well-structured paragraphing on the text

In every process of writing, the division of text into paragraphs is of great importance. This is because doing so creates order and organisation in a text. As Mossop (2010: 76) says: 'Paragraph divisions are important *markers* that guide the reader through the text's structure.'

A page cannot be one long paragraph: that would render a text daunting and unreadable and lead to unclear or miscommunication. It would, for one thing, not be clear what belongs to what and would be unhelpful in trying to get the reader to understand. The length of paragraphs therefore seems to have a noticeable effect on the ease with which text can be read (Mossop 2010: 76). Consequently, the text editor must have a keen sense of what paragraphing entails and how it should work in practice in order to remedy what is structurally incorrect.

'Good' paragraphing is necessary for a text to communicate effectively and to make the reading process efficient. Writers should not want to overload their readers with information, so they should divide their text up into easily digestible units. Since they aim at persuading their audience to go along with the message they want to convey, presenting the arguments in an easily accessible (and recognisable) way is important. However, few people really know what is meant by a 'paragraph' or what effects paragraphs have on both writer and reader, and on the reading process (Enquist & Oates 2009: 33–34; Murphy 2011: 130). So what makes a paragraph well-structured and meaningful to a reader?

Text editors would do well to bear in mind the contribution that well-structured paragraphs make to text and the fundamental difference they can make to the reader's experience of it.

Paragraphs:
- help writers to organise what they write.
  In this way they help to divide the text *thematically* into blocks ('tiny boxes', according to Enquist & Oates 2009: 33).
- help writers to build up their *argumentation*.
  Keep track of the constituent arguments and their internal relationships.
- help readers to understand the *organisation* of the text.
  One part succeeds another and there are logical connections.
- give readers an indication of logical *interruptions* in the text.
  They can then either accept such interruptions or become irritated by them.
- help to make the page *layout* more attractive and support the reading process.
  Paragraphs (especially block paragraphs, as in this book) serve to create white space on a page. This provides a breathing space and helps to prevent reader fatigue.

The text editor should therefore use this as a checklist, if necessary, against which to justify editorial changes they feel should be made with respect to paragraphing.

2.2 Insights into paragraphing

It is possible to learn how to paragraph well; it is a skill that can be acquired and put into practice fairly easily if a few straightforward pointers are followed (text editors take note):

Paragraph content:
- Murphy (2011) views the ideal paragraph as being organised with a topic sentence containing a guiding idea, some sentences that support it and which are linked appropriately, and a final sentence that pulls the paragraph together *and* points to the guiding idea in the next paragraph. Paragraphs, she says, need to be varied in length, and there is nothing wrong with a single-sentence paragraph occasionally to make a strong point. Likewise, there is nothing wrong with a much longer paragraph where a lengthier explanation or argument is required (2011: 130).

Paragraph length:
- Paragraphs should preferably not have a fixed or uniform length – the length should vary (Murphy 2011: 130). In a sense, this variation of paragraph length is a visual element that makes pages more appealing and seemingly more readable (see chapter 10). There is a school of thought which says that, on average, paragraphs should not be longer than 100 words. (If comprising four sentences, the average of 25 words per sentence is too high; if comprising five sentences, the average of 20 words per sentence is approaching a more readable and acceptable length. Six sentences of about 16 words each on average would be best for most adult readers.) However, this guideline should really be reader-driven: in some genres longer paragraphs are customary, for example legal or academic texts; in others, such as information leaflets and brochures aimed at consumers, paragraphs should be somewhat less than 100 words long.

- Extremes of length are also unsatisfactory: paragraphs that are *too short* are difficult to follow and can usually consist of only one idea each, leading to a staccato, disconnected effect that detracts from fluent reading and comprehension. Such paragraphs can leave the readers to make the connection(s) themselves if they don't make a point emphatically. Paragraphs that are *too long* tire readers unnecessarily and also reduce comprehension. Variety is therefore important because when the length of consecutive paragraphs is unpredictable, the reader's attention is retained (Murphy 2011: 130).

Paragraph structure:

- Paragraphs have a typical structure: the first sentence in a paragraph is the *theme*, *topic* or *key sentence* (that is, the sentence that indicates the subject of the paragraph). The next sentence is the *plan* or *structure sentence* (ie the sentence which indicates how the theme is going to develop further), and that is followed by the *supporting sentence(s)*, that is, that sentence (or those sentences) which helps to develop the theme further and provide support for the opening statement. The final sentence should summarise the theme ('clincher') and point the reader to the next paragraph or idea. Mackenzie (2011: 76) underlines research findings that paragraph length should be varied to ensure an optimal effect (see also Helen Jenkins' 1992 linguistic analysis of Stephen Hawking's *A brief history of time*). A word of advice: 'A paragraph may be several hundred words in length, but an occasional one-sentence paragraph can make a pleasing effect' (Mackenzie 2011: 76). Whatever the length of your paragraph, a 'paragraph is tied together by a single coherent idea' (Mackenzie 2011: 76).
- Paragraphs must be *coherent*, that is, the parts must connect to one another logically so that the reader can easily follow the development of the writer's ideas (see below on the role of coherence). One paragraph should typically connect to the previous and the next paragraphs. Paragraphs that are coherent (ie bound by content or theme) will connect to each other, will be relevant to the build-up of the argument, will be organised (eg the placement of causes ahead of consequences), will give sufficient information to support the theme, but will also not be longwinded.

Paragraph linking:

- Paragraphs must follow one another *logically*.
- Paragraphs are supposed to have mutual *cohesion*, that is, they display a formal connection (Halliday & Hasan 1976). This means that consecutive sentences will be connected by means of a few acquired techniques, including:
    - reference: referring back (where structural words such as *it*, *this* or *that* or *see above* refer back to *the book*); referring forward;
    - ellipsis: used when some words are omitted or when something is repeated
    - conjunctions between two clauses expressing different relationships (*and, then, but, first, finally*, etc);
    - lexical cohesion: repetition of core words or phrases (or their synonyms), highlighting key words (which could be *italicised*);

- substitution: pronouns replacing nouns (*he, who,* etc);
- grammatical cohesion when certain syntactic patterns are repeated (parallel forms).

What follows are some guidelines for practitioners for identifying and editing paragraphs so as to render them well structured:

Checklist 7.1 Identifying and editing paragraphs

✓ Read the text and find the main idea.
✓ Identify the topic sentence in each paragraph, the supporting sentences (do they focus on the main idea?) and the closing sentence (with clincher).
✓ Check whether the facts and ideas are organised in such a way that they develop the main idea.
✓ Check that every paragraph supports the text's main idea.
✓ Check whether the author has used clear and simple sentences to express their meaning (chapter 8).

As indicated above, it is important for the text editor to pay attention to the *links* within and between paragraphs, as it falls to them to repair those that are not appropriate or are absent. The links could perform any of the following functions:

- Introducing new ideas or supporting facts (*in the first instance, on the one hand, for one thing*).
- Building on previous ideas or supporting facts (*in addition, next, moreover*).
- Indicating the opposite of a previous idea or contrary facts (*conversely, however, on the other hand*).
- Indicating a sequence of steps or events (*first, secondly, thirdly, finally*).
- Clarifying a previous statement (*in other words, stated differently*).

Linking words (or logical operators) are used to link ideas when writing. They enable the writing to flow from one idea to the next in a logical and cohesive way. There are three main types of linking word:

- *conjunctions* (to coordinate two parts of a sentence: *and, but, so,* etc);
- *sentence connectors* (to link ideas from one sentence to the next and to give paragraphs coherence: they introduce, order, contrast or sequence ideas, theory, data, etc: *first, however, thus*).
- *sentence subordinators* (to join clauses and express comparison/contrast, cause/effect, time, possibility, place and manner: *although, when, since, if, where*).

Paragraphs must follow one another in such a way that the *full picture* is clear and the entire story makes sense. As text editor, you should make it easy for the reader to follow the author's train of thought throughout the whole text. The links must also be grammatically correct (in person and number), they must not bore the reader, and the use of synonyms should not cause confusion. Connections between paragraphs must also not disrupt linkages; they should also not interrupt the flow of ideas or information between paragraphs.

Typographically, paragraphs can be indicated in two ways:
- by indenting the first word of the first line, or
- by leaving a blank line between paragraphs (in which case the first line is not indented – the 'block' paragraph), or by a combination of these two paragraph styles. Most journal, magazine and book publishers have a style sheet that defines this.

Style guides give useful tips in this respect. Some examples: Quirk 1982; *Chicago manual of style* 1993; *The Cambridge Australian style guide* 1995; *The little book of style* 1998; *The New York Times manual of style and usage* 1999; *Style manual* (Australian) 2002, *MHRA styleguide* 2002; *The Oxford style manual* (since 2003) comprises *The Oxford dictionary for writers and editors* 2000 and *The Oxford guide to style* 2002 which was the successor to *Hart's rules,* published since 1893; Marsh & Marshall 2004; *The Associated Press stylebook* 2004; Lynch 2008; Linnegar, Shamberger & Bishop 2009; *MLA style manual* 2009.

With the above we have tried to show that text editors must know what paragraphing entails. In reality, text editors owe it to their clients to offer the best possible service and advice regarding effective paragraphing, and this can be done only if they are fully conversant with the techniques of good paragraphing.

3 Argumentation: the need for coherence

> I have defined *incoherence* as writing in which separate, unrelated ideas appear to be juxtaposed: *they are next to, but not connected to each other ... coherence* exists in a sequence of *words, sentences* and *paragraphs* in which the reader can perceive *connections* ... To produce a coherent stretch of discourse, writers use basic thought patterns, or logical patterns, in both simple and complex ways.
> *Brostoff*

> The hanging together of a text with relation to its *context* or situation or *culture* is called coherence.
> *Taboada*

> Writing a coherent text longer than a sentence is one of the hardest of all of the skills schools set out to teach.
> *Davies*

3.1 Coherence as a founding principle of argumentation

In chapter 2 section 7 the importance of coherence was introduced when the development of textual understanding and textual fluency was discussed. All effective communication has to abide by the requirement of coherence, that is, texts have to communicate in such a way that there are smooth transitions between the different parts (from sentence to sentence, and from paragraph to paragraph) and that all the parts connect to one another (Billingham 2002: 48–53).

Coherence normally refers to discourse relationships that may or may not be explicitly signalled; cohesive devices are surface, textual indicators of interconnectedness. Used well, these devices can contribute greatly to text readability (Essem Educational Limited: 2011).

In a way, it can be said that coherence is the most important criterion for determining a text's quality; Lourens (2007) summarises this assertion as follows: '*Coherence* can even be labelled as *the* attribute that a text must possess in order to be a text.'

Coherence ensures, as it were, that the bigger picture is clear (Perelman, Paradis & Barrett 2001). Without coherence, the structure of ideas and the logical flow of ideas will not make a text a readable text, since it will not be a communicative *unity*. Kies (2003) explains it as follows:

> Coherence is a product of many different factors, which combine to make every paragraph, every sentence, and every phrase contribute to the meaning of the whole piece. Coherence in writing is much more difficult to sustain than coherent speech simply because writers have no nonverbal clues to inform if their message is clear or not. Therefore, *writers must make their patterns of coherence more explicit and much more carefully planned*. Coherence itself is the product of two factors – paragraph unity and sentence cohesion.

If a text is logical and well structured, the reader may experience it as 'making sense', namely that what is being transmitted is understandable and connected. Coherence is therefore in effect an inherent characteristic of texts: without coherence a written piece of text is not really a text.

What has been said about coherence above also holds for argumentation patterns, that is, that the order of ideas and thoughts has to create the impression of being well thought out and rounded off. Arguments will typically be constructed to support a statement about a certain topic which, in turn, will be supported by further statements based on facts, reasons, ideas, values, invitations for action, examples, and the like, that aim to make the statement accessible and acceptable to the recipient.

As far as *structure* is concerned, the author's point of view is presented at the beginning of the text or paragraph and is then supported in logically connected sentences (see paragraph structure above). The first sentence (or sentences in a longer text) is also called a 'hook', and it functions as an eyecatcher and teaser that draws the reader into the piece. Last but not least, the argumentation has to be concluded with a final or concluding sentence, which restates the main idea of the introductory sentence and emphatically brings the message of the paragraph or text home to the reader. It is sometimes referred to as a 'clincher' or a 'conclusive argument' and, together with the first sentence, it forms the 'filling' or main substance of the piece.

Argumentation is vital in any form of communication. Sometimes the author shares a point of view and at other times the argumentation takes the form of elucidation. Whatever the case may be, it is important for text editors to understand this argumentation so that the development of the arguments – whether factual statements, opinions, value statements or invitations to act, motivate or convince – is conceptually sound, which means that the arguments will make sense for the reader and can be understood. As indicated above, effective argumentation is structured and organised and consists of two key elements: a thesis statement and support:

1. A *thesis statement* is a clear, one-sentence statement of the writer's main argument.
2. *Support* is the material – the evidence – a writer uses to convince their reader that the writer's argument is valid (Van de Poel & Gasiorek 2006: 35, 36).

It is not enough, however, merely to have a list of reasons why your argument is valid. In order for the support to be effective, it needs to be (explicitly) structured and organised. To this end, the text will make use of structuring or planning sentences that, through their linking words, for example, indicate the flow of the argumentation.

In any case, the requirements of the genre in which the argumentation takes place will have to be taken into account. The development of arguments in an academic article takes a different form than, for instance, the narrative in a novel. The editor is expected to judge the value of the argumentation, which can be achieved by evaluating the role of coherence in the development of the arguments. In this way the text editor will help to create a well-structured text that appears to be a coherent unity and which will create a positive reading experience. Lourens (2007: 5) suggests a simple reason for this: readers have a need, either consciously or unconsciously, for structure, order and organisation. It is the task of the writer (and, in the editing process, that of the text editor) to fulfil this very basic need. Vivanco (2005: 1234) adds that, by definition, a reader will actually search for coherence:

> On reading a new text, even though it may not make any sense, the reader *tries to look for*, *discover*, or *disclose* coherence. We even look for it so desperately that, sometimes, we use our own, subjective interpretations of the text in order to clarify its obscure meanings. *In this way, looking for coherence becomes a path to the understanding of a text* ...

Text editors play the role of facilitators because it is their primary task to evaluate whether the author's structuring and argumentation are appropriate to the audience with a view to determining whether the message being conveyed via the text will be communicated as easily as possible.

3.2 Pitfalls in argumentation structure

The vigilant text editor should be on the lookout for problems with the author's argumentation. Since the structure of logical arguments depends greatly on linguistics but also to some extent on philosophy, it will suffice (and probably be simpler and more effective) to summarise some of the major pitfalls that have to be avoided when an author constructs an *argument* (cf Jansen & Steehouder 2001; Van Eemeren, Grootendorst & Kruiger 1987; Van Eemeren & Houtlosser (eds) 2005; Van Eemeren & Garssen (eds) 2006, 2009; Van Wijk 1999; Walton 2004). The fallacies below are logical arguments that appear to be correct but that turn out to be incorrect when examined more closely. The text editor should be alert to them, and not simply accept them at face value:

- *Argumentum ad populum*
  This is known as Playing to the Gallery or Appealing to the People. To commit this fallacy is to attempt to win acceptance of an assertion by appealing to a large group of people. This form of fallacy is often characterised by emotive language.
  Example: Pornography must be banned. It constitutes violence against women.

- *Ad hominem*/emotional appeal
  The author argues their point through an emotional appeal based almost entirely on personal opinion or bias unsubstantiated by facts.
  Example: Although Ferguson's book on the Belgian Congo is well researched, I doubt that an American scholar can contribute much to our understanding of the Belgian colonial past.

- *Converse accident/hasty generalisation*
  This fallacy occurs when an author forms a general rule by examining only a few specific cases that are not representative of all possible instances.
  Example: All of my blind dates have been embarrassing disasters, so I know this one will be too.
  Example: Everyone in my class agreed that the latest Ian McEwan novel was pretty bad, which shows that McEwan is not a popular writer among students.

- The 'slippery slope' argument
  This argument states that should one event occur, so will other harmful events. No proof is offered that the harmful events are caused by the first event.
  Example: If we legalise marijuana, then we would have to legalise crack and heroin and we will have a nation full of drug addicts on welfare. Therefore we cannot legalise marijuana.
  Example: The acceptance of abortion does not end with the killing of unborn human life. It then goes on to affect our attitude toward all aspects of human life. This is most obvious in how quickly, following the acceptance of abortion, the practice of infanticide is accepted – the killing of babies who after birth do not come up to someone's standard of life worthy to be lived – and then of euthanasia of the aged. If human life can be taken before birth, there is no logical reason why human life cannot be taken after birth.

- *Plurium interrogationum*/many questions
  This fallacy occurs when a questioner demands a simple answer to a complex question. It is committed when someone asks a question that presupposes something that has not been proven or accepted by all the people involved. In the first example below, the presupposition is that Mary wears dresses; but if she never does, then this question is a case of plurium interrogationum. In the second, the underlying assumption is that the addressee has assaulted their children at some stage prior to now. Both questions tend to force a 'no' or 'yes' answer, each of which is incriminating.
  Example: Does Mary prefer wearing a blue or a red dress?
  Example: Have you stopped assaulting your children?

- Faulty cause-and-effect reasoning
  The fact that event B follows event A does not necessarily mean that A caused B.
  Example: Oil prices were at an all-time high before Barack Obama's election brought them back to a reasonable level.
  Example: I drank bottled water and now I am throwing up all the time, so the water must have made me sick.

- Begging the question/circular reasoning
  Begging the question is a way to avoid formulating an actual argument: rather than support the conclusion, the writer essentially restates it in different terms.
  Example: Faculty administrators should not be permitted to come to student council meetings because student council meetings should be for students only.

- *Non sequitur*
  A non sequitur is an argument where the conclusion is drawn from premises that are not logically connected with it.
  Example: If the mill were polluting the river, we would see an increase in fish deaths. Fish deaths have increased. Thus, the mill is polluting the river.

- Red herring (disambiguation)
  This fallacy is committed when irrelevant material is introduced to the issue being discussed, so that everyone's attention is diverted away from the points being made towards a different conclusion.
  Example: It took us an hour to travel to the airport: have you seen the new Air France A380 aircraft? It landed as we arrived.
  Example: We admit that this measure is unpopular. But we also urge you to note that there are so many local issues in this ballot that the whole thing is getting ridiculous.

- The extended analogy
  The fallacy of the extended analogy often occurs when some suggested general rule is being argued over. The fallacy is to assume that mentioning two different situations, in

an argument about a general rule, constitutes a claim that those situations are analogous to each other.

Example: From a debate about anticryptography legislation: 'I believe it is always wrong to oppose the law by breaking it.'

Example: 'Are you saying that cryptography legislation is as important as the struggle for Black liberation? How dare you!'

- **Ad hoc**

  There is a difference between argument and explanation. If we are interested in establishing A, and B is offered as evidence, the statement 'A because B' is an argument. If we are trying to establish the truth of B, then 'A because B' is not an argument, it is an explanation.

  The ad hoc fallacy is to give an after-the-fact explanation that does not apply to other situations. Often this ad hoc explanation will be dressed up to look like an argument.

  Example: If we assume that God treats all people equally, then the following is an ad hoc explanation:

  'I was cured of cancer.'

  'Praise the Lord, then. He is your healer.'

  'So, will He heal others who have cancer?'

  'Er ... The ways of God are mysterious.'

- **Either ... or fallacy**

  An either ... or fallacy suggests that there are only two alternatives when there are in fact more.

  Example: The war on drugs has not worked. Either we should legalise drugs or we should turn the drug war over to our armed forces and let them fight it.

The following short checklist may be used to make dealing with an author's argumentation easier, leading to greater coherence:

Checklist 7.2 How to check for coherence

✓ Ensure that the overall text is coherent.
✓ Check that the paragraphs are internally coherent.
✓ Check that consecutive paragraphs are connected when necessary.
✓ Check that the correct linking words are being used.
✓ If necessary, as text editor, discuss the problem with the author so you obtain an insight into their textual intentions and can adapt the text accordingly.

4 Summary and conclusion

In this chapter, we have drawn closer to the practice of text editing by dealing with the topics central to structure: paragraphing and coherence. In the next chapter, we consider more 'micro' aspects of text editing in practice: grammar, meaning, style and register.

Text editing in practice: wording

Too much importance is still attached to grammarians' fetishes and too little to choosing right words. But we cannot have grammar jettisoned altogether; that would mean chaos.
Gowers

… the sequence of words must not give rise to the 'huh?' reaction. Readers should not have to go over a sentence two or three times just to see how the parts of the sentence are connected to each other and to get the basic point.
Mossop

You should not confuse the different varieties of English with levels of formality, or what linguists call register. Even within Standard English there are different levels of formality reflected in the vocabulary, grammar, and style of the language used.
Allen

Contents

Objectives

After having introduced the application of text-editing principles in the areas of *text types* and *content* in chapter 6, we moved on to *text structure* and its effect on argumentation in chapter 7. The current chapter focuses on *wording* and, more particularly, on how *knowledge* of normative grammar (syntax and morphology) and text linguistics (style and register), as introduced in chapter 2, should be applied to produce an effective text. We (a) provide guidelines for putting knowledge in practice, (b) indicate where there are *tensions* and problems and (c) provide tips on and insights into how to deal with these prescriptive and descriptive aspects of wording. Chapters 9 and 10 – the final, practical chapters – focus on the textual level of presentation, starting with aspects of spelling and punctuation that affect text quality (chapter 9) and then considering how typography and layout can aid a reader's understanding of a text (chapter 10).

1 Introduction

> Arguments over grammar and style are often as fierce as those over IBM versus Mac, and as fruitless as Coke versus Pepsi and boxers versus briefs.
> *Jack Lynch*

The most verbal aspect of textual quality is to be found at the *word level* (see chapter 2). This is the most normative of all the five textual levels and the least tolerant of deviation (as introduced in chapter 6). This is because deviations from the norm at this level can lead to ambiguity, inaccuracy and also the insufficiency of the text and the communication. Therefore, a knowledge of wording – grammar, meaning, style and register – empowers the practitioner to analyse and enhance texts systematically.

One of the challenges facing many text editors, however, is being able to distinguish between style and register, and in this chapter we hope not only to clarify the difference between them, but also to demonstrate just how closely interconnected they are.

2 Consider the normative grammar

> An active knowledge is always operating in the background, activating itself when it's needed.
> *Campbell*

During the Salem witch trials of 1692, Rebecca Nurse would have been set free except for her words, 'She is one of us,' spoken about another woman. She meant that the woman was a fellow defendant, but the judge thought she meant that the

woman was a fellow witch. Rebecca Nurse was hanged because the antecedent of a pronoun was misunderstood. She died because of a mistake in grammar.
http://www.dailywritingtips.com/is-there-really-room-for-error-in-writing/

As an editor, when you correct a grammatical mistake or infelicity, you must be able to *explain why* you have done so in the correct terminology. ... The rules of good writing are the foundation of your editing ...
Mackenzie

Practitioners will rarely encounter a written text that is error-free. Apart from misspellings, the most obvious errors – and often the least tolerated – are *grammatical*. Grammatical errors are usually experienced as a writer's lack of knowledge and, by implication, perhaps even the copy editor's, if they are allowed to slip through to the proof or print.

Traditionally, *grammar* means the set of *rules* of a language that regulates the formation of words, phrases and sentences. These rules are usually limited to a particular language – which means that each language has its own system of *internal* norms for its phonology (the use of sounds), morphology (the construction of words) and syntax (the construction of phrases and sentences) as well as its phonetics (the production, transmission and perception of sounds), semantics (the study of meaning), and pragmatics (the study of context) (compare sections 6.1 and 6.2.1 in chapter 2).

For the text editor who works in English, it is important to consider the particular aspects of syntax and morphology of a text to ensure that it conveys its message(s) directly, clearly and unambiguously.

Mossop (2010: 40–46) distinguishes between the errors made by native speakers and those committed by NNSs. For example, attempts to use the correct idiomatic prepositions gives rise to considerably more problems for speakers of English as a foreign language than for native speakers (witness: he is responsible *for* the human resources function; he is responsible *to* me; that is the responsibility *of* human resources!).

The above, of course, does not mean that native speakers are always able to justify their choice (Ellis 2005; Ellis et al 2009), but they are more likely to select the correct preposition intuitively, because they would in all probability have grown up with the correct idiomatic usage. For their part NNSs will, quite naturally, apply the idiomatic usage of their own native tongue – often with unfortunate or discordant results (Linnegar 2009b: 9–10, 45–66)!

2.1 Knowledge of grammar

English grammar is probably the best studied component of the English language and it has been covered in different types of publication, from research-focused to pedagogic, from descriptive to prescriptive (see section 3 below). In more recent grammatical descriptions of the language, it can be noted that usage heavily informs the theoretical rules, which in turn influences the effect linked to grammar. Thus, in written texts it is no longer regarded as grammatically criminal to split an infinitive, to end a sentence with a preposition, or to use 'will' instead of 'shall' together with the pronouns 'I' and 'we'; and 'their' may now be used as a singular pronoun where its use leads to a less clumsy construction than the 'politically correct', gender-sensitive he/she ... him/her ... himself/herself combinations. Language usage sometimes allows the 'rules' of grammar to be 'bent', and text editors should keep abreast of and be sensitive to such adaptations and modifications.

The particular aspects of grammar we're concerned with here (as the text editor should be) are syntax (and common syntactical errors) and morphology (and common morphological errors).

2.1.1 Knowledge of syntax

English, like the other Germanic languages, 'makes very little use of word structure, or morphology, to express the meanings that Latin conveys in its word endings (to love: *amo*, *amas*, *amat*, *amamus* ...). Most of English grammar is taken up with the rules governing the order in which words can appear: the field of syntax. Word order is crucial for English ... where the meaning of the sentence alters dramatically once the order varies' (Crystal 1990: 21) – for example, *The dog bit the man* vs *The man bit the dog*: the same words are used, but in different arrangements, leading to different messages.

Word order also becomes important in the fixed patterns involving adjectives. For example, qualitative adjectives (*tall*, *diminutive* in the sentence below) should precede classifying (*foreign*, *French*) adjectives:

> The tall foreign gentleman ordered a pizza while his diminutive French poodle waited patiently outside.[1]

It would sound unnatural in English to say or write 'foreign tall gentleman' and 'French diminutive poodle'. Similarly, adjectives of size should precede adjectives of colour:

> I bought a large green balloon for my daughter, a smaller yellow one for my son.

2.1.1.1 Word order and meaning

What follows are a number of instances of where the order of words can affect the meaning conveyed by a sentence.

---

[1] Note that a comma should not be inserted between qualitative and classifying adjectives when they occur together. However, a comma should be inserted between two or more qualitative and between two or more classifying adjectives.

› *Only:* In the use of 'only', word order is fundamental to conveying the correct meaning; haphazard or incorrect placement can lead to ambiguity (Kahn 1985: 406–410):

> 'The researchers only injected rats in the morning' could mean that only rats were injected or that only in the morning rats were injected – or that only the researchers did the injecting, or that they didn't trap or shoot them.

A general convention to follow is to ensure that 'only' describes (or limits) the word(s) immediately to the *right* of it. And depending upon its position in the sentence, it can change its function too (see 2.1.1.3 Word classes below):

> *Only* I attended the cocktail party that evening. (an adjective describing the pronoun 'I' – nobody else attended)
> I *only* attended the cocktail party that evening. (an adverb describing the verb 'attended' – I didn't do anything else)
> I attended *only* the cocktail party that evening. (an adjective describing the noun phrase 'cocktail party' – I attended no other function)
> I attended the cocktail party *only* that evening. (an adverb describing the adverb phrases 'that evening' – at no other time)

› *Adverbs and modal verbs:* When adverbs are combined with modal verbs (see Word classes below), they normally do so in a specific order:

> I have *always* admired his work.
> She is *constantly* being complimented for her exquisite taste.

In general, words that belong together should be placed as close together as possible. So:

> – when an auxiliary and a past participle (see Word classes below) are modified by an adverb, the adverb is usually inserted between them: 'have always admired' (an alternative is to place 'always' at the end of the sentence, provided it is not then too far removed from the verb);
> – when two auxiliaries precede a past participle, the adverb sits most comfortably between the two auxiliaries: 'is constantly being complimented).

› *Prepositions* are, by convention, usually placed before the noun or noun equivalent: *in* the summer; *on* the roof; *in spite of* his rantings; *upon* realising his mistake. But it is also quite permissible to place a preposition at the end of a sentence, as in:

> Is this the room you sleep *in*?

>>

This word order sounds more natural, more conversational. A more formal (though not any more 'correct') word order would be:

Is this the room *in* which you sleep?

› *Adverbs of place, time and manner*: The order in which we place adverbs of place, time and manner (see Word classes below) has also become governed by convention:

He marched <u>into my classroom</u> <u>at 12 noon precisely</u> <u>brandishing an encyclopaedia</u>.

The three separately underlined phrases follow the order place (where?), time (when?) and manner (how?); to change the order would sound awkward or unnatural to a native English speaker.

› *Sentence order – inversion*: The normal word order of an English sentence is subject–verb–object (Suzi ate her sandwich; The men rode their bicycles that morning). However, parts of a sentence may be inverted for effect – usually to change the focus of the content or to shift the emphasis to the front of a sentence.

Inversion is also a useful device for changing the rhythm or pace of a passage of text, to counteract the monotony of the normal word order being used repeatedly. It is therefore another aspect of word order that often requires the text editor's sympathetic attention:

The men rode their bicycles in the afternoon.
In the afternoon the men rode their bicycles.
In the afternoon, the men rode their bicycles.

In the first sentence, the focus is on the men; in the second and third sentences it is placed on the time of the action. The comma inserted in the third sentence separates the adverbial phrases more emphatically, heightening the effect of the inversion (Allen 2005: 108–109).

The normal sentence order is also often reversed in questions:

Statement: The exercise was strenuous.
Question: Was the exercise strenuous?

But the order sometimes remains unchanged when the question begins with an interrogative pronoun (see Word classes below) such as *who*:

Who wrote this? I wrote this.

2.1.1.2 Word combinations and meaning

As can be seen from the examples cited above, the study of *syntax* as a discipline includes studying the ways in which *words* are combined to form *sentences* that make sense to speakers of a language. This applies also to verbs, including phrasal verbs:

>Julian *broke* the glass by dropping it. (smashed, shattered)
>Sally *broke* the record for the 100 metres sprint. (surpassed or bettered)
>'Will has *broken* my heart,' wept Kate. (emotionally upset)
>Sam *broke down* when he heard the news. (lost control of emotions)
>Eliot *broke down* the door. (tore it off its hinges; smashed it)
>My car *broke down* on my way to you. (stopped operating)
>After threats of torture, they *broke* the spy *down*. (force someone to give up and tell secrets)

In each case, while the words 'broke' and 'broke down' are identical, they take on a different meaning, determined in large part by the words surrounding them, which combine to convey different meanings or messages as a whole. And, of course, the denotations (meanings, as distinct from implications) of 'broke' and 'broke down' are themselves different too.

If we consider the sentence 'Eliot broke down the door', for instance, we see here a fairly typical group of words arranged as a simple sentence comprising actor (Eliot), action (broke down) and person or thing acted upon (the door) or, using more traditional labels, subject, (phrasal) verb and object. By combining these words in this way, we convey the writer's message most directly and clearly.

2.1.1.3 Word classes (parts of speech)

On the basis of their *form* and the *function* that they fulfil, words are classified in clearly distinguishable *parts of speech* or *word classes*. These parts of speech or word classes are combined with one another in unique ways, according to particular *patterns of usage* (the so-called *rules* of a language) that have to be adhered to if good, clear phrases, clauses and sentences are to be formed. If sentences are formed according to applicable rules, it is to be expected that these sentences in combination with each other will contribute to effective communication.

For example, adjectives perform the function of describing nouns and pronouns:

>*Silly old* Eliot broke down the *front* door.

And, in English, when we make a general statement or we have to be vague, we use the determiner (or indefinite article) 'a' or 'an':

>Where can I find *a* branch of ABC bank?

Once we get down to specifics, we use the determiner (or definite article) 'the':

>*The* nearest branch is round the corner in Short Street.

Traditionally, the following two word classes are distinguished:

- Open word classes are *lexical items*, which are defined by their syntactic or morphological behaviour. Common linguistic categories include *noun* and *verb*. Open word classes constantly acquire new members, whereas normally no new items can be added to closed word classes.
- Closed word classes usually contain a relatively small number of items and these are typically *determiners, prepositions, pronouns* and *conjunctions.*

List 8.2 Word classes in English

Closed word classes:

› *Determiners* 'occur before [a] noun acting as head of the noun phrase' (Quirk et al 1985: 253). They include the definite and indefinite articles:
   – the, a, an, that, every, some, three, none, most, all …

› *Prepositions* are connecting words that show the relationship between a pronoun or a noun and another word. The nine most frequent prepositions are:
   – at, by, for, from, in, of, on, to, with.

There are also phrasal prepositions such as:
   – because of, with regard to, in spite of.

› *Pronouns* are traditionally said to 'stand in the place of' nouns. They include personal, possessive, demonstrative, reflexive, relative, and interrogative pronouns:
   – Personal: I, you, we, they – Between you and me, I think she's wrong.
   – Possessive: my, your, his/hers/its, theirs – The dog wagged its tail.
   – Demonstrative: this/that, these/those – These are my car keys.
   – Reflexive: myself, themselves – At the buffet I helped myself to salad.
   – Relative: who/whom, which, that – He is the person whom I respect most.
   – Interrogative: who?, where?, when? – When will I see you again?

› *Transition words* or *conjunctions* have either a coordinating or a subordinating function:
   – and, that, when, although, however
   – I gave him some money, *although* I hardly trusted him. (subordinating)
   – She is short *and* he is tall. (coordinating)

>>

> *Interjections* are typical of spoken language:
>   – No!, oh!, don't!, exactly!

> *Numerals*, cardinal and ordinal numbers, can belong either to the open or to the closed classes:
>   – one, thousand, one million; first, second, third, …

Open word classes:

> *Nouns* can be subdivided into proper nouns (referring to specific people), common nouns, collectives, abstracts and verb-nouns (gerunds):
>   – Proper: Duncan Dock, London Eye, Eisenhower
>   – Common: boy, building, (a specific) crime
>   – Collective: flock, gaggle
>   – Abstract: truth, honesty, crime (generally)
>   – Verb-nouns (gerunds): I like *walking*. She does *typing* for a *living*.

Nouns can also be viewed as either countable or uncountable:
   – Countables: rocks, motor cars, bottles of water, people
   – Uncountables: sand, sugar (grains), water
        We use many and few(er) with countables:
        There were *many* people at the meeting.
        We consumed *fewer* bottles of water than expected. (not much or less)
        I don't have *much* sugar in my coffee.
        There is *less* water in that jug than in this one. (not many or fewer)

> *Adjectives* describe nouns and pronouns. They can be single words, phrases or clauses, and can be used either at the head of a noun phrase (attributive form) or predicatively as a subject or an object complement:
>   – The *real* reason is this. The *well-known* author gave us his *latest* novel. (attributive form, before a noun)

The pupil *over there* looks *unhappy*. (predicative, after the noun or pronoun, or after a verb, complement) Adjectives also take the form of *participles* (past and present):
   – Present participles: A *walking* stick; *running* shoes
   – Past participles: a *heated* debate; a *frought* situation; *burnt* toast

Compound adjectives also deserve a mention here, because of the problem of knowing when to hyphenate them or not. Consider these:

>>

- The *much-admired* poet held us enthralled as she read her poems.
- That artist's work is much admired.
- The *highly respected* artist assessed our drawings and paintings.

The first compound adjective is hyphenated because it occurs attributively (in front of the noun, 'poet'), adverb and adjective forming a unit.

The second follows the verb 'is', so it occurs predicatively (as a complement) and therefore can safely be written as two words.
The third involves an adverb ending in -*ly*, and such adverbs should not be compounded.

› *Verbs* are traditionally divided into three major groups. A distinction is made between full verbs, auxiliaries or primary verbs, and modal verbs. Within the first category we can distinguish, for instance,
  - transitive and intransitive verbs: Mike *plays* bridge. (verb takes an object in this instance = transitive) That *helps* a lot. (verb has no object in this instance = intransitive)
  - prepositional verbs: *Tune in* to his radio station. *Move on* to better things.
  - phrasal verbs: He *broke up* with his girlfriend. The plane *took off* late.
  - auxiliaries *(be, have, do)* and modals *(can, must, will, should)* are regarded as a closed class of verbs:
    She *has been* there before.
    We *should be walking* home instead.

› *Adverbs* describe or intensify verbs, adjectives and other adverbs. They can be single words, phrases or clauses and are classified as adverbs of
  - time (when?): He arrived *a minute ago*.
  - place (where?): The meeting took place *at the airport*.
  - manner (how?): Tell me *plainly*.
  - reason (or cause) (why?): He did it *because he was frustrated*.
  - degree (how much?, to what extent?): I like that *very much*.
  - condition (if what?): *If you do that*, I shall disown you.

Another way of distinguishing adverbs is as simple (*just, well*), compound (*therefore, somewhere*) or derivational (*interestingly, oddly*) (see Quirk et al 1985).

2.1.2 Potential syntactical errors

Writers of English texts are usually able to arrange the above parts of speech in the correct order and usually succeed in forming the correct combinations of words in simple, compound or complex sentences by means of main and subordinate clauses (subject, verb and object; adjectival clause, adverbial clause, etc):

> Sarah, who is my friend, sings as if she were a nightingale.

Here, 'Sarah sings' is the main idea and therefore the main clause; 'who is my friend' describes the noun 'Sarah', so it is an adjectival clause; 'as if she were a nightingale' tells us more about how she sings, so it is an adverbial clause of manner. Both the adjectival and the adverbial clauses are subordinate to the main clause.

Through sentence construction, active voice and passive voice can be conveyed:

> *We think* that he is incorrect. (active)
> *It is thought* that he is incorrect. (passive)
> *The artist completed* her painting. (active)
> *The painting was completed* by the artist. (passive)

In most writing, the active voice is preferred because it is more direct and clearer, largely because subject, verb and object are in the correct logical order. This sequence is particularly important in helping non-native speakers (NNS) of English comprehend the messages conveyed through sentences.

Through sentence construction, furthermore, defining as opposed to non-defining relative clauses (with the help of a relative pronoun) can be created:

> My brother *who lives in LA* turns 40 today. (defining the brother, presumably because there are two or more)
> My brother, *who lives in LA,* turns 40 today. (non-defining, incidental information, possibly because there is only one brother)
> The guide book, which I have now bought, is very useful. (non-defining, incidental information)
> The guide book that I have bought is very useful. (defining the guide book, distinguishing it from all others)

In practice, however, writers do not always follow the rules of English syntax and grammar, which results in syntactical errors that can adversely affect both the grammatical soundness of sentences and the readers' understanding of them.

A further example of such a lack of grammatical soundness is the absence of subject–verb agreement caused by the intervention of a plural noun between the two parts:

> The noise of the pneumatic drills are deafening. (this should be 'is deafening', the subject being the singular noun, 'noise')

The performance of the massed choirs have improved since yesterday. (this should be 'has improved', the subject being the singular noun, 'performance')

Mathematics are a difficult subject. (mathematics 'is' because the subject is a singular concept)

See also Congruence below.

2.1.3 Syntax in practice

Research into language usage has revealed potential pitfalls regarding a number of syntactic structures. We present them below in a top-down order from sentence level to word level. For each pitfall, we provide an explanation and an example. The example often contains an error, in which case the carrier phrase is preceded by an ✽ (asterisk). It is then followed by an → (arrow) introducing a correct version:

List 8.3 Potential syntactic problem areas

› *Run-on sentences* are sentences that should have been two or even three sentences:
  ✽ Run-on sentences are sentences that are too long, they are sentences that ought to have been two or even three sentences but the writer didn't stop to sort them out, potentially leaving the reader feeling exhausted and confused by the end of the sentence – which took too long to arrive.
  → Run-on sentences are too long. They ought to have been two or even three sentences, but the writer didn't stop to sort them out. Instead, they risked leaving the reader feeling exhausted and confused at the end of the endlessly long sentence.

› *Fused sentences* occur when two independent clauses are put together without a comma, semi-colon, or conjunction:
  ✽ Researchers investigated several possible vaccines for the virus then they selected one.
  → Researchers investigated several possible vaccines for the virus; then they selected one.

› Sentence *fragments*:
  A sentence must have a subject and a finite verb if it is to make sense:
  ✽ The book, being interesting and a bestseller.
  → The book is interesting and a bestseller.

  A subordinate clause is not a complete sentence if it does not relate to a main clause, even though it may have a subject and a verb:
  ✽ Because it is a bestseller.
  → We bought the book because it is a bestseller.
  → Because it is a bestseller, we were persuaded to buy the book.

>>

> *Linking sentences*: the effect of using incorrect *connectors* such as conjunctions and relative pronouns on a sentence, in combination with the use of *punctuation* (commas, colons, semicolons) (see chapter 9), can affect the meaning being conveyed:

    ✳ Anyhow, we hypothesise that a higher ambient temperature and higher wind speed are to a lesser or greater extent combined in the agricultural landscape, and in more open conditions, *what we predict to result in* a larger variation of chill distances and heating rates.

    → … which we predict will result in …

> *Adverbs and verbs:* adverbs such as 'already', 'never', 'always' are placed between the auxiliary and the past participle of the verb in the perfect tense:

    → She has *never* been regarded as a second-rate writer.

Where there is only an auxiliary and a past participle, the adverb is placed between them:

    → He was *always* regarded as a mediocre pupil.

'Both' occurs after the verb and before the noun it refers to:

    → They are *both* sonnets.

In a sentence starting with 'not only', subject and verb are inverted:

    → Not only *does she focus* on the negative aspects, but she also explains in detail why they are negative.

If a sentence starts with one of the following negative adverbs, then subject and verb are inverted: *seldom, rarely, never, hardly (when), scarcely (when), no sooner (than), by no means, little, neither, nor*

    → Very seldom *do we* get a second chance.

> *Congruence* (or agreement) in person and number between pronoun subjects and verbs, especially when the subject and verb are separated by an intervening clause or phrase:

    → *I am, she is,* but *they are* – I, but not my wife, *am attending* your party. (I … am)

When two or more singular nouns or pronouns are connected by *or* or *nor*, use a singular verb:

    → Neither Alison nor Helen *has* a close relationship with Steven.

>>

Units usually take singular verbs:
→ 150 ml of blood *was* sampled.
→ Five months' maternity leave *is* a long time.

Fractions are regarded as singular:
→ Three-quarters of the sample *was* defective.

Singular concepts that have a plural form are singular:
→ The news *is* not good.
→ Logistics *is* my area of expertise.

When a compound subject contains both a singular and a plural noun or pronoun joined by *or* or *nor*, the verb should agree with the part of the subject that is nearer the verb:
→ It is clear that neither the critics nor the writer *uses* notes.
→ It is clear that neither the writer nor the critics *use* notes.

› *Congruence* (or agreement): nouns and pronouns that refer to each other must agree in number and gender (cf Einsohn 2000: 361–364, 2005; Kahn 1985: 31–32; 466–467; Ridout & Clarke 1989: 283–285):
  ∗ I don't understand what the *chap* wants. *She* mumbles and on top of that *she* also stutters.
If the pronoun *she* (× 2) in the second sentence refers to the antecedent *the chap* in sentence 1, then there is no gender congruence between the two sentences, that is, a female pronoun *she* refers to the male antecedent *the chap*.
  → I don't understand what the chap wants. He mumbles and on top of that he also stutters.
Gender congruence restored.
  ∗ *The hijackers* struck at the traffic lights on the corner of Camp and Burg streets, but fortunately *he was* caught red handed by police who were passing, and he was arrested at once.
There is no agreement in terms of number.
  → *The hijackers* struck at the traffic lights on the corner of Camp and Burg streets, but fortunately *they were* caught red-handed by police who were passing, and they were arrested at once.
The agreement in terms of number has been restored.

Congruence (or agreement): The words *each, each one, either, neither, everyone, everybody, anybody, anyone, nobody, somebody, someone,* and *no one* are singular and require a singular verb:
  Nobody likes to criticise her.
  Everyone is invited.

>>

In sentences starting with *It is*, the verb form of *is* is always in the singular, regardless of the number of the noun that follows the verb:
→ *It is* the critics who made a fuss. The audience loved it.

Congruence (or agreement): collective nouns are words that imply more than one person but that can be considered singular in certain contexts. These include: *group, team, committee, class*, and *family*. They can take a singular verb:
→ The committee *wants* to award a prize for his new novel. (singular)

But the plural verb is used if the individuals in the group are thought of and specifically referred to:
→ The committee *are* voting on whether to award him the prize. (plural)

(Hint: If you can place 'the members of' in front of the collective noun and the sentence makes sense, then the plural is intended.)

Compare the following sets of sentences:
→ *Province take* on Bulls
the team members collectively are meant, so plural
→ *Province overspends* health budget
the provincial government as an entity is meant, so singular
→ *The government is* not always given credit for what *it* does to ensure the safety of *its* citizens.
the government as an entity, so singular
→ *The crowd* got out of control when *they* heard that the trains were running late yet again. *They* set fire to two railway carriages in the process and so the police had to intervene to prevent *them* causing any further damage.
The word *crowd* is understood as a large group (here of individual commuters), so plural referents.

› Ensure that the correct pronoun is used to refer to *objects*. Vessels and vehicles, for example, are generally *she* or *it* in English:
→ *The Queen Mary 2* lay at anchor in the bay; *she's* a real beauty!
→ I love my new motor car – *it's* a nippy little thing!

› Make sure you use the correct form of Latin and Greek nouns such as data, medium, criterion and phenomenon:
→ Data *are* presented and two phenomena *were* classified using one criterion.

› Note that 'data is' is usually reserved for use in an IT context or for non-technical usage (where 'data are' would seem out of place),

List 8.3 continued

whereas 'data are' is the usual academic or scientific form (in such circles, 'data is' may possibly appear to be uninformed).

› *Noun-appositional constructions*: These usually involve a (job) title and a noun being placed side by side, either bracketed off from the other with a pair of commas (non-restrictive apposition), or not (restrictive apposition):
   → *Mr Jensen*, our *jeweller*, demonstrated how to make a brooch.
   → The *investigating officer, PC Reynolds,* asked me searching questions.
   → Her *husband, Mike,* joined us for lunch.
   → *Author JK Rowling* was present at the launch of her latest book.

Usually, where the title is preceded by an article or a possessive pronoun, the commas around one of the pair of appositionals are required (the first three examples); if there's no article or possessive pronoun, there's usually no need for commas (fourth example, an example of restrictive apposition (Quirk et al 1985: 9.56, 9.57). An important use of restrictive apposition is found with citations and names of books, films, etc:
   → the term 'heavy water'
   → the novel *Crime and punishment*

› *Dangling participles* (usually at the beginning of a sentence) apparently modify a word other than the word intended:
   ✶ *Playing with the ball in the park, a dog bit me.*
   → *Playing with the ball in the park, I was bitten by a dog.*
   → *A dog bit me as I played with the ball in the park.*

› *Ambiguous referents:* when it is not clear which of two or three earlier nouns a pronoun (usually it, they or them) stands for:
   ✶ The files arranged by the temps were out of order, so we sent *them* back to the main office. (Who or what was sent back?)
   → The files arranged by the temps were out of order, so we sent the entire stack back to the main office.

› Lack of *parallelism* in word-pair constructions (either ... or; neither ... nor; both ... and; not only ... but also) and lack of *parallelism and/or concord* in vertical lists:
   ✶ The main character experiences a series of losses: she loses her husband, her youth, her physical attractiveness and a purpose in life, after having lost job and house.
   → The main character experiences a series of losses: she loses her

husband, her youth, her physical attractiveness and *her* purpose in life, after having lost *her* job and house.

› The use of the *subjunctive* (as opposed to the indicative) mood:
   ∗ I wish I was rich.
   → I wish I *were* rich.
   ∗ If only he can have visited us.
   → If only he *could* have visited us.

› The place of *adverbs* (especially in verb phrases) and *adverbials:* manner-place-time
   ∗ He *always* has been doing that.
   → He has *always* been doing that.
   ∗ Let's get together *tomorrow morning informally at my office.*
   → Let's get together *informally* (manner) *at my office* (place) *tomorrow morning* (time).

› The idiomatic use of *prepositions,* difficult at all times, is a significant problem for NNSs of English:
   ∗ The interest rate increased *with* 1.5% last week.
   → The interest rate increased *by* 1.5% last week.
   ∗ *On* the end, he agreed with me.
   → *In* the end, he agreed with me.

› The use of *relative pronouns*, especially *which* vs *that; who* vs *that; who* vs *whom* (slightly outdated according to some sources), and *what* versus *which:*
   Which vs that: Which is used largely to introduce non-defining (non-limiting) relative clauses; that is used to introduce defining (or limiting) relative clauses:
   → The Victorian house, which is painted green, is mine. ('which is painted green' is incidental information)
   → In Bread Street, the house that is painted green is mine. ('that is painted green' identifies, defines or limits the house being referred to)

   Who vs that: Who is associated with people, that with animals and things:
   ∗ He is a person that is fun to be with.
   → He is a person who is fun to be with.

   Who vs whom:
   ∗ The woman *who* you have spoken to is my yoga teacher.
   → The woman *whom* you have spoken to is my yoga teacher.

List 8.3 continued

Conversational uses:
→ The women *to whom* you have spoken is my yoga teacher.
→ The woman *who* you have spoken to is my yoga teacher.

What vs which:
→ What flight are you booked on? (the speaker has only the vaguest knowledge of the flight options)
→ Which flight are you booked on? (the speaker is better informed about the flight options)

› The use of *reflexive pronouns* in relation to their antecedent:
＊ My wife and *myself* would like to accept your invitation.
→ My wife and *I* would like to accept your invitation.
→ I have done that *myself* before now. (the reflexive used here for emphatic effect)

› The correct reference to gender through *personal pronouns*, for example, third person singular female or male or plural forms instead (he/she, he, she, them, their, they); and when do infants stop being referred to as *it*? Both of these are acceptable in context:
→ A researcher rarely steps outside *his or her* specific context or research specialty.
→ A researcher rarely steps outside of *their* specific context or research specialty.

› The use of accusative *pronoun* forms after *prepositions*:
＊ Between you and I we'll solve the problem.
→ Between you and *me* we'll solve the problem.

› The use of *articles* (especially when terminology is involved)*:* when to use *a* or *an*; when to use *the* or *a*; and to decide when an article is superfluous:
use *a* before a consonant sound – *a* biscuit; *a* European language; *a* university graduate; *a* historic moment.
use *an* before a vowel sound – *an* apple; *an* MP; *an* S-bend
use *a* or no article for general statements or generalisations:
→ We need *a* policy to deal with that.
→ editors should abide by *a* professional code of conduct.

Use *the* for specifics:
→ *The* industrial policy is not working in practice.
→ *The* players who broke *the* rules were disqualified.

Examples illustrating these problem areas were dealt with in a normative context in section 6.1.1 of chapter 2. They deserve serious attention as part of the training of prospective editors and the lifelong learning process of their more experienced peers.

2.1.4 Knowledge of morphology

The study of morphology as a discipline broadly encompasses the study of a *word*, its unique *structure* and the *processes* by which new words can be *created* (cf Aronoff & Fudeman 2010; Quirk et al 1985; Huddleston & Pullum 2002, 2005). When studying words, particular emphasis is placed on the way in which they are structured and how the different kinds of *morpheme* (the smallest elements in a language that convey meaning; such elements can be lexical morphemes, derivational morphemes, inflectional morphemes; simplexes and complexes) are employed to create words. This includes the formation of plurals, compounds and derivatives and the creation of neologisms.

A phenomenon such as *analogy* (based on the power of the example) contributes to the fact that the word-building process is not always carried out correctly, because incorrect forms can be created on the basis of other supposedly correct forms, leading to over-generalisations. For example:

- *gooses*, could be based on a form such as *nooses*;
- *lay down* is formed instead of *lie down*, which might be based on a misunderstanding of the different denotations of *lay* and *lie*, etc.

In any normative study – as in the day-to-day work of the text editor – attention should be paid to the possible errors that can arise as a consequence and the effect they can have on the quality of the text.

2.1.5 Potential morphological errors

In English we can consider the following morphological problem areas, among a number of others:

List 8.4 Potential morphological problem areas

> *Plural* forms:
>   – Irregulars: mouse – mice; index – indices/indexes, foot – feet, person – people, etc.
>   – Foreign words: fait accompli – faits accompli; cul-de-sac – culs-de-sac/cul-de-sacs, etc.
>   – Titles: director-general – directors-general.

> *Possessive* forms of nouns: men's; children's; Jones'; the Joneses', etc.

> *Degrees of comparison*: we need to distinguish between morphological and syntactic grading systems:

>>

List 8.4 continued

- most *monosyllabic* and some *bisyllabic* adjectives have morphological degrees of comparison: *green* (positive), *greener* (comparative), *greenest* (superlative); *pretty, prettier, prettiest.*
- most polysyllabic adjectives use syntax: *complex, more complex,
  most complex; brilliant, more brilliant, most brilliant; endearing,
  more endearing, most endearing.*

› *Patterns of derivation for:*
  - Nouns and gerunds: walk – walking; ice – icing.
  - Adjectives and participles: burn, burning, burned, burnt; learn,
    learning, learned, learnt.
  - Verbs:
    Especially strong or irregular verbs: take – took, have taken; teach
    – taught; seek – sought; go – went, have gone; begin – began,
    have begun; to be – am, is, are.

The formation of verb tenses (past perfect (had walked) and present
perfect (have walked) vs simple past (walked):
  They *had hiked* five kilometres by the time the sun *rose.*
  They *have walked* that route many times before.

2.1.6 Morphology in practice

Below you will find some further *examples* of these problem areas (also revisit section 6.1.2
in chapter 2). Consult a reliable source if you are in any doubt about the correct form of:

List 8.5 More morphological problem areas

› *Plurals, derivatives* (nominalisations (or nounisms), adjectivisations),
  adverbials, and the like, especially plurals of words derived from Greek
  or Latin: *bacterium – bacteria; criterion – criteria; phenomenon – phenomena; medium – media; forum – forums* or *fora; stadium – stadiums*
  or *stadia; virus – viruses.*

› *Nominalisations* should be avoided wherever possible (though not
  always possible), because they tend to lead to passive voice constructions and longer sentences, both of which adversely affect the readability of sentences: *require* (verb) – *requirement* (nounism); *invite*
  (verb) – *invitation* (nounism). For example:
    ✻ *It is a requirement for* anyone taking up this position that they
      have a post-graduate degree.
    → For this position *we require* you to have a post-graduate degree.

>>

› *Verbalisations of nouns*: concrete – concretise (make concrete, give concrete form); operation – operationalise (put into operation).
  * We must *operationalise* our plans as soon as possible.
  → We must *put* our plans *into operation* as soon as possible.

› *Present and past participles*, also as part of collocations,[2] and idiomatic usage, as in:
  → burnt offerings; a burning question; the burned and charred body
  → a lesson learnt; but my learned colleague

Make sure you are comparing *similar items*:
  * The tusk of a mastodon is bigger than an elephant.
It sounds as if the writer is comparing the *tusk* with an *elephant.*
  → The tusk of a mastodon is bigger than the tusk of an elephant.
  → The tusk of a mastodon is bigger than *that* of an elephant.

Make sure your comparison is *balanced*. Use the same pattern on both sides of the comparison to make it readable and clear:
  * The tusk of a mastodon is bigger than an elephant's.
  → The tusk of a mastodon is bigger than that/the tusk of an elephant.

When comparing people or items that are grouped together, it may be necessary to use the word *other* or *else* to make the meaning clear:
  * The X-15 was faster than any airplane.
    The X-15 is an airplane. The sentence makes it sound as though it were some other kind of (air)craft.
  → The X-15 was faster than any other airplane.

› *Comparative and superlative forms of adjectives*. Be aware of the following in particular: avoid the double comparison:
  * That film was *more funnier* than the one we saw last week.
  → That film was funnier than the one we saw last week.
  * That's the *most clearest* example I can think of.
  → That's the clearest example I can think of.

2.2 Grammar in practice

Text editors are often expected to explain why they have made a certain grammatical correction; this is another reason for needing to use the appropriate terminology (Mackenzie 2011: 99). The following hints and tips regarding two broad areas of grammar may help when dealing with texts.

---

[2] A collocation is a habitual juxtaposition of a particular word with another word.

Structure

› If a sentence does not flow well (a very debatable concept), because it is too long (this is measurable), cut it in half (this is mathematics). Shorter sentences tend to communicate better (we know this from research).

    ＊ The Agency's finance unit, headed by a permanent chief financial officer is reportedly sufficiently-capacitated with qualified and experienced personnel both in the senior as well as lower ranked technical level to transact, manage, and administer revenue and expenditure processes, procedures and the overall accounts of SASSA.

    → The Agency's finance unit is headed by a permanent chief financial officer (CFO). The CFO is reported to have enough qualified and experienced staff to administer the overall accounts of SASSA.

› Effective argumentation follows the topic–comment structure. This means that the given or existing information comes first and the new information comes next or last. This given–new contract (Clark & Haviland 1974) reflects how the brain organises and retains information.

› Rule-of-thumb: one old idea, one new idea per sentence. Translated into syntactic terms, a sentence contains one main clause, one subclause:

    We can't leave for Hong Kong tomorrow, because our flight has been cancelled.

Reference

› Every personal pronoun (especially *it* and *they* when they occur in a subsequent sentence) must have an *antecedent*:[3] make *sure* that it is actually in the text.

› The antecedent should not be too far removed from the *anaphora*:[4]

    → *The president* arrived at the banquet late. I wonder what delayed *him*. *His* record in this regard is not very good. I think *he's* starting to make a habit of *it* already.

    → *The police investigation* into the murder began well, but in the course of time *it* lost momentum, until *it* was eventually called off.

---

[3] The antecedent of a pronoun is the item (a noun) earlier in the sentence or text that relates to the pronoun (as anaphora). In sentence such as: John took ill and he had to be admitted to hospital, John is the antecedent and the masculine pronoun he is the anaphora. On congruence between pronouns and their antecedents, compare Allen RE 2005: 72–78; Allen RE 2008; Einsohn 2005: 361–364; Kahn 1985: 466–467; Lester 2008: 80; Ridout & Clarke 1989: 283.

[4] An anaphor is a reference to a preceding or following utterance or a referent in the real world (Halliday & Hasan 1976).

3 Consider the meaning

> A word is not a thing, object or idea. It is only a symbol of some mental experience. ... A word only has full meaning in a context, ie when it is *used* in relationship with other words.
> *Ridout & Clark*

> Readers need to be able to process a text easily. They should not find the *wordings* getting in the way of the meanings. To put this in negative terms, the sequence of words must not give rise to the 'huh?' reaction. Readers should not have to go over a sentence two or three times just to see how the parts of the sentence are connected to each other and to get the basic point. *And they should not be distracted or misled by unintended ambiguities.*
> *Mossop*

> The primary job of a dictionary is to track how people actually use language.
> *Brians*

Semantics is that part of linguistics that is preoccupied with the use and meaning of *words* and *sentences* (cf Cann, Kempson & Gregoromichelaki 2009; Cruse 2011; Elbourne 2011; Goddard 2011; Maienborn, von Heusinger & Portner (eds) 2011; Murphy 2010; Riemer 2010). The study of semantics includes the study of how meaning is constructed, interpreted, clarified, obscured, illustrated, simplified, negotiated, contradicted and paraphrased. Language users communicate predominantly with one another through sentences or utterances (in discourse analysis sentences are referred to as utterances). Sentences in turn form a communicative whole that is interpreted as a whole, that is, a paragraph or a text. Sentences are actually made up of words, each of which has a particular value (meaning) of its own and which is interpreted according to the *context* in which it is used (see sections 7.1.2.5 and 7.2.3 in chapter 2 regarding the cardinal role of context in language use). In this way, meaning is a core concept in language usage, because the purpose of each communicative act is to convey information about something as effectively as possible. It is the text editor's role to ensure that errors which can affect meaning do not slip through.

3.1 Word usage and meaning

In order to convey meaning effectively, a writer must formulate a sentence in such a way that the reader will understand it. To this end, senders/writers and receivers/readers of a text have to adhere implicitly to a number of principles that underline the fact that meaning and word choice go hand in hand (Carstens 2011: 97–98). In this regard, it is often insightful to follow a functional model for effective communication (set out by its founding father, Roman Jakobson, in *The functions of language*, 1960):

- The writer must first *decide* precisely what is to be conveyed (the message).
- The writer must constantly take into account the reader's *context* and background (referential context).

- The writer should not be too worried that the reader will intentionally *misinterpret* the message – it happens, of course, but it should not put you off writing (psychological state of mind or channel).
- Both writer and reader should attach the *same value to the same words*, a coincidence that is determined by tradition, convention and general usage. This, of course, can never be guaranteed, but every step should be taken to ensure it does happen.
- Only then can the writer choose the appropriate words and register (code).
- Words must be used in the *correct context*, which means that readers must not be in any doubt about what is meant. They must be able to grasp the meaning immediately (instant decoding).

If these principles are not adhered to, it is possible that lapses in communication will occur that can lead to miscommunication and breaches of communication. Unstructured or poor thinking leads to the incorrect use of words and to weak sentence formulations. Classic examples are:

- ? Sometimes letters are sent to me in *typed handwritten* form.
- ? Dancing, singing and much wine and beer *will be consumed*.

3.2 Potential errors of meaning

When expressing a matter, idea or thought, words are sometimes incorrectly chosen, possible reasons for which are (a) ignorance, (b) inadequate knowledge, (c) laziness or (d) time pressure to check the meaning of the word in, for example, a dictionary or thesaurus. In this regard, the following aspects should be taken into account:

List 8.7 Potential errors of meaning

› Word choice closely relies on *pragmatic context* at all times, since the context determines which synonyms will be used in which context. When, for instance, do we use *food, meal, feed* or *fodder*? When do we say *get hitched, marry, enter into marriage* or *wed*? And when is it *aversion, dislike, hatred, repugnance, revulsion* or *antipathy*?

› *Malapropisms*, that is, words that sound approximately like the intended word, very often lead to the incorrect meaning being conveyed, often to humorous effect:
  - *perspire* vs *inspire*
  - *memorable* vs *memorial*
  - *diminished* vs *diminutive*.

› *Tautology*, that is, saying the same thing in two different ways, can occur unconsciously:
  - *set up and established*
  - *the two men shared a fear of heights*
  - *at 9 am in the morning*.

List 8.7 continued

Sometimes, the meanings of tautological forms such as these have become so entrenched that few users are able to make these fine distinctions, and commit tautology with aplomb!

› *Pleonasms*, that is, when one word repeats the meaning of the previous word and creates redundancy, as in:
  * a *necessary prerequisite*
  * her *emotional feelings*
  * the *semantic meaning* of a word
  * *retreat backwards*
  * *re-occur/recur again*
  * look *identically the same*
  * a *new innovation*.

› Words with *double meanings* occur frequently. This is mainly the result of poor sentence construction, which can be eliminated either by adjusting the sentence structure or by replacing the ambiguous word:
  * I am *quite* satisfied with her performance. (completely or partially?)
  * On this matter, Frank made a *fine* distinction. (a good one or a close one?)

› Poorly *constructed sentences* can also cause ambiguity (syntactical homonymy). Usually the sentence can be corrected by moving parts around, as in:
  * House to rent to young couple *near bus stop*.
  → *House to rent near bus stop, for young couple*. Or *House for young couple to rent near bus stop*.
  * I *only* eat bananas and dates. (You don't do anything other than eat them? Or You don't eat any other fruit?)

› Ignorance of variable plural forms (with different meanings) of *homonyms* (these are two words which have the same orthographical and phonological form) can lead to confusion in meaning. Examples:
  – *medium: mediums* (people who claim to communicate with the dead) vs *media* (newspapers and magazines – always plural)
  – *mouse: mice* (rodents) vs *mouses* (handheld electronic devices)
  – *life: still lifes* (paintings) vs people's *lives*:
  – *form: forms* (documents) vs f*orms* (shapes).

› *Homophones*, that is, words that are pronounced in the same way but which differ in their spelling, meaning and origin, can lead to many errors. Examples include:

>>

- *berth* vs *birth*
- *check* vs *cheque*
- *seen* vs *scene*
- *there* vs *their*
- *taut* vs *taught*
- *site* vs *sight*
- *plum* vs *plumb*
- *rain* vs *reign* vs *rein*.

For NNSs, there are other tricky pairs such as:
- *then* vs *than*
- *their, they're, there*
- *later* vs *latter*.

› *Doublets*, that is, words that have developed from the same root, but which gradually change in both form and meaning, can sometimes lead to problems. Examples are:
- *chef and chief*
- *fragile and frail*
- *host and guest*
- *warden and guardian*
- *secure and sure.*

› *Paronyms* are words that have developed from the same stem, and which sound similar, but which have different meanings. They often lead to tiresome malapropisms. Examples are:
- *affect* vs *effect*
- *farther* vs *further*
- *adopt* vs *adapt*
- *timely* vs *timeous*
- *practical* vs *practicable*
- *continuous* vs *contiguous* vs *continual*
- *ingenious* vs *ingenuous.*

› Sometimes a writer uses a word in a way that is not its *normal function*:
- an adjective as an adverb (*she sings beautiful,* instead of *beautifully*, for instance); or
- a verb as a noun (*to impact* instead of *to influence* or *to have an impact*);
- an adverb such as *presently* is often incorrectly used to mean *at present* or *currently*;
- a verb such as *aggravate* is used incorrectly to mean *irritate*.
- the adjective *alternate* to mean *alternative.*

› Often the influences on the spoken word are so strong that it is difficult to eliminate such grammatically 'incorrect' usage from writing, but for as long as such usage is not accepted or confirmed by dictionaries or grammars, it should be corrected:

* He performed magnificent at last night's concert. (*magnificently*)

* This policy is designed to impact the economy significantly. (*to have a significant impact on*)

* She is presently on sabbatical. (*currently* or *at present*)

* He aggravates me with his childish behaviour. (*irritates*)

* Lane closed. Please use alternate route. (*alternative*)

› *Vague words* are those that are used vaguely or inaccurately in that they do not convey the meaning they are supposed to. Such words have a general meaning, but a more specific meaning needs to be conveyed in a given context. Since the more specific words are often less frequently used they may be shunted into the background at the expense of the general word:

– *implement*, meaning *fulfil* (an undertaking);

– *complete* or *execute* (a contract, etc);

– *put* (a decision or plan into effect), and not *devise, originate, compose*;

– *transpire* means *emit* or *cause to pass as vapour through the walls of a body or vessel; emit vapour or perfume; give out an exhalation; leak out*; less commonly, it means *prove to be the case, turn out; happen, occur,* and

– *materialise* means *make material; represent in material form* – 'I tried to materialise my idea in words' – as opposed to the intransitive verb: *come into perceptible existence; become actual fact.* It does not mean *happen, arrive, take place.*

The reasons for this kind of verbal laziness are:

– the *convenient vagueness* afforded by the particular word chosen, and

– the pursuit of *highbrow* words to suit the circumstances.

› *Fashion words* are words that have been popular for a while and are used everywhere in language:

– *basically* (instead of *fundamentally,* but often used as a placeholder);

– *foundational*, when fundamental will do equally well;

– *huge* (for anything slightly out of proportion);

– *societal*, when social is actually intended;

>>

List 8.7 continued

     – *facilitate* (slightly more highbrow than *help*), and
     – *challenge* (instead of *problem* and with a positive ring to it).

Often there are better alternatives for these words, alternatives that are to be found in any thesaurus.

In summary, these instances of misuse or abuse of meaning can be avoided: simply looking up the meaning of a word in a reliable reference work (see chapter 11) will dispel any doubt about the inappropriateness or otherwise of one's word choice. Similarly, should you experience difficulty with homophones, homonyms, synonyms, malapropisms, plural forms of nouns, etc, consult a suitable reference work.

3.3 Meaning in practice

Some hints and tips that may help improve the quality of a text with respect to meaning:

- If you are in doubt (even in the slightest way) about the meaning of a word in a particular context, consult a reference work. Doing so will prevent the incorrect usage of homonyms, homophones, paronyms, doubles, synonyms and malapropisms.
- Ensure that the correct plural form of a particular noun is used.
- Ensure that the appropriate word is used in a given context.
- Avoid vague words; instead, use the specific word for a given context.
- Ensure that the meaning of a sentence is clear and unambiguous to you as the text editor (unless, of course, it is meant to be ambiguous, as, for example, in literature).

4 Consider the style

Style is definitely not garnishes sprinkled on our sentences to *impress* the reader. We should think of style, rather, as *all* the things we do to *express* our thoughts. ... style is intimately related to meanings and purpose.
Cheney

In its broadest sense, style refers to *the sound of the author's voice*. Here style is an amalgam of the word choices, word order, and rhythms the author employs.
Eisenberg

When you edit the style, you choose from a number of different ways of expressing the same thing. The decision you make will depend on your audience and your purpose.
Billingham

Choice of vocabulary is an important aspect of choosing the right style.
Allen

4.1 Style and language usage

Whereas syntax and morphology belong in the domain of grammatical rules and conventions or norms, style (and register) pertains to the field of text linguistics, where it is less bound by norms and more beholden to the author's purpose and the intended readers.

Style is core to any form of communication, especially when it applies to written texts (cf Quirk 1982; also Adey, Orr & Swemmer 1989; Dykman, Geldenhuys & Viljoen-Smook 2011; Enquist & Oates 2009; Lourens 2007; Lynch 2008; Ritter 2002, 2003, 2005; Sebeok (ed) 1960; Shober 2010; Siegal & Connolly 1999; Stilman 2010; Strunk & White 1979, 1999; Thomas 2009; Walker 1995). Despite this fact, there are many definitions around, and *style* is often best understood when juxtaposed with *register*. *Style* can be defined in terms of the tone, degree of formality, word choice and sentence structure of a document, whereas *register* has to do with the spectrum of writing from informal to formal, the author's tone, word choice, etc. (On register, see section 5 below.) As well as being clear, succinct and readable, a good style must be appropriate to the format or medium (email, formal report, legal document, etc); it also has to be tailored to the wider situation – the who?, when?, where? and why? of communication (Law (ed) 2001: 207).

Collins (in *Collins writing programme* 2010: 44, 45) says in answer to the question 'What is good style?':

> When people write with good style, their writing is clear, interesting, elegant and appropriate to their audience. The best style will vary according to the type of document ... original, descriptive writing you would use for a piece of creative writing would not be appropriate for a factual report. ... Think about the purpose of your document and the reader to help you choose the appropriate style and tone.

If the style of a text is considered *weak* or *inappropriate* (sometimes debatable qualities), the text will communicate poorly and then it becomes the task of the text editor to hone or shape the style so that optimal communication can take place and the receiver of the message will be able to *read* the text with the minimum of effort. In the course of the editing process, the text editor should therefore pay particular attention to the author's selection of words (the correct word or expression for a given context) and the formulation of sentences (including the effective use of punctuation) – two processes that largely belong to the area of grammar.

Often, the following functions have to be performed: superfluous elements (such as repetitions, fashion words, verbosity, clichés, malapropisms, overly long sentences, and instances of tautology (or redundancy) and pleonasm) must be removed or otherwise remedied, vague references made more specific, poor grammar corrected, inconsistent spellings and poor paragraphing repaired, inappropriate punctuation that does not support the writer's meaning fixed, and the like.

The test of effective editing is whether, after a document has been edited, the text communicates *unambiguously* and *directly*, and also whether it reads naturally. If this is the case, then the text will have been well edited. Try reading the edited text aloud: if the sentences are well structured, they will be easy to read and you will be able to pause in the right places (usually indicated by appropriate punctuation) (*Collins writing programme* 2010: 45; see also Collins 2011).

In the extensive literature on style, a text is described as 'good' if it meets specific requirements. When studying the list below, the attentive, observant text editor will notice that some of the attributes of well-written texts have already been dealt with at other levels; this is because writers use a broad array of definitions that all resort under the umbrella of 'style'.

4.2 Style in practice

Broadly speaking, the text editor's role is to clarify, simplify and tighten up text (Law (ed) 2001: 207; 2002), using the list below as a guideline.

List 8.8 Qualitative requirements of good writing style

> *Clarity*
>
> › The content of the text is *clear*. As a result, the reader will know what to expect in the text and what to get from it.
>
> › The words used are *clear* and are immediately *understood*. Root out instances of ambiguity, which can include the use of words that have more than one meaning, pronouns such as 'it' and 'they' that are ambiguous referents, confusion between the literal and figurative meanings of words, and uncertainty as to which noun an adjective is referring to (*Collins writing programme* 2010: 53–54).
>
> › Ideas, opinions and facts should be presented directly, not in vague and roundabout ways. Euphemisms should be replaced (*jobseekers* for *the unemployed*; *downsizing* when *firing staff* is meant, etc) (Allen 2005: 177–178).
>
> › Abbreviations should be *self-explanatory*; if not, they must be given in full. Wolff (2009) believes that abbreviations should be avoided or should at least be used sparingly. It is customary first to give an acronym's full form, accompanied by the acronym. The nature of a text will determine the convention to be adopted in the use of abbreviations.
>
> › The words and expressions are *appropriate* in the context in which they are used, and your reader will understand them as such. Jargon (terminology) is meant for specialists in the field and not for any other readers, so keep the readers uppermost in your mind when considering the inclusion (or not) of jargon and technical terminology.

>>

› There are no *unnecessary* elements in the text. Remove instances of redundancy (unnecessary words), tautology (saying the same thing twice) and 'empty' words (eg *in terms of*) in particular (*Collins writing programme* 2010: 51–52).

› The text has to be processed – that is, read and understood – *easily* (cf Allen 2005: 175–179; *Collins writing programme* 2010; 44–54; Lourens 2007; Mossop 2010: 64–66). In line with this, ensure that statements and opinions are expressed positively: when readers are faced with a negative, they must first imagine the positive alternative, then mentally cancel it out (Law (ed) 2001: 224).

› *Linguistic conventions* (grammar, spelling, punctuation, cohesion and coherence) are followed faithfully.

› *Plain English* principles are adhered to (cf Bailey 1997; Blamires 2000; Carr 2011; Cutts 2009; Dayanada 1986; Eagleson 1990; English Commission 2011):
   – use strong, active verbs instead of passive nounisms (nouns derived from verbs, eg entertainment, apprehension);
   – avoid unnecessary formality;
   – avoid unnecessary jargon;
   – sentences should, on average, be shorter rather than longer, simple rather than compound or complex.

› The text is devoid of *clichés*, which make text unoriginal, wordy and boring. Allow the author to use only as many words as they really need.

Consistency
› *Maintain the same style throughout* and do not allow sudden switches of style – especially when they affect the level of formality in a document.

› Choose *vocabulary* that is appropriate to the medium, its purpose and the readers.

› Ensure that gender-inclusive words (*police officer*, not *policeman*; *staff nurse*, not *nursing sister*) are used consistently and that idioms heavily dependent on gender/sex (*every man for himself*) are avoided (Allen 2005: 177–178).

› Ensure that the *tone* of a piece – as expressed through the author's attitude and vocabulary – is maintained throughout. Where a piece must be neutral, the editor must root out intrusions of the author's opinion (*Collins writing programme* 2010: 57–59).

Structure
› The *structure* and *organisation* of the writing is *logical* and *effective*.

› Sentence length *varies* according to the requirements of the text and the target audience.

› The *arguments* and *themes* in the sentences are interconnected, linking words being used for both sentences and paragraphs.

› There is *coherence* in the text in that all the components hang together logically and form a unitary whole that is easy to comprehend.

› *Paragraphs* are logically connected, through linking ideas and words.

› The level of presentation is *consistent*. The text does not jump from formal to informal, or vice versa, without good reason (Allen 2005: 176).

› Avoid *repeating words*. (Writing will sound dull and clumsy if the same words are used repeatedly. If you read aloud, you will notice whether your author has done this (*Collins writing programme* 2010: 44).

› *Vertical lists* help to break up complicated texts and present information in manageable chunks (Law (ed) 2001: 220–221); but you should ensure that the listed items share parallel constructions.

If the text meets the above requirements, it will in fact comply with the '4 C's', that is, *clarity, coherence, consistency* and *correctness*. In addition, it will also be *accurate, complete* and *appropriate*. (In this regard, see chapter 2, section 6.) Van de Poel & Gasiorek (2006: 76) maintain that a well-written text can be evaluated in terms of the '5 C's'; that is, a 'good' text:

- *communicates* – effectively and easily;
- *convinces* – the reader of the content;
- *is clear* – and intelligible;
- *is concise* – brief and to the point, and
- *is correct* – the content is factually accurate.

Elaborating on the 5 C's, text editors are able to compile and apply the following checklist to texts:

✓ The text should *communicate*:
  – Will the reader be engaged in the text?
  – A text must trigger the readers' interest in order to be *effective*. An easy and attractive style contributes considerably to the readers' feeling of involvement with the text and encourages them to read with attention and interest.

✓ The text should *convince*:
  – Is the argumentation coherent?
  – Are all the steps (arguments) clearly presented?
  – Is there a thesis statement and ample supporting statements or evidence?
  – Do the parts, sentences and words connect to each other easily and logically?

✓ The text should be *clear*:
  – Is the text intelligible?
  – Has the author chosen the best, most appropriate words to convey their meaning?
  – The *degree of difficulty* of a text is determined, among other ways, by the number of so-called *difficult words*, for example technical terms and jargon rather than common, everyday words. Where the former are neither necessary nor helpful, find suitable substitutes to suggest to your author.

✓ What is the text's ratio of *simple to complex sentences?*
  → If the sentences are long in general, your reader will take more time to understand the text, because longer sentences are more difficult to read and the reader may have to read them at least twice in order to comprehend their meaning. Variable sentence length is therefore recommended to hold the reader's interest and to make absorption of the message easier. One of the criteria of readability and accessibility of the Plain Language Movement may be helpful in this respect: for text to qualify as plain, a reader should be able to understand it at first reading. Moreover, Greer (2008: 184) advises that a sentence longer than 24 words must be looked at with great caution, because it may be too long for readers to parse, that is, to read and understand (this sentence contains 33 words).
  – Is the text vague?
  – A vague text conveys more than one message and should have any ambiguities removed.

✓ The text should be *concise:*
  – Is the text of an appropriate level of density?
  – The higher the *information density*, the higher the level of understanding required to grasp the message. Try to determine how many words are really needed to communicate a certain matter or fact. Do not allow authors' sentences to be constructed of multi-layered subordinate clauses – they are too dense.
  – How many passives are there in your text?
  – Voice can add to a text's degree of difficulty, especially the passive voice, because it tends to mask the actor (or subject) and leads to inverted sentence constructions (object, verb, subject). In general, the active voice is preferred above the passive voice. The active voice is 'shorter and stronger', punchier, more direct, engages the reader, and overall is easier to understand (see eg http://owl.english.purdue.edu).

✓ The text should be *correct:*
  – Is the text accurate, both factually and in other respects?
  – Is the grammar correct, and does punctuation contribute to conveying the author's meaning?
  – Is the language used appropriate to the text's purpose and the readership level?

As a topic and a discipline, style is not straightforward, and it can be approached from different angles. It follows, then, that there can be no final definition of the concept 'style', nor is there an irrefutable source that sets out what constitutes good writing. The vast number of sources on style as a *term* and a *concept* (see the references below) confirms this point. There is also no guarantee that those who are good at thinking will necessarily be good at writing. But there are certain steps involved in creating or following a style, as there are views on what constitutes style and what can be done to create a good piece of writing. What follows are some generally acknowledged observations about style in texts that editors would do well to consider.

In general, *style* is regarded as the outcome of the *linguistic choices* a writer makes in order to reach a certain goal, that is, the transfer of particular content, after having considered a number of aspects (such as the purpose of the text, the target audience, and the context (or medium or format) in which the text will be used). For the purposes of this book, the following are understood to be facets or determinants of style:

- the unique manner in which the writer formulates their thoughts and words;
- the manner in which the writer couches their thoughts, views and emotions through language (words and expressions), and
- the way in which all of these aspects are expressed in sentences and paragraphs.

For the text to communicate instantly, language and content must combine neatly and seamlessly to form a unit. It is the text editor's brief to tackle this aspect of the text if an appropriate end-product is to be created.

In principle, everyone can learn to spell fautlessly and learn to use grammar correctly. However, with style it is a different matter, because style is not a question of right or wrong but of the successful or less successful choices that an author makes to fulfil the purpose of the text. The context and purpose of the text therefore play a crucial role in determining its style.

In order to produce good style, the author needs the following:

- a good *command of the language* (if a writer cannot adequately use language, they cannot write coherently);
- the ability to *think clearly* (the writer must know what they want to say and think about the consequences), and
- *knowledge of the subject* on which they are writing (if they do not know what they are writing about, they will not necessarily be able to focus properly).

Text editors often find that authors generally fulfil the third requirement but fall short with the first two – which is where most of the text editor's input is required.

Style is often characterised according to a continuum from extremely formal to intimate.

For example, compare the use of expressions that refer to the concept 'marriage': *to get hitched, get a noose around the neck* (informal), *marry or get married* (neutral), or *enter into matrimony* (formal). The author will select the language according to the audience and context in which the text is situated, and according to the medium or format of the communication. When evaluating the manner in which authors have formulated their facts, ideas and emotions, the text editor must ensure that the *appropriate word or expression for a given context* has been selected. If not, editorial changes would have to be made.

Many errors of writing and formulation can be eliminated by the author or editor's paying attention to a number of factors that can hamper an otherwise good style of writing. So, the text editor should help the author to avoid:

List 8.9 Factors that hinder good writing style

› high-flown or inflated language (too many 'big' words hide a message: *endeavour* instead of *try*; *financial remuneration* instead of *pay* or *salary*).

› wordiness (say it more concisely, if you can). Too many words lead to boredom, and that is one thing that an author should avoid inducing in their readers above all else. For example, this sentence:
  – Register and style are in reality connected and the choice of style (eg formal or informal) to a large extent determines the choice of register, that is, the words and expressions that are used – in a particular text – to report on matters or to describe them.
  should be adapted along the lines of:
  – Register and style are in reality connected. The choice of style (eg formal or informal) to a large extent determines the choice of register: that is, the words and expressions used – in the particular context – to report on matters or to describe them.

› repeating words or phrases in consecutive sentences. Examples that occur regularly are the word 'thus' and the phrase 'with regard to'; alternate their use with synonyms instead: *therefore, consequently, as a result, accordingly.*

› subjective language. Use objective language instead in general texts.

› the use of too many adjectives (especially *very, huge, extreme*) and adverbs (*hugely, extremely*).

› non-significant or 'blank' words. These occur mainly in conversational language, but can easily spill over into the written word: 'I mean', 'like', 'in terms of'.

> clichés. These words and expressions once served a purpose, but through overuse they have lost their function and freshness. Eliminate them.

> fashion words (eg *huge, awesome, going forward*), otherwise in time they will become clichés.

> excessive metaphors (and similar imagery). If used, metaphors must serve a purpose; when metaphors are used, the text editor must make sure they are used correctly and appropriately (ie, make sure their literal meaning will be understood by the readers, especially NNSs). Metaphors should not be mixed.

> the use of inappropriate synonyms.

> slang in all but the most informal texts. The use of slang is largely determined by the target audience and the medium or format of the communication.

> using jargon when it is undesirable or ill-advised to use it in a given context. In such instances, wherever possible, use everyday words instead ('put into operation' or 'make happen' for *operationalise*; 'set aside for a specific purpose' for *ringfence*).

> using 'it' and 'they' without any antecedent. Pronouns are typically preceded by an antecedent (a noun), but often it is unclear to which preceding word or expression 'they' refers, which leads to ambiguity.

> misspelling – good style is characterised by correct spelling.

> a lack of punctuation or poor use of punctuation; it should be used functionally, and correctly. It must support the author's meaning; an excess of punctuation (especially commas) irritates and distracts modern readers.

> using the incorrect sense or meaning of words.

> malapropisms, pleonasms, tautology and doublets.

The context of a text will determine the purity of the words and expressions used. The more formal the text, the more important it is not to allow words to be used inaccurately or sloppily.

The context will determine whether a statement should be expressed in the active or the passive voice. Especially in technical manuals and legal texts, an important reason for using the active voice is often that the actor or the responsible person must be clearly identified. Ensure that the correct form is adopted.

In many reference works, it is recommended that the active voice be preferred to the passive form, but this is by no means a golden rule. The reason for using the active voice is that active sentences are mostly shorter and that writing becomes more concise as a result – making it generally easier to understand. The Plain Language Movement, in fact, strongly advocates the use of the active voice, for the reasons given above, and more (see Plain Language Association International, Plain Language Campaign 2011).

Just as the author should think before they write and about what they have written, so the text editor should think carefully before making changes. Is it actually what the author intended to write? Help the author to reshape their text by following the guidelines above.

4.3 The text editor's role regarding style

So what can the text editor do to deal with the style of a document? Well, first and foremost, read a lot, and widely, to learn what good style looks like (O'Connor 1978: 50). Then, when you engage with a text, treat the matter of style cautiously: first, be guided by the overall style of a publication (for example, an encyclopaedia does not contain any puffery or boasting; the style is entirely factual and dispassionate) (Fritze 2009) – and do so by reading the entire manuscript through at a macro level before micro-editing it. This means that, unless you are sure the text in its current form does not communicate effectively, be cautious about intervening in the document to change its style (unless there is no other solution, do not attempt to change the style).

Also, when you do begin to intervene, be careful not to impose your own preferences on a text simply for the sake of doing so. Remember, too, that if you start to change the style in one place, you must do so consistently throughout the text. Consistency is key here, so you have to keep the 'bigger picture' of the document as a whole in mind.

Another factor that can influence the style of a document, and possibly influence a text editor to change the style unnecessarily, is 'appropriateness'. Allen (2005: 179) states it as follows: 'No one style of vocabulary and grammar is superior to another; it is their appropriateness to the occasion that matters.' This usually differs between cultures (see Jansen & Neutelings (eds) 2001). You should therefore always take cultural differences and requirements into consideration when editing a manuscript.

5 Consider the register

> 'Register' is used to refer to variations in language according to *use*, 'in the sense that each speaker has a range of varieties and choices between them at different times'.
>
> *Halliday & Hasan*

The levels of formality in which English is used are called registers, which reflect the contexts in which they occur. ...
Allen

Halliday & Hasan (1976) interpret 'register' as 'the linguistic features which are typically associated with a configuration of situational features – with particular values of the field, mode and tenor ...'. 'Field' for them is 'the total event, in which the text is functioning, together with the purposive activity of the speaker or writer; includes subject-matter as one of the elements'. 'Mode' is 'the function of the text in the event, including both the channel taken by language – spoken or written, extempore or prepared, – and its genre, rhetorical mode, as narrative, didactic, persuasive ... etc'. 'Tenor' refers to 'the type of role interaction, the set of relevant social relations, permanent and temporary, among the participants involved'.

These three aspects – field, mode and tenor – are therefore the determining factors of the linguistic features of the text. 'The register is the set of meanings, the configuration of semantic patterns, that are typically drawn upon under the specified conditions, along with the words and structures that are used in the realization of these meanings.' Register, in the view of Halliday and Hasan (1976), is one of the two defining concepts of text:

A text is a passage of discourse which is coherent in these two regards: it is coherent with respect to the context of situation, and therefore consistent in register; and it is coherent with respect to itself, and therefore cohesive.

5.1 Register and language usage

In reality, register and style are closely related (Lourens 2007). The choice of style – for instance, on a scale from formal and technical at one extreme, via casual and consultative, to informal and intimate – to a large extent determines the choice of register, that is, the words and expressions used to report on or describe matters in the particular context in which writers find themselves. Thus, where style has to do with variations in formality, register is about variations in language usage connected to a specific topic. The type of communication can be a conversation, informal writing, journalism and broadcasting or formal writing such as essays, speeches, journal articles, academic texts and more learned works.

Conversation (informal):	Use of personal pronouns: I, you Use of contractions: I've, you're, don't Colloquialisms and slang words (on the up (successful), chill out (relax), aggro (aggression), biopic (biographical picture), etc) (Allen 2005: 180).
Formal writing:	Use of indefinite pronoun: 'one', one's Prepositions become more formal: 'upon' instead of 'on'; 'in respect of' instead of 'about' Use of more formal words: ascertain, endeavour, purchase (instead of find out, try and buy) (Allen 2005: 179).

Table 8.1 *The characteristics of informal vs formal writing*

A formal style will require a register that addresses technical or specialised vocabulary and needs exact definitions or specifications. Language specialists will typically use jargon (academic, legal, technical, and the like) to write about their subject (such as textbooks on subject-specific topics, proceedings, scripts, dissertations and academic articles), whereas non-specialists are more likely to use more general language. So, in short, register will refer to the use of specialist language related to a particular activity.

The register of the writer's language should match the type of writing: using an incorrect register can make writing sound odd and may even cause offence. Formal does not mean pompous, however: do not use very formal language to try to impress – it is more important to put your ideas across more clearly. Register can often be shown by the choice of words or phrases: ensure that each fits the communication medium and the proposed readers (Collins 2005: 55–56). For instance:

Formal	Neutral	Informal
of one's own volution (*Collins writing programme* 2010: 55)	voluntarily	off your own bat
in a state of euphoria	elated, extremely happy	on a high

Table 8.2 *Different types of register*

The writer's choice of grammar and the way they structure their sentences can also affect register. For example:

> There is the man to whom I gave my ticket.
> There is the man I gave my ticket to.
> We couldn't recommend that step; he'd simply not approve of it.
> We could not recommend that step; he would simply not approve of it.

In the first sentence, 'to whom' gives the sentence a formal register; in the second, the preposition is placed at the end, which is not only quite acceptable but is also appropriate to any document that is not formal (*Collins writing programme* 2010: 56).

In the third sentence above, the use of the contractions would be regarded as conversational, informal or not appropriate to more formal documents. The lack of contractions in the fourth sentence would be considered more suited to formal communications (Allen 2005: 179).

Register and style are not the same thing, though. The context will determine the style to be used in conveying a message, and the register mirrors this. Doctors will therefore use medical terms among themselves with ease (such as *carcinoma*, *intravenous* and *paranoia*) while they have to use more neutral (lay) terms with their patients (such as *cancer*, *into a vein* and *persecution complex*). As a further example, the word *abdomen* will change into *stomach* when addressing an adult patient with stomach pains, and *tummy* for a child with the same problems. Legal texts in turn are characterised by their formal language and style, longer sentences, Latin expressions, jargon (legal terminology), and so on. In reality, every subject area has its own way (that is, words, phrases and style) of expressing itself.

The text editor must know how to help the author use the appropriate words and expressions in the appropriate context (and replace inappropriate ones with more suitable synonyms) (Allen 2005: 179–191; *Collins writing programme* 2010: 56). This means in effect that text editors can be expected to know the reference works required to check particular information – for example, subject-specific dictionaries and explanatory dictionaries either in print or on websites (see chapter 11).

Although register affects word choice and placement most noticeably, it also influences the choice of grammatical form, for instance:
- *imperatives in recipes:* Add the flour and eggs. Whisk to a firm consistency. Bake for 40 minutes;
- *passives in technical papers:* The chemicals should not be combined before filtration has taken place; only the filtrates should be utilised in this process.

5.2 Register in practice

The following tips may help when dealing with register in practice:

Checklist 8.2 How to ensure that the register is appropriate to a text

✓ Ensure that you know in advance (based on your preliminary analysis of the text) which register a text *demands*, and maintain the chosen register consistently throughout the text.
✓ Allow yourself to be guided by the target readership of the manuscript when you have to decide upon the appropriate register. For example, sometimes words and phrases with a particular register are needed for specific types of writing – legal documents, for instance, often contain extremely formal language (*ex gratia, contra bonos mores, hereunder*). In scientific documents, the use of technical terms may be necessary to avoid any ambiguity: medical terminology such as *aetiology, vasodilation* and *appendectomy* is immediately understood by its readers.
✓ Choose words and construct sentences that create a register appropriate to the document, whether it is formal, neutral or informal.
✓ Ensure that every word is used *correctly*.
✓ If you doubt whether a word or expression suits a particular context, look it up in an appropriate dictionary.
✓ Avoid *contractions* when the text is intended for formal communications.
✓ Restrict *clichés* to a minimum.
✓ Take the emotional value of words into consideration:
 – *fatty* vs *overweight*;
 – *pimple* vs *chorb* vs *acne*;
 – *Miss Piggy* vs *glutton* vs *healthy appetite*.
✓ The use of informal language and sentence structures, and slang, in texts is wholly shaped by the target readership.

>>

Checklist 8.2 continued

✓ *Slang* does not belong in textbooks and similar formal documents, where reasonably formal language is required and the resultant register is more serious.

6 Summary and conclusion

In this chapter, we have focused on *wording* and, more particularly, on how the *knowledge* gained from normative grammar (syntax and morphology) and text linguistics (style and register) can be applied to produce or publish a text that communicates effectively with its readership. For the text editor, we have provided *guidelines* for implementing knowledge of grammar, meaning, style and register in order to improve documents through editorial intervention at this level, and we have indicated the potential *tensions* and *problems* that are likely to confront the editor. We hope, too, that in the process we have clarified the distinction between style, tone and register – a notoriously 'grey' area in the execution and analysis of written communication. In the next two chapters, we take the theme of text editing in practice one step further by focusing on presentation in its several manifestations.

Text editing in practice: presentation

Language changes, but it changes slowly. English speakers have been trying to agree on spelling and grammar for almost a millennium since the Norman Conquest, and a millennium and a half since the first Anglo-Saxons ... What's the most reliable way to say something important, if you want the most people to understand it: the way it's been written for five centuries, or the way it's been written for five years?
http://www.dailywritingtips.com/is-there-really-room-for-error-in-writing/

The rules for spelling and punctuation are set out ... in many grammar and usage books.
Mackenzie

A publication must be a showcase for the content, the meaning, the import, the substance, the usefulness, the significance of the story to the reader. The function of presentation is to expose them and bring them to the reader's attention.
White

9

Contents

Objectives

This penultimate chapter under the heading of Principles of text editing in practice deals with principles of presentation which have been touched upon in the document design section in chapter 2. After having introduced the application of text-editing principles in the areas of *text types* and *content* in chapter 6, we moved to *text structure* and its effect on argumentation in chapter 7, and on *wording* in chapter 8. In this chapter we aim to (a) provide guidelines, (b) indicate tensions and challenges, (c) highlight sources and (d) provide tips for and insights into how to deal with matters of spelling and punctuation. In the next, final chapter under the heading Principles of text editing and practice we do the same as we look at two other aspects of presentation with which text editors must equip themselves, namely, visual literacy in the form of typography and text layout.

1 Introduction

The last group of errors which influences text quality relates to how a text is presented, that is errors resulting from, for instance, weak spelling, unclear punctuation, conflicting typography, and untidy layout. We first discuss the text components that are more closely connected to the wording of the text and are surrounded by an aura of normativity (spelling and punctuation) and then approach the more arty and surface visual characteristics of typography and layout.

2 The approach to spelling

> ... a spelling error is a major fact error. It reflects harshly on the credibility of the (newspaper).
> *Berner*

> Many educated professional people in the English-speaking world have little confidence in their ability to spell and cling ever more desperately to the false security offered by the computer spellcheck.
> *Law*

> Editors are stuck with (English) as she is spelt, and you must be proficient. If you have the slightest doubt about a word, you will of course check it in a dictionary, but the trouble with spelling is that you don't know what you don't know.
> *Mackenzie*

> More than one-tenth of English words are not spelled the way they sound.
> *Taggart & Wine*

2.1 The history of spelling

> My spelling is Wobbly. It's good spelling but it Wobbles, and the letters get in the wrong places.
> *Winnie the Pooh, AA Milne*

> The traditional spelling system generally ignores both the changes in pronunciation over time and the variations in pronunciation through space; despite its notorious vagaries, it is a unifying force in world English.
> *Quirk et al*

Spelling or othography does not leave language users untouched. 'Good' spelling is often seen as a reflection of command of language and even intelligence. It is therefore important to pay attention to the textual aspect of spelling. In order to understand the spelling system of English, users of the language – especially when functioning as language practitioners – must understand the reasons why the spellings are as they are. It also helps to acquire an insight into how these spellings relate to the way words are pronounced, the more especially since English words are pronounced in thousands of different ways across the globe – from the United States and Canada in the west to Japan in the east, from Scotland in the north to South Africa and Australia in the south. Because such principles are not always taught, language practitioners who work in the medium of English – whether as first or a foreign language users – tend to be at a distinct disadvantage in this area. Since they often need to give explanations, too, we want to cast some light on the question of spelling in English beyond the mere surface of word forms.

2.1.1 The foundations of irregularities

Starting this section with a brief history of the development of the English language would therefore appear to be appropriate – if only to give the reader a sense of the reasons for the language's complexity so far as spelling is concerned.

The English spelling system is the result of a process of development that has been continuing for more than 1 000 years (cf Bryson 1991; Carney 1994; Crystal 1990, 2003; Scragg 1974; Upward & Davidson 2011; Waldman 2004). The spelling 'complications' (or irregularities) we have been bequeathed today are the result of the major linguistic and social events which took place during this time: first, when Old English was first written down by the Roman missionaries using the 23-letter Latin alphabet to cope with nearly 40 vowels and consonants (introducing the *th* sound and the *sc* combination of letters, for example); then, after the Norman Conquest (1066), the French scribes brought their own ideas about spelling to bear on the language (including the introduction of *qu* (queen), *gh* (night, enough), *ch* (church) and the 'soft' *c* (cell); they also replaced *u* with *o* (come) and introduced the *ou* spelling (house, mouse) (Bryson 1991: 115).

From the late fifteenth century, the many ways of spelling words then in existence came to be standardised after the introduction of printing in 1476. Standardising on the speech of the area around London, William Caxton stabilised the spelling of many words for the first time, and the notion of a 'correct' spelling began to develop (Crystal 1990: 74–76; Bryson 1991: 117, 118–119). During the same century, however, through a 'vowel shift', the pronunciation of English was transformed into its modern form, reflecting the way words were pronounced in Chaucer's time (accounting for the many 'silent letters' to be found in modern English spelling, such as the *k* in *knee* and *knowledge* and the *e* at the end of *bane* and *tone*). In the sixteenth century (the age of Queen Elizabeth I and Shakespeare), learned writers began showing the etymology of words in their spelling, which led to several of these new spellings becoming standard (the silent *b* was introduced, for instance, into words such as *debt* (*debitum*) as a reminder of their Latin roots). But even in its greatest flowering English was still considered in many respects a second-rate language, Latin being the language of scholarship, an area in which English use was experimental. Moreover, in Shakespeare's day, English was merely the language of England and lowland Scotland – it had yet to conquer the British Isles (Bryson 1991: 58).

From the late sixteenth century – an age of discovery and mercantile expansion – English received new waves of loan words from French, Latin, American Indian, Arabic, Chinese, Dutch, Greek, Spanish, Indian, Italian, Portuguese and African languages, including: *alkali, brusque, canoe, caucus, chutney, cocoa, dagga, intrigue, ketchup, moustache, potato, reign, shampoo, sofa, spaghetti, yacht* (Bryson 1991: 66; Crystal 1990: 77). Says David Crystal (1990: 77), 'some of the strangest spellings in the language stem from this period,' spellings that flout the usual English pattern.

Since the spelling of English words was finally fixed during the eighteenth century under the influence of people such as Samuel Johnson, their pronunciation has changed considerably. The etymological rather than the phonetic approach to spelling became entrenched, so that an Old English word like *rough*, for example, is now pronounced not with the gutteral *g* of *rug* but as if it were spelt *ruff*. Most of the difficulties of English spelling derive from this historical fact. Which is not to say that irregularity reigns supreme: in fact, more than 80% of all words follow a definite spelling pattern, even though more than one pattern may have to be learned for the same sound: '*ein*, for example, is to be found in cane, Dane, humane and sane, but also in gain, main, obtain, refrain, and in ballpein, rein' (Ridout & Clarke 1989: 337):

Even though this may seem utter chaos, it is helpful to be aware of the spelling patterns into which words can be grouped (see below).

2.1.2 UK vs US English

> England and America are two countries divided by a common language.
> *George Bernard Shaw*

Another factor complicating the spelling of English words is the split between American and British spellings. Until the eighteenth century, English spelling was not standardised on either side of the Atlantic. Then, in 1755, Samuel Johnson published his *Dictionary of the English language*, and in 1828, Noah Webster published *An American dictionary of the English language*.

Webster was an orderly minded man who disapproved of a lot of the spelling that Johnson had recorded. His dislike of words that were not pronounced the way they looked led him to decree that words such as *centre* and *theatre* should be spelled *center* and *theater*; he also dropped the silent *u* from words such as *colour* and *honour*. In fact, Webster was single-handedly responsible for most of the differences between British and American spelling that survive to this day (Taggart & Wines 2008: 17).

2.1.3 English going global

One further factor leading to the apparent randomness of English spelling is that it not only freely adopts words from other cultures and languages but also tends to preserve their spellings (eg *buffet*, *chutzpah*, *élan*, *garage*) (Bryson 1991: 119–120). The result is that English spelling is a curious mixture of different influences, which makes it enormously difficult to provide a comprehensive set of 'spelling rules' that can be applied absolutely. The truth is, there are usually many exceptions to the 20 or so 'rules' of English spelling; but by discerning patterns – and understanding them – we are more likely to detect and correct misspellings than without any such knowledge or comprehension.

2.2 The importance of spelling to text quality

According to Einsohn (2000: 121), good spellers not only know how to spell many commonly misspelled words but also:

- readily look up unfamiliar or unusual words;
- know which words they always have to look up;
- know that usage affects spelling;
- are not fooled by homophones;
- double-check a word in a dictionary before changing it in the manuscript;
- do not introduce misspellings into a manuscript.

In this section, then, for the benefit of those who fall short of Einsohn's list of criteria – possibly all of us – we consider the following aspects of English spelling along the lines of norm (2.2.1), variation (2.2.2) and mastering (2.2.3).

2.2.1 Norm

The following areas may require that you formulate your own position regarding norm and consistency in spelling (Brains 2008).

2.2.1.1 Compound words

There are three forms of compound words (mostly consisting of nouns and adjectives):

- closed form, for example *firefly, keyboard;*
- hyphenated form, for example *full-blown, ghost-writer, anti-social;*
- open form, for example the *middle class, mother tongue.*

The first form is the most uncommon. However, the rules are not clear-cut. So, for example, it is possible to have *airbase*, *air base* or *air-base*: all of them are correct and all these forms are found in usage. It is important, though, to ensure that individual forms are used consistently within a single text or range of texts. If you are in doubt, consult a dictionary. If you do not have a dictionary to hand, the safest is to use a space (the third form), because that is the most common form in English.

According to the *New Oxford dictionary for writers and editors* (OUP 2005: xi), there is a general tendency in modern English to avoid hyphenation for noun compounds. There is an additional preference in US English for the form to be one word and in UK English for the form to be two words: *end point* (British) vs *endpoint* (American). Both the *Oxford* and the *Collins dictionary for writers and editors* are invaluable references for the writer, editor and proofreader because they focus on 'words and names that cause difficulty or controversy' for us wordsmiths.

Many words that are still in a 'transitional' phase may be found hyphenated in dictionaries, but many editors and publishers will already have decided to make them one word for the sake of consistency (for instance, *cooperate, email, microorganism*).

2.2.1.2 Proper nouns

An important aspect of spelling is capitalisation: when to capitalise and when not to being the question. Nouns such as *king, president, chancellor* and *managing director* are generally written with a lower-case initial letter but may be capitalised with an uppercase in certain contexts:

> The *prince* arrived with his father, the *king*. (*prince* and *king* being functions)
> Then *Prince Igor* arrived with his father, *King Alphonso*. (*Prince* and *King* being titles)

2.2.1.3 Abbreviations and acronyms

An *abbreviation* is usually the first part of a word from which the remainder has been removed (Rev, Prof); a *contraction* comprises the first and last letters of a word (Dr, St); an *acronym* comprises the first letters of other words that as a group can be pronounced as words (Sita, Sabra); an *initialism* comprises the first letters of a name or title that can be said only letter by letter (EU, ILO, SADC).

Established acronyms and initialisms such as NATO, NASA, SABC and UCT are usually shown in capital letters, without full points. This is the usual style in UK and in South African English, though points are permissible if that is the house style. (In US English it is more usual to write such abbreviations with points.)

Acronyms are sometimes written with just an initial capital (*Nasa*). This is an acceptable house style that should be followed consistently.

2.2.1.4 Foreign words

Words and phrases that have come into English directly from other languages are traditionally written in italics to show that they are not fully established as English words (eg *cafard* (French for melancholia); *echt* (German for authentic)). As the word or phrase becomes more widely used, or naturalised, it may eventually become part of the standard vocabulary of English, and the italics may no longer be used. Some examples of naturalised words are given below; sometimes diacritics or capitals are dropped:

	Examples of naturalised words in English
From French:	carte blanche, de rigueur, déja vu, élan/elan, façade/facade, fait accompli, faux pas, hors d'oeuvre, laissez-faire, raison d'être, vis-à-vis
From German:	ersatz, gestalt, realpolitik, weltanschauung, zeitgeist
From Italian:	a cappella, al fresco, cappuccino, espresso, punctilio, virtuoso
From Japanese:	hara-kiri, hibachi, nigiri, samurai, sashimi, sushi, tempura
From Latin:	ad nauseam, agenda, de facto, in loco parentis, inter alia, modus operandi, sine qua non, sui generis
From Spanish/Portuguese:	aficionado, gringo, guerrilla, junta, padrão
From African languages:	kwaito, marimba, tsotsi, trek, takkie

Table 9.1 *Some naturalised words in English, with diacritic marks where retained*

Points of advice:

- Often the use of italics or not is a matter of gauging the readership: if the term is set in roman (ie unitalicised), will readers be confused? If the term is set in italics, will readers be surprised?
- If you are unable to verify the spelling and grammar of foreign words and phrases, remind your author to double-check quoted matter.
- When in doubt, use a reputable dictionary or word list as your guide to the use of italics.

2.2.1.5 Plurals

Plurals can cause problems, especially nouns that end in -o (hero), -ey (monkey) or Latin-based and French-based nouns that keep their own plurals (see the table below). All the major style manuals discuss the conventions regarding the formation of plurals.

When the dictionary lists two plurals for a common noun, read the entire entry to discover whether the two forms have different uses. For example: *appendices* and *appendixes*; *indexes* and *indices*; *mediums* and *media*; *mice* and *mouses*; *oxen* and *oxes*; *staffs* and *staves*.

Some traps:

Singular	Plural
Latin	
octopus	octopuses
cactus	cacti
fungus	fungi
addendum	addenda
minimum	minima
forum	forums/fora[1]
medium	media/mediums[2]
memorandum	memoranda/memorandums
stadium	stadiums/stadia[1]
Greek	
criterion	criteria
phenomenon	phenomena
French	
bureau	bureaux/bureaus
plateau	plateaux
Plurals of initialisms, letters and numbers	
NGOs	
1960s	
three l's in parallel	

Singular	Plural
-f	
life	lives/lifes[3]
scarf	scarves
roof	roofs
-o	
banjo	banjos
tomato	tomatoes
potato	potatoes
hero	heroes
-y	
baby	babies
money	monies/moneys[4]
monkey	monkeys
valley	valleys
Special plurals	
person	people/persons[5]
cupful	cupfuls
spoonful	spoonfuls
sister-in-law	sisters-in-law
fish	fish or fishes[6]
appendix	appendixes/appendices[7]
mouse	mice/mouses[8]

Table 9.2 *The plurals trap – how not to get caught*

Notes

1   The -*s* plural is the modern form; the -*a* plural is the classical form.
2   *Media* is the collective noun for newspapers, magazines, television and so on; *mediums* are people who claim to be able to communicate with those in the afterlife.
3   *Lives* is the common plural form; artists paint *still lifes*, though.
4   Both are acceptable; follow house style.
5   *People* is the common, everyday plural of *person*; *persons* is used in legal contexts (Alcohol may not be sold to persons under 18 years of age).
6   *Fish* is a mass plural (We netted many fish when we trawled); *fishes* is a count plural (He brought home five fishes that he'd caught);
7   *Appendixes* as bodily organs; *appendices* as addenda at the back of books.
8   The common plural is *mice*; the plural form of the electronic gadget is *mouses*.

2.2.1.6 Formation of possessives

Singular possessive – add 's:
>   the *child's* toy; the *horse's* mane; the *leader's* decision;
>   the *man's* watch; the *lass's* pigtails

Plural possessive – add ' unless an internal vowel change occurs:
>   the *horses'* manes; the *lasses'* pigtails;
>   the *children's* toys; the *men's* watches; the *people's* rights

Possessives of names:
>   *Jill's*; *Pete's*
If the final -*s* sound is soft, add 's:
>   *Barras's*; *Moss's*; *Francis's*
If the final sound is a hard *z*, add ':
>   *Moses'* life; the *Joneses'* car, *Jesus'* teaching, Cecil *Rhodes'* legacy

Names of French origin, where the final letter is not sounded – add 's:
>   *Du Toit's*; *Du Plessis's*; *Du Preez's*

Do not use the possessive apostrophe to form plurals (Truss 2003):
>   lady's; potatoe's; currant's; egg's, Sunday's; flower's are common errors.

2.2.1.7 Writing out numbers

Generally, 1–9 are spelt out in body text (not in tabular matter):
>   *nine* parents, *six* children and *11* friends attended.

Never start a sentence with a number – words only:
>   *The year 1992* got off to a good start. *Twelve* months seems a long time.

An estimated, approximate or rounded number should always be in words:
>   *about one thousand* residents attended the function.

Numbers such as twenty-six, seventy-nine and including -year-old(s) should be hyphenated: She's only a *16-year-old*; her boyfriend is twenty-three.

2.2.1.8 Formation of past tenses

The past tenses of verbs can be formed in five ways, ranging from simply regular (or weak) verbs through to irregular (or strong) verbs. There are nevertheless some patterns to discern and possibly learn (MacArthur 1992: 1083).

Regular verbs add *-ed* for the past tense and past participle: *talk, talked*; *cite, cited*; *lope, loped*. A number of verbs vary between *-ed* and *-t* endings (and in some cases change the vowel sound in the root): *burned, burnt*; learned, *learnt*; *dreamed, dreamt*; *spelled, spelt*; *kneeled, knelt*; *leaped, leapt*; *spoiled, spoilt.*

The *-t* form tends to be favoured when the past participle is used as an adjective: *spilt milk* but *I spilled the beans*; *burnt offerings* but *the house burned down*. The *-ed* form is usually retained in US English: She *spelled* better than she *punctuated.*

A number of verbs vary in the past participle only between the regular form and one ending in *-(e)n*: *hew, hewn*; *mow, mowed, mown*; *saw, sawed, sawn*; *rot, rotted, rotten*; *show, showed, shown*; *sow, sowed, sown*; *swell, swelled, swollen*. In most of these the *-(e)n* form is to be preferred; in UK English it is obligatory when the participle is used as an attributive adjective: *new-mown hay*; *one rotten apple*; *a sawn-off shotgun*; *a swollen gland.*

Irregular verbs are more complex and therefore often difficult to use correctly because they undergo a radical change to create their past tense forms: *forbid, forbade,* (have) *forbidden*; *go, went* (have) *gone*; *ring, rang,* (have) *rung*; *seek, sought,* (have) *sought*; *speak, spoke,* (have) *spoken*; *teach, taught,* (have) *taught*; *write, wrote,* (have) *written.*

2.2.1.9 Hyphenation and word breaks

There are two aspects of hyphenation to consider here: the use of a *hard* hyphen in compounded words such as *south-east*, *de-emphasise* or *co-ordinate* wherever they occur in a line of print; and the use of the hyphen to mark a word division or word break at the end of the line, because there is insufficient space for the whole of word to fit in.

Although standard spelling in English is fixed, hyphenation is not. The best advice we can give is to consult a reputable, recently published dictionary. It should reflect current usage regarding hyphenation and guide you, if only by analogy.

Word division generally improves the overall appearance of text that is justified (ie with the lines expanded to make the right-hand ends align vertically). In unjustified text (ie where the right-hand margin is irregular, also known as 'ragged right'), word division is less necessary, some would say less desirable. Word divisions are usually based on both the pronunciation of words (*finan-cial*) and their internal structure (*regret-table*; *ener-getic*).

However, when you are confronted with justified narrow-column setting, for instance, there are more, but 'less desirable' places to break (indicated by ~): *fi~nance, fi~nan-cial; re~gret, re~gret-table; en~ergy, en~er-get~ic*), so they reflect modern practice and are as unobtrusive as possible.

Sometimes the ugliness of a 'gappy' line of type (bad spacing, especially common in narrow columns) is less desirable than an 'impermissible' word division, and so the latter will be effected as a last resort if it is likely to contribute to the improved appearance of a page.

Another motivation for implementing word divisions could be the unfortunate patterns formed down the right margin owing to the repetition of words or characters: when three or more lines end in the same character(s), the inelegant pattern should be interrupted, as in the repetition of *and* below:

> Carrying out the Find *and*
> Replace sequences by *hand*
> all functions *beforehand*
> macro features are at times
> extremely helpful to the editor.

The usual solution to this type of problem is either to take over the middle word to the next line or to divide one of the words (if it is divisible).

For some simple rules for word division, see chapter 10 section 2.2.2.5.

2.2.1.10 Common confusables

Here are some words that writers (and even some editors) are prone to spell and use incorrectly:

accede	to agree	exceed	to surpass
accept	to receive	except	excluding
adapt	to adjust	adopt	begin to have, eg a new policy
affect	have an effect on	effect	to bring about
aid	help	aide	assistant
ambiguous	having two meanings	ambivalent	being in doubt: I am ambivalent about …
among	[more than two involved]	between	[two involved]
amount	[for non-countable things]	number	[for countable things]
ascent	rise	assent	consent

bazaar	market	bizarre	strange
beside	next to	besides	in addition to
blond	[male]	blonde	[female]
cite	to quote as example	site sight	position or place vision
coarse	rough in texture	course	grammar course racecourse
complement	complete	compliment	praise
continual	repeated	continuous	uninterrupted
co-operate	work together physically	collaborate	work together mentally, eg when doing research
councillor	council member	counsellor	advisor
dependant	[noun]	dependent	[adjective]
desert	sandy place to abandon	dessert	sweet course of a meal
disinterested	impartial	uninterested	lacking interest
economic	related to the economy	economical	cheap to operate
ensure	make certain	insure	getting financial protection
especially	particularly, more than other things	specially	for a special reason
historic	important	historical	old, belonging to history
opportunity	chance	possibility	option
principal	main, most important	principle	standard, rule
serial	series of episodes	cereal	edible grain

Table 9.3 Some common confusables

2.2.1.11 Cyberjargon

In the electronic age, copyeditors are encountering an increasing number of new terms, especially compounds of the form *e-learning, intra-net, internet, website, jpeg, pdf, url, uriel* and so on. In this melting pot, current practice is still fairly divided, and this jargon presents some new challenges, such as:

- E-mail, e-mail or email?
- Jpeg, JPEG or jpeg?
- URL or url?
- Website, web site or website?

- Internet or internet?
- Browsers and Crawlers or browsers and crawlers?
- PDf or pdf?

Increasingly – as both writers and readers become more familiar with this cyberterminology – we are moving towards solid spellings (one word) and initial lowercase. Acronyms and abbreviations are shifting from full caps to lowercase at the same time.

2.2.2 Variation

Language is a living entity and dynamic. Therefore, not everything is cast in stone. Variation can be interindividual, regional, georgraphic, social, text-based and genre-based. The main variation that can be described is regional in nature.

2.2.2.1 The Atlantic divide between British and American spellings

Noah Webster's seminal work in the early nineteenth century led to a parting of the ways between UK English spellings and those in US English. The sharp division has been in existence since his *Webster's dictionary* was published in 1828. The differences take a number of recognisable forms, illustrated below. Use the US variants only when working on texts specifically intended for the US and Canadian markets, or for clients who make it clear that they follow US English style and spellings.

-dg- versus -dge-
In US English *e* is dropped after *dg* and before a suffix beginning with a consonant:
> *abridgment, acknowledgment, judgment*

In UK English the *e* is retained, except for *judgment*, which is so spelled in legal works (though *judgement* is used with its general meaning).

-e (final silent)
This is often omitted in US spelling, as are the final silent *-ue* and *-me*:
> *adz, ax, analog, dialog, epilog, pedagog, program*

-ize versus -ise
The verbal ending *-ize* has been in general use since the sixteenth century. Today it is favoured in US English usage, and it is the preferred style of Oxford University Press for books published in Britain. However, in UK English *-ise* is also acceptable, provided that its use is consistent, and words which can be spelled *-ise* only (prise, comprise, exercise) do not have the *-ize* ending foisted upon them (Waite 2005: ix). (In UK English, *analyse* is always spelt thus.) Both Gowers (1969) and Treble & Vallins (1973) support standardisation on *-ise* as being more convenient to wordsmiths, although both Fowler (3rd edition by Burchfield 1999) and Partridge (1973) take the contrary view ('Where there are, in dictionaries, the alternatives -ise and -ize , use IZE' Partridge 1973: 160). South African publishers generally tend to follow the *-ise* style too.

l, single or double?

In US spelling *l* is usually double in:

> *enroll(ment), distill, enthrall, impell, instill*
> Exceptions: *annul(ment), extol*

-o- or -ou-

US spelling *-or* is usual in all cases except *glamour*:

> *color, favor, harbor, humor*

US spelling favours *o* alone instead of *ou* in:

> *mold, molder, molt, smolder*

2.2.2.2 English as a lingua franca (ELF), world English or international English

Despite the existence of 'standard' or 'correct' spelling, English spelling has never been fixed, alternative forms arising constantly. Take a word such as *minuscule*, for example. That's the correct spelling, derived from the Latin *minuscule* (somewhat smaller). However, because minuscule means 'very small', many people (52% of instances in the Oxford English Corpus) wrongly associate it with the well-known prefix *mini-* and spell it *miniscule* instead. While the lexicographers currently regard this newer spelling as an error to avoid, it may well become acceptable in the future and be added to the dictionary as a valid alternative spelling (DSAE 2006: SP11). This reinterpretation of spellings, in which a less familiar spelling is changed 'logically' to a more common one, is similar to the process known in linguistics as reanalysis. Many are the influences on English in this respect, not least of all because of its global spread and the emergence of English as an international language, influenced as it is by millions of non-native speakers of English (see chapter 6, section 1.2).

Guidance of sorts comes from an INTECOM International Technical Documentation Study Group conference in 2003 (Murphy 2011: 206–207). The study group's objective was 'to identify which spelling and usage we should recommend for documentation that would be written in English' but would 'receive worldwide distribution'. The upshot is a set of guidelines for three different situations:

1. for English-language documentation to be read primarily in countries where British-based spelling, terminology and usage are the norm;

2. for English-language documentation to be read primarily in countries where US-based spelling, terminology and usage are prevalent;

3. for English-language documentation to be read by people in a broader range of countries, with some accustomed to British and some to US usage.

Despite these options, the study group 'mostly suggested using US spelling and usage for English-language documentation that will have worldwide use'. This recognition of the pervasiveness of US English is perhaps understandable, particularly in the Asian context.

2.2.3 Mastering language

2.2.3.1 Lifelong learning

With time language users of course learn/have learned a lot about spelling. Meanwhile, here are some tips en route:

- Familiarise yourself with the spelling rules.
- Develop a reliance on dictionaries and other word lists.
- Get acquainted with spell-checkers and how to use them effectively.

(See chapter 11 on resources.)

Develop your own list of errors to check, according to what you find in the text, quite often as a result of mistyping. For example:

- Correct spelling but wrong word: *form/from*; *selling/spelling*; *then/them/than*; *trail/trial*
- Letters or punctuation repeated: *prooofs/prroofs*; *necesssary*; *in the end..*
- Miskeyed case: *aNNEXURE, fFrom*
- Missing letter in a word: *puntuate*
- Transposed or accidentally incerted letters: *fascinaiton*; *trouobled*; *referneces.*

Most of these will be highlighted in your spell-check, but do not rely on that to find them all.

Einsohn (2005: 122–124) gives some useful advice on how to improve your spelling skills – while at the same time urging you to become good friends with your dictionary:

- Stare at lists of difficult words.
- Keep a list of all the words you look up.
- Learn spelling rules and exceptions.
- Learn something about the etymology of difficult words.
- Pay special attention to suffixes that contain unstressed syllables.
- Learn some mnemonic devices.

2.2.3.2 The importance of consistency

Amid all these 'spelling decisions' you have to be cognisant of and implement, one message shines through crystal clear: while there may not be too many 'right' answers for you to rely upon, as long as you are following a particular standard and adhering to it consistently, you are doing your job as an editor and a proofreader (Linnegar, Shamberger & Bishop 2009). You cannot hope to know all the answers either; but you should know which resources to call on to find them.

What matters to the reader (and the reviewer), when all is said and done, is that every aspect of the text has been dealt with consistently, and no obvious errors of inconsistency

– whether of font choice, spelling, punctuation or anything else – are discernible to them. Ultimately, you the editor and proofreader are helping the author in a multitude of different ways to deliver a flawless product. And just as a diamond is only as valuable as the consistency of its colour and its flawless faceting, so a text will be judged by those who read it. Spelling – in all its facets, as outlined in this section – plays a signal role in presenting a text at its best.

2.2.3.3 House style

Whereas most aspects of spelling and punctuation are governed by rules, in many instances English offers the author and the text editor choices:

• scrutinize or scrutinise; no-one or no one; co-operate or cooperate; fulfil or fulfill;
• 'single quotation marks' or "double quotation marks"; e.g. and i.e. or eg and ie; 129,35 or 129.35.

For the practitioner, it's not so much a matter of allowing one alternative or another; it's more a case of abiding by your decision consistently, based upon what you perceive to be your author's preferences, or the preferences of a particular discipline (in some medical books, for example, microorganism and intrauterine are regarded as the norm in preference to their hyphenated alternatives; in history books, the style '19th century' would probably be preferred, whereas in a novel, say, 'nineteenth century' would be). And the number of decisions you're likely to make while editing a manuscript could be legion, involving much more than merely spelling and punctuation decisions (see the table below). So you have to have a systematic way of thinking about consistency, but also of recording your decisions for future reference. This systematic way is called 'house style' – something that publishers generally prize dearly, to the extent of producing a manual or guide about their preferences – and, compiled by the text editor as a book-specific supplement to the manual, a document called a 'style sheet'.

Consistency is a prized virtue in the copy editor's make-up. Perceived or actual inconsistency in a text's accuracy and presentation may have only a subliminal effect on a reader, but it is strange how the two merge: a few inconsistent spellings or use of punctuation marks in a text and a reader can't help themselves questioning whether the facts are also likely to be wrong or whether the careless author really knows their subject. In most texts, house style decisions abound.

Watch out for common name alternatives such as *Ann* or *Anne, McIntosh* or *Macintosh*, or in German history books *Frederic/Frederick/Friedrich*. In Switzerland the Germans spell the town *Basel*, the French use *Bâle* and the English will refer to it as *Basle*: all are correct, but only in their specific contexts.

Readers don't care much whether dates are given as *10 August 1998, August 10 1998* or *August 10, 1998*, but noticing the variation may still draw their attention from the text, ever so slightly, and these distractions can mount up, to the point of irritation and, sometimes, of outright rejection. Remember that our pass rate when it comes to imposing consistency on an author's manuscript is very high: we have to be 99.99% accurate.

The easiest way to ensure consistency is to make lists, as you go through the manuscript, of the author's way of dealing with punctuation, the use of uppercase, hyphens, italic, spellings, abbreviations and other elements of house style. Note unusual spellings, and record the folio number as they come up (for possible future reference); mark queries in the margin in pencil if it helps (delete all this before you pass the edited manuscript along), and use your notebook also to record your decisions.

Consistency should follow through from the text mark-up to the preliminary matter and even the text on the cover; it requires you to make sure the contents wording matches the chapters in the text, the footnotes or endnotes, the bibliography, and even the captions to illustrations.

Much of the text's structure is retained in the copy editor's short-term memory, and if you work on a manuscript in concentrated periods you'll remember the oddest things about spellings and italics. But wait a week and it all disappears (if you did retain it, that way leads madness!), so it pays you to keep fuller notes of house style decisions than you'd expect are necessary.

Useful resources to consult when having to make house style decisions include general dictionaries but also references such as the *Oxford dictionary for writers and editors* or its Collins or Penguin equivalents.

The sorts of house style decision you're likely to have to make as text editor could include any or all of the following:

Abbreviations

Gender-neutral words

Capitalisation of initial letters

Intext cross-references

Dates and time

Foreign languages

Hyphenation

Italics

Measurements (imperial/metric; conventions)

Currency

Numbers

Proper names

References

Spellings

Jargon

Parochialism and bias

Table and column headings

Punctuation (hyphen, dash (em- or en-rule, spaced or unspaced), quotation marks, decimal comma/point)

3 The approach to punctuation

> It is a sound principle that as few stops should be used as will do the work. ... stops are not to alter the meaning, but merely to show it up.
> *Fowler*

> The purpose of punctuation is to mark out strings of words into manageable groups and to show how these groups are related to each other. Correct punctuation clarifies both the meaning of the individual words and the construction of the sentence as a whole, so that even quite complex sentences can be understood at first reading ...
> *Law*

> A command of the full range of punctuation marks helps you to say more, and to say it more interestingly and effectively. Punctuation is ... essential ... as important as choosing the right words.
> *Law*

> A good copy editor, knowing the purpose for each punctuation mark, never relies simply on 'what sounds right'.
> *Bowles & Borden*

3.1 The importance of punctuation for text quality

> It is not just an optional frill: it is essential to the accurate exchange of written information, just as – in speech – intonation is a major clue to meaning. Ambiguity thrives on careless punctuation. Punctuate negligently, and you will communicate inefficiently and probably misleadingly.
> *Kahn*

> The purpose of punctuation is to make writing clear, by clarifying the structure of continuous writing and indicating how words relate to each other.
> *Oxford South African concise dictionary*

Punctuation is more a matter of convention, tradition and usage than of obligation. However, in the 1980s it was observed that the 'trend today is towards lighter punctuation than was the practice only a few years ago', but any potential defectors should be warned that this 'does nothing to lessen the writer's obligation to observe the accepted conventions' (Burton 1982: 159). Referring to 'well-recognised principles of punctuation', Kahn (1985: 500) expresses the position thus:

> Unfortunately, punctuation cannot be reduced completely to a system of rules. Its effective use requires an ability by the writer to put himself in the position of his readers and anticipate any likely difficulty or misunderstanding of theirs. ... So some aspects of punctuation are rule-governed, and some are matters of judgment and taste.

Punctuation depends to a large extent on taste and preference, on what the author considers will contribute best to making reading easier. Indeed, 'correct punctuation is essential for clarity' (Bowles & Borden 2011: 40). However, it is not an inter-individual tool to be switched on and off at will; some usages have in fact become so entrenched that any departure from them has come to be seen as erroneous. Examples of such entrenched usages in English sentences are that parenthetical phrases and clauses must be enclosed between a pair of punctuation marks (*commas*, *dashes* or *parentheses*), that abbreviations must take full points if the house style is to use full points for abreviations and contractions, that subordinate clauses have to be bracketed off with commas, and that a declarative sentence must terminate in a full point.

These accepted conventions of English often differ quite drastically from those of other languages. Therefore, the text editor is expected to know how to use the various punctuation marks correctly and functionally, so that they wil be able to serve as an aid rather than an obstacle to reading. That this is not always the case can be seen in the quotations with which we started this section.

Punctuation has four specific functions (Kahn (ed) 1985: 499):

- to end or round out: *Who says so? The boss does. How amazing!*
- to introduce: *He has one response to every request – blunt refusal.*
- to separate: *Those who can, do; those who can't, teach.*
- to enclose and set apart: *You, my fine fellow, are in serious trouble. 'I'll kill you,' he snarled.*

All these functions serve the higher purpose of punctuation – to clarify the writer's meaning (Kahn (ed) 1985: 499) and to communicate more effectively.

3.1.1 Markers at word, phrase and sentence level

There are two types of marker that help readers to decode written and spoken language: diacritics (or accents) are used at word level and punctuation marks are put to use at phrase and sentence level:

- The diacritics,[1] as in *é, à, Ö, ç, ñ* (*accent, diaresis, cedilla* and *tilde*), are seldom used in English, though copy editors and proofreaders should be familiar with their correct employment in Romance and Germanic languages. Their function is to help the reader identify a sound corresponding with a letter such as, for example, *n* versus *ñ*, *c* versus *ç*, *o* versus *ö*. They also operate as *phonetic symbols* that contribute to correct pronunciation, for instance, [u:] is the symbol for a long, rounded front vowel in which the colon denotes that [u] is lengthened.
- Punctuation marks are 'symbols that indicate the structure and organisation of written language, as well as intonation and pauses to be observed when reading aloud' (cf Kahn (ed) 1985: 499; McArthur 1992: 824). Punctuation, then, is 'the act or practice of inserting standardized marks or signs in written matter to clarify the meaning and separate structural units' (http://www.merriam-webster.com/dictionary/punctuation)

---

[1] A diacritic is an individual mark added to a letter indicating a difference in pronunciation.

3.1.2 Punctuation marks

Punctuation is used in written text to indicate natural breathing spaces, pauses and empha-sis (cf Crystal 1990: 93; Carey 1958; Field 2007: 65, 98–105, 122, 149; Kahn (ed) 1985: 499–502; Lukeman 2007; McArthur 1992: 824–826; Merriam-Webster 2001; Partridge 1955, 1973; Stilman 2010; Trask 1997; Truss 2003, 2008). In order from shortest to long-est pause or breathing space, the principal punctuation marks are the *comma, semicolon, colon/dash* and *full stop/period, question mark* and *exclamation mark*. These marks help to separate phrases, clauses and successive sentences with a view to making reading flow more easily. Here is a complete list of punctuation marks:

apostrophe (')	brackets ([ ], ( ), { }, ( ))	colon (:)
comma (,)	dash (en-rule/em-rule) (–, —)	ellipsis (…)
full stop/period (.)	guillemets (« »)	exclamation mark (!)
question mark (?)	quotation marks (' ', " ")	hyphen (-)
slash/oblique (/)	solidus (/)	semicolon (;)

3.1.3 Punctuation marks at word level

Even though most punctuation marks function at utterance level, some function at word level and are part of the conventional writing system: apostrophes, hyphens, accents, full stops in abbreviations and capitals (Trask 2008).

- The apostrophe (') used to occur in plurals such as banjo's, the 1920's and NGO's. In practice, however, this usage is largely falling away; where this happens, the apostrophe is left with but one function: to indicate the possessive case:
  John's trousers; the parents' dilemma; Du Plessis's husband; for goodness' sake.
- The hyphen is reserved for joining or compounding words (*well-being; a step-by-step process*) or joining prefixes to words (*co-ordinate; re-emerge; peri-urban, sub-Saharan*). A third useful function of the hyphen is to help avoid ambiguity in instances such as *re-cover* vs *recover* and *re-sign* vs *resign*.

3.1.4 The function of punctuation marks

All punctuation marks seem to serve a dual function:

- They are important stylistic devices. They ensure clarity of communication and convey the correct pauses or emphasis in the written word. This in turn contributes to the cor-rect sentence rhythm, which leads to greater clarity.
- They are functional. Their function is to facilitate reading and communication and thus contribute to a writer's ease of style (*Chicago manual of style* 1993: 158; *Merriam-Webster's guide to punctuation and style* 2001).

It is not only important that punctuation marks are used; it is especially important that they are used correctly where correct usage has become established, because the incorrect use of punctuation can lead to an incorrect interpretation of the text. A knowledge of punctuation marks also requires a knowledge of grammatical patterns and meaning potential, which are complementary. The following should be observed in this regard:

• Different style conventions have been captured in style books, manuals and inhouse 'brand books' or style sheets and are followed by different disciplines, regions, etc. The Modern Language Association's (MLA) conventions, for example, are accepted by most language and literature scholars. Alternatives are the APA style and publication manuals (by the American Psychological Association and most commonly used within the social sciences) and the *Chicago manual of style*, mainly used by professional text editors (Van de Poel & Gasiorek 2007: 59).

• The term 'brackets' in US English usually refers to square or box-type brackets, whereas in UK English usage it normally refers to round brackets. The different types are: parentheses or ( ), square brackets [ ], curly brackets { }, and angle brackets or chevrons ⟨ ⟩. Parentheses and (square) brackets should not be used interchangeably; whereas the former are used to separate parenthetical statements, the latter are reserved for editorial interpolations – for example, where an author has corrected an error in quoted matter. Curly brackets or braces are well known among mathematics authors and editors. The less than (<) and greater than (>) symbols are often used instead of angled brackets to indicate an email address or a url.

• Quotation marks or inverted commas are used to indicate matter quoted from other sources, dialogue (or direct speech), or words used in an unusual way (eg irony). The single styling is considered UK English, the double styling is standard in US English. Opening and closing quotation marks may be identical in form (*vertical, straight,* or *typewriter quotation marks*), or may be distinctly left-handed and right-handed (*typographic* or, colloquially, *curly quotation marks*). Quotation marks call for two styles of punctuation: the American style, in which commas and periods are almost always placed inside closing quotation marks, and the British style, which enables only those punctuation marks that appeared in the quoted material to occur within quotation marks. However, several sources permit stops/periods and commas outside the quotation marks when the presence of the punctuation mark inside the quotation marks will lead to ambiguity.

> She is known for her'eccentricity'.
> 'that is so,' he replied, 'but I still don't agree.'
> She yelled: 'Mike, don't do that!'

• The ellipsis serves two purposes: either to indicate where an author has intentionally omitted a word or words from a directly quoted passage or to show that the writer or speaker could or did not complete a sentence. An ellipsis should be spaced (see section 3.2.2).

• The solidus (or the *oblique* or *forward slash*, which usually stands for *or*) is most commonly used to separate alternatives (*he/she, and/or*). In expressions of time it can separate successive units: *2001/2003; 19/21 February* (instead of an en-rule). With non-metric units of measure, it is often used instead of the word *per*: *75 miles/hr*. Note that it is always unspaced.

3.2 Punctuation in practice

In practice, the following two pieces of advice may take you a long way:

- In general, be careful not to impose your personal preferences for punctuation usage on a text: 'You should not override the author's preference in your zeal to make the punctuation "correct"' (Mackenzie 2004: 87, 2011).
- Use fewer rather than too many punctuation marks – in other words, follow the conventions of open (or light) rather than closed (or heavy) punctuation (cf Law 2002: 90; Fowler, in Gowers 1969: 236; Kahn (ed) 1985: 500–501).

3.2.1 At word level

- Regarding the use of full stops together with abbreviations and acronyms, consult the relevant house style and follow it consistently. However, even if the house style is to have full points used with abbreviations, if the abbreviation ends in the last letter of the word, it will not terminate in a full stop. In general, though, the modern trend is to dispense with full points in abbreviations and acronyms.

    Examples: Mr JA Smithson; Prof Paul Cookson; Revd Dr Phipps; Ms Anne Rowlands; the SABC board; a website URL; she obtained a BA LLB last year; an MBChB requires seven years of study; Company ABC (Pty) Ltd.

As can be seen from these examples, acronyms never have full stops: NATO, Unisa, SANRAL.

- The apostrophe can sometimes give trouble to editors, in the following respects:
    - To indicate possession: to a singular noun add *'s* (*man's cap; James's pen*); to a plural noun not ending in s, add *'s* (*women's rights*); to a plural noun ending in s add only the apostrophe (*boys' shoes; teachers' classrooms*).
    - With multiple noun possessives: add the apostrophe to the latter noun if the two form a unit (*Boswell and Wilkie's circus*); but if the nouns are to be considered separately, add the apostrophe to both (*Jane's and Peter's iPods*).
    - Possessive adjectives and possessive pronouns are already possessive (*theirs, ours, his, hers, its*), so don't add an apostrophe.
    - In English, we tend not to use the apostrophe to indicate plurals (*tomatoes, banjos, echoes, peaches, beans, 1920s, NGOs, MPs*) – except for single letters, for the sake of clarity (*mind your p's and q's; there are two o's in loose*).
    - To mark contractions: use hasn't, didn't and so on only in informal and semi-formal writing.
- Do not confuse the hyphen, the en-rule (either as a dash or conveying the meaning 'to', 'and', or 'between') and the em-rule (dash). They are not generally interchangeable.

- The hyphen links together the elements of compound words: father-in-law; pre-eminent; peri-urban; re-enter. The hyphen is also necessary to distinguish different meanings:

  Is it true that all the footballers have re-signed/resigned?

  Have you re-covered/recovered your textbook?

- Do not, however, hyphenate phrasal verbs (or prepositional verbs) such as take off, look out, set up and wind up; only their noun forms warrant compounding:

  before *take-off*; he was our *look-out*; the computer *set-up* is easy; the *winding-up* of the company.

- The em-rule or em-dash is always only a dash, but it can have either spaces or no spaces either side of it, depending upon a publisher's or client's house style. It can be used in pairs instead of the parenthetical use of round brackets or commas:

  No future generation of English-speaking folks — for that is the tribunal to which we will appeal — will doubt that we were guiltless.

Alternatively, it can be used as a 'final summary' placed after a list of items:

  The layout, the circut, the components, the materials — all these add up to an entirely new concept for such a piece of equipment.

- The en-rule or en-dash can play the role of a dash (when it is invariably spaced, as in this book) or convey the meaning 'to', 'and' or 'between' (when it is always unspaced):

  1939–1945; pages 29–37; a Labour–Liberal alliance; the Cape–Cairo route; the Jones–Cameron method

  If a hyphen were used in this last case, it would convey a double-barrelled name.

3.2.2 At the end of a sentence

- Exclamation marks are seldom really necessary other than in dialogue. They serve only to indicate the emphasis that accompanies an exclamation as opposed to a statement. Avoid their excessive use – either yours or the author's – and never use more than one at a time. Never combine exclamation and interrogation marks.
- When an ellipsis is used, it should comprise no more than three dots, which should be spaced. Think of the ellipsis as a word: it should have a space to the right of it when it occurs at the start of a sentence; spaces either side of it when it stands for a word or words omitted mid-sentence, and it should have a space to the left of it when it occurs at the end of a quoted passage, thus:

  The author stated that '... in such an event it is ... their responsibility to make good the damage caused by their guests ...'.

The ellipsis can also be used to indicate suspense:

> And the winner is ... Cape Town, South Africa!

It is also used to indicate unfinished statements left dangling in mid-air:

> Unless, of course, he is the adulterer, after all ...

The ellipsis should not be used to indicate an interruption (that is the job of the dash):

> 'Mark, would you please mind –'
> 'I'm not going to!'

- If a complete or independent sentence is between brackets (or parentheses), the full stop should be inside the parentheses.

  > The hand that rocks the cradle rules the roost. (Every married man surely knows this.)

If, on the other hand, a sentence forms part of a 'bigger' sentence, then the full stop should follow the final parenthesis. In such sentences, moreover, the opening parentheses should never be preceded by punctuation.

> The hand that rocks the cradle rules the roost (according to the old saying).

3.2.3 In the middle of a sentence

- The comma is the punctuation mark indicating the least separation or pause, but it is a mark of great importance – and much misused! Incorrect uses include:

  - its use between two independent sentences not linked by a conjunction:

    > We wrote on 12 May asking for an urgent report about the contractor's complaint, this was followed up on 24 May by a telephone call.

    Replace the comma with either a semi-colon or a full point.

  - the use of only one instead of either a pair of commas or none:

    > Against all this must be set considerations which, in our submission are overwhelming.

    Omit the comma.

    > It will be noted that for the development areas, Treasury-financed projects are to be grouped together.

    Either omit the comma or insert one after *that*.

    > The first is the acute shortage that so frequently exists, of suitable premises.

    Omit the comma and move 'of suitable premises' to after 'shortage'.

  - the use of commas with defining or restricting relative (adjective) clauses: or of only one comma instead of a pair with commenting relative clauses;

    > Pilots, whose minds are dull, do not usually live long.

This should surely read:

> Pilots whose minds are dull do not usually live long.

The commas convert a truism into an insult!

> I find that the clerk, who dealt with your enquiry recorded the name of the firm incorrectly.

Omit the comma; the clause is defining. Inserting a comma after 'enquiry' would convert the clause into a commenting one, which is incorrect.

> Motorists who ignore traffic signs, are a menace.

This is a defining relative clause, so omit the comma.

– the insertion of a meaningless comma into an 'absolute phrase':
An absolute phrase (eg 'then, *the work being finished*, we rested') always has parenthetical commas around it. But there is no sense in the comma that so often carelessly appears inside it:

> The House, having passed the third reading by a large majority, the Bill was sent to the President for signature.

The first comma has been incorrectly inserted: it leaves the House waiting for a verb that never comes.

– to mark the end of the subject of a verb, or the beginning of the object:

> The question whether it is ligitimate to use a comma to mark the end of the subject, is an arguable one.

The comma is unnecessary. 'To use commas in this way is a dangerous habit; it encourages a writer to shirk the trouble of so arranging his sentences as to make their meaning plain without punctuation' (*The complete plain words* 1969: 245; Kahn (ed) 1985). The same may be said of the sentence

> I am now in a position to say that all the numerous delegates who have replied, heartily endorse the recommendation.

Omit the comma.

– before a clause beginning with *that*:
Nowadays, the insertion of the comma before *that* having gone out of fashion, in examples such as this it should be omitted:

> The true meaning is so uncertain and remote, that it is never sought.

– before *and* in certain parenthetical constructions:
In the following sentence, the comma is incorrectly placed before *and*:

> It has been found to be unacceptable, and as such, quite impermissible to serve alcohol on beaches.

The comma should be placed after *and*, because it is only *as such* that is parenthetical.

– either between different kinds of adjective or not between adjectives of the same kind. There are two types of adjective: classifying (Russian, triangular, mathematical) and qualitative (kind, quiet, rotund). Series of one type should be separated by commas; do not insert commas between the different types:

> He was a kind, gentle, compassionate man.
> She adored her lively, demanding French poodle.

Gowers (1969: 249; Seely 2007: 7) says of classifying adjectives: 'Where the final adjective is one that describes the species of the noun, it must of course be regarded as part of the noun, and not be preceded by a comma. Thus: "A silly, verbose, pompous official letter."'

– failure to use a comma to avoid ambiguity. Each of these is illustrated below. Consider these sentences – all of which are ambiguous as a result of the omission of a comma – and their remedies:

> The city is now without gas and elecricity and public services are seriously affected.

Insert a comma after *electricity* to avoid the false linking of it with *public services*.

> He contracted a heavy cold followed by penumonia after a night spent out in the open.

Insert commas around *followed by pneumonia*.

> The boy having tripped over the cat fell down the stairs.

Because *having tripped over the cat* separates subject (*boy*) from its verb (*fell*), it must be treated as parenthetical and be enclosed in a pair of commas for the sake of clarity.

– it is incorrect to join two or more complete sentences with commas alone, and without a suitable connecting word or coordinator (*and, but, …*). This very frequent error is known as the *comma splice*:

> I got up late this morning, I didn't have time for breakfast (Blue 2000).

It can be corrected in several ways:

> I got up late this morning. I didn't have time for breakfast.
> I got up late this morning; I didn't have time for breakfast.
> I got up late this morning, so I didn't have time for breakfast.
> I got up late this morning and I didn't have time for breakfast.

• The use of the serial comma (also the list or Oxford comma) is a matter of house style (or publisher's preference). Both of these sentences are correctly punctuated:

> Present at the opening of parliament were Ambassadors, Ministers, Bishops and Judges.
> Present at the opening of parliament were Ambassadors, Ministers, Bishops, and Judges.

Sometimes, however, the comma before *and* may be essential to avoiding ambiguity, as in:

> The company included the Bishops of Winchester, Salisbury, Bristol, and Bath and Wells.

Without the final comma, the reader is left wondering whether one bishop is responsible for Bristol, Bath and Wells or whether there's one for each of the dioceses. In this example, it's at least clear that there are two separate bishops for Bristol and for Bath and Wells.

- When *etcetera* or *etc* occurs at the end of a list, the comma before either is a matter of house style, and therefore optional.

- The colon is used either as an introducer of quoted matter or lists or to precede an explanation or particularisation (or, in the words of Fowler, 'to deliver the goods that have been invoiced in the preceding words' (Birchfield 1999)):

> News reaches a national paper from two sources: the news agencies and its own correspondents.
>
> The frog is a unique creature: it lives in water and on land.

- The semi-colon is used to divide main clauses for effect, and is useful when used as something less than a full stop and more than a comma.
  - It can, for example, be used to mark sharply the antithesis between two sentences:
    > In some cases the executive carries out most of the functions; in others the delegation is much more extensive.
  - It can be used instead of a conjunction:
    > To err is human; to forgive, divine.
    >
    > He is careless; not so Jim.
  - It can be used to separate items in a list when the individual items themselves contain commas:
    > Take the following with you: a clean shirt; a pair of shorts, though not too short; two towels, more if you have them; a thick jersey; a pair of shoes and several pairs of socks, as hard-wearing as possible.

- 'Do not be afraid of the *semi-colon* ... it marks a longer pause, a more definite break in the sense, than the comma; it is a stronger version of the comma' (Gowers 1969: 257–258). It is used to separate clauses having a strong connection with each other that would be broken if they were divided into separate sentences, but which require a slightly stronger connection than that offered by a comma. Looked at a little differently, semicolons are used to show that the second of two independent clauses follows from or is related to the first in a cause-and-effect relationship, or generalisation and example, or statement and response:

It rained all day; by evening the streets were flooded.

Baby giraffes are amazingly tall; their average height is two metres.

The immigrants have been led to believe that houses are easy to come by; however, six months of fruitless searching has convinced them that this is not the case.

Note that in all these examples a conjunction is absent: the semi-colon has taken its place.

• House style will dictate whether single or double inverted commas (or quotation marks, or quotes) are preferred in the first instance and doubles or singles are used within them. Formerly, double inverted commas were the convention, but the modern tendency is to use singles.

– Try not to use one type of inverted comma for quoted matter and another for unusual word usages – follow house style consistently.

– If the quotation is embedded in a sentence and is preceded by a punctuation mark (typically, a comma or a colon), the final punctuation is placed inside the inverted commas. In direct speech, the position of the punctuation relative to the inverted commas will resemble this:

'No,' I replied, 'I am quite used to that.'

'Are you certain?' Susan retorted. 'I've just the remedy for you.'

– Inverted commas should be the '6' orientation before quoted matter and the '9' configuration afterwards. This should be checked, especially at the proof-reading stage.

3.2.4 At the beginning of a sentence

When linking words or phrases introduce a sentence, they should be followed by a comma to separate them from the main clause to ensure transparency. The words or phrases are usually either conjunctions (eg 'however') or adverbs (eg 'alternatively') or prepositional phrases (eg 'in addition', 'on the one hand').

Words that build an argument:

• *Also*, the country's fairly developed infrastructure and robust economy facilitates this entry point into Africa.

• *In addition*, a more pertinent issue that must be evaluated is whether the recent economic boom is sustainable.

• *Moreover*, the country needs to understand how its economic relations with China will impact on its presence.

• *Similarly*, …

• *In conclusion*, …

• *Finally*, the country must remain conscious of its FTA with Europe and the trade deficit that exists between itself and Brussels.

Words that introduce a number of illustrations or examples, or a sequence:
- *First,/In the first place,* … *Second,* … *Third,* … *Finally,* …

Words that introduce the converse of a previous statement or scenario, or an alternative viewpoint:
- *However*, the concern is that South Africa remains a primary exporter of gold and needs to transform this advantage.
- *On the one hand,* … On the other hand, …
- *In contrast,* … (or: *By way of contrast,* …)
- *Alternatively,* …
- *Conversely,* …
- *Nevertheless*, it is still possible for the economy to achieve growth.

Words that indicate time:
- *Meanwhile*, South Africa became the first sub-Saharan African country to be granted approved destination status.
- *In the meantime,* …
- *At the same time*, the automotive industry is another sector that poses a challenge.
- *Simultaneously,* …

Words that clarify or restate differently:
- *In other words*, can the government afford to have another negative trade balance if it is to deliver on its contract with the people in 2014?
- *Expressed differently*, the problems will manifest themselves inevitably.

Others:
- *According to* the WTO, member countries have to comply with its trade and tariff agreements
- *Interestingly*, none of the money is being spent on the development of the textile industry as originally intended.
- *Inevitably*, fresh produce prices must rise after the serious losses that grain and fruit farmers have suffered.
- *Remarkably*, very little damage was caused to the building.

4 Summary and conclusion

This chapter has shown that it is not sufficient for wordsmiths such as text editors to confine themselves to words and words alone, or even to the meanings they convey, important as these elements undoubtedly are. An equally important contributor to the success of verbal communication is the way the text is punctuated, because punctuation both supports and conveys meaning in the written word in ways that largely reflect the manner in which people speak. Texts must also be punctuated consistently so that readers are not left confused by mixed messages.

Equally visible on the printed page are misspellings – a cause of irritation and derision among many readers, who then proceed to call the content of such 'carelessly produced' text into question. For the text editor (also when wearing their proofreader's cap), this entails developing an eagle eye for checking spelling and punctuation down to the finest detail to ensure correctness, coherence and consistency.

The remaining aspects of presentation – typography and layout – are dealt with in the next chapter, the final one under the heading Principles of text editing in practice.

10

Text editing in practice: presentation – visual literacy

Typography is the means by which a written idea is given a visual form.
Ambrose & Harris

Typography may be defined as the craft of ... so arranging the letters, distributing the space and controlling the type so as to aid to the maximum the reader's comprehension of the text.
Stanley Morison

Good design begins with you as the wordsmith. The editing process is part of the design and you, as the editor, are responsible for creating the best copy and for making your copy design-friendly.
Ferreira & Staude

What is printed should be so presented that in no other way will it be as clearly read and comprehended; it should not be ostentatious, either by ugliness or by excessive ornamentation; and it should acknowledge the reader's intelligence and taste ...
Style manual

10

Contents

Objectives

This is the final chapter under the heading of *Principles of text editing in practice*, dealing with the principles of presentation that have been touched upon in the document design section in chapter 2. After having introduced the application of text-editing principles in the areas of text types and content in chapter 6, we moved to text structure and its effect on argumentation in chapter 7, and on wording in chapter 8. Chapter 9 was devoted to spelling and punctuation as important – and obvious – elements of presentation. In this last chapter we (a) provide guidelines, (b) indicate tensions and challenges and (c) provide tips about and insights into how to deal with matters of spelling, punctuation, typography and text layout. We start with the effect of spelling and punctuation on text quality and study how typography and layout aid the reader's understanding of a text. At the end of this chapter we draw together the points discussed on text editing in practice in chapters 6 to 10.

1 Introduction

The accomplished text editor will also have a solid appreciation of the design aspects of documents, whether they be books, journals, magazines, reports or leaflets (cf Felker et al 1981; Kempton & Moore 1994; Maes et al 1999; White 1989: 7–12). Indeed, in some areas of publishing, the editor makes a significant collaborative contribution to the design by surveying the entire manuscript and assembling a set of manuscript pages that represent all the features in the proposed publication: chapter heads, drop caps, body text, text boxes, figures, tables, every level of subhead, special panels, footnotes, and so on. The designer then takes these together when considering an overall design for the book (Flann & Hill 2004: 15, 25; Mackenzie 2011: 62–64), bearing in mind also the subject-matter, the readership, the limitations of the printing process and the budgetary constraints.

2 Visual literacy: typography

> Knowledge of typography, the use of type and white space to convey meaning, is one of the core editorial skills, right up there with language and general knowledge.
> *Mackenzie*

2.1 Important design considerations

Design is important for text quality and communication (cf Tschichold, McLean & Kinross 1998; Walker 2001; Ambrose & Harris 2005; Baines & Haslam 2002; Evans 1974; Felici 2003; Mitchell & Wightman 2005). There are different types of error which result from weak typography and layout:

Visual problems	
Typographical errors	• Font types: roman, bold(face), italic • Typeface (family of fonts): Arial, Verdana, Times New Roman • Font size: point 10, 12 • Typos (typesetter's errors) • Consistency in choices
Layout problems	• Title page • Title • Table of contents • Page numbering • Titles and subtitles • Running title/head ((abbreviated) title at head or foot of each page) • Chapters • Sections • Paragraphs • Numbering • Page layout • Spacing (white space) • Use of colour and shadow • Columns • Margins • Widows (a paragraph last line at beginning of following page) • Orphans (a paragraph opening line or word, or subhead at bottom of page) • Paragraphs: alignment • Paragraphs: justification • Indenting paragraphs • Placement of quotes • Tables and titles • Illustrations • Sketches and photographs • End- and/or footnotes • Appendices • Format of bibliography • Format of index • Format of cross-references • Consistency in choices

Table 10.1 *Text presentation errors*

Document design achieves its purpose when it helps to make a book readable, physically attractive and suited to its particular purpose. Neither the author nor the text editor (nor the reader) should treat the text in isolation, without any consideration of design elements such as the font type and size, the text width, the leading (line spacing), the amount of white space on a page, and the typographical treatment and spacing of different features such as headings, extracts (long quotations), tables and boxes. All of these, in a harmonious whole, contribute to a readable publication or document.

Book design at its best is largely a matter of paying careful attention to minutiae (of type, spacing, etc) and of being a restrained mediator between author and reader precisely by making a book both physically attractive and readable. This is an approach that gives well-designed books their quiet good manners and simplicity.

At one level, the text editor may simply be expected to code the various design features (levels of heading, tables, etc) so that a designer can quickly decide on their typographical treatment. This coding or 'tagging' is also known as a 'production edit', which has become more or less an integral component of a text editor's job description as the nature of 'typesetting' has evolved increasingly towards pure layout since the advent of page make-up software such as InDesign. The designer may then do a detailed electronic typographical markup of the typescript.

Alternatively, or in addition, the designer may provide a typesetting specification (or type spec) for the typesetter to follow (cf Butcher, Drake & Leach 2006: 20–27, 36, 41, 2009; Flann & Hill 2004: 25, 342; Mackenzie 2011: 62–63), using the text editor's coding of the typescript, in the form of 'styles', which the typesetter simply imposes on the text in much the same manner in which MS Word's Styles functions.

Readability is a critically important concept in page makeup and layout. It is essentially a variable of established reading habits: what is easily readable (or legible) varies considerably among nations, changes from one decade to another, and obviously depends even upon the physical age, literacy level and condition of the prospective reader. Readability is an important term associated with reading any text (it is not synonymous with legibility, though it is closely associated with it: an illegible font (too small, all capitals or all italic, or in certain colours, for instance) will affect readability adversely). Moreover, the readability of a page of text is dependent upon several factors that must be considered both individually and collectively when selecting a typeface. These include the:

- texture and finish of the paper
- colour of the ink
- typeface itself
- size of type
- line length
- line spacing, and the width of gutters and margins.

Much about the *ink* on a page is about optics and optical illusion. *Paper* should be opaque (type on one side should not show through to the other) and even-textured so as not to distract the eye or reduce the impact of the ink. For body text, any colour other than black (and possibly deep blue) is unreadable. For text-heavy books, black–white contrast is also a strong contributor to readability.

Type should be set so as to be read with little effort or eyestrain: for most adult readers, a serif font such as Times Roman, Baskerville, Garamond is more suited to body text. For young readers, a sans serif font such as **Arial**, **Franklin Gothic**, **Trebuchet** or Gill Sans in 14 point size and larger is more recognisable, and therefore readable. On the other hand, a good guideline of book design is to use two different type families or typefaces (and possibly more in feature-rich school textbooks) – one for the body text, the other for display elements such as headings and subheadings, table text and the captions for illustrations. The essential concept at play here is contrast: for maximum impact, and to create the greatest interest on a page, ensure that the two fonts chosen have very little in common – yet they must complement each other.

Line length (or width), closely linked to type size, can be another important determinant of readability: the longer the lines of type, the larger the font should be, and vice versa. The eye really struggles to negotiate long lines of body text set in a small font, which tends to convey the message to the brain 'this is hard work, and therefore hard to read'. This is a particular hazard in publications produced to an A4 size, so a larger font, wider margins and a narrower line length, together with blocked paragraphs (a blank line between them, the first line not indented), make for a much more pleasing, inviting page.

Well-proportioned *leading* (line spacing), as well as adequate margins and gutters either between columns or around illustrations and text boxes, is another important contributor to readability: both too little and too much white space between lines of text can reduce ease of reading.

Achieving optimal leading can also be determined by the size of the type. Each document presents a different set of problems, depending on the type used, whether capital letters (or small caps) or lowercase letters are used, how much type there is on a page of a certain size, and so on.

Undoubtedly, the design of a document is influenced by the particular purpose of the volume. Given two manuscripts of the same length, one on economics of predictably limited circulation, say, the other a spy story with a large sales potential, the designer will surely want to handle them quite differently, aside from all considerations of readability and attractiveness.

It is often entirely a matter of taste as to what makes a book physically attractive. Is it the editor's, the designer's, the author's or the sales team's taste that should hold sway? Their various ideas about the look and feel of the end-product must at least be in harmony if an attractive book is to result.

As a go-between, as it were, between author/publisher and reader, the text editor as proofreader should voice their concerns about what is not working for them, either typographically or in terms of the layout of a particular title (Flann & Hill 2004). In multi-featured publications, another challenge facing the text editor is being able to keep track of all the features and deal with each one consistently throughout the manuscript and/or proofs, but also to identify opportunities to turn plain text into a feature such as a list or a table or some other, more readable, graphic alternative.

Whereas it is the designer in whose hands lies the ultimate responsibility for converting the raw materials of manuscript, type, paper, ink, photography and drawing them together in a coherent document of some kind, the text editor can also make a significant contribution by knowing how each of the features of the book needs to be dealt with typographically and to implement them in the manuscript. The text editor as proofreader then needs to read each of the features systematically to ensure that the typesetter has treated them consistently.

Many of the typographical and design principles described here for a print environment apply equally to an onscreen or digital context. Important differences include font style (must be sans serif in a digital environment), text width (narrower columns are more easily read and scanned onscreen, and there is less scrolling), and the use of vertical lists and subheadings to break up continuous text.

2.2 Typographical aspects of text editing

Typography is the process of setting and arranging types and printing from them; it also refers to the style and appearance of printed matter. It is a fundamental aspect of document production that the text editor cannot ignore. So he or she needs to have a good knowledge of and feel for it.

As stated above in this section, the signature of well-designed books is their quiet good manners and simplicity. However, text editors often have to deal with texts that do not pass muster as tools for effective communication, not because of the language or the syntax or the register but simply because they are typographically so ugly or unattractive or confusing that people are put off reading them.

There are several causes of this unsatisfactory state of affairs, including: authors uninitiated into the fundamentals of good typography having too much say in the end-product's appearance or not adopting a reader-centred approach; 'typesetters' who have learnt their craft not from years of contact with master craftsmen but at, say, a three-day beginners' course (and therefore lacking the all-important background knowledge and skills); publications designed by a committee whose members are 'not on the same page' regarding their vision for the look and feel of the title. In such circumstances, those responsible for the choice of type and the layout tend to overlook the simple fact that 'Good documents get us to read them, and when they do so, they communicate'. 'Good', in this context, means both good writing that is well edited (that is, the grammar, style and register are all ship-shape) and good visual design, the latter enhancing the former. As Ferreira & Staude (1991: 63) put it simply: 'Words are written to be read and *good design* helps you get your message across ... Design is therefore graphic communication.' This is particularly true of digital media, where design and functionality are critically important to the success of the user's interaction with a digital interface.

When a typographer (one who sets and arranges types and printing from them (*OED* 11 ed 2006)) tackles a text to design it in such a way that it communicates easily and effectively, he or she considers the overall design of the document, which is based on the use of type as well as the layout (which includes the use of white space, as indicated above). The typography and the page layout of a document must complement and reinforce the subject-matter of the publication; they should make it easier for the reader to unlock the content and meaning of the text.

Typical typographical errors that occur include the inconsistent use of type sizes, typefaces and weights, or variants, of type (eg bold type and italics) and type families (eg Arial, Times New Roman in all their variant forms). On top of these inconsistencies or incorrect usages, typing (or typesetting) errors are an annoying occurrence. These aspects are important to the text editor as proofreader especially, because by rectifying them they are able to contribute to a more attractive, more consistent, more perfect end-product – even though they are not expected to be a typographer or a layout artist themselves, of course (Murphy 2011: 4–5).

2.2.1 Some general typographical conventions

Depending upon the projected age group at which the publication is aimed, and whether the publication is word processed or typeset, different font families may be indicated in the design specification. Typically, these could be:

- A serif font for text-heavy published books and magazines, the body text usually between 10 point and 12 point in size.
- A sans serif font for published works aimed at younger readers (up to, say, age 10–12) and for word-processed documents a body text of usually between 12 point and 16 point in size.
- Shorter quotations embedded in text are set in the same type and size as the body text. For displayed extracts (longer quotations) set apart from the body text, the convention is to use a type size one point smaller than the body text.
- The typeface for chapter titles, subheadings, tabular matter (but often not table captions/ headings) and figure/artwork labels (but not their captions/headings) should contrast

with the body text typeface sufficiently for the difference to be noticeable to the reader. One typeface family should be used for all such features. In the case of a serif body text, it's usually advisable to select a contrasting (but complementary) sans serif typeface.

- The narrower the text or column width, the smaller the typeface and type size should be. Also, the greater the need to left justify text rather than (fill) justify it. The reason for this is that justified text in a narrow width text leads to two undesirable outcomes: lines of text with very wide word spaces and so-called 'rivers of white' running down pages (especially if word division (or hyphenation) is not permitted); and/or a host of word divisions at the end of lines, if word division is permitted. (See section 2.2.2.4 below.)
- It is widely held that left justified (and ragged right) text is much more readable than justified text on a narrow measure (line length). This is because practised readers do not read letter by letter or word by word but by recognising the visual pattern made by several words at a time, simultaneously absorbing whole phrases and short sentences. If too much space is inserted between words, this pattern is destroyed and reading becomes slower. On the other hand, if the space between words is too small, one word will appear to run into the next, again affecting legibility and readability.
- For footnotes and endnotes, it is usual to select a typeface two points smaller than the body text typeface, usually somewhere between 7 point and 9 point.
- Running heads and footers should be set in the same font as the body text, or at least one that's sympathetic to it. Running heads are usually set in uniform SMALL CAPS (Butcher et al 2006: 210, 2009).

2.2.2 Specific typographical conventions

2.2.2.1 For extracts (longer quotations)

Extracts from other sources cited by the author should be treated in a special way to differentiate them from the body text or the author's own words. They are usually displayed (that is, set apart from the body text), with the quoted text being indented (either left or both left and right, depending on the publisher's house style) and a blank line being inserted above and below the extract. It is usually a matter of individual choice whether displayed extracts are set between quotation marks or not. If they are, the use of singles or doubles will be determined by house style. In extracts that comprise more than one paragraph, only the final paragraph ends in a close quotation mark; each paragraph should start with an open quotation mark, if that is house style; otherwise not.

Italic type should be avoided for long extracts, because it tends to be much less readable than roman (ie upright) text.

If a footnote number is attached to quoted matter, its position should always be *after* the final punctuation – whether that's a full stop, a semicolon or colon, or close quotation marks. The only time a footnote number would precede a close parenthesis or a close dash is when the note refers specifically to what is between the parentheses or dashes.

2.2.2.2 For vertical lists

Generally, if the bulleted items run on grammatically from the lead-in (or introductory) sentence, they should commence with a lowercase letter and terminate in a semicolon (or no punctuation – again, house style will prevail). If, however, each bulleted item is a complete, standalone sentence, then they should all start with an uppercase letter and terminate in a full stop. Really short items (one word or a brief phrase) should start with a lowercase letter and not terminate in punctuation at all – except, perhaps, the final bullet.

Do we number or bullet the listed items? Number them only when a sequence of steps is indicated or the reader is required to remember the number of items. Where neither of these requirements exists, use bullets instead.

Onscreen, lists should be short and simple to minimise scrolling; it may be better to present some of the information in the list by means of hyperlinks (Mackenzie 2011: 111).

2.2.2.3 For tabular matter

We live in an age where readers prefer to digest and recall information in graphic or visual form far more than as mere text. The text editor should therefore approach texts from a much more 'visual' perspective and, accordingly, seek out opportunities for converting text to vertical lists, tables or graphics (such as bar graphs and pie charts) wherever appropriate.

The components of tables to consider here are:

Type size/-face Usually one point size down from the body text, and possibly a contrasting typeface from that of the body text that is also clear and easily readable.

Heading Must be set above the table, so as not to compete with source and note information, which is placed below the table. In works with a large number of tables, they should preferably be numbered per chapter (eg Table 3.1, Table 3.2) rather than throughout the text. 'Table' should be either upper and lower case or caps and small caps; either roman/regular or bold type. Headings should either consistently end in a full stop or not.

Column heads These signal to the reader the content of each column and should be brief and pithy. If two levels, the lower level is usually italic, the upper level bold – either left aligned or centred. To ensure consistency within and between tables, column heads should not take their cue from the alignment of the data, but be uniformly aligned. If a third level is necessary, it should be bold italic. Follow the minimum caps/sentence case style. All column heads should be aligned from the top of a cell down, not from the bottom up. Units (such as ($), (000s)) should be given as such in a column head, not repeated in the data section of a table.

Side heads	Side heads (to the left of each row) should be left aligned and usually neither bolded nor italicised.
Column data	Alignment and capitalisation are the main issues here. Words should be either left aligned or centred and min caps/sentence case style should be followed. The alignment of numerals will be determined largely by their nature: whole numbers should be right aligned as an entire column, then centred using the widest number as one's guide; amounts involving decimals should be decimal (or right) aligned, then centred as a column on the widest number. Use initial capitals or lowercase consistently throughout all the tables in one document.
Rules	Minimise the use of vertical and horizontal rules in tables (use MS Word's Borders function to do this). Try to limit the horizontal rules to those above and below the column heads, and below the last row of the table. Vertical rules should be regarded as largely unnecessary clutter. Use shading (tints) carefully – they should not be so heavy as to compete with the text, rendering it unreadable.
Source(s)	These should be set immediately below a table, left aligned, the word 'Source:' usually in italic type. Type size is usually one point down from the table text size.
Note(s)	In the table itself, any data worth noting should have a lowercase superscript a, b, c, etc attached to it. Especially if the body text is footnoted (using 1, 2, 3, etc), using a different noting notation in tables is imperative. The notes are then listed below the table and the source(s) under their own heading 'Notes:'.

2.2.2.4 For figures and other graphics

Captions and labels require special treatment in figures and graphics. First, they should be typeset in a font that contrasts with the body text font (usually sans serif). The labels are usually set a typesize down from the caption font size or the body text size.

To aid readability, labels should preferably be set horizontally rather than at angles to the horizontal. As far as possible, they should also be distributed evenly to the left and right of the illustration or graphic. Any pointer lines between illustration and label should not pass over the width of the illustration; rather move the label to the opposite side of the illustration.

2.2 2 5 For word division

In typesetting justified text it is sometimes necessary to break a word at the end of a line because there is not sufficient space for the whole word, and to take it onto the next line would result in excessive spacing between the remaining words in the line. Although words should not be divided unnecessarily, some division is unavoidable, especially when the measure (or line length) is narrow (Waite (ed) 2005: ix–xi).

The division of words should follow certain rules of sound and sense. As far as possible, the part of the word before the hyphen at the end of the line should suggest the remainder of a word, so that the reader's thought is carried on logically without the interruption that the divided word would otherwise cause.

The following general rules should be observed when dividing words in English:

List 10.1 Some general rules for word division

> › Do not break words of one syllable: *wound, salt, thought.*

> › Do not break short words of two syllables unless a narrow measure makes this unavoidable: *never, eldest, sudden.*

> › Do not make a break which would result in fewer than three letters being carried over to the next line – or fewer than three letters being left behind.

> › Derivatives break where the root word ordinarily would be divided, or before the prefix or suffix: *know-ledge-able*; *rest-less-ness.*

> › Hyphenated words: words such as after-party can be divided at the hyphen under almost any circumstances. Take care, then, that it is not assumed to be a solid word (eg *re-sent* vs *resent*). Should it be necessary or unavoidable to divide hyphenated words at points other than the hyphen, there should generally be at least six letters after the hyphen: *self-govern-ment*; *self-seeded* should not be divided before -*ed*. Take care not to produce an unacceptably obtrusive or misleading result in the process: *cot-ton-picking.*

> › Where possible, the part of the word carried over should begin with a consonant rather than a vowel: *fic/tion, not fict/ion; regu/late, not reg/ulate.* But this rule should not be applied where to do so would mislead the reader: *draw/lings, not dra/wings.*

> › The two divisions should not lead to the creation (misleadingly) of two new words or a misunderstanding of the first part of the word: *leaden, leg-end, pis-ton*; 'lead' could be either *leed* or *led* when read in isolation.

> › Divide between two consonants when they occur together between vowels: *pic/ture; plat/form.*

>>

› When a word has double consonants, place the break between them: *admit/tance*; *transmis/sion* (unless the consonants are part of the same root: *tell/ing*; *pass/ing*).

› Divide a word after a prefix: *proto/type*; *sub/ject*; *uni/lateral*.

› Avoid as far as possible dividing off prefixes and suffixes (or word parts) of fewer than three characters, and then only if the word is of at least six letters:
> -ed and -ing:
> Permissible: *part-ing*, *calm-ing*
> Impermissible: *part-ed*, *end-ed*, *calm-ed* (one syllable); *buy-ing*
>
> -er and -est:
> Permissible: *calm-est*, *short-est*
> Impermissible: *odd-er*, *dry-er*

› Avoid hyphenation in more than two successive lines.

› Avoid breaking a figure or separating it from its associated word or symbol: 30,000; 100 km; 17 June (but a break between month and year is permissible). In MS Word, inserting a non-breaking space instead of a normal 'soft' space prevents such breaks occurring (press Shift+Ctrl+Spacebar).

› Avoid breaking abbreviations and acronyms: *UNICEF*, *Dept*, *Unisa*.

› Avoid splitting a person's name and initials, or the initials themselves.

› Personal names: some writers and typesetters prefer not to divide personal names at all. Advice: follow house style.

3 Visual literacy: text layout

> Good layout relaxes a reader's mind: New paragraphs make text orderly and digestible; in lists, consistent organization allows the reader to know the order of things; and dependable alignment creates a subconscious trust on the reader's part.
> *Gilad*

> … apart from visual design elements, one can also get creative with the layout of the site – its structure and the way the information is presented and communicated.
> *Vitaly Friedman*

> Use as much white space as you can afford to use. It minimizes distraction and draws attention to what matters most.
> *NAA Ad elements study*

3.1 Making text more visual (visualisation)

We live in a visual age where, for many people, the less reading that has to be done, the better. The popularity of picture-led magazines, website 'scanning' habits and handheld devices are to some extent responsible for this phenomenon. So text editors should be helping authors (who, as skilled users of words, naturally think in words, sentences and paragraphs to communicate their messages) to present their information more visually, parcelling it up in neat, easily digestible 'packages' and giving strong clues as to the content along the way (cf Delin, Bateman & Allen 2002; Evans 1974; Hazelton 2009). This approach has become especially critical in digital environments.

Also, in a visual age it has become all the more important that what is printed should be easily and clearly read and comprehended. Achieving these ends requires the text editor to think laterally about the manuscript before them: about logical structuring of information; about applying the principle of parallelism to similar features in chapters (subheadings, tables and figures, exercises, and quoted matter, for instance); about converting text into vertical lists and either tables or graphical devices (such as pie charts, graphs and spider-grams or mind-maps).

The layout of text on a page helps to make the information on it accessible to the reader. It is a broad but cardinal function/purpose of any process of preparing a manuscript and it takes special expertise to do it well though this does not mean that the text editor has to be a typographer or a page layout artist; but a knowledge of the facets that could have an impact on the outcome (in particular those related to the design and page layout) could help them make a meaningful contribution to a more polished editing process and end product.

3.1.1 The process of visualisation

The text editor's involvement in this process often begins when they're asked to supply a set of manuscript pages on which the different features of the document occur: chapter titles, headings and subheadings, body text, bulleted lists, graphics and their captions and labels, figures and tables and their heads, displayed quotations, footnotes or endnotes, and so on. They should be selecting examples of the shortest and longest chapter titles, for example, and the shortest and longest headings and subheadings, to give the designer a good idea of the typefaces and type sizes that will work for a particular document and page design. These various features will then be incorporated into the design specification for the publication – the blueprint for the printed or web-based work (see Brinck, Gergle & Wood 2002).

Once the design specification has been signed off (including by the author), it becomes the text editor's task to implement all the specifications in the manuscript so that what the typesetter produces as proofs (having applied the Styles for the particular document) is true to the design specification. In this regard, the typographical and layout aspects of textbook editing, setting and proofreading are particularly challenging, because of the large number of features typical of this genre. The only way to ensure consistency is to edit each feature separately in one pass (over and above editing the text as a whole). This places a heavy burden on the text editor, particularly when deadlines are already tight.

3.1.2 Text editors as systematic proofreaders

The text editor should check – and edit – as many of the following aspects as possible at manuscript stage. Then, once the text has been typeset into laid-out pages, their task as proofreader begins, and the following details need to be checked carefully and systematically in several passes through a set of proofs:

Checklist 10.1 Details a proofreader should check

Preliminary pages

Title page
✓ Check that the title is the latest and that it mirrors the title on the cover and on all the left-hand (verso) pages.
✓ Ensure correct spelling of the author's or authors' names, and that either first names or initials (as preferred) are reflected there. They should also mirror what's on the cover, the spine and the back cover.
✓ Ensure that the correct publisher's imprint has been inserted.

Imprint page
✓ Check that the correct month and year are given as the publication date and that the copyright holder(s) is correctly cited.
✓ Is the ISBN correct?

Table of contents
✓ Does it reflect the actual page proofs exactly? Update the contents list in line with the edited and typeset proofs – checking both wording and page numbers.
✓ It should be laid out clearly and pleasantly, and should be as detailed as possible. It should be an accurate chronological road map of the book's content.

Foreword
✓ Is the wordcorrectly spelt? Is the author's name correct? Has the date been updated?

List of abbreviations
✓ Check that the alphabetical order of abbreviations is correct. Run a random check to confirm both that all those listed are in the text and that any in the text have not been omitted.

Part titles
✓ If there are meant to be part titles interspersed between groups of chapters, check that they are in place. Check, also, that they are included in the page count (usually two pages per part title, including the blank verso).

>>

Text pages

Headers and footers
✓ Left-hand (verso) pages usually show the book title or the section title; right-hand (recto) pages usually display the current chapter title. Check every chapter's headers and footers, because copying and pasting often leads to previous chapters' headers appearing incorrectly.
✓ Footers usually comprise a folio (page number). Check that every page that ought to have a page number on it does have one; in the same format; the same type size; to the same alignment (left, centred or right); and that the sequence of folios is consecutive. (Chapters are often set up as discrete documents, and typesetters sometimes forget to reset the start number correctly.) Remember that the text proper always starts on page (Arabic) 1; the end-matter pagination simply continues where the last page of the text left off. The preliminary pages are numbered from (Roman) i (to, say, xvi) so as not to upset the pagination of the text itself. The only pages in the preliminaries to carry folios are those with readable text (Foreword, Preface, Introduction, Acknowledgements, Contents).
✓ Check that the other pages (title, imprint, dedication) do not have folios on them but that they are in the correct sequence.

Page depth
✓ Ensure that, where required, every page ends with the last line at the same position (say the 38th line). Mathematics and science texts are exceptions, as are heavily illustrated texts, where 'floating' page depths are permitted, for practical reasons; heavily footnoted texts are another exception.

Page layout
✓ Do the different elements (text, illustrations, headings, captions) fit together as a balanced whole, especially if a publication has been designed to double-page spreads (DPSs)?

Chapter titles
✓ Are they all in the same display type and size, aligned the same, numbered correctly (in sequence)? Is the white space (the 'drop') below them the same in every chapter (ie does line 1 of the body text start at the same point throughout the chapter)?

Leading (line spacing)
✓ Is the leading constant and consistent within and between chapters for each different feature?
✓ Spacing before and after tables and figures: Is it uniform (usually one blank line)? Is the white space around photographs and other artwork sufficiently wide so as not to make the page appear cramped?

Paragraphing
✓ This should be consistently one style only: either blocked and spaced or first line indented (except the first line of a chapter or below a subhead) and unspaced.

Displayed quotations
✓ These should be consistently downsized and indented (either from the left, or from

left and right). There should be a blank line space above and below each displayed quotation. Quotation marks should be consistently either in or out.

Quotation marks
✓ Check that either double quotes or singles are consistently used throughout.

Tables
✓ Tables should be placed as closely as possible after the text that describes them. If possible, try not to allow a table to break between pages, especially not between a right-hand followed by a left-hand page. Tables that have to be split should have the column heads repeated above the second part; at the foot of the first part there should be an indication that the balance of the table follows overleaf.
✓ If a table is too wide in portrait format, it should be landscaped (turned 45 degrees to the left). No other text (other than a caption or heading, perhaps, should appear on the landscape page). Usually no header or footer appears on such a turned page.
✓ Numbering of tables/figures: check that the numbering is sequential per chapter, and that heads are consistently treated throughout (eg alignment, final full stop).

Bullets/numbers
✓ In vertical lists, are the bullets the same size throughout? Are the numbers sequential? Is the space between bullets/numbers and text uniform throughout? Are the turnover lines correctly aligned?

Captions
✓ Check that the correct caption appears alongside an illustration, and that the caption refers correctly to the subject of the illustration (eg 'the man on the left' is actually on the right in the illustration).

Diagram labels
✓ The font should be uniform in style and size, and either in minimal caps or significant caps style.

Word divisions
✓ In justified text, are the divisions correct? If there are more than two in succession, it's usually best to try to eliminate the middle one to remove the problem.

Cross-references
✓ In first proofs highlight these in the text for future reference (**000** or **XXX**); in second and third proofs keep checking that the cross-references to page numbers and figure/table numbers are correct. These can never be checked frequently enough (especially 'on the facing page', 'on page 39', 'below', and so on).

Footnotes/endnotes
✓ Is the numbering system consistent; are all the footnotes in place; do the numbers correspond exactly to the notes attached to them? Are the numbers all superscripted?

References
✓ Is one system/style used consistently: eg Harvard, AMA, short title?
✓ Are authors' names spelt correctly/consistently?

>>

✓ Are publication dates correct, and do they agree with the information in the bibliography/list of references?

✓ Is there consistently a space after colons (or no space at all)?

House style

✓ Check to see whether the editor's house style decisions have been consistently implemented throughout.

Widows and orphans[1]

✓ Watch out for these in one separate pass of the proofs (otherwise you're bound to miss a couple) and edit them out as necessary.

End-matter

Glossary

✓ Check the alphabetical order of the entries. That the headwords are all bolded or italicised consistently, and that they either start with an initial capital or are lowercase throughout.

✓ Check that the glosses are all punctuated correctly and start with either a capital letter or with lowercase.

Bibliography

✓ Is it a full Bibliography or simply a List of References (ie only those works cited in the present text)? Check that the authors are correctly sequenced alphabetically, or alphabetically and then in date order (in the case of several works published by one author in the same year).

✓ Check the punctuation throughout carefully and systematically (especially full stops). Is 'and' or '&' used consistently for joint authors? And (ed.) but (eds), where the house style is to include full stops with abbreviations?

List of authors

✓ The authors' names should be in the correct alphabetical order, at the very least.

Index

✓ Check the alphabetical order of both headwords and subentries/subcategories very carefully.

✓ Check that commas and spaces are correctly inserted between locators (page numbers).

✓ Check that subentries are correctly indented below headwords. If italics and/or bold are used to indicate folios on which illustrations occur, is an explanation included below the title 'Index'?

✓ Check that lists of subentries are broken usefully, not badly, between columns.

✓ Spot check locators to ensure that the index is an accurate reflection of the location of the topics in the pages (you must have a set of the latest page proofs to hand when you proofread an index – otherwise it's impossible to do the job thoroughly).

---

[1] Widows are the last line of a paragraph at the top of a page; orphans are the first line of text, or a subheading, separated at the bottom of a page from the remainder of the paragraph. Widows are also the very short last lines of paragraphs.

3.2 Layout aspects of text editing

Layout helps the reader to access the information on a page. It is a comprehensive and important task in the preparation of a manuscript that requires specific skills. Of course, a text editor does not have to be a layout specialist, but a knowledge of the processes involved in typography and layout will help to round off the editing process. The following checklist will ensure that no aspects are forgotten in the course of the editing process:

Checklist 10.2 Typography and layout checklist

Typography and layout checklist

Preliminary pages
✓ Do the details on the title page mirror those on the cover: font and layout of title, authors' names, imprint?
✓ Does each component start on a right-hand page, where required?
✓ Is the contents list clearly laid out, broken well between pages, leaders correctly aligned?
✓ Do the page numbers in the contents list correspond to the pagination of the latest set of proofs?
✓ Are Foreword, Preface and other titles in the same font and format as the chapter titles?
✓ Are the pages correctly folioed (or blind folioed)?
✓ Is the body text font in the preliminary matter consistent with that of the text itself?

Footnotes/endnotes
✓ Is a consistent font, downsize from the body text used for all footnotes and endnotes?
✓ Are the note numbers all superscripted?
✓ Do any two notes have the same number?

Pagination and folios
✓ Do the chapters all begin on a new page (right-hand if part of the design; left-hand if chapter openers are double-page spreads)?
✓ Is there a header and a folio on every page?
✓ Do page numbers follow in the correct sequence?
✓ Are the headers and page numbers throughout given in the same font and manner and are they consistently aligned (left, centred, right; in header or footer)?
✓ Are the running heads or footers consistently in the same format? Rectos and versos different? Correct headers/footer for each chapter?

Structure: chapter heads and subheads
✓ Are the chapter numbers preceded by 'Chapter' or not? Are they in the same font style and size throughout?
✓ Are chapter heads in the same font, same size, same alignment?
✓ Is there the same amount of white space (drop) between chapter heads and first line of body text?
✓ Author attributions: are they in a consistent style using the same footnoting device?

>>

✓ Does the first line of the body text start at the same point in each chapter?
✓ Are there part or section title pages; and do they fall on right-hand pages followed by blank versos? Are they blind folioed?
✓ Are the type style and type size for heads and subheads the same throughout?
✓ Are heads and subheads clearly distinguished?
✓ Are bullets for list items consistently the correct size and style?
✓ Do chapters open on new pages (or recto pages, if desired)?
✓ Are the running heads and footers formatted and justified consistently?
✓ Have widows and orphans been eliminated (at proofreading)?

Illustrations and tables
✓ Have tables been placed in the correct position on each page, especially in relation to the relevant text?
✓ Have illustrations been consistently left aligned or centred?
✓ Are sketches and photographs correctly positioned, and the right way round?
✓ Have the tables, illustrations, sketches and photographs been broken in an acceptable manner?
✓ Are the tables, illustrations, sketches and photographs accompanied by captions in the correct positions?
✓ Have the captions been formatted and placed consistently?
✓ Are the labels for figures and tables in a consistent font style and size, and alignment?
✓ Are the column heads in tables in a consistent font style and size, and alignment?
✓ When shading is used in figures and tables, are the percentages consistent?

Body text (both text editing and proofreading)
✓ Is the page layout and appearance clear?
✓ Is the text justified or ragged right?
✓ Are the word breaks/divisions correct?
✓ Are paragraphs indented or blocked?
✓ Is the leading (line spacing) correct and consistent?
✓ Have all orphans been eliminated (at proofreading)?
✓ Have all widows been eliminated (at proofreading)?
✓ Is the spacing (above subheads, between paragraphs, around lists and displayed quotations, and around illustrations) even and consistent?
✓ Is italics used minimally/meaningfully and consistently?
✓ Is bold used minimally/meaningfully and consistently?
✓ Has underlining been eliminated, or used very sparingly/specifically?
✓ Is the use of different forms of emphasis restrained? Is bold italic used effectively?
✓ Is displayed quoted matter treated consistently throughout?
✓ Is embedded quoted matter treated consistently throughout?
✓ Are intext examples, exercises and case studies treated in the same way throughout?
✓ Are those sections that should be highlighted by means of colour or shading all correctly and consistently highlighted?
✓ Are all rules and frames of a consistent weight?

Checklist 10.2 continued

End-matter: references and bibliography; index

✓ Does the end-matter start on the correct page number? Does each part of the end-matter start on a right-hand page, or should they simply flow?

✓ Are all the heads (Bibliography, Index, etc) treated typographically as chapter heads?

✓ Are all references/sources treated in the same manner?

✓ Are the turnover lines all indented consistently?

✓ For the given discipline/subject-matter, has the bibliography been set out correctly?

✓ Are the font styles correctly applied to the different elements of the references (eg roman, italic)?

✓ Is the spacing in the bibliography consistent?

✓ Is the index in the correct font, column width and number of columns?

✓ Are the alphabetical letters preceding each alphabetical section all in place and in the correct typeface? Is the spacing between alphabetical sections consistent?

✓ Are the headwords in the correct alphabetical order, and either all taking an initial uppercase, or only proper nouns?

✓ Are the subentries/subcategories correctly/uniformly indented?

✓ Where lists of subentries/subcategories run over more than one column, is their headword repeated at the head of the next column?

✓ Are turnover lines (of long lists of locators) correctly indented, so as not to line up with either headwords or subentries/subcategories?

✓ Are lists of locators correctly spaced and punctuated, including commas between them and en-rules for page ranges?

✓ Are cross-references (see, see also) correctly italicised?

✓ Do the columns on the last page end evenly (or as evenly as possible)?

It is possible to amend this checklist to suit your own needs or the nature of the text editing and proofreading work you do – you are encouraged to do so to make the task of checking manuscripts and proofs easier for yourself. We hope that this checklist makes your task as text editor and proofreader much easier – and more watertight. Your reputation as a text editor could depend upon it.

4 Summary and conclusion

In this chapter we showed in more detail how typography and layout contribute to text quality and to more effective communication. An inventory of visual problems led to an overview of general and specific typographical considerations and conventions. The second part of the chapter described how a text can be made more visual. It was further explained how a knowledge of the process of laying out text, together with typography, can support the editor's work.

5 Overall summary and conclusion for text editing in practice

In chapters 6 through to 10, we have tried to come closer to the practice of text editing. During education and training the editor will be confronted with many topics that have to be mastered, but en route theory and practice will start to merge. This is why these chapters were devoted to the application of knowledge and the means that are required to facilitate the day-to-day life of a text editor. We hope that we have succeeded in showing that theory and practice are merely two sides of the same coin.

11

Resources

In the 1890s, a proofreader at the University of Chicago Press prepared a single sheet of typographic fundamentals intended as a guide for the University community. That sheet grew into the *Chicago manual of style*, an essential reference for authors, editors, and publishers in any field.

… editors have enough reasons to reject your work; don't let sloppy inconsistencies be one of them.
The New York Times manual of style & usage

Who can exhaust a man? Who knows a man's resources?
Jean-Paul Sartre

11

Contents

Objectives

In this chapter we present the main resources which a text editor can rely on. First, standards for editing practice are described. Next, different general and specific tools for text editing are introduced. A large number of extremely useful references are available electronically. These vary from spell-checkers to grammar- and style-checkers to CD-ROM and internet editions of dictionaries. Because of the dynamic nature of the electronic environment, this market segment is experiencing exceptionally strong growth, with the result that new materials are constantly becoming available, and the serious text editor will have to keep a lookout for them. The chapter concludes with some reflections on how to refer to sources.

1 Standards for editing practice, and editing practice generally

The resources listed immediately below have to do with the standards which professional associations in English-speaking countries have set for practitioners to aspire to and work towards, as a guide to employers and clients as to the standard of workmanship they can expect of text editors. Also included in this list are the textbooks and guides that deal with text editing and what it means to be a text editor more generally. (A section later in this chapter headed 'In practice' contains a selection of more practically oriented publications aimed at text editors.)

Australia:
- *Australian standards for editing practice,* compiled by the Council of Australian Societies of Editors 2001. Revised edition published in 2011 by the Institute of Professional Editors (IPEd). <www.iped-editors.org>.
- Flann, E & B Hill 2004. *The Australian editing handbook* (2 ed). Milton: Wiley & Sons Australia.
- Mackenzie, J 2011. *The editor's companion.* Cambridge University Press.
- Manning Murphy, E 2011. *Working words.* Canberra Society of Editors.
- McMurrey, DA 2004. *Online technical writing: Power-revision techniques – sentence-level revision.* <www.io.com/~hcexres/textbook>.
- McMurrey, DA. McMurry newsletters. *Copyediting: Because language matters.* Bimonthly newsletter. <http://wwwcopyediting.com>.
- Sabto, M 2003. *The on-screen editing handbook.* Melbourne: Tertiary Press.
- Canberra Society of Editors Commissioning Checklist 2009. <www.editorscanberra.org/?s =commissioning+checklist>.

Canada:
- Editors' Association of Canada/Association Canadienne des Révisieurs. <http://www.editors.ca/>.
- Editors' Association of Canada/Association Canadienne des Révisieurs 2009. *Professional editorial standards.*
- Editors' Association of Canada/Association Canadienne des Révisieurs 2010–2011. *Meeting professional editorial standards* (4 vols).
- Editors' Association of Canada/Association Canadienne des Révisieurs 2011. *So You want to be an editor: Information about a career in editing.*

United Kingdom:
- The Society for Editors and Proofreaders. <http://www.sfep.org.uk/>.
- Butcher, J; C Drake & M Leach 2009. *Butcher's copy-editing* (4 ed). Cambridge: Cambridge University Press.

United States:
- The American Copy Editors Society. <http://www.copydesk.org>.
- Editorial Freelancers Association. <http: //www.the-efa.org/>.
- *Copyediting: Because language matters.* Bimonthly newsletter published by McMurry newsletters. <http://wwwcopyediting.com>.
- EEI Communications Staff 1996. 'Estimating editorial tasks: A five-step method' In *Stet again! More tricks of the trade for publications people; selections from 'The Editorial Eye'* 279–281. Alexandria, VA: EEI Press.
- Einsohn, A 2011. *The copyeditor's handbook: A guide for book publishing and corporate communications* (5 ed). Berkeley: University of California Press; also at <http://copyedit.ucpress.edu>.
- Northwest Independent Editors Guild. *Experienced editors wisdom.* <http://edsguild.org/wisdom.htm>.
- Gross, G (ed) 1993. *Editors on editing: what writers need to know about what editors do* (3 ed). New York: Grove.
- Hart, G. *Effective on-screen editing.* <http://www.geoff-hart.com>.
- Judd, K 2001. *Copyediting: A practical guide* (3 ed). Menlo Park, CA: Crisp Learning.
- Plotnik, A 1982. *The elements of editing: A modern guide for editors and journalists.* New York: Collier/Macmillan.
- Ross-Larsen, B 1996. *Edit yourself: A manual for everyone who works with words.* New York: WW Norton & Co.
- Saller, CF 2009. *The subversive copy editor: Advice from Chicago.* Chicago & London: University of Chicago Press.
- Sharpe, LT & I Gunther 1994. *Editing fact and fiction: A concise guide to book editing.* Cambridge: Cambridge University Press.
- Myers Stainton, E 2002. *The fine art of copyediting* (2 ed). New York: Columbia University Press.

- Tarutz, JA 1992. *Technical editing: The practical guide for editors and writers.* Reading, MA: Addison-Wesley.
- Walsh, B (since 1995) *The slot.* <http//www.theslot.com>.

2 Tools facilitating text editing

Copyeditors buy reference books the way some people buy clothes or compact discs. Although you needn't rival your local library branch with your collection, *certain reference books are absolutely indispensible,* and others, according to the kind of copyediting you do, may be desirable or have specific uses.
Judd

Every craft or profession requires tools.
Landers

... my bookshelves contain classics by authors including Strunk and White, Gowers, Fowler and the like, editing handbooks by Butcher, Flann and Hill, Mackenzie and others, grammar and style books. This doesn't mean that the beginning editor should go on a shopping spree, but do own the essentials and do refer to them while editing.
Murphy

2.1 The usefulness of tools

It should be obvious that practitioners need to have at their disposal and make use of a diverse range of tools to check language usage, just as any other professionals find the tools of their trade indispensable. These form the subject-matter of this chapter.

No one possesses a complete knowledge of a language (thanks, largely, to a limited memory), and so in order to use language well or to improve their usage of it they have to use sources with ease. It therefore makes sense to focus on accumulating a knowledge of the kinds of tool available and where to find them when you need them. There is in fact a tool available for every type of problem, in the form of dictionaries, encyclopaedias, language guides and textbooks as well as online sources on the Web.

Landers (2001: 171–172) warns against arrogance when using references: if there's one thing that text editors (and language practitioners generally) have in common, it is the realisation that they don't monopolise wisdom and that they therefore have to take the trouble to acquire and use reliable reference materials:

If we are honest with ourselves, we are constantly reminded how inadequate our final product is, how far from perfection our best efforts leave us. While a library full of reference works will not make one into a (translator), a decent respect for our own limitations obliges us *to equip ourselves with the best possible tools to exercise our profession.*

We practitioners all have so much to learn and a modicum of modesty will lead us to seek the best possible support (that is, references that will supplement our limited knowledge and also enable us to check texts) in resolving problems that arise during the editing process. This is precisely why one can claim that text editors' training is never complete: and why they should place more emphasis on ongoing training, keeping abreast of the latest developments both in language usage and in the world around us (including technological change). A well-rounded text editor should read widely: newspapers, advertising billboards, specialist magazines and journals and internet sites in order to build up their vocabulary and to remain abreast of new words acquired by or introduced into a language.

Text editors also have to be aware that (1) a single reference seldom provides adequate answers to problems or (2) that there is usually not only one correct answer to a question (Einsohn 2005: xii). This means that practitioners should consult more than one reference work, that sometimes conflicting opinions regarding an answer have to be weighed up one against the other and that practitioners have to be able to make an informed and deliberate decisions about when to apply, adapt or ignore conventions and rules. This is a skill that has to be acquired, so be receptive to the suggestions of new sources, including this one.

The next question is this: what kinds of reference work should an English-speaking text editor have at their disposal? In practice, the following should be regarded as a minimum (Einsohn 2011; Murphy 2011: 19):

List 11.1 Minimal references required for text editing

> › Good mid-range to upper-range dictionaries: both explanatory/defining and, in multilingual Europe and South Africa, translating types; either reflecting US English or UK English; either printed, on CD-ROM or online (the latter two for ease of access and for being more up to date).

> › Appropriate subject-specific dictionaries: medicine, law, finance and accounting, banking, psychology, geography, electronics, and so on.

> › At least two good, recent language usage guides.

> › A reliable language textbook that will help to resolve problems of a grammatical nature.

> › A thesaurus or synonym dictionary, or reverse dictionary.

> › Access to internet-based sources (dictionaries, thesauruses, encyclopaedias, lists of abbreviations and acronyms).

> › The style guide of the particular institution/client, if they have one, supplemented by the *New Oxford dictionary for writers and editors,* the *Penguin dictionary for writers and editors* or the *Collins dictionary for writers and editors* (for publications that follow UK English conventions) or the *Chicago manual of style* or *Words into type* (for publications that follow US English conventions).

In the sections that follow we explore the various tools briefly and provide examples of each of them.

2.2 The abundance of tools

There is a wealth of English-language reference works that cover virtually every facet of the text editor's intervention in authors' documents. Whereas many of them are still available as printed publications (and some of the classics are even out of print, available only secondhand with difficulty), yet others are also available in digital format. Both formats can be purchased on the internet, through online bookstores such as Amazon.com (www.amazon.com), Foyles (www.foyles.co.uk), Waterstones.com (www.waterstones.com/waterstonesweb).

It is true that some of the references have become dated to varying degrees – which affects their validity and reliability – particularly in the modern, technologically driven period that is the twenty-first century (think of the plural of mouse: until the 1980s it was indubitably mice; but since the invention of the now-ubiquitous electronic device associated with PCs and laptops, mouses has come into use as an alternative plural form). In what follows, we survey some of the categories of reference work that should prove to be indispensable to text editors and other language practitioners.

2.3 Dictionaries

> A good dictionary does not necessarily contain an abundance of abstruse words that nobody ever comes across: it must contain those words that you are looking for.
> *Andries*

> Copyeditors working for book and journal publishers must also have access to a recent edition of a good unabridged dictionary – and must always keep this volume to hand.
> *Einsohn*

A wide variety of dictionaries are available for editors of English texts: unilingual, bilingual and multilingual; unilingual explanatory/descriptive dictionaries and translating dictionaries, and specialised dictionaries (eg subject-specific dictionaries, subject-specific word lists, and thesauruses (or reverse or synonym dictionaries). What follows are some brief comments on each of the different types, illustrated with examples of each.

As Einsohn emphasises (2000: 58), it's a mistake to think of a dictionary simply as a spelling list with definitions. Dictionaries usually also contain the following features and information that's extremely useful to wordsmiths of all kinds:

- irregular forms (eg irregular plurals for nouns, past tense and past participles for verbs);
- guidelines on capitalisation, hyphenation, syllabification and pronunciation;
- usage notes, usage examples, and synonyms;
- scientific (Latin) names for plants and animals;

- spelled-out forms of common acronyms, abbreviations, signs, symbols;
- biographical information for well-known people,
- geographical information (location, population) for major cities and countries;
- translations of foreign words and phrases commonly used in English;
- Lists of common and scientific abbreviations and symbols.

2.3.1 Explanatory/descriptive dictionaries

Some examples illustrating the wide variety and increasing specialisation of dictionaries:

Australian English:
- *Macquarie dictionary* 2012. (4 ed). <www.macquariedictionary.com.au/>.
- *The Australian national dictionary: A dictionary of Australianisms on historical principles* 1989. Melbourne: Oxford University Press.
- *The Macquarie A–Z people and place* 2009. (5 ed). Sydney: Macmillan Publishers.

UK English:
- *Cambridge advanced learners' dictionary* 2012. (3 ed). Cambridge: Cambridge University Press.
- *Chambers English dictionary* 2011. (12 ed). London: Chambers.
- *Collins COBUILD advanced learner's English dictionary* 2010. London: Heinle ELT.
- *Collins COBUILD English grammar* 2011. (3 ed). London: HarperCollins.
- *Collins COBUILD English usage* 2012. (3 ed). London: Collins Cobuild.
- *Collins concise encyclopaedia of knowledge* 1987. MW Dempsey (ed).
- *Collins English dictionary* 2011. <http://www.Collinslanguage.com>.
- *Concise/shorter Oxford English dictionary* 2009. (11 ed). Oxford: Oxford University Press (also on CD-ROM).
- *Longman dictionary of common errors* 2003. (2 ed). London: Longmans.
- *Oxford advanced learners' dictionary.* Oxford: Oxford University Press (also on CD-ROM).
- *Oxford dictionary of new words* 2010. Oxford: Oxford University Press.
- *The Penguin dictionary of troublesome word.* 1987. B Bryson. London: Penguin.

US English:
- *American heritage dictionary of the English language* 2011. (5 ed). New York: Houghton Mifflin Harcourt.
- *Cambridge academic content dictionary* nd. Cambridge: Cambridge University Press.
- *Fowler's modern English usage dictionary* 1983. (2 ed). Oxford: Clarendon Press.
- *Merriam-Webster's concise dictionary of English usage* 2002. Springfield, MA: Merriman-Webster.
- *Merriam-Webster's manual for writers & editors* 1998. Springfield, MA: Merriman-Webster
- *Random House Webster's unabridged dictionary* 2005. (2 ed). Springfield, MA: Random House Reference.

- *The facts on file student's dictionary of American English* 2008. New York: Facts on File.
- *Webster's dictionary of English usage* 2009. Springfield, MA: Merriman-Webster.
- *Webster's third new international dictionary* 2004. (4 ed). Springfield, MA: Merriman-Webster.

South African English:

- *A dictionary of South African English on historical principles* 1996. Cape Town: Oxford University Press.
- *Oxford concise South African dictionary* 2010. (2 ed). Cape Town: Oxford University Press.
- *Oxford South African English dictionary* 2010. (2 ed). Cape Town: Oxford University Press.
- *Pharos dictionary of new words/nuwe woorde woordeboek* 1999. Cape Town: Pharos.
- *Pharos English dictionary for South Africa* 2011. Cape Town: Pharos (including CD-ROM).

2.3.2 Bilingual or multilingual dictionaries

These dictionaries give a word or term in one language (such as English) and its equivalent in another language (from Arabic to Urdu). Such dictionaries can include both classical and contemporary languages and can be bilingual (such as English–Swahili, Latin–English and English–Classical Greek) or even multilingual (such as English–French–Portuguese and the Pharos multilingual illustrated dictionary (seven of the official languages of South Africa, including English)). Some of these dictionaries are now also available as ebooks.

2.3.3 Specialised dictionaries

No text editor worth their salt can do a competent job without having some knowledge of these dictionaries and also without using any of them on certain projects – especially if they specialise in a particular subject area. Despite the fact that some of them are outdated or out of print also doesn't exactly make the text editor's task any easier at times, the enterprising language practitioner will take the trouble to trace these sources wherever they may be available, including on publishers' websites (see the list below), or via, for instance, *My big sourcebook: For people who work with words or pictures* (1996, Alexandria, VA: EEI Press) or Evan Morris's (1998) *The book lover's guide to the internet* (New York: Fawcett Books).

2.3.4 Unilingual subject-specific dictionaries

In these unilingual editorial tools the vocabulary of a particular subject area is explained: mathematics, physics, electronics, idioms, and so on. Collectively, the range of subject areas they cover is wide enough to satisfy most text editors' needs:

Abbreviations
Accounting
Archaeology
Architecture
Art and Artists
Biology
Botany
Building
Business
Business Management
Chemistry
Civil Engineering
Classical Mythology
Computers
Design and Designers
Economics
Electronics
English and European
History
English Idioms

Environment and
Conservation
Finance and Banking
for Writers and Editors
French
Geography
Human Geography
Information Technology
Law
Literary Terms and Literary
Theory
Mathematics
Medicine
Modern History
Modern Quotations
Music
Nursing
Philosophy
Phrase and Fable
Physical Geography

Physics
Proverbs
Psychology
Quotations
Religions
Rhyming Dictionary
Saints
Science
(Historical) Slang
Sociology
Spanish
Spelling
Statistics
Surnames
Telecommunications
The Theatre
Troublesome Words
Twentieth-century
Weather

Examples include:
- Dale, D & S Puttick 1999. *Dictionary of abbreviations & acronyms*. United Kingdom: Wordsworth Editions.
- De Klerk, J 1999. *Illustrated mathematics dictionary*. Cape Town: Longman.
- *Geddes & Grosset classical mythology: A dictionary of the tales, characters and traditions of classical mythology* nd. New Lanark: Geddes and Grosset.
- Ryan, C 1989. *McGregor's dictionary of stock market terms*. Cape Town: Juta.

Biographical dictionaries:
- *Chambers biographical dictionary* 2011. (9 ed). London: Chambers.
- Sonderling, N (ed) 1999. *New dictionary of South African biography.* Pretoria: HSRC. <http://www.hsrcpress.ac.za>.

Etymological dictionaries:
- Barnham, RK & S Steinmetz 1999. *Chambers dictionary of etymology*. Edinburgh: Chambers.
- Hoad, TF 1996. *The concise Oxford dictionary of English etymology.* Oxford: Oxford University Press.
- Merriman-Webster 2004. *Webster's new explorer dictionary of word origins.* Springfield, MA: Merriman-Webster.

- Onions, CT (ed) 1996. *The Oxford dictionary of English etymology.* New York: Oxford University Press.
- *Online etymology dictionary.* <www.etymonline.com>
- Partridge, E 1988. *Origins: A short etymological dictionary of modern English.* New York: Random House Value Publishing.
- <www.putlearningfirst.com/language/04change/etmol.html>.
- < www.filestube.com/e/english+etymology+dictionary>.
- < http://rapidshare.com/files/245516316/_A_dictionary_of_English_etymology_.pdf>.

Dictionaries of prefixes, suffixes and combining forms:
- < www.learningnerd.wordpress.com/2006/08/27/english-etymology/>.
- < www.oxforddictionaries.com/words/prefixesandsuffixes>.
- < www.merriam-webster.com/help/dictnotes/combi.htm>.
- Biological and medical prefixes and suffixes: *Suffix prefix dictionary.* <www.macroevolution.net/suffix-prefix-dictionary.html>.
- Edmonds, D (ed) 1999. *The Oxford reverse dictionary.* Oxford: Oxford University Press.

Thesauruses and synonym/antonym dictionaries:
Many language practitioners do not know precisely how to use a thesaurus, but it is a skill that must be acquired if the correct word in a given context is to be used. Some include:

- MS Word's Thesaurus and Research features, which are quick and easy to access and use.
- *Collins thesaurus A–Z* 2006. (2 ed). New York: Harper Collins (also www.collinsdictionary.com/english-thesaurus).
- *Collins thesaurus of the English language* 2010. New York: Harper Collins (also http://www.collinslanguage.com).
- Edmonds, D (ed) 1999. *Oxford reverse dictionary.* Oxford: Oxford University Press.
- Kipfer, BA (ed) 2006. *Rogers 21st century thesaurus: In dictionary form* (rev ed). London: Bantam Doubleday Dell.
- Kirkpatrick, B (ed) 2000. *Oxford paperback thesaurus.* Oxford: Oxford University Press.
- LaRoche, N 1986. *The synonym finder* (2 ed). New York: Grand Central Publishing.
- Lindberg, CA (ed) 2008. *Oxford American writer's thesaurus.* New York: Oxford University Press.
- *Oxford dictionary of synonyms and antonyms.*
- *Oxford thesaurus of English* 2009. (3 ed). Oxford: Oxford University Press.
- Princeton Language Institute. *21st century synonym and antonym finder (21st century reference).* Princeton: Dell.
- *Reader's Digest reverse dictionary* 1989. New York: Reader's Digest.
- Roget, P & GW Davidson (eds) 2002. *Roget's thesaurus of English words and phrases* (150th anniversary ed). London: Penguin.

Proverb and idiom dictionaries:

These can be used to check that an author has used the correct form and is conveying the desired meaning in context through the use of a particular idiom:

- Ayto, J 2010. *Brewer's dictionary of phrase and fable* (18 ed). New York: Collins Reference.
- *Brewer's dictionary of phrase and fable* 2000. (online) Bartelby.com.
- Freeman, W 1967. *A concise dictionary of English idioms*. The English Universities Press Ltd.
- Manser, MH 2006. *Dictionary of idioms.* United Kingdom: Wordsworth Editions.
- *McGraw-Hill's essential American idioms dictionar.* 2006. New York: McGraw-Hill.
- *Spears, RA* 2008a. *McGraw-Hill's essential American idioms dictionary* (2 ed). New York: McGraw-Hill.
- *Spears, RA* 2008b. *McGraw-Hill's essential American slang dictionary.* New York: McGraw-Hill.
- Stiefring, J 2005. *The Oxford dictionary of idioms* (2 ed). Oxford: Oxford University Press.

Pronouncing dictionaries:

United Kingdom:
- Burchfield, R 1981. *The spoken word: A BBC guide.* London: BBC Publications.
- Jones, D et al 2011. *Cambridge English pronouncing dictionary with CD ROM* (18 ed). Cambridge: Cambridge University Press.
- Sangster, C 2006. *Oxford BBC guide to pronunciation.* Oxford: Oxford University Press.
- Wells, J 2008. *Longman pronunciation dictionary.* London: Pearson Longman.

United States:
- Ehrlich, EH; R Hand & JF Bender 2006. *The NBC handbook of pronunciation*. New York: Harper & Row.

Preposition dictionaries:
- *Oxford dictionary of prepositions.*
- <www.englishpage.com/prepositions/verb_html>.
- <www.englishpage.co/prepositions/phrasaldictionary.html>.
- <www.thefreedictionary.com/prepositions>.

Phrasal verb/verb–preposition dictionaries:
- Cowie, AP 1975. *Oxford dictionary of current idiomatic English: Verbs with prepositions and particles.* Oxford: Oxford University Press.
- Spears, RA 2008c. *McGraw-Hill's essential phrasal verb dictionary: The practical guide to American English phrasal verbs* (2 ed). New York: McGraw-Hill.
- <www.englishpage.com/prepositions/verb_prepositions,html>.
- <www.englishpage.co/prepositions/phrasaldictionary.html>.

Unusual words and names:

- Ehrlich, E 1987. *Le mot juste: The Penguin dictionary of foreign terms and phrases.* London: Penguin.
- Foyle, C 2007. *Foyle's philavery: A treasury of unusual words.* Edinburgh: Chambers Harrap.
- Geddes & Grosset classical mythology nd. *A dictionary of the tales, characters and traditions of classical mythology.* New Lanark: Geddes and Grosset.
- Johnson, M 1990. *Business buzzwords: The tough new jargon of modern business.* Oxford: Blackwell.
- *McGraw-Hill's essential American slang dictionary* 2008.
- Quinion, M 2008. *Gallimaufry: A hodgepodge of our vanishing vocabulary.* Oxford: Oxford University Press.
- Room, A 1993. *Brewer's dictionary of names: people & places & things.* Oxford: Helicon.
- Spears, RA 2008. *McGraw-Hill's essential American slang dictionary.* New York: McGraw-Hill.

Internet terms:

- Geer, S 2000. *Pocket internet* (2 ed). London: The Economist Books.

Spelling:

- *Collins Webster's easy learning. English spelling* 2011 (also available as an ebook).
- Dale, R & S Patrick 1999. *Dictionary of abbreviations & acronyms.* United Kingdom: Wordsworth Editions.
- King, G 2004. *Collins good punctuation: The one-stop punctuation problem solver.* Glasgow: HarperCollins Publishers.
- Soanes, C & S Ferguson 2007. *Oxford A–Z of spelling.* Oxford: Oxford University Press.
- Stilman, A 2010. *Grammatically correct: The essential guide to spelling, style, usage, grammar, and punctuation* (2 ed). Cincinnati, OH: Writer's Digest Books.
- Waite, M (ed) 2005. *New Oxford spelling dictionary. The writers' and editors' guide to spelling and word division.* Oxford: Oxford University Press.
- West, W 1964. *A dictionary of spelling: British & American.* London: Longman.

2.4 Language textbooks/manuals/guides

> Anyone who takes language seriously will have to fork out the money, every few years, for updated dictionaries and language guides.
> *Niewoudt*

The textbooks, manuals and guides on English language and its usage and abusage are legion, the greatest challenge to practitioners being which to choose for their particular purposes. While some of them are somewhat dated, others, on the other hand, are also available in up-to-date digital format. Included here are both those that have stood the test of time and more contemporaneous titles that reflect current usage:

- Allen, R 2005. *How to write better English*. London: Penguin Group.
- Baxter, P 2010. *Theses and dissertations: Checking the language*. London: Society for Editors and Proofreaders.
- Bryson, B 1987. *The Penguin dictionary of troublesome words*. London: Penguin.
- Bryson, B 1991. *Mother tongue: The English language*. London: Penguin Books.
- Bryson, B 1994. *Penguin dictionary for writers and editors*. London: Penguin Books.
- Burchfield, RW (ed) 2004. *Fowler's modern English usage* (3 ed). Oxford University Press.
- Butterfield, J (ed) 2007. *Oxford A–Z of English usage*. Oxford: Oxford University Press.
- Carter, R & M McCarthey 2006. *Cambridge grammar of English. A comprehensive guide: Spoken and written English grammar and usage*. Cambridge University Press.
- Cheney, TAR 2005. *Getting the words right: 39 ways to improve your writing* (2 ed). Cincinnati, OH: Writer's Digest Books.
- Cochrane, J 2004. *Between you and I: A little book of bad English*. Naperville, IL: Sourcebooks Inc.
- *Collins COBUILD guide to English usage* 2012.
- Dornan, EA & CW Dawe 1987. *The brief English handbook* (2 ed). Boston: Little, Brown.
- Dornan, EA & CW Dawe 1987. *The brief English handbook* (9 ed). Boston & Toronto: Little, Brown.
- Field, M 2007. *Improve your punctuation and grammar* (2 ed). Oxford: Howtobooks.
- Fowler HW & FG Fowler 1979. *The King's English* (3 ed). Oxford: Oxford University Press.
- Foyle, C 2007. *Foyle's philavery: A treasury of unusual words*. Edinburgh: Chambers Harrap.
- Garner, BA 2003. *Garner's modern American usage* (2 ed). New York: Oxford University Press.
- Gowers, E 1996. *The complete plain words* (revised by S Greenbaum & J Whitcut) (3 ed). London: Penguin Books.
- Huddleston, R & GK Pullum 2002. *The Cambridge grammar of the English language*. Cambridge: Cambridge University Press.
- Huddleston, R & GK Pullum 2005. *A student's introduction to English grammar*. Cambridge University Press.
- Hudson, N 1997. *Modern Australian usage* (2 ed). Melbourne: Oxford University Press.
- Hughes, B; Drury, J & M Barrett (eds) 1991. *The Penguin working words: An Australian guide to modern English usage*. Melbourne: Viking.
- Law, J (ed) 2001. *Oxford language reference*. Oxford: Oxford University Press.
- Law, J (ed) 2002. *The language toolkit*. New York: Oxford University Press.
- Linnegar, J 2009. *Engleish, our Engleish: Common problems in South African English and how to resolve them*. Cape Town: Pharos.
- Locher, MA & J Strässler (eds) 2008. *Standards and norms in the English language*. Berlin/New York: Mouton de Gruyter.
- Lynch, J 2008. *Guide to grammar and style*. <http://andromeda.rutgers.edu/~jlynch/Writing>.

- Marsen, S 2007. *Professional writing: The complete guide for business, industry and IT* (2 ed). London: Palgrave Macmillan.
- Murphy, EM 2011. *Working words*. Canberra: Canberra Society of Editors.
- Nesfield, JC 1961. *Outline of English grammar*. London: Macmillan & Co Ltd.
- Partridge, E 2000. *Usage and abusage: A guide to good English*, revised by J Whitcut. London: Penguin Books.
- Peters, P 2004. *The Cambridge guide to English usage*. Cambridge University Press. <www.cambridge/org/peters>.
- Pullum, G 2009. 50 years of stupid grammar advice. *The chronicle review*, 17/04/2009. <http://chronicle.com/free/v55/i32/32b01501.htm> (Accessed April 2009).
- Reader's Digest (Kahn (ed)) 1985. *Right word at the right time: A guide to the English language and how to use it.*
- Sebeok, TA (ed) 1960. *Style in language*. Cambridge, MA: MIT Press.
- Seely, J 2007. *Oxford A–Z of grammar & punctuation*. Oxford: Oxford University Press.
- Strunk, W & EB White nd. *The elements of style*. London: Penguin Books.
- Swan, M & B Smith (eds) 1987. *Learner English: A teacher's guide to interference and other problems*. Cambridge: Cambridge University Press.
- Taggart, C & JA Wines. 2008. *My grammar and I (or should that be 'me'?): Old-school ways to sharpen your English*. London: Michael O'Mara Books Limited.
- Thomas, C 2009. *Your house style: Styling your words for maximum effect*. London: Society for Editors and Proofreaders.
- Trask, RL 2000. *The Penguin dictionary of English grammar*. London: Penguin Group.
- Trask, RL 2001. *Mind the gaffe: The Penguin guide to common errors in English*. London: Penguin Books.
- Treble, HA & GH Vallins. 1973. *An ABC of English usage*. Calcutta: Oxford University Press.
- Van de Poel, K 2006. *Scribende: Academic writing for students of English*. Leuven/Voorburg: Acco.
- Van de Poel, K & J Gasiorek 2007. *All write: An introduction to writing in an academic context*. Leuven/Voorburg: Acco.
- Walter, E & K Woodford. 2010. *Easy learning writing*. Glasgow: HarperCollins.
- Yagoda, B 2007. *When you catch an adjective, kill it*. New York: Broadway Books.

There are, naturally, many more sources than the examples listed above. These types of source are easy to use to check queries you may have regarding word choice and spelling, and also a wide variety of matters regarding language usage. They are especially useful for resolving any confusion surrounding the meaning of a word, phrase or sentence. The fact that the information they contain is often arranged alphabetically makes them that much more accessible; language practitioners (including text editors, subeditors and teachers) therefore find it easier to look up information in them.

One downside, however, is that they can – and do – become out of date fairly soon after publication, with new information not being incorporated as soon as it ought. This is a particular problem for the text editor who wants to ensure that the solution or advice they receive is based on the latest, most-up-to-date usage conventions and authorities. Interestingly, the older publications tend to contain more reliable information than their most recent successors or competitors.

An important aspect of language usage – particularly on either side of the Atlantic Ocean – is spelling, and regarding misspellings both publishers and readers exercise zero tolerance, which means that the text editor and proofreader simply have to ensure that words are correctly spelt, even after a spell-checker has been run through a text (see the section on spell-checkers below in this chapter). Apart from the standard mid-range dictionaries, there are some reliable and useful spelling dictionaries and manuals for those whose ability to spell or to recognise misspellings is not what it ought to be:

Some help for spelling and punctuation:

- Carey, GV 1986. *Mind the stop: A brief guide to punctuation, with a note on proof correction*. London: Penguin.
- King, EG 2004. *Good punctuation: The one-stop punctuation problem solver*. Glasgow: HarperCollins Publishers.
- Lukeman, N 2007. *The art of punctuation*. Oxford & New York: Oxford University Press.
- *Merriam-Webster's guide to punctuation and style* 2001. (2 ed). Springfield, MA: Merriam-Webster.
- Partridge, E 1955. *You have a point there: A guide to punctuation and its allies*. London: Hamish Hamilton.
- *Pharos English pocket speller* 2005. Cape Town: Pharos.
- Soanes, K & S Ferguson 2007. *Oxford A–Z of better spelling*. Oxford University Press.
- Trask, RL 1997. *The Penguin guide to punctuation*. London: Penguin Group.
- Truss, L 2003. *Eats, shoots and leaves: The zero tolerance approach to punctuation*. London: Profile Books.
- Waite, M (ed) 2005. *New Oxford spelling dictionary: The writers' and editors' guide to spelling and word division*. Oxford: Oxford University Press.
- West, M 1964. *A dictionary of spelling: British & American*. London: Longman.

Text editors who have the slightest flaws or weaknesses where spelling is concerned must get into the habit of not trusting their own judgement and checking every single spelling with which they're not 100% comfortable or familiar.

2.5 Style guides

> Style manuals do not cover everything, but only what their authors preceive to be the most important patterns.
> *Crystal*

> Most offices have a style book or style sheet, although in many cases it may only be a few pieces of paper to supplement some agreed work of reference.
> *Morrish*

> Style manuals and style sheets help to create a distinctive institutional voice and visual image for a publication – a 'house style'. They also create consistency among all the texts produced by a given publisher.
> *Mossop*

> ... style rules ... are often by nature arbitrary and changeable. ... they aren't used because they're 'correct'. They're used for your convenience in serving the reader.
> *Saller*

2.5.1 National style guides

A style manual or guide should be the next tool in the text editor's and proofreader's arsenal. It should be regarded as a basic guide, as a resource that can be followed, adapted or ignored on given points, depending upon the client's (or text editor's) own preferences, and not as a source to be followed slavishly. Bear in mind that its primary purpose is to help enforce well-informed consistency in a document.

Australian English:
- Peters, P 1995. *The Cambridge Australian English style guide*. Cambridge University Press.
- Purchase, S (ed) 1997. *The Australian writers' dictionary*. Melbourne: Oxford University Press.
- Purchase, S (ed) 1998. *The little book of style*. Canberra: AusInfo.
- Snooks & Co 2003. *Style manual for authors, editors and printers* (6 ed). Brisbane: John Wiley & Sons.

UK English:
- Isaacs, A, J Daintith & E Martin (eds) 1991. *The Oxford dictionary for scientific writers and editors*. Oxford: Oxford University Press.
- Linnegar, J; P Schamberger & J Bishop 2009. *Consistency, consistency, consistency: The PEG guide to style guides*. Johannesburg: Professional Editors' Group.
- Manser, MH 2007. *Collins dictionary for writers and editors: Essential reference for writers, editors and proofreaders*. London: Collins.
- *MHRA style guide: A handbook for authors, editors and writers of theses* 2002. Modern Humanities Research Association.
- *New Hart's rules: The handbook of style for writers and editors* 2005. Oxford: Oxford University Press.
- *New Oxford dictionary for writers and editors*. Oxford: Oxford University Press.
- *The Oxford guide to style* 2000. Oxford: Oxford University Press.
- Strunk, W & EB White 2007. *The elements of style*. London: Penguin.
- Walker, D (ed) 1995. *Do it in style: The editorial style guide of the Independent Newspapers*. Johannesburg: Independent Newspapers Holdings Limited.

US English:
- *APA style* (American Psychological Association) Publication Manual 2003. <http://www.apastyle.org>.

- *The Associated Press stylebook and briefing on media law* 2011. New York: Basic Books. <http://www.apstylebook.com/>.
- *Chicago manual of style: The essential guide for writers, editors, and publishers* 2010. (16 ed). Chicago: University of Chicago Press.
- *Chicago manual of style online.* <http://www.chicagomanualofstyle.org>.
- Copperud, RH 1980. *American usage and style: The consensus*. New York: Van Nostrand Reinhold.
- Editorial Freelancers Association. <http://www.the-efa.org/>.
- Editorium. <http://www.editorium.com/>.
- Editors' Association of Canada/Association Canadienne des Réviseurs. <http:www.editors.ca/>.
- EEI Communications Staff (eds) 2000. *E-what? A guide to the quirks of new media style and usage: How to handle inconsistencies in punctuation, capitalization, internet addresses, and more.* Alexandria, VA: EEI Press.
- Gibaldi, J (ed) 1998. *MLA style manual and guide to scholarly publishing* (2 ed). New York: Modern Language Association of America.
- Marsh, D 2003. *Keeping our house style in order.* <http://www.guardian.co.uk>.
- MLA (Modern Language Association of America) 2009. *MLA style manual and guide to scholarly publishing* (3 ed). New York: MLA.
- *Scientific style and format: The CBE manual for authors, editors, and publishers* 2006. (7 ed). Compilers the Style Manual Committee of the Council of Science Editors. Reston, VA: Council of Science Editors in cooperation with the Rockefeller University Press.
- Siegal, AM & WG Connolly 1999. *New York Times manual of style and usage*. New York: Times Books.
- Skillin, M 1974. *Words into type* (based on studies by Marjorie E Skillin, Robert M Gay et al) (3 ed). Englewood Cliffs, NJ: Prentice Hall.

2.5.2 Broad style guides

It is fairly general practice for businesses and institutions such as publishers and newspapers – when it comes to writing – to adopt a house style of their own for written materials. This is a kind of institutionalised language usage that takes the form of a guide that applies to a particular organisation. It relates to those established usages and decisions (the latter often taken by mutual agreement and sometimes imposed autocratically – and sometimes a 'law of the Medes and Persians') relating to language and allied matters when people resort to writing for such institutions. The purpose behind doing so is simply that through the uniform use of language rules and usage writers and editors (and publishers) save time, leading to greater effectiveness) and in the process greater consistency can be achieved (cf Billingham 2002: 26–27; Bishop 2009; Flann & Hill 2004: 48; Merriam-Webster 2001: 240–243; Saller 2009: 29; Tarutz 1992: 186). Writing doesn't have to be laboriously 'corrected'; by following a house style, every writer is able to use the same sort of language in a comparable context, which leads to good communication. In the first instance, publishers require their authors to observe the house rules, or house style when they are writing.

But what exactly is 'house style'? And how does it differ from a style sheet? And from an author's style of writing?

House style is an organisation's list of preferences in respect of spellings, capitalisation, hyphenation/one word/two words, punctuation, the use of numbers, dates and currencies, and so on, where there are two or more choices. A house style guide can be a few roughly put together pages or a formal manual, or any document in between; and it can develop organically from an informal set of notes to a formal, bound manual as an editorial department's output grows. It aims to be comprehensive without being overly prescriptive and inflexible. It also tends to have general application, because such a guide cannot hope to cover all the specifics of every single subject published.

That's where the editorial style sheet (or word list) comes into its own. Below are two examples of a style sheet – the one alphabetically arranged, the other arranged according to categories of decision.

Examples of house style decisions – sample style sheets (word lists):

Example A: Alphabetical arrangement of style decisions

AN Author	Title of manuscript		
ABC and, not & comma: no list comma	**DEF** decimal comma, not decimal stop dates: 14 June 2018	**GHI** italics for: emphasis *coup de main*	**JKL** km, kg, kWh
MNO M = mega; m = metre	**PQR** per cent (2 words)	**STU** thousands space, not comma	**VWXYZ** X-ray (cap X)

Example B: Arrangement by category of decisions

AN Author	Title of manuscript		
One word	**Hyphenated** health-care (adj) well-known (attrib)	**Two words** health care (n) well known (pred)	**Numbers, time, dates** 18:03 14 January 2016
Italics	**Special spellings** enquiry, not inquiry microorganism multidisciplinary	**Initial uppercase**	

For each specific title a text editor is likely to work on, style issues specific to the subject-matter will have to be decided upon (eg should microorganism be one word or hyphenated?). This is where flexibility is called for (Saller 2009: 27–28). According to Saller, 'the inability to identify the difference between negotiable matters of style and non-negotiable matters of standard English is perhaps the most common cause of grief' among editors who approach the University of Chicago Press staff for advice. What text editors must understand is that editorial styles can differ from one genre to another: compare the house style for an academic journal with that of a daily newspaper aimed at the masses against children's books. Different readerships, and different subject-matter, requires varying styles. By compiling a style sheet, the editor working on a specific text keeps a running record of decision made on particular questions of style, having found that a dictionary or other standard reference work was unable to give guidance; nor was the institution's house style guide of any help. It is helpful to use one dictionary as a basis for these decisions, both to give a rationale for explaining them to the author and to save time agonising over which of the author's three styles to favour (Flann & Hill 2004: 49).

At first, it is advisable for the text editor to note the manuscript page numbers against style decisions taken, in case such decisions have to be revised or overturned later on, once the author's preferences are discerned. This raises another aspect of flexibility: you should not be reluctant or afraid to revisit your earlier style decisions, and certainly don't make decisions (however correct you think they are) that fly in the face of an author's or a discipline's preferences (Saller 2009: 28–29). For example, if doctors and chemists commonly use 'microorganism', don't attempt to hyphenate the word if you find many occurrences of the single-word spelling throughout the manuscript. Sensitivity is definitely required here, and it should be borne out by an initial overview of the manuscript (Flann & Hill 2004: 48).

Moreover, flexibility in imposing style is one of the key tools in managing good relationships with your writers. By indicating that your editing will be open to discussion, you give a writer reassurance that will inform your relationship from the start' (Saller 2009: 30). And once you show your author the sources in support of your decisions, and if you make a habit of enclosing your style sheet with the manuscript, you'll usually win the author over to your side.

Compiling your style sheet on your computer makes alphabetical listing and reordering easy. It also enables you to print out or email copies for the author and proofreader, and use it for later reference when briefing the designer (Flann & Hill 2004: 51).

How, then, does house style differ from style of writing? Well, the latter expression refers to the way in which an author writes, and is usually appropriate to the genre and the audience. This links style closely to register – the degree of formality or informality with which an author writes, that is, their diction, their turn of phrase, and their sentence construction. Writers who interpret laws, for example, write in a distinctive style, as do psychologists and psychiatrists who write textbooks adopt a style of their own. Recipe book authors compose their text and use a vocabulary and sentence structure that is entirely different from those used in other books and certainly specific to the way they have to communicate the information in recipes.

The savvy text editor will therefore tap into an author's particular style of writing and work at ensuring that it is sustained throughout. Whereas there are no alternatives to consider when considering an author's writing style, the text editor who is having to make house style decisions is dealing exclusively with choices that have to be made between variants to ensure that whenever they occur in the text they will be treated consistently.

The great advantage of having a house style in place is twofold: (1) it helps to project an impression of uniformity and polish to one's audience (Mossop 2007: 39) and (2) it indicates that the institution took care in producing the communication and therefore takes seriously the public with which it communicates. Billingham (2002: 27; also Mossop 2007: 39) adds that the consistency that's achieved in the process in texts that the organisation (eg publisher and newspaper) puts out helps to create a professional image for it.

Institutions in the publishing and newspaper industries worldwide are characterised by the guides they generate, known as house style guides. For example, text editors and proofreaders can choose between the *Oxford manual of style*, *New Hart's rules*, the *Collins* or *New Oxford dictionary for writers and editors*, the *Chicago manual of style*, and the style manuals of *The Guardian*, the *New York Times*, the *Economist* and *The Times* of London – just to name a few. Journalists and publishers who work for these organisations check their own writing and that of others largely against these guides, supplemented by other reference works such as dictionaries of various kinds and subject specialisations (eg advanced learners' dictionaries; science, physics and mathematics dictionaries). The content of these guides and other reference works serves primarily to guide the practitioner when decisions have to be made between different options – for example, the way of writing abbreviations and acronyms, of numerals and quantities, the use or not of capital letters, whether words must be written as two words, one word or hyphenated, and so on.

Such a style guide is often the product of a long process of development and decision-making about language usage and relevant issues in an organisation. It comes into existence as a result of a need for guidance leading to standardisation and uniformity regarding ways of writing. Billingham (2002: 26–27) points out that these guides differ between organisations – in length, complexity and degree of formality. A style guide can also take the form of a book (such as the *Oxford manual of style* and the *Chicago manual of style* and the *Collins dictionary for writers and editors*) or a number of printed pages – depending upon the needs of and value attached to them by the organisation in question. These types of guide obviously come to contribute to a greater common consistency in written communications; for example, that official titles are spelt consistently with an initial uppercase letter, that many words of Latin origin (and not yet fully embraced by another language) are consistently italicised, that the full expressions (for example, that is) and not the abbreviated forms (eg, ie) are consistently used, and that the names of places such as Munich, Basel, Venice and Antwerp are spelt consistently in these anglicised ways. This involves making choices based on preferred forms for the sake of conveying meaning uniformly.

Any text editor worth their salt will therefore find out from the client beforehand (1) what the requirements of the inhouse writing style that have to be met are and (2) whether a guide dealing with this is available for use as a reference to check against during the editing process. It is a characteristic of these kinds of guide that they often take the form of a published book. Sometimes they can even act as a supplement to an existing source, for example a dictionary in a specific language.

Text editors are also advised to compile their own style guides and not to rely only on those put together by the organisations they work for (which are often outdated). Obviously an institution's guide takes precedence when the text editor does work for it, but it will be to the benefit of text editors if they record their experiences with language and language practice for their own use when they become involved in future manuscripts (Billingham 2002: 28–29). The house style guide therefore becomes a generally useful reference on usage that will be updated constantly and in the process enable the text editor to keep up with developments in the area of language usage.

It is therefore important to know that:

- House style guides help text editors to restrict the choices they have to make.
- House style guides mainly give only guidelines and cannot explain all occurrences (Butcher et al 2006: 117, 2009). The principle of analogy also applies here.
- House style guides give quick answers to routine questions and give guidelines on how to handle more difficult issues (Tarutz 1992: 185).
- House style guides are in reality a list of do's and don'ts (Einsohn 2005: 6). This helps with making important decisions about language practice.
- House style guides sometimes support existing standard publications (Flann & Hill 2004: 48; Morrish 1998: 106, 2003: 39).
- House style guides aim at consistency in the choices that have to be made while writing; in that way, uniformity of writing can be sustained (Mossop 2010: 38–39; Linnegar 2008: 39).
- The consistent application of a style guide can give a publication credibility.
- A large number of institutions have their own house style guide and that that must be followed when work is done for them.
- A large number of institutions' house style guides have become publications in their own right.
- A large number of text editors compile their own style guides to ensure consistency in the choices they make and in usage when they edit texts.
- For some manuscripts a unique style guide has to be developed out of a need to deal with

technical language usage (such as chemistry terminology) (Morrish 1998: 106, 2003; Flann & Hill 2004: 49).

- These types of guide sometimes become part of the tradition and growth of a particular institution.
- These types of guide are mostly the outcome of collective editorial decisions and usage over a long period in an institution.
- Immediately after a contract is accepted, the text editor should ask the client whether they have a house style guide (Billingham 2002: 26–27: Flann & Hill 2004: 48–49).
- If such a guide exists, it must be used to deal with the writing style and language usage at the institution concerned.
- Freelance editors who may be working on several different manuscripts and house styles are advised to keep a copy of each set of styles with each manuscript (Flann & Hill 2004: 49; Saller 2009: 104).
- In the electronic era, printed house style guides are just about out of date as soon as they appear (Marsh 2003). In future, an effort will have to be made to make these kinds of resource available electronically.
- Asking the authors up front about house style/consistency decisions/conventions; determining the discipline's or author's preferences and either retaining them or at least imposing consistency regarding their preferences (noting the page numbers on which instances occur (Merriam-Webster 2001: 241).
- The style sheet/word list will accompany the text through the production process to the author, the typesetter and the proofreader (Merriam-Webster 2001: 240, 243); even the indexer should receive a copy, so that when they come across discrepancies or inconsistencies, they will know which the correct alternative is.

2.5.3 House style requirements

Typically, what can we expect to include in a house style guide? The following list indicates the information that should be included. It could, of course, have been extended considerably, and it does not claim to be complete. The items included below are purely illustrative of what could be included in a house style guide.

Point of departure: The guide begins with a statement indicating the primary source to be used in the first instance or upon which the particular style guide is based (for example, a dictionary or a published house style guide). House style should also not be implemented in book, article and journal titles, or in quotations, except an author's own translation.

List 11.2 Suggested content for a house style guide or a style sheet[1]

› Abbreviations and acronyms
  – Are unfamiliar ones explained in a list in prelims or at first occurrence?
  – Replace all common Latin abbreviations with English equivalents (that is, not ie; for example, not eg) – except in parenthetical expressions and in notes
  – %, not per cent
  – No full point in contractions that end in the last letter of the word: St, Dr
  – No full points: NATO, IMF, MBChB, eg, ie (or follow author's preference throughout)
  – Initial capital letter for acronyms pronounced as words (Nafta, Basic, Unesco, Opec, Nasdaq); but either AIDS or Aids, depending on the particular publishing house's style
  – All caps for acronyms pronounced letter by letter (IMF, HIV, UNO)
  – On first mention of a term, introduce its acronym in parentheses; non-governmental organisations (NGOs) are … (the term is all lowercase, unless a name of an institution)
  – When the acronym is better known, mention it first followed by the full term in parentheses
  – Spell out in parentheses only those acronyms likely to be unfamiliar to readers.
  – If a term is mentioned only once, do not provide its acronym, unless the acronym will aid recognition of the term
  – AD, BCE, BP (small caps) for time periods

› Ampersand
  – Only where & is part of a registered name; otherwise do not use instead of 'and'
  – In joint-author citations, use '&' only within parentheses and in bibliographies, 'and' in run of text

› Bias and parochialisms
  – Watch out for bias and stereotypes: especially male-female stereotypes; racial stereotypes
  – Change 'this country', 'this province', 'this year' (change 'one year ago' to actual year)
  – Spell out abbreviations likely to be unfamiliar to overseas readers

› Bold
  – In text, use for key words or glossed words only.
  – Use for subheadings and column headings (if a level is required above italicised column heads)

---

[1] Butcher, Drake & Leach 2009: 434–436; Linnegar, Schamberger & Bishop 2009: 22–24.

>>

› **Brands**
  – DaimlerChrysler; smart (car); Mercedes-Benz
  – Verb forms: hoover, google, tippex

› **Capitalisation versus lowercase**
  – Small caps vs full caps (BCE, AD, BP or BCE, AD or BCE?)
  – Lowercase vs full initial cap (the pope vs Pope Benedict XVI)
  – Special terms: capitalisation consistent (Balkanisation; Russification); but to google/bostik/hoover (verbs)
  – Min caps, not sig caps for headings and subheadings; captions, labels
  – southern Africa (when geographical region, not part of a title)

› **Contractions**
  – Spell out all contractions (except for the expression 'do's and don'ts'
  – Follow author's preference (depend upon degree of formality required)

› **Cross-references**
  – Standard format: (see page 45); in Chapter 5; see Table 3.4; see Fig 12.1
  – Arabic, not roman numerals where necessary
  – Page cross-refs: change numbers to **00** or **000** so that they can be picked up at proof stage

› **Currencies**
  – USD450, not US$450
  – $4.50: 50c

› **Dates and time**
  – 15 September 2012
  – 15:30 but 3.30 pm (not 15h30 nor 3:30 pm) (am, pm, not small caps)
  – 1.4.2011 means 1 April in Britain, 4 January in USA
  – Change 'one year ago' to actual year
  – 1960s, the Sixties
  – AD, BCE, BP (small caps) for time periods

› **Extracts – see Quoted matter**

› **Foreign words and phrases**
  – Spelling, accenting, italicisation should be consistent
  – Use English-style plurals, not Latin or Greek-influenced forms: syllabuses (not syllabi), memorandums (not memoranda), stadiums (not stadia), forums (not fora)
  – 'Data' is singular in an IT context; plural everywhere else
  – 'Media' is the plural of medium

List 11.2 continued

– Do not italicise the names of foreign buildings or institutions: the Volksraad; Hôtel de Ville
– Do not italicise a quotation in a foreign language – place it in quotation marks

› **Gender neutrality**
– Use 'they' and 'them' in preference to 'he/she' or 'he or she' and 'his or her'. Never 's/he' or '(s)he'.

› **Hyphen/one word/two words**
– Follow any reputable style manual/dictionary for hyphenation guidance
– At first appearance, record decisions about one word, two words or hyphenated
– Hyphenate compounds in which the last letter of the prefix and the first letter of the root are identical vowels: intra-arterial; pre-empt; anti-intellectual; micro-organism
– Treat 'mid' as a prefix: mid-nineteenth century; mid-1960s
– Fractions: one-half, three-quarters
– Sub-Saharan; trans-Siberian
– Co-operate; co-ordinate
– Health care (n); health-care professional (adj)
– No one
– Wellbeing

› **Intext citations (Harvard style)**
– If a work has many authors, list the first three and then 'et al'.
– Arrange multiple intext citations alphabetically, not in date order or in order of value to the reader: Adams 1979; Butler 1977; Smithson 1990
– Style of citation in parentheses: (Jones & Black 2010: 63–9)
– Names of authors in run of text: Jones and Black (2010) …
– Subsequent editions: 2 ed, 16 ed
– Editor/editors: (ed)/(eds)
– Reference to page numbers: 63–9, not pp 63–9

› **Italics or not (roman)**
– For foreign words: consult your standard English dictionary for guidance (eg, coup d'état, zeitgeist, but *coup de main*)
– Check plural 's' italic, possessive 's' Roman: *The Times*'s editor
– With *(a)*, *(b)*, *(c)* the parentheses must also be italics
– Titles in italics: published books, journals, magazines, poetry anthologies; operas, ballets, dramas, CD collections, TV soaps and other programmes, works of art

– Titles Roman and quoted: chapters titles in books; journal articles; individual poems (unless they are long enough to constitute a book); unpublished theses; government/official reports

› **Lists**
  – Use bullets as default.
    Use numbers only when there's a need for numbering the items (eg, a sequence of steps; things to remember)
  – Single- or two-word lists: start each item with a lowercase letter (except for proper nouns and proper adjectives) and terminate each item without punctuation
  – Independent, full-sentence items: start with an uppercase letter and terminate each in a full stop
  – Sentences that run on from and complete the introductory sentence: start with a lowercase letter and terminate each (except the last) in a semicolon

› **Names of people and places**
  – Clark or Clarke
  – Jameson or Jamieson
  – Ladismith or Ladysmith
  – Romania or Rumania
  – Philip or Phillip
  – Pyotr or Peter
  – Lyn, Lynne or Lynn
  – Jane or Jayne

› **Numbering of divisions of a document, tables, figures**
  – Divisions of a document: metric numbering 1, 1.1, 1.1.1, 1.1.1.1 (no final stop)
  – Number figures, tables by chapter: Figure 2.1, 2.2, Table 3.1, 3.2 etc

› **Numbers, units, etc**
  – Lining or non-lining figures?
  – For plurals of numbers and acronyms, add 's': 1980s, NGOs (no apostrophe)
  – 000,87 (thousands space; decimal comma)
  – Nine, 10
  – One-half, three-quarters
  – 1st, 3rd
  – 1967–69, 2010–12; but financial years: 2010/2011
  – 20–1, 101–17
  – 0,79, not ,79
  – En-rule for number/date ranges

- Numbers with units of measurement: 69 km (not kms; symbols lowercase; number and unit spaced); 225 K (kelvin); 24 ms^{-1}
- Large numbers: $60 million
- Tbl, tsp for tablespoon, teaspoon

› Punctuation
- Apostrophe: do's and don'ts
- No apostrophe: NGOs; 1980s
- Apostrophe for p's and q's; i's and t's (single letter plurals)
- List comma: in or out? (red, white, and blue or red, white and blue?)
- No comma before 'etc'
- No stops for abbreviations and acronyms
- Position of " in relation to final punctuation
- Misplaced commas
- Possessives: Thomas' or Thomas's; Rhodes' or Rhodes's?
- En-rule for ranges, not hyphen or em-rule – unspaced
- Em-rule unspaced for dash
- Accents used correctly and consistently
- Subordinate clauses: use comma both at beginning and at end (except with defining clauses – no commas at all)
- Style for bibliography?

› Quoted matter
- Embedded in text (fewer than 40 words): single quotation marks, doubles inside singles
- Displayed (40 or more words): spaced above and below; down 1 pt size; indented on left; no quotation marks
- Spacing
- One space between sentences
- One hard (non-breaking; Ctrl+Shift+Spacebar) space between number and symbol: 145 km/h

› Spelling
- Correct spelling errors: separate; accommodation; liquefy; a lot; necessary
- UK: fulfil; marvellous; biased; focused/focusing
- US: fulfill, color, program
- Foreign words and names
- US or UK spellings: Pearl Harbour vs Pearl Harbor but International Labor Organisation vs International Labour Organisation; Lincoln Center
- Foreign or anglicised spellings: Basel or Basle; München or Munich; Ivory Coast or Côte d'Ivoire

We want to note once again that this list is given simply as an example of what could be included in a house style guide; it is by no means comprehensive. Such lists should be amended for each new manuscript and depending upon the available references for particular subject-matter.

In summary, some suggested content for a house style guide or style sheet:

Text facet	Kind of information to be included Requirement concerning …
Text type	• Gender neutrality: he, she, they, … • Bias and parochialisms • Intext citations (Harvard style, short title, APA, MLA, …)
Content	• Cross-references • Names of people and places • Foreign words and phrases
Structure	• Numbering of divisions of a document, tables, figures • Quoted matter and extracts
Wording	• Abbreviations and acronyms • Brands

Language presentation	• Spelling in general:
	  Hyphen/one word/two words
	  Names of people and places
	  Numbers, units, etc
	  Currencies
	  Dates and time
	  Uppercase vs lowercase
	  Contractions
	• Punctuation: comma, colon, ampersand

Visual presentation	• Typography
	  Italics or not (roman)
	  Bold
	• Layout
	  Spacing
	  Lists

Table 11.1 *The minimum content for a house style guide*

Examples of language guides in English which take a broad approach to house style:

› Abbott, B 2010. *Reference*. Oxford: Oxford University Press.
› Arnold, GT 2007. *Media writer's handbook. A guide to common writing and editing problems* (4 ed). New York: McGraw-Hill.
› Baskette, FK; JZ Sissors & BS Brooks 1986. *The art of editing*. New York: Macmillan.
› Bowles, DA & DL Borden 2011. *Creative editing* (6 ed). Boston, MA: Thomson/Wadsworth.
› Brooks, BS; JL Pinson & JG Wilson 2006. *Working with words. A concise handbook for media writers and editors*. New York: St Martin Press.
› Burchfield, RW 2004. *Fowler's modern English usage* (3 ed). London: Clarendon Press.
› Butcher, J 1993. *Copy-editing: The Cambridge handbook for editors, authors and publishers* (3 ed). New York/Cambridge: Cambridge University Press.
› Butcher, J; C Drake & M Leach 2009. *Butcher's copy-editing* (4 ed). Cambridge: Cambridge University Press.
› Butterfield, J (ed) 2007. *Oxford A–Z of English usage*. Oxford: Oxford University Press.
› Carter, R & M McCarthey 2006. *Cambridge grammar of English. A comprehensive guide: Spoken and written English grammar and usage*. Cambridge: Cambridge University Press.
› Clark, GN 2001. *Inside book publishing*. London: Routledge.
› Davies, G & R Balkwill 2011. *The professionals' guide to publishing: A practical introduction to working in the publishing industry*. London/Philadelphia/New Delhi: Kogan Page.
› Dykman, DJ; JDU Geldenhuys & EE Viljoen-Smook 2011. *The write stuff: The style guide with a difference*. Cape Town: Pharos.
› Einsohn, A 2011. *The copyeditor's handbook. A guide for book publishing and corporate communications* (3 ed). Los Angeles: The University of California Press.
› Eisenberg, A 1992. *Guide to technical editing: Discussion, dictionary, and exercises*. New York: Oxford University Press.
› Flann, E & B Hill 2004. *The Australian editing handbook* (2 ed). Milton: John Wiley & Sons Australia Ltd.
› Foster, C 1993. *Editing, design and book production*. London: Journeyman.
› Garner, BA 2003. *Garner's modern American usage* (2 ed). New York: Oxford University Press.
› Grossman, J (ed) 1993. *Chicago manual of style* (14 ed). Chicago: Chicago University Press.

> Law, J (ed) 2001. *Oxford language reference*. Oxford: Oxford University Press.
> Legat, M 1991. *An author's guide to publishing* (revised and expanded ed). London: Robert Hale.
> Leiter, K; J Harriss & S Johnson 2000. *The complete reporter. Fundamentals in writing and editing*. Massachusetts: Allyn & Bacon.
> Lynch, J 2008. *Guide to grammar and style*. <http://andromeda.rutgers.edu/~jlynch/Writing>.
> Mahan, M (ed) 2003. *Chicago manual of style* (15 ed), also available as CD-ROM and online. <http://www.chicagomanualofstyle.org/home.html>.
> Manser, MH 2011. *Good word guide: Answers everyday language problems* (rev ed). London: A & C Black.
> Manser, MH 2006. *Dictionary of idioms*. Hertfordshire, UK: Wordsworth Editions.
> Manser 2007. *Collins dictionary for writers and editors*.
> McKernan, J 1991. *The writer's handbook* (2 ed). New York/Chicago: Holt, Rinehart and Winston.
> Merriam-Webster's online. <http://www.m-w.com/>.
> MLA 2008. *The MLA style manual* (3 ed).
> MLA (Modern Language Association of America) 2009. *MLA handbook for writers of research papers* (7 ed). New York: MLA.
> Mossop, B 2010. *Revising and editing for translators* (2 ed). Manchester: St Jerome Publishing.
> *The Cambridge guide to English usage* 2004.
> *The Oxford guide to style* 2002.
> *The Oxford style manual* 2003.
> *New Oxford dictionary for writers and editors* 2005 (Adaptation of 2 ed of *The Oxford dictionary for writers and editors*).
> *New Hart's rules* 2005.
> *Style manual for authors, editors and printers of Australian government publications* 2002 (6 ed).
> <http://www.en.wikipedia.org/wiki/Manual_of_Style>.
> <http://www.en.wikipedia.org/wiki/Style_guide>.

List 11.3 continued

This section indicates that house style guides and style sheets (word lists) play a cardinal role in the day-to-day practice of text editing, mainly because they contribute towards consistency (one of the core requirements of text editing) in texts and also help the text editor to save time (by having fewer choices to make). The extent and nature of reference works in this field is discussed further and illustrated by means of examples in chapters 5/6.

2.6 Electronic sources

> Wordprocessing and email are indispensable for the editor.
> *Mackenzie*

> [People] recognize that computers can do a lot of intellectual heavy lifting but rather little creative work.
> *Anonymous*

> Although a computer is a useful tool for the copy-editor, it cannot read for sense, repetition or ambiguity.
> *Butcher et al*

> Computers are superb workhorses but cannot judge quality, spot libel, or tactfully negotiate a problem with an author.
> *Waddingham*

In Chapter 4.8.1 the use of technological tools in support of text editing was discussed in detail. There, emphasis was placed on the role that word processing software in general, and spell- and grammar-checkers and online dictionaries and thesauruses specifically (where available), play to make text editing appreciably easier and to save time in the process. Computers are in fact superb workhorses (Sunshine 2009; Waddingham 2006: 401). It is important that the role of the following are highlighted briefly:

- Take advantage of the functionality that spell- and grammar-checkers, online dictionaries and thesauruses have to offer (for more, see chapter 4 and this chapter 2.6.1).
- Exploit the full potential of your word processing software (Billingham 2002: 96–100). Are you able to exploit the necessary shortcuts (of which there are many if you know how to harness the computer's full potential) to save yourself time and effort? Microsoft's example of this is the AutoCorrect function, which can be set to recognise errors and correct them automatically as the text continues.
- The *internet* can be used supportively and comprehensively for research purposes. Morrish (1998: 252; 2003: 123) says that the information explosion during the past 20 years – which is largely the consequence of the potential and expansion of the internet (cf, among others, Bidgoli (ed) 2004; Bradley 2002; Craig 2005; Deitel & Deitel 2008; Dorner 2000; Mates 2000; Sunshine 2009; Whittaker 2002; Wiggins 1994; Windeatt 2000; Zittrain 2008) – has made knowledge and information available at an unbelievable speed.
- The internet has become the hub of a global marketplace of information and commerce (Craig 2005: xi).
- It is in fact important to realise that not all the information on the internet is reliable (it is certainly not always the gospel truth) and the text editor will have to learn to distinguish between what is available and trustworthy, on the one hand, and what is available but not to be trusted, on the other. For text editors, the internet is also a medium through which further training happens when, for example, they learn about websites that contain relevant information (such as about dictionaries that are out of print) or through

which opportunities for training can be made available. For more about this topic see chapter 5, including the examples that illustrate it.

- *Electronic mail (email)* serves as a really useful and fast communications channel between the text editor and the client and the author (Dorner 2000; Rooksby 2002; Whelan 2000). Nowadays, no text editor can afford to be without an email connection. Email is, in particular, also a way of taking part in internet chat groups, a place where language practitioners, for example, can send their questions about language issues or where they can test their ideas and opinions, problems with language, and terminology and problems against a wide, like-minded audience.
- *The management of electronic documents:* how documents are received, formatted (if necessary, so that they are compatible with your computer's software and programs), and stored in an ordered and organised manner; how documents are safely stored; how backup copies are made; how documents are sent out again; how attachments are received, stored and processed (Gilad 2007; Mackenzie 2004, 2011).
- *Electronic sources of information*, such as dictionaries, are of enormous value to the text editor for their easy availability as much as for their speed. Electronic sources of information are also discussed further in chapter 5, section 14.6. A number of examples of such sources are also provided there.

In conclusion: electronic tools definitely make the life of the contemporary text editor appreciably easier. However, this is the role that electronic development continues to play – for those who have to use it, as a means of getting work done. For now, it has not supplanted human beings in the realm of decision-making.

MS Word

- *Editorium Update*. Newsletter at <http://www.editorium.com/newsletr.htm>.
- Lockwood, B 2001. *Editing documents for publication using Microsoft Word for the IBM/PC*. Melbourne: Brett Lockwood. Also at <http://www.wordbytes.com.au>.
- Powers, H 2007. *Making Word work for you: An editor's intro to a tool of the trade*. New York: Editorial Freelancers Association.
- Tyson, H 2007. *Microsoft Word 2007 Bible*. Indianapolis: John Wiley.
- TheWord MVP Site: <http://word.mvps.org/>. Tips and tutorials on using MS Word for PC and Mac; includes a troubleshooting section.

Language references (some examples)

- <www.askoxford.com>.
- <www.collinslanguage.com>.
- <www.dailywritingtips.com>.
- <www.grammarforgrownups.wordpress.com>.

2.6.1 Spell-checkers, grammar-checkers and style-checkers

Practically speaking, spell-checkers, and also grammar- and style-checkers, can make a significant contribution to the text editor's productivity, level of accuracy and thoroughness.

In the first instance, they are a quick way of checking the spelling in a document. Secondly, they are thorough: they don't miss a single instance of genuine misspellings, typing errors and breaches of grammar rules. Thirdly, when they do detect errors, all it takes for the text editor to correct them onscreen is to press a couple of keys.

There are three obvious limitations of the checking facilities available to users of MS Word which make intelligent human intervention critical to successful outcomes:

- The spell-checker is fallible in that it doesn't detect correct spellings that are actually the incorrect word choice in a particular context: *form* vs *from*, for instance, or homophone pairs such as *there* vs *their,* or will not account for spellings determined by usage such as *all together* vs *altogether;* and *no-one* vs *no one* (this last a house style choice).
- This limitation requires the text editor to be additionally vigilant when running a spell-check on a document; and possibly to use the Find/Replace function to help detect occurrences of incorrect word usage. It also makes a thorough knowledge of the rules of spelling essential on those occasions when the spell-checker is unable to recognise words as misspelt/mistyped or to correct them.
- The grammar checker applies US English grammar conventions and rules, some of which don't apply to UK and other Englishes: for example, the use of *which* vs *that* and the use or omission of prepositions American-style (I wrote my sister; we visited *with* our parents at the weekend). This requires the text editor to be sufficiently au fait with the grammar rules and conventions to be able to determine whether occurrences of 'errors' detected by the system should be ignored or corrected.
- 'Good style' tends to be measured fairly mechanically in terms of sentence length (ie number of words per sentence) and word difficulty (ie words comprising three or more syllables). Sometimes, the style checker's interpretation of an 'overlong' sentence doesn't quite fit the typical reader of a text, so due allowance has to be made for that; and on occasion, according to Plain Language principles, the longer word may be clearer and more accurate than the suggested (much) shorter synonyms.

2.6.2 Spell-checkers and how to use them effectively

All wordprocessing programs include a spell-checking function, a device that will inform you that certain words you have written *do not appear in its dictionary* and then suggest plausible alternatives. For checking relatively short documents free of technical terms, proper names, abbreviations not in general use and/or jargon, they offer a speedy way of detecting and correcting spelling errors; but they are not entirely reliable – as indicated above, they'll not guarantee accurate spelling or detect misspellings that are themselves legitimate words (such as those listed above); they'll also not distinguish between homophones, will not account for spellings determined by usage, and may allow variant spellings and hyphenations that might not be compatible with the preferred spellings listed in the house style.

For long documents that contain many unusual (ie jargon or technical) words and abbreviations, spell-checking can be tedious and a nuisance. In such cases, after happening upon a particular word that you know is correct for the style or idiom of the publication, you could save yourself some time by clicking the Ignore All button, which instructs the computer to ignore all subsequent instances of the word in the current document.

Alternatively, at this point you could click on Add, which adds the word either to the system's main dictionary or to a custom dictionary that you have created (you can create one custom dictionary for each different subject area you work in). This option having been selected, added words will be skipped in later spell-checking.

Hint: Use the English (UK) or English (South Africa) dictionary for all documents intended for the British and South African markets; however, if you work on a document destined for the North American market, use the English (US) dictionary, which is usually the default for most word processing and spell-checking software.

In the case of texts that contain many brand names (for example), bibliographies, reference lists and some indexes, which tend to be filled with proper names the spell-checker won't recognise, spell-checking is likely to be a slow process: you have to decide whether you can rely on your eyes alone to pick up spelling inconsistencies or take the time to do it digitally.

When the copy-editor works onscreen, running the spell-checker should be one of their routine tasks (just as checking for double and triple word spaces and converting them to single spaces should be), because no error is more obvious than spelling errors or inconsistencies and therefore more potentially damaging to an editor's reputation. Ideally, a document should be spell-checked at least twice: once at the start of the editing process or sometime during it; then again during the final tidy-up, after the author's changes have been incorporated.

Even if the copy-editor has to work on hard copy, obtaining the author's disk and running the spell-checker on their file will at least help the editor to detect those hard-to-spot typos (Einsohn 2011: 145). From this perspective, it is also possible to check spellings in PDF-format documents by running the Find/Search facility expertly through a PDF.

Spell-checking lists of names (most of which will not be in the system's dictionary initially) can turn out to be a tedious undertaking, so many text editors avoid carrying out this essential check electronically, either abandoning the Search altogether or resorting to a paper-based check instead (Einsohn 2011: 144).

Note: Never hand a document back to a client without it first having been spell-checked at least once.

2.6.3 Imposing consistency via the Search or Find function

As an alternative to the spell-checker, when you have to check for spelling and other inconsistencies in a document, most wordprocessors usually have a Search or Find function that enables you to root out, for example, all instances of no one (that should be no-one), an historian (a historian), organize (organise), programme (program), off (of), AIDS (Aids), i.e. (ie), *ersatz* (ersatz), "crazy" ('crazy'), and so on.

Using this function in this way will not only save the text editor time (hunting for those needles in the haystack) but also greatly enhance the consistency of the text – you couldn't wish for a more reliable tool to preserve your reputation in this area. One caution, though: when using this function, do not use the Change All option – it could lead to all sorts of unforeseen changes being made that not even the Undo button will help you to reverse!

Also be especially careful to specify a search word exactly, with a space either side of it (or, if a fragment of a word, either spaced or unspaced as appropriate): you will want to narrow the search as much as possible to avoid a search for 'dog' leading you to 'dogged', 'dogfish', 'dogma' and 'endogenous'.

The available spell-checkers vary from extremely useful to less user friendly (Murray & Johanson 2006). Each individual text editor's specific requirements will probably determine which of the spell-checking software packages are acquired.

2.7 Internet sources

> The day will come when on-line dictionaries will replace many if not most of those in use today, whether in book form or as computer software.
> *Landers*

The internet is a resource where information can be found and checked quickly and easily, provided you have a computer with a fast internet connection. As Landers (2001: 178) points to the power of the internet so well: 'there are times when the Internet can bring to bear resources unavailable elsewhere to address a ... problem.' In this way, the internet holds many advantages for the text editor, including (1) the convenience and usefulness of the accessability of information that make it possible; and (2) a savings of time and money which information that carries the cost of paper, printing and distribution does not hold for users.

The adept text editor will harness the advantages of the internet to look up and check troublesome names, dates, people, events and addresses that seem doubtful or to survey uncharted territory briefly. In short, they will make their life a lot easier, and work more efficiently, by tracking down information much more quickly on this powerful resource.

2.7.1 Editorial resources

The following resources are a representative sample of helpful guides to using the internet as an editorial resource – it is impossible to provide a complete list together with their links, and in any event each text editor will in all likelihood have their own list of favourites to add:

- Harnack, A & E Kleppinger 2001. *Online! A reference guide to using internet sources.* Boston: Bedford/St Martin's.
- Walker, JR & T Taylor 1998. *The Columbia guide to online style.* New York: Columbia University Press.
- Modern Language Association of America (www.mla.org) provides examples of MLA style for citing electronic documents.
- American Psychological Association website (www.apa.org/journals/webref.htm) provides examples of the APA style for citing electronic documents.
- <http://www.google.co.za> or <http://www.google.com> – this is the easiest way of finding anything on the internet.
- <http://en.wikipedia.org> – for general information on aspects of the English language and its usage. Note, however, that the information on Wikipedia is not authoritative (anybody can contribute to the content on this site and the quality control, such as it is, leaves much to be desired), so it should always be verified by checking it against similar information on other, more authoritative websites.
- <http://www.woes.co.za> – a website that contains numerous links to other websites.
- <http://www.loc.gov/rr/international/portals.html> – the Library of Congress 'Portals to the World'; it has numerous links to other useful websites.
- <http://www.accurapid.com> – for 'Translators'on-line resources.'
- <http://www.refdesk.com> – for fact-checking.
- <http://www.answers.com> – for fact-checking.
- <http://www.hyperhistory.com> – for checking historical information covering 3,000 years.
- <http://www.well.com> – a chat group worth subscribing to.
- <http://www.fnt.co.za> – about finance and matters financial.
- <http://www.symbols.com/> – a linked encyclopaedia of graphic symbols.
- <http://www.alltheweb> – another resource for tapping into useful information.
- <http://www.chicagomanualofstyle.org> – a useful online resource when you're struggling to deal with style issues.
- <http://www.electriceditors.net> – a resource with numerous references to other sites in and about English.
- <http://www.theslot.com> – an important site for text editors.
- <http://www.allwords.com> – useful for checking words from foreign languages – follow the link to 'Links for Word lovers', which will unlock a host of sources.

2.7.2 Online dictionaries

- <http://www.gotranslators.com> – for word lists, dictionaries, and so on, that are pertinent to translators.
- <http://www.onelook.com> – for dictionaries.
- <http://www.dictionary.com> – about numerous English-language dictionaries.
- <http://www.hyperdictionary.com> – for links to dictionaries.
- <http://www.ilovelanguages.com/> – about dictionaries in other languages, plus numerous other useful links.
- <http://dictionary.oed.com> – the *Oxford English dictionary* 2009; use it to check the correctness of English words and expressions.
- <http://www.merriam-webster.com> – the Merriam-Webster online; use it to check the correctness of American English words and expressions.
- <http://www.dictionary.cambridge.org> – the well-known *Cambridge advanced learners dictionary* can be used to check English words and expressions.
- <http://www.ldoceonline.com> – the site of *Longman's dictionary of contemporary English.*
- <http://www.oxforddictionaries.com> – the site of the suite of dictionaries from Oxford University Press.
- <http://www.oxfordreference.com> – a collection of reference works in electronic format. Users are required to subscribe to the website before they can gain access to the resources on it.

The above is a random selection of the available internet resources; there are, of course, many more. Text editors quickly learn what works and what doesn't – and also which resources need to be added to their resource base.

2.8 Encyclopaedias

For language practitioners, encyclopaedias (whether in print or electronic format) serve as useful general resources for checking the information given by authors. Text editors must have at least one at their disposal to be able to conduct random verifications or to check information that gives cause for doubt or suspicion. Much more compact and user-friendly – and up to date – than their paper-based equivalents, the recent generation of online versions make the editor's task so much easier.

Print format
- Bidgoli, H (ed) 2004. *The internet encyclopedia*. Hoboken, NJ: John Wiley & Sons.
- Mallory, J 1987. *Collins concise encyclopedia*. New York: HarperCollins.
- Law, J 2007. *Oxford concise encyclopaedia* (2 ed). Oxford: Oxford University Press.
- *Reader's Digest guide to places of the world: A geographical dictionary of countries, cities, natural and man-made wonders* 1987. New York: Reader's Digest.
- *Reader's Digest library of modern knowledge* 1981. New York: Reader's Digest.

CD-ROM/Internet format

- <http://en.wikipedia.org> – for general information about the English language and usage.
- <http://www.britannica.com> – an exceptionally useful general resource that covers a wide variety of topics.
- <http://www.encyclopedia.com> – another internet site on which to find information of a general nature.
- <http://www.noodletools.com/> – an excellent resource for finding solutions.
- <http://www.libraryspot.com/encyclopedias.htm> – to find out where to find online encyclopaedias.
- <http://www.pantheon.org> – the *Encyclopedia mythica* for (among others, Greek) mythology and religion.

2.9 Atlases

- Andromeda 2001. *Cassell's atlas of world history*. London: Weidenfeld & Nicolson.
- *Collins world atlas* 2011. New York: HarperCollins.
- <http://www.worldatlas.com/>.
- <http://www.infoplease.com/atlas/>.

2.10 Plain language

- Bailey, EP Jr 1997. *The plain English approach to business writing*. Oxford: Oxford University Press.
- Blamires, H 2000. *The Penguin guide to plain English*. London: Penguin Books
- Carr, S 2011. *Editing into plain language. Working for non-publishers*. London: Society for Editors and Proofreaders.
- Center for Plain Language. Various useful resources: <centreforplainlanguage.org/>. Washington, DC.
- Charrow, RP & V Charrow 1979. 'Making legal language understandable: A psycholinguistic study of jury instructions.' *Columbia law review* 79: 1306–1374.
- Clarity International. *Clarity* and other resources: <www.clarity-international.net>.
- Cutts M 2000. *Lucid law* (2 ed). <clearest.co.uk/publications/books/lucid law>.
- Cutts, M 2008. *Writing by numbers: Are readability tests to clarity what karaoke is to song?* <www.clearest.co.uk/files/WritingByNumbersKaraoke.pdf>.
- Cutts, M 2009. *The Oxford guide to plain English*. Oxford: Oxford University Press.
- Dayananda, J 1986. 'Plain English in the United States.' *English today* 5: 13–16.
- Eagleson, RD, assisted by G Jones & S Hassall 1990. *Writing in plain English*. Canberra: Australian Government Publishing Service.
- English Commission. 2011. *Plain English lexicon*. <www.clearest.co.uk/pages/publications/plainenglishlexicon>.
- European Commission *How to write clearly* <http://ec.europe.eu/translation/>.
- Felker, DB; F Pickering, VR Charrow, VM Holland & JC Redish 1981. *Guidelines for document designers*. Washington: American Institutes for Research.

- Gowers, E 1969. *The complete plain words*. London: Penguin.
- Jarrett, C & G Gaffney 2008. *Forms that work: Designing Web forms for usability*. Burlington, MA: Morgan Kaufmann.
- Kempton, K & N Moore 1994. *Designing public documents: A review of research*. London: Policy Studies Institute.
- Kimble, J 2003. Answering the critics of plain language. <www.plainlanguagenetwork. org/kimble/critics.htm>.
- Kimble, J 2006. *Lifting the fog of legalese: Essays on plain language*. Durham, NC: Carolina Academic Press.
- Mills, G & M Duckworth. 1996. *The gains for clarity: A research report on the effects of plain-language documents*. Centre for Micro-economic Policy Analysis and Centre for Plain Legal Language, University of Sidney.
- Murphy, EM 2008. *Effective writing: Plain English at work*. Melbourne: Pitman.
- Plain Language Association International (PLAIN). <http://www.plainlanguagenetwork. org/>.
- Plain Language Campaign 2011. *The A to Z of alternative words*.
- <www.plainenglish.co.uk/files/alternative.pdf>.
- Schriver, K 1997. *Dynamics in document design: Creating text for readers*. New York: Wiley.
- Stephens, C 2011. *Plain language, then and now*. <http://www.Themediaonline.co.za/ 2011/plain-language-then-and-now>.
- US Federal Government. Plain Language site. <www.plainlanguage.gov/resources/index. cfm>.

2.11 Networks

The usefulness of networks – that is, groups of contact people at certain institutions, including universities – cannot be underestimated. Networking is the current new way of exchanging ideas with kindred spirits and making important new contacts, sometimes with a view to doing business together or collaborating on projects – or even passing business or projects on to others. Every language practitioner (including text editors) should nurture their contacts (those who choose not to network are foolishly shortsighted), because at some time or other they'll need to call upon such contacts for advice, information or assistance of some kind related to language practice. Being a member of a professional association offers many networking opportunities, however informally.

There are also radio programmes to tune into, or participate in, on the subject of language that serve to stimulate interest in the subject or to provide solutions to language problems. Such programmes often involve discussions by and interviews with experts in some or other language-related area, and therefore offer unique, free opportunities to obtain information from the horse's mouth, as it were. They also provide opportunities for practitioners to learn about the latest publications in the field of language practice, text editing, linguistics and lexicography.

2.12 In practice

First and foremost, as text editor you'll need to have to hand the latest edition of any publication on editing practice, for example:

- Allen, RE (ed) 1991. *The Oxford writers' dictionary*. Oxford: Oxford University Press.
- American Copy Editors Society. <http://www.copydesk.org>.
- Council of Australian Societies of Editors 2001. *Australian standards for editing practice*. <www.iped-editors.org>.
- AVS 2006. *Proofreading and copy editing*. <http://www.gotlinks.com/earticles/ 108636-proofreading-and-copy-editing.html>.
- Baskette, FK; JZ Sissors & BS Brooks 1986. *The art of editing*. New York: Macmillan.
- Beene, L 2009. *Most bang for the buck. An editor's workbook. A reference text with exercises for beginning proofreaders, copyeditors, and developmental editors*. <http:// www.faculty.washington.edu/pheld/tcxg482/Beene.pdf>.
- Butcher, J; C Drake & M Leach 2009. *Butcher's copy-editing: The Cambridge handbook for editors, authors and publishers* (4 ed). Cambridge: Cambridge University Press.
- Cranford, RJ 1967. *Copy editing workbook*. New York: Holt, Rinehart & Winston.
- Critchley, W 2007. *The pocket book of proofreading: A guide to freelance proofreading and copy-editing*. London: First English Books.
- Editors' Association of Canada 2000. *Editing Canadian English*.
- Editors' Association of Canada 2010–2011. *Meeting professional editorial standards*.
- Einsohn, A 2011. *The copyeditor's handbook. A guide for book publishing and corporate communications* (3 ed). Los Angeles: The University of California Press.
- Eisenberg, A 1992. *Guide to technical editing: Discussion, dictionary, and exercises*. New York: Oxford University Press.
- Glover, A 1996. 'In search of the perfect copy editor: 10 copy editor traits that guarantee you success.' <http://poynter.org/content>.
- Gross, G (ed) 1993. *Editors on editing. An inside view of what editors really do* (3 ed). New York: Harper Row.
- Guy, ME (ed) 1990. *Ethical decision making in everyday work situations*. Connecticut: Quorum Books.
- Harris, N 1991. *Basic editing: A practical course*. London: Book House Training Centre.
- Hart, G 2007. *Effective onscreen editing: New tools for an old profession*. Pointe-Claire, Quebec: Diaskeuasis Publishing. <http://www.geoff-hart.com>.
- Horwood, T 1995. *Freelance proofreading and copy-editing: A guide*. Beaworthy, UK: Action Print Press.
- Kerzner, H 2004. *Advanced project management: best practices in implementation*. Hoboken, NJ: Johan Wiley.
- Lunsford, A & R Connors 2001. *The new St Martin's handbook* (5 ed). Boston: Bedford/ St Martin's.
- Mackenzie, J 2004. *The editor's companion*. Cambridge: Cambridge University Press.

- Miller, K; K Swift & S Dowrick 1995. *The handbook of non-sexist writing for writers, editors and speakers* (3 ed). London: Women's Press.
- Moffett, H 2008. *Advice from an editor*. Cape Town: Centre for the Book.
- Montagnes, I 1991. *Editing and publication: A training manual*. Manilla, Phillipines: International Rice Research Institute.
- Murphy, EM 2011. *Working words – for editors, writers, teachers, students of English grammar and wordsmiths all*. Manuka, Australia: Canberra Society of Editors.
- O'Connor, M 1986. *How to copyedit scientific books and journals*. Philadelphia: ISI Press.
- Orr, AD 2004. *Advanced project management: A complete guide to the key processes, models and techniques*. London: Sterling.
- Samson, D 1993. *Editing technical writing*. Oxford: Oxford University Press.
- Small, I & M Walsh (eds) 1991. *The theory and practice of text-editing*. Cambridge: Cambridge University Press.
- Society for Editors and Proofreaders. <http://www.sfep.org.uk/pub/faqs/fedit.asp>.
- Van Buren, R & MF Buehler 1991. *The levels of edit* (2 ed). Arlington, VA: Society for Technical Communication.
- Zook, LM (ed) 1976. *Technical editing: Principles and practices*. Washington: Society for Technical Communication.

In the process of equipping yourself with suitable resources, you'll need to ensure that you observe the following guidelines:

Checklist 11.1 Choosing suitable resources

✓ Ensure that you always have the most recent resource(s) to hand. If a new edition becomes available, it is unforgivable not to have taken note of it.

✓ Purchase as many dictionaries as you can afford, always purchasing the latest edition.

✓ Ensure that you really do know how to make optimal use of dictionaries. It is possible to acquire this skill over time.

✓ Never rely on only one dictionary, even if it is your favourite! Get into the habit of consulting more than one as a double-check of any decisions you have to make or solutions you have to arrive at.

✓ Acquire the large, well-known dictionary (see the list above). School dictionaries are unsuitable for professional text editors, because among their limitations is the fact that the vocabulary they contain is too limited.

✓ Keep an eye out for the launch of newer resources – on the radio, via media releases, on websites and by being linked to key websites (ie of publishers and professional associations).

✓ Ascertain which resources work the best for you and the kind of work you do. Keep them close at hand whenever you are working on a text.

✓ Remember that the first meaning given in a list in a dictionary is not necessarily the correct one in the context in which you are working. It is possible that only the third or fourth meaning will fit into a particular context. Do not accept a purely mechanical meaning of a word without considering its context (Landers 2001: 175–176).

✓ Use internet resources such as Wikipedia and Google with care and circumspection. The information such resources contain is only as reliable as the person who put together the content – everything you'll find on the internet is not necessarily the truth.

3 Tools dealing specifically with proofreading

Many practitioners begin their careers in communications and publishing as proofreaders before migrating to the more exacting (for many) craft of copy-editing. Others never move beyond proofreading, having found their niche there – those with an eagle's eye fit very comfortably in this niche. Texts that deal exclusively with proofreading are few and far between (it's often considered to be part and parcel of the copy-editor's skills set), but there are those aimed specifically at proofreaders, including:

- Anderson, L 1990. *Handbook for proofreading*. Lincolnwood: NTC Business Books.
- AVS 2006. 'Proofreading and copy editing.' <http://www.gotlinks.com/earticles/108636-proofreading-and-copy-editing.html>.
- British Standards Institution. 2005. BS 5261C: *Marks for copy preparation and proof correction.*
- Beene, L 2009. *Most bang for the buck. An editor's workbook. A reference text with exercises for beginning proofreaders, copyeditors, and developmental editors.* <http://www.faculty.washington.edu/pheld/tcxg482/Beene.pdf>.
- Butcher, J; C Drake & M Leach 2009. *Butcher's copy-editing: The Cambridge handbook for editors, authors and publishers* (4 ed). Cambridge: Cambridge University Press.
- Gilad, S 2007. *Copyediting and proofreading for dummies*. Indianapolis, IN: Wiley.
- Horwood, T 1995. *Freelance proofreading and copy-editing: A guide.* Beaworthy, UK: Action Print Press.
- Linnegar, J 2008. *Manual on basic copy editing and proofreading*. Cape Town: McGillivray Linnegar Associates. <info@editandtrain.com>.
- Linnegar, J 2009. *Manual on advanced copy editing and proofreading*. Cape Town: McGillivray Linnegar Associates. <info@editandtrain.com> & <www.editandtrain.com>.
- Markman, T 2008a. Critical differences between proofreading, copy editing and rewriting. <http://www.bizcommunity.com> (Accessed October 2008).
- Smith, DA & HA Sutton 1994. *Powerful proofreading skills: tips, techniques and tactics.* Menlo Park: Crisp Publications.
- Souder, SA & CC White 1995. *Proofreading – skills for success.* New York: Houghton Mifflin.

4 Referring to sources (citation)

Academic institutions and scientific publications require writers of scientific works to refer to the sources they have consulted.
Lourens

4.1 Rationale for using sources

One of the characteristics of discursive texts is that they are usually accompanied by a *list of references* (that is, only those sources that are referred to in the text) or a *bibliography* (that is, all the sources that the authors consulted, some of which may not be referred to in the text). It is important to compile and arrange this list of sources in the correct manner, following accepted conventions, which are often spelt out in an organisation's house style guide or manual.

Two further aspects of intext referencing should be mentioned at this stage: (1) *references to the full titles* of the works cited in the bibliography (such as the one at the back of this book, which comprises all the titles we authors consulted but did not necessarily quote specifically at any point in the text) and (2) *references using an abbreviated mode of citation* (or short title) rather than the full details given in the bibliography.

Writers refer to other people's writing because they reckon that those people's research or writing (be it an article, a report, a conference paper, a book or an internet source) will help to strengthen their case or support their hypothesis. This was also the case with this book: we as authors have freely made use of a large number of sources because we believed that the works consulted would help us to formulate our own arguments and also to substantiate them. Throughout the process, we felt it important to indicate those sources we used, and we did so by adopting the abbreviated Harvard method (Lourens 2007: 104) – a method used a great deal in academic writing. In this way we tried to achieve the following objectives (as indicated by Lourens 2007: 104):

› We wanted to acknowledge all the information and opinions that were not our own.

› We wanted to provide support to or offer proof of assertions we made so that the reader(s) could see we hadn't made them up and that other thinkers and researchers' views accord with our own.

› We wanted to help the reader(s) to locate the sources easily.

› We wanted to give the reader(s) the opportunity to be able to access and read the sources independently.

› We wanted to illustrate the fact that we can also participate in the academic discourse on the subject-matter of this book.

› We wanted to give credence to our own writing by referring to the highly reputable sources on the topics dealt with in our book that we were able to obtain, read and reflect on.

› We also wanted to ensure that we did not commit plagiarism, so we ensured our references are both cautiously and accurately cited. We adopted this approach in order that work of other researchers was not seen to be ours: that is not only unethical and unacceptable but also a breaches the law of intellectual property and of copyright.

List 11.4 Why we have to indicate sources of citations

>>

According to the available sources on the subject of referencing, there are three main methods of indicating one's sources:

1. the Harvard method (a more characteristic style of the humanities – which in fact also includes the Modern Language Association (MLA) of America's way of doing things);
2. the APA (American Psychological Association) method – which tends to be used more in the social and behavioural sciences; or
3. the Vancouver method (a type of numerical referencing system more characteristic of the mathematical sciences).

How do a knowledge and an understanding of these methods of referencing affect the text editor?

List 11.5 How does a knowledge of references benefit a text editor?

› The text editor must know which method the author of the text has chosen. The choice of method has implications for the way in which the text is read and for checking the abbreviated citations.

› The chosen method must be maintained consistently during the editing process.

› Give particular attention to the spelling, punctuation, font size and font style in the bibliography or list of references.

› Run at least a random check of the abbreviated citations to ensure that they correspond correctly to the corresponding reference in the bibliography or list of references. It is usually not possible to check an entire bibliography or list of references because doing so is very time-consuming.

› The bibliography or list of references can be viewed as a kind of style guide that can be used to check intext references against.

4.2 Resources about citations

On the subject of methods of referencing sources there are a large number of references in English. Those listed below are some of the texts worth consulting:

- Association of Legal Directors & D Dickerson 2010. *ALWD citation manual: A professional system of citation* (4 ed). New York: Aspen Publishers.
- Harvard Law Review Association 2005. *The Bluebook: A uniform system of citation* (18 ed). Boston, MA: Harvard Law Review.
- British Standard 1629: 1989 *References to published materials.*
- British Standard 5605: 1990 *Recommendations for citing and referencing.*
- Burger, M 2010. *Bibliographic style and reference techniques.* Pretoria: Unisa Press.

- Butcher, J; C Drake & M Leach 2009. *Butcher's copy-editing: The Cambridge handbook for editors, authors and publishers* (4 ed). Cambridge: Cambridge University Press.
- *Canadian guide to uniform legal citation* 2002. (5 ed). *Carswell/McGill law journal.*
- *Chicago manual of style online.* <http://www.chicagomanualofstyle.org>.
- Einsohn, A 2011. *The copyeditor's handbook: A guide for book publishing and corporate communications* (3 ed). Berkeley: University of California Press.
- Gibaldi, J (ed) 1998. *MLA style manual and guide to scholarly publishing* (2 ed). New York: Modern Language Association of America.
- *Publication manual of the American Psychological Association* 2001. (5 ed). Washington, DC: American Psychological Association.
- *Scientific style and format: the CBE manual for authors, editors, and publishers.* 2006. Compiled by the Style Committee of the Council of Science Editors (7 ed). Reston, VA: Council of Science Editors in cooperation with the Rockefeller University Press.
- Turabian, KL 2007. *A manual for writers of research papers, Theses, and dissertations: Chicago style for students and researchers* (7 ed). Chicago: University of Chicago Press.
- *The University of Chicago manual of legal citation* 2000. Edited by the staff of the University of *Chicago law review* and of the University of Chicago Legal Forum (2 ed). Chicago: University of Chicago.
- Most universities, publishers and other organisations have their own house style preferences for referencing and bibliographies. Obtain a copy of their house style before starting to edit the references and bibliography to ensure that you do not have to make counter-productive and time-consuming amendments in line with their specific preferences – which can often be hybrids of established styles such as Harvard, APA, uniform legal citation conventions, and so on.

4.3 In practice

The references listed above offer a large number of extremely practical hints regarding the complexity of referencing, including the use of punctuation marks and capitalisation and the use of italics. Readers are advised to consult these (and other similar) sources regularly. A number of internet sources that deal with referencing are also available (some include references to other sources), as indicated in the selected list below:

- <http://www.apastyle.org>.
- <http://www.mla.com/style/>.
- <http://www.bridgew.edu/Library/styleman.cfm/>.
- <http://www.mckendree.edu/academics/bibliographic_style.aspx/>.
- <http://owl.english.purdue.edu/>.

Here follows a selection of tips from these sources:

- Bibliographical references must be as complete as possible so that the reader is able to go directly to the correct place without any effort (Butcher 1992; 1993: 64; Butcher, Drake & Leach 2006; 2009).

- If in a text there is a reference to a source that is given in a language other than the language in which the document has been written (in the case of this book, a reference to a text in Afrikaans, Dutch, Italian or Spanish, for instance), the reference must be given in the original language. Consequently: (*ed*) should be (*red* – Dutch or Afrikaans) or (*réd* – French); *Munich* should become *München*.
- If there is a cross-reference to one specific sentence, it will form a part of that sentence, and the punctuation that terminates the sentence should follow the close parenthesis:

    It would seem that punctuation could be a problem with references. *(British Standard 1629: 1989).*

- If there is a cross-reference to a preceding section or chapter, it should be positioned after the sentence and therefore after the final punctuation. This matter has already been discussed elsewhere. (See chapter 5.)
- When an ellipsis is used to indicate that a section or sections of a quoted excerpt has or have been omitted from the original, it should comprise only three spaced stops; if the ellipsis falls at the start of the excerpt, it should be followed by a single space; if it falls mid-sentence, it should have a space either side of it; if it falls at the end of an excerpt, it should be preceded by a space and there should be no space between the ellipsis and the final punctuation:

    '... it is said that Jones (1998: 24) is incorrect in ... insisting that hurricanes happen frequently ...'.

- Italicise the titles of *published* works: books and anthologies, periodicals and journals, and newspapers.
- When one author has published more than one work in the same year and such works are cited in the text and listed in a bibliography or list of references, the works should be differentiated by means of the lowercase letters a, b, c, etc, appended to the date:

    Botha (2005a) ... Botha (2005c)

in both the intext references and the bibliography or the list of references.

- In a list of two or more references cited in one place a semicolon should separate the references from one another. The references should be arranged in ascending alphabetical order by author and then chronologically by date.

A number of useful *plagiarism detection software packages* can also be downloaded at little or no cost from the web. These have been taken at random after a Google search:
- <www.turnitin.com>.
- <www.duplichecker.com>.
- <www.dustball.com/cs/plagiarism.checker>.
- <www.grammarly.com>.

5 Summary and conclusion

On a page on the Canadian Association of Editors' website the words 'Editing is an art as well as a discipline' are displayed. There is more than a mote of truth in this statement, as is borne out by the many editing resources listed in this chapter. As professional editors we probably have an innate 'talent' (art) for our craft, but we also have to be aware of our limitations and wise enough to know, first, that there are resources available to check, verify and, if necessary, double-check the content of whatever we're editing and, secondly, to have to hand such resources and consult them whenever necessary.

These resources – both in print format and internet-based – are essential tools to have at one's disposal to consult whenever the need arises, whether it's to resolve a procedural problem, to apply a rule or convention of grammar, to apply house style consistently, or to check an author's facts. It is not expected of a text editor to know everything; what is expected, however, is that they know where to look for information, which is where the meaning of 'discipline' referred to above fits in.

In this chapter we've surveyed the key tools to consult: professional guidelines for editors; mid- to upper range dictionaries in whatever language(s) you edit in; subject-specific dictionaries; encyclopaedias; grammars and language-usage guides; thesauruses, and style guides. We've also considered the resources that will support text editors when they are editing for plain language and also when dealing with citations.

While both print and electronic media have been considered, we're aware that it's not possible either to know about every possible resource or to include them all in a text of this nature. We would welcome any contributions you'd like to see included in future editions of *Text editing*.

12

Text editing in practice: a comparative analysis of texts

Übung macht den Meister.
Practice makes perfect.
Experience is the best teacher.
German idiom

If the proof of the pudding is in the eating,
then *Übung macht den Meister* is an as-good-as-homemade dessert.
Ian Emerson

12

Contents

Objectives

In this chapter we integrate the knowledge, skills, tips and suggestions of chapters 4 to 10 into the facets of text editing described in chapter 3. We do so by applying both to the editing of some of the types of text highlighted in chapter 2. In doing so, we follow the CCC model described in chapter 2, fleshed out in the form of an evaluation grid that meshes the five facets (or 'lenses') through which the text editor could/should view a text – text type, content, structure, formulation, presentation – with each of the three criteria – correspondence, consistency and correctness.

We present this grid for the purpose of achieving an optimal level of text editing in every document you the text editor are likely to tackle; by so doing, we hope to help you cover all bases when working on a text, that is, to approach your intervention systematically and thoroughly, and to leave no stone unturned in the process. We hope that, through this handbook, and especially through this chapter, we have been able to offer a workable, integrated example of text editing in practice.

Accordingly, the central question in this chapter is this: What exactly is it that the text editor requires in order to proceed from one text to another and yet still perform a thorough editing job on both?

1 Introduction: a question about practice

1.1 A request to text editors

Even though we have spent 11 chapters describing what makes a successful, communicative text, we authors are aware that several roads usually lead to Rome. Therefore, we invited text editors to bring their wealth of collective wisdom and experience to this final chapter. However, our invitation had a sting in its tail: we asked the 11 who volunteered to critically analyse the texts – all but one of which had already been published and, by implication, edited. The fact that the texts under scrutiny have been made public has made it easier for us to use them for our present educative purposes.

The 11 text editors[1] were asked to reconstruct the editorial intervention required to get the texts up to their published standard. Thus, our brief to those who volunteered to participate in the exercise was to do the opposite of editing, namely, to examine the texts or text fragments and to point out potential problems that could typically occur in these types of

---

1 The 11 volunteers who went the extra mile and are greatly acknowledged here are: Wendy Barrow, John Deane, Anne Denniston, Eldene Eyssel, Joan Fairhurst, Denise Fourie, Catherine Grady, Jean Kilroe, Marina Pearson, Anni Protti and Pauline Visser.

text and which would require editorial intervention of some sort to be remedied. We are most grateful to all of them for their willing participation in this project – their contributions have made this chapter and analysis possible and constitutes the final piece and the *pièce de résistance* of this book.

Because one of the purposes of this book is to make a contribution to the training of text edtitors (including proofreaders), the present authors thought it could benefit from some hands-on experience from professionals in the field presented systematically. We therefore not only presented the editors with some sample texts, we also gave them an inventory of errors based on the available literature on the subject: (1) Content errors; (2) Text-structural errors; (3) Language/grammar problems, and (4) Visual/presentation errors (including graphics, spelling and punctuation). This inventory was summarised as table 6.1. and further illustrated in chapters 6 to 10.

1.2 The reactions of the text editors

Most of the participating editors tackled the texts thoroughly and with considerable commitment, and we thank them sincerely for that. However, we take responsibility for the manner in which the texts were selected and arranged, and the editors' collective responses have been employed and analysed in this chapter.

All the sample texts were intended for publication (either on the internet or in print), and therefore we felt that they were appropriate for our pedagogical purposes. The fact that the texts have been published implies that an attempt has been made to make them communicate as optimally as possible, which entails that they have been improved – to a greater or lesser extent. This made the materials serve our purpose all the more. Because one of the aims of this book is to serve as an educational text, we tried to highlight and group together a number of possible errors. In practice, though, text editing is a more holistic undertaking (see section 5 at the end of this chapter for two examples of holistic editing in practice), but in a training situation it's sometimes not a bad idea to turn likely errors and problems into abstractions of what could have been the case. We also had to make some choices because we could not include every possible text, error, problem or challenge in the available space. In the end, only five of the six texts were used in our analysis of errors.

2 Types of text for editing

For this chapter about the application of editing theory and the well-defined editing skills covered in the previous chapters, we chose texts from a variety of text types (please refer back to the complete overview in chapter 2). Some texts clearly belong to only one type, but the others fall into two or more categories. We consciously excluded literary texts from this exercise (that is, literary, expressive and rhetorical texts), because in that genre the collaboration between the source text and the target text is exceptionally intense and such texts normally undergo an extensive editing process; in this exercise, therefore, we have specifically focused on non-fiction. In addition, texts that are merely a written version of an oral interaction have also not been included. In summary, then, the texts can be divided up as follows:

Main text type

1. Referential texts (descriptive)

SECONDARY TYPE	TEXT AIM	EXAMPLES	SAMPLE TEXTS
Informative	Presenting information: factual messages	• Travel guides • Pamphlets • News messages • Articles (journals & newspapers) • Newspapers & journals • Dictionaries	• Estuary Villa • How do I claim maintenance?
Argumentative	Presenting information: well-reasoned relation-ships between facts	• Academic articles • Reports • Essays • Theses • Memorandums • Specialised books	• Multilingualism in South Africa
Instructive	Presenting information: systematically broadens knowledge	• Handbooks • Manuals • Directories • DIY books • Sports rules • Descriptions • Lists	• Induction of labour
Narrative/ descriptive	Presenting information: retells what happened	• Children's and other stories • Logbooks • Novels • Short stories • Reports	

2. Appellative texts

SECONDARY TYPE	TEXT AIM	EXAMPLES	SAMPLE TEXTS
Evaluative	Influencing opinions, thoughts, ideas: judgemental	• Reviews (of books, plays, etc) • Speeches • Legal judgments • Political pamphlets	
Directive	Influencing opinions, thoughts, ideas: change in attitude and behaviour	• Advertisements • Consumer guides • Lectures (teaching) • Fundraising letters • Election speeches • Political texts	• LiceBGone
Rhetorical	Influencing opinions, thoughts, ideas: provoking reflection (and action)	• Debates • Speeches • Literary texts • Church sermons	

Table 12.1 *Overview of sample texts according to text types*

The first text was the first draft of a text intended for the online holiday accommodation/ resort portal, www.safarinow.com (http://www.safarinow.com/go/EstuaryVilla5/) but not yet posted to the website (the final well-edited version can now be viewed). It features details of the guesthouse in KwaZulu-Natal province named Estuary Villa (retrieved first quarter 2011). It is essentially an online advertisement (one of many on this website) and constitutes text about travel/destinations. Its function is both to inform and to persuade, as visitors to the webpage must be attracted to the total package being offered through a stay at Estuary Villa, having learned what it and its surroundings have to offer the tourist or holidaymaker. One of this text's major challenges is to describe local activities, facilities and destinations without using local terms that non-local tourists are likely not to understand while at the same time describing them accurately and attractively. We refer to the text as Estuary Villa.

Essentially a fairly academic article, the piece about Multilingualism in South Africa was taken off the website <http:////scnc.ukzn.ac.za/doc/Lang/Broeder-P_Multilingualism_in_ SA_KwaZulu_Natal_Durban_OccPap7.pdf>. Its purpose is largely informative, and it is aimed at quite a wide audience of people who would be interested in the status quo of the major (official) languages of South Africa since 1994. This piece focuses exclusively on the major languages spoken in the province of KwaZulu-Natal. In a sense it is also argumentative in that it provides a number of views or opinions on the factors leading to the status of isiZulu and the position the language currently finds itself in. Perhaps the single biggest challenge for the authors was how to refer to the local languages (ie what labels to use for them consistently). This text is referred to as Multilingualism.

One informative consumer-oriented text was taken directly off the web: LiceBGone (http://www.licebgone.co.za/; http://www.licebgone.com/). Besides providing important health-related information in a systematic manner, it is also intended to be both instructive and persuasive. The LiceBGone text takes the form of an advertisement, the purpose of which is to influence the purchasing behaviour of the reader through the claims it makes (there is a more elaborate and narrative website too). The delivery of the essential information proved to be the major difficulty the authors of this text has encountered, including the most appropriate way of laying out and sequencing the text. We will refer to the text used in this example as LiceBGone.

The writers and designers of the citizen's guide to understanding an aspect of the law, in the form of the information booklet *'How do I claim maintenance?'* (2009) (in short *Maintenance*), faced the challenge of writing simply and clearly about a highly complex legal topic. This is a printed eight-page booklet. The topic and process of claiming maintenance from former spouses or partners has very practical implications for ordinary citizens (especially people who cannot afford access to legal counsel and who themselves are either illiterate or semi-literate and certainly are unable to understand legal process and terminology). Clarifying and simplifying a complex topic required the use of plain language, the logical sequencing of information, and a clear, unequivocal layout.

The textbook material entitled *'Induction of labour'*, an edited chapter from an academic textbook aimed at nursing students (now published), most of whose native language is not English, was the last of the texts to be scrutinised by the editor team. It epitomises the publication comprising highly specialised subject-matter written by a non-native speaker of the language of publication and intended for largely non-native speaking readers – a really challenging combination which stretches correspondence to the limits.

3 Textual analysis following the CCC model

3.1 A systematic approach to text evaluation

For a text to be communicative it has to correspond and be consistent and correct for all five textual facets. These criteria for analysis are the basis for evaluating text quality. Each of the criteria when applied to each text facet generates a specific evaluation point [EP]. The facets, criteria and evaluation points do not occur in isolation and are not finely delineated. The boundaries between them are not hard-and-fast and even though a certain evaluation point is highlighted there may well be an overlap with others or a trickling down effect from one into another.

3.2 The five facets of texts

The quality of a text can be determined by analysing it from five different textual angles or perspectives (or through different lenses), namely text type, content, structure, formulation or wording, and presentation. In this section we study how a focus on one facet influences the text as a whole.

Text type (textual facet A):

Every text belongs to a particular text type (book, thesis, advertisement, web page) that has to be appropriate to a predetermined public; it also has to possess the characteristics of a particular type of text (genre) in which the rules and conventions have to be applied correctly. The *Estuary Villa* text, for instance, is an online advertisement. The wording has to be persuasive in nature and has to breathe what is expected from an advertisement selling a tourist service while at the same time informing the visitor to the website.

Content (textual facet B):

Not only must every text convey adequate and sufficient information, there must also be agreement between various facts, while the content must also be factually correct. In the *Maintenance* text the facts have to be represented correctly, but they also have to be understandable to the readers, since the text functions as a bridge between the Maintenance Court and the citizens confronted with having to claim maintenance payments.

Structure (textual facet C):

A text has to be logically structured (both in its argumentation and in being in the correct sequence) and there must be a visible link/connection between the parts of the text (continuity). In other words, the structure must provide cohesiveness to the content so that it appears logical, uniform and as a unit. In *Estuary Villa*, as much convincing information as possible has to be provided in a predefined small space (the webpage). It is a question of drawing the reader's attention and standing out among competitors. There is a risk that, in the process of focusing on one aspect, logical structure may have been compromised. The compiler of the *Maintenance* text certainly began well by structuring information in the very accessible question-and-answer format, but at times couldn't sustain the structural approach in the presentation of the information.

Wording (textual facet D):

It goes without saying that grammar and word choice have to be correct, but style and register must also match the knowledge and ability of the target group and they must be maintained throughout the text. The *Induction of labour* text is informative and instructive in nature, as textbook material should be, a genre which requires the consistent use of terminology when presenting facts and procedures. Everything has to be sufficiently defined, explained and supported (argumentation).

Presentation (textual facet E):

Last but not least, there is the facet of presentation, which concerns the editing and polishing of a text so that the average reader is able to understand what is intended. Presentation not only supports the readablility process; it often complements and reinforces it. When presentation and wording clash, the text will not communicate. It is important to be consistent when undertaking the editing of a text, which must include a consideration of the choice of typography, a supportive layout, on the one hand, and the meaningful, correct spelling and punctuation in the text, on the other. The *Maintenance* text is rather interesting in this respect, since it presents complicated legal matters which have to be communicated in plain language with as little terminology as possible, since most of its readers do not have the technical background knowledge but are often emotionally tied up in the topic. Moreover, it can be assumed that most of the pamphlet's audience does not use the text's language as a first language, and most are semi-literate and might not be familar with the visual conventions used in the text. This eight-page informative pamphlet thus serves a complicated communicative purpose.

Now let's see how the three evaluation criteria are carried through in the five text facets, using four of the sample documents as the vehicles for our analysis.

3.3 Three criteria for analysing text quality

The starting point for our quest to achieve a text that communicates optimally is captured in the three criteria of correspondence, consistency and correctness (for more information consult section 3.3 in chapter 2). A text should show:

- *Correspondence* or agreement between the needs and expectations of the author and the recipient of the text.
- *Consistency* of choices made during the creative process and throughout the text.
- *Correctness* in reproducing factual content accurately and faithfully and in applying the rules of the language.

Each of the criteria serves as a basis for analysing the quality of a text and is below illustrated in excerpts from the sample texts. In this first part we will not tamper too much with the text extracts and will indicate where the published texts have been adapted for our purposes.

3.3.1 Correspondence in an informative pamphlet

The extract below – a black-and-white reproduction from a printed official document intended to inform citizens what their rights to maintenance payment are and how they should go about obtaining payment through the official channels (*'How do I claim Maintenance?'*) – shows how a lack of *correspondence* can cause a document to communicate less effectively and/or meet the needs of the targeted recipients to a lesser extent than would be wished for.

Since correspondence plays at different textual levels, we will work our way bottom up, starting with the text facet of presentation (E) and ending with text type (A) (see figure 12.2 below). But first a small sample of the text:

What steps do I take if I do not receive the money in my bank account?

- Request a detailed statement (not a mini statement) of your bank account at your local bank counter or ATM.
- Bring the bank statement together with your ID Book to the Court.
- The Court will issue summons to institute criminal charges against the person responsible for the payment.

If I am the person paying the Maintenance money, what do I need to do?

You can use the following methods of paying:
- Garnishee order - the company you work for takes the money directly from your salary.
- Cash payment – you come to the Court and pay the money over the counter.
- Direct payment into the bank account – you make a deposit into the bank account of the person entitled to the money.

Your method of payment must be recorded on the Court Order.

Remember:
- The Reference Number provided by the Court must always be given when making a direct payment into the bank account or over the counter.
- Always fax the proof of payment (deposit slip or receipt) to the Court when paying directly into the bank account of the Court.

(Taken from pp 7–8 of the pamphlet)

The pamphlet is issued by the Department of Justice and Constitutional Development, Chief Directorate: Promotion of the Rights of Vulnerable Groups and it aims to communicate people's rights and offer support when their rights are violated. For the recipients the primary need is advice which is easily accessible. Appropriate wording is the key.

The overall formulation of this document promotes accessibility and readability, through the question-and-answer technique, in particular, and the bulleted responses consisting of simple and short sentences. At first sight and keeping the audience in mind, text quality seems to be guaranteed at the level of text type and presentation. However, when looking deeper, the document fails to establish a meaningful connection between sender/author and recipient/ reader with respect to sufficient information, appropriate wording and presentation [EP4/10/13].

The layout [EP13] is not geared to an audience with minimal literacy skills. Important words, like 'remember', are not bolded or highlighted to draw attention to them. There are no line breaks at 'natural' boundaries, ie end of sentences or end of phrases to enhance text understanding. The line breaks seem accidental and inspired by the length of a printed line. In some instances there are white spaces where they should not be. Every page is presented with a different colour background (eg page 7 is purple and page 8 is yellow), but the colours serve no apparent purpose. Even though a font has been selected with a sympathetic feel to it, it does not enhance the readability and clashes with the text type. Moreover, with some questions ill-considered illustrations seem to have been added to the text at a later stage. It is clear that the text production process has not been the subject of integrated document design.

Structurally [EP7], consistency is lacking in that sometimes an explanation is given in brackets (eg 'a detailed statement is not a mini-statement of your bank account'), and sometimes the explanation follows after after a dash, (eg *Garnishee order – the company you work for takes the money directly from your salary*).

The lack of correspondence can most readily be seen in the wording of the text. There are quite a number of words and expressions which are regarded as 'difficult' and which the typical readers of the document are unlikely to understand. Moreover, they are not consistently explained or glossed anywhere in the text. In particular, examples of legalese such as *Garnishee order, to issue summons, and to instittute [sic] criminal charges against someone* are not likely to be understood by the typical citizen who has to approach the courts to have maintenance payments enforced on the other parent of their children (EP10 wording and EP12 meaning don't score well here and they in turn reflect on the unity of style [EP11]). But even apart from the legal jargon and terminology, the style is rather elevated (eg *request* instead of *ask*, *provided* instead of *given*, *recorded* instead of *written*, *furnish* instead of *give*). This probably means that the writer of the document, to whom the words and phrases are familiar (probably a lawyer or a legal drafter), did not or was not able to adopt a reader-centred approach when compiling the text.

Text facets	Criteria for analysis of text quality		
	Correspondence	Consistency	Correctness
A. Text type	1. Appropriate text	2. Unity of genre	3. Application of genre rules
B. Content	4. Appropriate and sufficient information	5. Congruence of facts	6. Facts
C. Structure	7. Sufficient cohesion	8. Uniformity of structure	9. Linking words and argumentation
D. Wording	10. Appropriate wording	11. Unity of style	12. Syntax, vocabulary and meaning
E. Presentation	13. Appropriate layout and typography	14. Congruence between text and layout	15. Spelling, punctuation, layout and typography
	15 evaluation points		

Figure 12.1 *Dominant points for evaluating correspondence in informative texts*

From the above quick and partial analysis it can be seen that the information provided is not appropriate or sufficient for the intended readership [EP4] and consequently the text itself will not communicate as effectively as it should and, ultimately, it will miss the point of helping the group of people who need help most [EP1].

Errors that are characteristic of informative texts can be evaluated by focusing mainly on the dark grey evaluation points [EP4/10]. Such errors will have an immediate knock-on effect on the lighter grey points [EP1/7/13] in figure 12.1 above.

3.3.2 Correspondence in an informative/persuasive online advertisement

Mainly in a different way – through text-structural disorganisation [EP7/8/ 9] – the *Estuary Villa* text, which aims at attracting tourists, also fails to fulfil the criterion of *correspondence* in the following excerpt – which is the first unpublished draft version of the text (for convenience of reference we have numbered the paragraphs):

1.	The Villa is situated in very secure surroundings on a Country Estate, a short stroll to the beach. All three bedrooms are en-suite with a shower and a toilet. The kitchen is fully equipped with a glasstop stove, oven, microwave, fridge/freezer, dishwasher, kettle, toaster, pots, pans and cooking utensils. Cutlery, crockery and glassware are provided for 6 guests. The bedrooms are fully equipped with sheets, blankets, duvets and pillows. Please bring your own towels. There is a TV with a DSTV decoder, please bring your own smart card. Braai facilities are situated outside the villa. Strictly no pets allowed. No Smoking.
2.	Port Edward and the surrounding district have a large variety of activities that cater to all tastes and requirements. The close proximity to the Wild Coast Sun Country Club (10 minutes) and San Lameer Country Club (15 minutes), keeps the pros and amateurs out of mischief. Port Edward also has a nine-hole golf course that is a great way to relax.
3.	There is a game reserve Lake Eland (35 minutes) and the Umtamvuna Nature Reserve offers a variety of trails for outdoor enthusiasts and those keen to get fit . The flora and fauna in this reserve is outstanding and the scenery is spectacular. There is horse riding in the vicinity and a huge variety of adventure activities ranging from 4x4 trails to the highest abseil in the country.
4.	There is on-site parking for 2 cars.
5.	A full or part-time maid service and laundry arrangements can be made. sheets and towels are changed twice a week for longer-staying guests. Culinary afficonados and nightclub-'jollers' are also catered for with a large variety of restaurants and eateries. The Wild Coast Casino (5 minutes) also offers something for the young and old, big and bold!
6.	Port Edward has all the necessary daily shopping facilities with two large supermarkets, bottle stores, garages, a post office and a variety of other shops and restaurants.

(first draft)

There are what technically looks like six paragraphs. *Structurally*, the first paragraph explains what the Villa has to offer. However, there is so much detail that the reader easily loses track. Port Edward is mentioned in the second paragraph together with other examples for sightseeing (paragraphs 2 and 3), and it is mentioned again at the end of the text in connection with shopping. Paragraph 4 is an isolated sentence and it probably belongs to paragraph 1. Paragraph 5 then is a weird mix of the extra services provided and the activities available in the region. The final paragraph – one sentence – deals with shops and eating out (but that was also named in the previous paragraph).

Here the *content* is jumbled up [EP7]: accommodation, equipment, facilities, sightseeing and activities are not grouped logically and there is little logical flow of information [EP4/9]. Moreover, this also gives rise to some confusion: you are requested to bring your own towels in the first paragraph, but towards the end of the text (paragraph 5) it says that sheets and towels are changed twice a week.

The use of *local words* or words [EP 12] with a specific local meaning (*Country Estate, braai, garages, 4x4 trails, smart card*) indicates that the author gave little thought to the readership – which, for a tourist website, is likely to be international, and likely either to misunderstand the jargon or not grasp it at all [EP10]. But also the use of trendy words such as *culinary afficonados* (which should be *aficionados*) and *nightclub-'jollers'* (South African slang for revellers) may attract a specific audience and exclude another. The style adopted sends out conflicting messages and it is not clear who exactly is targeted: *very secure surroundings, keeps the pros and amateurs out of mischief, the golf course is a great way to relax, the highest abseil in the country, outdoor enthusiasts, those keen to get fit, the scenery is spectacular, the Casino offers something for the young and old, big and bold!*

Text facets	Criteria for analysis of text quality		
	Correspondence	Consistency	Correctness
A. Text type	1. Appropriate text	2. Unity of genre	3. Application of genre rules
B. Content	4. Appropriate and sufficient information	5. Congruence of facts	6. Facts
C. Structure	7. Sufficient cohesion	8. Uniformity of structure	9. Linking words and argumentation
D. Wording	10. Appropriate wording	11. Unity of style	12. Syntax, vocabulary and meaning
E. Presentation	13. Appropriate layout and typography	14. Congruence between text and layout	15. Spelling, punctuation, layout and typography
	15 evaluation points		

Figure 12.2 *Dominant points for evaluating correspondence in persuasive texts*

Again, in this case, the text as it stands here does not communicate optimally for its intended clientele. The fact that the text is to be published online changes the nature and quality of the readership (we have to stress, once again, that the excerpt above was a first draft only).

Errors that are characteristic of informative/persuasive texts can be evaluated by focusing mainly on the darkened CCC evaluation points, which will have an immediate knock-on effect on the lighter coloured points.

3.3.3 Correspondence in an informative/instructional handbook

When, as often happens, the author of a text intended to inform or instruct is a non-native speaker (NNS) of a language and also a subject expert in a highly specialised field, almost inevitably there will be barriers in the way of correspondence between author's meaning, content and wording and the readers' understanding and interpretation of what they read. The text editor therefore has to exercise additional diligence and proceed extra cautiously to ensure that the identified readers will be able to receive the communication clearly and correctly.

Induction of labour (taken from a text on pharmacology aimed at nurses) is a good example of such a document: it is a mix of NNS writing and highly specialised medical content and terminology, including a host of abbreviations and acronyms. The potential for miscommunication is therefore high:

---

1.   Introduction

Induction of labour (IOL) is the commonest obstetric intervention performed on a daily basis in the labour wards after 24 weeks' of gestation, for a variety of reasons. It is often undertaken in instances when continuation with pregnancy poses a risk to either the mother or the fetus or both and the benefits of early delivery far outweigh the risks.

2.   Definition

IOL refers to the process of artificially initiating uterine contractions and effecting cervical effacement and dilatation using pharmacological agents before the onset of labour resulting in delivery of a live healthy baby vaginally within a specified period of 24 hours. ...

3.   Incidence

It is a common procedure done in 10-15% of term pregnancies. ...

5.   Maternal indications

Pre-eclamptic toxaemia (PET) is a common indication as it poses serious health risks to both the mother and the fetus. The risks to the mother from PET include intra-cerebral haemorrhage, eclampsia, abruption placenta, pulmonary oedema, renal and liver failure (HELLP syndrome). Delivery may be indicated at early gestational age resulting in prematurity. If, however, blood pressure is well controlled delivery after 34 weeks is recommended to reduce the risk of prematurity.

In this text, with few exceptions, the sentence and paragraph length are exemplary, given the complexity of the information being communicated; they communicate complex information in small doses. Its primary weakness, however, lies in the facets of wording, content and structure [EP4/7/10], in that order, via congruence of facts [EP5] and unity of style [EP11] to linking words and argumentation [EP9], syntax, vocabulary and meaning [EP12] and spelling and punctuation [EP15].

The following cause a delay in text comprehension: *on a daily basis* could have been shortened to *daily* [EP12]; *after 24 weeks' of gestation* is an incorrect double-possessive construction and it should have been either *after 24 weeks' gestation* or *after 24 weeks of gestation* [EP12/15]; *for a variety of reasons* is misplaced where it is at the end of the sentence, because it appears to refer to *period of gestation* and it should refer more directly to *instances when continuation with pregnancy poses a risk* and for this reason, it would be better placed at the start of the sentence [EP7/9]; *continuation* should be *continuing* [EP12]; *or both* would read better if it were enclosed within parentheses [EP15].

This being chapter 7 of the textbook, one would hope that the terminology in the second paragraph (cervical *effacement*; *dilatation*) has been glossed or explained previously, otherwise this paragraph will make for very difficult reading. The word *resulting* is a poor choice because it leads to a long sentence that contains dense information and also because, ending in *-ing*, it naturally links up with *initiating, effecting* and *using*, which it should not. This very long, dense sentence is likely to lead to information overload, reducing the effectiveness of the paragraph considerably. It's best to start a new sentence with *This results in* … [EP9/12].

10–15% of term pregnancies: this is a bland, unsubstantiated statement – among which population, for example?

The second sentence of the final paragraph (*The risks to the mother … (HELPP syndrome)*) is ambiguous in its construction – there should be an *and* before *renal* because *renal and liver failure* form a unitary item at the end of the sentence. Again, this being chapter 7, one would hope that the terminology in this sentence (*intra-cerebral haemorrhage, eclampsia, abruptio placenta, pulmonary oedema*) have been glossed or explained previously. The acronym HELLP is not explained, nor is the full name given [EP4/7].

The third sentence of the final paragraph is missing the indefinite article *an* before *early*: *at early gestational age resulting in prematurity*; moreover, the word *resulting* should read either … *and results in* … or … *; it results in* … [EP9/10/12].

The final sentence requires the insertion of the definite article *the* before *blood pressure* and a comma to be inserted between the main clause and the conditional clause, that is, after *controlled* [EP7/12].

3.3.4 Consistency in an informative legal pamphlet

As regards consistency, in the *Maintenance* text congruence between words and layout could be easily achieved by highlighting certain key terms and important information (*Remember*) could be set apart [EP14].

You can use the following **methods of paying:**
- Garnishee order - the company you work for takes the money directly from your salary.
- Cash payment – you come to the Court and pay the money over the counter.
- Direct payment into the bank account – you make a deposit into the bank account of the person entitled to the money.

Your method of payment must be recorded on the Court Order.

Remember:
- The Reference Number provided by the Court must always be given when making a direct payment into the bank account or over-the-counter.
- Always fax the proof of payment (deposit slip or receipt) to the Court when paying directly into the bank account of the Court.

The above text can easily suffer from a lack of unity of style [EP11] as a result of the mixing of the active and the passive voice. Of the six sentences in the short extract only three are active (eg *you use/can make*), one is a directive or imperative (*fax*) and two are passives (eg *the number must be given, payment must be recorded*). In texts for academic and professional communication this mix of active and passive voice is encouraged to provide variety. In this text, however, the absence of an identifiable subject (as is the case in passive and imperative) may result in the person who has to pay the maintenance money not feeling addressed.

In view of the target readership, the sentences should be kept as short and direct as possible, which only an active voice construction is able to achieve effectively, indicating to readers exactly who is responsible for what. This direct approach will also draw the responsible addressee into the text (it should be mentioned, for completeness' sake, that, according to the title of the pamphlet (*How do I claim Maintenance?*), this person is not the intended addressee of this paragraph). Because of the inconsistency, the text will not achieve unity of style [EP11].

As for the language, there are small inconsistencies: the list with the methods of payment is not symmetrical, different terms are used (*methods of paying* vs *method of payment*) and the phrase *into the bank account* (which is elliptic when it first occurs) is repeated:

Direct payment into the bank account - you make a deposit into the bank account of the person entitled to the money

---

Instructive texts require consistency in the use of terminology and the explanation of the terms used, or more broadly, the text needs to contain sufficient and appropriate information [EP5]. Again, whereas in academic texts the use of synonyms is applauded, it may be confusing for this text's intended audience. Congruence of facts and unity of style could be improved in the extract above. In the text, three methods of payment are mentioned: *Garnishee order* (which should come last), *cash payment, direct payment into bank account of the beneficiary.* And when administrative details are given, a fourth method follows, ie *direct payment into the Court's bank account.* Moreover, the text makes mention of *The Reference Number* (capitalised!) *provided by the Court,* but it is not clear what it is or where it can be found. The text also tells the reader always to fax the proof of payment to the Court, but the number is first provided right at the end of the pamphlet (which may be difficult for a semi-literate reader to find). All of these aspects can slow down the reading process since they are problematic with respect to EP5 (no congruence of facts).

Alternative spellings for terminology, such as *payment over-the-counter* or *over the counter* represent a typical problem of English spelling, which has closed, open and hyphenated forms. Whatever form is selected, it has to be used consistently [EP14]. Many writers are not always consistent when using capital letters: *Reference Number, reference number, Court Order, a file for the court.*

All of the instances of (in)consistency mentioned above – from layout and spelling to wording, structure and congruence of information – have an effect and, in good cases, will support the unity of the genre [EP2], as indicated by the shaded cells in figure 12.3:

Text facets	Criteria for analysis of text quality		
	Correspondence	Consistency	Correctness
A. Text type	1. Appropriate text	2. Unity of genre	3. Application of genre rules
B. Content	4. Appropriate and sufficient information	5. Congruence of facts	6. Facts
C. Structure	7. Sufficient cohesion	8. Uniformity of structure	9. Linking words and argumentation
D. Wording	10. Appropriate wording	11. Unity of style	12. Syntax, vocabulary and meaning
E. Presentation	13. Appropriate layout and typography	14. Congruence between text and layout	15. Spelling, punctuation, layout and typography
	15 evaluation points		

Figure 12.3 *Dominant points for evaluating consistency in informative texts*

3.3.5 Consistency in an instructive advertisement

In the *LiceBGone* text certain words are *inconsistently* treated, by randomly giving them uppercase and lowercase initial letters [EP11–15]. This is especially apparent when the phrases are meant to be slogans (*Buy Now; it's a safe and effective Alternative!*):

Buy Now R74,95 Plus Postage (Special Offer: Postage included for batches of 24 bottels)

We Introduce ... **Lice B Gone**

1. • Lice B Gone is a safe, non-toxic, multi-enzyme shampoo made from natural vegetable extracts.

2. • It is totally effective in removing head lice.

3. • It is equally effective on nits, loosening the glue that bonds them to the hair shaft for easy removal with a nit comb.

4. • Lice B Gone solves the worst of head lice and nit problems *without* the dangers normally associated with toxic, pesticide containing products.

5. • Use it with confidence because; it's a safe and effective Alternative!

Even the brand name *LiceBGone* is treated inconsistently: it is sometimes presented as a logo, sometimes as *LiceBGone*, but it is also given as *Lice B Gone* [EP11].

The use of full caps for certain words is arbitrary:

Previouesly it made sense to kill the head lice with pesticides BUT that was not the
best solution, that was BEFORE Lice B Gone was developed.

Generally, a lack of cohesion and of adequate linking of words and argumentation complicates the reading process [EP7/8/9], as illustrated by the following two examples:

---

3. • It is equally effective on nits, loosening the glue that bonds them to the hair shaft for
     easy removal with a nit comb.

In this example, the syntax suggests that the glue that bonds the lice also facilitates their removal – which is, of course, illogical. A clearer sentence construction would be: *loosening the glue that bonds them to the hair so that they can easily be removed with a nit comb.* The illogical syntax has now been removed.

With Lice B Gone, one application gets rid of head lice and the nits:
1.   because it softens the glue that holds the nits to the hair shaft,
2.   allowing them to be easily combed and rinsed away. .

In the second example, one continuous sentence has been artificially turned into an introduction plus a numbered list. This does not work. The clearer, more logical result is: *With LiceBGone, one application gets rid of head lice and nits by softening the glue that holds the nits to the hair shaft and allowing them to be easily combed and rinsed away.* By changing the verb form to *softening* you would also introduce verbal parallelism into the sentence, which enhances understanding.

> **LiceBGone**
> **– HOW IT WORKS**
> To successfully treat someone, you have to understand the two distinctly different problems you are trying to solve simultaneously:
> • kill the head lice and kill
> • remove the nits.

The placement of *simultaneously* also leads to ambiguity: do you have to understand and solve simultaneously, or solve two problems simultaneously?

Errors of consistency that are characteristic of informative/persuasive web-based texts can be evaluated according to the shaded evaluation points:

Text facets	Criteria for analysis of text quality		
	Correspondence	Consistency	Correctness
A. Text type	1. Appropriate text	2. Unity of genre	3. Application of genre rules
B. Content	4. Appropriate and sufficient information	5. Congruence of facts	6. Facts
C. Structure	7. Sufficient cohesion	8. Uniformity of structure	9. Linking words and argumentation
D. Wording	10. Appropriate wording	11. Unity of style	12. Syntax, vocabulary and meaning
E. Presentation	13. Appropriate layout and typography	14. Congruence between text and layout	15. Spelling, punctuation, layout and typography
		15 evaluation points	

Figure 12.4 *Dominant points for evaluating consistency in instructive advertisements*

3.3.6 Correctness

In informative texts problems with correctness – of content, structure, and presentation – can be typically identified at genre and wording level. They have an immediate effect on the readability and communicative force of the text. Correctness also exercises a major influence on the text's surface validity and the reader will take the author(s) and the message more seriously if no critical errors occur.

LiceBGone wants to be an advertisement and to capture the audience's attention in bulleted lists and slogans. The licebgone.com website takes a completely different, more narrative approach. This choice entails the danger of oversimplifying the text with respect to:

• the rules of the genre, ie a website and an advertisement; as it stands the text may not reach its objective of being a serious communication [EP3];
• the use of argumentation (through appropriate linking words); the argumentation process lacks clarity [EP9];
• appropriate syntax: a lack of clear thinking about what a process involves combined with a lack of command of the target language may result in some misleading constructions and muddled argumentation [EP12];
• spelling, punctuation, layout and typographical errors may creep in because of a lack of time, original knowledge, and the like [EP15].

Text facets	Criteria for analysis of text quality		
	Correspondence	Consistency	Correctness
A. Text type	1. Appropriate text	2. Unity of genre	3. Application of genre rules
B. Content	4. Appropriate and sufficient information	5. Congruence of facts	6. Facts
C. Structure	7. Sufficient cohesion	8. Uniformity of structure	9. Linking words and argumentation
D. Wording	10. Appropriate wording	11. Unity of style	12. Syntax, vocabulary and meaning
E. Presentation	13. Appropriate layout and typography	14. Congruence between text and layout	15. Spelling, punctuation, layout and typography
		15 evaluation points	

Figure 12.5 *Dominant points for evaluating correctness in informative texts*

In the *Estuary Villa* original draft text this takes the following form:

• The writer breaks the rules of the genre (website) by composing dense, continuous prose rather than a series of brief paragraphs and vertical lists, and also not presenting the information it contains in a logical sequence [EP3/9].
• The text is, however, factually correct (although it might be slightly embellished as an advertisement for the services on offer) [EP6].

>>

- Regarding the wording and presentation, there are numerous errors of syntax, vocabulary, meaning, spelling, punctuation and typography [EP12]: double spaces between words, a space before full stops; comma splices; 'afficonadoes'; DSTV (instead of the brand name DStv)
- Word choice [complete facet D Wording] also leads to an uneven tone in this text, ranging as it does from formal/informative/imperative (*Strictly no pets allowed. No smoking*) to too informal (*the young and old, big and bold; jollers*), creating a general identity problem for this text type [EP1/2/3].

From the above it would seem that variances in text quality will – and do – occur in texts and that correctness in texts can be viewed from different perspectives.

4 Types of problem that become apparent during the editing process

By way of illustration, we want to distinguish between a number of categories of error from the angle of the textual facets by citing a number of examples in each. We use the texts introduced above. In section 5 we show how they intertwine in the process of editing.

4.1 Content errors

Content errors deal with the kind (correct) and amount (appropriate and sufficient) of information and how it is organised (consistently). In more detail, it concerns among others:

B Content		
Correspondence	**Consistency**	**Correctness**
EP4 Appropriate and sufficient information	EP5 Congruence of facts	EP6 Correct facts
• TERMINOLOGY - Defined - Explained - Supported - Appropriate to audience • WORD CHOICE - Readability - Accessibility (facilitated) - Written-spoken language continuum - Appropriate to audience	• ETHICS - Plagiarism - Defamation or libel/slander - Copyright (ICP) • PRESENTATION of FACTS - Consistency	• WORD LEVEL - Facts, events, dates - Names of people, institutions, companies, places - Titles of books, films, ... - Addresses - Figures, tables, ... - Mathematics (numbers, calculations) - Statistics • TEXT LEVEL - Quotations & sources - Cross-references

Table 12.2 *Quality evaluation of the content of a text*

In the following example from *Multilingualism*, facts have to be presented correctly:

> They have their major regional base in Kwa-Zulu Natal[1] and Eastern Cape, respectively.
> Louw and Finlayson (1990) focus on southern Bantu[2] origins as represented by Xhosa[3] and Setswana, whereas Harries (1995) deals with the historical origins of Xitsonga. ... The main regions for Sesotho (previously Southern Sotho) and Setswana are the Free State and the North-West Province[4], respectively.

1 KwaZulu-Natal 2 Southern Bantu 3 isiXhosa and Setswana (mind the spelling) *4 North West*

In the first instance, the name of the province KwaZulu-Natal is not spelt correctly. Secondly, the name of the language group is Southern Bantu with Southern being an integral part of the name. The Constitution of South Africa lists the eleven official languages as isiZulu, isiXhosa, Afrikaans, Sepedi, Setswana, English, Sesotho, Xitsonga, siSwati, Tshivenda and isiNdebele and South African Sign Language and any variants of those spellings (eg Xhosa or Northern Sotho) are incorrect. The name North-West Province is incorrect: in the Constitution it is given as North West.

4.2 Structural errors

The evaluation of structural errors is catered for by the following:

C Structure		
Correspondence	**Consistency**	**Correctness**
EP7 Sufficient cohesion	**EP8 Uniformity of structure**	**EP9 Linking words and argumentation**
- Appropriateness to the intended audience - Expectations & knowledge of text components - Expectations & knowledge of text structure - Sufficient coherence of macro & micro structure for optimal readability - Type, order & flow of argumentation	- Introduction, middle, conclusion - Consistency of choices	• PARAGRAPHING ERRORS - Length of paragraphs - Thesis statement (hook), supportive sentences summative sentence - Number of themes - Transitions within & between paragraphs; linking words • COHERENCE ERRORS - Choice of genre structure - Identification of themes - Logical sequencing of argument - Thread of arguments

Table 12.3 *Quality evaluation model for text structure*

Example:

> The Villa is situated in very secure surroundings on a Country Estate, a short stroll to the beach. All three bedrooms are en-suite with shower and toilet. The kitchen is fully equipped with a glasstop stove, oven, microwave, fridge/freezer, dishwasher, kettle, toaster, pots, pans and cooking utensils. Cutlery, crockery and glassware provided for 6 guests. The bedrooms are fully equipped with sheets, blankets, duvets and pillows. Please bring your own towels. There is a TV with DSTV decoder, please bring your own smart card. Braai facilities outside. Strictly no pets allowed. No Smoking. Port Edward and the surrounding district have a large variety of activities that cater to all tastes and requirements. Close proximity to the Wild Coast Sun Country Club (10 minutes) and San Lameer Country Club (15 minutes), keep the pros and amateurs out of mischief. Port Edward also has a nine-hole course that is a great way to relax. There is a game reserve Lake Eland (35 minutes away) and the Umtamvuna Nature Reserve offers a variety of trails for enthusiasts and the fitness challenged. The flora and fauna seen in this reserve is outstanding and the scenery is spectacular.

In the above example, the first part describes the house, the second the tourist attractions in the neighbourhood. Here, the information provided lacks cohesion and uniformity of structure but it also contains fundamental paragraphing errors, with a whole lot of disparate facts thrown together in no clear groupings or order. Themes are not clearly identified; logical sequencing is largely missing. The single paragraph is also too long, especially for the genre of website and onscreen reading.

4.3 Language errors

Language errors can be categorised as syntactic, lexical (word choice and meaning), register, style, spelling and punctuation errors. Since spelling and punctuation have an immediate bearing on the text's surface level, these errors are dealt with under Presentation (section 4.4).

D Wording		
Correspondence	**Consistency**	**Correctness**
EP10 Appropriate wording	EP11 Unity of style	EP12 Syntax, vocabulary and meaning
- Appropriateness to the intended audience - Appropriate to audience's language skill & knowledge - Appropriate to audience's education background - Appropriate to audience's expectations	• STYLE AND REGISTER ERRORS - Length of sentences - Vague or clumsy language - Empty sentences - Level of formality - Stiltedness - Bombast - Longwindedness - Ambiguity - Treatment of clichés - Figurative language - Humour & irony	• GRAMMAR ERRORS - Formulation - Simple & complex sentences - Verb tenses & forms - Phrasal verbs - Congruence (person-number) - Present participles & gerunds - Group vs mass nouns - Plurals - Adjectives & adverbs - Attributive/predicative adjectives

Correspondence	Consistency	Correctness
EP10 Appropriate wording	EP11 Unity of style	EP12 Syntax, vocabulary and meaning
	- Jargon & slang - Active vs passive voice - Elimination of repetition - American vs British English • WORD BORROWINGS/FOREIGN WORDS - Lexical, idiomatic, phonetic, syntactic & graphic borrowings - Words of foreign origin - Loanwords & their variants - Mixed metaphors	- Conjunctions - Adverbs as linking words - Pronouns: personal, possessive, demonstrative, interrogative, reflexive, relative - Prepositions - Determiners (including articles) • ERRORS OF MEANING - Correct word choice - Ambiguous meaning - Appropriate synonyms - Parts of speech - Malapropisms - Tautology/redundancy - Pleonasms - Homonyms, homophones - Paronyms - Doublets - Figures of speech - Clichés, mixed metaphors - Foreign words

Table 12.4 *Model for the assessment of the wording facet of a text*

What follows are some examples of the most obvious and disturbing of the errors likely to occur in texts.

4.3.1 Style and register

Example 1

> **What if the bank account where the money was supposed to be paid in has been closed?**
> • Furnish[1] the Court with new banking details.
> • The Maintenance Officer will advise[2] the Respondent of your new banking details and the amount owed by him.

1 Provide or You should give …
2 inform

Furnish, as used in this context, comes across as vague, high-sounding and stilted as against the use of the exhortative (or highly persuasive) *You should ....* Also, this word would probably be misunderstood by the average reader, being more closely associated with furniture and furnishing a home. This sentence is also constructed in the imperative form, which adds to its high-blown tone; this is inappropriate to a document purporting to help the average citizen.

Advise is a vague word, a synonym for *tell* in this instance (not for *counsel*), which is more accessible and no less accurate.

Example 2

> Culinary afficondos[1] and nightclub-'jollers'[2] are also catered for with a large variety of restaurants and eateries. The Wild Coast Casino (5 minutes) also offers something for the young and old, big and bold[3]!

All these words are inappropriate to the intended audience:
1 afficondos (enthusiasts)
2 nightclub-'jollers' (party-goers)
3 the young and old, big and bold (large and striking)

There are two levels of formality in this excerpt, taken from a passage that is informative, first and foremost, and so it needs to be fairly serious if it is to be believable to the respondent looking for holiday accommodation. *Nightclub-'jollers'* and *the young and old, big and bold* are too informal ('jollers' is also South African slang for *revellers*) for a text and medium of this nature, and so it detracts from the text and the offering as a whole.

4.3.2 Grammar

The sampled texts abound with grammatical errors, but we have selected some representative ones to illustrate the nature of this particular problem.

Example 1

> Braai facilities outside.[1] Strictly no pets allowed. No Smoking. The close proximity to the Wild Coast Sun Country Club (10 minutes) and San Lameer Country Club (15 minutes), keep[2] the pros and amateurs out of mischief.
> The flora and fauna in the reserve is[3] outstanding and the scenery is spectacular.

1. Braai facilities are situated outside the villa.
2. keeps
3. are

In this first passage there are two principal errors: *Braai facilities outside* is an elliptic or incomplete sentence, lacking a finite verb. It opens a row of three short sentences, two of which are prohibitions and not in the kindest tone of voice. Secondly, there's a lack of subject–verb concord between *close proximity* and *keep* and *The flora and fauna* and *is*.

Example 2

> There is a TV with a DSTV decoder,[1] please bring your own smart card.

1 There is a TV with a DSTV decoder; please bring your own smart card.
or:
There is a TV with a DSTV decoder. Please bring your own smart card

In this sentence we find an example of the comma splice – two complete sentences simply joined by a comma. Either a semicolon or a full stop would correct this problem.

Example 3

> Previously it made sense to kill the head lice with pesticides BUT that was not the best solution, that was BEFORE Lice B Gone was developed.

another example of the comma splice.

Example 4

> The entire process of[1] applying for maintenance to receiving the first payment[2] might[3] take several week's[4], depending on the co-operation[5] of both parties.

1 from
2 ,from applying for maintenance to receiving the first payment,
3 could
4 weeks
5 level of

The preposition *of* following *the entire process* is incorrect. Furthermore, the entire phrase *for applying for maintenance to receiving the first payment* should be inserted between commas since it is an explanation of what the process consists of. The modal verb *might* expresses a very weak probability and should be replaced by *could* (it is more certain that it well take less time) to make the meaning clearer. Several *week's* is not possessive, so the apostrophe should be deleted to make way for the plural form, *weeks*.

Example 5

> Moreover, there is a lack or rejection of standardised Zulu texts for educational purposes among both teachers and children.

There is an ungrammatical construction in the phrase *a lack or rejection of* in particular, but the whole sentence, written in the passive voice, is substandard. It should read something like: *Moreover, standardised Zulu texts for educational purposes aimed at teachers and children are in short supply and they are often rejected.*

Example 6

> Payment cannot be traced due to[1] incorrect reference number been supplied.[2]

1 an   2 having been supplied

There are two grammatical errors in this sentence: an indefinite article should be inserted before *incorrect reference number*. The verb form *been supplied* is a passive but needs an auxiliary verb to indicate a continuous action in the past.

Example 7

> Induction of labour (IOL) is the commonest[1] obstetric intervention performed daily in the labour wards after 24 weeks' of gestation[2] for a variety of reasons[3]. It is often undertaken in instances when continuation with pregnancy[4] poses a risk to either the mother or the foetus or both and the benefits of early delivery far outweigh those risks[5].

1 most common
2 either 24 weeks' gestation or gestation of 24 weeks
3 for a variety of reasons is misplaced; it should start the sentence
4 continuing with pregnancy
5 a risk or that risk

There are several problems with respect to grammar (morphology and declination) in this short two-sentence extract. The National Health Service in its online *Pregnancy care planner* aimed at mothers-to-be (http://www.nhs.uk/Planners/pregnancycareplanner/Pages/PregnancyHome.aspx) puts it in the following way:

> Inducing labour
> Sometimes labour can be induced (started artificially) if your baby is <u>overdue</u> or there is any sort of risk to you or your baby's health, for example if you have <u>high blood pressure</u> or if your baby is failing to grow and develop.

Clinical guideline D, *Induction of labour*, issued in 2008 by the National Institute for Health and Clinical Excellence (NICE) (downloadable from www.nice.org.uk/CG070) is written for health care staff and introduces the topic as follows:

> Induction of labour is a relatively common procedure. In 2004 and 2005, one in every five deliveries in the UK was indiced. This includes indiction for all medical reasons.

4.3.3 Meaning

Example 1

> Both parents are responsible for the care of their child whether the child is borne[1] in or out of marriage. If the person responsible for paying maintenance does not pay, a compliant[2] can be made at the Maintenance Court.

1. born
2. complaint

The two words used here look very much like what they should be, but both misspellings happen to convey completely different meanings from the correct words. *Borne* is the past tense of *bear* (to hold or carry); *compliant* means to conform or meet the requirements of someone or something.

Example 2

> The Villa is in close proximity to the Wild Coast Sun Country Club (10 minutes) and[1] San Lameer Country Club (15 minutes), keeps the pros and amateurs out of mischief[2]. Port Edward also has a nine-hole course that is a great way to relax[3]. There is a game reserve Lake Eland (35 minutes) and the Umtamvuna Nature Reserve offers a variety of trails for outdoor enthusiasts and the fitness challenged[4].

1 insert: the
2 replace by: amused or occupied
3 insert: playing on a nine-hole course is a great way to relax
4 replace by: those who need to get fit

The omission of *the* before *San Lameer Country Club* is slightly misleading in that it creates the impression that the two country clubs are one, possibly contiguous, entity whereas in fact they are separate clubs. Inserting the definite article will create a symmetrical list and remove any ambiguity. The phrase *that is a great way to relax* is indirectly linked to *course*; what it should be related to is missing from the sentence: *playing on a nine-hole course is a great way to relax*. Referring to a group of people as *the fitness challenged* is an example of euphemism and irony (*fitness challenged* meaning *unfit*, presumably). It would be clearer and more direct to write something *like those who need to get fit* or *those who need to improve their level of fitness*.

Example 3

> With Lice B Gone, one application gets rid of head lice and the nits:
> 1. because it softens the glue that holds the nits to the hair shaft,
> 2. allowing them to be easily combed and rinsed away.

As indicated earlier, incorrectly listing what is an otherwise continuous sentence serves to cloud the meaning being conveyed, because the bulleted construction does not work in the usual way. The numbering also suggests a staged process, which is not the case here. Undoing the bullets leads to the following sentence: *With LiceBgone, one application gets rid of head lice and the nits, because it softens the glue that holds the nits to the hair shaft, allowing them to be easily combed and rinsed away*. With a little more grammatical improvement, the sentence could read more clearly: *One application of LiceBgone eliminates both head lice and nits, because it softens the glue that binds the nits to the hair shaft and enables you to comb and rinse them away easily*.

Example 4

> LiceBGone
> – HOW IT WORKS
> To successfully treat someone, you have to understand the two distinctly different problems you are trying to solve simultaneously:
> *   kill the head lice and kill.
> *   remove the nits.

This poor construction, with incorrect punctuation, and the inclusion of redundant and otherwise unnecessary words, serves to cloud the meaning being conveyed in this sentence. For greater clarity, it should read:

> LiceBGone
> HOW IT WORKS
> To treat someone successfully, you have to understand the two distinct problems you are trying simultaneously to solve:
> *   to kill the head lice, and
> *   to remove the nits.

Example 5

> The entire process of applying for maintenance to receiving the first payment might take several weeks, depending on the co-operation[1] of both parties.

1 degree of co-operation

It's really the extent of the co-operation between the parents that will either speed up or slow down the process, not the co-operation per se. For this reason, *co-operation* should read *degree of co-operation* or *level of co-operation* to convey the meaning clearly and unambiguously.

Example 6

> The risks to the mother from PET include intra-cerebral haemorrhage, eclampsia, abruption placentae, pulmonary oedema,[1] renal and liver failure (HELLP syndrome)[2].

1 Insert and
2 (the symptoms of the HELLP syndrome, characterised by haemolysis, elevated liver enzymes and a low platelet count)

Renal and liver failure is the last item in this list of conditions, so it should be linked with the previous items in the list by *and*. The meaning behind the phrase *HELLP syndrome* is doubly unclear: first, does it refer only to renal and liver failure or to the list of conditions as a whole? Then, the acronym HElPP is not explained at this point, so the reader (a learner) is left in the dark, unable to fathom out the significance of the expression in parentheses.

4.4 Visual presentation errors

The final group of errors relates to the presentation of a text, that is, errors of poor typography, inadequate layout and wording-related spelling and punctuation

E Presentation		
Correspondence	**Consistency**	**Correctness**
EP13 Appropriate layout and typography	**EP14 Congruence between text and layout**	**EP15 Spelling, punctuation, layout and typography**
- Appropriateness to the intended audience - Degree of visual literacy - Experience & background - Correspondence between visual (typography & layout) and textual aspects (wording, text type & text structure)	• TYPOGRAPHICAL ERRORS - Type size, style, weight: regular, … - Consistency of choices • LAYOUT ERRORS - Title & contents page - Preface & foreword - Acknowledgements - Lists of figures, tables, maps - Publisher's imprint (cover, title, …) - ISBN & copyright statement - Date of publication - Dedication/epigraph - Appendices/addenda/annexures - Bibliography, glossary, index, credits - Headings & subheadings - Running heads & footers - Widows & orphans - Paragraph style - Numbering - Format of cross-references - Page layout/design - Page numbers - Spacing & margins - Indenting of paragraphs - Treatment of quoted matter - Use of colour & shading/tints - Tables, column heads, side heads, alignment & numbering - Illustrations, labels & captions - Sketches & diagrams (DTP artwork) - Photographs - Footnotes and/or endnotes	• SPELLING ERRORS - Hyphen/one word/two words - Abbreviations & acronyms - Word breaks - Plural forms - Diminutive forms - Uppercase vs lowercase - Accents/diacritics - Numbers & symbols - Decimal point/comma - Percentages - Consistency of choices -American vs British English • PUNCTUATION ERRORS - Spaces around punctuation marks - Full stops, question & exclamation marks - Commas - Semicolons - Colons (uppercase?) - Ellipsis - Hyphen/en-rule/em-rule (dash) - Parentheses - Brackets - Quotation marks: singles or doubles?

Table 12.5 *Assessment model for the quality of the presentation facet of a text*

4.4.1 Spelling

Example 1

> Culinary afficonados

Correct spelling: *aficionados*, but the question is whether the readership will understand.

Example 2

> Zulu (when referring to the language); North-West Province

Correct spellings: *isiZulu; North West.*

Example 3

> The payment date is dependant on the court order.

Dependent is the correct adjectival form that should have been used here; *dependant* is the noun form.

Example 4

> Previouesly it made sense to kill the head lice with pesticides.

The correct spelling is *previously*.

Example 5

> **The best way to collect Maintenance is by the direct payment into your bank account.**
>
> The advantages are
> • No traveling to the COURT
> • No transport oncosts
> • No standing in queues
> • No lost time of work.

The spelling of *traveling* is US English and it is not consistent with the spelling system used in the rest of the text. Surely there's little reason to capitalise COURT here?

Example 6

> Evaluation of pre-requisites before induction of labour.

The correct spelling is prerequisites.

Example 7

> Confirm fetal[1] cephalic presentation and a Longitudinal[2] lie.
> In some instances (as in diabetes) a Lung[2] maturity test may be required.

1 foetal
2 longitudinal
3 lung

Fetal is a US English spelling; *foetal* is a UK English spelling. The publisher and author will have to decide which of the two spellings to standardise on, depending largely upon the readership and the conventions of the discipline. There seems to be little reason to upper-case the first letter of *longitudinal* and *lung*, because they are not used as proper nouns here.

4.4.2 Punctuation

Example 1

> In the case of death, the Executor of the applicant's estate or Guardian of the child, is given permission to collect the money.

Under the influence of syntax rules alien to English, the comma has been inserted after *child*. It should be removed, because it is separating the subject (*Executor*) from its verb (*is*).

Example 2

> A Maintenance Order may be made for :

There is an unwarranted space before the colon. It should be deleted.

Example 3

> Office hours: Monday - Friday: 7h45 - 16:15

To be typographically correct and consistent, the hyphen should be an en-rule. The times should read *07:45–16:15*.

Example 4

> Previously it made sense to kill the head lice with pesticides BUT that was not the best solution, that
> was BEFORE liceBgone was developed.

There should be a full stop after *pesticides*; the comma after *solution* (a comma splice) should be either a semicolon or a full stop.

4.4.3 Typography and layout

Example 1

<u>Buy Now</u> R75,95 Plus Postage

Underlining for emphasis is not a sound typographical convention; remove it and leave the bold in place.

Example 2

We Introduce

1. Lice B Gone is a safe, non-toxic, multi-enzyme shampoo made from natural vegetable extracts.
2. It is totally effective in removing head lice.
3. It is equally effective on nits, loosening the glue that bonds them to the hair shaft for easy removal with a nit comb.
4. Lice B Gone solves the worst of head lice and nit problems **without**[1] the dangers normally associated with toxic, pesticide containing products.
5. Use it with confidence because; it's a safe and effective Alternative!

Previouesly it made sense to kill the head lice with pesticides BUT[2] that was not the best solution, that was BEFORE[3] Lice B Gone was developed.

1 **without**
2 **but**
3 **before**

Both bold lowercase and regular uppercase are used for emphasis here, which sends out mixed messages to the reader as they conflict with each other. Bold would be the more usual typographical treatment for emphasis.

Example 3

This overview includes *nine* indigenous African languages. Taken together, *(isi)Zulu* and *(isi)Xhosa* are the home languages of about *40%* of South Africans. They have their major regional base in *KwaZulu-Natal* and Eastern Cape, respectively. Five other African languages are mainly spoken in the Northern Province *and/or Mpumalanga, i.e.*, *Sesotho* sa Leboa (previously Northern Sotho), *Xitsonga*, *siSwati*, Tshivenda and isiNdebele. The main regions for Sesotho (previously Southern Sotho) and *Setswana* are the Free State and the North-West Province, respectively. For a detailed description of the geographical concentration of these *nine* African languages, we refer to the *Language Atlas of South Africa,* published by *Van der Merwe* and *Van Niekerk* (1994). All in all, these *nine* languages are spoken at home by about *75%* of the entire South African population. In spite of their spread, the available sociolinguistic knowledge about the African languages of South Africa is astonishingly meagre, compared to what is known about South African (*White*) English (SAE), South African Black English (SABE) and Afrikaans. The term *Bantu* as an overarching concept for these African languages was invented by Bleek (1862), who described *Xhosa* as a member of the *Bâ-ntu* family of languages. Most of the work on Bantu languages is based on typological classifications and genetic relationships (cf. Guthrie, 1948, revised 1967–71; Bailey, 1995a). Louw and Finlayson (1990) focus on Southern Bantu origins as represented by *Xhosa* and *Setswana*, whereas Harries (1995) deals with the historical origins of *Xitsonga*. ...

Here the paragraphs are not distinguished from one another, either by inserting a line space between them or by indenting the first line of each paragraph. Also, a carriage return (Enter) has been inserted at the end of every line, forcing a ragged right-hand margin! This typographical style is eccentric and doesn't aid readability.

Example 4

The best way to collect Maintenance is by the direct payment into your bank account.

The advantages are
- No traveling to the COURT
  - No transport oncosts
  - No standing in queues
  - No lost time of work.

The problem here, typographically, is that by centring the items in the bulleted list, reading is made more difficult. The solution would be to left align the list. Inserting a colon after *are* would help to introduce the list more clearly by differentiating the lead-in line from the listed items.

5 The holistic text editing process

Text editing is a process and a holistic one at that: when text editors work on a document, in reality they work simultaneously according to different evaluation points and on diverse categories of error. It is well-nigh impossible to describe the process from all the different angles; in fact, we believe it is more important and useful to give you, the reader, insight into how experienced text editors engage with a text.

For this reason, we now shift our focus to two of the texts that the group of volunteer editors critiqued and edited. Even though the genesis of the two texts is very specific, they are representative of any text in similar domains: the online *Estuary Villa* text advertises a South African venue, but is illustrative of countless online advertisements; equally so, the *Maintenance* text is characteristic of many official-legal pamphlets that communicate with a particular audience, in this case ordinary citizens.

First we consider the original documents; then we look at a version of each document that incorporates the full range of errors that the volunteers introduced, commented on or corrected. The final version of each document is then displayed to show the product and effect of their editorial intervention at the level of text type, content, structure, wording, and presentation by applying – wittingly or unwittingly – the three criteria of analysis of correspondence, consistency and correctness of the CCC model.

We hope that some positive messages will emerge from this final exercise about applying the 15 evaluation points in the CCC model systematically to every document that you, the text editor, are likely to engage with. And that, having witnessed what others have done to improve others' texts, you will be suitably inspired to deliver work of the highest professional quality – and nothing less.

5.1 Text 1: Estuary Villa

5.1.1 Version 1: The original first draft

Estuary Villa

The Villa is situated in very secure surroundings on a Country Estate, a short stroll to the beach. All three bedrooms are en-suite with a shower and a toilet. The kitchen is fully equipped with a glasstop stove, oven, microwave, fridge/freezer, dishwasher, kettle, toaster, pots, pans and cooking utensils. Cutlery, crockery and glassware are provided for 6 guests. The bedrooms are fully equipped with sheets, blankets, duvets and pillows. Please bring your own towels. There is a TV with a DSTV decoder, please bring your own smart card. Braai facilities are situated outside the villa. Strictly no pets allowed. No Smoking.

Port Edward and the surrounding district have a large variety of activities that cater to all tastes and requirements. The close proximity to the Wild Coast Sun Country Club (10 minutes) and San Lameer Country Club (15 minutes), keeps the pros and amateurs out of mischief. Port Edward also has a nine-hole golf course that is a great way to relax.

There is a game reserve Lake Eland (35 minutes) and the Umtamvuna Nature Reserve offers a variety of trails for outdoor enthusiasts and those keen to get fit . The flora and fauna in this reserve is outstanding and the scenery is spectacular. There is horse riding in the vicinity and a huge variety of adventure activities ranging from 4x4 trails to the highest abseil in the country.

There is on-site parking for 2 cars. A full or part-time maid service and laundry arrangements can be made sheets and towels are changed twice a week for longer-staying guests. Culinary afficonados and nightclub-'jollers' are also catered for with a large variety of restaurants and eateries. The Wild Coast Casino (5 minutes) also offers something for the young and old, big and bold!

Port Edward has all the necessary daily shopping facilities with two large supermarkets, bottle stores, garages, a post office and a variety of other shops and restaurants.

5.1.2 Version 2: The annotated text

This text is very incoherent and lacks a thorough structure. In this next version, some annotations and editing have been carried out. They are not complete; they indicate the worst of the challenges. In general, the text is in need of fundamental restructuring and subheadings and bulleted lists will have to be inserted as an aid to the online reader. We have provided the comments in the margin preceded by the evaluation point that is under scrutiny.

Estuary Villa

The Villa is situated in very secure surroundings on a Country Estate, a short stroll to the beach. All three bedrooms are en-suite with a shower and a toilet. The kitchen is fully equipped with a glasstop stove, oven, microwave, fridge/freezer, dishwasher, kettle, toaster, pots, pans and cooking utensils. Cutlery, crockery and glassware are provided for 6 guests. The bedrooms are fully equipped with sheets, blankets, duvets and pillows. Please bring your own towels. There is a TV with a DSTV decoder, please bring your own smart card. Braai facilities are situated outside the villa. Strictly no pets allowed. No Smoking.

Port Edward and the surrounding district have a large variety of activities that cater to all tastes and requirements. The close proximity to the Wild Coast Sun Country Club (10 minutes) and San Lameer Country Club (15 minutes), keeps the pros and amateurs out of mischief. Port Edward also has a nine-hole golf course that is a great way to relax.

There is a game reserve Lake Eland (35 minutes) and the Umtamvuna Nature Reserve offers a variety of trails for outdoor enthusiasts and those keen to get fit . The flora and fauna in this reserve is outstanding and the scenery is spectacular. There is horse riding in the vicinity and a huge variety of adventure activities, ranging from 4x4 trails to the highest abseil in the country. There is on-site parking for 2 cars. A full or part-time maid service and laundry arrangements can be made sheets and towels are changed twice a week for longer-staying guests.

Culinary aficionados and nightclub-'jollers' are also catered for with a large variety of restaurants and eateries. The Wild Coast Casino (5 minutes) also offers something for the young and old, big and bold! Port Edward has all the necessary daily shopping facilities, with two large supermarkets, bottle stores, garages, a post office and a variety of other shops and restaurants.

Comment: [1] EP7-EP9 – fundamental restructuring with subheadings and bulleted list needed

Comment: [2] EP11 – non-uniform style

Comment: [3] EP7/8- bedroom and kitchen information should be regrouped and structure made consistent

Comment: [4] EP15 - misspelling; word difficult to recognise

Comment: [5] EP11 - inconsistency in use of numbers less than 10

Comment: [6] EP4 – insufficient information – pillow-cases?

Comment: [7] EP9 – incorrect connectors/lacking

Comment: [8] EP4 – insufficient information – where is the TV? In each bedroom, or only in the sitting room or TV room?

Comment: [9] EP12 – incorrect sentence construction (comma splice)

Comment: [10] EP1 – text not well matched to international readers (correspondence wrong) (*decoder, smart card, braai?*)

Comment: [11] EP11 - change of tone: imperious

Comment: [12] EP15 – incorrect punctuation

Comment: [13] EP11 - change of tone: informal/humorous

Comment: [14] EP11 – inconsistency in use of numbers less than 10

Comment: [15] EP12 – what is relaxing?

Comment: [16] EP11 – non-uniform style

Comment: [17] EP11 – unity of style

Comment: [18] EP12 – grammar!

Comment: [19] EP11 – non-uniform style

Comment: [20] EP12 – wrong v ... [1]

Comment: [21] In this context, ... [2]

Comment: [22] EP12 - grammar

Comment: [23] EP12 – syntax: ... [3]

Comment: [24] EP7 - In the wr ... [4]

Comment: [25] EP15 – misspelling

Comment: [26] EP1/2 – text n ... [5]

Comment: [27] EP11 – repetiti ... [6]

Comment: 28] EP10 – inapprop ... [7]

Comment: [29] EP1 – unsuitabl ... [8]

5.1.3 Version 3: The 'ideal' product of editing

By accepting the changes proposed in version 2, the edited text becomes visible. Using the same information but rearranging it, giving the terms used a more international English flavour and providing some subheadings, and applying a more even tone and register to the passage, our team of volunteer editors has created a new text, which looks like this:

Estuary Villa

Estuary Villa is situated in very secure surroundings on a country estate, a short stroll to the beach and in close proximity to the coastal town of Port Edward and a number of game or nature reserves.

Accommodation and facilities

All three bedrooms are en-suite with a shower and a toilet. The bedrooms are fully equipped with sheets, pillow cases, blankets, duvets and pillows. Please bring your own towels. A full- or part-time maid and a laundry service are available on request. For guests who stay longer than a week, the bed linen is changed weekly.

The kitchen is fully equipped with a glass-top stove, oven, microwave, fridge-freezer, dishwasher, kettle, toaster, pots, pans and cooking utensils. Cutlery, crockery and glassware are provided for six guests.

In the living room, there is a TV with a DSTV decoder, but please bring your own smart card. There are braai (barbecue) facilities for guests to use on the terrace. Please note that we do not accept pets, nor is smoking allowed on the property. There is on-site parking for two motor vehicles.

Outdoor attractions to view and relax at

Port Edward and the surrounding district offer our guests a large variety of activities that cater to all tastes and requirements. For sports enthusiasts of varying abilities there are the Wild Coast Sun Country Club (10 minutes) and the San Lameer Country Club (15 minutes). Port Edward also has a nine-hole golf course, which is a great way to relax.

For wildlife and outdoors enthusiasts the Lake Eland game reserve is only 35 minutes away by car, and the Umtamvuna Nature Reserve offers a variety of trails – a great way to keep fit. The flora and fauna in this reserve are outstanding and the scenery spectacular. Horse riding in the vicinity is popular, while a wide variety of adventure activities – ranging from 4x4 trails to the highest abseil in the country – are right on your doorstep.

Wining, dining, gambling and shopping

Culinary aficionados and the nightclub set are also catered for by the large selection of restaurants and eateries nearby. An added attraction is the Wild Coast Casino (5 minutes away), which offers a different experience for young and old.

Port Edward has all the daily shopping needs at heart, with its two large supermarkets, liquor outlets, service stations, post office and variety of shops and restaurants.

Whether you arrive to relax or play, Estuary Villa offers the ideal breakaway.

Comment: [1] Original opening statement lacked punch or persuasion, and didn't really set the scene for Estuary Villa.

Comment: [2] EP13/14 - Appropriate illustrations are needed to accompany this text, so that text and illustrations complement each other.

Comment: [3] Introduction of subheadings to draw the reader into the web text and signpost the text to follow was deemed necessary. Also, like things needed to be grouped together, and the subheadings help promote cohesiveness.

Comment: [4] This word hyphenated is easier on the eye and more accessible as a result.

Comment: [5] 'Braai' was left in to cater for South Africans and add some local flavour, but 'barbecue' was added because that's how it's commonly known among international tourists.

Comment: [6] Home-based sources of entertainment grouped together. The tone of the original prohibition of animals and smoking was in consistent with the purpose and tone of the website, so it has been couched more gently, in full sentences.

Comment: [7] All the outdoor activities grouped together under this subheading.

Comment: [8] This replaces 'amateurs and pros', which is inappropriate and also out of kilter with the remainder of the text.

Comment: [9] For this web page to be really useful/informative, there should be a map of the area.

Comment: [10] Reworded the original text to raise the tone to that of the rest of the text (consistency).

Comment: [11] Replaced the incorrect 'is' with 'are' to restore subject-verb agreement.

Comment: [12] Originally misspelt

Comment: [13] Replaced 'jollers' as contributing an inappropriate tone and being a foreign word to many website visitors.

Comment: [14] South African terms (bottle store, garage) replaced with international English terms to cater for the needs and limitations of non-SA visitors to the website.

Comment: [15] This concluding sentence was added because the original ended up in the air. The ... [1]

5.1.4 Version 4: Estuary Villa 5 – The published text

Below, for the sake of comparison, we have reproduced the *Estuary Villa* text as it is currently available online (http://www.safarinow.com/go/EstuaryVilla5/). Critical minds will notice that some of the editing comments above were in fact implemented by the client, whereas some others haven't been, while some new tourist information has been added. The reasons for the divergence between our editors' final version and the online presentation can be many and would certainly have included limitations of space, time and resources (after all, who could afford to have 11 editors working on their web text?; and what may look like 'ideal' text will not always be feasible).

Estuary Villa 5

Description

This beautiful villa is located on a secure country estate. The house accommodates six guests in three bedrooms and is the ideal venue for a family or small group of friends.

All the bedrooms have en-suite bathrooms and sheets, blankets, duvets and pillows are provided. Guests are requested to bring their own towels. The kitchen is fully equipped for self-catering purposes and comprises a stove and oven, a microwave oven, a fridge-freezer, a kettle, a toaster, cooking utensils and all crockery and cutlery. The lounge area contains a TV with a DStv connection; guests can bring their own decoders and smart cards.

The Estuary Villa is situated within 30 minutes of the Wild Coast Sun Country Club and Casino, the San Lameer Country Club and the Lake Eland Game Reserve. The Umtamvuna Nature Reserve close by offers a variety of hiking trails and the resident flora and fauna contribute to the spectacular scenery.

In the area guests can enjoy horse riding, swimming, fishing, 4x4-ing and the highest abseil in the country. A large number of easily accessible restaurants and nightclubs serve as dining and entertainment options. The operating lighthouse is a must-see and this seven-storey building provides visitors with arguably the most beautiful coastal view in South Africa. This site also hosts the Maritime Museum which specializes in 16th century wrecks, some of them of immense significance to South African and Portuguese history. Lectures can be arranged on request.

Supermarkets, bottle stores, fuel stations and a post office are conveniently located for necessities. The villa offers secure off-street parking for two vehicles. A cleaning service can be provided on request and bedding will be changed twice a week for longer stays.

5.2 Text 2: How do I claim maintenance?

The original text follows first, then a version in which the problems in the text are pointed out; finally, a third version reflects the 'ideal' edited text.

5.2.1 Version 1: The original text

How do I claim Maintenance? What are my rights?
- It is the duty of both parents to support their child financially.
- This includes contributions towards paying for food, clothing, accommodation, medical care and education.
- The amount of maintenance will be determined in proportion to each parrents income.
- Both parents are responsible for the care of their child whether the child is borne in or out of marriage.
- The person responsible for paying the maintenance has the right to appeal against the Maintenance Order.
- If the person responsible for paying maintenance does not pay, a compliant can be made at the Maintenance Court.
- A Maintenance Order may be made for :
- Expenses in connection with the birth of the child
- Expenses in connection with the maintenance of the child from the date of the childs birth to the date of the enquiry
 - In the case of a divorce, the ex spouse is entitled to receive maintenance if it was included as part of the Divorce Court procedure.

When can I approach the Maintenance Court?
- When the other party does not provide for the maintenance of the child or family.
- When applying for maintenance for the first time.
- When the Divorce Court has made an order; to open a file for the court to inform the person responsible when, how and where payments are made.
- When applying for an increase or decrease of an existing Maintenance Order.

Which Court should I go to in order to apply for Maintenance money?
Please contact your nearest Court by telephone as they will be able to assist you with the correct information. (The Court in the district in which the child or person to be maintianed resides.)

Please note:

The entire process of applying for maintenance to recieving the first payment might take several week's, depending on the co-operation of both parties

I need to claim Maintenance money: how do I go about to apply for it?
- Phone your local Court to find out which court is the correct one to go to for maintenance.

>>

• Phone that Maintenance Court and confirm what you will need to bring with you in order to apply for maintenance money.
• Come to the Court and complete an application form.
• The Court will provide you with a date on which you and the Respondent (the other parent) will need to come to Court.
• The Court will issue a subpoena to the Respondent (the other parent) to appear in Court on a specific date.

...

I need to go to the Maintenance Court, what do I need to take with me?
Make sure you bring the following with you: • Identity book
• ID nr and photo of parent / person responsible for paying the maintenance money.
• Bank statement if you have a Bank Account.
• List of expenses describbing the childs needs.
• Documents to prove these expenses, e.g. water and lights bill, grocery tillslips, clothing accounts etc.
• Current payslip of both parties who earn an income.
• Physical, residential and work address of the person who needs to pay the money.
• Physical, residential and work address of a family member or next of kin.
• Court date (if already determined) .
• Reference number (if already allocated).
• Court Order (if already granted).
• Divorce Agreement (in the case a divorce).
• Payment date

What expenses can be listed as the child's needs
• Accomodation • Skool fees
• Water and Lights (Electricity bills) • Medical costs
• Food and other groceries • Travel costs
• Clothes

You will need to bring supporting documentation for each of these expenses, otherwise THE COURT CANNOT INITIATE PROCEEDINGS, eg: pay slip, electericity bills, school fees and receipts of medicinal costs

---

...

How long will I wait for a Court Order to be issues?
This depends on the cooperation of both party's. Should the Party's reach an agreement, the first payment should be done as specified by the Court order

What are the different ways that I can collect Maintenance money?
• Garnishee order – the company takes the money directly from the responsible person's salary and pays it into the Court's bank account.
• Cash pay ment – you collect the money over the counter at the Court.

>>

• Direct payment into your bank account – the respondent makes a deposit into your bank account.

The best way to collect Maintenance is by the direct payment into your bank account.

The advantages are
• No traveling to the COURT
• No transport oncosts
• No standing in queues
• No lost time of work.

5.2.2 Version 2: The annotated text

How do I claim Maintenance?

What are my rights?
• It is the duty of both parents to support their child financially.
• This includes contributions towards paying for food, clothing, accommodation, medical care and education.
• The amount of maintenance will be determined in proportion to each parents income.
• Both parents are responsible for the care of their child whether the child is borne in or out of marriage.
• The person responsible for paying the maintenance has the right to appeal against the Maintenance Order.
• If the person responsible for paying maintenance does not pay, a compliant can be made at the Maintenance Court.
• A Maintenance Order may be made for :
- Expenses in connection with the birth of the child
- Expenses in connection with the maintenance of the child from the date of the childs birth to the date of the enquiry
- In the case of a divorce, the ex spouse is entitled to receive maintenance if it was included as part of the Divorce Court procedure.

When can I approach the Maintenance Court?
• When the other party does not provide for the maintenance of the child or family.
• When applying for maintenance for the first time.
• When the Divorce Court has made an order; to open a file for the court to inform the person responsible when, how and where payments are made.
• When applying for an increase or decrease of an existing Maintenance Order.

Which Court should I go to in order to apply for Maintenance money?
Please contact your nearest Court by telephone as they will be able to assist you with the correct information. (The Court in the district in which the child or person to be maintianed resides.)

Please note:

The entire process of applying for maintenance to recieving the first payment might take several week's, depending on the co-operation of both parties

Comment: [1] EP7 - Overall, the question and answer approach in this document works well, so it is not going to be changed, just refined/improved on.
EP13 – not ideal presentation for a semi-literate audience

Comment: [2] EP11 – consistency of spelling: why a capital letter?

Comment: [3] EP12 - towards the cost of

Comment: [4] EP12 - according to

Comment: [5] EP5 - misspelling and possessive apostrophe missing

Comment: [6] EP15 - comma missing

Comment: [7] EP12 - incorrect word choice – should be 'born'

Comment: [8] EP12 - incorrect article for a general statement – should be 'a'

Comment: [9] EP4 – insufficient information (too complicated a term)

Comment: [10] EP15 - misspelling

Comment: [11] EP11 - for the sake of consistency and because it's common in legal documents to use an initial uppercase C in Court, this will be the style applied throughout this document; also Maintenance Cou ... [1]

Comment: [12] EP9/12 - passive voice doesn't address the reader ... [2]

Comment: [13] EP15 - unnecessary space before colon

Comment: [14] EP15 - possessive apostrophe missing

Comment: [15] EP1/12 - maintenance enquiry

Comment: [16] EP12 - bulleted list: lack of grammatical concord; this ... [3]

Comment: [17] EP11 - Court/court inconsistent usage

Comment: [18] EP12 - insert 'a'

Comment: [19] EP12 - incorrect preposition (should be 'in')

Comment: [20] EP11 - Court/court inconsistent usage

Comment: [21] EP15 - should be lowercase

Comment: [22] EP12 - 'they' should be 'the court staff' or 'informatic ... [4]

Comment: [23] EP15 - misspelling

Comment: [24] EP1/12 - tending towards 'officialese', which the r ... [5]

Comment: [25] EP15 - misspelling

Comment: [26] EP15 - incorrect plural form – no apostrophe required –

Comment: [27] EP12 - incoherent sentence construction: 'dependir ... [6]

>>

I need to claim Maintenance money: how do I go about to apply for it?

• Phone your local Court to find out which court is the correct one to go to for maintenance.

• Phone that Maintenance Court and confirm what you will need to bring with you in order to apply for maintenance money.

• Come to the Court and complete an application form.

• The Court will provide you with a date on which you and the Respondent (the other parent) will need to come to Court.

• The Court will issue a subpoena to the Respondent (the other parent) to appear in Court on a specific date.

...

I need to go to the Maintenance Court, what do I need to take with me?

Make sure you bring the following with you:

• Identity book

• ID nr and photo of parent / person responsible for paying the maintenance money.

• Bank statement if you have a Bank Account.

• List of expenses describing the childs needs.

• Documents to prove these expenses, e.g. water and lights bill, grocery tillslips, clothing accounts etc.

• Current payslip of both parties who earn an income.

• Physical, residential and work address of the person who needs to pay the money.

• Physical, residential and work address of a family member or next of kin.

• Court date (if already determined) .

• Reference number (if already allocated).

• Court Order (if already granted).

• Divorce Agreement (in the case a divorce).

• Payment date

What expenses can be listed as the child's needs

• Accomodation

• Skool fees

• Water and Lights (Electricity bills) • Medical costs

• Food and other groceries • Travel costs

• Clothes

Comment: [28] EP15 - should be lowercase

Comment: [29] EP12 - the gerund 'applying', not the infinitive, is grammatically more correct here

Comment: [30] EP15 - double space between words

Comment: [31] EP15 - double space between words

Comment: [32] EP12 - this is not about a need, but an obligation: wrong word

Comment: [33] EP14 - legalese used – inaccessible to readers

Comment: [34] EP12 - this is not about a need, but an obligation: wrong word

Comment: [35] EP12 - unexplained legalese – inaccessible to readers

Comment: [36] EP12 - this is not about a need, but an obligation: wrong word

Comment: [37] EP15 - comma splice – incorrect sentence construction

Comment: [38] EP12 – not need, but obligation

Comment: [39] EP12 - inconsistent reference to 'identity/ID'; 'nr' is the incorrect abbreviation for 'number'; EP15 – full word would in any event probably be understood more easily

Comment: [40] EP15 - should be lowercase

Comment: [41] EP15 - misspelling; EP12 - also incorrect word choice (indicating, supporting your claim for)

Comment: [42] EP15 - incorrect form of the possessive

Comment: [43] EP9/12 - incorrect wording: 'whichever of the parents or parties earns an income'

Comment: [44] EP15 - delete comma to convey correct meaning

Comment: [45] EP12 - addresses – plural form required

Comment: [46] EP12 - address ... [1]

Comment: [47] EP12 - difficult ... [2]

Comment: [48] EP12 - difficult ... [3]

Comment: [49] EP15 - space b ... [4]

Comment: [50] EP12 – 'of' missing

Comment: [51] EP15 - full stop ... [5]

Comment: [52] EP15 - question ... [6]

Comment: [53] EP12 - incorre ... [7]

Comment: [54] EP15 - misspelling

Comment: [55] EP12/15 - wro ... [8]

Comment: [56] EP11 - unneces ... [9]

>>

• Water and Lights (Electricity bills) • Medical costs

• Food and other groceries • Travel costs

• Clothes

You will need to bring supporting documentation for each of these

expenses, otherwise THE COURT CANNOT INITIATE PROCEEDINGS, eg: pay slip,

electericity bills, school fees and receipts of medicinal costs

...

How long will I wait for a Court Order to be issues?

This depends on the cooperation of both party's. Should the Party's reach an agreement, the

first payment should be done as specified by the Court order.

What are the different ways that I can collect Maintenance money?

• Garnishee order – the company takes the money directly from the responsible person's

salary and pays it into the Court's bank account.

• Cash pay ment – you collect the money over the counter at the Court.

• Direct payment into your bank account – the respondent makes a deposit into your bank

account.

The best way to collect Maintenance is by the direct payment into your bank account.

The advantages are

• No traveling to the COURT

• No transport oncosts

• No standing in queues

• No lost time of work.

Comment: [56] EP11 - unnecessary use of capital letters (not proper nouns)

Comment: [57] EP8 - structure is overall consistent, but maybe this text should be placed outside the box

Comment: [58] EP10/1 - inappropriate word choice for the audience with an immediate effect on the appropriacy of the text

Comment: [59] EP1 - inappropriate word usage for the readers

Comment: [60] EP15 - misspelling

Comment: [61] EP12 - incorrect word choice (should be 'medical')

Comment: [62] EP12 - wrong form of verb (should be 'issued')

Comment: [63] EP15 - inconsistency – co-operation used elsewhere

Comment: [64] EP11, EP12/15 - incorrect plural form ('parties'); inconsistent use of lower and uppercase

Comment: [65] EP12 - incorrect verb – evidence of a non-English speaker's hand in drafting this document (should be 'made')

Comment: [66] EP15 - unnecessary/inconsistent use of uppercase

Comment: [67] EP1 - legalese, not explained to the reader anywhere

Comment: [68] EP15 - should be one word

Comment: [69] EP12 - deposits

Comment: [70] EP15 - unnecessary/inconsistent use of uppercase

Comment: [71] EP15 - insert a colon before a bullet list

Comment: [72] EP11 - non-consistent US spelling

Comment: [73] EP12 - evidence of a non-English speaker's hand in drafting this document

Comment: [74] EP1/12 – unidiomatic and undecipherable ('No loss of work time')

5.2.3 Version 3: The 'ideal' product of editing

This is the version that incorporates all the comments, suggestions and editing of the team of volunteer text editors.

How do I claim maintenance? What are my rights?
- It is the duty of both parents to support their child financially.
- This includes contributions towards food, clothing, accommodation, medical care and education.
- The amount of maintenance will be determined according to each parent's income.
- Both parents are responsible for the care of their child, whether the child is born in or out of marriage.
- The person responsible for paying the maintenance has the right to appeal against a Maintenance Order.
- If the person responsible for paying maintenance does not pay, a complaint can be laid at the Maintenance Court.
- A Maintenance Order may be made for:
    - Expenses in connection with the birth of the child.
    - Expenses in connection with the maintenance of the child from the date of the child's birth to the date of the maintenance enquiry.

In the case of a divorce, the ex-spouse is entitled to receive maintenance if it was included as part of the Divorce Court process.

When can I approach the Maintenance Court?
- When the other party does not provide for the maintenance of the child or the family.
- When applying for maintenance for the first time.
- When the Divorce Court has made an order, to open a file for the Court to inform the person responsible when, how and where payments are to be made.
- When applying for an increase or a decrease in an existing Maintenance Order.

Which Court should I go to in order to apply for maintenance money?
Please contact your nearest Court by telephone as the staff there will be able to help you obtain the correct information. (This is the Court in the district in which the child or person to be maintained lives.)

I need to claim maintenance money - how do I go about applying for it?

> Please note:
>
> The entire process from applying for maintenance to receiving the first payment might take several weeks, depending on how well the parties co-operate.

- Phone your local Court to find out which courtroom is the correct one to go to for a maintenance hearing.
- Phone that Maintenance Court and confirm what you will need to bring with you in order to apply for maintenance money.
- Come to the Court and complete an application form.
- The Court will provide you with a date on which you and the other parent will have to come to Court.

>>

- The Court will issue a subpoena (a letter ordering someone to appear in court) to the other parent to appear in Court on a specific date.

I have to go to the Maintenance Court; what must I take with me?
Make sure you take the following with you:
- Identity book
- Identity number and a photograph of parent or person who will be paying the maintenance money.
- A recent bank statement, if you have a bank account.
- A list of items your child needs and how much you spend on each of them (for example, clothing, milk, baby food).
- Documents to prove these expenses, for example, your monthly water and lights bill, grocery till slips, clothing accounts.
- The current payslips of either or both parents, depending upon who earns an income.
- Physical residential and work address of the person who has to pay the money.
- Physical residential and work address of a family member or next of kin.
- Court date (if already set).
- Case reference number (if already allocated).
- Court Order (if already granted).
- Divorce Agreement (in the case of a divorce).
- Payment date.

What expenses can be listed as those necessary to meet the child's needs
- Accommodation • School fees
- Water and electricity bills • Medical costs
- Food and other groceries • Travel costs
- Clothing

You will need to bring proof of payment for each of these expenses, otherwise THE COURT CANNOT START PROCEEDINGS: your pay slip, rental payment receipt, water and electricity bills, school fees and receipts for medicines.

How long will I have to wait for a Court Order to be issued?
This depends on how well the two parents co-operate. Should the two parents reach an agreement, the first payment should be made as specified in the Court Order.

What are the different ways that I can collect Maintenance money?
- Garnishee order – the employer takes the money directly from the salary of the person paying maintenance and pays it into the Court's bank account. You then claim the money from the Court.
- Cash payment – you collect the money over the counter at the Court.
- Direct payment into your bank account – the person paying maintenance deposits the money into your bank account.

The best way to collect Maintenance is by direct payment into your bank account.
The advantages of this payment method are:
- No travelling to the Court
- No transport costs
- No standing in queues
- No work time lost.

6 In conclusion

We hope that that we've been able to clarify the editing process through these few real-life examples. We also trust, through the pages of this book, and especially of this chapter, that you've come to realise that text editing is a process, because editing typically takes the form of a series of steps or phases. Our wish is that the extent of these steps is now a lot clearer to you, now that you've been able to witness almost first hand the contributions of a group of editors to the improvement of a range of texts.

As a last 'goodie' for your editorial backpack we have pasted together the entire evaluation scale, which includes all the types of error you the text editor are likely to encounter as you work through documents great and small.

A Text Type		
Correspondence	**Consistency**	**Correctness**
EP1 Appropriate text	EP2 Unity of genre	EP3 Application of genre rules
- Expectations & knowledge of the world - The audience's background	- Consistency in text type - Function - Length - Structure	- Genre - Carrier: pen-and-paper, electronic medium

B Content		
Correspondence	**Consistency**	**Correctness**
EP4 Appropriate and sufficient information	EP5 Congruence of facts	EP6 Correct facts
• TERMINOLOGY - Defined - Explained - Supported - Appropriate to audience • WORD CHOICE - Readability - Accessibility (facilitated) - Written-spoken language continuum - Appropriate to audience	• ETHICS - Plagiarism - Defamation or libel/slander - Copyright (ICP) • PRESENTATION of FACTS - Consistency	• WORD LEVEL - Facts, events, dates - Names of people, institutions, companies, places - Titles of books, films, ... - Addresses - Figures, tables, ... - Mathematics (numbers, calculations) - Statistics • TEXT LEVEL Quotations & sources - Cross-references

C Structure		
Correspondence	**Consistency**	**Correctness**
EP7 Sufficient cohesion	**EP8 Uniformity of structure**	**EP9 Linking words and argumentation**
- Appropriateness to the intended audience - Expectations & knowledge of text components - Expectations & knowledge of text structure - Sufficient coherence of macro & micro structure for optimal readability - Type, order & flow of argumentation	- Introduction, middle, conclusion - Consistency of choices	• PARAGRAPHING ERRORS - Length of paragraphs - Thesis statement (hook), supportive sentences and summative sentence - Number of themes - Transitions within & between paragraphs - Linking words • COHERENCE ERRORS - Choice of genre structure - Identification of themes - Logical sequencing of argument - Thread of arguments

D Wording		
Correspondence	**Consistency**	**Correctness**
EP10 Appropriate wording	EP11 Unity of style	EP12 Syntax, vocabulary and meaning
- Appropriateness to the intended audience - Appropriate to audience's language skill & knowledge - Appropriate to audience's education background - Appropriate to audience's expectations	• STYLE AND REGISTER ERRORS - Length of sentences - Vague or clumsy language - Empty sentences - Level of formality - Stiltedness - Bombast - Longwindedness - Ambiguity - Treatment of clichés - Figurative language - Humour & irony - Register - Jargon & slang - Active vs passive voice - Elimination of repetition - American vs British English • WORD BORROWINGS/ FOREIGN WORDS - Lexical, idiomatic, phonetic, syntactic & graphic borrowings - Words of foreign origin - Loanwords & their variants - Mixed metaphors	• GRAMMAR ERRORS - Formulation - Simple & complex sentences - Verb tenses & forms - Phrasal verbs - Congruence (person-number) - Present participles & gerunds - Group vs mass nouns - Plurals - Adjectives & adverbs - Attributive/predicative adjectives - Degrees of comparison - Conjunctions - Adverbs as linking words - Pronouns: personal, possessive, demonstrative, interrogative, reflexive, relative - Prepositions - Determiners (including articles) • ERRORS OF MEANING - Correct word choice - Ambiguous meaning - Appropriate synonyms - Parts of speech - Malapropisms - Tautology/redundancy - Pleonasms - Homonyms, homophones - Paronyms - Doublets - Figures of speech - Clichés, mixed metaphors - Foreign words

E Presentation		
Correspondence	**Consistency**	**Correctness**
EP13 Appropriate layout and typography	**EP14 Congruence between text and layout**	**EP15 Spelling, punctuation, layout and typography**
- Appropriateness to the intended audience - Degree of visual literacy - Experience & background - Correspondence between visual (typography & layout) and textual aspects (wording, text type & text structure)	• TYPOGRAPHICAL ERRORS - Type size, style, weight: regular, ... - Consistency of choices • LAYOUT ERRORS - Title & contents page - Preface & foreword - Acknowledgements - Lists of figures, tables, maps - Publisher's imprint (cover, title, ...) - ISBN & copyright statement - Date of publication - Dedication/epigraph - Appendices/addenda/annexurres - Bibliography, glossary, index, credits - Headings & subheadings - Running heads & footers - Widows & orphans - Paragraph style - Numbering - Format of cross-references - Page layout/design - Page numbers - Spacing & margins - Indenting of paragraphs - Treatment of quoted matter - Use of colour & shading/tints - Tables, column heads, side heads, alignment & numbering - Illustrations, labels & captions - Sketches & diagrams (DTP artwork) - Photographs - Footnotes and/or endnotes	• SPELLING ERRORS - Hyphen/one word/two words - Abbreviations & acronyms - Word breaks - Plural forms - Diminutive forms - Uppercase vs lowercase - Accents/diacritics - Numbers & symbols - Decimal point/comma - Percentages - Consistency of choices - American vs British English • PUNCTUATION ERRORS - Spaces around punctuation marks - Full stops, question & exclamation marks - Commas - Semicolons - Colons (uppercase?) - Ellipsis - Hyphen/en-rule/em-rule (dash) - Parentheses - Brackets - Quotation marks: singles or doubles?

Table 12.6 *Integrated assessment model for text quality*

Appendices

There are many different varieties of English – including British, American, Australian, Indian, South African – that have developed into established and acceptable standards in their own right. There's also English used as a lingua franca (ELF), spoken or written as the common language among people who, but for English, would otherwise not be able to communicate with one another. However, since English is not governed by hard-and-fast rules laid down by an academy, it presents additional challenges for its users: lexicon and idiom are but two aspects that present speakers with difficulties, whatever native varieties we speak of; the grammar of English (including morphology, semantics and syntax) is another.

The extent to which a text editor may intervene in texts is at any time a vexed question and will also depend upon the editor's command of either Standard English or International English or a local variety, or simply their sensitivity to maintaining the author's voice and native tongue. It will almost certainly also be determined by the intended readership of a particular document: the greater the disjuncture between the writer's English and that of their audience (and the cultural differences between them), the more the editor will have to adjust their author's text. In books destined for an international market, occurrences of the vernacular, for example, may have either to be omitted from texts or else explained – an editorial decision taken in careful consultation with the author.

For writers publishing for an international audience this poses a real dilemma: Which 'English' should we be adopting? Our own variety, or an international (or world) English? And what are the characteristics of this variety, so that we might apply them in our writing? Here, the problem is more complex than merely deciding whether to follow US or UK English conventions: as these appendices illustrate, questions of the differences in vocabulary, grammar, punctuation, style and register, and idiom all come into play.

For those writers for whom English is a foreign language the challenges are more complex, since they have learned the rules and conventions of their target language and often those are at odds with the rules and conventions of their native language. For their text editors the challenges of editing their writings and communicating the effected changes can be equally formidable.

This brings us to the reason why we have included these appendices in this volume (and we intend adding to them in time): we are attempting to sensitise you as a language practitioner and/or text editor to some of the characteristics of the Englishes to which you are likely to be exposed, and to offer you some sort of guidance as to how to approach your task when you edit these types of text.

Appendix A

Text editing for the multinational client

Catherine Grady

Translation into English makes one aware of the remarkable elasticity of the language. If only it could be reduced to an orderly set of rules. An editor receives an email from a translation agency needing a quick revision: '*The client asks if this sentence is correct. Could you please let me know ASAP as they are about to print this out?*'

Working in Belgium, what I find is often behind the above request is the reality that a non-native speaker (NNS) working in an international context can develop an excellent ear for 'correct' English. Like any writer, they rely on an inner voice telling them when something doesn't sound quite right.

Under the pressure of deadlines, '*make sure the English translation is done by a native speaker*' occasionally breaks down into a surly '*whoever translated this can't possibly be a native speaker, it's full of errors!*' and you are faced with a pre-press emergency. That's when a second translator or editor will be called in to 'fix' the wretched text. If only it were as simple as sending it back to the kitchen, however ...

This may be far more likely to occur in those parts of Europe (which may correspond somewhat to the distribution of Germanic languages, but not necessarily strictly so, as I would include many French-speakers here) where the general knowledge of English is extremely good. Translators in Belgium rarely have the opportunity to be amused by NNSs' comical attempts! But the very fact that English has become entrenched as the corporate and institutional lingua franca creates a situation in which an idea of what proper English should be, as learned at school by a very well-educated population, will face off with the authentic native speaker (NS) who is suspected of being unreliable, unprofessional and unprintable!

While elsewhere English-language publishers may be wrinkling their noses at the efforts of NNSs, a reverse situation can occur in the commercial sector. A NNS client will be responsible for production, and this includes penalising suppliers who deliver shoddy linguistic merchandise.

Often, the client is justified and there is something unnatural-sounding about the text. But equally often, in the very same set of comments, the client will see grave errors where there is nothing of the sort. In fact, this is as good as always the case. It is perhaps a part of the mastery of a language to assume the authority to judge when someone else strikes a note off key.

In a recent such emergency, some of the choices the other translator had made sounded 'wrong' or 'awkward' to my ear initially, causing me at first to nod vigorously in agreement with the client. But as I looked at each case more closely, it became clear that the other translator was obviously an NS who just happened to choose different expressions than I might do. In the internet age, one can look up a questionable usage and instantly discover that, in fact, for some people out there at least, it is the standard.

If the client in question is a multinational corporation whose Board of Directors includes two Belgians, a Swiss, a Norwegian, a South African and an American, they would presumably be looking for an English that is acceptable to all. Those who associate entrepreneurship with the United States might be tempted to think that American usage would be the default for all such clients. It is true that the 'corporate' style employs a language that recalls the American mass media, a sort of 'business-casual' tone that comes across as polished and professional yet direct and appealing, the linguistic equivalent of the proverbial firm handshake (sentences such as *'We offer a challenging and rewarding career in a global company that focuses on growth, operational excellence and industry leadership'.* Note the heavy use of abstract nouns such as excellence, leadership, growth.) Yet in Continental Europe at least, this is complicated by an image of British English as being more refined. Plus, the entire official apparatus of the European Union applies British English, and it is traditionally taught in schools, making the default English for translators working in Belgium effectively 'UK English'. My impression is that in a European corporate context that familiar American *tone* is often desired, but this by no means implies a preference for idiomatic American English.

The majority of the basic corrections in the work of NNSs have to do with prepositions, those little in-between spaces, together with the occasional 'false friends', where the Dutch or French word resembles something else. These are the parts I would strip out when going over a text.

Often, the client wants to insert 'corrections' which, while not necessarily completely unacceptable, do give the text a distinctly non-native ring.

> *Rinse thoroughly in an eye-wash fountain with your eyes open.*
> (the orignal NS version).
> *Rinse thoroughly using an eye-wash fountain with your eyes open.*
> (the NNS's 'correction')

Also, what can be left out, those places where one can omit words that are simply implied in the phrase, is often read as an error by non-natives:

> *Before you start work check where the safety provisions and escape routes are.*
> (the original NS version)

Before you start working/start to work check where the safety provisions and escape routes are.
(the NNS's suggested 'corrections')

Some Dutch 'false friends':

These are the core features of our *offering* (range) as a specialised service provider to investors.

Our independence also makes us an *interesting* (attractive) partner for many industry players.

As a non-executive partner, Paul *overlooks* (oversees) Investor Relations

Cases in which the client suspects the translator of falling prey to 'false friends':

'Keep away from **naked flame***'* (Dutch: *naakte vlam*).

My own initial reaction (as a US NS):

*'I've never heard of "***naked flame***" in my life, what a silly error on the part of the translator!'*

Yet in an online translators' forum discussion about the use of '**naked flame**' vs '**open flame**' to translate the German '**offene Flamme**' a UK NS says:

*'"**Naked flame**" looked right as soon as I saw it, but surprisingly gets an awful lot fewer hits ... Hmmmm!'*

As an NS looking at a text, there is, admittedly, the inward cringe at a choice of words that sounds out of place. It makes the writer sound childish or primitive – not the image one wants to project in the business marketplace, where an aura of competence and finesse is a very real, if intangible, asset.

An example is the idiomatic expression *to hold someone in good stead/stand someone in good stead.* On the website of the same multinational corporation, an Australian metal worker is quoted:

'The skills learnt in the graduate program held me in good stead ...'

My own inward reaction (as a US NS):

'Ouch, a bit of a malapropism there, but we get the idea!'

However, on the internet:

(in an online translation forum, a native UK English speaker asks): *'How do you translate the phrase "to hold (someone) in good stead" into French?'*

(a native French speaker's reply): *'That's a new one to me – I just knew* to stand in good stead. *Is it somehow akin to* to hold ... ?'

And on a different online forum: *'How can you translate: "to hold someone in good stead"?'*

(a native German speaker's reply): *'I only know "to stand s.o. in good stead", which means* zu gute kommen.'

There is no academy dictating which choices should be made, and ultimately it is a matter of developing an ear based on a wide exposure to different writers; yet increasingly this includes NNSs who are naturally going to have a different background from the respective NSs around the world (however one wishes to define the term).

The NNSs have much to contribute to a language that has long been an international currency. In this context, however, the professional English editing marketplace becomes one in which a translation agency and a client can end up haggling over the quality of the goods. The text editor then becomes the negotiator who is expected to maintain the utmost integrity, but regarding a language in which many rules can be bent.

Appendix B

Aspects of South African English, suggesting the challenges facing text editors

John Linnegar

In South Africa, though it has always been a minority language, English is spoken by a number of significant groups: the roughly 8% of the population who speak it as their first language; and the varieties spoken as Cape Flats English, Black South African English, Afrikaans English and Indian English. According to Onraët (2011: 13), considering the 11 different languages from five different language families with limited mutual intelligibility, the need for a widely used lingua franca is clear. South African English (SAE) is strongly influenced by at least each of these local Englishes, but will continue to function as an important lingua franca between speakers who do not share a first language (Crystal 2003: 46).

Since the early nineteenth century, when the British first began to govern the Cape Colony, English (in a variety of dialectal forms) has been a dominent language in South Africa, alongside first Dutch and then its successor from 1925, Afrikaans. For 92 years, then, two European languages, English and Afrikaans, were the dominant official languages (Onraët 2011: 13), though during the period 1948 to 1990 apartheid society was dominated by Afrikaans. Whereas during this period Afrikaans came to be perceived by the black majority as the language of authority and oppression, English was perceived by the government as the language of protest, opposition and self-determination (Crystal 2003: 45). Meanwhile, a number of varieties of English had evolved: Cape Flats English developed among the so-called Coloured community and is strongly influenced by Afrikaans and local idiom; an African variety of English also developed, spoken by black people who had learned the language mainly in mission schools but influenced in different ways by the various language backgrounds of the speakers (eg isiZulu, Sesotho). From 1860, English was also adopted by immigrants from India who settled on the plantations of what was then Natal and most of whom had no knowledge of the language. This variety of English illustrates the unusual sociolinguistic complexity that can be encountered in South Africa (Mesthrie 1987, 1993, in Crystal 2006). From the 1950s, the language came to be taught to children in Indian schools, and within a generation a process of language shift was taking place, with English becoming the first language of the majority. Moreover, because these children were separated by apartheid from UK-English speaking children, their English developed in very different ways from mainstream South African English. The result is a variety of English which mixes features of Indian, South African and Standard British, creole and foreign Englishes in a fascinating way.

As a result of these cultural and linguistic influences, SAE has contributed a number of uniquely South African words and expressions to the language, some of which are little understood (or likely to be misunderstood) by speakers of other Englishes[1]. For example:

SAE word	Origin/meaning	Non-SAE equivalent
bakkie	a light delivery vehicle; Afrikaans *bak* = container	light delivery vehicle
bottle store	SAE: euphemism for liquor store	off licence, liquor store
braai	Dutch/Afrikaans: short for *braaivleis* = an informal outdoor gathering at which meat is grilled over an open fire; the grilled food	barbecue
bunny chow	Hindi: *banya* = merchant, trader; Chinese: *chow* = spicy food; take-away food consisting of a hollowed-out half-loaf of bread filled with vegetable or meat curry	–
donga	isiZulu/isiXhosa for a deep, dry watercourse	gully
garage	SAE: place where one fills up with petrol or diesel	petrol station; service station
garam masala	Hindi: *garam* = hot + *masala* = spices; a mix of curry spices and herbs	curry powder
gogga	Khoisan: collective term for creeping and slithering creatures	'creepy-crawly', insect, bug
indaba	isiZulu, isiXhosa: important, lengthy meeting	meeting, discussion
informal settlement	SAE: of a settlement erected in an unregulated and unplanned manner upon unproclaimed land, with no infrastructure provided by the local authority	shackland, shanty town
just now	SAE, from Afrikaans *netnou*	in a while, presently, directly, immediately
kwela	isiZulu, isiXhosa: 'jump', 'climb on'	music played by a pennywhistle, dance style
laani, larney	from Malay *rani* = rich or Hindi *rani* = queen	white man, boss; uppercrust, posh; smart, elegant
lekker	Dutch/German/Afrikaans: tasty, delicious (of food); also a term of general approval	tasty, enjoyable, nice, pleasant, good, lovely
padkos	Afrikaans/Dutch: 'road' + 'food'	food for a journey; provisions
robots	SAE, from UK English, from Czech *robota* = forced labour	automatic traffic lights traffic signals
shebeen	From Anglo-Irish *shebeen*, modern Irish *sibín* = a drinking establishment, usually in a private home in a township, where liquor is sold and consumed	a low public-house, tavern

[1] Penny Silva (ed) 1996. *A dictionary of South African English on historical principles*. Oxford: Oxford University Press in association with the Dictionary Unit for South African English; Rajend Mesthrie with Jeanne Hromnik 2011. *Eish, but is it English?* Cape Town: Zebra Press.

In the 21st century, SAE continues to reflect the changes in the country after the past decades. As can be expected, when first and second language varieties are as closely in contact as they are in South Africa, some mutual influence is bound to take place, a process that is already well advanced. Grammar (including verb, adverb and preposition usage, and structural deviations), pronunciation (a continuum of accents exists (Crystal 2003: 45)) and lexicon have been particularly affected.

But as barriers between the speakers of different languages have begun to break down, English is being enriched with increasing numbers of words from South Africa's other languages: *nè*, *nogal*, *letsema* and *mashonisa*; *eish!*, *vuvuzela*, *tshakalaka* and *makoya*, for example (DSAE 2006: SP7). The practices of code-switching (using two or more languages alternately in separate communications) and code-mixing (using two or more languages in a single communication) in both popular television series and current literature are promoting this process of familiarisation and borrowing.

On the other hand, the users of English as a lingua franca – whether belonging to the Cape Flats, the Afrikaans, the Black or the Indian varieties – have experienced the challenges of using Standard English/SAE in practice, both the spoken word and in writing. A selection of these are highlighted below.

Among Afrikaans-speakers, the typical errors committed in English usage (and for which text editors should be on the lookout) are (Linnegar 2009):

- a lack of subject–verb agreement, or concord, especially with the verbs is/are and have/has: *My friend have three children. They is all boys.*
- difficulty with using strong (irregular) verbs (eg *sing*, *sang*, *have sung*) in their correct tense form: *They sung the song perfectly.*
- verbs used incorrectly, based on Afrikaans usage: *Borrow me your pen, please.*
- the infinitive form of verbs used instead of the gerundive form: *We look forward to see everyone at the event.* (We look forward to seeing everyone at the event.)
- the comma that's obligatory between two clauses in Afrikaans sentences is not used in English: *Some people who learn a language, find that they can master it easily.*
- prepositions not used idiomatically correctly, as a result of direct translation from Afrikaans: *The interest rate increased with one per cent. He threw me with a stone.* (The interest rate increased by one per cent. He threw a stone at me.)
- the word order of personal pronouns being the opposite of Afrikaans usage: *I and my friend went shopping. Me and my sister listened to music together.* (My friend and I went shopping. My sister and I listened to music together.)
- the use of adjectives where adverbs are required: *He played fantastic well in yesterday's match. She dances so beautiful.* (He played fantastically well in yesterday's match. She dances so beautifully.)
- the use of 'it' in the same way as 'dit' is used in Afrikaans (ie both singular and plural forms): *Those principles: we can't uphold it.* (Those principles: we can't uphold them.)

- the influence of the tendency towards combining words to create a single word for a concept: *A strategic change attempt was recently launched at our hospital.* (An initiative to implement strategic change was released at our hospital. – from '*strategiese veranderingsaksie*')
- the literal translation of Afrikaans words into English: *concept report* (draft report, from *konsepverslag*); *instance* (institution, from *instansie*).

Typical of Cape Flats English (strongly influenced by Afrikaans idiom; Linnegar 2009) in the Western Cape province are:

- the *-d* and *-ed* endings are usually clipped off the ends of past participles such as *minced*, *curried*, *pickled* and *sundried* when they qualify nouns, with the result that, even in print, we see examples such as: *mince meat*, *curry beans*, *pickle fish* and *sundry apricots*.
- in addition, the 'auxiliary' verb *did* has become fairly entrenched in many a statement (not necessarily for emphasis), as in *I did go to the disco last night* (I went to the disco last night).
- the replacement of the reflexive pronoun *myself* with the first person singular pronoun *me*: *I did go shopping and I did buy me a dress* (I went shopping and I bought myself a dress). This is probably due to the influence of the Afrikaans '*my*', which can mean either 'my' or 'myself'.
- the use of the singular form of nouns that are normally plural in English but singular in Afrikaans: *I tried on a trouser first and then a jean.* (I tried on (a pair of) trousers and then (a pair of) jeans, from Afrikaans *Ek het eers 'n broek aangepas en daarna 'n jean*).

Speakers of South Africa's nine indigenous African languages experience particular difficulty with (Linnegar 2009):

- the use of the feminine third person singular pronoun (she), usually, for either males or females, because the indigenous languages do not have the same pronounal distinction (nouns are used to indicate gender);
- pronunciation: lengthening short internal vowel sounds (*sheep* for *ship; feel* for *fill*) and shortening long internal vowel sounds (*hit* for *heat; siriyas* for *serious*) (this results in real problems of misinterpretation and misunderstanding in public forums, where oral representations have to be transcribed);
- misplaced syllabic emphasis, following mother-tongue stress patterns or mother-tongue vowel sounds (the bold characters indicate where the stress falls): cir**cum**stances; de**fic**it; con**sti**tion for constitution; de**tter**mined for de**ter**mined; ita**lise** for italicise;
- the use of the present continuous tense instead of the simple present: *She is saying* ...; *I am thinking that* ... *He is having* ... (She says ...; I think that ...; He has ...);
- the incorrect usage of prepositions, usually an unidiomatic choice: *Please ask to him* ... (Please ask him ...);
- the use of 'very much' as an adverbial phrase intensifier: *I am very much glad for the opportunity* ....

South African Indian English has acquired well over a thousand distinctive items, at least in informal speech, including loan words from Indian languages: *thanni* (a card game), *dhania* (coriander) and *isel* (flying ant); and adaptations of many native English words: *proposed* (engaged), *future* (husband/wife-to-be) and *cheeky* (stern), for example (Mesthrie 1987, 1993, in Crystal 2003). But the most notable feature of this variety is its syntax, including:

- reduplication: *fast-fast* (very fast), *different-different* (many and different);
- rhetorical use of question-words: *Where he'll do it!* (He certainly won't do it!), *What must I go?* (Why should I go?).
- pronoun omissions: *If you got, I'll take. Where you bought?*
- tag questions: *He came there, isn't it?*
- end-placed verbs: *Customer you got.*
- relative clauses: *Who won money, they're putting up a factory next door* (The people who won money are ...).
- postpositions: *Durban-side* (near Durban), *afternoon-time it gets hot* (in the afternoon ...).
- final use of some conjuctions and adverbials: *She can talk English but*; *I made rice too, I made roti too* (I made both rice and roti).

Understandably, then, in a multilingual society such as South Africa's, where 'historical, racial, tribal and political factors have combined to produce a sociolinguistic situation of stunning intricacy' (Crystal 2006), the normative and text-linguistic challenges that face the text editor of English-language texts are as stimulating as they are great.

Appendix C

Editing Strine: challenges facing Australian editors

Janet Mackenzie, DE, and Elizabeth Manning Murphy, DE

Australian English resembles British English in many respects. There are no differences in grammar, but accent and vocabulary combine to produce a distinctive variant. The spoken form is colloquially known as Strine, from the purported pronunciation of 'Australian'.

Australian vocabulary

Much Australian public discourse is indistinguishable from other varieties of English but despite global influences the Australian vernacular stubbornly retains many peculiarities. Fiction writers and their editors have to decide how much of this vocabulary to use, and how much to explain, in books destined for an international market.

Words such as *digger*, a serving soldier or veteran, and *tucker*, food, carry a great weight of history and sentiment. There are many survivals from English dialects, such as *dunny* for an outdoor lavatory and *dag* for an eccentric person. The huge influence of the wool industry in Australian history is apparent in the continuing Australian preference for the strong form of the verb *to shear*: its past forms are generally *shore* and *shorn*, where other varieties of English prefer *sheared*. Common English words such as *bush*, *mate*, *battler* and *mob* take on particular resonance in Australian English.

At times Australians choose eclectically between British and American words, preferring *petrol* to *gasoline* but *kerosene* to *paraffin*. Sometimes they simply create a term: what the British call a *cafetière* and the Americans a *French press* is known as a *coffee plunger*; the British *sweets* and American *candy* are *lollies*; the British *4x4* and American *SUV* is a *4WD* or *four-wheel drive*.

The peculiarities of Strine are most apparent in colloquial speech. Some Cockney rhyming slang survives, such as *dead horse* for tomato sauce, *porkies* (from *pork pies*) for lies and *billy lids* for kids. Diminutives are abundant and new ones are constantly being coined: *firie* for firefighter, *ambo* for ambulance officer, *servo* for service station, *possie* for position, *arvo* for afternoon, *pokie* for poker machine, *super* for superannuation pension. Slang is vigorous and often humorous, as with the term *budgie smugglers* for a brief, tight male swimming costume (in reference to *budgerigar*, a small native parrot). A *dummy-spit* is an angry outburst, with the implication that it is no more than a childish tantrum. *To drop one's bundle* is to go to pieces. Our current female prime minister is unmarried; her de facto partner has no official title but is widely known as *the First Bloke*.

There is some regional variation in the vocabulary of Australian English and the terms that differ can rouse considerable emotion, particularly in pubs: a half-pint glass of beer is a *schooner* in New South Wales but a *pot* in Victoria.[1]

A nation of immigrants

Since its colonisation by people of British and Irish descent, successive waves of immigrants and refugees have contributed to Australia. Immigration has been especially rapid in the past few decades: as much as one-quarter of the present population was born overseas, and about 20 per cent speak a language other than English at home. The largest immigrant groups are from the United Kingdom, New Zealand, Italy, Vietnam and China, and there are identifiable communities from more than 100 countries.[2] The government provides various services for people of non-English-speaking background, such as English-language instruction, a telephone interpreter service and news broadcasts in community languages. Australia has been comparatively successful in creating a multicultural society out of this mix, as demonstrated by the invention of the *burkini*, a modest swimming costume for Muslim women. Despite the numbers, most Australians are monolingual and Australian English has adopted little from the languages of its immigrants except for food names, which are plentiful. *Babyccino*, a modified version of cappuccino coffee served to children, shows linguistic invention at work in this area.

The huge variety of cultural backgrounds among authors presents challenges for editors. Often authors unwittingly use the grammar of their first language with English vocabulary, or make mistakes in idioms. For instance, among those whose first language is Mandarin or Korean common errors include a lack or misuse of articles, wrong construction of tenses, misuse of prepositions, misplacement of adverbs and the lack of a plural marker on nouns, as well as semantic mistakes.

Editors must be both alert and tactful in working with non-native speakers. Just correcting the English is little help; such authors need to understand the reasons for the corrections, so that they learn from the editorial experience.

Indigenous influences

At the time of white settlement in 1788, more than 200 Aboriginal languages were spoken. In a sad loss to humanity, most of them are now defunct. Some words were preserved as settlers adopted the names of animals (*kangaroo*, *koala*), plants (*coolibah*, *mulga*) and artefacts (*woomera*, a spear thrower; *coolamon*, a wooden or bark vessel). A few, such as *boomerang*, *didgeridoo* and *corroboree*, are recognised beyond Australia.[3]

People who identify as Indigenous comprise a little over 2% of the population. Many speak standard Australian English, but some are fluent in several Indigenous languages.

---

[1] See *Australian national dictionary* (1989) Melbourne: Oxford University Press.
[2] Department of Immigration. <http:// www.immi.gov.au/media/statistics>.
[3] *Australian national dictionary.*

Indigenous people have enlisted the help of linguists to preserve these languages, and some schools use the local language for teaching.

Australian Aboriginal English is a distinct dialect. It has given us terms such as *whitefella* and *walkabout* and is still influencing standard Australian English with phrases such as *sorry business* (mourning ceremonies), *welcome to country* and *speaking language*. In court-room transcriptions of Aboriginal English it may be necessary to elicit the precise meaning intended by the witness. For instance, 'They lock him up' might be meant in the past tense because consonant clusters such as /kt/ in *locked* are often elided. The whitefella failure to recognise the distinct nature of Aboriginal English can lead to serious misunderstandings.

Cross-cultural editing is a maze of negotiation. When preparing Indigenous authors' writing for publication, editors need to take care to preserve the original voice and to respect Indigenous understandings of authorship and copyright, which may be communal.[4] Government communication with Indigenous people should take into account their linguistic needs. One successful example of this was the 2001 Census, in which the standard form asked 'Where does the person usually live?', but the Indigenous form worded this as 'Do you live at this place most of the time?' Indigenous respondents are interviewed individually by trained Indigenous census collectors, so 'you' and 'this place' had direct referents.

Editors in Australia

Australia has a vigorous publishing industry, producing fiction, non-fiction and educational materials for local and export markets. Major publishing houses have Australian branches with local publishing programmes, and there are many independent firms. Editors also find employment in commercial and government publishing.

Australian editors are fortunate to have the *Macquarie dictionary*, which records the English language as used in Australia, and the *Australian national dictionary*, which lists distinctively Australian words and usages.

The seven state-based societies of editors federated in 2008 to become the Institute of Professional Editors (IPEd), whose aim is 'to advance the profession of editing'. IPEd has published *Australian standards for editing practice* and conducts national examinations for accredited status.[5]

As elsewhere, electronic publishing presents enormous challenges for Australian editors. They are beginning to realise that they work in a global industry where outsourcing to low-wage countries is easy. Their professional future depends on high standards of work and a thorough understanding of Australian and international English.

---

[4] Australia Council for the Arts 2008. *Writing: Protocols for producing indigenous Australian writing* (2 ed). <www.australiacouncil.gov.au/research>.

[5] <http://iped-editors.org>. It awards the post-nominals:AE – Accredited Editor and DE – Distinguished Editor.

Appendix D

'Southwest-European English' and the challenges facing editors of this 'variety'

David Owen

This short account refers to written English texts produced by non-native speakers (NNSs) in France, Portugal, Spain and Italy. Strictly for the purposes of this discussion, this form of English is termed *Southwest-European English*.

At a taxonomic level, it makes no sense to speak about this 'type' of English as if any such variant really existed in the way that British English, or South African English or Indian English exists: put simply, there is no such thing as Southwest-European English. In addition, though this goes without saying, the English produced in southern European countries is influenced at the usual levels of phonetics, syntax, semantics and morphology by the various languages of the speakers in this area (French, Portuguese, Spanish, Italian, Catalan, Galician, Basque, among others), languages – chiefly Romance – that are often similar to one another, though equally often are substantially different. This gives rise to a considerable variety of typical second- or foreign-language (L2) errors, depending on the underlying first language (L1). So we might begin by saying that any discussion of the English produced in this area is a rather thankless task in that perhaps little can be said of it that is both useful and relevant, yet also generally valid.

But, in all events, our concern here is not to attempt the description of the many forms and applications of what is, in effect, a pseudo-variant. Instead, for the purposes of editorial guidelines, we begin with the important constraint of focusing only on formal written language. And in this ambit, several things can be observed.

At the broadest level, what might be called the *rhetorical tradition*s of discourse in this part of Europe are rather distinct from those of the English-speaking world. We are necessarily generalising here, but – for a native English speaker – the stylistics of formal written French, Spanish or Catalan, to give only three examples, frequently appears to be extraordinarily *ornate* in its use of lengthy phrases and subordinate clauses, its penchant for what can seem to be hugely complex syntactic arrangements, its battery of subjunctives, its bewildering passive constructions.

Much of this derives from earlier traditions and unquestionably has its linguistic and aesthetic merits; but it is quite dramatically counter-current to the more prosaic, direct and transparent rhetorical tradition (if this is what we can call it) that we now see favoured in much English writing.

The simple practical upshot of this is that editors of Southwest-European English will almost certainly need to adjust their authors' texts – to a greater or lesser extent – to suit them to differing reader expectations of style and form. Often this will mean breaking paragraph-length sentences down into far smaller units of meaning; another probable intervention will be the disentangling of subordinate clauses and their rearrangement, with respect to their main clause, into more readily comprehensible sentences. An editorial insistence on a basic SVO structure (subject + verb + object) will generally clarify syntactic difficulties, as will an insistence – where reasonable or expected – on using the active rather than the passive voice.

At a more mechanical level, as we have already observed, it is difficult to make observations of much validity without engaging more directly with the specifics of the underlying L1 that influence the production of written English in this area. Nevertheless, there are some general issues that will probably need some attention. These include the following:

- **Punctuation**
  The use of word-initial capitals in English is often significantly at variance with the languages of southwest Europe. Typical problems are with days of the week and months; nationality adjectives and languages, which may be erroneously written with a lower-case initial letter. The distribution of commas may also require attention, as it is common in many Romance languages to use these as clause separators/markers, where modern English may no longer use them (eg 'some of the students who were at the lecture, thought that this was too difficult').

- **Grammar**
  The use and restrictions of stative and dynamic verbs in English rarely coincide with those of Romance languages, which can lead to constructions that accurately reflect L1 usage but which are unusual or incorrect in English (eg 'I am thinking that this is a good opportunity').

Countable and uncountable nouns, and most especially the grammatical consequences that these nouns bring with respect to related verbs, determiners and quantifiers, may cause difficulties (eg 'there are too few money').

The use and omission of the definite article is a perennial difficulty in English for Southwest-European English authors. In general, English makes use of this to emphasise, and omits it in generalisations; for most Romance speakers, nouns almost always require an article, and generalisations always take the definite article. This understandably leads to an over-use of such forms (eg 'the main purpose in this man's life was the power, the money and the reputation').

The use of the indefinite article is less problematic, though use of a/an may be affected by a failure to perceive certain word-initial sounds in nouns as semi-vowels, leading to errors (eg 'this is an European problem').

Romance languages have grammatical gender, though this will rarely affect the form of written English that its speakers produce (however, French speakers in particular have a certain tendency in English to refer to inanimate nouns by the animate pronouns *he*, *she* and *they*). But one general area of confusion may be more frequent, which is the relationship between possessor and possessed in pronoun forms. In English, the form of the possessive pronoun is determined by the gender of the subject, or *possessor* ('John and <u>his</u> sister'); in Romance languages, it is the gender of the *possessed* noun that determines the form of the possessive pronoun. This may therefore lead to sentences such as, for the same example given above, 'John and <u>her</u> sister'.

In general, prepositional use and, especially, collocation is a minefield! Essentially, prepositions that may correspond directly to their English counterpart in translation will nevertheless be distributed distinctly in the writers' L1, leading to erroneous constructions (eg 'they live at Paris'; 'they travelled home in train').

Verbal forms may also be incorrectly produced, largely because of a certain morphological similarity between English forms and those of the speakers' L1 that are actually used in rather distinct ways. This not only concerns the various uses of simple tenses in English, but more usually also relates to perfective aspect in English, particularly the present perfect, which may be confused with a true past form (eg 'when I was young, I have lived in Africa').

Conditional structures are often morphologically similar between English and Romance languages – though many important distinctions hold – and may have similar uses. However, a distrust of the flexibility of English verbal form (in which, for instance, the form of the past simple and the subjunctive is the same (eg *would*, *could*, *were*)) may lead to rather convoluted structures that will need some sorting out.

- **Lexis**

  An obvious point to make about Romance languages (and so this emphatically does not concern Basque) is that they are Latin-derived and therefore have a huge Latinate word store. For the production of formal written English texts, this is sometimes a considerable advantage for non-native authors, but – depending on the nature, purpose and content of the text in question – this lexical feature can also produce a degree of formality that may not be suitable to the target readership. Intervention in this sense could often involve an editor in a good deal of judicious fine-tuning of the author's level of style.

Finally, given the Latin foundations of Romance languages and the enormous influence of Latin on English, there is a vast range of cognateness between English and these languages, though much of it is in the shape of false friends. Considerable lexical confusion in English texts produced by Southwest-European English authors derives from these deceptive 'equivalences', and editors working with such texts should make the effort to obtain a detailed and reliable list of such false cognates for their authors' L1. It is worth observing that native-English speakers resident in Romance-language territories have often become desensitised to this question and therefore may not be the best source of problem-resolution for editors!

In lieu of what would necessarily be a lengthy bibliography of reference works allowing editors to compare and contrast the features of English with the languages of southwest Europe, and then to decide on potential problems for non-natively produced English, a simpler option is to defer to the insights of the excellent handbook *Learner English: A teacher's guide to interference and other problems* (Michael Swan & Bernard Smith (eds) 1987. Cambridge: Cambridge University Press).

Appendix E

Aspects of Academic ELF: Most commonly occurring errors in academic writing

Kris Van de Poel

A study carried out in 2010 among undergraduate students of English at the University of Antwerp has shown that the students have embraced some aspects of the English as a lingua franca or ELF phenomenon due to their contacts with it as a global or international language, but they retain a strong belief in the native standard norm as practised in education (Xu & Van de Poel 2011). This has consequences for language teaching and learning in general and writing and editing in particular.

A 2001 US nationwide study by Andrea Lunsford and Robert Connors showed that 20 different mistakes comprise 91.5% of all errors in student texts. On <www.dartmouth. edu/~writing/materials/student/ac_paper/write.shtml> the 20 errors are listed according to the frequency with which they occur.

Flemish students studying English language and literature at university seem to have more problems formulating their thoughts than getting, for instance, their pronouns right. On the basis of a critical error analysis of 250 literary essays and more than 200 undergraduate examination papers (2002–2012), the following list of errors has been composed which could form the backbone for (self-)editing academic texts.

A Text type

- Academic tone
  No *elliptic* sentences, CAPITALS or emotives!
- Text coherence
  Use *conjunctions* and provide transitions between sentences and paragraphs.
  Bulleted lists in academic texts will not do.
  → Pay attention to academic style (by, for instance, reading more).

B Text structure

- Fragments
  Be sure all of your sentences are complete. *Fragments* are sentences that are incomplete, ie missing either a main subject or a main verb.
- Run-ons
  Run-ons are sentences that contain two or more complete sentences without appropriate conjunctions or punctuation to link them properly; the most common type of run-on

sentence is called a *comma splice*. This is where two complete sentences are separated only by a comma.

→ If replacing the comma with a period (or semicolon, or conjunction such as *and, but, however*) leaves you with two complete sentences, you need to fix the original sentence.

• Linking words

Linking words make the structure of essays more transparent and the relationships between ideas clearer. This makes essays easier to read and the writer's train of thought easier to understand.

→ Proofread critically to disentangle any structural problems.

C Word choice

• Specificity

Try to be as *specific* as possible in your word choice. While general terms can be useful in certain situations, precise, accurate words are always best in an academic context.

→ Use verbs rather than nouns (avoid nounisms especially).

• Variation

Try to *vary* your word choice.

→ Use pronouns, synonyms and hyponyms[1] to avoid repeating the same word or phrase.

• Wordiness

Try to be as *economical* as possible in your use of words. In an effort to demonstrate their knowledge of the English Language or to explain their ideas as completely and precisely as possible, students in higher education often write very long, dense, wordy sentences, the ideas in which can be expressed more clearly with fewer words.

→ When revising, constantly ask yourself, 'Is this the best way to say this? Could I say it more concisely?' In writing, less is often more.

D Grammar

• Consistency

Be consistent throughout your entire text in the use of both *tense* and *person*. If your text begins in the present tense, it should continue and end in the present tense (unless you are specifically referring to another point in time). If you use 'I' in the first sentence of your introduction, you must use 'I' throughout the paper.

→ A stubborn error requires focused proofreading.

• Subject–verb agreement

This is a stubborn error, especially in *complex sentences*.

→ Close reading is required, especially focusing on the verbs and then identifying their subjects.

---

[1] Words whose meaning implies or is included in that of another (eg *scarlet* in relation to *red*).

- The perfect tense
  To be used to highlight the relationship with the moment of *speaking*:
    - to indicate that the action lasts up to now;
    - to focus on the result of the action, etc.
  → Critical re-reading is required in order to apply the rules properly.

- Articles
  Use definite articles instead of demonstratives.
- Genitives
    - are frequently used in academic English;
    - possessive apostrophe error: Johns' book, her's, their's, etc. Its/it's.
  → Critically proofread and be careful when using a spell-checker.
- Pronoun references
    - Be sure your pronouns always match your antecedent and that it is always clear to your reader what that antecedent is.
    - Other problems may be: ambiguous pronoun reference, pronoun agreement error or dangling, misplaced modifier.

E Presentation

- Capitalisation
  Capitalisation rules in English differ considerably from those of other languages.
  → Keep a list of your own frequent words.
- Punctuation
  Avoid using (too many) *exclamation* and *question* marks in academic essays.
  → In general, if you are unsure about usage rules or punctuation in a specific situation, consult an English grammar manual.
- Commas
    - Try not to miss a comma after introductory phrases, in compound sentences, in non-restrictive relative clauses, in a series.
    - Remove unnecessary commas with restrictive clauses.
    - Be aware of the comma splice (yes, again).
  → Proofreading (applying the rules) and practice

Since writing is a form of communication, paying attention to the details of writing style removes potential stumbling blocks between your reader and your ideas, so you will communicate as clearly and as effectively as possible.

Based on research carried out for *Scribende* (2006) and *All write* (2007).

Bibliography

This bibliography contains full bibliographic references for all the works which have been cited in the course of this book, apart from the resources which have been listed in chapter 11.

Abbott, A 1988. *The system of professions*. Chicago/London: The University of Chicago Press.

ACES, 1999. *The American copy editors society 1999 conference*. <www.copydesk.org/> (Accessed September 2003).

Adey, D; M Orr & D Swemmer 1989. *Word power: The South African handbook of grammar, style, and usage*. Johannesburg: AD Donker.

Alamargot, D & L Chanquoy 2001. *Through the models of writing*. Dordrecht: Kluwer Academic Publishers.

Alba Juez, L 2009. *Perspectives on discourse analysis: Theory and practice*. Cambridge: Cambridge Scholars Publishing.

Allen, RE 2005. *How to write better English*. London: Penguin Group.

Allen, RE (ed) 2008. *Pocket Fowler's modern English usage* (2 ed). Oxford: Oxford University Press.

Ambrose, G & P Harris 2005. *Typography: the arrangement, style and appearance of type and typefaces*. London: Thames & Hudson.

The American Copy Editors Society. <www.copydesk.org>.

American Copy Editors Society 1999 Conference. <www.copydesk.org/> (Accessed September 2003).

American Copy Editors Society 2009. <www.copydesk.org/conference/2009/minne/entry/aces-survey/>.

American Psychological Association (APA) 2003. *APA style* (5 ed). <www.apastyle.org>.

Anderson, J & M Poole 2009. *Assignment & thesis writing* (South African ed). Cape Town: Juta.

Anonymous 2006a. *What copy editors do*. <www.luc/edu/faculty/owitte/copyedit/> (Accessed January 2012).

Anonymous 2006b. *Problem-solving for copy editors*. <www.luc/edu/faculty/owitte/copyedit/> (Accessed November 2011).

Anonymous 2006c. *BigBrainEditing: Why work with us*. <bigbrainediting.com/why.html> (Accessed February 2012).

Anonymous 2006d. *BigBrainEditing: How we work*. <bigbrainediting.com/how.html> (Accessed November 2011).

Anonymous 2008. *Current courses*. <www.socedvic.org/cms/public_php/training.php> (Accessed January 2008).

APA, 2001. *Manual of the American Psychological Association* (5 ed). Washington, DC: American Psychological Association.

Arms, J 2005. How to succeed as a freelancer editor, in J Mackenzie (ed) *At the typeface. Selections from the newsletters of the Victoria Society of Editors*. Melbourne: Victoria Society of Editors Inc.

Arnold, GT 2007. *Media writer's handbook. A guide to common writing and editing problems* (4 ed). New York: McGraw-Hill.

Aronoff, M & K Fudeman 2010. *What is morphology?* London: Wiley-Blackwell.

Associated Press 2011. *The Associated Press stylebook and briefing on media law 2011*. New York: Basic Books. <www.apstylebook.com/>.

Attwell, A *What e-books mean for professional editors.* <arthurattwell.com/2010/05/29/what-ebooks-mean-for-professional-editors/> (Accessed March 2010).

Auman, A 2000. *Who would want to be a copy editor? The industry and academe should work to raise the value of editing.* <www.copydesk.org/words/ASNEJanuary.htm> (Accessed November 2011).

Auman, AE; FE Fee & JT Russial 2001. *Creating new value for copy editing instruction in the curriculum and the university.* Association for Education in Journalism and Mass Communication Convention Newspaper Division. Research paper abstracts, September 2003. <www.aejmc.org/convention/2001conabs/index.html>.

AVS 2006. *Proofreading and copy editing.* <www.gotlinks.com/earticles/108636-proofreading-and-copy-editing.htm> (Accessed November 2011).

Bailey, EP Jr 1997. *The plain English approach to business writing*. Oxford: Oxford University Press.

Baines, P & A Haslam 2002. *Type & typography*. London: King.

Baker, M 1992. *In other words. A coursebook in translation*. London/New York: Routledge.

Barber, B 1963. Some problems in the sociology of professions. *Daedalus* 92(4): 669–688.

Bartsch, R 1987. *Norms of language: Theoretical and practical issues*. London: Longman.

Baskette, FK; JZ Sissors & BS Brooks 1986. *The art of editing*. New York: Macmillan.

Becker, HS; B Geer; EC Hughes & AL Strauss 2009. *Boys in white: Student culture in medical school*. Chicago, IL: University of Chicago Press.

Beene, L 2009. *Most bang for the buck. An editor's workbook. A reference text with exercises for beginning proofreaders, copyeditors, and developmental editors.* <www.faculty.washington.edu/pheld/tcxg482/Beene.pdf> (Accessed December 2009).

Bell, R 2000. Pseudo-, para-, or proto-: what kind of a professional is the translator or interpreter? Professionalism and translators & interpreters. *The linguist* 39(5): 147–150.

Berner, TR 1982. *Editing*. New York: Holt, Rinehart & Winston.

Bhatia, VK; J Flowerdew & RH Jones 2008. Approaches to discourse analysis, in VK Bhatia; J Flowerdew & RH Jones (eds) *Advances in discourse studies*. London/New York: Routledge, 1–17.

Bhatia, VK; J Flowerdew & RH Jones (eds) 2008. *Advances in discourse studies*. London/New York: Routledge.

BigBrainEditing. <Bigbrainediting.com/> (Accessed June 2011).

Billingham, J 2002. *Editing and revising text*. New York: Oxford University Press.

Bisaillon, J 2007. Professional editing: Emphasis on the quality of a text and its communicative effectiveness, in D Alamargot; P Terrier & JM Cellier (eds) & G Rijlaarsdam (series ed) *Written documents in the workplace*. Amsterdam: Elsevier, 75–95.

Bishop, CT 1984. *How to edit a scientific journal*. Philadelphia: ISI Press.

Bishop, J 2009. *Creating and updating a house style*. Johannesburg: PEG.

Bishop, J; J Linnegar & L Pretorius 2011. *The business of editing*. North Riding: PEG.

Blaauw, JWH 2001. The design of a code of ethics for text editors. MA dissertation, Potchefstroom University for Christian Higher Education, Potchefstroom.

Blaauw, JWH & E Boets 2003. Towards a code of ethics for text editors, in K Van de Poel (ed) Text editing – from a talent to a scientific discipline. *Antwerp papers in linguistics (APIL)* 103: 64–82.

Blake, BJ 2008. *All about language*. Oxford: Oxford University Press.

Blamires, H 2000. *The Penguin guide to plain English*. London: Penguin Books.

Blijzer, F & L Kloet 1999. Problemen by het categorisering van commentaren. Internal report, University of Tilburg, Netherlands.

Bloor, M & T Bloor 2007. *The practice of critical discourse analysis. An introduction*. London: Hodder Arnold.

Blue, T 2000. *What is a comma splice, and how do I fix it?* <grammartips.homestead.com/splice.html> (Accessed February 2012).

Boland, B 2008. A good year (… contemplating the transition to the life of a freelancer). *Muratho* 2008(April): 15–16.

Bolter, JD 1991. *Writing space – the computer, hypertext, and the history of writing*. Hillsdale, NJ: Erlbaum.

Bornstein, G 1994. Why editing matters, in G Bornstein (ed) *Representing modernist texts: Editing as interpreting*. Ann Arbor: University of Michigan Press, 1–16.

Bornstein, G (ed) 1994. *Representing modernist texts: Editing as interpreting*. Ann Arbor: University of Michigan Press.

Botha, L 2008. Ups and downs of owning a language agency. *Muratho* 2008 (April): 21–22.

Bowles, DA & DL Borden 2010. *Creative editing* (6 ed). Boston: Thomson/Wadsworth.

Bradley, P 2002. *The advanced internet searcher's handbook*. London: Library Association.

Brains, P 2008. *Common errors in English usage* (2 ed). Wilsonville, OR: William, James Co.

Brains, P 2011. *Common errors in English usage*. <www.wsu.edu:8001/~brians/errors> (Accessed September 2011).

Breeze, R 2011. Critical discourse analysis and its critics. *Pragmatics* 21(4): 493–525.

Brinck, T; D Gergle & SD Wood 2002. *Usability for the Web*. San Francisco: Morgan Kaufmann.

Brown, G & G Yule 1983. *Discourse analysis*. Cambridge: Cambridge University Press.

Bryson, B 1991. *Mother tongue: The English language*. London: Penguin Books.

Bühler, K 1933. Die Axiomatik der Sprachwissenschaften. *Kant-Studien* 38: 19–90.

Burchfield, R (ed) 1996. *The new Fowler's modern English usage*. Oxford: Oxford University Press.

Burchfield, RW 2004. *Fowler's modern English usage* (3 ed). London: Clarendon Press.

Burton, B 1991. Ten points for proofreaders, in J Mackenzie (ed) *Representing modernist texts: Editing as interpreting*. Ann Arbor: University of Michigan Press, 74.

Burton, SH 1982. *Mastering English language*. London: Macmillan.

Butcher, J 1992. *Copy-editing: The Cambridge handbook for editors, authors and publishers*. New York: Cambridge University Press.

Butcher, J; C Drake & M Leach 2006. *Butcher's copy-editing*. Cambridge: Cambridge University Press.

Butcher, J; C Drake & M Leach 2009. *Butcher's copy-editing: The Cambridge handbook for editors, authors and publishers* (4 ed). Cambridge: Cambridge University Press.

CALD (*Cambridge advanced learners dictionary*) online. <dictionary.cambridge.org/>.

Cambridge dictionaries. <dictionary.cambridge.org>.

Campbell, CS 1995. *Using transformational grammar as an editing tool*. <infohost.nmt.edu/~cpc.trangram.html> (Accessed January 2010).

Campbell, KS 1995. *Coherence, continuity, and cohesion: Theoretical foundations for document design*. Hillsdale, NJ: Erlbaum.

Canagarajah, S 2010. Internationalizing knowledge construction and dissemination. *The modern langauge journal* 94(4): 661–664.

Canberra Society of Editors 1994. *Commissioning checklist*. <www.editorscanberra.org/?s=commissioning=checklist>.

Candlin, CN & S Sarangi (eds) 2011. *Handbook of communication in organisations and professions*. Amsterdam: De Gruyter Mouton.

Cann, R; R Kempson & E Gregoromichelaki 2009. *Semantics. An introduction to meaning*. Cambridge: Cambridge University Press.

Capstick, F 2008. Letter to the editor. *Muratho* 2008(April): 25.

Cardinal, M 1992. Stylistic editing, in GHJ Sándor & I Higgins (eds) *Thinking translation: A course in translation method: French–English*. London: Routledge, 189–199.

Carey, GV 1958, 1986. *Mind the stop: A brief guide to punctuation, with a note on proof correction*. London: Penguin Books.

Carney, E 1994. *A survey of English spelling*. London: Routledge.

Carr, S 2011. *Editing into plain language. Working for non-publishers*. London: SfEP.

Carstens, WAM 1997. *Afrikaanse tekslinguistiek. 'n Inleiding*. Pretoria: JL van Schaik Akademies.

Carstens, WAM 2003. Text linguistics and text editing, in K Van de Poel (ed) *Text editing – from a talent to a scientific discipline*. *Antwerp papers in linguistics (APIL)* 103: 22–35.

Carstens, WAM 2011. *Norme vir Afrikaans. Enkele riglyne by die gebruik van Afrikaans* (5 rev ed). Pretoria: Van Schaik.

Carter, R & M McCarthey 2006. *Cambridge grammar of English. A comprehensive guide: Spoken and written Fnglish grammar and usage*. Cambridge: Cambridge University Press.

Catalano, K 1987. Righting words. *Journal of language and editing* I: 13–17.

Cataldo, M & J Oakhill, 2000. Why are poor comprehenders inefficient searchers? An investigation into the effects of text representations and spatial memory on the ability to locate information in text. *Journal of education psychology* 92(4): 791–799.

Chen, H & K Cruickshank 2009. Conceptualising the field of applied linguistics from a Bernsteinian perspective: Challenges and opportunities, in H Chen & K Cruickshank (eds) *Making a difference. Challenges for applied linguistics*. Cambridge: Cambridge Scholarly Publishing, 1–20.

Chen, H & K Cruickshank (eds) 2009. *Making a difference. Challenges for applied linguistics*. Cambridge: Cambridge Scholarly Publishing.

Cheney, TAR 1990. *Getting the words right: How to rewrite, edit & revise*. Cincinnati, OH: Writer's Digest Books.

Cheney, TAR 2005. *Getting the words right: 39 ways to improve your writing* (2 ed). Cincinnati, OH: Writer's Digest Books.

Chicago manual of style: The essential guide for writers, editors, and publishers 2010. (16 ed). Chicago: University of Chicago Press.

Chicago manual of style online. <www.chicagomanualofstyle.org>.

Christiansen, T 2011. *Cohesion: A discourse perspective*. Berlin: Peter Lang.

Clark, GN 2001. *Inside book publishing*. London: Routledge.

Clark, RP & D Fry 1992. *Coaching writers. The essential guide for editors and reporters*. New York: St Martin's.

Clark, HH & SE Haviland 1977. Comprehension and the given-new contract, in RO Freedle (ed) *Discourse production and comprehension*. Norwood, NJ: Ablex, 1–40.

Cleaveland, J 1999. *Copy editors want to tackle credibility*. <www.copydesk.org/words/ASNEMay99.htm> (Accessed November 2011).

Clouse, BF 1992. *The student writer. Editor and critic*. New York: McGraw-Hill.

Coffin, C; T Lillis & K O'Halloran (eds) 2010. *Applied linguistics methods: A reader. Systemic functional linguistics, critical discourse analysis and ethnography*. London/New York: Routledge.

Collins, J 2010. *Collins writing programme*. <wwwcollinseducationassociates.com/> (Accessed January 2012).

Combrink, AL & JWH Blaauw 1998. Professionalization of the language practitioners' occupation, in A Kruger; K Wallmach & M Boers (eds) *Language facilitation and development in southern Africa*. Paper delivered at a congress on 'An International Forum for Language Workers', 6–7 June 1997, Pretoria. Pretoria: SAVI.

Combrink, AL & MM Verhoef 2002. The professionalisation of language practice in South Africa. Paper read at the 16th International FIT Conference, Vancouver, Canada, August 2002.

Commonwealth of Australia 1990. *Style manual for authors, editors and printers of Australian government publications* (3 ed). Canberra: Australian Government Printing Services.

Conley, D & S Lamble 2006. *The daily miracle: An introduction to journalism* (3 ed). Oxford/ New York: Oxford University Press.

Cook, BB & SR Banks 1993. Predictors of job burnout in reporters and copy editors. *Journalism quarterly* 70: 108–17.

Cook, G 2003. *Applied linguistics*. Oxford: Oxford University Press.

Cook, G & S North (eds) 2009. *Applied linguistics in action: A reader*. London/New York: Routledge.

Cook, G & B Seidlhofer (eds) 1995. *Principle & practice in applied linguistics. Studies in honour of HG Widdowson*. Oxford: Oxford University Press.

Copydesk 2009. <www.copydesk.org/guidelines.htm/>.

Corder, SP 1981. *Error analysis and interlanguage*. Oxford: Oxford University Press.

Cotter, C 2010. *News talk. Investigating the language of journalism*. Cambridge: Cambridge University Press.

Council of Australian Societies of Editors 2001. *Australian standards for editing practice*. Australia: CASE. <www.iped-editors.org>.

Craig, R 2005. *Online journalism. Reporting, writing and editing for new media*. Belmont, CA: Thomson Wadsworth.

Cruse, AD 2011. *Meaning in language. An introduction to semantics and pragmatics*. Oxford: Oxford University Press.

Crystal, D 1990. *The English language*. London: Penguin Books.

Crystal, D 2003. *English as a global language* (2 ed). Cambridge: Cambridge University Press.

Crystal, D 2003. *The Cambridge encyclopaedia of the English language* (2 ed). Cambridge: Cambridge University Press.

Crystal, D 2004. The BBC Voices project website, November 2004. <www.davidcrystal. com/DC_articles/English6.pdf> (Accessed December 2011).

Crystal, D 2007. *English as a global language* (3 ed). Cambridge: Cambridge University Press.

Crystal, D 2008. *A dictionary of linguistics and phonetics*. London: Blackwell.

Crystal, D 2010. *The Cambridge encyclopaedia of the English language* (3 ed). Cambridge: Cambridge University Press.

Cutts, M 2009. *The Oxford guide to plain English*. Oxford: Oxford University Press.

Daniëls, W 2011. *Teksten redigeren*. Houten-Antwerpen: Unieboek.

Davies, A 2004 (1999). *An introduction to applied linguistics*. Edinburgh: Edinburgh University Press.

Davies, A 2007. *An introduction to applied linguistics: From practice to theory*. Edinburgh: Edinburgh University Press.

Davies, A & C Elder 2006. Applied linguistics: Subject to discipline? in A Davies & C Elder (eds) *The handbook of applied linguistics*. Oxford; Blackwell, 1–15.

Davies, A & C Elder (eds) 2006. *The handbook of applied linguistics*. Oxford, Blackwell.

Davies, G & R Balkwill 2011. *The professionals guide to publishing: A practical introduction to working in the publishing industry*. London/Philadelphia/New Delhi: KoganPage.

Dayananda, J 1986. Plain English in the United States. *English today* 5: 13–16.

De Beaugrande, RA & WU Dressler 1981. *Introduction to text linguistics*. London: Longman.

De Beaugrande, RA 1995. Text linguistics, in J Verschueren; J Östman & J Blommaert (eds) *Handbook of pragmatics. Manual*. Amsterdam: John Benjamins, 536–544.

De Beaugrande, RA 2004. *A new introduction to the study of text and discourse*. <www. beaugrande.com/new_intro_to_study.htm>.

De Beaugrande, RA 2009. *Ground rules for text linguistics*. <www.beaugrande.com/ GroundRulesTextLinguistics.htm> (Accessed September 2009).

De Jong, M & PJ Schellens 1997. Reader-focused text-evaluation: An overview of goals and methods. *Journal of business and technical communication* 11: 402–432.

Deitel, PJ & HM Deitel 2008. *Internet & World Wide Web: How to program*. Upper Saddle River, NJ: Pearson Prentice Hall.

Delin, J; J Bateman & P Allen 2002. A model of genre in document layout. *Information design journal* 11(1): 54–66.

Demoor, M; G Lernout & S van Peteghem (eds) 1998. *Editing the text: essays presented at the tekst/texte/text-conference*, Ghent, 1995. Tilburg: Tilburg University Press.

Derricourt, R 1996. *An author's guide to scholarly publishing*. Princeton, NJ: Princeton University Press.

De Stadler, L 2004. Assessing document quality: Not as easy as one might think. *Information design journal & document design* 13(1): 70–73.

De Stadler, L 2005. *Issues in document design, Volume 1*. Stellenbosch: Stellenbosch University Language Centre.

De Stadler, L; E Basson & L Luttig 2005. *Making your documents work: Document design in a multicultural society*. Stellenbosch: Stellenbosch University Language Centre.

Donnelly, C 1994. *Linguistics for writers*. Buffalo: SUNY Press.

Dontcheva-Navratilova, O & R Povolna (eds) 2009. *Coherence and cohesion in spoken and written discourse*. Cambridge: Cambridge Scholars Publishing.

Dorner, J 2000. *The internet: A writer's guide*. London: ABC Black.

Du Plessis, C 2007. Myth management: The me-too professional. *Altitude* 2007(October): 114.

Du Plessis, M (ed) 1999. *New words and previously overlooked ones*. Cape Town: Pharos.

Dykman, DJ; JDU Geldenhuys & EE Viljoen-Smook 2011. *The write stuff: The style guide with a difference*. Cape Town: Pharos.

Dytel, M (ed) 2009. *Advances in discourse approaches*. Cambridge: Cambridge Scholars Publishing.

EAC (The Editors' Association of Canada/Association Canadienne des Révisieurs) 2006. *The voice of Canadian editors* <www.editors.ca> (Accessed November 2006).

EAC 2009. *Professional editorial standards*. <www.editors.ca/>.

EAC 2010–2011. *Meeting professional editorial standards* (4 vols). <www.editors.ca/>.

EAC (Editors' Association of Canada) 2011. *So you want to be an editor: Information about a career in editing*. <www.editors.ca/> (Accessed November 2011).

Eagleson, RD; assisted by G Jones & S Hassall 1990. *Writing in plain English*. Canberra: Australian Government Publishing Service.

Editorial Freelancers Association 2011. .

EEI Communications Staff (eds) 1996. *Stet again! More tricks of the trade for publications people; selections from 'The editorial eye'*. Alexandria, VA: EEI Press.

EEI Communications Staff (eds) 1998. *My big sourcebook: For people who work with words or pictures*. Alexandria, VA: EEI Press.

Einsohn, A 2011. *The copyeditor's handbook. A guide for book publishing and corporate communications* (3 ed). Los Angeles: The University of California Press.

Eisenberg, A 1992. *Guide to technical editing: Discussion, dictionary, and exercises*. New York: Oxford University Press.

Elbourne, PD 2011. *Meaning. A slim guide to semantics*. Oxford: Oxford University Press.

Elling, E & L Lentz 2003. De voorspellende kracht van het CCC-model. *Tijdschrift voor taalbeheersing* 25: 221–235.

Ellis, R 2005. Principles of instructed language learning. *Asian EFL journal* 7(May) Special edition, conference proceedings.

Ellis, R (with S Loewen; C Elder; R Erlam; J Philp & H Reinders) 2009. *Implicit and explicit knowledge in second language learning. Testing and teaching*. Bristol, Multilingual Matters.

English Commission 2011. *Plain English lexicon*. <www.clearest.co.uk/pages/publications/plainenglishlexicon>.

Enkvist, NE 1991. On the interpretability of texts in general and of literary texts in particular, in R Sell (ed) *Literary pragmatics*. London/New York: Routledge, 1–25.

Enquist, A & LC Oates 2009. *Just writing. Grammar, punctuation and style for the legal writer*. New York: Aspen Publishers.

Encyclopaedia Britannica. <www.britannica.com>.

Essem Educational Limited 2011. <www.readability.biz/index.html> (Accessed November 2011).

Etymology dictionary online. <www.etymonline.com//>.

Evans, H 1974. *Editing and design: A five volume manual of English typography and layout. (Book two: Handling newspaper texts)*. London: Heinemann.

Fairclough, N 1995. *Critical discourse analysis. The critical study of language*. Harlow: Longman.

Felici, J 2003. *The complete manual of typography: A guide to setting perfect type*. Berkeley, CA: Peachpit Press.

Felker, DB; F Pickering; VR Charrow; VM Holland & JC Redish 1981. *Guidelines for document designers*. Washington: American Institutes for Research.

Ferreira, T & I Staude 1991. *Write angels. The a b c for house journals*. Johannesburg: Write Minds.

Ferris, DL 2002. *Treatment of error in second language student writing*. Ann Arbor: Michigan University Press.

Fetzer, A & E Oishi (eds) 2011. *Context and contexts. Part meets whole?* Amsterdam: John Benjamins.

Field, M 2007. *Improve your punctuation and grammar* (2 ed). Oxford: Howtobooks.

Firth, A 1996. The discursive accomplishment of normality. On 'lingua franca' English and conversation analysis. *Journal of pragmatics* 26: 237–259.

Flann, E & B Hill 2004. *The Australian editing handbook* (2 ed). Milton: John Wiley & Sons Australia Ltd.

Flowerdew, J 2001. Attitudes of journal editors to nonnative speaker contributions. *TESOL quarterly* 35: 121–150.

Flowerdew, J 2008. Scholarly writers who use English as an additional language: What can Goffman's 'Stigma' tell us? *Journal of English for academic purposes* 7: 77–86.

Forey, G & G Thompson (eds) 2008. *Text type and texture.* London: Equinox.

Foster, C 1993. *Editing, design and book production.* London: Journeyman.

Fowler, HW 1954. *A dictionary of modern English usage.* Oxford: Clarendon Press.

Fowler, HW & FG Fowler 1979. *The King's English* (3 ed). Oxford: Oxford University Press.

Freidson, E 1983. The theory of professions: state of the art, in R Dingwall & P Lewis (eds) *The sociology of the professions: Doctors, lawyers and others.* London: Macmillan, 19–37.

Freidson, E 1994. *Professionalism reborn: Theory, prophecy and policy.* Cambridge: Polity.

Fryer, C 1988. Wat verwag die uitgewer van die taalversorger? *The language practitioner* 1988(1): 27–46.

Fryer, C 1997. Jongleur, chirurg en koppelaar. *Insig*, 30 September 1997.

Game, C 2005. Freelancing: how to do it, in J Mackenzie (ed) *At the typeface. Selections from the newsletters of the Victoria Society of Editors.* Melbourne: Victoria Society of Editors Inc, 128–133.

Garbers, K 2007. My life as a technical editor at the SABS. *Muratho* 2007(April): 17–18.

Gardiner, D 2010. Discovering XML for editing. *The Canberra editor*, May 2010. <www.editorscanberra.org/may2010/>, in J Mackenzie (ed) *At the typeface. Selections from the newsletters of the Victoria Society of Editors.* Melbourne: Victoria Society of Editors Inc, 92–93.

Gee, JP 2010. *How to do discourse analysis: A toolkit.* London: Routledge.

Geldenhuys, JDU & EE Viljoen-Smook 2009. *Business dictionary/sakewoordeboek.* Cape Town: Pharos.

Gibaldi, J (ed) 1998. *MLA style manual and guide to scholarly publishing* (2 ed). New York: Modern Language Association of America.

Gilad, S 2007. *Copyediting and proofreading for dummies.* Indianapolis, IN: Wiley Publishing.

Gile, D 1995. *Basic concepts and models for interpreter and translator training.* Amsterdam: John Benjamins.

Glamann, H 2000. *How papers can find and retain copy editors.* <www.copydesk.org/words/ASNEFebruary.htm> (Accessed November 2006).

Glover, A 1996. *In search of the perfect copy editor: 10 copy editor traits that guarantee you success*. <poynter.org/content> (Accessed November 2008).

Goddard, P 2011. *Semantic analysis. A practical introduction*. Oxford: Oxford University Press.

Goode, WJ 1969. The theoretical limits of professionalization, in A Etzioni (ed) *The semi-professions and their organization*. NewYork: Free Press, 266–313.

Gouadec, D 2007. *Translation as a profession*. Amsterdam/New York: John Benjamins.

Gowers, E 1969. *The complete plain words*. London: Penguin.

Gowers, E 1996. *The complete plain words* (3 ed). Revised by S Greenbaum & J Whitcut. London: Penguin.

Grabe, W 2002. Applied linguistics: An emerging discipline for the twenty-first century, in RB Kaplan (ed) *The Oxford handbook of applied linguistics*. New York: Oxford University Press, 3–12.

Greco, AN 2005. *The book publishing industry*. London: Lawrence Erlbaum.

Greer, G (ed) 2008. *Introducing journalism and media studies*. Cape Town: Juta.

Grice, HP 1989. Logic and conversation, in P Cole & J Morgan (eds) *Studies in the way of words*. Cambridge, MA: Harvard University Press, 22–40.

Grossman, J 1993. Preface, in J Grossman (ed) *Chicago manual of style*. Chicago, IL: Chicago University Press, vii–ix.

Grossman, J (ed) 1993. *Chicago manual of style* (14 ed). Chicago, IL: Chicago University Press.

Gump, D 1997. *Project report*. The Knight Foundation Fellowship for Copy Editors, 12 December 1997. <www.ibiblio.org/copyed/gump-proj.html> (Accessed September 2003).

Hall, CJ; PH Smith & R Wicaksono 2011. *Mapping applied linguistics. A guide for students and practitioners*. London: Routledge.

Halliday, MAK & R Hasan 1976. *Cohesion in English*. London: Longman.

Harris, N 1991. *Basic editing: A practical course*. London: Book House Training Centre.

Harris, Z 1952. Discourse analysis. *Language* 28: 1–30.

Hart, C (ed) 2011. *Critical discourse studies in context and cognition*. Amsterdam/New York: John Benjamins.

Hart, G 2007. *Effective onscreen editing: New tools for an old profession*. Pointe-Claire, Quebec: Diaskeuasis Publishing. <www.geoff-hart.com>.

Hart, J 2005. Computer technology at Lonely Planet, in J Mackenzie (ed) *At the typeface. Selections from the newsletters of the Victoria Society of Editors*. Melbourne: Victoria Society of Editors Inc, 289–291.

Hatch, E 1992. *Discourse and language education*. Cambridge/New York: Cambridge University Press.

Hatim, B & I Mason 1990. *Discourse and the translator*. London: Longman.

Haynes, A 2010. *Writing successful academic books*. Cambridge: Cambridge University Press.

Hazelton, M 2009. Basic layout tips for MS Word. *PEGboard* 16(3): 6.

Hendry, O 2011. *The (essential) companion for writers & editors*. Cape Town: Pharos.

Hermans, T 1996. *Translation's other*. London: University College, London.

Hinkkanen, S 2006. The triangle of professional ethics. *Muratho* 2006(December): 38–39.

Holden, M & F Hardie 2005. Guess what: You're freelance!, in J Mackenzie (ed) *At the typeface. Selections from the newsletters of the Victoria Society of Editors*. Melbourne: Victoria Society of Editors Inc, 133–136.

Honey, J 1997. *Language is power. The story of standard English and its enemies*. London: Faber & Faber.

Hope, K 2005. *Bad spelling and grammar hurts the bottom line*. <www.texttrust.com> (Accessed May 2009).

Horn, B 2006. *Editorial project management*. London: Horn Editorial Books.

House, J 2002. Communicating in English as a lingua franca. *EUROSLA yearbook* 2: 243–261.

House, J 2009. *Translation*. Oxford: Oxford University Press.

Howes, RF 1965. *Historical studies of rhetoric and rhetoricians*. New York: Ithaca.

Hubbard, EH 1989. *Reference cohesion, conjunctive cohesion and relational coherence in academic student writing*. DLitt & Phil dissertation, Unisa, Pretoria.

Huddleston, G & GK Pullum 2002. *The Cambridge grammar of the English language*. Cambridge: Cambridge University Press.

Huddleston, R & GK Pullum 2005. *A student's introduction to English grammar*. Cambridge: Cambridge University Press.

Hudson, D 1999. *Applied linguistics*. <www.phon.ucl.ac.uk/home/dick/AL.html> (Accessed April 2009).

Hughes, EC 1963. Professions. *Daedalus* 92(4): 655–668.

Hunston, S & D Oakey 2009. *Introducing applied linguistics. Concepts and skills*. London: Routledge.

Hyde-Clarke, N 2011. *Communication and media ethics in South Africa*. Cape Town: Juta.

Institute of Professional Editors (IPEd), Australia nd. <www.iped-editors.org>.

Institute of Professional Editors (IPEd) 2011. *Australian standards for editing practice* (rev ed). <www.iped-editors.org>.

Jackson, H 1990. *Grammar and meaning. A semantic approach to English grammar*. London/New York: Longman.

Jakobson, R 1960. Closing statement: Linguistics and poetics, in TA Sebeok (ed) *Style in language*. Cambridge, MA: The MIT Press, 350–377.

James, C 1997. *Errors in language learning and use – exploring error analysis*. Edinburgh: Longman.

Jansen, C & A Maes 1999. Document design. *SA journal of linguistics and applied language studies* 17(4): 234–255.

Jansen, CJM & MF Steehouder 2001. How research can lead to better government forms, in D Janssen & R Neutelings (eds) *Reading and writing public documents*. Amsterdam: Benjamins, 12–36.

Janssen, D & R Neutelings (eds) 2001. *Reading and writing public documents*. Amsterdam: John Benjamins.

Jenkins, J 2000. *The phonology of English as an international language*. Oxford: Oxford University Press.

Jenkins, J 2002. A sociolinguistically based, empirically researched pronunciation syllabus for English as an international language. *Applied linguistics* 23(1): 83–103.

Jenkins, HR 1992 On being clear about time. An analysis of a chapter of Stephen Hawking's *A brief history of time. Language sciences* 14: 529–544.

Jones, J 2005. The freelance experience, in J Mackenzie (ed) *At the typeface. Selections from the newsletters of the Victoria Society of Editors*. Melbourne: Victoria Society of Editors Inc, 144–146.

Judd, B 2007. A full and varied day working for the state. *Muratho* 2007(April): 29–30.

Judd, K 1990. *Copyediting: A practical guide* (2 ed). Menlo Park, CA: Crisp Publications, Inc.

Judd, K 2001. *Copyediting: A practical guide* (3 ed). Menlo Park, CA: Crisp Learning.

Kachru, BB 1985. Standards, codification and sociolinguistic realism in the English language in the outer circle, in R Quirk & HG Widdowson (eds) *English in the world: Teaching and learning the language and literatures.* Cambridge: Cambridge University Press, 11–30.

Kahn, JE (ed) 1985. *The right word at the right time: A guide to the English language and how to use it.* London: Reader's Digest.

Kastely, JL 1997. *Rethinking the rhetorical tradition: From Plato to postmodernism.* New Haven, CT: Yale University Press.

Kemisho, S 2006. Professionalism. *Muratho* 2006(December): 39.

Kempton, K & N Moore 1994. *Designing public documents: A review of research*. London: Policy Studies Institute.

Kibrik, A 2011. *Reference in discourse*. Oxford: Oxford University Press.

Kies, D 2000. Coherence in writing. The HyperTextBooks, in KB Yancey. Looking for sources of coherence in a fragmented world: Notes towards a new assessment design. *Computors and composition* 21: 102.

Knowles, M 2011. Digital manager at Oxford University Press, addressing a seminar at the SfEP annual conference, Oxford, 27 September 2011.

Kotze, AD 1998. Die teksversorger as spookskrywer: Christelike uitgewersmaatskappye as 'n gevallestudie. MA dissertation, Potchefstroom University for Christian Higher Education, Potchefstroom.

Kotze, AD 2012. Die professionalisering van taalpraktisyns in Suid-Afrika en Vlaandere: 'n vergelykende studie. PhD dissertation, North West University.

Kotze, A & MM Verhoef 2003. The text editor as a ghost-writer: Scrutinizing the theory and the profession, in K Van de Poel (ed) Text editing – from a talent to a scientific discipline. *Antwerp papers in linguistics (APIL)* 103: 36–47.

Krüger, F (ed) 2004. *Black, white and grey: Ethics in SA journalism*. Cape Town: Double Story.

Kruger, H 2007. Training text editors as part of a general programme in language practice: a process-oriented approach. *South African linguistics and applied language studies* 2(1): 1–16.

Kruger, H 2008. Training editors in universities: considerations, challenges and strategies, in J Kearns (ed) *Translator and interpreter training: Issues, methods and debates*. London: Continuum, 39–65.

Lancashire Grid for Learning (LGfL) 2012. *Lancashire primary literacy.* <www.lancsngfl. ac.uk/nationalstrategy/literacy/index.php?category_id=72> (Accessed January 2012).

Landers, CE 2001. *Literary translation: A practical guide*. Clevedon/Buffalo, NY: Multilingual Matters Ltd.

Langley, GJ; KM Nolan, TW Nolan, CL Norman & LP Provost 1992. *The improvement guide: A practical approach to enhancing organisational performance*. New York: John Wiley & Sons.

Larson, MS 1977. *The rise of professionalism: A sociological analysis*. Berkeley, CA: University of California Press.

Law, J (ed) 2001. *Oxford language reference*. Oxford: Oxford University Press.

Law, J (ed) 2002. *The language toolkit*. New York: Oxford University Press.

Law, MA & H Kruger 2008. Towards the professionalisation of editing in South Africa. *Southern African linguistics and applied language studies* 26(4): 479–493.

Lee, J 2005. A chip on your shoulder: publishing in the electronic age, in J Mackenzie (ed) *At the typeface. Selections from the newsletters of the Victoria Society of Editors.* Melbourne: Victoria Society of Editors Inc, 302–309.

Lefevere, A 1999. Composing the other, in S Bassnett & H Trivedi (eds) *Post-colonial translation: Theory and practice*. London: Routledge.

Legat, M 1991. *An author's guide to publishing* (rev & exp ed). London: Robert Hale.

Leiter, K; J Harriss & S Johnson 2000. *The complete reporter. Fundamentals in writing and editing*. Massachusetts: Allyn & Bacon.

Liebenberg, W 2008. Running a freelance practice in South Africa: Challenges and opportunities. *Muratho* 2008(October): 15–19.

Lightfoot, H 2005. Production for editors, in J Mackenzie (ed) *At the typeface. Selections from the newsletters of the Victoria Society of Editors*. Melbourne: Victoria Society of Editors Inc, 295–302.

Lih, A 2009. *The Wikipedia revolution*. New York: Hyperion.

Linnegar, J 2008. *Manual on basic copy editing and proofreading*. Cape Town: McGillivray Linnegar Associates. <info@editandtrain.com>.

Linnegar, J 2009. *Engleish, our Engleish: Common problems in South African English and how to resolve them*. Cape Town: Pharos.

Linnegar, J; P Schamberger & J Bishop 2009. *Consistency, consistency, consistency: The PEG guide to style guides*. Johannesburg: Professional Editors' Group (PEG).

Linnegar, J; L Marus & J de Wet 2012. *Marketing your freelance services* Johannesburg: Professional Editors' Group (PEG).

Lipson, C 2011. *Cite right: A quick guide to citation styles – MLA, APA, Chicago, the sciences, professions, and more* (2 ed). Chicago: Chicago University Press.

Literacy Education Online (LEO) 2007a. *General strategies for revising and editing on computers.* <leo.stcloudstate.edu/acadwrite/computerediting.html> (Accessed May 2007).

Literacy Education Online (LEO) 2007b. *Editing and proofreading strategies for specific sentence-level errors.* <leo.stcloudstate.edu/acadwrite/editing.html> (Accessed May 2007).

LLT 2006. *Copy editing.* <dictionary.laborlawtalk.com/copy_editing> (Accessed November 2006).

Locher, MA & J Strässler (eds) 2008. *Standards and norms in the English language.* Berlin/New York: Mouton de Gruyter.

Lourens, A 2007. *Scientific writing skills. Guidelines for writing theses and dissertations.* Stellenbosch: African Sun Media.

Lowenstein, W 2005. Self-publishing, in J Mackenzie (ed) *At the typeface: Selections from the newsletters of the Victorian Society of Editors.* Melbourne: Victoria Society of Editors Inc.

Lukeman, N 2007. *The art of punctuation.* Oxford & New York: Oxford University Press.

Lynch, J 2008. *Guide to grammar and style.* <andromeda.rutgers.edu/~jlynch/Writing> (Accessed November 2008).

Lyons, W 2001. *Matters of the mind.* Edinburgh: Edinburgh University Press & New York: Routledge.

McArthur, T (ed) 1992. *The Oxford companion to the English language.* Oxford: Oxford University Press.

Macdonald, KM 1995. *The sociology of the professions.* London: Sage.

Mackenzie, J 2004. *The editor's companion.* Cambridge: Cambridge University Press.

Mackenzie, J (ed) 2005. *At the typeface. Selections from the newsletters of the Victoria Society of Editors.* Melbourne: Victoria Society of Editors Inc.

Mackenzie, J (ed) 2011. *The editor's companion* (2 ed). Melbourne: Cambridge University Press.

Maes, A; H Hoeken; LGM Noordman & W Spooren 1999. *Document design. Linking writers' goals to readers' needs.* Tilburg: Tilburg University Press.

Mahan, M (ed) 2003. *Chicago manual of style* (15 ed). Chicago, IL: Chicago University Press.

Maienborn, C; K von Heusinger & PH Portner (eds) 2011. *Semantics. An international handbook of natural language meaning.* Amsterdam: De Gruyter Mouton.

Marsen, S 2007. *Professional writing: The complete guide for business, industry and IT* (2 ed). London: Palgrave Macmillan.

Marsh, D & N Marshall 2004. *The Guardian stylebook.* Cambridge: Cambridge University Press.

Massey, G 2005. Process-oriented translator training and the challenge for e-learning. *Meta* 50(2): 626–633.

Mates, BT 2000. *Adaptive technology for the internet: Making electronic resources available to all*. Chicago, IL: American Library Association.

Mauranen, A 2003. The corpus of English as lingua franca in academic settings. *TESOL quarterly* 37(3): 513–527.

Mellet, S & D Longrée (eds) 2009. *New approaches in text linguistics*. New York/Amsterdam: John Benjamins.

Merriam-Webster's online. <www.m-w.com/> (Accessed September 2003).

MHRA style guide: A handbook for authors, editors and writers of theses 2002. New York: Modern Humanities Research Association.

Mišak, A; M Marušić & A Marušić 2005. Manuscript editing as a way of teaching academic writing: experience from a small scientific journal. *Journal of second language writing* 14(2): 122–131.

Mitchell, M & S Wightman 2005. *Book typography: A designer's manual*. Marlborough: Libanus.

Modern Language Association of America (MLA) 2009. *MLA style manual and guide to scholarly publishing* (3 ed). New York: MLA.

Modern Language Association of America (MLA) 2009. *MLA handbook for writers of research papers* (7 ed). New York: MLA.

Morris, E 1998. *The book lover's guide to the internet*. New York: Fawcett Books.

Morrish, J 1998. *Magazine editing: How to develop and manage a successful publication* (2 ed). London: Routledge.

Morrish, J 2003. *Magazine editing: How to develop and manage a successful publication* (3 ed). London: Routledge.

Mossop, B 2001. *Revising and editing for translators*. Manchester: St Jerome Publishing.

Mossop, B 2007a. *Revising and editing for translators* (2 ed). Manchester: St Jerome Publishing.

Mossop, B 2007b. Empirical studies of revision: what we know and need to know. *The journal of specialised translation* [on-line serial] 8. <www.jostrans.org> (Accessed July 2007).

Murphy, EM 2011. *Working words – for editors, writers, teachers, students of English grammar and wordsmiths all*. Manuka, Australia: Canberra Society of Editors.

Murphy, ML 2010. *Lexical meaning*. Cambridge: Cambridge University Press.

Murray, S & L Johanson 2006. *Write to improve: A guide to correcting and evaluating written work*. Randburg: Hodder & Stoughton.

Nel, F 2001. *Writing for the media in Southern Africa* (3 ed). Oxford: Oxford University Press.

Neubert, A & G Shreve 1992. *Translation as text*. Kent, OH: Kent State University Press.

New Hart's rules 2005. (RM Ritter (ed)) Oxford: Oxford University Press.

Newmark, P 2003. *A textbook of translation*. Harlow, England: Pearson Education.

NHS nd. *Pregnancy care planner*. <www.nhs.uk/Planners/pregnancycareplanner/Pages/PregnancyHome.aspx> (Accessed January 2012).

Norrish, J 1983. *Language learners and their errors*. London: Macmillan Press.

Nyssen, H 1993. *Du texte au livre, les avatars du sens*. Paris: Nathan.

Ochs, E 1985. Variation and error: A sociolinguistic approach to language acquisition in Samoa, in D Slobin (ed) *The crosslinguistic study of language acquisition*. Hillsdale, NJ: Lawrence Erlbaum Associates, 783–833.

O'Connor, M 1978. *Editing scientific books and journals*. London: Pittman Publishing.

O'Connor, M 1986. *How to copyedit scientific books and journals*. Philadelphia: ISI Press.

O'Connor, M 1993. *Writing successfully in science*. London: Chapman & Hall.

O'Connor, PJ 1990. Normative data: their definition, interpretation, and importance for primary care physicians. *Family medicine* 22(4): 307–311.

O'Halloran, K 2003. *Critical discourse analysis and language cognition*. Edinburgh: Edinburgh University Press.

Online etymology dictionary. <www.etymonline.com> (Accessed November 2011).

Onraët, LA 2011. *English as a lingua franca and English in South Africa: Distinctions and overlap*. MA dissertation, University of Stellenbosch

Owen, A 2003–2012. *Editing services*. <www.writershelper.com> (Accessed November 2011).

The Oxford dictionary for writers and editors 2000. Oxford: Oxford University Press.

The Oxford guide to style 2002. Oxford: Oxford University Press.

The Oxford style manual 2003. Oxford: Oxford University Press.

Painter-Morland, M 2011. *Business ethics as practice: Ethics as the everyday business of business*. Cambridge: Cambridge University Press.

Partridge, E 1955a. *Usage and abusage: A guide to good English*. London: Hamish Hamilton.

Partridge, E 1955b. *You have a point there: A guide to punctuation and its allies* (with a chapter on American practice by John W Clark). London: Hamish Hamilton.

Partridge, E 1973. *Usage and abusage*. London: Penguin Books in Association with Hamish Hamilton.

Partridge, E 2000. *Usage and abusage: A guide to good English* (rev ed by J Whitcut). London: Penguin Books.

Pennycook, A 2001. *Critical applied linguistics. A critical introduction*. Mahwah, NJ/London: Lawrence Erlbaum.

Perelman, LC; J Paradis & E Barrett 2001. *The Mayfield handbook of technical and scientific writing*. New York: McGraw-Hill. <books.google.be/books?id=102APQAACAAJ&dq=The+Mayfield+Handbook+of+Technical+and+Scientific+Writing&hl=en&sa=X&ei=C-tmT9R_0aE6r5v1-wc&ved=0CDEQ6AEwAA> (Accessed June 2009).

Phillipson, R 1992. *Linguistic imperialism*. Oxford: Oxford University Press.

Phillipson, R 1997. Realities and myths of linguistic imperialism. *Journal of multilingual and multicultural development* 18(3): 238–248.

Plotnik, A 1982. *The elements of editing. A modern guide for editors and journalists*. New York: Macmillan.

Pöhland, J. *Learning English online*. <www.englisch-hilfen.de> (Accessed April 2011).

Poole, D 2002. Discourse analysis and applied linguistics, in RB Kaplan (ed) *The Oxford handbook of applied linguistics*. New York: Oxford University Press, 73–84.

Professional Editors' Group (PEG). <www.editors.org.za>.

Publishers' Association of South Africa (PASA) 2011. *Copyright*. <www.publishsa.co.za/copyright/> (Accessed November 2011).

Pym, A 2000. *Globalization and segmented language services*. <usuaris.tinet.cat/apym/on-line/translation/segmentation.htm> (Accessed January 2011).

Quinn, S 2001. *Digital sub-editing & design*. Oxford: Focal Press.

Quinn, S 2003. *10 things to know and love about copy editors*. <poynter.org/content> (Accessed November 2006).

Quirk, R 1982. *Style and communication in the English language*. London: Longman.

Quirk, R 1985. The english language in a global context, in R Quirk & HG Widdowson (eds) *English in the world: Teaching and learning the language and literatures*. Cambridge: cambridge University Press, 1–6.

Quirk, R; S Greenbaum, G Leech & S Svartvik 1985. *A comprehensive grammar of the English language*. London: Longman.

Rae, W 1952. *Editing small newspapers: A basic handbook for journalists*. New York: Mill.

Renkema, J 1987. *Tekst en uitleg. Een inleiding in de tekstwetenschap*. Dordrecht: Foris.

Renkema, J 1996. Over smaak valt goed te twisten. Een evaluatiemodel voor tekstkwaliteit. *Tijdschrift voor taalbeheersing* 4: 324–338.

Renkema, J 2000. *Tussen de regels. Over taalgebruik in bijsluiters, belastingformulieren en bybelvertalingen*. Utrecht: Het Spectrum.

Renkema, J 2001. Undercover research into text quality as a tool for communication management: The case of the Dutch tax department, in D Janssen & R Neutelings (eds) *Reading and writing public documents*. Amsterdam: John Benjamins, 37–57.

Renkema, J 2004. *Introduction to discourse studies*. Amsterdam: John Benjamins.

Renkema, J 2005. *Schrijfwijzer compact*. The Hague: SDU.

Renkema, J 2008. *Schrijfwijzer* (4 ed). The Hague: SDU.

Renkema, J 2009. *The texture of discourse. Towards an outline of connectivity theory*. Amsterdam: John Benjamins.

Renkema, J (ed) 2009. *Discourse, of course*. Amsterdam: John Benjamins.

Renkema, J & L Kloet 2000. De toestand van een tekst. Een diagnose volgens het CCC-model. *Management & communication* 6(December).

Ridout, R & DW Clarke 1989. *A reference book of English: A general guide for foreign students of English*. London: Macmillan.

Riemer, N 2010. *Introducing semantics*. Cambridge: Cambridge University Press.

Ritter, RM 2002. *The Oxford guide to style*. Oxford: Oxford University Press.

Ritter, RM 2003. *The Oxford style manual*. Oxford: Oxford University Press.

Ritter, RM 2005. *New Oxford dictionary for writers and editor*. (adapted from *The Oxford dictionary for writers and editors* (2 ed)). Oxford: Oxford University Press.

Ritter, RM 2005. *New Hart's rules*. Oxford: Oxford University Press.

Roberts, R 2004. *Why train?* <www.sfep.org.uk/pages/why_train.asp> (Accessed November 2006).

Robinson, P nd. In the matter of: The gatekeeper: The gate contracts. Unpublished humorous book.

Rooksby, E 2002. *E-mail and ethics: style and ethical relations in computer-mediated communication*. London/New York: Routledge.

Ruddock, A 2001. *Understanding audiences*. London: Sage Publications.

Saller, CF 2009. *The subversive copy editor: Advice from Chicago*. Chicago/London: University of Chicago Press.

Schiffrin, D 1994. *Approaches to discourse*. Oxford: Basil Blackwell.

Schiffrin, D; D Tannen & H Hamilton (eds) 2001. *The handbook of discourse analysis*. Oxford: Blackwell.

Schriver, KA 1997. *Dynamics in document design: Creating text for readers*. New York: Wiley.

Scragg, DG 1974. *A history of English spelling*. Manchester: Manchester University Press.

Sebeok, TA (ed) 1960. *Style in language*. Cambridge, MA: The MIT Press.

Seely, J 2007. *Oxford A–Z grammar & punctuation*. Oxford: Oxford University Press.

Seidlhofer, B 2001a. Closing a conceptual gap: The case for a description of English as a lingua franca. *International journal of applied linguistics* 11(2): 133–156.

Seidlhofer, B 2001b. Towards making 'Euro-English' a linguistic reality. *English today* 17(4): 14–16.

Seidlhofer, B (ed) 2003. *Controversies in applied linguistics*. Oxford: Oxford University Press.

Seidlhofer, B 2004. Research perspectives on teaching English as a lingua franca. *Annual review of applied linguistics* 24: 209–239.

Seidlhofer B 2005. English as a lingua franca. *ELT journal* 59(4) October.

Seidlhofer, B; A Breiteneder & A Pitzl 2006. English as a lingua franca in Europe: Challenges for applied linguistics. *Annual review of applied linguistics* 26: 3–34.

Selyer, C 2008. Time management and the art of saying no. *Muratho* 2008(October): 20.

Shober, D 2011. *Writing English with style*. Pretoria: JL van Schaik.

Shorter Oxford dictionary 2007. <ukcatalogue.oup.com/product/>.

Sidnell, J (ed) 2009. *Conversation analysis. Comparative perspectives*. Cambridge: Cambridge University Press.

Sidnell, J 2010. *Conversation analysis. An introduction*: London: Wiley-Blackwell.

Siegal, AM & WG Connolly 1999. *The New York Times manual of style and usage*. New York: Random House.

Simpson, J (ed) 2011. *The Routledge handbook of applied linguistics*. London: Routledge.

Skehan, P 1995. Analysability, accessibility, and ability for use, in G Cook & B Seidlhofer (eds) *Principle & practice in applied linguistics. Studies in honour of HG Widdowson*. Oxford: Oxford University Press, 91–106.

Slembrouck, S 2007. Intertextuality, in J Östman; J Verschueren & E Versluys (eds) *Handbook of pragmatics*. Amsterdam/Philadephia: John Benjamins.

Small, I 1991. The editor as annotator as ideal reader, in I Small & M Walsh (eds) *The theory and practice of text-editing*. Cambridge: Cambridge University Press, 186–199.

Small, I & M Walsh 1991. Introduction: the theory and practice of text-editing, in I Small & M Walsh (eds) *The theory and practice of text-editing*. Cambridge: Cambridge University Press, 1–13.

Small, I & M Walsh (eds) 1991. *The theory and practice of text-editing*. Cambridge: Cambridge University Press.

Society for Editors and Proofreaders (SfEP) <www.sfep.org.uk/pub/faqs/fedit.asp>.

Society for Editors and Proofreaders (SfEP) 2009. *21 top tips to make the most of your freelance copy-editor of proofreader.* <www.sfep.org.uk.pub.faqs/toptips/21tips_freelances.asp> (Accessed September 2010).

Society for Editors and Proofreaders (SfEP) 2011. *Proofreaders help to protect the bottom line.* <www.sfep.org.uk/pdocs/sfep-release-20110715.pdf> (Accessed July 2011).

South African Translators' Institute (SATI). <www.translators.org.za/>.

Spits. <www.collegasintekst.org/> (Accessed March 2012).

Spivey, NN 1997. *The constructivist metaphor. Reading, writing and the making of meaning*. San Diego/London: Academic Press.

Stepp, CS 1989. *Editing for today's newsroom. New perspectives for a changing profession*. London: Lawrence Erlbaum.

Stilman, A 2010. *Grammatically correct: The essential guide to spelling, style, usage, grammar, and punctuation* (2 ed). Cincinnati, OH: Writer's Digest Books.

Strunk, W & EB White 1979. *The elements of style*. New York/London: Macmillan.

Strunk, W & EB White 1999. *The elements of style* (3 ed). New York: Bartleby.com

Style manual for authors, editors and printers of Australian government publications 2002. (6 ed). Queensland: John Wiley & Sons.

Sunshine, C 2009. *Copyediting in the digital age. How computor technology has changed the editing process.* <www.suite101.com/content//copyediting-in-the-digital-age-a 184421>.

Svartvik, J & G Leech 2006. *English: One tongue, many voices*. Basingstoke: Palgrave Macmillan.

Swan, M 1980. *Practical English usage*. Oxford: Oxford University Press.

Swan, M 2005. *Practical English usage* (3 ed). Oxford: Oxford University Press.

Swanepoel, P 2005. Stemming the HIV/AIDS epidemic in South Africa: Are our HIV/AIDS campaigns failing us? *Communicatio* 31(1): 61–93.

Swanepoel, P & H Hoeken (eds) 2008. *Adapting health communication to cultural needs: optimizing documents in South-African health communication on HIV and AIDS*. Amsterdam: John Benjamins.

Swann, J; A Deumert; T Lillis & R Mesthrie 2004. *A dictionary of sociolinguistics*. Edinburgh: Edinburgh University Press.

Taggart, C & JA Wines 2008. *My grammar and I (or should that be 'me'?): Old-school ways to sharpen your English*. London: Michael O'Mara Books Limited.

Tarutz, JA 1992. *Technical editing: The practical guide for editors and writers*. Reading, MA: Addison-Wesley.

The Learning Centre nd. *Academic skills at the University of New South Wales 'avoiding plagiarism – What is plagiarism?'* <www.lc.unsw.edu.au/onlib.plag.html> (Accessed October 2004).

Thill, JV & CL Bovee 2002. *Excellence in business communication* (5 ed). New Jersey: Pearson/Prentice Hall.

Thill, JV & CL Bovee 2005. *Excellence in business communication* (6 ed). New Jersey: Pearson/Prentice Hall.

Thomas, C 2009. *Your house style: Styling your words for maximum effect*. London: SfEP.

Torstendahl, R & Burrage, M (eds) 1990. *The formation of professions: Knowledge, state and strategy*. London: Sage.

Toolan, M 1997. What is critical discourse analysis and why are people saying such terrible things about it? *Language and literature* 6(2): 83–103.

Trappes-Lomax, H 2006. Discourse analysis, in A Davies & C Elder (eds) *The handbook of applied linguistics*. Oxford; Blackwell, 133–164.

Trask, RL 1997. *Penguin guide to punctuation*. London: Penguin Group.

Trask, RL 2008. *Phonetics & linguistics*, UCL. <www.phon.ucl.ac.uk/>.

Treble, HA & GH Vallins 1973. *An ABC of English usage*. Calcutta: Oxford University Press.

Truss, L 2003. *Eats, shoots & leaves. A zero tolerance approach to punctuation*. London: Profile Books.

Truss, L 2008. *The girl's like spaghetti – Why, you can't manage without apostrophes!* London: Profile Books.

Tschichold, J; L McLean & R Kinross 1998. *The new typography: A handbook for modern designers*. Berkeley, CA: University of California Press.

Tseng, J 1992. Interpreting as an emerging profession in Taiwan – a sociological model. MA dissertation, Fu Jen Catholic University, Taiwan.

Turabian, KL 2007. *A manual for writers of research papers, theses, and dissertations: Chicago style for students and researchers* (7 ed). Chicago: University of Chicago Press.

Turabian, KL 2010. *Student's guide to writing college papers* (4 ed). Chicago: University of Chicago Press.

Upward, C & G Davidson 2011. *The history of the English spelling*. London: Wiley-Blackwell.

US Department of Labor 2006. *Writers and editors*. <www.bls.gov/oco/ocos089.htm> (Accessed November 2006).

Van de Poel, K (ed) 2003. Text editing – from a talent to a scientific discipline. *Antwerp papers in linguistics (APIL)* 103. University of Antwerp. <webh01.ua.ac.be/apil/>.

Van de Poel, K 2006. *Scribende. Academic writing for students of English*. Leuven/Voorburg: Acco.

Van de Poel, K & J Gasiorek 2007. *All write. An introduction to writing in an academic context*. Leuven/Voorburg: Acco.

Van Dijk, TA 1972. *Some aspects of text grammars. A study in theoretical linguistics and poetics*. The Hague: Mouton.

Van Dijk, TA 2000. Theoretical background, in R Wodak & TA van Dijk (eds) *Racism at the top. Parliamentary discourses on ethnic issues in six European states*. Klagenfurt: Drava Verlag, 13–30.

Van Dijk, TA 2008. *Discourse and power*. London: Palgrave Macmillan.

Van Dijk, TA 2010. *Discourse and context. A socio-cognitive approach*. Cambridge: Cambridge University Press.

Van Dijk, TA (ed) 1985. *Handbook of discourse analysis. Volume I–IV*. London: Academic Press.

Van Dijk, TA (ed) 2007. *Discourse studies. Volume I–V*. Los Angeles/London: SAGE.

Van Eemeren, FH & B Garssen (eds) 2006. *Argumentation in context*. Amsterdam: John Benjamins.

Van Eemeren, FH & B Garssen (eds) 2009. *Pondering on problems of argumentation. Twenty essays on theoretical issues*. Berlin: Springer.

Van Eemeren, FH; R Grootendorst & T Kruiger 1987. *Handbook of argumentation theory. A critical survey of classical backgrounds and modern studies*. Dordrecht: Foris.

Van Eemeren, FH & P Houtlosser (eds) 2005. *Argumentation in practice*. Amsterdam: John Benjamins.

Van Rooyen, B 2005. *Get your book published in 30 (relatively) easy steps*. Johannesburg: Penguin.

Van Wijk, C 1999. Conceptual processes in argumentation: A developmental perspective, in M Torrance & D Galbraith (eds) *Knowing what to write: Cognitive perspectives on conceptual processes in text production*. Amsterdam: Amsterdam University Press, 31–50.

Vivanco, V 2005. The absence of connectives and the maintenance of coherence in publicity texts. *Journal of pragmatics* 37: 1233–1249.

Waddingham, A 2006. On-screen editing, in J Butcher; C Drake & M Leach *Butcher's copy-editing*. Cambridge: Cambridge University Press, 400–430.

Waddingham, A 2008. *Editor and client: Building a professional relationship*. London: SfEP.

Waite, M (ed) 2005. *New Oxford spelling dictionary. The writers' and editors' guide to spelling and word division*. Oxford: Oxford University Press.

Waldman, NM 2004. *Spelling dearest: The down and dirty, nitty-gritty history of English spelling*. London: Authorhouse.

Walker, D (ed) 1995. *Do it in style: The editorial style guide of Independent Newspapers*. Johannesburg: Independent Newspapers Holdings Limited.

Walker, J 2002. Hiring and training copyeditors. *Science editor* 25(6): 190.

Walker, S 2001. *Typography and language in everyday life: Prescriptions and practices*. New York: Longman.

Wallace, PM 2004. *The internet in the workplace: How new technology is transforming work*. Cambridge/New York: Cambridge University Press.

Wallraff, B 2004. *How to edit copy and influence people*. <poynter.org/content> (Accessed November 2006).

Walton, D 2004. *Relevance in argumentation*. Mahwah, NJ: Erlbaum.

Wasserman, H 2008. International journalism ethics, in AS de Beer & JC Merrill (eds) *Global journalism: Topical issues and media systems*. Boston: Pearson.

Webster's dictionary of English usage 2009. Springfield, MA: Merriam-Webster.

Webster's third new international dictionary 2004. (4 ed). Springfield, MA: Merriam-Webster.

Wei, L & VJ Cook (eds) 2009. *Contemporary applied linguistics. Volume 1 & 2*. London: Continuum.

Werth, P 1984. *Focus, coherence and emphasis*. London: Croom Helm.

Whelan, J 2000. *E-mail@work. Get moving with digital communication*. Harlow: ft.com.

Whittaker, J 2002. *The internet*. London: Routledge.

White, JV 1989. *Thoughts on publication design*. Johannesburg: JRS Publishing.

White, L 2005. So you want to be a freelancer?, in J Mackenzie (ed) *At the typeface. Selections from the newsletters of the Victoria Society of Editors*. Melbourne: Victoria Society of Editors Inc, 125–127.

Wiggins, RW 1994. *The internet for everyone*. Maidenhead: McGraw-Hill.

Wikipedia. *Style guide*. <en.wikipedia.org/wiki/Style_guide> (Accessed June 2009).

Wikipedia. *Manual of style*. <www.en.wikipedia.org/wiki/Manual_of_Style> (Accessed January 2012).

Wilensky HL 1964. The professionalization of everyone? *American journal of sociology* 70(2): 137–158.

Wilkinson, P 2006. Professionalism. *Muratho* 2006(December): 39–41.

Williams, H 2006. *When the 'last line of defence' failed*. <www.theslot.com/captain.html> (Accessed November 2006).

Windeatt, S 2000. *The internet*. Oxford/New York: Oxford University Press.

Wizda, S 1997a. Parachute journalism. *American journalism review* July–August: 40–44. <www.uvm.edu/~tstreete/readings/Parachute_Journ.txt> (Accessed September 2003).

Wizda, S 1997b. Copy desk blues. *American journalism review* 19(September).

Wodak, R & M Meyer (eds) 2009. *Methods of critical discourse analysis*. Los Angeles: SAGE.

Wodak, R & TA van Dijk (eds) 2000. *Racism at the top. Parliamentary discourses on ethnic issues in six European states*. Klagenfurt: Drava Verlag.

Wood-Ellem, E 2005. A freelance editor's charter, in J Mackenzie (ed) *At the typeface. Selections from the newsletters of the Victoria Society of Editors*. Melbourne: Victoria Society of Editors Inc, 140–141.

Woods, N 2006. *Describing discourse*. London: Hodder Arnold.

WordNet. Princeton University. <http://wordnet.princeton.edu> (Accessed November 2010).

Xu, J & K Van de Poel 2011. English as a lingua franca in Flanders. A study of university students' attitudes. *English text construction* 4(2): 257–278.

Yancey, KB 2004. Looking for sources of coherence in a fragmented world: Notes towards a new assessment design. *Computers and composition* 21: 89–102. <papyr.com/hypertextbooks/engl_101/coherent.htm>.

Zittrain, J 2008. *The future of the internet: and how to stop it*. New Haven, CT: Yale University Press.

Index

A page number in a bolder font indicates that the topic is to be found in a checklist, a figure, a list or a table on that page.